Proceedings of the
13th INTERNATIONAL
CONFERENCE
ON
RESEARCH AND DEVELOPMENT
IN
INFORMATION RETRIEVAL

BRUSSELS-BELGIUM
5-7 September 19S

Edited by : Jean-Luc VIDICK
              Université Libre de Bruxelles
              CP 142
              avenue Fr. Roosevelt, 50
              1050 Bruxelles (Belgique)

The Association for Computing Machinery
11 West 42nd Street
New York, New York 10036

ISBN 0-89791-408-2

Additional copies may be ordered prepaid from :

ACM Order Department   Price :
P.O. Box 64145   Members........ $18.00
Baltimore, MD 21264   All others $24.00

ACM Order Number : 606900

Dépôt légal Bruxelles : D/1990/0098/069

PREFACE

— — — — — — — —

This book contains the papers presented at the 13th International Conference on Research and Development in Information Retrieval held in Brussels, Belgium, september 5th trough 7th 1990.

For the first time, this annual ACM Sigir Conference was organized in Belgium. It was for me a great honour to undertake this responsibility.

I'm very grateful to Gerard Salton and Leo Egghe who, as co-chairmen of the program committee, helped greatly in the success of this Conference. I would also like to thank the program committee members, the session chairmen and the authors.

I'm also very grateful to Yves Chiaramella and Bruce Croft for their support.

Jean-Luc VIDICK
Conference Chairman

CONFERENCE ORGANIZATION

CONFERENCE COMMITTEE

Conference Chairman
Jean-Luc Vidick — Section de Science de l'Information et de la Documentation
Université Libre de Bruxelles (B)

Programme Chairmen
Leo Egghe — Limburgs Universitair Centrum (LUC) (B)
Universitaire Instelling Antwerpen (UIA) (B)

Gerard Salton — Cornell University, Ithaca (USA)

Tutorials Chairman
Georges Van Slype — Bureau Marcel van Dijk
Université Libre de Bruxelles (B)

Local arrangements
Pierre Geilfus — SIE, Brussels (B)

Publicity
Egbert De Smet — Universitaire Instelling Antwerpen (UIA) (B)

Treasurer
Jean-Luc Vidick — Université Libre de Bruxelles (B)

CONFERENCE SECRETARIAT

CONFERENCE OFFICE BRUSSELS
rue de l'Orme 19 Olmstraat
1040 BRUSSELS - BELGIUM

Tel. : (32/2) 736.03.35 - 736.03.05
Fax : (32/2) 734.67.02
Telex : 61473

PROGRAMME COMMITTEE

TABLE OF CONTENTS

I

SIGNATURES

Chair : S.T. Klein, University of Chicago (USA)

KNOWLEDGE BASED INFORMATION RETRIEVAL

Chair : G. Brajnik, University of Udine (Italy)

INFORMATION RETRIEVAL MODELS (2)

Chair : N. Fuhr, Technische Hochschule Darmstadt (Germany)

IV

Inference Networks for Document Retrieval

Howard Turtle and W. Bruce Croft
Computer and Information Science Department
University of Massachusetts
Amherst, MA 01003

Abstract

The use of inference networks to support document retrieval is introduced. A network-based retrieval model is described and compared to conventional probabilistic and Boolean models.

1 Introduction

Network representations have been used in information retrieval since at least the early 1960's. Networks have been used to support diverse retrieval functions, including browsing [TC89], document clustering [Cro80], spreading activation search [CK87], support for multiple search strategies [CT87], and representation of user knowledge [OPC86] or document content [TS85].

Recent work suggests that significant improvements in retrieval performance will require techniques that, in some sense, "understand" the content of documents and queries [vR86, Cro87] and can be used to infer probable relationships between documents and queries. In this view, information retrieval is an inference or evidential reasoning process in which we estimate the probability that a user's information need, expressed as one or more queries, is met given a document as "evidence." Network representations show promise as mechanisms for inferring these kinds of relationships [CT89,CK87].

The idea that retrieval is an inference or evidential reasoning process is not new. Cooper's logical relevance [Coo71] is based on deductive relationships between representations of documents and information needs. Wilson's situational relevance [Wil73] extends this notion to incorporate inductive or uncertain inference based on the degree to which documents support information needs. The techniques required to support these kinds of inference are similar to those used in expert systems that must reason with uncertain information. A number of competing inference models have been developed for these kinds of expert systems [KL86,LK88] and several of these models can be adapted to the document retrieval task.

In the research described here we adapt an inference network model to the retrieval task. The use of the model is intended to:

- Support the use of multiple document representation schemes. Research has shown that a given query will retrieve different documents when applied to different representations, even when the average retrieval performance achieved with each representation is the same. Katzer, for example, found little overlap in documents retrieved using seven different representations, but found that documents retrieved by multiple representations were likely to be relevant [KMT+82]. Similar results have been obtained when comparing term- with cluster-based representations [CH79] and term- with citation-based representations [FNL88].

- Allow results from different queries and query types to be combined. Given a single natural language description of an information need, different searchers will formulate different queries to represent that need and will retrieve different documents, even when average performance is the same for each searcher [MKN79,KMT+82]. Again, documents retrieved by multiple searchers are more likely to be relevant. A description of an information need can be used to generate several query representations (e.g., probabilistic, Boolean), each using a different query strategy and each capturing different aspects of the information need. These different search strategies are known to retrieve different documents for the same underlying information need [Cro87].

- Facilitate flexible matching between the terms or concepts mentioned in queries and those assigned to documents. The poor match between the vocabulary used to express queries and the vocabulary used to represent documents appears to be a major cause of poor recall [FLGD87]. Recall can be improved using domain knowledge to match query and representation concepts without significantly degrading precision.

The resulting formal retrieval model integrates several previous models in a single theoretical framework; multiple document and query representations are treated as evidence which is combined to estimate the probability that a document satisfies a user's information need.

In what follows we briefly review candidate inference models, present an inference network-based retrieval model, and compare the network model to current retrieval models.

2 Inference networks

The development of automated inference techniques that accommodate uncertainty has been an area of active research in the artificial intelligence community, particularly in the context of expert systems [KL86,LK88]. Popular approaches include those based on purely symbolic reasoning [Coh85,Doy79], fuzzy sets [Zad83], and a variety of probability models [Nil86,Che88]. Two inference models based on probabilistic methods are of particular interest: Bayesian inference networks [Pea88,LS88] and the Dempster-Shafer theory of evidence [Dem68,Sha76].

A Bayesian inference network is a directed, acyclic dependency graph (DAG) in which nodes represent propositional variables or constants and edges represent dependence relations between propositions. If a proposition represented by a node p "causes" or implies the proposition represented by node q, we draw a directed edge from p to q. The node q contains a *link* matrix that specifies $P(q|p)$ for all possible values of the two variables. When a node has multiple parents, the link matrix specifies the dependence of that node on the set of parents (π_q) and characterizes the dependence relationship between that node and all nodes representing its potential causes.[1] Given a set of prior probabilities for the roots of the DAG, these networks can be used to compute the probability or degree of belief associated with all remaining nodes.

Different restrictions on the topology of the network and assumptions about the way in which the connected nodes interact lead to different schemes for combining probabilities. In general, these schemes have two components which operate independently: a *predictive* component in which parent nodes provide support for their children (the degree to which we believe a proposition depends on the degree to which we believe the propositions that might cause it), and a *diagnostic* component in which children provide support for their parents (if our belief in a proposition increases or decreases, so does our belief in its potential causes). The propagation of probabilities through the net can be done using information passed between adjacent nodes.

The Dempster-Shafer theory of evidence, although not originally cast as a network model, can be used as an alternative method for evaluating these kinds of probabilistic inference networks. Rather than computing the belief associated with a query given a set of evidence, we can view Dempster-Shafer as computing the probability that the evidence would allow us to prove the query. The degree of support parameters associated with the arcs joining nodes are not interpreted as conditional probabilities, but as assertions that the parent node provides support for the child (is *active*) for some proportion p of the time and does not support the child for the remainder of the time. For an *and*-combination we compute the proportion of the time that all incoming arcs are active. For an *or*-combination we compute the proportion of the time that at least one parent node is active. To compute the provability of the query given a document, we examine all paths leading from the document to the query and compute the proportion of time that all of the arcs on at least one proof path are active. Given the structure of these networks, this computation can be done using series-parallel reduction of the subgraph joining the document and query in time proportional to the number of arcs in the subgraph.

The Bayesian and Dempster-Shafer models are different and can lead to different results. However, under the assumption of disjunctive rule interaction (so called "noisy-OR") and the interpretation of an arc from a to b as $P(b|a) = p$ and $P(b|\neg a) = 0$, the Bayesian and Dempster-Shafer models will produce similar results [Pea88, page 446]. The document retrieval inference networks described here are based on the Bayesian inference network model.

The use of Bayesian inference networks for information retrieval represents an extension of probability-based retrieval research dating from the early 1960's [MK60]. It has long been recognized that some terms in a collection are more significant than others and that information about the distribution of terms in a collection can be used to improve retrieval performance. The use of these networks generalizes existing probabilistic models and allows integration of several sources of knowledge in a single framework.

---

[1] While this probability specification is generally referred to as a link matrix, it is actually a tensor.

3

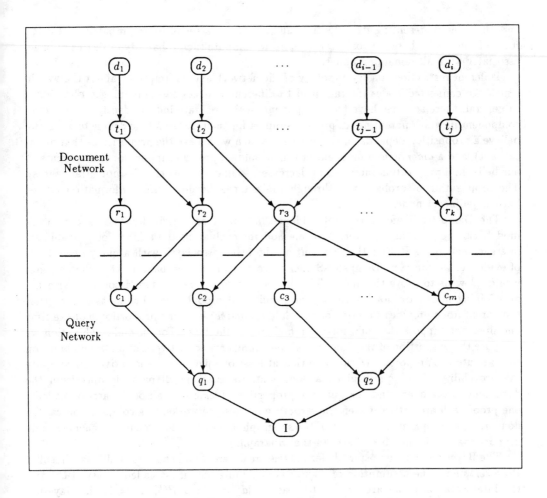

Figure 1: Basic document inference network

3 Basic Model

The basic document retrieval inference network, shown in Figure 1, consists of two component networks: a document network and a query network. The document network represents the document collection using a variety of document representation schemes. The document network is built once for a given collection and its structure does not change during query processing. The query network consists of a single node which represents the user's information need and one or more query representations which express that information need. A query network is built for each information need and is modified during query processing as existing queries are refined or new queries are added in an attempt to better characterize the information need. The document and query networks are joined by links between representation concepts and query concepts. All nodes in the inference network take on values

4

from the set {*false,true*}.

3.1 Document network

The document network consists of document nodes (d_i's), text representation nodes (t_j's), and concept representation nodes (r_k's). Each document node represents a document in the collection. A document node corresponds to the event that a specific document has been observed. The form of the document represented depends on the collection and its intended use, but we will assume that a document is a well defined object and will focus on traditional document types (e.g., monographs, journal articles, office documents).

Document nodes correspond to abstract documents rather than their physical representations. A text representation node or text node corresponds to a specific text representation of a document. A text node corresponds to the event that a text representation has been observed. We focus here on the text content of documents, but the network model can support documents nodes with multiple children representing additional component types (e.g., figures, audio, or video). Similarly, a single text might be shared by more than one document. While shared components is rare in traditional collections (an example would be a journal article that appears in both a serial issue and in a reprint collection) and is not generally represented in current retrieval models, it is common in hypertext systems. For clarity, we will consider only text representations and will assume a one-to-one correspondence between documents and texts. The dependence of a text upon the document is represented in the network by an arc from the document node to the text node.

The content representation nodes or representation nodes can be divided into several subsets, each corresponding to a single representation technique that has been applied to the document texts. For example, if a collection has been indexed using automatic phrase extraction and manually assigned index terms, then the set of representation nodes will consist of two distinct subsets or content representation types with disjoint domains. Thus, if the phrase "information retrieval" has been extracted and "information retrieval" has been manually assigned as an index term, then two representation nodes with distinct meanings will be created. One corresponds to the event that "information retrieval" has been automatically extracted from a subset of the collection, the second corresponds to the event that "information retrieval" has been manually assigned to a (presumably distinct) subset of the collection. We represent the assignment of a specific representation concept to a document by a directed arc to the representation node from each text node corresponding to a document to which the concept has been assigned. For now we assume that the presence or absence of a link corresponds to a binary assigned/not assigned distinction, that is, there are no partial or weighted assignments.

In principle, the number of representation schemes is unlimited; in addition to phrase extraction and manually assigned terms we would expect representations based on natural language processing and automatic keyword extraction. For any real document collection, however, the number of representations used will be fixed and relatively small. The potential domain of each representation scheme may also be unlimited, but the actual number of primitive representation concepts defined for a given collection is fixed by the collection. The domain for most automated representation schemes is generally bounded by some function of the collection size (e.g., the number of keywords cannot exceed the number of words in a collection). For manual representation schemes the domain size is limited by the number of documents, the representation scheme itself (e.g., a controlled vocabulary), and the amount of time a human expert can spend analyzing each document.

The basic document network shown in Figure 1 is a simple three level DAG in which document nodes are roots, text nodes are interior nodes, and representation nodes are leaves. Document nodes have exactly one text node as a child and each text node has one or more representation nodes as children.

Each document node has a prior probability associated with it that describes the probability of observing that document; this prior probability will generally be set to 1/(collection size) and will be small for real collections. Each text node contains a specification of its dependence upon its parent; by assumption, this dependence is complete, a text node is observed ($t_i = true$) exactly when its parent document is observed ($d_i = true$).

Each representation node contains a specification of the conditional probability associated with the node given its set of parent text nodes. This specification incorporates the effect of any indexing weights (e.g., term frequency for each parent text) or term weights (e.g., inverse document frequency) associated with the representation concept. While, in principle, this would require $O(2^n)$ space for a node with n parents, in practice we use canonical representations that allow us to compute the required conditional probabilities when needed. These canonical schemes require $O(n)$ space if we weight the contribution of each parent or $O(1)$ space if parents are to be treated uniformly.

3.2 Query network

The query network is an "inverted" DAG with a single leaf that corresponds to the event that an information need is met and multiple roots that correspond to the concepts that express the information need. As shown in Figure 1, a set of intermediate query nodes may be used when multiple queries express the information need. These nodes are a representation convenience; it is always possible to eliminate them by increasing the complexity of the distribution specified at the node representing the information need.

In general, the user's information need is internal to the user and is not precisely understood. We attempt to make the meaning of an information need explicit by expressing it in the form of one or more queries that have formal interpretations. These queries may be generated from a single natural language description (e.g., keywords or phrases for a probabilistic search, a Boolean representation, sample documents, ...) or they may represent additional sources of information (e.g., an intermediary's description of the user or of the information need, or feedback provided by the user). It is unlikely that any of these queries will correspond precisely to the information need, but some will better characterize the information need than others and several query specifications taken together may be a better representation than any of the individual queries.

The roots of the query network are query concepts; they correspond to the primitive concepts used to express the information need. A single query concept node may have several representation concept nodes as parents. Each query concept node contains a specification of its dependence on the set of parent representation concepts. The query concept nodes define the mapping between the concepts used to represent the document collection and the concepts used in the queries. In the simplest case, the query concepts are the same as the representation concepts so each query concept has exactly one parent. In a slightly more complex example, the query concept "information retrieval" may have as parents both the node corresponding to "information retrieval" as a phrase and the node corresponding to "information retrieval" as a manually assigned term. As we add content representations to the document network and allow query concepts that do not explicitly appear in any document representation, the number of parents associated with a single query concept will increase.

A query concept is similar to a representation concept that is derived from other representation concepts (see section 5 for a discussion of derived representation concepts) and in some cases it will be useful to "promote" a query concept to a representation concept. For example, suppose that a researcher is looking for information on a recently developed process that is unlikely to be explicitly identified in any existing representation scheme. The researcher, if sufficiently motivated, could work with the retrieval system to describe how this new concept might be inferred from other representation concepts. If this new concept definition is of general interest, it can be added to the collection of representation concepts. This use of inference to define new concepts is similar to that used in RUBRIC [TS85].

The attachment of the query concept nodes to the document network has no effect on the basic structure of the document network. None of the existing links need change and none of the conditional probability specifications stored in the nodes are modified.

A query node represents a distinct query form and corresponds to the event that the query is satisfied. Each query node contains a specification of the dependence of the query on its parent query concepts. The link matrices that describe these conditional probabilities are discussed further in section 3.4, but we note that the form of the link matrix is determined by the query type; a link matrix simulating a Boolean operator is different than a matrix simulating a probabilistic or weighted query.

The single leaf representing the information need corresponds to the event that an information need is met. In general, we cannot predict with certainty whether a user's information need will be met by a document collection. The query network is intended to capture the way in which meeting the user's information need depends on documents and their representations. Moreover, the query network is intended to allow us to combine information from multiple document representations and to combine queries of different types to form a single, formally justified estimate of the probability that the user's information need is met. If the inference network correctly characterizes the dependence of the information need on the collection, the computed probability provides a good estimate.

3.3 Use of the inference network

The retrieval inference network is intended to capture all of the significant probabilistic dependencies among the variables represented by nodes in the document and query networks. Given the prior probabilities associated with the documents (roots) and the conditional probabilities associated with the interior nodes, we can compute the posterior probability or belief associated with each node in the network. Further, if the value of any variable represented in the network becomes known we can use the network to recompute the probabilities associated with all remaining nodes based on this "evidence."

The network, taken as a whole, represents the dependence of a user's information need on the documents in a collection where the dependence is mediated by document and query representations. When the query network is first built and attached to the document network we compute the belief associated with each node in the query network. The initial value at the node representing the information need is the probability that the information need is met given that no specific document in the collection has been observed and all documents are equally likely (or unlikely). If we now observe a single document d_i and attach evidence to the network asserting $d_i = true$ we can compute a new belief for every node in the network given $d_i = true$. In particular, we can compute the probability that the information need is met given that d_i has been observed in the collection. We can now remove this evidence and instead assert that some d_j, $i \neq j$ has been observed. By repeating this process we can compute the probability that the information need is met given each document in the collection and rank the documents accordingly.

In principle, we need not consider each document in isolation but could look for the subset of documents which produce the highest probability that the information need is met. While a general solution to this best-subset problem is intractable, in some cases good heuristic approximations are possible. Best-subset rankings have been considered in IR [Sti75], and similar problems arise in pattern recognition, medical diagnosis, and truth-maintenance systems. See [Pea88] for a discussion of the best-subset or belief revision problem in Bayesian networks. At present, we consider only documents in isolation because the approach is computationally simpler and because it allows comparison with earlier retrieval models that produce document rankings consistent with the Probability Ranking Principle [Rob77] in which documents are considered in isolation.

The document network is built once for a given collection. Given one or more queries representing an information need, we then build a query network that attempts to characterize the dependence of the information need on the collection. If the ranking produced by the initial query network is inadequate, we must add additional information to the query network or refine its structure to better characterize the meaning of the existing queries. This feedback process is quite similar to conventional relevance feedback.

3.4   Link matrix forms

For all non-root nodes in the inference network we must estimate the probability that a node takes on a value given any set of values for its parent nodes. If a node a has a set of parents $\pi_a = \{p_1, \ldots, p_n\}$, we must estimate $P(a|p_1, \ldots, p_n)$.

The most direct way to encode our estimate is as a link matrix. Since we are dealing with binary valued propositions, this matrix is of size 2×2^n for n parents and specifies the probability that a takes the value $a = true$ or $a = false$ for all combinations of parent values. The update procedures for Bayesian networks then use the probabilities provided by the set of parents to condition over the link matrix values to compute the predictive component of our belief in a or $P(a = true)$. Similarly, the link matrix is used to provide diagnostic information to the set of parents based on our belief in a. As mentioned earlier, encoding our estimates in link matrix form is practical only for nodes with a small set of parents, so our estimation task has two parts: how do we estimate the dependence of a node on its set of parents and how do we encode these estimates in a usable form?

We will describe four canonical link matrix forms, three for the Boolean operators and a fourth for simple probabilistic retrieval. For illustration, we will assume that a node Q has three parents A, B, and C and that

$$P(A = \text{true}) = a, \quad P(B = \text{true}) = b, \quad P(C = \text{true}) = c.$$

For or-combinations, Q will be true when any of A, B, or C is true and false only when A, B, and C are all false. This suggests a link matrix of the form

$$L_{\text{or}} = \begin{pmatrix} 1 & 0 & 0 & 0 & 0 & 0 & 0 & 0 \\ 0 & 1 & 1 & 1 & 1 & 1 & 1 & 1 \end{pmatrix}.$$

Using a closed form of the update procedures, we have

$$
\begin{aligned}
P(Q = \text{true}) &= (1-a)(1-b)c + (1-a)b(1-c) + (1-a)bc + a(1-b)(1-c) \\
&\quad + a(1-b)c + ab(1-c) + abc \\
&= 1 - (1-a)(1-b)(1-c)
\end{aligned}
$$

which is the familiar rule for disjunctive combination of events that are not known to be mutually exclusive. Similar matrix forms can be developed for and ($P(Q = \text{true}) = abc$) and not ($P(Q = \text{true}) = 1 - a$).

If we restrict the parent nodes for any of these logic operators to values 0 or 1 then Q must also have a value of 0 or 1. If we allow terms to take on weights in the range $[0, 1]$ and interpret these weights as the probability that the term has been assigned to a document text, then these inference networks provide a natural interpretation for Boolean retrieval with weighted indexing. The use of these canonical forms to simulate Boolean retrieval is discussed in section 4.3

For probabilistic retrieval each parent has a weight associated with it, as does the child. In this weighted-sum matrix, our belief in Q depends on the specific parents that are true – parents with larger weights have more influence in our belief. If we let $w_a, w_b, w_c \geq 0$ be the parent weights, $0 \leq w_q \leq 1$ the child weight, and $t = w_a + w_b + w_c$, then we have a link matrix of the form

$$
\begin{pmatrix}
1 & \frac{(w_a+w_b)w_q}{t} & \frac{(w_a+w_c)w_q}{t} & \frac{w_a w_q}{t} & \frac{(w_b+w_c)w_q}{t} & \frac{w_b w_q}{t} & \frac{w_c w_q}{t} & 1 - w_q \\
0 & \frac{w_c w_q}{t} & \frac{w_b w_q}{t} & \frac{(w_b+w_c)w_q}{t} & \frac{w_a w_q}{t} & \frac{(w_a+w_c)w_q}{t} & \frac{(w_a+w_b)w_q}{t} & w_q
\end{pmatrix}.
$$

Evaluation of this link matrix form results in

$$P(Q = \text{true}) = \frac{(w_a a + w_b b + w_c c)w_q}{t}.$$

This link matrix can be used to implement a variety of weighting schemes, including the familiar term weighting schemes based on within-document term frequency (tf), inverse document frequency (*idf*) or both (*tf.idf*). To illustrate a *tf.idf* weighting, let Q be a representation node and let A, B, and C be document nodes. Let w_a, w_b, and w_c be the normalized *tf* values for A, B, and C, let idf_q be the normalized *idf* weight for Q, and let

$$w_q = idf_q \cdot (w_a + w_b + w_c). \tag{1}$$

Given our basic model, when A is instantiated, belief in Q is given by

$$
\begin{aligned}
\text{bel}(Q) \;&=\; \frac{w_a w_q}{w_a + w_b + w_c} \\
&=\; \frac{tf_a \cdot idf_q \cdot (w_a + w_b + w_c)}{w_a + w_b + w_c} \\
&=\; tf_a \cdot idf_q
\end{aligned}
$$

which is a form of *tf.idf* weight. In general, when a document is instantiated all representation concept nodes to which it is attached take on the *tf.idf* weight associated with the document/term pair.

The weight at Q has two distinct parts. The first part (idf_q in our example) acts to set the maximum belief achievable at a node. If, for some combination of parent values, our belief in Q is certain then this component disappears. Note that in this formulation, the *idf* component is dependent only upon the distribution of the term in the collection, not on the distribution of the term in relevant and non-relevant subsets. Relevance feedback is modeled as part of the query network and does not affect belief in representation concepts.

The second part ($w_a + w_b + w_c$ in our example) acts to normalize the parent weights. Equation 1 is appropriate for the basic model in which only one document is instantiated at a time. In the extended model of section 5 where multiple roots can be instantiated, this component is adjusted to normalize for the maximum achievable set of parent weights. In the general case, where all parents can take any value in the range $[0, 1]$, this normalizing component disappears.

These canonical forms are sufficient for the retrieval inference networks described here, but many others are possible (see section 4.3 for other examples). Further, when the number of parents is small (say, less than 5 or 6) we can use the full link matrix if the dependence of a node on its parents does not fit a canonical form.

4 Comparison with other retrieval models

The inference network retrieval model generalizes both the probabilistic and Boolean models. Inference networks can be used to simulate both probabilistic and Boolean queries and can be used to combine results from multiple queries.

In this section we compare the inference network model with probabilistic (sections 4.1 and 4.2) and Boolean (section 4.3) models and show how inference networks can be used to simulate both forms of retrieval. We then consider how the probabilities required by the model can be estimated (section 4.4); the estimation problems are essentially equivalent to those encountered with probabilistic or vector-space retrieval.

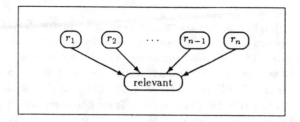

Figure 2: Inference network for binary independence model

4.1 Probabilistic retrieval models

Conventional probabilistic models [vR79,SM83] rank documents by the probability that each document would be judged relevant to a given query, $P(\text{relevant}|d_i)$.[2] This is, in many ways, similar to computing the probability that a user's information need is met given a specific document, $P(I|d_i)$. The principal differences between conventional probabilistic models and the model described here are: 1) most probabilistic models do not explicitly represent the query, 2) conventional probabilistic models do not distinguish between a document and its representations but treat a document as a single vector, and 3) the inference network model depends less upon Bayesian inversion than probabilistic models, Bayesian inversion is just one way to estimate $P(I|d_i)$ (or $P(Q|d_i)$ in the case of a single query).

In this section we summarize the major differences between the inference network and conventional probabilistic models by comparing the network model to the binary independence model. In the next section we provide a formal comparison of the inference network model with a recent probabilistic model that explicitly represents documents and queries.

An inference network that corresponds to the binary independence model [vR79] is shown in Figure 2. A document is represented by a vector whose components are indexing or representation concepts ($d_i = \{r_1, \ldots, r_n\}$). The set of concepts considered is generally restricted to the subset that actually occurs in the query. Comparing this network with that shown in Figure 1, we see that in the binary independence model, the document network is represented by a single level of representation nodes and the query network consists of a single relevance node. In order to implement this network we must somehow estimate the probability of relevance given the set of parent representation concepts and this estimate must incorporate all of our judgments about the probability that a representation concept should be assigned to a document, about the semantic and stochastic relationships between representation concepts, about the relationship between concepts named in the query and assigned to documents, and about the semantics of the query itself. This dependence is complex and its estimation is not a task we could expect users to perform willingly or

---

[2]Most probabilistic models do not actually compute $P(\text{relevant}|d_i)$, but simply rank documents using some function that is monotonic with $P(\text{relevant}|d_i)$. Like Fuhr ([Fuh89]), we believe that an estimate of the probability of relevance is more useful than the ranking by itself. A ranked list of documents in which the top ranked document has a probability of relevance of 0.5 should be viewed differently than a similar list in which the top ranked document has a probability of relevance of 0.95.

reliably.

One approach to simplifying the estimation task is to invoke Bayes' rule so that we need only estimate the probability that each representation concept occurs in relevant or non-relevant documents. This approach does not help to provide initial estimates of the probability distributions since these "simpler" estimates must still incorporate all of the judgments required for the "hard" estimate. The advantage of this approach is that, given samples of relevant and non-relevant documents, it is easy to compute $P(r_i)$ for the relevant sample and to use the result as an estimate of $P(r_i|\text{relevant} = true)$. We can use a similar estimate for $P(r_i|\text{relevant} = false)$. Given a set of independence assumptions and estimates for $P(d_i)$ and $P(\text{relevant} = true)$ we can compute $P(\text{relevant}|d_i)$.[3] Estimating $P(\text{relevant}|d_i)$ without the use of Bayes' rule would be extremely difficult.

Essentially the same procedures can be used to estimate $P(Q|d_i)$. The main difference between the two estimates is that instead of using the representation concepts directly we must compute $P(c_j|\pi_{c_j})$ and compute an expected value for $P(c_j|d_i)$ in order to estimate $P(Q|d_i)$.

The question remains, however, whether estimates of $P(\text{relevant}|d_i)$ or $P(Q|d_i)$ obtained in this way match users' intuition about the dependence. The fact that relevance feedback does improve retrieval performance suggests that the estimates of $P(\text{relevant}|d_i)$ do capture at least some of the dependence, but these estimates are generally based on a small number of relevant documents and are necessarily rather coarse.

While it is clear that estimating $P(\text{relevant}|d_i)$ directly from a small number of documents is impractical, it may be possible to obtain estimates of $P(Q|\pi_Q)$. Users may, for example, be able to assign importance to the concepts in their query and may be able to identify significant interactions between concepts. These estimates could improve the initial estimate and might be used in conjunction with the estimates derived from training samples.

A second approach to simplifying the estimation task is to identify the different types of judgments that enter into the overall estimate and to develop estimates for each type of judgment separately. The model presented here represents one decomposition in which the task of estimating the probability that a given document satisfies an information need consists of judgments about the relationship of a document to its text, the assignment of representation concepts to the text, the relationships between query and representation concepts, and the relationship between queries, query concepts, and the information need. Other decompositions are certainly possible and can be accommodated within the same general framework. The set of relationships presented here incorporates those judgments most important for current generation document retrieval systems.

When viewed this way, the probabilistic and inference models use two similar approaches to the same estimation problem. The probabilistic model uses a single, general purpose rule and makes assumptions about term dependence in order to estimate $P(\text{relevant}|d_i)$. The model presented here views the problem of estimating $P(I|d_i)$ as consisting of a set of logically related estimates. Each estimate is made independently using procedures specific to

---

[3] $P(d_i)$ and $P(\text{relevant} = true)$ do not play a major role in probabilistic models that only produce a document ranking but are required to compute $P(\text{relevant}|d_i)$.

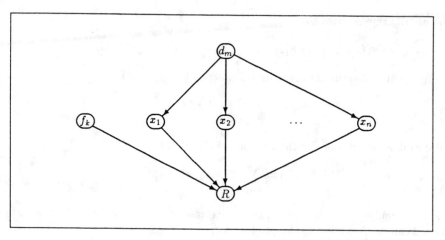

Figure 3: Inference network for the RPI model

the type of estimate; the "probabilistic" estimate of $P(Q|\pi_Q)$ is simply one component of the overall estimate. The component estimates are then combined in a manner consistent with the dependence relationships represented in the inference network to provide an estimate of $P(I|d_i)$.

4.2   Comparison with the RPI model

To further clarify the relationship between the inference network model and the probabilistic model, we will compare the inference network model with Fuhr's model for retrieval with probabilistic indexing (RPI model) [Fuh89]. To simplify the comparison, we will temporarily adopt Fuhr's notation. Let

d_m represent a document in the collection,

x   be the binary vector $(x_1, x_2, \ldots, x_n)$ in which each x_i

       corresponds to a document descriptor (representation concept),

f_k represent the query, and

R represent the event that a document is judged relevant to a query.

All variables are binary valued. In this model, $P(x_i = 1|d_m)$ is interpreted as the probability that a descriptor r_i is a "correct" indexing of d_m. Let X be the set of possible values for **x**, where $|X| \leq 2^n$.

The network shown in Figure 3 corresponds to the probability distribution

$$\begin{aligned} P(R, f_k, x_1, \ldots, x_n, d_m) &= P(R|f_k, d_m) \\ &= P(R|f_k, x_1, \ldots, x_n)P(x_1|d_m)\ldots P(x_n|d_m)P(f_k)P(d_m). \end{aligned}$$

We will evaluate this expression for a given document and query so f_k and d_m are known and the distribution reduces to

$$P(R|f_k, d_m) = P(R|f_k, x_1, \ldots, x_n)P(x_1|d_m) \ldots P(x_n|d_m).$$

Assuming that the descriptors are assigned independently, that is

$$P(\mathbf{x}|d_m) = \prod_{1 \leq i \leq n} P(x_i|d_m),$$

the basic ranking expression for the network of Figure 3 is

$$P(R|f_k, d_m) = \sum_{\mathbf{x} \in X} P(R|f_k, \mathbf{x})P(\mathbf{x}|d_m). \tag{2}$$

Equation 2 is equivalent to the basic ranking expression used by Fuhr [Fuh89, equation 9]. Equation 2 can be expanded to the product form

$$P(R|f_k, d_m) = P(R|f_k) \prod_{1 \leq i \leq n} \left(\frac{p_{ik}}{q_i} u_{im} + \frac{1 - p_{ik}}{1 - q_i}(1 - u_{im}) \right) \tag{3}$$

where

$$\begin{aligned} p_{ik} &= P(x_i = 1|R, f_k) \\ q_i &= P(x_i = 1) \\ u_{im} &= P(x_i = 1|d_m). \end{aligned}$$

(Strictly speaking, the network corresponding to equation 2 should have a single node $\mathbf{x}$ in place of $x_1, \ldots, x_n$ since equation 2 makes no independence assumptions. Independence is, however, assumed in all derivations based on equation 2 so we have chosen to show it in the network.)

Using the same notation and variables, the network of Figure 1 can be reduced to the network of Figure 4. This inference network is described by the probability distribution

$$\begin{aligned} P(R, f_k, x_1, \ldots, x_n, d_m) &= P(R|d_m) \\ &= P(R|f_k)P(f_k|x_1, \ldots, x_n)P(x_1|d_m) \ldots P(x_n|d_m)P(d_m). \end{aligned}$$

Comparing Figure 4 with Figure 3 we see that in the inference network model the query does not appear as a separate prior (root) but is explicitly conditioned on the representation concepts. Again, d_m is given, so we have

$$P(R|d_m) = P(R|f_k)P(f_k|x_1, \ldots, x_n)P(x_1|d_m) \ldots P(x_n|d_m).$$

Applying Bayes' rule we get

$$P(R|d_m) = P(R|f_k)\frac{P(x_1, \ldots, x_n|f_k)P(f_k)}{P(x_1, \ldots, x_n)}P(x_1|d_m) \ldots P(x_n|d_m).$$

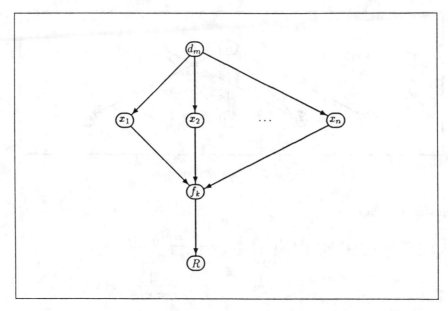

Figure 4: Example inference network

Assuming that the x_i are distributed independently in documents (4) and that the assignment of the x_i is independent of the query (5)

$$P(x_1, \ldots, x_n) = \prod_{1 \leq i \leq n} P(x_i) \tag{4}$$

$$P(x_1, \ldots, x_n | f_k) = \prod_{1 \leq i \leq n} P(x_i | f_k) \tag{5}$$

we have

$$P(R|d_m) = P(R|f_k)P(f_k) \sum_{\mathbf{X} \in X} \prod_{1 \leq i \leq n} \frac{P(x_i|f_k)}{P(x_i)} P(x_i|d_m). \tag{6}$$

The application of Bayes' rule essentially inverts the network of Figure 4 to obtain the equivalent network shown in Figure 5[4]. Note that the use of Bayes' rule here is to allow us to derive a closed-form ranking expression that can be compared with the RPI model. In practice, we would use an estimate of $P(f_k|x_1, \ldots, x_n)$ and would not invert the network.

---

[4]While the networks in Figures 4 and 5 are equivalent in the sense that the computed probability distributions are the same, Figure 5 does not lend itself to normal belief network updating procedures. In order to produce the new $P(x_i|f_k, d_m)$ link matrix and the new prior $P(f_k)$ we must make use of the assumed value of $P(d_m)$. In essence, when we invert the network we fold the prior probability of d_m into the new link matrix and extract a new prior for the query. This means that to test the effect of a change in $P(d_m)$, we would have to recompute the link matrices at each x_i and compute a new $P(f_k)$. With the network in Figure 4, we can change our assumed value for $P(d_m)$ without changing the probability information stored at each node.

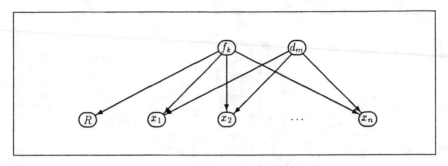

Figure 5: Effect of inversion

Equation 6 reduces to

$$P(R|d_m) = P(R|f_k)P(f_k) \prod_{1 \leq i \leq n} \left(\frac{P(x_i = 1|f_k)}{P(x_i = 1)}P(x_i = 1|d_m) \right.$$
$$\left. + \frac{P(x_i = 0|f_k)}{P(x_i = 0)}P(x_i = 0|d_m) \right).$$

If we let

$$\begin{aligned} p_{ik} &= P(x_i = 1|f_k) \\ q_i &= P(x_i = 1) \\ u_{im} &= P(x_i = 1|d_m) \end{aligned}$$

we get the ranking expression

$$P(R|d_m) = P(R|f_k)P(f_k) \prod_{1 \leq i \leq n} \left(\frac{p_{ik}}{q_i}u_{im} + \frac{1 - p_{ik}}{1 - q_i}(1 - u_{im}) \right) \qquad (7)$$

Equation 7 differs from equation 3 in that p_{ik} is conditioned only on the query and not on R and the resulting probability is normalized by $P(f_k)$. The difference in conditioning for p_{ik} arises because the network of Figure 4 implicitly assumes that $\mathbf{x}$ and R are conditionally independent given the query, that is, $\mathbf{x}$ cannot influence our assessment of relevance except through its effect on the query. The network of Figure 3 assumes that $\mathbf{x}$ and f_k are independent, but not necessarily conditionally independent given R, that is, $\mathbf{x}$ and the query can influence our assessment of relevance independently. Under the assumption of conditional independence

$$P(\mathbf{x}|R, f_k) = P(\mathbf{x}|f_k)$$

and the p_{ik} terms are identical. $P(f_k)$ is constant for a given query and does not affect the ranking so, under the assumption of conditional independence, the rankings produced by the two models are identical.

The networks in Figures 3 and 4 help to clarify the differences between the probabilistic and inference network retrieval models. In the network of Figure 3, the query is modeled as a separate variable that is related to the possible document descriptions through the specification of $P(R|\mathbf{x}, f_k)$. The network of Figure 4 explicitly models the dependence of the query on the document representation and the dependence of relevance on the query. Again, the network of Figure 4 asserts the independence of the document representation and relevance given the query; the document representation cannot influence the probability of relevance except through its influence on the query.

The principal difference between the two models, then, lies in the dependencies assumed. While we have chosen Fuhr's model as the basis for comparison, network forms could be developed for the many other probabilistic formulations. The chief advantage of the inference network model is that it allows complex dependencies to be represented in an easily understood form and it allows networks containing these dependencies to be evaluated without development of a closed form expression that captures these dependencies.

4.3 Boolean retrieval

Using the canonical link matrix forms of section 3.4 we can implement Boolean retrieval as follows. For clarity, we assume that the query and representation vocabularies are identical so we can omit query concepts from the network. We also assume that when one document is instantiated all remaining documents are set to false.

1. Use a canonical *or* matrix at each representation node. When a document is instantiated, all representation concepts to which it has been attached will have $\text{bel}(r_i) = 1$. All remaining representation concepts have $\text{bel}(r_j) = 0$.

2. Build an expression tree for the query. The root of the tree is the query and all arcs in the tree are directed toward the root. The leaves of this tree will be representation concepts and the interior nodes will correspond to expression operators. At each operator node use the canonical link matrix form for that operator. Attach this tree to the document network.

3. Using the evaluation procedure described in section 3.3, instantiate each document in turn and record the belief in the query node. Any document for which $\text{bel}(Q) = 1$ satisfies the query, any node for which $\text{bel}(Q) < 1$ does not.

Under the assumptions above and using binary indexing, $\text{bel}(Q)$ can only have values 0 or 1 and the inference network simulates a conventional Boolean system exactly. If we relax the requirement that all uninstantiated documents be set to 0, then only documents for which $\text{bel}(Q) = 1$ satisfy the query and all remaining documents have a small but non-zero $\text{bel}(Q)$.

The same probabilistic interpretation of the Boolean operators applies equally well to weighted indexing. Using the approach described in section 3.4 we can incorporate indexing weights by replacing the *or* link matrix at the representation concept nodes with a weighted-sum matrix incorporating the appropriate *tf* and *idf* weights. In this case, when a document is instantiated, all representation nodes to which it is attached take on the *tf.idf* weight for that term/document pair and all remaining representation nodes take on $\text{bel} = 0$. These weights are then combined using the closed-form expressions of section 3.4. In short, the *tf.idf* weights are interpreted as probabilities and are combined using the normal rules for negation and for disjunctive or conjunctive combination of sets in an event space. As a result, the inference network model provides a natural interpretation of Boolean operations in probabilistic terms and of the meaning of indexing weights.

The binary nature of the retrieval decision in Boolean systems is frequently cited as a drawback [Cro86,SM83,Sal88]. We can relax our strict interpretation of the probabilistic semantics of the Boolean operators by allowing the number of parents=true to influence our belief. For example, we can choose a value $n \leq c \leq \infty$ and interpret the *and* operator to mean

$$P(Q_{and} = \text{true}|n \text{ parents} = \text{true}) = 1$$

$$P(Q_{and} = \text{true}|k \text{ parents} = \text{true}) = 1 - \frac{n-k}{c}, \quad 0 < k < n$$

$$P(Q_{and} = \text{true}|\text{no parents} = \text{true}) = 0$$

and the *or* operator to mean

$$P(Q_{or} = \text{true}|n \text{ parents} = \text{true}) = 1$$

$$P(Q_{or} = \text{true}|k \text{ parents} = \text{true}) = \frac{k}{c}, \quad 0 < k < n$$

$$P(Q_{or} = \text{true}|\text{no parents} = \text{true}) = 0$$

Since a node implementing the *not* operator has exactly one parent, its interpretation is unchanged. Under this interpretation, when $c = \infty$ the operators have their normal Boolean interpretation. As c decreases, our belief in Q depends increasingly on the number of parents that are true. When $c = n$ the distinction between *and* and *or* has disappeared and the link matrices for both operators are the same. The use of this parent weighting scheme is quite similar to the extended Boolean retrieval or p-norm model [Sal88,SM83]. The two approaches are equivalent when $c = n$ and $p = 1$ and when $c = p = \infty$; the resulting probability and similarity functions are monotonic for $n < c < \infty$ and $1 < p < \infty$.

4.4 Estimating the probabilities

Given the link matrix forms of section 3.4, we now consider the estimates required for the basic model of Figure 1. The only roots in Figure 1 are the document nodes; the prior probability associated with these nodes is set to 1/(collection size). Estimates are required for five different node types: text, representation and query concepts, query, and information need.

Text nodes. Since text nodes are completely dependent upon the parent document node, the estimate is straightforward. Since there is a single parent, a matrix form can be used; t_i is true exactly when d_i is true so

$$L_{\text{text}} = \begin{pmatrix} 1 & 0 \\ 0 & 1 \end{pmatrix}.$$

This matrix form is the inverse of that used for *not*.

Note that the distinction between document and text nodes is not required for the basic model and we often ignore text nodes for clarity. Text nodes are required if we support sharing of text by documents and to support the extended model of section 5 which includes citation links and document clustering. If we allow document nodes to share text nodes, then an *or* matrix is appropriate, t_i is true when any parent is instantiated.

Representation concept nodes. Link matrix forms for representation concepts were discussed in section 3.4. For binary indexing and unweighted terms an *or*-combination can be used. For *tf*, *idf*, or *tf.idf* weights a weighted-sum link matrix is used.

Query concept nodes. As we have seen, previous indexing research can be incorporated directly in the document network. The query network, particularly the links between representation and query concepts is less well understood. Here we are interested in estimating the probabilistic dependence of concepts mentioned in the user's query upon the representation concepts. Most current retrieval models view these two sets of concepts as identical under the assumption that the user knows the set of representation concepts and can formulate queries using the representation concepts directly. Under this assumption, the same link matrix as for text nodes should be used.

Research suggests, however, that the mismatch between query and indexing vocabularies may be a major cause of poor recall [FLGD87]. While our initial implementation is limited to linking query concepts to "nearly" equivalent representation concepts using a weighted-sum combination rule, it would appear that improved estimates of the dependence of query concepts on representation concepts could markedly improve performance. Two areas of research bear directly on improving the quality of these estimates: automatic thesaurus construction and natural language research aimed at extracting concept descriptions from query text, identifying synonymous or related descriptions, and resolving ambiguity.

Query nodes. The dependence of query nodes on the query concepts is more straightforward. For Boolean queries we use the procedure described in section 4.3. For probabilistic queries we use a weighted-sum matrix. In both cases we can adjust link matrix values if we have information about the relative importance of the query concepts.

Information need. The information need can generally be expressed as a small number of queries of different types (Boolean, m-of-n, probabilistic, natural language, ...). These can be combined using a weighted-sum link matrix with weights adjusted to reflect any user judgments about the importance or completeness of the individual queries.

5 Extensions to the basic model

The basic model described in section 3 is limited in at least two respects. First, we have assumed that evidence about a variable establishes its value with certainty. Second, we have represented only a limited number of dependencies between variables. In this section we will see that these limitations can be removed.

5.1 Uncertain evidence

The only use of evidence in the basic model is to assert that a document has been observed ($d_i = true$). During query processing we assert each document true and rank documents

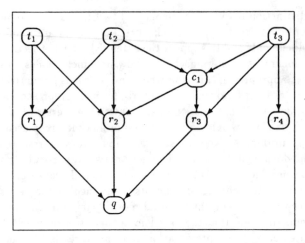

Figure 6: Document clustering model

based on the probability that the information need is met. Evidence is attached to a node a in a Bayesian network by creating a new *evidence* node b as a child of a. This new node b then passes a likelihood vector (both components of a likelihood ratio) to a. Since evidence is expressed in terms of likelihood we are not restricted to the values *true* and *false* but need only specify the likelihood of $a = true$ and $a = false$ given the evidence summarized at b. Thus we can "partially" instantiate nodes in the network when the evidence we have is not sufficient to establish the value of a proposition with certainty. This uncertain evidence can be used to model citation and document cluster information.

Document clustering. A variety of document clustering techniques have been developed for information retrieval [vR79]. Document clustering is generally used to find documents that are similar to a document that is believed relevant under the assumption that similar documents are related to the same queries. Our use of cluster information is somewhat different since we do not retrieve clusters, but we can incorporate cluster information by treating cluster membership as an additional source of evidence about document content. In the fragment shown in Figure 6, document texts t_1, t_2, and t_3 are indexed using representation concepts r_1, r_2, r_3, and r_4. Documents t_2 and t_3 have been identified as part of cluster c_1; both texts are linked to a cluster node and the cluster node is linked to the representation concepts that define the cluster. The cluster node is similar to a conventional cluster representative. Documents t_1 and t_2 are indexed by the same representation concepts (r_1 and r_2) and, if we assume equivalent conditional probabilities, would be ranked equivalently in the absence of the cluster node. With the addition of the cluster node, however, a new representation concept (r_3) is associated with t_2 by virtue of its cluster membership. Assuming that r_3 contributes positively to the belief in q, t_2 would be ranked higher than t_1. In practice, the links between documents and clusters are not represented in the network; evidence is attached to all clusters to which a document has been assigned when that document is instantiated.

Citation and nearest neighbor links. A variety of asymmetric relationships between pairs of documents can also be represented. These relationships are similar to clustering in that they use an assumed similarity between documents to expand the set of representation concepts that can be plausibly associated with a text. They differ in that they are ordered relations defined on pairs of documents rather than an unordered, set membership relationship between documents and clusters.

One example of this kind of relationship is the nearest neighbor link in which a document is linked to those documents judged to be most similar to the original. A second example is based on citations occurring in the text. Citation links may be useful if the type of reference can be determined to allow estimation of the probabilistic dependence between the nodes. Again, these links are not explicitly represented in the network; evidence is attached to a document's nearest neighbors and citation partners when the document is instantiated.

5.2   Additional dependencies

In the basic model, we assume that there are no dependencies between documents, between texts, between representation concepts, between query concepts, or between queries. While independence assumptions like these are common in retrieval models, it is widely recognized that the assumptions are unrealistic. In addition to the document cluster and citation information which is modeled as evidence, we would like to explicitly represent the term dependencies embodied in conventional term clusters and thesauri.

The basic mechanism for representing these dependencies is unchanged, we identify the set of nodes upon which a given node depends and characterize the probability associated with each node conditioned on its immediate parents. When adding these new links, however, we must be careful to preserve the acyclic nature of the inference network. Bayesian inference networks cannot represent cyclic dependencies, in effect evidence attached to any node in the cycle would continually propagate through the network and repeatedly reinforce the original node. In the basic model, no cycles are possible since nodes are only linked to node types that are lower in the DAG. The introduction of these new dependencies makes cycles possible.

Inference networks provide a natural mechanism for representing dependencies between representation concepts and between query concepts. Several automatic clustering techniques produce structures that can be used in an inference network. For example, dependence trees or Chow trees [vR79,Pea88] contain exactly the term dependence information required for an inference network in a form that is guaranteed to be cycle-free.

These networks can also be used to represent probabilistic thesaurus relationships. These relationships extend those of a conventional thesaurus by including conditional probability information. For example, a conventional thesaurus might list "house pet" as a broader term for "dog" and "cat"; the network representation will include a specification of the probability that "house pet" should be assigned given a document containing "dog" or "cat" in isolation, neither term, or both terms.

Synonyms, related terms, and broader terms can be represented by creating a new node to represent the synonym or related term class or the broader term and adding the new node as a child to the relevant representation concept nodes. We will generally prefer to add these nodes as part of the query network since their presence in the document network would represent a computational burden even when not used in a query. Although generally less useful, narrower term relationships can also be represented.

6 Conclusion

The retrieval model presented here provides a framework within which to integrate several document representations and search strategies. We are currently refining the model and conducting experiments to compare search performance based on this model with that of other models and to compare performance of potential representations and search strategies.

Acknowledgments

This work was supported in part by OCLC Online Computer Library Center, by the Air Force Office of Scientific Research under contract 90-0110, and by NSF Grant IRI-8814790.

References

[CH79]   W. Bruce Croft and D. J. Harper. Using probabilistic models of document retrieval without relevance information. *Journal of Documentation*, 35:285–295, 1979.

[Che88] Peter Cheeseman. An inquiry into computer understanding. *Computational Intelligence*, 4:58–66, February 1988. Article is part of a debate between logic and probability schools in AI.

[CK87]   Paul R. Cohen and Rick Kjeldsen. Information retrieval by constrained spreading activation in semantic networks. *Information Processing and Management*, 23(2):255–268, 1987.

[Coh85] Paul R. Cohen. *Heuristic Reasoning About Uncertainty: An Artificial Intelligence Approach*. Pitman, Boston, MA, 1985.

[Coo71] W. S. Cooper. A definition of relevance for information retrieval. *Information Storage and Retrieval*, 7:19–37, 1971.

[Cro80] W. Bruce Croft. A model of cluster searching based on classification. *Information Systems*, 5:189–195, 1980.

[Cro86] W. Bruce Croft. Boolean queries and term dependencies in probabilistic retrieval models. *Journal of the American Society for Information Science*, 37(2):71–77, 1986.

[Cro87] W. Bruce Croft. Approaches to intelligent information retrieval. *Information Processing and Management*, 23(4):249–254, 1987.

[CT87]   W. Bruce Croft and Roger H. Thompson. I^3R: A new approach to the design of document retrieval systems. *Journal of the American Society for Information Science*, 38(6):389–404, November 1987.

[CT89]   W. Bruce Croft and Howard Turtle. A retrieval model incorporating hypertext links. In *Hypertext '89 Proceedings*, pages 213–224, 1989.

[Dem68]   A. P. Dempster. A generalization of Bayesian inference. *Journal of the Royal Statistical Society B*, 30:205–247, 1968.

[Doy79]   John Doyle. A truth maintenance system. *Artificial Intelligence*, 12(3):231–272, 1979.

[FLGD87] G. W. Furnas, T. K. Landauer, L. M. Gomez, and S. T. Dumais. The vocabulary problem in human-system communication. *Communications of the ACM*, 30(11):964–971, November 1987.

[FNL88]   Edward A. Fox, Gary L. Nunn, and Whay C. Lee. Coefficients for combining concept classes in a collection. In *Proceedings of the Eleventh Annual International ACM SIGIR Conference on Research and Development in Information Retrieval*, pages 291–308, New York, NY, 1988. ACM.

[Fuh89]   Norbert Fuhr. Models for retrieval with probabilistic indexing. *Information Processing and Management*, 25(1):55–72, 1989.

[KL86]   Laveen N. Kanal and John F. Lemmer, editors. *Uncertainty in Artificial Intelligence*. North-Holland, Amsterdam, 1986.

[KMT+82] J. Katzer, M. J. McGill, J. A. Tessier, W. Frakes, and P. DasGupta. A study of the overlap among document representations. *Information Technology: Research and Development*, 1:261–274, 1982.

[LK88]   John F. Lemmer and Laveen N. Kanal, editors. *Uncertainty in Artificial Intelligence 2*. North-Holland, Amsterdam, 1988.

[LS88]   S. L. Lauritzen and D. J. Spiegelhalter. Local computations with probabilities on graphical structures and their application to expert systems. *Journal of the Royal Statistical Society B*, 50(2):157–224, 1988.

[MK60]   M. E. Maron and J. L. Kuhns. On relevance, probabilistic indexing and information retrieval. *Journal of the ACM*, 7:216–244, 1960.

[MKN79]   Michael McGill, Mathew Koll, and Terry Noreault. An evaluation of factors affecting document ranking by information retrieval systems. Technical report, Syracuse University, School of Information Studies, 1979. Funded under NSF-IST-78-10454.

[Nil86]   Nils J. Nilsson. Probabilistic logic. *Artificial Intelligence*, 28(1):71–87, 1986.

[OPC86]   Robert N. Oddy, Ruth A. Palmquist, and Margaret A. Crawford. Representation of anomalous states of knowledge in information retrieval. In *Proceedings of the 1986 ASIS Annual Conference*, pages 248–254, 1986.

[Pea88]   Judea Pearl. *Probabilistic Reasoning in Intelligent Systems: Networks of Plausible Inference*. Morgan Kaufmann Publishers, 1988.

[Rob77]   S. E. Robertson. The probability ranking principle in IR. *Journal of Documentation*, 33(4):294–304, December 1977.

[Sal88]   Gerard Salton. A simple blueprint for automatic boolean query processing. *Information Processing and Management*, 24(3):269–280, 1988.

[Sha76]   Glen Shafer. *A Mathematical Theory of Evidence*. Princeton University Press, 1976.

[SM83]   Gerard Salton and Michael J. McGill. *Introduction to Modern Information Retrieval*. McGraw-Hill, 1983.

[Sti75]   K. H. Stirling. The effect of document ranking on retrieval system performance: A search for an optimal ranking rule. *Proceedings of the American Society for Information Science*, 12:105–106, 1975.

[TC89]   Roger H. Thompson and W. Bruce Croft. Support for browsing in an intelligent text retrieval system. *International Journal of Man-Machine Studies*, 30:639–668, 1989.

[TS85]   Richard M. Tong and Daniel Shapiro. Experimental investigations of uncertainty in a rule-based system for information retrieval. *International Journal of Man-Machine Studies*, 22:265–282, 1985.

[vR79]   C. J. van Rijsbergen. *Information Retrieval*. Butterworths, 1979.

[vR86]   C. J. van Rijsbergen. A non-classical logic for information retrieval. *Computer Journal*, 29(6):481–485, 1986.

[Wil73]   Patrick Wilson. Situational relevance. *Information Storage and Retrieval*, 9:457–471, 1973.

[Zad83]   Lotfi A. Zadeh. The role of fuzzy logic in the management of uncertainty in expert systems. *Fuzzy Sets and Systems*, 11:199–228, 1983.

A Retrieval Model based on an Extended Modal Logic and its Application to the RIME Experimental Approach

Yves Chiaramella, Jianyun Nie
Laboratoire IMAG-Génie Informatique
BP 53X - 38041 Grenoble Cedex - France

Abstract:

This paper focuses on the query processing module of RIME, an experimental prototype of an intelligent information retrieval system designed to manage high-precision queries on a corpus of medical reports. Though highly specific this particular corpus is representative of an important class of applications: information retrieval among full-text specialized documents which constitute critical sources of information in several organizations (medicine, law, space industry..). This experience allowed us to design and implement an elaborate model for the semantic content of the documents which is an extension of the Conceptual Dependancy approach.The underlying retrieval model is inspired from the Logic model proposed by C.J. VanRijsbergen, which has been considerably refined using an Extended Modal Logic. After presenting the context of the RIME project, we briefly describe the models designed for the internal representation of medical reports and queries. The main part of the paper is then devoted to the retrieval model and its application to the query processing module of RIME which has a natural language interface. Processing a query involves two main phases: the interpretation which transforms the natural language query into a search expression, and the evaluation phases which retrieves the corresponding medical reports.We focus here on the evaluation phases and show its relationship with the underlying retrieval model. Evaluations from practical experiments are also given, along with indications about current developments of the project.

I. Introduction - the RIME project:

RIME is an experimental prototype of an intelligent information retrieval system able to process high-precision queries on a corpus of medical reports related to radiographic images. This project has been developped in the particular context of a multimedia database environment in which textual data (medical reports) and iconographic data (X-ray pictures) are associated in a one-to-one way. Every medical report describe the observations, and possibly the diagnosis, made by the physician about the patient's disease while analysing a given X-ray picture. A medical report may thus be considered as a kind of indexing document of the associated picture. The main goal of the project is to design a retrieval model and implement a corresponding retrieval system enabling physicians to retrieve this textual data and its associated iconographic data, using natural language queries. A particular feature of the queries is that they may be either very accurate and complex in terms of medical concepts (physicians, surgeons looking for previously observed particular medical cases) or more thematic queries (users looking for broader classes of medical cases). A consequence is that the retrieval model must be more precision-oriented than recall-oriented.

Medical reports are structured, one-page documents written using a natural language the characteristic of which are also important: it is a technical language based on a simple syntax and a mostly technical vocabulary. These particular features allowed us to design and implement an elaborated model to describe the semantic content of the documents, which is an extension of the Conceptual Dependancy approach [Schank]. In sections II and III we present the proposed models for documents and queries. The semantic model used to describe semantic content of the medical reports and the corresponding indexing technique are due to C. Berrut [Berrut89]. We shall briefly present this semantic model in section II in order to facilitate the understanding of this paper which makes intensive reference to it.

Considering the retrieval process which is the main topic of this paper, the underlying retrieval model is inspired from the Logic Model proposed by C.J. VanRijsbergen [Rijs86] and has been considerably refined by J. Nie [Nie88] using an Extended Modal Logic. Section IV below gives the main features of this model in order to help understanding the retrieval process which is presented in section V of the paper. Finally, evaluations from practical experiments are given in section VI, and we conclude with indications about current developments of the project.

II. The Medical Reports Model:

Medical reports are viewed are sets of two kinds of attributes:

- *the external attributes (EXT-ATT)*:: these attributes describe the context of the medical information: date of examination, patient name, physician name.. Most of these attributes correspond to classical database attributes, except for physician's names which may be multivalued. Hence in most cases access to medical reports using these attributes may be based on classical database access techniques.

- *the content attribute (CONT-ATT):* this unique attribute is intended to give a description of the semantic content of the document, according to a semantic model. It corresponds to a *set of Semantic Expressions* (SE) each of them being the interpretation of a sentence of the medical report according to the semantic model.

A medical report (MR) may then be described as below (where [x] denotes a non-empty list of items of type x):

MR ::= [EXT-ATT] CONT-ATT

EXT-ATT ::= (ATT-NAME , att-value)

CONT-ATT ::= [SE]

The semantic model which describes SE is more extensively defined in [Berrut89]. We restrict ourselves to a short presentation of this model here.

Every semantic expression SE may be represented as a binary tree made of two kinds of elements:

- *the terminal nodes:* they correspond to elementary (i.e atomic) concepts in the medical field, such as "lung", "opacity".. . They mainly reflect basic domain knowledge about anatomy and radiology.

- *the non-terminal nodes:* they correspond to three kinds of *operators*, each category having its own semantics:

- the semantic operators: they are binary operators and their name denote a particular *semantic relationship* between the two dependant subtrees, such as "bears-on", "has-for-location",..The model contains a predefined set of such operators. They are noted between square brackets: [bears-on], [has-for-location]..

- the uncertainty operators: they are unary operators which denote the uncertainty of the dependant subtree. There are four of them "t" (for "certain"), "p" (for "possible"), "pf" (for "possibly false", or uncertain) and "f" (for false). For example, [p](cancer) denotes the possibility of a cancer (as part of a diagnosis in this case).

-the boolean operators: they correspond to the binary operators "and" and "or", and are used to reflect conjunctions or disjunctions of events (occurrences of concepts not related by an explicit semantic relationship).

Each semantic expression (possibly reduced to a basic concept) belongs to a *semantic class* which expresses a semantic classification of the concepts in the model. As for the set of basic concepts, the definition of these classes of course depend on the particular application domain. In RIME we shall have classes such as SGN (for "observed sign"), LOC (localization), DIAG (diagnosis)... Semantic classes will always be noted using upper case characters.

Thus if defined using the classical prefixed notation for trees, a semantic expression will always have the following format:

$$\{[op2](se1, se2), C\} \qquad \{[op1](se3), C\} \qquad \{term, C\}$$

where [op2] represents an arbitrary binary operator [op1] an unary operator, se1, se2 and se3 are semantic expressions which constitute the arguments of [op], "term" is a basic concept, and C is the semantic class of the expression. The definition is recursive considering se1, se2 and se3. Of course an equivalent tree representation may be used. Depending on the purpose, we shall either indicate or not the semantic class of each node (concept) for the readability of the figure.

example: the sentence "an opacity affecting probably the lung and the trachea" will be interpreted as follows:

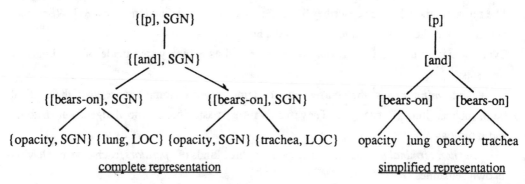

complete representation   simplified representation

This tree reformulates the initial statement in this way: "there is an opacity affecting the lung [and] an opacity affecting the trachea, with certainty [p] (probable)".
Of course any interpretation involves some deformation considering the meaning of the initial natural language sentence: there are neither perfect understanding process nor perfect semantic model for a textual document. In the example above, the given interpretation losses the initial fact that there was seemingly only one opacity observed by the physician.
These trees are defined using a syntax. Hence the set of possible semantic expressions correspond to an *indexing language*. For example RIME contains the two following rules:
(1) SGN ::= [has-for-value](CHARACTER,QUAL-VAL)
(2) SGN ::= [bears-on](SGN,LOC)
These rules are used in the following way. For example if the sentence "lung opacity" is found in a report, the consultation of RIME's dictionary gives the two elementary expressions {lung, LOC} and {opacity, SGN} for these two words. Due to their syntactical relationship in the original sentence, a new concept is derived from the two original concepts of respective semantic classes SGN and LOC, by connecting them with the semantic operator [bears-on].

Rule 2 above then assigns the semantic class SGN (the left side of rule 2) to this new concept, giving the final expression:

{[bears-on]({opacity, SGN}, {lung, LOC}), SGN}

Considering rules involving *semantic operators*, there are two kinds of them in the model which define the way expressions such as {[op]({t1,C1}, {t2, C2}), C3} are built:
- two terms of semantic classes CLASS1 and CLASS2 are connected by a semantic operator, giving a term of a *different* semantic class (CLASS3):

   CLASS3 ::= [op](CLASS1,CLASS2)

   where CLASS1 ≠ CLASS2 ≠ CLASS3

   For example rule 1 above is of this kind. They generate terms of the kind:

   {[op]({t1, CLASS1}, {t2,CLASS2}), CLASS3}

- a term belonging to CLASS1 is connected with a second term by a semantic operator, giving a term of the same class CLASS1:

   CLASS1 ::= [op](CLASS1, CLASS2)

   For example rule 2 above is of this kind. They generate terms of the kind:

   {[op]({t1, **CLASS1**}, {t2,CLASS2}), **CLASS1**}

The second type of rule has interesting properties because the *resulting term has the same semantic class as its first component*. This applies for example to the term {[bears-on]({opacity, SGN}, {lung, LOC}), SGN} given above, which has the same semantic class (SGN) as its component term "opacity". According to the semantic model, the component term can occur everywhere the resulting term can. In other words, the substitution of the resulting term by its first component in a tree does not violate the constraints of the semantic model, because they have the same semantic class. An other property is that the resulting term is more *specific* than the component term ("lung opacity" is more specific than "opacity"). We call this term the *governor* of the resulting term because the resulting term inherits its semantic class. These properties will be used while defining transformation rules for trees in section V below.

An other important fact is that these interpretations have to be *standardized* in some way in order to represent the common meaning of semantically equivalent sentences (paraphrasing), and also to improve the performances of the matching process between semantic expressions and content requirements (see the next section). An aspect of this standardization is that semantic operators always have the lowest level in the trees, then when needed we found boolean and certainty operators at the upper levels, as in te example above.

This process of transforming every sentence of a medical report into such a representation constitutes the indexing process of RIME, which is in this case closely related to natural language understanding techniques (see [Berrut89]).

III. The Query Model:

Because the end users of RIME are non-specialists considering information retrieval, we choosed to design a natural language interface. Syntactically speaking, a query is then a french sentence based on a restricted syntax which has been estimated powerful enough for this particular application. Considering the semantic level, we consider that every query may refer to one or both of the two kinds of documents' attributes (external and content attributes). The processing of a query is then divided in two main phases: the interpretation phase which transforms the natural-language query into a Search Expression (an expression made of search operators and search arguments), and the evaluation phase which executes the search expression on the corpus of medical reports.

A Search Expression (SRE) may then be viewed according to the following syntax which combines boolean expressions of *external requirements* (EXT-REQ), which are requirements about external attribute values of searched documents, and *content requirements* (CONT-REQ) which are requirements about the content attribute of searched documents ({x} denotes a possibly empty list of items of type **x**):

    SRE::= EXT-REQ | CONT-REQ | EXT-REQ and CONT-REQ
    EXT-REQ::= EXT-ATT-COND {BOOL-OP EXT-ATT-COND}
    CONT-REQ::= SE {BOOL-OP SE}

Where BOOL-OP stands for a boolean operator and SE is a semantic expression such as those presented in the previous section. The metasymbol EXT-ATT-COND stands for a classical condition on the value of an external attribute, such as PATIENT-NAME = "Jones", DATE>1987 etc..

If the search expression contains both types of requirements its evaluation involves two phases:

- the evaluation of the external requirement which may be processed using classical database access techniques as far as the attributes are single-valued. This evaluation may be viewed as a preselection of the medical reports using external attributes.

- the evaluation of the content requirement: this implies a matching process between semantic expressions of the documents and the content requirement of the query which will be presented below in section V.

Example: from the query "give me the report number of all medical reports, dated after 1987, concerning lung cancer", we may imagine a SQL-like interpretation as below:

    SELECT report-number FROM medical-report
                WHERE (DATE > 1987) and (TALKS-ABOUT = "lung cancer")

where the DATE clause expresses the external requirement which will have to be matched to the DATE attribute of the documents, and the TALKS-ABOUT clause expresses the content requirement of the query, which will have to be matched to the content attribute of the documents.

IV. The Retrieval Model

In [Rijs86], a new retrieval model is proposed which suggests that the relevance between a document (D) and a query (Q) is determined by the strength P of the implication between D and Q: P(D→Q). Given a document in its initial state, it is often impossible to directly evaluate this implication. In [Nie88], this model is further developped using Modal Logic. Since we have to limit ourselves in this paper we shall give here only a general presentation of what should need otherwise a complete formal presentation. When the direct evaluation (exact match) fails between a document's content and the content requirement of a query, the evaluation consists in transforming the initial document into other related interpretations which may match the query (the *possible worlds* of Modal Logic). If the transformation mechanism can drive the initial document to a *final* state which satisfies the query we may say that the document is *relevant*. An evaluation of the system relevance is also introduced which takes into account the validity of the transformations and the certainty of the asserted facts in the medical reports (remain the uncertainty operators in the semantic model). Hence the classic operators of Modal Logic have had to be extended to cope with RIME's four uncertainty operators.

It is clear however that the relevance measure must be a function of the number and the validity of the transformations which have been carried out and which have changed the original document's content. Given a sequence of transformations from an initial document to a final document satisfying the query, the more the sequence changes the initial document, the less this initial document may be evaluated as relevant by the system. The same observation applies considering the *validity* of each transformation. The key problem is then to determine how much a transformation changes the content. According to our model, this determination is based on what we call the *system's knowledge* (SK) which may be roughly defined as the set of *rules* on which the system relies to infer possible transformations of documents' content and to evaluate their validity. As a consequence we may say that in the retrieval model we evaluate the certainty of $D \rightarrow Q$ in the context of SK, which we note P(D→Q | SK).

In general, this knowledge may be represented by a set of logical implications between terms, such as: (A⇒B,v), which means that when the term A occurs in a document, then the term B implicitly occurs, with the certainty value "v" (which is generally bound within [0,1] or [false,true], or any other *certainty domain*). An other interpretation of this implication is that A is a specific term for B, or that B is a generic term for A with a given *certainty value*.

As a consequence it is necessary to evaluate the implication D→Q that D talks about the *same* subject or a more *specific* subject than Q. Thus if a final document satisfying the query can be obtained by transforming the initial document's content to an *equivalent* or more *generic* (less *specific*) one, then the initial document is *certainly* relevant to the query.

Example: suppose a query limited to the term "database", and a document indexed by the term "deductive database" this document does not match the query. If SK contains the rule:

("deductive database"⇒"database", true), we can transform the document's content into a *more generic* one - "database"- which satisfies the query. The original document may thus be considered as relevant to the query with certainty "true".

But if the transformation leads to a not strictly equivalent or more specific document, then the relevance of the initial document is *uncertain*.

Example: Suppose now the same query as above and an other document indexed by "computer science". In order to match it with the query, its content has to be changed into a *more specific* one - "database"- using an other rule: ("database"⇒"computer science", true). Because "computer science" is a generic term for "database" the relevance of this document will be thus considered as *uncertain*.

Hence given a document and SK, a valid transformation will consist in replacing any part of its content (keyword, semantic expression..) corresponding to the left side of an implication rule of SK, by the right side of the rule: if (A⇒B,v) ∈ SK and if A occurs in D, then replace A by B and assign the uncertainty value "v" to this transformation.

Several rules may be simultaneously applicable, giving different interpretations of the initial document. The set of possible transformations from the initial document may be viewed as a *transformation tree*, the root being the initial document, and the leaves being final documents which can or cannot satisfy the query. Among all paths from the root to the leaves satisfying the query, there is (are) one (or more) transformation path(s) which correspond to the minimal number of changes from the initial document's content, and which may be considered as optimal. This notion of optimal path has in turn to be chosen as a basis for measuring the relevance between the initial document and the query.

V- Application to RIME:

Considering the chosen models for documents and queries, the retrieval process will have to prove the implication between expressions such as:

Q = EXT-REQ and CONT-REQ
and
D = [EXT-ATT] and CONT-ATT

In the general case where the query contains external requirements, it is clear that D→Q is equivalent to:

([EXT-ATT] →EXT-REQ) and (CONT-ATT →CONT-REQ)

The evaluation of the first implication refers to the classical evaluation of boolean expressions of external attributes which can thus be carried on using classical boolean search (based on standard database access techniques for example).

The evaluation of the second implication concerns only the evaluation of the content requirement of the query . According to the retrieval model, this evaluation consists in *transforming the semantic expressions* which constitute the document's content until they match the *content requirement* of the query. In other words, for every semantic expression in a report, the evaluation consists in replacing in the corresponding tree an element A which corresponds to the left side of a rule by the right side of the rule, say B, (A⇒B,v) being a rule of the system's knowledge. If this kind of transformation can drive the initial tree to a final tree which matches the query, then the initial tree is considered as *implying* the query, and the report is considered as relevant, with the uncertainty measure "v".

5.1- The system knowledge of RIME:

RIME's knowledge is a set of implications such as: (A⇒B,v) where v may have the following values: "t" (true), "p" (possible), "pf" (possibly false, or uncertain), and "f" (false), and where terms A and B are semantic expressions of the kind presented in section II. Because the way operators occur in the hierarchy of every expression is standardized (see section II), the matching of subtrees may be evaluated level by level among trees of the same kind (i.e having the same type of operators). This allows us to consider only four basic cases which we shall separately study in the remaining of this section: trees made of semantic operators only, trees made of uncertainty operators (t, p, pf, f) only, trees made of boolean operators (and, or) only, and finally the limit case where trees are reduced to elementary terms.

a). Implication between trees containing semantic operators:
Medical reports provide *assertion*s about medical facts. For example, when the term "opacity" occurs in a medical report, the *existence* of an "opacity" is asserted. When the term "lung opacity" occurs, the existence of an "opacity" is asserted, this fact being in the relationship "[bears-on]" with "lung". Two types of assertions can then be distinguished: the first one concerns the simple notion of *existence*, while the second concerns not only the notion of existence but also the *semantic relationship* with other terms. We call them respectively *existential assertion* and *relational assertion*.
We can then establish two notions of *implication*: when the existence of a term implies the existence of a second term: when the first term *extentially implies* the second (noted ⇒), and when a term *relationally implies* the second term (noted ⇛).
Relatively to trees made of *semantic operators*, we can establish the following implications:
   • Consider a term {[op]({t1,C1}, {t2, C2}), C3}. When this term occurs in a report the existence of the term is asserted and also the existence of "t1" and "t2". For example, when {[bears-on]({"opacity", SGN}, {"lung", LOC}), SGN}

occurs in a report, the report can also be considered as a report on "opacity" or a report on "lung". So {[op]({t1,C1}, {t2, C2}), C3} *extentially implies* {t1, C1} and {t2, C2}, and we have the general rule:

$$({[op]({t1,C1}, {t2, C2}), C3} \Rightarrow {t1,C1},t)$$
$$({[op]({t1,C1}, {t2, C2}), C3} \Rightarrow {t2, C2},t)$$

These implications are certain (with uncertainty value "t").

• When a report asserts a relationship involving a term having a *governor term* (see section II above), it is then implicit that this relationship is also asserted on its governor. In other words, the term relationally *implies* its governor:

$$({[op]({t1,CLASS1}, {t2, CLASS2}), CLASS1} \Rightarrow {t1, CLASS1}, t)$$

An example of this implication is:

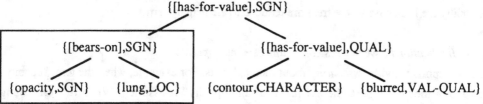

As said in section II, this means that the governor may replace its embedding term because they have the same semantic class. Given the example above, when the following tree occurs in a report:

{[has-for-value],SGN}

{[bears-on],SGN} {[has-for-value],QUAL}

{opacity,SGN} {lung,LOC} {contour,CHARACTER} {blurred,VAL-QUAL}

the following term (obtained by the substitution of "lung opacity" by "opacity") is relationally implied:

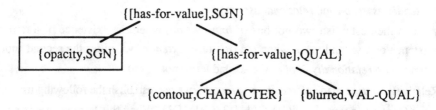

Remark that one cannot replace "lung opacity" by "lung" to transform the initial tree, despite the *existential* implication between "lung opacity" and "lung" (their semantic classes are different).

The key difference between the two kinds of implications is that the existential implication does not take care of the semantic property of terms, whereas the relational one does.

It can be easily shown that the relational implication is stricter than the existential implication. So we have the following property:

$$A \Rightarrow B \text{ if } A \Rrightarrow B$$

b. Implication between trees containing uncertainty operators:

Assertions from medical reports may also be uncertain in sentences such as "the examination shows that a lung cancer is possible". In RIME, four unary uncertainty operators : [t], [p], [pf], [f] are associated to the four uncertainty values "t", "p", "pf" and " f".

The following implication is directly obtained for any certainty operator [cert]:

$$([\text{cert}](\{t, C\}, C\} \Rightarrow \{t, C\}, \text{cert})$$

which means that we may substitute an uncertain term by a certain one by assigning its former uncertainty value to the substitution itself.

c. Implication between trees containing boolean operators

Assertions from medical reports can be linked by boolean operators (and, or). For example, a sentence such as "the lung opacity affecting the front and lower lobes" will be represented as below:

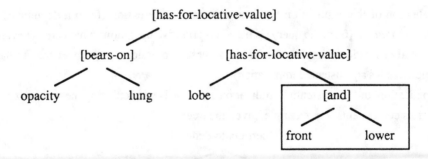

Similarly to classical logic, the implications relatively to boolean operators are the following (note that for each rule, all semantic classes are identical):

$([\text{and}](\{t1, C\}, \{t2, C\}), C\} \Rightarrow \{t1, C\}, t)$ $([\text{and}](\{t1, C\}, \{t2, C\}), C\} \Rightarrow \{t2, C\}, t)$

$(\{t1, C\} \Rightarrow \{[\text{or}](\{t1, C\}, \{t2, C\}), C\}, t)$ $(\{t2, C\} \Rightarrow \{[\text{or}](\{t1, C\}, \{t2, C\}), C\}, t)$

$(\{[\text{or}](\{t1, C\}, \{t2, C\}), C\} \Rightarrow \{t1, C\}, p)$ $(\{[\text{or}](\{t1, C\}, \{t2, C\}), C\} \Rightarrow \{t2, C\}, p)$

The two last implications come from the following hypothesis: if two facts are asserted in a disjunctive expression in a report, it is implicit that the connected facts are not certain, but possible.

In RIME, the set of elementary terms (the basic domain knowledge) is organized in a hierarchical way, expressing classical specificity and genericity relationship among these concepts.

<u>example:</u>

level1	level2	level3
tumor	cancer	sarcoma
	hygroma	
	kyste	polykystosis
	pseudokyst	
	polyp	polyposis

For example, a "sarcoma" is a "cancer" which is a "tumor".

Terms related by this kind of implication are of the *same semantic class* and thus the implication is *relational:*   sarcoma⇒cancer, cancer⇒tumor.

5.2- Transforming a semantic expression to match a semantic requirement:

The evaluation of the implication between a semantic expression (from a document) and a semantic requirement (from the query) is based on primitive operations which are the evaluation of existential or relational implication between these expressions (remember that a relational implication implies an existential implication):

- The application of the existential implication rule consists in replacing the whole expression by one of its components. For example, given the tree:

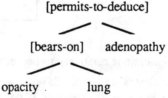

this expression can be transformed into "[bears-on](opacity,lung)" or into "adenopathy". So two different transformations are possible at this state:

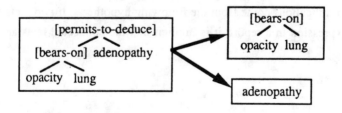

If one of the two obtained expressions exactly matches the query, the transformation is achieved with the certainty value "t" (because the existential implication rule always give "t" as uncertainty value). Otherwise, the expressions have to be transformed again (if not possible the process fails and the expression cannot match the query).

- The application of the relational implication rule consists in replacing the left subtree of the expression by its governor.

Example:

In the above example, there is a relational implication which corresponds to (([bears-on]({opacity, SGN},{lung, LOC}), SGN}≡>{opacity, SGN}, t), the initial tree has thus a third possible transformation:

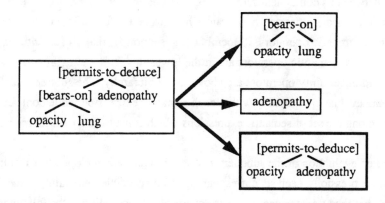

The evaluation process in RIME is based on these tree transformations which are organized in transformation paths. This transformation continues until obtaining all the final trees matching the query expression (success), or until none of the final trees can satisfy the query and none of them can be further transformed (failure). At each step of the process an uncertainty value is given to the corresponding transformation, according to the rule which is applied and the current certainty value of the considered expression. When a transformation path is made of several steps between the initial expression and the final one, we thus obtain a sequence of uncertainty measures (one at each step), of decreasing value from the initial expression to the final one. We may thus define the minimal certainty value of the sequence as the certainty measure of the transformation path. Among the certainty values obtained for all the successful transformation paths, the maximal value is the relevance measure considered for the expression.

5.3 - The evaluation of a content requirement:

Given the content requirement (CR) of a query, every document containing an expression or a set of expressions which exactly match the CR or which implies the CR, is considered as relevant. In other words, the document is relevant when, in an explicit or implicit way the CR *exists* in this document.

Given a document D, its content attribute is a conjunction of semantic expressions. On the other hand, the content requirement is also a boolean expression of semantic expressions. The global evaluation of the content requirement may thus be viewed as the classical evaluation of a boolean query, except that the term matching is much more complex here: it consists in the matching of semantic expressions described above. Moreover the process also handles uncertainty values.

 In this case, the correspondence between a tree and the query is 4-valued ("t","p","pf","f"). The relevance of a document takes the maximal value among the correspondence measures evaluated between its component semantic expressions and the query.

Boolean operators and uncertainty operators have to be evaluated in a different way from the evaluation of semantic operators. Remember (see section II) that all semantic expressions are *standardized*, so semantic operators are at the lowest levels in the expressions while boolean operators and uncertainty operators are above in the hierarchy. The subtrees made of semantic operators are evaluated separately within each semantic expression while boolean operators are evaluated among the set of semantic expressions which constitutes a medical report.

The separated evaluation of the subquery restricted to its semantic operators results in four sets of semantic expressions, each set corresponding to one possible uncertainty value. These sets of expressions are then transformed into four document sets according to the following criterion:

   Given a subquery, the uncertainty value assigned to a report (and hence the report set
   assigned to that report) is the maximal one among those found for its component
expressions.

Defining t-set(A), p-set(A), pf-set(A) and f-set(A) as the four document sets, the boolean operators and the certainty operators are then evaluated as follows:

  - t-set([and](A,B)) = t-set(A) $\cap$ t-set(B)
  p-set([and](A,B)) = p-set(A) $\cap$ p-set(B) $\cup$ (p-set(A) $\cap$ t-set(B)) $\cup$ (p-set(B) $\cap$ t-set(A))
  pf-set([and](A,B)) = (pf-set(A) $\cup$ pf-set(B)) – f-set([and](A,B))
  f-set([and](A,B)) = f-set(A) $\cup$ f-set(B)

  - The evaluations for the operator "or" are similar.
  - The following evaluations about uncertainty operators ([p] and [pf]) are obtained
  intuitively, because there have no equivalent in classical logic:

$$t\text{-set}([p](A)) = p\text{-set}(A)$$
$$p\text{-set}([p](A)) = t\text{-set}(A) \cup pf\text{-set}(A)$$
$$pf\text{-set}([p](A)) = f\text{-set}(A)$$
$$f\text{-set}([p](A)) = \emptyset$$

$$t\text{-set}([pf](A)) = pf\text{-set}(A)$$
$$p\text{-set}([pf](A)) = p\text{-set}(A) \cup f\text{-set}(A)$$
$$pf\text{-set}([pf](A)) = t\text{-set}(A)$$
$$f\text{-set}([pf](A)) = \emptyset$$

$$t\text{-set}([f](A)) = f\text{-set}(A)$$
$$p\text{-set}([f](A)) = pf\text{-set}(A)$$
$$pf\text{-set}([f](A)) = p\text{-set}(A)$$
$$f\text{-set}([f](A)) = t\text{-set}(A)$$

Four report sets are thus built from a query, which give a final relevance measure to each obtained report according to the four-valued uncertainty measure of the model.

5.4 - optimisation of the evaluation process:

It is clear that the above transformation and uncertainty evaluation process is very time consuming because every semantic expression of every medical report has to be matched to the content requirement. Some optimization must obviously be designed in order to speed up the process and make it applicable to real-size corpuses. We have already said in section III that the external requirement of a query (if existing) may be used as a preselection criterion before the evaluation of the content requirement. The key problem is now to limitate the number of evaluations within these preselected documents. We present below two ways for implementing this secondary optimization which have proved very efficient in our experimentations.

a) preselection on the content attribute:

An other kind of preselection may be processed from the content requirement of a query. Given an expression A of the content requirement, a necessary condition for any semantic expression for document expressions to match A is that all elementary terms of A must *explicitely* or *implicitely* occur in the semantic expression. For example, considering a query about "lung tumor", every matching expression will have either to contain the elementary terms "lung" and "tumor", or to contain terms which logically imply these concepts. A preselection base don this condition is then suggested in the following way:

Suppose TERM(B)={b1,...,bn} to be the set of the elementary terms of a semantic expression B, and TERM(A)={a1,...,am} to be the equivalent for the query expression A. We can then express the preselection condition as:

$((a1 \in TERM(B)$ or $(\exists b \in TERM(B) \mid b \Rightarrow a1))$ and $((a2 \in TERM(B)$ or $(\exists b \in TERM(B) \mid b \Rightarrow a2))$ and ...and $((am \in TERM(B)$ or $(\exists b \in TERM(B) \mid b \Rightarrow am))$

<u>Example:</u> Given A=[bears-on](tumor, lung), every document with a content attribute B satisfying the following condition will be preselected:

((tumor∈ TERM(B) or (∃b∈ TERM(B) | b⟹tumor))

and ((lung∈ TERM(B) or (∃b∈ TERM(B) | b⟹lung))

This condition may be implemented using a classical database query except for the second arguments of the "or" operators which imply a deduction on the query's terms. A deductive step has thus to be processed prior to the formulation of the database query, which finds all the possible terms "b" of the condition and which will allow the formulation of the complete query. This process of course uses the system's knowledge as presented in the sections above.

The formal expression (∃b∈ TERM(B) | b⟹a) is implemented using a disjunctive expression of conditions, one for every term "b" which implies "a" (where b⟹a is found in the knowledge base):

(∃b∈ TERM(B) | b⟹a)⟺(t1∈ TERM(B)) or ....or (tn∈ TERM(B)) where t1⟹a,...,tn⟹a

<u>Example:</u>

Suppose that TERM(expr) is the set of elementary terms in an semantic expression "expr", we can express the condition for the above example as:

(("lung"∈ TERM(expr)) and ["tumor"∈ TERM(expr) or "xanthoma" ∈ TERM(expr) or "hygroma" ∈ TERM(expr) or...or "teratoma" ∈ TERM(expr)]

The last member of this condition is the result of the deductive preprocessing which succeeded in expanding the term "tumor" to a set of implying terms extracted from the knowledge base.

As described above, the implication relations between elementary terms are defined hierarchically in the knowledge base which, in RIME, has at most four levels in the hierarchy.

This condition is implementable using a standard SQL query for example:

SELECT report-number FROM medical-report MR

WHERE

("lung" IN TERM(MR))

and

("tumor" IN TERM(MR)

or "xanthome" IN TERM(tree) or "hygroma" IN TERM(tree) or...or "teratoma" IN TERM(tree))

Given the optimal performances of the database selection, this operation improves the verification process despite the apparent complexity of the query.

b) compatibility test on semantic classes:

Considering two semantic expressions A and B the consideration of their semantic class may help in deciding wether there is a possibility to demonstrate that A implies B or not. If the impossibility may be stated this allows to substancially limitate the expansion of the solution space by pruning branches of the corresponding tree. The semantic model presented in section II defines constraints about the construction of semantic expressions. These rules may also be seen in the following way: a term of a given semantic class (the left side of the rule) can be formed using component terms belonging to given semantic classes (the right side of the rule).

<u>example:</u>
Rule 1 in section II asserts that a term of class SGN (sign) can be built using a term of class CHARACTER (physical character) and a term of class QUAL-VAL (qualitative value). If we consider the entire set of rules having SGN as their left side, we observe that LESION for example never occurs in the right side of these rules. This means that a semantic expression of class SGN cannot contain a subexpression of class LESION. So if a query concerns a LESION and if the current semantic expression examined if of class SIGN it is not worth to continue the derivation process in order to try to establish a semantic equivalence which is impossible.

This property may thus be used to foresee the possibility or impossibility of a match between two semantic expressions. Analysing in this way the set of all the rules we can define a *compatibility relation* CR among the predefined semantic classes which is defined as below:

(C1,C2) ∈ CR if a term of class C1 may be built using a term of class C2.

<u>example:</u> according to the semantic model of RIME the following elements belong to CR:
(SGN, CHARACTER), (SGN, QUAL-VAL)
Considering this relation, the compatibility test becomes obvious: given a content requirement A of class C1, all semantic expressions B of class C' such as (C, C') ∉ CR cannot match with A.
Only if (C, C') ∈ CR shall we continue the matching process between A and B using the procedure described above.

VI. Implementation and conclusion:

The above evaluation strategy has been implemented in a UNIX environment using C-PROLOG on a Gould machine. The test corpus was made of 36 medical reports amounting to about 300 semantic expressions. At the moment the prototype does not integrate a real database facility to store the medical reports and efficiently retrieve them using external attributes. This will be done in a next step of the project, the planned database system being ORACLE. So every storage and access facility have been coded in PROLOG for simulation purposes, which is of course not realistic considering full-scale applications (up to tens of thousands medical reports). Our main goal was of course to validate the global strategy of successive preselections.

It should be clear that the most important aspect considering performances concerns the evaluation of content requirements. We have run a set of 200 queries having only content requirements on this small corpus and, as expected, we have obtained very good precision ratios.

The response times that we effectively obtained are summarized in the figure below:

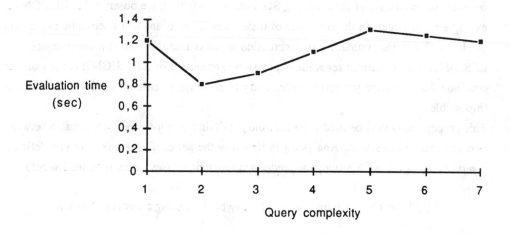

From these preliminary results the following comments can be given:
- the cost of the evaluation does not increase proportionally to the complexity of the query (measured considering the number of elementary terms in the query). This is due to the preselection on terms: the more a query is complex the more the preselection is effective, and the less semantic expressions are submitted to the matching process. The total cost is thus a compromise between the cost of the preselection and the cost of the matching process.
- what was more surprising was the average response time of one second that we effectively obtained for a query despite the simulation of the database operations in PROLOG. If we accept that the response time is proportional to the number of documents, then the evaluation of a content requirement using our experimental system on a corpus of 10,000 medical reports

would require about 5 minutes. Considering that in the next version of RIME term preselection will be processed using ORACLE we consider that this performance is quite encouraging.

- aside improvements about the implementation further work has to be done to improve the deductive capabilities of the prototype, i.e to integrate deductive knowledge (which is in fact expert knowledge) such as: "a lung opacity the diameter of which is greater than 10mm is a pathologic opacity". It seems clear that this kind of knowledge is an extension of the implication between elementary terms which is used in the prototype. It will meanwhile be used in the same way: from a query involving "pathologic opacity", we shall be able to retrieve medical reports containing observations such as "lung opacity the diameter of which is greater than 10mm".

BIBLIOGRAPHY

[Berrut88] C. Berrut *Une méthode d'indexation fondée sur l'analyse sémantique de documents spécialisés - Le prototype RIME et son application à un corpus médical"*
PhD thesis - Université Joseph Fourier, December 1989.

[Ber-Chia89] C. Berrut, Y. Chiaramella *Indexing medical reports in amultimedia environment - The RIME experimental approach*
Proc. of the 12th ACM-SIGIR International Conference on Research and Development in Information Retrieval. Boston, June 1989.

[Deo-Rag88] J.S. Deogun, V.V. Raghavan *Integration of information retrieval and database management systems*
Information Processing and Management, Vol. 24, N° 3, 1988.

[Hug-Gre68] G. Hugues, M. Gresswill *An Introduction to Modal Logic*
Methuen, 1968

[Minker88] J. Minker *Perspectives in deductive databases*
Journal of Logic Programming, Vol. 5, pp 33-60, 1988

[Nie88] J. Nie *An outline of a general model for information retrieval*
Proc of the 11th ACM-SIGIR International Conference on Research and Development in Information Retrieval. Grenoble, June 1988.

[Sal-McG83] G. Salton, M.J. McGill *Introduction to Modern Information Retrieval*
International Student Edition, 1983

[Schank80] R. Schank *Language and memory*
Cognitive Science, Vol 4, pp 243-284, 1980

[Rijsbergen86] C. J. VanRijsbergen *A non classical logic for information retrieval*
Computer Journal, Vol. 29, N° 6, 1986.

Probabilistic Document Indexing from Relevance Feedback Data

Norbert Fuhr
TH Darmstadt
Darmstadt
West Germany

Chris Buckley *
Cornell University
Ithaca, NY
USA

Abstract

Based on the binary independence indexing model, we apply three new concepts for probabilistic document indexing from relevance feedback data:

1. Abstraction from specific terms and documents, which overcomes the restriction of limited relevance information for parameter estimation.

2. Flexibility of the representation, which allows the integration of new text analysis and knowledge-based methods in our approach as well as the consideration of more complex document structures or different types of terms (e.g. single words and noun phrases).

3. Probabilistic learning or classification methods for the estimation of the indexing weights making better use of the available relevance information.

We give experimental results for five test collections which show improvements over other indexing methods.

1 Introduction

Document indexing is the task of assigning terms to documents for retrieval purposes. In an early paper on probabilistic retrieval [Maron & Kuhns 60], an indexing model was developed based on the assumption that a document should be assigned those terms that are used by queries to which the document is relevant. With this model, the notion of weighted indexing (instead of binary indexing), that is the weighting of the index terms w.r.t. the document, was given a theoretical justification in terms of probabilities. In [Fuhr 89a], this approach is generalized to all models of probabilistic indexing by introducing the concept of "correctness" as the event to which the probabilities relate.

The Maron and Kuhns model assumes that the probabilistic indexing weights for a document can be estimated on the basis of relevance information from a number of queries w.r.t. the specific document. However, in real applications there is hardly ever enough relevance information for a specific document available in order to estimate the required probabilities. For this reason, retrospective experiments based on this model (or related ones) might show its feasibility [Kwok 89] [Gordon 88], but are of little value with regard to real applications. The model described in [Kwok 86] overcomes this problem by regarding document components as units to which the index term weights relate to; however, experimental evaluations showed that this model is inferior to non-probabilistic indexing approaches [Kwok & Kuan 88]. A different model for using probabilistic indexing weights in retrieval is described in [Robertson et al. 81] as the "2-Poisson-Independence" model, but also

---

*This study was supported in part by the National Science Foundation under grant IRI 87-02735

---

had little success (mainly because of parameter estimation problems). In contrast to these results, the approaches developed in [Croft 81] [Croft 83] [Wong & Yao 89] show improvements over binary indexing; however, these models lack an explicit notion of an event to which the probabilistic weights relate.

In this paper, we present a radically different approach to probabilistic indexing. We introduce the concept of "relevance description" as an abstraction from specific term-document relationships. As different term-document pairs may have the same relevance description, we overcome the problems of parameter estimation mentioned above by estimating probabilities for relevance descriptions instead of specific term-document pairs. Furthermore, this concept is flexible w.r.t. the representation of documents. For the computation of the indexing weights, we use probabilistic classification procedures instead of simple estimation schemes.

In the following, we first give a brief introduction to the binary independence indexing model, which forms the theoretical justification for our probabilistic indexing weights. Then we describe the basic concepts and procedures of our indexing approach. Section 4 outlines the test setting and the parameters investigated in our experiments, followed by the presentation of the experimental results in section 5.

2 The binary independence indexing model

The binary independence indexing model described in the following is based on the indexing model from [Maron & Kuhns 60] (see also [Fuhr 89a]).

Let $\underline{Q} = \{\underline{q}_1, \underline{q}_2, \underline{q}_3, \ldots\}$ denote the set of queries, where a query $\underline{q}_k$ is regarded as being unique, that is, two requests submitted to an IR system at different times are always treated as different queries. The same approach is taken in the derivation of the "unified model" [Robertson et al. 82], where a single query $\underline{q}_k$ is termed an "individual use". With $\underline{D} = \{\underline{d}_1, \underline{d}_2, \underline{d}_3, \ldots\}$ denoting the set of documents in a collection, the event space of the BII model is $\underline{Q} \times \underline{D}$. As in any probabilistic model the probabilities relate to representations of documents and queries instead to the objects itself (see [Fuhr 89b]), let $Q = \{q_1, q_2, q_3, \ldots\}$ and $D = \{d_1, d_2, d_3, \ldots\}$ denote the corresponding sets of representations of queries and documents. (In the unified model, the set of queries having the same query representation q_k is called the "class of similar uses"). In the case of the BII model, query representations are sets of terms. As a consequence, the BII model will yield the same ranking for two different queries which use the same set of terms. With $T = \{t_1, \ldots, t_n\}$ as the set of index terms in our collection, the query representation of q_k of a query $\underline{q}_k$ is a subset $q_k^T \subset T$. Below, we will also use a binary vector $\vec{x}_k = (x_{k_1}, \ldots, x_{k_n})$ instead of q_k^T, where $x_{k_i} = 1$, if $t_i \in q_k^T$, and $x_{k_i} = 0$ otherwise. The document representation is not further specified in the BII model, and below we will show that this is a major advantage of this model. In the following, we will assume that there exists a set $d_m^T \subset T$ of terms which are to be given weights w.r.t. the document. For brevity, we will call d_m^T "the set of terms occurring in the document" in the following, although the model also can be applied in situations where the elements of d_m^T are derived from the document text with the help of a dictionary or knowledge base (see e.g. [Fuhr 89a]). Let us further assume that we have a binary relevance scale $\Re = \{R, \overline{R}\}$ denoting relevant/non-relevant query-document relationships. Then each element $(\underline{q}_k, \underline{d}_m)$ of the event space has associated with it the sets q_k^T, d_m^T and a relevance judgement $r_{km} = r(\underline{q}_k, \underline{d}_m) \in \Re$.

The BII model now seeks for an estimate of the probability $P(R|q_k, d_m) = P(R|\vec{x}_k, d_m)$ that a document with the representation d_m will be judged relevant w.r.t. a query with the representation $q_k = q_k^T$. Applying Bayes' theorem, we first get

$$P(R|\vec{x}_k, d_m) = P(R|d_m) \cdot \frac{P(\vec{x}_k|R, d_m)}{P(\vec{x}_k|d_m)} \tag{1}$$

Here $P(R|d_m)$ is the probability that document d_m will be judged relevant to an arbitrary request. $P(\vec{x}_k|R, d_m)$ is the probability that d_m will be relevant to a query with representation $\vec{x}_k$, and $P(\vec{x}_k|d_m)$ is the probability that such a query will be submitted to the system.

Regarding the restricted event space consisting of all documents with the same representation d_m and all queries in the collection, first two independence assumptions are made:

- The distribution of terms in all queries is independent:

$$P(\vec{x}_k|d_m) = \prod_{i=1}^{n} P(x_{k_i}|d_m)$$

- The distribution of terms in all queries to which a document with representation d_m is relevant is independent:

$$P(\vec{x}_k|R, d_m) = \prod_{i=1}^{n} P(x_{k_i}|R, d_m)$$

With these assumptions, (1) can be transformed into

$$
\begin{aligned}
P(R|\vec{x}_k, d_m) &= P(R|d_m) \cdot \prod_{i=1}^{n} \frac{P(x_{k_i}|R, d_m)}{P(x_{k_i}|d_m)} \\
&= P(R|d_m) \cdot \prod_{x_{k_i}=1} \frac{P(x_{k_i}=1|R, d_m)}{P(x_{k_i}=1|d_m)} \prod_{x_{k_i}=0} \frac{P(x_{k_i}=0|R, d_m)}{P(x_{k_i}=0|d_m)}
\end{aligned}
\tag{2}
$$

Now we make an additional simplifying assumption that is also used in [Maron & Kuhns 60]:

- The relevance of a document with representation d_m with respect to a query q_k depends only on the terms from q_k^T, and not on other terms.

This assumption means that the last product in formula (2) has the value 1 and thus it can be omitted. We can transform the elements of the first product by using the relationship

$$\frac{P(x_{k_i}=1|R, d_m)}{P(x_{k_i}=1|d_m)} = \frac{P(R|x_{k_i}=1, d_m)}{P(R|d_m)} = \frac{P(R|t_i, d_m)}{P(R|d_m)}$$

Here $P(R|t_i, d_m)$ is the probabilistic index term weight of t_i w.r.t. d_m, the probability that document d_m will be judged relevant to an arbitrary query, given that it contains t_i. From our model, it follows that d_m^T should contain at least those terms from T for which $P(R|t_i, d_m) \neq P(R|d_m)$. Assuming that $P(R|t_i, d_m) = P(R|d_m)$ for all $t_i \notin d_m^T$, we get the final BII formula

$$P(R|q_k, d_m) = P(R|d_m) \prod_{t_i \in q_k^T \cap d_m^T} \frac{P(R|t_i, d_m)}{P(R|d_m)}. \tag{3}$$

In this form it is nearly impossible to apply the BII model, because there hardly will be enough relevance information available to estimate the probabilities $P(R|t_i, d_m)$ for specific term-document pairs. All attempts in this direction are doomed to fail ([Maron 83] [Kwok 89]).

3   New indexing concepts

The basic ideas for our new approach stem from the Darmstadt Indexing Approach (DIA) [Fuhr 89a] [Biebricher et al. 88]. This approach has been developed for automatic indexing with a prescribed indexing vocabulary. We will show how the concepts developed within the DIA can be applied to all kinds of probabilistic indexing.

In the DIA, the indexing task is subdivided in a description step and a decision step. First, attribute values of the term t_i, the document d_m and their relationship are collected in the *relevance description* $x(t_i, d_m)$. Our approach makes no additional assumptions about the choice of the attributes and the structure of x. So the concrete definition of relevance descriptions can be adapted to the specific application context. Examples for possible elements of x are

- dictionary information about t_i, e.g. its inverse document frequency,

- parameters describing d_m, e.g. its length or the number of different terms in it,

- information about the *form of occurrence* of t_i in d_m (see [Fuhr 89a]), e.g. the parts of the document in which t_i occurs (title vs. abstract), the within-document-frequency of t_i in d_m, or in the case of t_i being a noun phrase, the word distance in d_m between the first and the last component of t_i.

In the decision step, a probabilistic index term weight based on this data is assigned. This means that we estimate instead of $P(R|t_i, d_m)$ the probability $P(R|x(t_i, d_m))$. In the former case, we would have to regard a single document d_m with respect to all queries which contain t_i in order to estimate $P(R|t_i, d_m)$. Now we regard the set of all query-document pairs in which the same relevance description x occurs. Here the probability $P(R|x(t_i, d_m))$ is the probability that a document will be judged relevant to an arbitrary query, given that one of the document's index terms which also occurs in the query has the relevance description x.

There are two advantages from the introduction of the concept of relevance description:

- By abstracting from specific document-term pairs, we do not need relevance information about the specific document d_m or the specific term t_i for the estimation of $P(R|x(t_i, d_m))$. According to the definition of the relevance description, document-term pairs with different documents or terms can be mapped onto the same relevance description. For this reason we can use relevance information from other documents or even from queries q_k with $t_i \not\in q_k^T$ for the estimation of $P(R|x(t_i, d_m))$, too. This is a major improvement over other probabilistic IR models, which yield either document- or query-specific estimates. These models can only use the relevance information that is available for the specific document (query), and no information about other documents (queries) is considered by these models. In our approach, the amount of relevance data that is available for the estimation of a specific indexing weight is not restricted by the number of queries for the specific document (or documents for the specific query) for which we have relevance information. In a system running an application, the amount of relevance data from which the indexing weights are computed will always increase and therefore improve the probability estimates.

- Relevance descriptions can be defined for different forms of representation. Most other probabilistic IR models are based on a specific form of representation of documents or queries, and for every new form of representation, a different model has to be developed. The independence of our approach from a specific form of representation offers the following possibilities:

  - The representations can be adapted to the amount of relevance information that is currently available: The more data we have, the more detailed we can choose our representations.

- We can consider new forms of representations that are based on techniques from artificial intelligence or computational linguistics. Now the restricted view of regarding a document as a set of terms with multiple occurrences can be abandoned (some concepts for a more detailed document representation are described in [Fuhr 89a]). On the other hand, our approach provides a solid theoretical background and an easy-to-apply method for the effective integration of these new types of representation in IR.

- We can develop relevance descriptions for different types of terms or documents. Several authors have investigated the benefit of using noun phrases in addition to single words as index terms [Salton et al. 75], [Croft 86], [Smeaton 86], [Fagan 87], [Fagan 89]. However, none of them could devise a theoretical basis for the computation of document-oriented probabilistic index term weights for this new type of terms. The probabilistic foundation of our approach gives us a kind of objective weighting scheme for all types of terms. In a similar way, one could differentiate between several types of documents that are stored in the same database. This possibility of handling heterogeneous document collections becomes important in new application areas of IR systems, e.g. in the office environment.

In the decision step, estimates of the probabilistic index term weights $P(R|t_i, d_m)$ are computed. These estimates are derived from a learning example $L \subset \underline{Q} \times \underline{D} \times \Re$ of query-document pairs for which we have relevance judgements, so $L = \{(\underline{q}_k, \underline{d}_m, r_{km})\}$. By forming relevance descriptions for the terms common to query and document for every query-document pair in L, we get a multi-set of relevance descriptions with relevance judgements $L^x = [(x(t_i, d_m), r_{km})|t_i \in q_k^T \cap d_m^T \wedge (\underline{q}_k, \underline{d}_m, r_{km}) \in L]$. This set with multiple occurrences of elements forms the basis for the estimation of the probabilistic index term weights. However, there is a minor problem with the definition of the event space in the probability estimation process: According to the definition of the BII model, a single event is a query-document pair, so all query-document pairs should be equiprobable. We will denote this event space by E_{BII} in the following. On the other hand, the definition of L^x suggests a different event space E_x in which the triples (query, document, term) are equiprobable events. As different query-document pairs will have different numbers of relevance descriptions, it is obvious that the equiprobability assumption on L implies non-equiprobability on L^x. So there is an error in using E_x instead of E_{BII}. However, the choice of E_x eases the process of probability estimation (see below), therefore we will regard both definitions in the following and investigate whether this difference has any influence on the experimental results.

Following the concepts of other probabilistic IR models, we would estimate the probability $P(R|x(t_i, d_m))$ as the relative frequency from those elements of L^x that have the same relevance description (in the case of E_x). (Attributes with continous values would have to be discretized for this purpose, see e.g. [Wong & Chiu 87]). As a simple example, assume that the relevance description consists of two elements defined as

$$x_1 = \begin{cases} 1, & \text{if } t_i \text{ occurs in the title of } d_m \\ 0, & \text{otherwise} \end{cases}$$

$$x_2 = \text{number of occurrences of } t_i \text{ in } d_m.$$

Furthermore, assume that we have relevance information about two query-document pairs as shown in table 1. From this table, we can estimate $P(R|(0, 1)) = \frac{2}{3}$ by using E_x and $P(R|(0, 1)) = \frac{1}{2}$ based on E_{BII}

Now, the second important concept of the DIA comes into play: It is the task of an *indexing function* $e(x(t_i, d_m))$ to estimate the probabilities $P(R|x(t_i, d_m))$. As indexing functions, different probabilistic classification (or learning) algorithms can be applied. The general advantage of these probabilistic algorithms over simple estimation from relative frequencies is that they yield better estimates, because they use additional (plausible) assumptions about the indexing function.

query	document	r_{km}	term	x
q_1	d_1	R	t_1	(0,1)
			t_2	(0,1)
			t_3	(1,2)
q_2	d_2	$\overline{R}$	t_1	(0,2)
			t_4	(0,1)

Table 1: Example for simple estimation of indexing weights

Within the application of the DIA for indexing with a controlled vocabulary, we have investigated several probabilistic classification algorithms as indexing functions. (Most of these algorithms are restricted to a vector form $\vec{x}$ of the relevance description):

- The so-called Boolean approach developed by Lustig [Beinke-Geiser et al. 86] exploits prior knowledge about the relationship between single elements of the relevance description x and the corresponding probability $P(R|x)$ for the development of a discrete indexing function.

- The probabilistic learning algorithm ID3 developed by Quinlan [Quinlan 86] seeks for significant components of $\vec{x}$ that form a probabilistic classification tree [Faißt 90].

- By assuming only pair-wise dependencies among the components of $\vec{x}$, one can apply the tree dependence model [Chow & Liu 68] [Rijsbergen 77] as indexing function [Tietze 89].

- Using logistic regression [Freeman 87] the indexing function yields $e(\vec{x}) = \frac{exp(\vec{a}^T \cdot \vec{x})}{1+exp(\vec{a}^T \cdot \vec{x})}$, where $\vec{a}$ is a coefficient vector that is estimated based on the maximum likelihood method [Pfeifer 90].

- In this paper, we will use least square polynomials (LSP) [Knorz 83] [Fuhr 89a] as indexing functions. This method is described in more detail in the following.

For the LSP approach, we first have to choose the class of polynomials from which the indexing function is to be selected. Based on the relevance description in vector form $\vec{x}$, a polynomial structure

$$\vec{v}(\vec{x}) = (1, x_1, x_2, \ldots, x_N, x_1^2, x_1 x_2, \ldots)$$

has to be defined (where N denotes the number of dimensions of $\vec{x}$). Then our indexing function yields $e(\vec{x}) = \vec{a}^T \cdot \vec{v}(\vec{x})$, where $\vec{a}$ is the coefficient vector to be estimated.

Let $y(q_k, d_m) = y_{km}$ denote a class variable for each element of L with

$$y_{km} = \begin{cases} 1 & \text{if } r_{km} = R \\ 0 & \text{else} \end{cases}$$

Then the coefficient vector $\vec{a}$ is estimated such that it minimizes the squared error

$$E((y - \vec{a}^T \cdot \vec{v}(\vec{x}))^2).$$

Here E(.) denotes the expectation based on a uniform distribution within E_x or E_{BII}, respectively. $\vec{a}$ can be computed by solving the linear equation system [Fuhr 89a]

$$E(\vec{v} \cdot \vec{v}^T) \cdot \vec{a} = E(\vec{v} \cdot y). \tag{4}$$

As an approximation for the expectations, the corresponding arithmetic means from the learning sample are taken. The momental matrix M which contains both sides of the equation system (4) is computed according to the underlying event space:

- In the case of E_{BII}, we have

$$M_{BII} = \frac{1}{|L|} \sum_{(\underline{q}_k, \underline{d}_m, r_{km}) \in L} \frac{1}{|q_k^T \cap d_m^T|} \sum_{t_i \in q_k^T \cap d_m^T} (\vec{v}_{im} \cdot \vec{v}_{im}^T, \vec{v}_{im} \cdot y_{km})$$

where $\vec{v}_{im} = \vec{v}(\vec{x}(t_i, d_m))$.

- For the event space E_x, the matrix M_x is computed as

$$M_x = \frac{1}{|L^x|} \sum_{(x_{im}, r_{km}) \in L^x} (\vec{v}_{im} \cdot \vec{v}_{im}^T, \vec{v}_{im} \cdot y_{km})$$

The momental matrix M can then be solved to yield the coefficient vector $\vec{a}$.

For most of the experiments described here, we used a relevance description of four elements and a polynomial structure $\vec{v}(\vec{x})$ of length five (i.e. an additional constant for a linear function). So we had to compute five coefficients $a_1, \ldots, a_5$. Each of these parameters is estimated for a collection rather than a particular query term (as in conventional probabilistic retrieval), and is therefore based on much more evidence. In our experiments, the smallest learning sample L has about 400 elements. In comparison, in conventional probabilistic retrieval, a typical feedback query might be 20 terms long, and thus you must estimate 40 probabilistic parameters, each one based on perhaps 15 elements. On the other hand, our approach considers interdependencies between all the parameters, and other experiments [Knorz 83] [Fuhr 88] have shown that we need about 50–100 elements per parameter in order to achieve reliable estimates.

4   Test setting

Some experiments with a preliminary version of our approach in combination with controlled vocabulary indexing have been described in [Fuhr 88, pp. 146-150]. In this paper, we apply our approach to the task of free term indexing and compare it with the standard SMART indexing procedures as described in [Salton & Buckley 88]. We use the same representation of queries and documents as the SMART approach here. For this reason, our evaluation should be regarded as a starting point for further experiments in which improved representations of documents (e.g. with noun phrases as index terms) are considered.

For our experiments, we used the five experimental collections shown in table 2. In order to perform predictive experiments, the set of queries of each collection was split into halves. Because of the limited number of queries in our collections, a random sampling technique might have split the queries into two very different samples; therefore we used the number of relevant documents for a query as a criterion to get two disjoint, but similar query sets for each collection. Table 2 shows for both sets the number of queries and the average number of terms as well as the average number of relevant documents per query. From these two query sets, we used one for the estimation of the probabilistic indexing function, which is called learning sample in the following. With the second set, called test sample below, only predictive retrieval runs were performed, that is, no relevance information from this set has been used for the estimation of the indexing function. In additional retrospective experiments the learning sample was used for retrieval runs, too.

Besides the choice of the query set, we also had to decide which documents should be considered in the learning set L. In our experiments, we investigated two possibilities:

- Full relevance information: All documents retrieved for the queries from the learning sample are considered. A document d_m is retrieved with respect to a query q_k if $d_m^T \cap q_k^T \neq \emptyset$.

collection	CACM	CISI	CRAN	INSPEC	NPL
#documents	3204	1460	1398	12684	11429
#learning queries	26	38	113	39	47
#test queries	26	38	112	38	46
avg. length learning	11.1	25.7	9.1	15.8	7.2
avg. length test	10.5	19.9	9.2	15.8	7.1
avg. rels. learning	14.8	39.8	8.3	33.2	22.8
avg. rels. test	15.8	42.1	8.1	32.8	22.0

Table 2: Collections used for experiments

- Top 15 documents: Only the top 15 documents for each query (by applying the retrieval function ϱ_{tfidf} with $tf \times idf$ indexing weights, see below) are included in L.

The first variant follows from the BII model which is based on the event space $|Q| \times |D|$; the additional assumptions restrict this event space to a set of all query-document pairs which have at least one term in common. The second case is more realistic for applications, because mostly a user will only judge the top ranking documents.

For the development of the LSP indexing functions, we first had to define a relevance description $\vec{x}$. Here we consider only information that is also used in the standard SMART indexing procedures [Salton & Buckley 88], which are based on the following parameters:

$$
\begin{aligned}
tf_{mi}: &\quad \text{within-document frequency (wdf) of } t_i \text{ in } d_m. \\
max\,tf_m: &\quad \text{maximum wdf } tf_{mi} \text{ of all terms } t_i \in d_m^T. \\
n_i: &\quad \text{number of documents in which } t_i \text{ occurs.} \\
|\underline{D}|: &\quad \text{number of documents in the collection.} \\
|d_m^T|: &\quad \text{number of different terms in } d_m.
\end{aligned}
$$

With these parameters, we defined the components of the relevance description:

$$
\begin{aligned}
x_1 &= tf_{mi} \\
x_2 &= 1/max\,tf_m \\
x_3 &= \log(n_i/|\underline{D}|) \\
x_4 &= \log|d_m^T|
\end{aligned}
$$

Based on this relevance description, three different indexing functions e_L, e_Q and e_{tfidf} were developed by defining the polynomial structures

$$
\begin{aligned}
\vec{v}_L &= (1, x_1, x_2, x_3, x_4) \\
\vec{v}_Q &= (1, x_1, x_2, x_3, x_4, x_1^2, x_1x_2, x_1x_3, x_1x_4, x_2^2, x_2x_3, x_2x_4, x_3^2, x_3x_4, x_4^2) \\
\vec{v}_{tfidf} &= (1, x_1x_2x_3, x_1x_2, x_3, x_4)
\end{aligned}
$$

So we have the indexing functions

$$
\begin{aligned}
e_L &= a_0 + a_1\,tf_{mi} + a_2/max\,tf_m + a_3 \log(n_i/|\underline{D}|) + a_4 \log|d_m^T|, \\
e_Q &= .\;\; a_0 + a_1\,tf_{mi} + a_2/max\,tf_m + a_3 \log(n_i/|\underline{D}|) + a_4 \log|d_m^T| \\
&\quad + a_5(tf_{mi})^2 + a_6\,tf_{mi}/max\,tf_m + a_7\,tf_{mi} \cdot \log(n_i/|\underline{D}|) \\
&\quad + a_8\,tf_{mi} \cdot \log(|d_m^T|) + a_9/(max\,tf_m)^2 \\
&\quad + a_{10}/max\,tf_m \cdot \log(n_i/|\underline{D}|) + a_{11}/max\,tf_m \cdot \log(|d_m^T|) \\
&\quad + a_{12}(\log(n_i/|\underline{D}|))^2 + a_{13} \log(n_i/|\underline{D}|)\log|d_m^T| + a_{14}(\log|d_m^T|)^2, \\
e_{tfidf} &= a_0 + a_1\,tf_{mi} \log(n_i/|\underline{D}|)/max\,tf_m + a_2\,tf_{mi}/max\,tf_m + a_3 \log(n_i/|\underline{D}|) + a_4 \log|d_m^T|.
\end{aligned}
$$

e_L is a linear function of $\vec{x}$, while e_Q is a so-called "complete quadratic polynomial" of $\vec{x}$. $e_{tf \cdot idf}$ was defined in order to get a function similar to the best SMART indexing function called $tf \times idf$ [Salton & Buckley 88].

The retrieval results for the LSP indexing functions are compared with those of the $tf \times idf$ indexing function described in the following (for further details, see [Salton & Buckley 88]). In contrast to our indexing method, the SMART approach does not consider any relevance information for the computation of the indexing weights. With the parameters as defined above, first a preliminary indexing weight α_{mi} for each term in a document is computed:

$$\alpha_{mi} = (0.5 + 0.5 \frac{tf_{mi}}{maxtf_m}) \cdot \log \frac{n_i}{|D|}.$$

These weights are further normalized by the factor

$$w_m = \sqrt{\sum_{t_i \in d_m^T} \alpha_{mi}^2}$$

So the final indexing weight for a term t_i in a document d_m according to the $tf \times idf$ formula yields

$$u_{mi} = \frac{\alpha_{mi}}{w_m}.$$

In the retrieval process, the indexing weights u_{mi} are used by the retrieval function $\varrho(q_k, d_m)$ which computes a relevance value for each query-document pair. Then the documents are ranked by decreasing relevance values. In our experiments, we only considered the scalar product as retrieval function with

$$\varrho(q_k, d_m) = \sum_{t_i \in q_k^T \cap d_m^T} c_{ki} \cdot u_{mi}.$$

Here c_{ki} denotes the weight of the term t_i with respect to the query q_k. As mentioned in [Wong & Yao 89], this retrieval function can be given a utility theoretic interpretation in the case of probabilistic indexing weights u_{mi}: The weight c_{ki} can be regarded as the utility of the term t_i, and the retrieval function gives the expected utility of the document with respect to the query.

For the computation of the query term weights c_{ki}, three different possibilities were considered in our experiments. In the following, we denote these weighting schemes as subscript of the retrieval function:

- ϱ_{bin}: Binary query term weights are used with $c_{ki} = 1$ for all $t_i \in q_k^T$.

- ϱ_{tf}: The query terms weight c_{ki} is set equal to the number of occurrences tf_{ki} of t_i in the query formulation q_k.

- $\varrho_{tf \cdot idf}$: The query term weights are computed in the same way as the $tf \times idf$ document term weight, except that the within-query frequencies tf_{ki} (and $max\, tf_k$) are regarded instead of the within-document frequencies.

For evaluation, the standard SMART evaluation routines were taken, and then the average precision value at the recall points 0.25, 0.50 and 0.75 is considered as global retrieval measure.

5 Experimental results

With the test parameters described before, we performed a number of retrieval runs according to a factorial test plan; that is, we tested (almost) all possible parameter combinations. In the following, we will present the experimental results grouped by the different parameters, in order to show the influence of each parameter on the final retrieval quality. Unless mentioned otherwise, all probabilistic indexing functions are based on the event space E_x.

Learning vs. test sample

Before presenting results of predictive retrieval runs for probabilistic indexing, we want to discuss the sampling problem: Our approach requires a representative sample of the collection as learning sample. With the limited number of queries available in our collections, we had to split the query sets into similar halves instead. Now we want to investigate how similar these two samples really are. It is obvious that this is still an open research problem in IR: having experimental results for a collection A, for which other collections is A representative (so that one can conclude that the experimental results hold for this set of collections)?

collection	learn. sample	test sample	relative difference
CACM	0.3046	0.2963	- 2.7%
CISI	0.1358	0.2099	+ 54.6%
CRAN	0.3634	0.3816	+ 5.0%
INSPEC	0.2214	0.2489	+ 12.4%
NPL	0.1505	0.2138	+ 42.1%

Table 3: Average precision values for learning and test samples (ϱ_{tfidf}, $tf \times idf$)

As a very simple measure of the similarity of two collections, we use the results of the retrieval function ϱ_{tfidf} in combination with $tf \times idf$ indexing weights here. Table 3 shows the average precision values for the learning and the test samples of each collection, and the relative difference between the two results. It can be seen that we have the best sampling for the CACM collection, and for the CRAN and INSPEC collection, the two query sets also seem to be quite similar. In the case of the CISI collection, the difference is much larger (see also the average query lengths in table 2); in the following, we will see that this may account for some strange results that we got for the CISI collection. We have the biggest difference for the NPL collection; however, as claimed in [Salton & Buckley 88], the combination of ϱ_{tfidf} and $tf \times idf$ is not appropriate for the NPL collection, since terms occur at most once in the queries of this collection, and are possibly from a controlled vocabulary. Therefore, our measure of similarity may be invalid for the NPL collection. This assumption is also supported by the results presented in the following.

Documents in the learning set

Using either the top 15 ranked documents or all documents retrieved as elements of L, we show the retrieval results for the different indexing functions in tables 4 and 5. It can be seen that the differences in the retrieval results caused by the choice of L are the smallest for the indexing function e_L; this may be due to the fact that the estimation of the coefficient vector $\vec{a}$ is less crucial for e_L than for e_Q and e_{tfidf}, since e_L is the only linear function. With the exception of the CISI collection, most of the results for the indexing functions based on the top 15 documents are worse than those based on full relevance information. On the other hand, the loss in retrieval quality by restricting to the top 15 documents is not too large to make our approach infeasible for practical applications. Following this point of view, we will discuss only results of indexing functions based on the top 15 ranked documents in the following.

collection	e_L		e_Q		e_{tfidf}	
	full	top	full	top	full	top
CACM	0.2889	0.3024	0.3260	0.3187	0.3010	0.3167
	+ 4.7%		- 2.2%		+ 5.2%	
CISI	0.1034	0.1159	0.1094	0.1231	0.1012	0.1180
	+ 12.1%		+ 12.5%		+ 16.6%	
CRAN	0.3741	0.3786	0.3534	0.3386	0.3493	0.3372
	+ 1.2%		- 4.2%		- 3.5%	
INSPEC	0.1960	0.2033	0.2228	0.1847	0.2093	0.2105
	+ 3.7%		- 17.1%		+ 0.6%	
NPL	0.2109	0.1705	0.1750	0.1285	0.1975	0.1237
	- 19.2%		- 26.6%		- 37.4%	

Table 4: Retrieval results using either the top 15 ranked documents or full relevance information (learning sample, ϱ_{bin}, E_x)

collection	e_L		e_Q		e_{tfidf}	
	full	top	full	top	full	top
CACM	0.3078	0.3003	0.3669	0.3540	0.3352	0.3234
	- 2.4%		- 3.5%		- 3.5%	
CISI	0.1378	0.1677	0.1542	0.1918	0.1406	0.1711
	+ 21.7%		+ 24.4%		+ 21.7%	
CRAN	0.4157	0.4252	0.4062	0.3924	0.3895	0.3749
	+2.3%		- 3.4%		- 3.7%	
INSPEC	0.2316	0.2286	0.2449	0.2108	0.2031	0.1884
	- 1.3%		- 13.9%		- 7.2%	
NPL	0.2391	0.2777	0.2068	0.1745	0.2709	0.1934
	+ 16.1%		- 15.6%		- 28.6%	

Table 5: Retrieval results using either the top 15 ranked documents or full relevance information (test sample, ϱ_{bin}, E_x)

Event space

Tables 6 and 7 show the difference in the retrieval quality by using either the event space E_x or E_{BII}. For e_L, the differences are negligible, while the other indexing functions are again more sensitive to small changes in the learning samples. In general, one can say that the choice of the event space is not crucial for the development of probabilistic indexing functions.

collection	e_L		e_Q		e_{tfidf}	
	E_x	E_{BII}	E_x	E_{BII}	E_x	E_{BII}
CACM	0.3024	0.3117	0.3187	0.3001	0.3167	0.3097
	+ 3.1%		- 5.8%		- 2.2%	
CISI	0.1159	0.1142	0.1231	0.1192	0.1180	0.1166
	- 1.5%		- 3.2%		- 1.2%	
CRAN	0.3786	0.3764	0.3386	0.3279	0.3372	0.3251
	- 0.6%		- 3.2%		- 3.6%	
INSPEC	0.2033	0.2063	0.1847	0.1797	0.2105	0.2021
	+ 1.5%		- 2.7%		- 4.0%	
NPL	0.1705	0.1655	0.1285	0.1205	0.1237	0.1184
	- 2.9%		- 6.2%		- 4.3%	

Table 6: Retrieval results using either E_x or E_{BII} (learning sample, top, ϱ_{bin})

collection	e_L		e_Q		e_{tfidf}	
	E_x	E_{BII}	E_x	E_{BII}	E_x	E_{BII}
CACM	0.3003	0.2980	0.3540	0.3068	0.3234	0.3252
	-0.8%		- 13.3%		+ 0.6%	
CISI	0.1677	0.1606	0.1918	0.1824	0.1711	0.1599
	- 4.2%		- 4.9%		- 6.5%	
CRAN	0.4252	0.4196	0.3924	0.3710	0.3749	0.3514
	- 1.3%		- 5.5%		- 6.3%	
INSPEC	0.2286	0.2318	0.2108	0.2049	0.1884	0.1764
	+ 1.4%		- 2.8%		- 6.4%	
NPL	0.2777	0.2743	0.1745	0.1644	0.1934	0.1843
	- 1.2%		- 5.8%		- 4.7%	

Table 7: Retrieval results using either E_x or E_{BII} (test sample, top, ϱ_{bin})

Indexing functions

In tables 8 and 9, we compare the retrieval results of the probabilistic indexing functions with those of the $tf \times idf$ formula. At first glance, these results seem to be inconsistent: With the learning samples, there is a different indexing function for each collection which yields the best retrieval results. We would expect that e_Q always performs better than e_L here: Since e_Q contains all the parameters of e_L plus all quadratic combinations of elements of $\vec{x}$, it can be adapted closer to the learning sample. As this assumption does not hold for three of the five collections, the deviations between the theoretical model and our experiments, namely the choice of the retrieval function, should be considered in further experiments. Furthermore, we should investigate the influence of the independence assumptions of our model on these results.

Looking at the test samples, we get more uniform results: For three of the five collections e_L yields the best retrieval results or all indexing functions considered. The CISI and the CACM collections behave differently, and for both collections the similarity between learning and test sample may be the reason: With the CISI collection, the results for the probabilistic indexing functions in comparison to the $tf \times idf$ formula are better for the test sample than for the learning sample. In the

collection	$tf \times idf$	e_L	e_Q	e_{tfidf}
CACM	0.2604	0.3024 + 16.1%	0.3187 + 22.4%	0.3167 + 21.6%
CISI	0.1188	0.1159 - 2.4%	0.1231 + 3.6%	0.1180 - 0.7%
CRAN	0.3567	0.3786 + 6.1%	0.3386 - 5.1%	0.3372 - 5.5%
INSPEC	0.1706	0.2033 + 19.2%	0.1847 + 8.3%	0.2105 + 23.4%
NPL	0.1580	0.1705 + 7.9%	0.1285 - 18.7%	0.1237 - 21.7%

Table 8: Probabilistic indexing functions vs. $tf \times idf$ formula (learning sample, top, E_x, ϱ_{bin})

collection	$tf \times idf$	e_L	e_Q	e_{tfidf}
CACM	0.2674	0.3003 + 12.3%	0.3540 + 32.4%	0.3234 + 21.6%
CISI	0.1407	0.1677 + 19.2%	0.1918 + 36.3%	0.1711 + 21.6%
CRAN	0.3841	0.4252 + 10.7%	0.3924 + 2.2%	0.3749 - 2.4%
INSPEC	0.1848	0.2286 + 23.7%	0.2108 + 14.1%	0.1884 + 1.9%
NPL	0.2141	0.2777 + 29.7%	0.1745 - 18.5%	0.1934 - 9.7%

Table 9: Probabilistic indexing functions vs. $tf \times idf$ formula (test sample, top, E_x, ϱ_{bin})

case of the CACM collection, the better performance of e_Q (in comparison to e_L) can be explained by the small difference between learning and test sample. Here we get good estimates for the larger number of parameters of e_Q. With the other collections, the (relatively) small learning samples yield only good estimates for the indexing function with the lowest number of parameters and a linear structure, namely e_L. In the case of e_{tfidf}, we have the same number of parameters as for e_L, but the elements of the polynomial structure $\vec{v}_{tfidf}$ are strongly dependent on each other, which makes this function rather sensitive to differences between learning and test sample. So, with the size of the collections available, only e_L seems to be appropriate.

Comparing the results of the probabilistic indexing functions with those of the $tf \times idf$ function, one can see that the probabilistic functions outperform the SMART function in most cases.

Retrieval functions

If one is interested in good retrieval results, the comparison of indexing functions by using a simple retrieval function like ϱ_{bin} may not be appropriate. Table 10 shows the results for the indexing function e_L in combination with the three retrieval functions ϱ_{bin}, ϱ_{tf} and ϱ_{tfidf}. It can be seen that ϱ_{tf} yields the best results among the retrieval functions (only for the CACM collection ϱ_{tfidf} is slightly better). As ϱ_{tf} performs better than ϱ_{bin}, the information about the within-query frequency of the search terms seems to be useful in consideration with probabilistic document indexing. This result confirms the utility-theoretic justification of linear retrieval functions. On the other hand, there is no improvement by using ϱ_{tfidf} instead of ϱ_{tf} for the probabilistic indexing weights: This is plausible, since the information about the inverse document frequency of the terms has been considered already in the document indexing process.

collection	$tf \times idf$ ϱ_{tfidf}	e_L		
		ϱ_{bin}	ϱ_{tf}	ϱ_{tfidf}
CACM	0.2963	0.3003 + 1.3%	0.3210 + 8.3%	0.3286 + 10.9%
CISI	0.2099	0.1677 - 20.1%	0.2169 + 3.3%	0.2089 - 0.5%
CRAN	0.3816	0.4252 + 11.4%	0.4280 + 12.2%	0.3929 + 3.0%
INSPEC	0.2489	0.2286 - 8.2%	0.2583 + 3.8%	0.2491 + 0.1%
NPL	0.2138	0.2777 + 29.9%	0.2777 + 29.9%	0.2354 + 10.1%

Table 10: Comparison of different retrieval functions (test sample, top, E_x)

The retrieval results for the probabilistic indexing functions are compared with those of the $tf \times idf$ indexing weights and the ϱ_{tfidf} retrieval function. In [Salton & Buckley 88], this combination proves to be – more or less – the best SMART indexing and retrieval method. The comparison of this method with e_L in combination with ϱ_{tf} shows that the probabilistic indexing function yields better retrieval results for all collections. This finding is not surprising: The SMART approach offers a general indexing function which is applicable to a broad range of collections, whereas our approach can be adapted to each specific collection. On the other hand, the development of probabilistic indexing function requires learning data which has to be collected from the running retrieval system, but the SMART indexing functions can be applied without having any relevance information at all. For this reason, with regard to applications, the two approaches are complementing each other: When a new collection is set up, first the SMART approach should be applied and relevance information should be collected. After a while, when there is enough learning data available, the probabilistic approach can be applied. As more and more relevance information is collected, the probabilistic indexing can be further improved by choosing more detailed relevance descriptions and more complex indexing functions (polynomial structures).

6 Conclusions

In this paper, we have devised a new probabilistic indexing approach which is feasible for real applications. The major concepts of our approach are the following:

- Definition of a probabilistic indexing model in terms of the BII model: In contrast to non-probabilistic indexing models (like e.g. [Salton & Buckley 88]) or earlier probabilistic models [Croft 81], the indexing weights of the BII model have a clear notion as probabilities in a well-defined event space. For retrospective experiments, the estimation of these probabilistic indexing weights is trivial.

- Abstraction from specific term-document pairs by definition of relevance descriptions: Unlike many other probabilistic IR models, the probabilistic parameters do not relate to a specific document or query. This feature overcomes the restriction of limited relevance information that is inherent to other models, e.g. by regarding only relevance judgements with respect to the current request. Our approach can be regarded as a long-term learning method (similar approaches have been investigated in [Yu & Mizuno 88] and [Fuhr 89c]) which complements the short-term learning method of relevance weighting of search terms. For the latter problem, the retrieval-with-probabilistic-indexing (RPI) model [Fuhr 89a] has been developed. This model allows to distinguish between two queries q_1, q_2 with $q_1^T = q_2^T$ by regarding query-specific relevance feedback information (similar to model 3 in [Robertson et al. 82]). Consequently, the query representation of the RPI model is a pair $q_k = (q_k^T, q_k^J)$, where q_k^J denotes a set of documents with relevance judgements w.r.t. q_k.

- Flexibility of the form of representation of term-document relationships in relevance descriptions: While other probabilistic models relate to specific forms of representation (which is also a reason for the large number of models published), our approach can be easily adapted to new forms of representation. This is very important for new text analysis and knowledge-based methods, which have not been considered by probabilistic models yet. Now we have devised an easy-to-apply model for the integration of these methods in IR systems.

- Probabilistic learning (or classification) methods as indexing functions instead of simple parameter estimation method: This way, we can make better use of the available learning data, and we can choose the complexity of the indexing function according to the size of the learning sample.

The experimental results indicate that our approach can be applied in running IR systems and that it is superior to other indexing methods. Currently, the size of the available test collections puts some difficulties on the testing of the probabilistic indexing approach, as the results for the nonlinear indexing functions show. In contrast to other probabilistic models, this problem can be neglected in real applications, as the learning sample size is a function of the total number of queries with relevance judgements available. Furthermore, we have shown that the restriction of the learning sample to the top ranking documents is not a serious impediment for the applicability of our method.

With the concepts described in this paper, we have given a framework for the development of probabilistic indexing functions. Besides the investigation of different probabilistic learning and classification methods for the development of indexing functions, the consideration of improved document representations will be a prospective field of research.

Acknowledgement

We thank Keith van Rijsbergen for his constructive comments on an earlier version of this paper.

References

Beinke-Geiser, U.; Lustig, G.; Putze-Meier, G. (1986). Indexieren mit dem System DAISY. In: Lustig, G. (ed.) : *Automatische Indexierung zwischen Forschung und Anwendung*, pages 73–97. Olms, Hildesheim.

Biebricher, P.; Fuhr, N.; Knorz, G.; Lustig, G.; Schwantner, M. (1988). The Automatic Indexing System AIR/PHYS — from Research to Application. In: Chiaramella, Y. (ed.) : *11th International Conference on Research and Development in Information Retrieval*, pages 333–342. Presses Universitaires de Grenoble, Grenoble, France.

Chow, C. K.; Liu, C. N. (1968). Approximating Discrete Probability Distributions with Dependence Trees. *IEEE Transactions on Information Theory 14(3)*, pages 462–467.

Croft, W. B. (1981). Document Representation in Probabilistic Models of Information Retrieval. *Journal of the American Society for Information Science 32*, pages 451–457.

Croft, W. B. (1983). Experiments with Representation in a Document Retrieval System. *Information Technology: Research and Development 2*, pages 1–22.

Croft, W. B. (1986). Boolean Queries and Term Dependencies in Probabilistic Retrieval Models. *Journal of the American Society for Information Science 37(2)*, pages 71–77.

Fagan, J. (1987). Automatic Phrase Indexing for Document Retrieval. In: Yu, C. T.; van Rijsbergen, C. J. (ed.) : *Proceedings of the Tenth Annual ACM SIGIR Conference on Research & Development in Information Retrieval*, pages 91–101.

Fagan, J. L. (1989). The Effectiveness of a Nonsyntactic Approach to Automatic Phrase Indexing for Document Retrieval. *Journal of the American Society for Information Science 40(2)*, pages 115–132.

Faißt, S. (1990). *Development of Indexing Functions Based on Probabilistic Decision Trees (in German)*. Diploma thesis, TH Darmstadt, FB Informatik, Datenverwaltungssysteme II.

Freeman, D. H. (1987). *Applied Categorial Data Analysis*. Dekker, New York.

Fuhr, N. (1988). *Probabilistisches Indexing und Retrieval*. Dissertation, TH Darmstadt, Fachbereich Informatik.

Fuhr, N. (1989a). Models for Retrieval with Probabilistic Indexing. *Information Processing and Management 25(1)*, pages 55–72.

Fuhr, N. (1989b). Optimum Polynomial Retrieval Functions. In: Belkin, N.; van Rijsbergen, C. J. (ed.) : *Proceedings of the Twelfth Annual International ACMSIGIR Conference on Research and Development in Information Retrieval*, pages 69–76. ACM, New York.

Fuhr, N. (1989c). Optimum Polynomial Retrieval Functions Based on the Probability Ranking Principle. *ACM Transactions on Information Systems 7(3)*, pages 183–204.

Gordon, M. (1988). Probabilistic and Genetic Algorithms for Document Retrieval. *Communications of the ACM 31(10)*, pages 1208–1218.

Knorz, G. (1983). *Automatisches Indexieren als Erkennen abstrakter Objekte*. Niemeyer, Tübingen.

Kwok, K. L.; Kuan, W. (1988). Experiments with Document Components for Indexing and Retrieval. *Information Processing and Management 24(4)*, pages 405–417.

Kwok, K. L. (1986). An Interpretation of Index Term Weighting Schemes Based on Document Components. In: Rabitti, F. (ed.) : *Proceedings of the 1986 ACM Conference on Research and Development in Information Retrieval*, pages 275–283. ACM, New York.

Kwok, K. L. (1989). A Neural Network for Probabilistic Information Retrieval. In: Belkin, N.; van Rijsbergen, C. J. (ed.) : *Proceedings of the Twelfth Annual International ACMSIGIR Conference on Research and Development in Information Retrieval*, pages 21–30. ACM, New York.

Maron, M. E.; Kuhns, J. L. (1960). On Relevance, Probabilistic Indexing, and Information Retrieval. *Journal of the ACM 7*, pages 216–244.

Maron, M. E. (1983). Probabilistic Approaches to the Document Retrieval Problem. In: Salton, G.; Schneider, H.-J. (ed.) : *Research and Development in Information Retrieval*, pages 98–107. Springer, Berlin et al.

Pfeifer, U. (1990). *Development of Log-Linear and Linear-Iterative Indexing Functions (in German).* Diploma thesis, TH Darmstadt, FB Informatik, Datenverwaltungssysteme II.

Quinlan, J. R. (1986). The Effect of Noise on Concept Learning. In: Michalski, R. S.; Carbonell, J. G.; Mitchell, T. M. (ed.) : *Machine Learning: An Artificial Intelligence Approach , Vol. II*, pages 149–166. Morgan Kaufmann, Los Altos, California.

van Rijsbergen, C. J. (1977). A Theoretical Basis for the Use of Co-Occurrence Data in Information Retrieval. *Journal of Documentation 33*, pages 106–119.

Robertson, S. E.; Van Rijsbergen, C. J.; Porter, M. F. (1981). Probabilistic Models of Indexing and Searching. In: Oddy, R. N.; Robertson, S. E.; Van Rijsbergen, C. J.; Williams, P. W. (ed.) : *Information Retrieval Research*, pages 35–56. Butterworths, London.

Robertson, S. E.; Maron, M. E.; Cooper, W. S. (1982). Probability of Relevance: A Unification of Two Competing Models for Document Retrieval. *Information Technology: Research and Development 1*, pages 1–21.

Salton, G.; Buckley, C. (1988). Term Weighting Approaches in Automatic Text Retrieval. *Information Processing and Management 24(5)*, pages 513–523.

Salton, G.; Yang, C. S.; Yu, C. T. (1975). A Theory of Term Importance in Automatic Text Analysis. *Journal of the American Society for Information Science 36*, pages 33–44.

Smeaton, A. F. (1986). Incorporating Syntactic Information into a Document Retrieval Strategy: an Investigation. In: *9th International Conference on Research & Development in Information Retrieval*, pages 103–113. ACM, New York.

Tietze, A. (1989). *Approximation of Discrete Probability Distributions by Dependence Trees and their Application as Indexing Functions (in German).* Diploma thesis, TH Darmstadt, FB Informatik, Datenverwaltungssysteme II.

Wong, A. K. C.; Chiu, D. K. Y. (1987). Synthesizing Statistical Knowledge from Incomplete Mixed-Mode Data. *IEEE Transactions on Pattern Analysis and Machine Intelligence 9(6)*, pages 796–805.

Wong, S. K. M.; Yao, Y. Y. (1989). A Probability Distribution Model for Information Retrieval. *Information Processing and Management 25(1)*, pages 39–53.

Yu, C. T.; Mizuno, H. (1988). Two Learning Schemes in Information Retrieval. In: Chiaramella, Y. (ed.) : *11th International Conference on Research & Development in Information Retrieval*, pages 201–218. Presses Universitaires de Grenoble, Grenoble, France.

EXPRESS: An Experimental Interface for Factual Information Retrieval

Heinz Ulrich Hoppe, Karin Ammersbach, Barbara Lutes-Schaab, Gaby Zinßmeister
GMD-IPSI, Dolivostr. 15, D-6100 Darmstadt (FRG)
e-mail: hoppe@darmstadt.gmd.dbp.de

Paper submitted to SIGIR 90

Abstract

The EXPRESS system has been designed and implemented in order to explore methods for user assistance in accessing complexly structured factual databases, e.g. relational product databases. Terminological support in this area has to take into account that different controlled vocabularies may be used in a variety of attributes spread over several relations. In our approach, traditional thesaurus structures are extended in order to cope with these problems and to encode further domain-specific knowledge. User support in query reformulation is based on this enriched thesaurus as well as on the local evaluation of the retrieved data sets. Concepts for the representation of retrieval strategies in the form of plans and their potential use in future systems are discussed.

1 Introduction

Intelligent interfaces for Information Retrieval (IR) can be based on different sorts of knowledge, such as knowledge about the user and his or her information need, expert strategies and tactics for query planning and reformulation, terminological knowledge, or even content-oriented, semantic descriptions of the objects gathered in the database. Significant progress in supporting direct end-user access to public databases may be expected from any of these knowledge bases and it is therefore desirable that an intelligent retrieval system should use all these in an integrated form. On the other hand, none of the different approaches mentioned is already able to offer well-established and easily applicable engineering methods in order to incorporate the respective features into a retrieval system. There are still open research issues in the different relevant fields. In spite of integration being desirable, significant advances of the basic mechanisms towards the development of a practical methodology may also be achieved through a "divide and conquer" strategy, i.e. by means of elaborating on a subset of the approaches separately.

A considerable amount of work in the area of intelligent retrieval interfaces focuses on user modeling (e.g. Brajnik et al., 1987; Brooks et al., 1985). There are different notions of user models (cf. Kobsa, 1989), which are all relevant to IR. Rich's GRUNDY system (Rich , 1979) is an early example for user modeling based on stereotypes. The stereotype approach views a specific user as a representative of a category or class which is predefined in terms of several long-term characteristics and typical preferences. In its simplest form, such an approach can hardly be flexible enough to capture individual differences. More flexibility is achieved by allowing individual refinements of predefined prototypes and multiple inheritance from different classes.

A more fundamental problem with the use of stereotyped user models in IR systems originates from the possibility that one and the same individual may show qualitatively very different information needs over time, even within one session. There is a dynamic interaction between the problem context which gives rise to the information need, the user's role in this problem context, and the user's articulated problem description. In many cases, the information need is much less determined by the relatively permanent individual characteristics of a user than by the problem context or task. Task modeling in its different forms (e.g. Card et al., 1983; Payne & Green, 1986; Hoppe, 1988) can be used to represent fixed operational schemata which apply to certain problem classes. Request of some specific information may be one step in such an operational schema for attaining a task such as e.g. travel planning. Inside the information retrieval task, operational schemata have also been identified in terms of search tactics and strategies (e.g. Bates, 1987; Fidel, 1985). Existing task modeling approaches are not directly applicable in order to represent tactics and strategies in IR, because here the final actions are not yet determined when "the procedure is entered". This is due to the fact that "goals" in IR cannot be simply defined in terms of state changes in the underlying system, but have to be regarded as changes in the user's knowledge state. Therefore, a continuous evaluation of system feedback is necessary in order to pursue a certain strategy and determine the next action. One of our current research goals is to combine user support mechanisms based on task models with more flexible planning methods (e.g. Hayes-Roth & Hayes-Roth, 1979; Mannes & Kintsch, 1989).

The notion of retrieval tactics and strategies constitutes a specific aspect of the expert system approach to intelligent IR (cf. Brooks, 1987), since these are typical components of the expertise provided by professional search intermediaries. The expert knowledge encoded in intelligent retrieval interfaces also includes simple procedures (e.g. connection to the host) and conversion from a standardized representation of Boolean expressions to the specific query languages. For this part of the job, there are already acceptable engineering solutions. More "intelligent" features comprise the elaboration of a Boolean query from an unstructured list of natural language terms (as e.g. in EP-X, cf. Smith et al., 1989) or from a partial analysis of free natural language input (as e.g. in PLEXUS, Vickery & Brooks, 1987) as well as the construction of a plan for the incremental evolution of queries, as done in EURISKO (cf. Barthès & Glize, 1988). A common shortcoming of this category of intelligent retrieval interfaces may be attributed to the paradigm of simulating the reasoning of a human expert. Such systems (like human intermediaries) are usually not equipped with mechanisms for performing exhaustive analyses of the retrieved data sets. Although the analysis of term frequencies in given response sets is already supported by existing technology (for example in the retrieval languages MESSENGER and QUEST), the logical next step of using regularities in a given data set as clues for system-supported query reformulation is generally not taken, e.g. to assist the user in broadening as well as narrowing or a change of focus. One exception is the EUROMATH interface for bibliographic retrieval in the domain of mathematics (McAlpine & Ingwersen, 1989). This interface provides access to the results of host frequency analyses as additional information for the user; however, it does not utilize them in its internal search strategy.

Most of the existing intelligent retrieval interfaces support only the retrieval of bibliographic references or full text documents. In these areas, terminological knowledge is available in the form of thesauri, which can be used as additional knowledge sources. Traditional thesauri have been replaced by richer knowledge structures, such as semantic networks or frames (Monarch & Carbonell, 1986; Shoval, 1983; Smith et al., 1989). Accordingly, indexing is seen as a semantic representation of the document content. The issue of "natural" or commonsense semantics in user utterances or texts leads to open problems in AI and computational linguistics. In order not to overload the strive for intelligent IR with these "heavy" problems, we consider it appropriate to further exploit the notion (and use) of thesauri as terminological knowledge bases. This seems to be particularly valid in the somewhat neglected, but practically very relevant domain of factual databases, such as chemical or materials databases. In these areas there is a clearly defined technical terminology. A deeper understanding of this terminology usually requires a thorough scientific background. It is questionable if an attempt should be made to provide the retrieval interface with this kind of deep knowledge, as long as there are open problems which can be solved on the terminological level. Using current technology, information about materials or chemical substances can be adequately stored in relational format, each attribute representing a particular feature expressed in terms of a numerical value or range, a formula, or a textual description. We will show that access to this kind of information system can be supported by an enriched thesaurus which contains not only taxonomic but also domain-specific relations and reflects the attribute structure of the underlying relations by means of different facets.

Based on this critical view of existing approaches to intelligent IR, we have focused our research on the following open problems:

- terminology support for information retrieval from complexly-structured factual databases,

- the implementation of query planning and reformulation mechanisms using this kind of terminological knowledge bases as well as mechanisms for an exhaustive analysis of the retrieved data sets,

- the relevance of task models and planning mechanisms for user guidance in IR.

In order to put our ideas into practice, we have implemented a prototype called EXPRESS (EXperimental PRototype for Exploring Support Strategies in factual IR). The following sections will be successively devoted to an overview of the functionality and architecture of EXPRESS at a global technical level, a brief description of the specific problems involved in fact retrieval, a structural description of the underlying terminological knowledge base, and the query evaluation and reformulation mechanism in its current form as well as envisaged extensions. Particularly in the latter aspect, we will assume a cognitive science point of view in that we regard information retrieval as a planning or problem solving activity.

2 The EXPRESS system

As a testbed for intelligent assistance in information retrieval, we have implemented a prototype
system which supports users in accessing a factual database of products for wood protection. The
EXPRESS (EXperimental PRototype for Exploring Support Strategies in factual IR) system
provides terminological support during the process of (re-)formulating queries to satisfy users'
information needs.

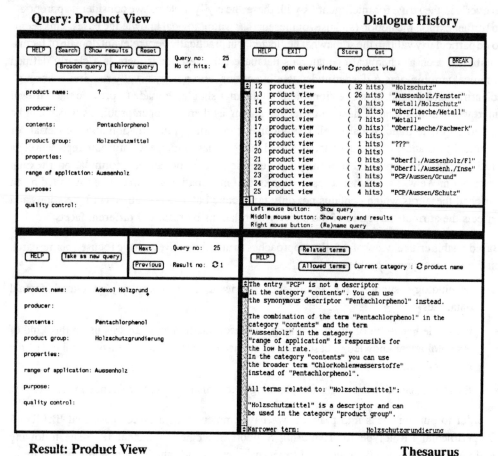

Figure 1 : The surface of the EXPRESS system

Figure 1 shows the surface of the system. In the upper left window, queries are constructed by
filling out an onscreen form. Such a form represents a predefined view of the database. This can
be seen as a simple **query-by-example** (QBE) interface as presented in (Zloof, 1983). At the
moment, users may choose from two such views: the product view, which describes specific
products; and the content view, which can be used to place queries concerning the ingredients of
products and their potential effects. In implementing this type of access to the database, the
intention was to avoid the typical problems end users encounter with any given
command-oriented retrieval language.

Query results are then presented successively in the lower left window in a form similar to that of the query. Any given document in an answer set may be transferred to the query window and used as the basis for a new query (using the 'take as new query'-button).

In the window on the upper right the dialogue history is recorded. The user is able to assign meaningful catchwords to former queries. Following the paradigm of **'query-by-reformulation'**, former queries as well as answers can be used as a basis for developing new queries. This paradigm has been used in some other prototypes such as the HELGON system (Fischer & Nieper-Lemke, 1989).

One of the main problems of casual users of a retrieval system is to find the 'right' terms to describe their information need. The trouble lies in the discrepancy between the user's personal vocabulary usage and the terminology used to index the objects in the database. Therefore EXPRESS supports users in mapping user terms onto system terms. Once the (controlled) vocabulary has been found, the response to a query might nevertheless be unsatisfying in that the hit rate is too small or too large. To overcome these difficulties, the EXPRESS system offers help in the form of suggestions as to which terms in the query could be replaced during reformulation in order to arrive at a satisfactory answer set. In the current system version, the user judges whether or not a given answer set is satisfactory, and then explicitly invokes the broadening/narrowing algorithms to receive reformulation suggestions. The main knowledge base for (re-)formulation purposes is an **enriched thesaurus** implemented as a semantic network. The thesaurus is described in detail in Chapter 4, the **broadening** and **narrowing** functions are explained in Chapter 5.

A **'check-value' function** supports the mapping of terms on the level of morphological similarity. Starting from the user-given term T in a category C, the algorithm checks the following conditions in the given order and suggests the derived descriptor D and additional information depending on the valid case:

(1) Is T a descriptor D in the category C?

(2) Is T a synonym for a descriptor D in C?

(3) Is T morphologically similar to a descriptor D in C?

(4) Is T morphologically similar to a synonym S of descriptor D in C?

Steps (1) to (4) are then performed on all other categories with controlled vocabularies, which can, for example, result in the information that the requested term is a descriptor in a category other than the one in which it was requested. To check these conditions the algorithm uses the faceting in the thesaurus (see Chap. 4), the synonymy relationship, and a method for assessing morphological similarities between terms.

Apart from the help described above, where the system uses the thesaurus as a knowledge base to deduce the appropriate search terms, the user can **browse in the thesaurus** independently of the ongoing search. On the one hand, all the allowed terms for any category (attribute) can be looked at alphabetically. On the other hand, starting from a user term, EXPRESS will display all the information it can derive from this term using the thesaurus links and by means of the same

67

algorithms as mentioned above. I.e. synonyms, related descriptors in the same or other categories, and textual definitions of terms are presented in the thesaurus window.

The goal in designing the EXPRESS system was to explore ways to automate various user support functions. For purposes of experimentation and transparence, in the current version, all support mechanisms are semi-automatic, i.e. available upon user request, usually by means of a labeled button. This provides users with easy and direct access to all options and alternatives onscreen. To achieve this, we have used the top level control mechanism of event handling as offered by SunView. Thus, SunView events trigger the invocation of the functions performed by the underlying Prolog programs.

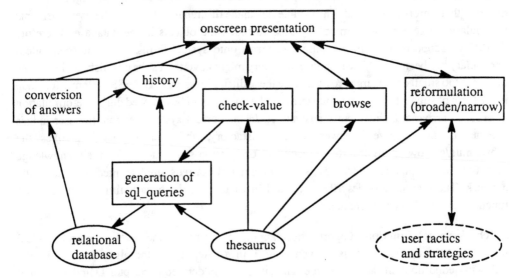

Figure 2 : The components of EXPRESS

In Figure 2 the system components are shown from the functional point of view. The ovals designate knowledge bases and the boxes the methods to be applied to them. In placing a query, the system checks the terms and generates an SQL-query which is sent to the relational database. The database response is converted into a representation which can easily be used in the onscreen, form-oriented presentation. At the moment, the reformulation functions are implemented implicitly in the program, each reformulation rule being a specific Prolog clause. In the future, they will be represented more explicitly to separate the inference engine from the knowledge base. The advantages are obvious: the knowledge base can easily be modified, extended and improved without changing the control mechanism. Beginning with a small knowledge base, one can experiment with the system and incrementally extend it. The other components of the figure should be clear from previous explanations.

The interface with its help facilities is independent of the specific data base. A second relational data base with SQL-access and an available thesaurus has been connected to EXPRESS as well. The database itself is implemented using Sybase; the thesaurus and the interface are implemented in Prolog; the system runs on Sun workstations.

3 Specific problems encountered in retrieval from factual databases

The choice of fact retrieval (e.g. in materials or product databases) as domain for the EXPRESS prototype poses a number of problems which differ from those encountered in bibliographic retrieval. Empirical evidence for some of these problems is provided by analyses of the behavior of professional intermediaries during their interaction with clients in online retrieval sessions using bibliographic and factual databases (Ammersbach, 1986; Ammersbach et al., 1988). The main problems observed and the way in which they are being taken into account in the EXPRESS interface are described in this section.

Attribute selection

In bibliographic databases, the structure of the records is straightforward and the categories used are clear, i.e. author, abstract, etc. The data type used to describe the categories is also generally intuitive; e.g. abstract and title are text strings, publication year is an integer, and so on. In product or materials databases, often a very large number of attributes (sometimes more than 100) and a variety of attribute types (e.g. intervals, integers, text) are used to describe each documented entity. This is a source of difficulty, since confusion may arise as to the meaning of the attribute labels (field names), and as to which attribute to search in for a given information need. The problems include nonintuitive field labeling and the fact that nuances of the same phenomenon may be described in different places in a given record. Both these characteristics lead to ambiguity and uncertainty as to where to search for what. In the EXPRESS system, we have partially countered this problem by using a QBE interface reflecting predefined views of a relational database, and by referral to an online thesaurus for an onscreen display of attribute values (see below).

Attribute-specific terminology support

Solving the problem of selecting the right attribute does not solve the terminological problems within the attribute. Searching in factual databases still shares many of the terminological pitfalls of bibliographic databases. Here, too, polysemy and synonymy abound, insofar as attributes are described using natural language terms. This is compounded by the fact that thesauri are often unavailable. In the case of attributes containing numerical values, users sometimes express their information need as a natural language circumscription of information which is numerically coded in the database. Another problem is that search queries may be posed in terms of different units of measure than those used in the database. This is especially true for attributes containing ranges of values (e.g. temperature range). The empirical data shows that especially in the latter cases, query reformulation often involves an iterative change of ranges or discrete values within the chosen attribute, and if the response set is still too small, a decision is made to switch to a different, related attribute, usually in hopes of broadening the search. The decision is based on the knowledge of the professional intermediary about cross-attribute relationships.

Thus, different attribute types require different kinds of terminological support. The provision of an online thesaurus which is referred to by the check-value algorithm already described helps solve lexical problems and synonymy in natural language fields. In addition, EXPRESS offers pop-up menus for each attribute which display a partial alphabetical list of allowed terms, thus providing users with examples. A complete list of allowed terms for a given attribute is available in the thesaurus window. A planned rule-based expansion of the equivalency relationship to link natural language terms to numerical values and ranges of values and these to each other will alleviate the problems arising from different data types. The introduction of faceting and a cross-attribute relationship in the thesaurus, which is described in more detail in the next chapter, allows the simulation of expert knowledge in broadening and narrowing unsuccessful queries.

Precision-oriented search

Another empirical finding is that when describing their information need, clients of fact databases usually have a concrete application in mind which implies that the target of the search has to comply with more rigid constraints than is usually the case in literature search. In some cases this can even be a performance specification of a sought-for material, in contrast to the subject description typical of pre-search interviews during bibliographic retrieval. Still, due to the plethora of attributes and lack of controlled vocabularies described above, this does not mean that mapping the information need onto system terminology is easier. The formulation of a search query on the same level of specificity as the user's information need often leads to a very small or even null response set. Thus, the strategy of first employing the tactic of broadening is often used as an interim step to achieve a hit rate large enough to enable further narrowing in order to iteratively achieve the desired precision. EXPRESS supports both narrowing and broadening, described in Chapter 5.

4 The thesaurus knowledge base in EXPRESS

In the EXPRESS interface, the terminological knowledge base plays a central role in supporting the user during both initial query formulation and query reformulation. The thesaurus at the core of the terminology base provides a pool of networked terms whose various links are exploited by the check-value algorithm described in Chapter 2, and by the algorithms for broadening and narrowing the scope of a query as described in Chapter 5. It can also be easily referred to for browsing independently of a specific query. As a pragmatic departure point in designing the terminological knowledge component, we have chosen to enhance traditional thesaurus structure in compliance with the exigencies of the chosen domain of fact (here product) retrieval described in Chapter 3. In the following, the most important enhancements of conventional thesaurus structure and their relevance for the support algorithms are described.

Faceting for fact retrieval

The EXPRESS thesaurus device described in this section is a type of faceting intended to counter the problems caused by the large number of attributes used to describe any one documented entity in a factual database, as described in the previous chapter. The explicit assignment of each controlled term to a particular facet in the thesaurus is used by both the check-value and the broadening algorithms.

In bibliographic indexing and retrieval, the object to be described and retrieved is generally a document as a whole. Postable terms from a thesaurus, or descriptors, are often only located in a single category for thesaurus index terms. If a classification scheme or subject indexing scheme other than a thesaurus is used, these terms may also be located in their own fields. Still, the terms selected from each of the ordering systems refer to the entire document. To counter the fact that any object to be indexed can be described from various points of view, or aspects, the concept of a faceted classification was devised. A facet, in this sense, is a semantic cluster, i.e. a set of associated terms with a basic semantic affinity.

In a highly structured factual database, much of what is achieved in a thesaurus by clustering into facets has already been performed and is reflected in the fine structure of the records; i.e. various attributes (equivalent to facets) are used to describe the substance, material, object, etc. undergoing the documentation process. Each attribute is described using a set of terms or values which already share a semantic affinity, i.e. their membership in the semantic cluster represented by the attribute. In EXPRESS we have made this implicit semantic categorization explicit by partitioning the controlled vocabulary according to the attributes it is used for. Thus the facets in the thesaurus are derived from the underlying attribute structure of the database. We assume these classes to be mutually exclusive. Thus a separate thesaurus is implemented for each attribute, i.e. hierarchization takes place within the cluster allowed for each attribute, respectively. Any given postable term's membership in a particular partial thesaurus is indicated by a special thesaurus relationship named 'facet'. This means that when a term is looked up in the thesaurus, it becomes immediately apparent which attribute the term can be used to describe. This is a condition for the functioning of the check-value algorithm described in the previous chapter. The coding of each term with a tag indicating its facet (i.e. allowed attribute) is also a prerequisite for the cross-attribute relationship to be described in the next section.

In the product view of the current EXPRESS database, for example, eight attributes are used to describe each documented product: *product name, producer, contents, product group, properties, range of application, purpose,* and *quality control.* The choice of attributes as well as the terminology associated with each attribute were derived from standard technical specification sheets available from the manufacturers of the described products. With the exception of *product name* and *producer,* which are proper names, and of the freetext attribute *properties,* each of these attributes is terminologically controlled, and each allowed term is linked in the thesaurus to the attribute (facet) which it can be used to describe. Thus a thesaurus search for, for example, the term *insecticide* will reveal that this term can be used to instantiate the attribute *product group*; looking up *wood pests* will lead to the attribute *range of application.* The fact that these two terms, although in different facets, are obviously related, inspired the associative relationship described in the next section.

Cross-attribute relationship

One specific type of semantic knowledge possessed by experts in the domain of factual databases is that of likely associations between an allowed term for one attribute and a term allowed for another attribute. In the EXPRESS system we have devised a cross-attribute relationship which reflects this association. A typical example of this:

- *hydrogen fluoride* is an allowed term for the attribute *contents*
- *wood pests* is an allowed term for the attribute *range of application*
- *insecticide* is an allowed term for the attribute *product group*

Since the three terms *hydrogen fluoride, wood pests* and *insecticide* are members of different facets in the thesaurus (*contents, range of application,* and *product group* respectively), there would normally be no link between them, as hierarchization takes place solely within the vocabulary of a single facet. However, a product which contains hydrogen fluoride (a poison) is likely to be effective against wood pests, and is likely to be an insecticide. It is therefore compatible with domain knowledge to code a link between the terms indicating just this (see Fig. 3). While investigating the vocabulary in the thesaurus with a view to establishing this relationship between hitherto unlinked terms, it became apparent that in most cases a prognosis could be made as to the direction in which a query would be influenced by changing to the related term. In the example above, switching to the attribute *range of application* and searching for the term *wood pests* will be likely to produce a larger response set than *hydrogen fluoride* in *contents* (since other products which could be used to combat wood pests contain other pesticides). The cross-attribute relationship is therefore always directed (the first argument is assumed to be the more specific term), and thus can be used by the broadening/narrowing algorithms to suggest terms for search reformulation.

Thus thesaurus-based help for a typical search situation is possible: a user specifies a value in a specific attribute as a search parameter, and the expert intermediary informs him or her that a term in a different field would be also/more likely to lead to success, while still retaining the essential sought-for characteristics.

```
facet('insecticide', 'product group').
facet('wood pests', 'range of application').
facet('hydrogen fluoride', 'contents').

cross–attribute('hydrogen fluoride', 'wood pests').
cross–attribute('hydrogen fluoride', 'insecticide').
```

Figure 3 : Excerpt from the EXPRESS thesaurus

Domain-specific associative relationships

The terms within each facet are interrelated by means of the standard thesaurus relationships (generic, partitive, equivalence, associative). If the semantics of the documented domain make it seem expedient, a domain-specific differentiation of the associative relationship can, of course, also be incorporated. Examples for such relationships included in the prototype EXPRESS thesaurus are the 'can-be-made-of' relationship and the 'can-be-treated-with' relationship. The reasoning for the inclusion of these domain-specific associative relationships was pragmatic, the assumption being that a differentiation would allow operationalization for the broadening and narrowing support functions. For example, if a user is searching for a product with which a *compost fence* can be treated, he or she would probably retrieve more hits using the related term *wood with earth contact*. These two terms are related by the 'can-be-made-of' relationship, which is always consulted by the broadening algorithm.

The embedment of the thesaurus in the EXPRESS system

Figure 4 shows which of the relationships contained in the thesaurus knowledge base are mainly exploited in order to support the three main thesaurus-based functions offered by EXPRESS, i.e. initial query formulation, query reformulation, and browsing. Browsing independently of a given query can, of course, involve all relationships, and can take place concurrently with (re-)formulation. The check-value mechanism otherwise associated with initial formulation can also be invoked during the reformulation process, thus the initial formulation box is contained in the reformulation box.

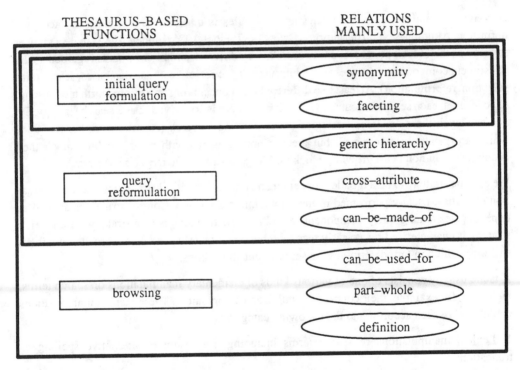

Figure 4 : Correlation between support functions and thesaurus relations used

The thesaurus knowledge base currently contains 347 unique terms, which are interlinked using the eight types of relationships shown in the above diagram. Of these, the generic and partitive relationships are partially defined by means of Prolog rules, i.e. the general *broader-term* relationship is defined recursively as the transitive closure of the explicit, one-step *broader-term1* relationship, and narrower terms are derived by inverting the *broader-term* relationship. Thus, the entire subterm/superterm tree can be retrieved recursively from any given starting point. In indexing the products in the database, the principle of assigning the most specific (narrowest) descriptor was strictly adhered to. This, together with the recursive expansion, are the basis for the feature that an EXPRESS search query also retrieves all products indexed with the generic narrower terms of the specified search term. When translating a QBE query into SQL, all narrower terms of controlled input terms are retrieved and ORed with the original term. This is an important prerequisite for the functioning of the narrowing algorithm described in the next chapter.

To date the database contains descriptions of 94 wood treatment products. The addition of many more products is planned, whereas the thesaurus has probably achieved its saturation point as far as further growth is concerned. The fact that almost no additional terms were added to the thesaurus during the indexing of the last ca. 20 products tends to confirm that the terminological description of the domain is now comprehensive enough to encompass many additional products.

5 Retrieval tactics and strategies

A common feature of retrieval tactics and strategies is that they lack a generally-accepted definition. Although several definitions (Bates, 1987; Fidel, 1985; Linden, 1987) share a view of strategy as the overall plan of an entire search, they differ essentially in what is regarded as the constituent components (e.g. pre-search interview, selection of hosts and databases, search term selection, reformulation). At least two different basic concepts of strategy are worth mentioning. On one level, each search executed in an online database is conceived of as a search strategy. On another level, there are three strategies for conducting a search (Armstrong & Large, 1988) which are generally recognized, but are not homogeneous with regard to how much they encompass: citation pearl growing, block building, most specific term (facet) first.

We assume strategy to be a broader concept than tactics. A retrieval strategy is thus a combination of tactics, usually performed in more than one search step. Control structures as well as dependencies among query components are characteristic features of a strategy. Moreover, a strategy is characterized by a clearly recognizable direction (i. e. narrowing, broadening, focus shifting), which in turn determines the set of applicable tactics.

A tactic usually consists of one of various kinds of elementary manipulations on search terms, including, for example, their connection with Boolean operators. These tactical manipulations could be classified according to the following categories:

1. Lexical manipulations of search terms including, for example, alternative spelling or truncation;

2. Syntactical manipulations involving the use of Boolean and adjacency operators or alternative spacing;

3. Semantic manipulations using broader, narrower or related thesaurus terms or classification codes; and

4. Functional manipulations on search queries. These include narrowing or broadening of a range of measured values, or a switch to a different attribute in case of functional dependencies

between attributes. The latter plays an important role especially in factual database structures (see previous section on thesaurus).

In our experimental prototype we concentrate on semantic and functional tactics to support the user's reformulation.

Broadening

In order to give advice on how to broaden a query, two main steps have to be performed. First the most appropriate term to broaden has to be detected, whereas there may be more than one. Then a suitable broader term has to be deduced using the various relationships in the thesaurus. In the following, the algorithm is described in more detail:

A) Finding the most appropriate term to broaden:

Examine individual terms

> For all the terms with hit rate 0 check if they are allowed terms using the check-value function (see Chapter 2). If they are not, give the appropriate hints and stop. Otherwise search for all terms with a hit rate less than a given threshold[1] and broaden them ($\rightarrow$ B).

> If all individual hit rates exceed the threshold continue with the next step.

Examine binary combinations of terms

> For all those pairs which have a hit rate below a given threshold perform the appropriate of the following steps:

> – If both terms are descriptors compare the individual hit rates and the sum of the hit rates of their binary combinations and broaden the most restrictive term ($\rightarrow$ B).

> – If one of the terms is an entry in an uncontrolled and the other one in a controlled attribute then broaden the descriptor ($\rightarrow$ B).

> – If both terms are entries in uncontrolled attributes, propose deleting the one with the lower individual hit rate from the query.

B) Proposing a suitable broader term for the term(s) detected in A:

> Consult the thesaurus and select a relationship according to the following preference list: domain-specific before generic before cross-attribute relationships. Propose using the thus-found term instead of the previous one. If no 'broader' term can be found the term might have to be deleted from the query.

There are some implicit decisions within this algorithm which should be made explicit. For example, descriptors are preferred to non-descriptors because meaningful advice can be given only for them, since only descriptors are interrelated in the thesaurus. It is important to examine

---

1. The threshold can either be defined as a constant or as a variable which depends on the size of the answer set of the query to be broadened.

combinations of terms because it is often the case that only the combined use of terms restricts the hit rate. On the other hand, for reasons of combinatorial explosion, it is unreasonable to take into account larger subsets of terms than pairs.

Narrowing

The narrowing of a query based on generic thesaurus relations is more difficult to perform than broadening, because it involves selecting from among a potentially large number of more specific terms. It is also not as easy to select the appropriate attribute in which to narrow. An analogous application of the principle used for broadening would be: Select those attributes and terms with the highest individual hit rates. But often these specifications are only used to delimit a certain general area (e.g. a product group), whereas the essential characteristics are specified in attributes which are already more selective, but not selective enough. In light of these problems, we have not yet implemented a sufficiently complete narrowing function in EXPRESS. But, on the other hand, we have exploited some internal mechanisms of EXPRESS, namely the indexing with most specific terms and the automatic recursive term expansion described in Chapter 4, in order to achieve an elegant partial solution.

A) Analysis of the result set:

> For the controlled attribute fields, collect resulting terms which differ from the input term. (The query mechanism ensures that these are more specific!)

> For all these controlled terms, calculate their relative frequency in the entire answer set.

> Select attributes with subterms that exceed a certain minimal relative frequency ($\rightarrow$ B).

B) Present the selected attributes and terms with respective relative frequencies to the user.

> Order attributes by maximal ratio.

> Within an attribute order terms by ratio.

This information allows the user to select appropriate narrower terms according to their relative frequency in the response set for the respective attribute. This criterion, which is independent of the total hit rate, can guide the choice of tactics, for example substitution of a broader term by a narrower term (semantic) or dropping of OR-ed terms (syntactical). In case of absence of suitable narrower terms or rejection by the user, the cross-attribute relation can be used for further suggestions.

Query reformulation as described in the previous sections takes place on the tactical level. The narrowing and broadening support mechanisms which are offered in EXPRESS support the user's decisions as to how the query could be reformulated in order to get a better result. This is based on the assumption that the user's goal, i.e. a specific information need, does not change, and that only the means have to be better adapted to the system. As long as broadening and narrowing are not performed automatically by the system, this is not problematic. But there are important aspects in the evolution of queries which are not captured by these basic functions. The user may subsequently try to pursue different goals in order to extract portions of information and integrate them later on. The general strategy of block building is an example of this kind of search behavior, but we can also imagine domain-dependent procedures which can only be interpreted and explicitly supported if we know what the information is to be used for. This point is of particular interest for highly structured factual databases.

Specific query patterns and plans

As already pointed out, we assume the database to consist of various relations, each containing a number of attributes. Relational database technology already offers the possibility of defining certain views reflecting specific information needs. A view allows us to combine and select pieces of information in a way which is different from the actual representation in the database. Nevertheless, in order to be useful, a view has to serve a certain class of information needs. Specific information needs have to be mapped onto an adequate view by means of instantiating certain attributes with values and requesting the values of some other selected attributes. Following the "query by example" approach, EXPRESS offers easy-to-use query forms in order to specify such a request. We found that the notion of a **"specific query pattern"** (SQP), defined in terms of a view with a selection of specified and requested attributes, is a useful basis for further examining the role of procedural task knowledge in retrieval from highly structured databases. Figure 5 illustrates the basic structure of such an SQP, where the attributes to be specified are subdivided into those with constant and those with variable values. Of course, the possible choices of attributes are predetermined by the view.

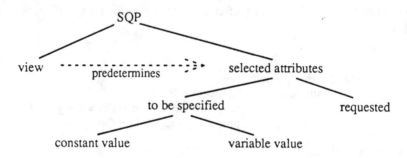

Figure 5 : Structure of a "specific query pattern"

In a small empirical evaluation of protocolled EXPRESS search histories, some SQPs could be identified. The simplest frequent pattern consists of a single requested attribute (*product name* or *effect*) and a single specified attribute (e.g. *range of application* is specified and *product name* is requested in the *product view*). More complex patterns usually evolve as extensions of simpler ones. In the example, the most probable later attribute to be specified in addition to *range of application* is *product group*, followed by *contents*. The specification of additional attributes represents a specific narrowing tactic. Similar tactics based on cross-attribute relationships lead to transitions in which a specified attribute is replaced by another one. But we can also find transitions between SQPs which cannot be interpreted as narrowing or broadening steps. Such transitions agglomerate several SQPs in the form of a task-specific procedural pattern. As yet, SQPs have only been extracted "manually" from dialogue histories. But it should not be too difficult to use machine-learning techniques in order to extract and generate frequently used SQPs and associated transitions from given protocols automatically. It is one of our current research goals to adapt existing methods for the inductive acquisition of procedural task knowledge (cf. Hoppe & Plötzner, 1989) to the specific requirements of IR.

In order to describe SQPs formally, we suggest the following **notational conventions**: An SQP is defined as a term with two arguments; in the first argument the view is specified and in the second a list of attributes. Within the attribute list, attribute names are identified with variables to be instantiated (in case of requested or user-specified values) or constants (in case of a specified attribute with a constant constraint). Variable names must begin with a capital letter. To-be-specified attributes are marked with the prefix '!'; requested attributes by the prefix '?'. Furthermore, it is useful to distinguish single-valued from list-valued attributes. The latter will be indicated by the suffix '*'. For list-valued attributes which are to be specified, it is important to know their logical connection. If the connection is uniform, e.g. always OR, this is indicated in brackets after the attribute name, otherwise the variable has to be replaced by a pattern containing variable names and logical operators. In the uniform case, the logical operation is interpreted as a prefix operator applied to the list of arguments, so that [NOT OR] is interpreted as a negated disjunction, whereas the specification [OR NOT] would generally not make sense for a list of arguments. Figure 6 shows an example of such a formal description specifying a query in the product view where *product* (the product name) is requested, a disjunction of *ranges of application* may be specified together with a negative specification of a *product group*. Of course, the formal specification of logical operators does not imply that the user has to use the same formal notation. The system may offer the user much easier ways of specifying logical connections.

```
SQP ( view: product-view,
        attributes:    ?product* = Prod,
                       !range-of-application*[OR] = Range,
                       !product-group[NOT] = Group )
```

Figure 6 : An example SQP

Compositions of several SQPs can be regarded as **plans** in the sense of Sacerdoti (1977). The components of such a plan may be partially organized in sequential form, but may also contain order-independent and optional elements. An adequate representation of plans has to account for these possible control structures as well as for hierarchically-nested plan structures and dependencies between parameters (cf. Hoppe, 1988; Schwab, 1989).

The following sequence gives an example of such a plan in the EXPRESS environment: Assume that the user first selects the product view, specifies a product, and requests its contents, purpose(s), and possible range(s) of application. The information on contents, i.e. a set of substances, is then used for specifying the content in the content/effect view in order to obtain a set of possible effects (requested attribute). For a subset of these effects, which are considered to be particularly critical, the user may invert this query pattern by specifying effects and asking for the complete set of critical substances. In the last step, the product view is queried by specifiying purpose and range as elements of the initially found value sets and specifying the contents as the negated disjunction of critical substances.

Such a plan could be employed to perform the task of assessing the environmental compatibility of some given product and finding less dangerous substitutes. Figure 7 shows how this plan can be represented as a sequence of SQP's with certain parameter constraints expressed in the "where" clause. It is important to note that the final actions are, although highly constrained, not completely determined by the initial query. The concrete instantiation of parameters depends on decisions on the part of the user and has to be handled interactively. Schemata like the one in Figure 7 can be used to monitor the user's task performance, detect potential errors, and suggest further steps or modifications. Suggestions may be presented in the form of optional selection menues.

A plan like "find-substitutes" is clearly domain-specific and should not be confounded with a general retrieval strategy. Nevertheless, general retrieval strategies like block-building or citation pearl growing can be modeled in a similar way.

```
find-substitutes ::=
    sequence-of (    SQP-1 (    view: product-view,
                                attributes:  !product = Prod1,
                                             ?content* = Cont1,
                                             ?purpose* = Purp1,
                                             ?range-of-application* = Rang1 ),
                     SQP-2 (    view: content/effect-view,
                                attributes:  !content*[OR] = Cont2,
                                             ?effect* = Eff2 ),
                     SQP-3 (    view: content/effect-view,
                                attributes:  !effect*[OR] = Eff3,
                                             ?content* = Cont3 ),
                     SQP-4 (    view: product-view,
                                attributes:  !content*[NOT OR] = Cont4,
                                             !purpose = Purp4,
                                             !range-of-application = Rang4,
                                             ?product* = Prod4 ) )
    where        ( Cont2 ⊆ Cont1, Eff3 ⊆ Eff2, Cont4 ⊆ Cont3,
                 Purp4 ∈ Purp1, Rang4 ∈ Rang1 ).
```

Figure 7 : Plan "find-substitutes"

Epilogue: An example dialogue

In order to illustrate the potential benefit of providing interfaces like EXPRESS with a knowledge base of SQPs and plans, let us follow a hypothetical natural language dialogue based on the *find-substitute* plan. We assume that the user has already completed SQP-1 (specifying some product ABC) and the next step SQP-2 (looking at the effects of ABC's contents), which makes it probable that something like *find-substitute* could be intended. So, the system may present the effects (Eff2) and suggest:

.....

System: "Amongst these effects, select those you would like to focus on."

User: (selects some effects)

System: "Would you like to see a complete list of substances which might produce these effects?"

User: Yes.

System: (shows the list)
"Would you like to find other products which do not contain any of these substances and could be used instead of ABC?"

User: Yes.

System: (presents the previous results Rang1 and Purp1)
"Please select the range of application and the purpose for the substitute."

.....

Obviously, this kind of user support is not bound to a natural language interface but could also be provided using graphical presentation and interaction techniques together with "canned text". And of course, the same precautions which apply to any intelligent user interface will have to be taken, e.g. avoid being intrusive, or: do not overload the user with information unless it is really needed in order to perform the task. But considering the current reality of factual Information Retrieval, we find good reasons to try to construct better interfaces for the end user. Providing the interface with more knowledge about terminology, tactics, and strategies might help.

To evaluate and extend the knowledge base in the next version of the EXPRESS system, we plan to empirically identify SQP's by means of automatically analyzing protocols of user queries. This will allow us to assess transition probabilities between tactical moves or shifts of focus, which will then provide a further basis for user support.

Acknowledgements

We would like to thank our colleagues Bernd Kostka and Sylvie Tschumakoff for the implementation of the SunView interface to EXPRESS and other valuable technical support.

6 References

Ammersbach, K. (1986): *Benutzermodelle für Information-Retrieval-Systeme*. Diplomarbeit, Technische Hochschule Darmstadt, Fachbereich Psychologie, Februar 1986.

Ammersbach, K.; Fuhr, N. & Knorz, G. (1988): *Empirisch gestützte Konzeption einer neuen Generation von Werkstoffdatenbanken*. In: Strohl-Goebel, H. (ed.): Deutscher Dokumentartag 1987, Weinheim.

Armstrong, C. J. & Large, J. A. (1988): *Developing search strategies*. In: Armstrong, C. J. et al. (eds.): Manual of online search strategies. Aldershot et al. (Gower), pp. 1-43.

Barthès, C. & Glize, P. (1988): *Planning in an Expert System for Information Retrieval*. In: Proceedings of ACM SIGIR '88, Grenoble, pp. 535-550.

Bates, M. (1987): *How to use Information Search Tactics online*. In: ONLINE, May 1987.

Brajnik, G.; Guida, G. & Tasso, C. (1987): *User Modeling in Intelligent Information Retrieval*. In: Information Processing & Management, Vol. 23, No 4, pp. 59-63.

Brooks, H.M., Daniels, P.J. & Belkin, N.J. (1985): *Problem Descriptions and User Models: Developing an Intelligent Interface for Document Retrieval Systems*. In: Advances in Intelligent Retrieval, Proceedings of Informatics 8, London: Aslib, 1985, pp. 191-214.

Brooks, H.M. (1987): *Expert Systems and Intelligent Information Retrieval*. In: Information Processing & Management, Vol. 23, No 4, pp. 367-382.

Card, S.K., Moran, T.P. & Newell, A. (1983): *The Psychology of Human-Computer Interaction*. Hillsdale, NJ: Erlbaum.

Fidel, R. (1985): *Moves in Online Searching*. In: Online Review 1985, Vol. 9, No 1, pp. 61-74.

Fischer, G. & Nieper-Lemke, H. (1989): *HELGON: Extending the Retrieval by Reformulation Paradigm*. In: Proceedings of ACM SIGCHI Conference on Human Factors in Computing Systems, Austin, Texas, April/May 1989, pp. 357-362.

Hayes-Roth, B. & Hayes-Roth, F. (1979): *A Cognitive Model of Planning*. In: Cognitive Science, Vol. 3/4, pp. 275-310.

Hoppe, H.U. (1988): *Task-Oriented Parsing – A Diagnostic Method to be Used by Adaptive Systems*. In: Proceedings of ACM SIGCHI Conference on Human Factors in Computing Systems, Washington D.C., May 1988, pp. 241-247.

Hoppe, H.U. & Plötzner, R. (1989): *Inductive Methods for Acquiring Task-Knowledge in Adaptive Systems*. GMD-Tech. Report No. 392, Birlinghoven, FRG.

Kobsa, A. & Wahlster, W. (eds.) (1989): *User Models in Dialogue Systems*. Berlin-Heidelberg-New York: Springer.

Linden, F. (1987): *Wissensgestützte Datenbankauswahl und Recherche*. WBS-Bericht 5/87, TU Berlin, Inst. f. Angewandte Informatik.

Mannes, S. & Kintsch, W. (1989): *Action Planning: Routine Computing Tasks*. In: Proceedings of 10th Conference of the Cognitive Science Societ,. Montreal, Canada, August 17-19, 1988, pp. 97-103.

McAlpine, G. & Ingwersen, P. (1989): *Integrated Information Retrieval in a Knowledge Worker Support System*. In: Proceedings of ACM SIGIR '89, Cambridge, MA, June 25–28, 1989, pp. 48–57.

Monarch, I. & Carbonell, J. (1986): *CoalSORT: A Knowledge-Based Interface to an Information Retrieval System*. Tech. Report, Carnegie-Mellon University, Pittsburg, PA.

Payne, S.J. & Green, T.R.G. (1986): *Task-Action Grammars – a Model of the Mental Representation of Task Languages*. In: Human-Computer Interaction, Vol. 2, pp. 93-133.

Rich, E. (1979): *Building and Exploiting User Models*. PhD Thesis, Computer Science Department, Carnegie-Mellon University, Pittsburg, PA.

Sacerdoti, E. (1974): *A Structure for Plans and Behavior*. Amsterdam: North-Holland.

Schwab, T. (1989): *Methoden zur Dialog- und Benutzermodellierung in adaptiven Computersystemen*. PhD Thesis, Univ. Stuttgart: Inst. f. Informatik.

Shoval, P. (1983): *Knowledge Representation in Consultation Systems for Users of Retrieval Systems*. In: The ·Application of Mini- and Micro-Computers in Information, Documentation and Libraries. Amsterdam: North Holland, pp. 631-643.

Smith, P.J.; Steven, J.S.; Galdes, D. & Chignell, M.H. (1989): *Knowledge-Based Search Tactics for an Intelligent Intermediary System*. In: ACM Transactions on Information Systems, Vol. 7, No 3, pp. 246-270.

Vickery, A. & Brooks, H.M. (1987): *PLEXUS – the Expert System for Referral*. In: Information Processing & Management, Vol. 23, No 2, pp. 29-117.

Zloof, M.M. (1983): *The Query-by-Example Concept for User-Oriented Business Systems*. In: Sime, M.E. & Coombs, M.J. (1983): Designing for Human-Computer Communication, London: Academic Press, pp. 285-309.

Hypertext, Full Text, and Automatic Linking

Dr. James H. Coombs
Institute for Research in Information and Scholarship
Box 1946, Brown University
Providence, RI 02912

ABSTRACT

Current computing systems typically support only mid-century information structures: simple hierarchies. Hypertext technologies enable users to impose many structures on document sets and, consequently, provide many paths to desired information, but they require that users work their way through some structure. Full-text search eliminates this requirement by ignoring structure altogether. The search strategy can also be restricted to work within specified contexts. The architecture provided for search readily supports automatic linking. These ideas have been tested in IRIS Intermedia.

INTRODUCTION

Most microcomputers and personal workstations provide direct support for a single organization and retrieval method: the hierarchical file system. The limitations of this method were well known in 1945, when Vannevar Bush published "As We May Think." Briefly, the searcher is constrained to a single access path for each item, in spite of the fact that the human mind maintains many access paths. Moreover, locating one item does not necessarily help one locate other items. Bush proposed an "associative indexing" in which one follows trails of links from one item to the next related item.

In the 1960's, researchers such as Engelbart, Nelson, and van Dam responded by acting upon Bush's call for associative indexing. The hypertext systems that have evolved provide users with the ability to record connections between items and, consequently, to structure the same information in many different ways. Along with this multiplicity of structures, one gains a multiplicity of access paths.

In the late 1950's, H. P. Luhn initiated a second line of research—automatic indexing of document content. Automatic indexing systems cut across document hierarchies, enabling one to locate quickly all documents that contain the word "profit," for example. In effect, the index provides a representation of the documents without any of the original organization, either within or between documents. The index may be organized in any way that supports the quick location of a term; typical structures include b-trees and hash tables.

Recently, the hypertext and search technologies have begun to merge. At Hypertext '87, Frank Halasz noted the limitations of navigating through hypertext networks and called for the elevation of "search and query" to a "primary access mechanism on par with navigation" [1987, 353-54]. Indeed, SuperBook had already made some efforts in this direction but only for a single static document at a time [Remde 1987]. Two years later at Hypertext '89, a number of researchers presented their latest results.

These efforts make important contributions to our knowledge, but they do not address the need for the synergistic integration of search and manual linking in large, multi-user, dynamic databases. First, I provide a brief survey of the recent research. Then I describe the effort at IRIS to develop fully integrated capabilities.

THE STATE OF THE ART: HYPERTEXT '89

Frisse and Cousins: Information Retrieval From Hypertext

Frisse and Cousins report progress in creating a hypertext of the *Manual of Medical Therapeutics* (Frisse 1989). They decomposed the manual into card-sized units, organized hierarchically. Key terms from each card have been indexed, and the index terms have also been organized hierarchically, according to probabilistic dependencies. As users traverse the network of linked cards, they can indicate whether they Like or Don't Like the current card, causing the recomputation and possible restructuring of the index. The values assigned to each index node will then be used as a sort of relevance metric. As the authors state, the approach offers many interesting possibilities, but they have limited themselves so far to "small information spaces" in laboratory settings.

Before the research can be transferred into a less restricted environment, several issues must be addressed. First, the computation of probabilistic dependencies appears to rely on tightly constrained indexing of cards. The example card presented in the paper consists of approximately sixty word types, but only three have been indexed. This procedure opens the door to the well-known difficulties of manual indexing and has not been supplemented by full-text indexing. Such selective indexing appears to be required by the algorithm for updating the belief network, which applies the user's evaluation of the card to all indexed terms. Second, the approach appears to militate heavily against the sort of lengthy documents that people typically read and write. This paper, for example, lives in a single document, and it would be unnatural to split the document up into many small units. I want to focus on the ideas and their expression, not in accommodating myself to the requirements of the system. Finally, it remains to be seen how users will respond to the evaluation buttons. The system relies on a binary vote, but this requires an extra decision that many users may find burdensome. We can predict that people will be frustrated by the requirement that they map an analogic evaluation onto a binary evaluation. A Don't Care button might alleviate this response, even if the system simply ignores the selection. Even without this placebo, the consequences of voting will frequently lead to no observable consequences, and we can predict that people will simply stop voting.

Croft and Turtle: A Retrieval Model Incorporating Hypertext Links

Like Frisse and Cousins, Croft and Turtle use Bayesian inference networks [Croft 1989]. Instead of attempting to exploit a belief network based on elicited testimony, however, they seek to describe a model that "appears to capture the major aspects of previous probabilistic IR models and can easily be extended to include hypertext links" [1989, 214]. In short, one has a variety of reasons to infer that a particular node, or document, is about a particular topic. Crucially, if node 1 is about concept C and node 2 is linked to node 1, then there is some reason to believe that node 2 is also about concept C. To accommodate a variety of information retrieval techniques in this model, Croft and Turtle extend the notion of link to include statistically derived nearest neighbors, direct citations, and structural hierarchies as well as the manual links that one normally associates with hypertext.

In many ways, the Croft-Turtle model is exemplary in its integration of hypertext information with traditional information retrieval techniques. Moreover, the network does not require elicitations of information from the user. On the other hand, the lack of information on how the system is performing eliminates the possibility for adapting automatically to users' needs. More seriously, the authors note that Bayesian inference networks are directed, acyclic dependency graphs, creating a topology restriction that has no meaning to most users. For example, two documents could not cite each other; yet one often sees such mutual citations in collections of papers, especially where the papers take conference discussion into account. Such restrictions would have to be addressed before the model could be tested in an implementation.

Crouch, Crouch, and Andreas:
The Use of Cluster Hierarchies in Hypertext Information Retrieval

Crouch, Crouch, and Andreas favor a more limited approach to the enhancement of information retrieval [Crouch 1989]. They reject the Boolean model because of the difficulty of query formulation and the lack of control over results. Instead, they find the vector space model conceptually simpler and "better suited for use in hypertext retrieval systems" [1989, 227]. In the vector space model, a document is represented as a set of term-weight pairs. In response to a query, the engine searches for the vectors that are most similar to the query vector. A relevance-feedback loop may easily be implemented by searching for the documents most similar to a document that the user selects. The authors extend this well established retrieval technique by automatically computing a hierarchy of document clusters. An interactive browser then assists the user in traversing the hierarchy. Working with the MEDLARS collection, the authors found that they were able to retrieve 55% of the relevant documents for the queries in the test set.

This research project has the major virtue of having been carried through to implementation and testing, although the reported testing has been limited to the use of the system by the researchers themselves. Whatever the success rate achieved by the researchers, one has to be particularly concerned by the complexity of the browser interface, which, among other things, presents to users lists of numbers representing concepts and documents. As the authors explain, "Clicking on a concept number reveals the word forming that concept and the document frequency of the concept." Thus, clicking on the number 3340 reveals "les 90," where "les" is supposed to represent the concept *lesion*. These seem to be system internals instead of user-level abstractions. Just as serious, there is no provision for user-created links, so one wonders to what extent this is a hypertext system. Finally, the value of a computed hierarchy is suspect in an environment that supports a hierarchical file or folder system maintained by human intelligence.

Summary

The three papers described so far have the most bearing on the present discussion. To fill out the picture, however, I should mention the equally valuable papers presented in the second session. Consens and Mendelzon described GraphLog, a graph-based language for querying the structure of a hypertext [Consens 1989]. Clitherow, Riecken, and Muller described preliminary work in the development of an intelligent assistant for the construction of hypertexts [Clitherow 1989]. Finally, Michael Lesk found that card-sized hypertext systems might benefit from the techniques that he has developed for library catalogs [Lesk 1989].

Taken as a whole, the papers presented at Hypertext '89 indicate considerable progress in the development of individual techniques.[1] One does not find, however, a full system that attempts to integrate the essential features of hypertext and traditional information retrieval: manual linking and content-based searching. Moreover, one does not find systems that have proven useful to a large number of people in their daily work.

IRIS INTERMEDIA

IRIS Intermedia provides a multi-windowed, desktop environment supporting the creation and manipulation of documents with a variety of editors [Meyrowitz 1986; Yankelovich 1988; Walter 1989]. In addition to text and graphics, users can create time-lines and animations, and they can control video disk players. An annotation facility supports cooperative work on all types of documents. A Selection Manipulation Protocol supports the exchange of data between applications, permitting the use of a spelling corrector, for example, on text in graphics documents as well as word documents [Coombs 1989]. Finally, a lexical reference (InterLex) enables users to search the *American Heritage Dictionary* and *Roget's II: The New Thesaurus*.[2]

Document Hierarchy

IRIS Intermedia provides two primary methods for organizing information: a hierarchical document system and a hypertext network. The document hierarchy is presented as a desktop, with direct manipulation of folders and their documents. This approach has the advantage of familiarity and simplicity, enabling us to present the system to faculty and students with minimal training. In addition to making the system readily available for real work, by adopting the hierarchical filesystem we directly address the dominant issues of information retrieval in the 20th century. As Vannevar Bush said at mid-century, the organization of information into hierarchies buries important information in "the mass of the inconsequential." Nonetheless, such organizations have proven so compelling that we can expect them to be dominant well into the 21st century, and no one is well served by research that fails to make the most of the structures that people typically create.

Hypertext Network

As a first approach to breaking the tyranny of the absolute hierarchy, Intermedia provides hypertext networks, enabling users to superpose an indefinite variety of structures on a single document set. This mechanism introduces three major concepts into the system: anchors, links, and webs.

At the foundation of the network, one finds **anchors**, which have two functions. First, anchors serve as the end-points of links. Second, they provide a mechanism for attaching a persistent selection and brief annotation to some document content. To create an anchor

---

[1] Historical note—the work described in this paper was demonstrated at Hypertext '89 but was not sufficiently advanced in time for the call for papers.

[2] See Coombs [1990] for information on InterLex. *The American Heritage Dictionary*, College Edition, © 1988, 1985 Houghton Mifflin Company. *Electronic Thesaurus*, © 1986, 1987, 1988 Houghton Mifflin Company.

in Intermedia, one selects some symbol—a square in a structured graphic, a word or a paragraph in a text—and picks the Create Anchor menu item. An optional dialog enables the user to specify an "explainer." The scholar of English literature, for example, might annotate an allusion in Wordsworth's *Prelude* by selecting the passage "The earth is all before me" and providing the explainer "allusion to end of Milton's *Paradise Lost.*"

To **link** two selections together, the user picks the Start Link menu item, traverses to the destination, selects the endpoint, and picks the Complete Link menu item. Anchors can be selected as end points, or the user can leave it to Intermedia to create anchors automatically. Continuing with the previous example, the scholar of English literature would select the anchor just created in *The Prelude,* pick the Start Link menu item, open Book XII of Milton's *Paradise Lost,* select the passage "The World was all before them," and complete the link.

An icon appears above the text, indicating the presence of the link. To traverse from one anchor to the other, the user selects the link icon and picks the Follow menu command (or just double clicks on the icon). Because links are **bidirectional**, the user can quickly traverse back and forth between the end points—perhaps to simplify comparison, perhaps just to return to the previous context.

All anchors and links are collected into **web** documents, permitting the creation of multiple, shared hypertexts from a single document set. The Wordsworth scholar, for example, would create a "Wordsworth" web, and the Milton scholar would create a "Milton" web. Thus, the link from *The Prelude* to *Paradise Lost* would not be imposed upon the Miltonist, although the web could be shared if so desired.

Note that the system does not restrict the network to particular topologies. Users can create cycles if they so desire, and they can create links between anchors in the same document. They can also link selections into sequences, and they frequently impose an informal hierarchy through "overview" documents.

In addition to the link icons that direct attention to adjacent nodes in the network, Intermedia provides a history of recent document events and a local map of links [Utting 1989]. Thus, users can find documents by remembering that they worked with them recently, and they can browse the network directly.

Figure 1 shows penetration into the document hierarchy down to the folder /int/dickens2/Dickens Web 22. The user has opened the documents "DICKENS OVERVIEW" and "19C HISTORY OVERVIEW", which provide alternative structural interpretations of the document database. The arrow icons (in the upper left corners of the boxes) represent links to more information on major topics. In addition to the overview documents, the user has opened the Dickens web. The Web View reveals the scope of the web: 245 documents and 681 links. The history at the top of the document shows the most recent document events and a map of the documents that are linked to the current document. The user can open documents from the history or the map simply by clicking on the document icon.

Evaluation

The hypertext network relieves many of the restrictions of the single document hierarchy. Moreover, the Intermedia approach keeps the users in control; instead of attempting to compute optimal organizations based upon document attributes, the system supports users in creating the organizations that best suit their needs.

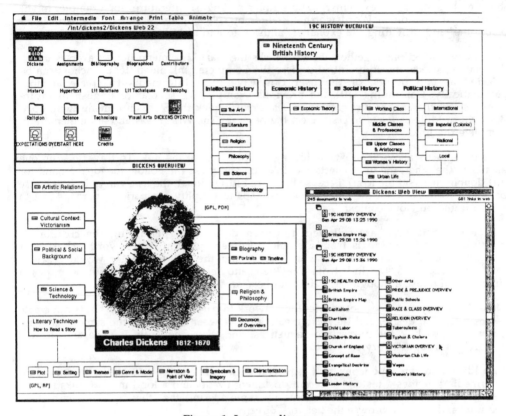

Figure 1. Intermedia screen.

Finally, we must bear in mind that such organizations often have educational value that cannot be achieved by computation. In English courses at Brown University, George Landow [1989a, 1989b] finds that he can instruct students in the need to take a global view of literature by presenting structures that represent the place of an author or a work from many different perspectives at once. Moreover, students add new perspectives to the communal whole by creating their own anchors and links; in the process, they enjoy the advantages of the generationist effect—students who generate their own answers retain knowledge of a field longer than those who receive and memorize.

This is not to say that the automatic computation of structures has no value. In our philosophy at least, all users participate actively in the creation and structuring of information. Without a doubt, they do so mentally even in systems that prohibit them from directly recording some persistent representation of their work. Any technique that helps people find information must be valued, but a system that helps them quickly *re-find* that information may be even more valuable. Manually created links help people re-find information by enabling them to create trails through information that they have found valuable. In sum, automatic structuring techniques should be deployed, but support for manual and personal structuring must take priority.

FULL TEXT

Although such a hypertext model enables users to create many structures, they must still traverse *some* structure in order to locate desired information. In an unfamiliar document set, they may be guided by such informal techniques as Overview and Start Here documents, and they will certainly be helped by the combination of the hierarchical file system with the hypertext structures. One cannot assume, however, that a document set will be carefully authored for presentation to all users. In fact, the assumption must be the opposite: that the database contains useful information organized uselessly.

The need is clear. Users must be able to break through structural boundaries to locate information. As a first step, I have implemented content-based searching in Intermedia.

Acquisition: Invisibility and Currency

First, in order to respond to queries within a few seconds on the average, the system maintains an inverted index with term-frequencies in a b-tree database. An indexer runs constantly for each Intermedia database. When a document is added, modified, or deleted, the Intermedia link server records the appropriate information in a shared table and wakes up the indexer, which immediately updates the database. This technique provides the crucial characteristics of *invisibility* and *currency*. Users neither know nor need to know that the system maintains an index; and in most cases, one has to rush in order to execute a query before the indexer has completed its update.

In addition, the system works with all types of documents. For each document type, we have a document reader that extracts all text. During indexing, the indexer invokes the appropriate document reader and processes the results. New document types can be added to the system simply by adding a document reader; the indexer need not be updated for each format. This approach contributes to a seamless integration, in which users can be sure that they are searching all and only the text in the document database.

Query

To query the index, users initiate a dialog by picking the Full Text menu item. The dialog contains two text-edit fields: one for the search text and the other for the search context. The search text may be a boolean expression, a natural-language expression, or some combination of the two. In short, the user is always right (almost), and the query engine can work out some reasonable strategy. The search context can be the name of any folder that the user wants to treat as the Root of the hierarchy to be searched.

SEARCH TEXT

First, for the *booleans*, the query engine supports *and, or, not,* and parenthetical scoping. Many people claim that these operators are too obscure and arbitrary for naive users, but many users are logically sophisticated and only computationally naive. Booleans, then, have been provided for those who want to use them; compared to the natural language expressions in the system, booleans provide faster response and greater control.

Figure 2. Full Text dialog.

Natural language queries, however, tend to be the first choice. Briefly, users can enter anything they want to, whatever is comfortable; the practice tends toward a list of terms instead of complete sentences. The query engine treats the specification as a disjunct but manipulates the ranking so that the documents with the most matching terms will be ordered first. I had originally intended to implement a quorum-level search, which, given three terms A, B, and C, searches for the conjunct A & B & C and progressively relaxes the query to the disjunct A | B | C. I found, however, that I could compile and execute a complete disjunct faster than a series of more constrained queries. With document ranking and the ability to manipulate the list of results directly, there seems to be little need to artificially limit the size of the result set.

The *ranking* scheme is currently the term frequency times inverse document frequency; specifically, the number of times the term occurs in the document times the log of the number of documents in the database divided by the number of documents that contain the term [Salton 1989]. Because automatic ranking is a relatively rough affair, I do not currently normalize for document length, and the ranking of a boolean is just the maximum of all term rankings for that document. To a large extent, these decisions have been motivated by the need for simplicity and high performance; because information is currently distributed between the full-text and the hypertext databases, normalization would require an extra query for each document. Specifically, I retrieve document ids from the Words table, and then I retrieve the information about documents (name, path, etc.) from the hypertext database. To determine the number of words in the document, I would also have to retrieve the record from the Full Text Documents table. When the query locates several hundred documents to be sorted by relevance, these extra record retrievals could cause a significant performance penalty.

More interesting, perhaps, is the manipulation of natural language queries, where the number of matched terms takes precedence over the ranking of any individual term. This decision may be motivated best by example. Let us say that two literary scholars, a Romanticist and a Miltonist, share an interest in prophetic poetry. The Miltonist, who has assembled a considerable database, offers to share the information with the Romanticist. The Romanticist enters the reasonable query "prophecy Wordsworth Milton." The query engine finds many documents on prophecy and Milton, but few on Wordsworth; moreover, the documents on Wordsworth actually discuss his theory of poetry and provide no discussion of his prophetic attempts or his emulation of Milton.[3] A traditional ranking algorithm would favor the rare term Wordsworth and force these irrelevant documents to the top of the list, ahead of those that discuss prophetic poetry. We could have had our Romanticist assign weights to the query terms to indicate their relative importance, but the poor fellow has not mastered propositional logic much less probability theory. The current algorithm alleviates this problem somewhat by ordering first those terms that contain both "prophecy" and "Milton." Notice that the results of the ranking approximate the results of a quorum-level search.

MORPHOLOGICAL ANALYSIS

Each term in the query may optionally be expanded into its full inflectional set or its full derivational set. Most users seek information on a topic, not information on the use of particular forms of words. Thus, there should be no need for them to generate the likely forms of a word; they should be able to keep their minds on the current task. Our Romanticist, for example, should not have to specify the inflection "prophecies" or the derivationally related words "prophet," "prophetic," etc. Unlike suffix stripping, this analysis is based on information derived from *The American Heritage Dictionary*, ensuring an unusually high accuracy [Coombs 1990]. Moreover, the system analyzes prefixes as well as suffixes, enabling one to locate such terms as "pseudoprophet" and "antiprophet."

By default, the system applies full derivational analysis, and users generally accept the setting. The ability to restrict the analysis to inflections provides users with some control in cases where the derivational analysis seems to have gone awry. In addition, the system supports full regular expressions, so users can use the equivalent of the traditional "truncation operators" if they so choose.

SEARCH CONTEXT

In addition to the search text, users can specify a context by restricting the search to a particular branch of the document hierarchy. Without worrying about database organization then, a user can restrict the search to Shakespeare, or to the Unix man pages, or to the filtering team's design documents, etc. This capability can be exploited to home in on a section of the document hierarchy. Interested in the web concept, for example, the user might search the entire database, locating over two-hundred documents. In the list, the user spots Vannevar Bush's "As We May Think" and discovers that there is a "Hypertext History" folder. Since that folder provides a promising area for further exploration, the user clicks on the folder name, establishing a new search context. Further

---

[3] This is an imaginary example to illustrate the point. In the Dickens database, the query actually locates only 11 documents.

searches will not be cluttered with design documents from the filtering team or chapters of a medical textbook. Moreover, the user can simply click on the folder "Hypertext History" to switch from the full text to the folder browsers. Alternatively, the folder could be opened by clicking on the title bar of the "As We May Think" document.

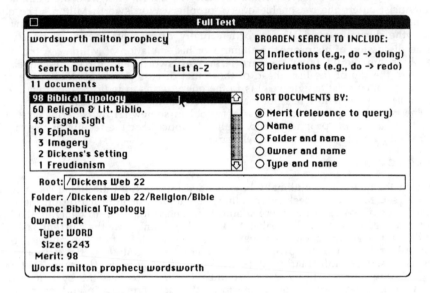

Figure 3. Document Search dialog with controls displayed.

In addition to focusing the search, such context restrictions are taken into account during query optimization and frequently provide faster response. For example, searching the 5024 documents in our main database for all forms of *web* locates 228 documents in 9 seconds. Restricting the search to the 33 documents in the Hypertext History branch locates 7 documents in 1 second.

In some cases it might be useful to restrict a search to sets of folders or even to sets of documents. The interface would be significantly complicated by this additional power, however, and we do not believe that users would frequently take advantage of such capabilities.

Document List

In many ways, the display and manipulation of the results is as important as the query itself. The dialog displays the results in a sorted, scrollable list. Figure 3 shows the dialog expanded to reveal the complete set of controls.

The list may be sorted by any of five criteria, each designed to meet a typical need:

- Merit, or computed relevance—for topic-oriented searching. This is the default and by far the favorite among users.

- Document name—for assistance in recall of a document whose location has been forgotten.

- Folder name then document name—to examine the results by project area, etc. This sort can provide a quick way to determine the density of documents in a particular branch of the hierarchy and provides a good preliminary to context-restricted searching.

- Document owner then name—to find one's own documents in particular, or perhaps those of team members.

- Document type then name—to locate graphics documents, for example.

For each sort, the list changes to display the attributes that the user has chosen. This approach reduces the display required for the list and eliminates the complexity of introducing a horizontal scroll bar. Moreover, such adaptive display guarantees that the information of interest remains in view. To display extended information on a document, the user need only click on the item in the list; the bottom of the dialog then displays the document's folder, name, owner, type, size, and merit as well as a list of the terms located in the document.

Perhaps most important, this ability to sort the list provides an unusually intuitive second-stage query capacity. If I am looking for one of my own documents, for example, I can search for a term, sort by owner, and then scroll to the portion of the list containing my documents. In order to retrieve the same information in a static list, the system would have to provide the capability to specify the values of many different properties in a single query. The result will be either a query language that is too complicated for all but expert users or a massive property sheet with fields for all possible properties.

Document Manipulation

To open a document in the list, the user need only select the item and pick the Open menu command, or just double-click on the item. The system launches the document with its normal application and appearance. The Find command is fed a list of the terms located in the search, which the user can then locate by executing the command. There has been some interest in having the document scroll immediately to the first occurrence of a term, but one does not always want to skip over the introductory information, which generally provides the best indication of what the document is really about. In addition, the system could highlight all occurrences of the located terms, but doing so can make the document hard to read when the terms occur in dense patterns. A useful option might be to toggle exhaustive highlighting on and off, but users seem to consider this more of an interesting possibility than something that would help them in their work.

Evaluation

The Full Text application provides Intermedia users with a simple tool for breaking structural boundaries and locating information quickly. Figure 4 illustrates the close integration of Full Text with other Intermedia capabilities. In this example, the user has recognized the importance of overview documents in the Dickens database. In order to get a quick sense of the entire database, the user brings up Full Text and searches for the word "overview," which generates a list of all overview documents in the database.

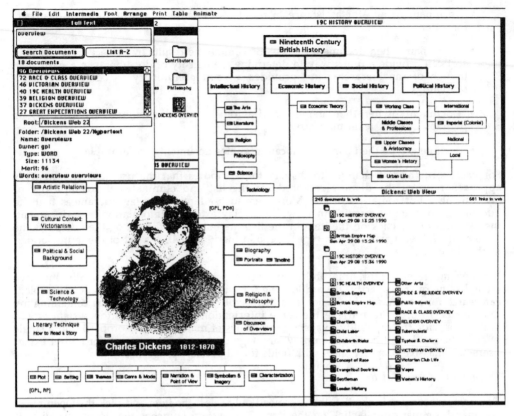

Figure 4. Intermedia screen with Full Text dialog

In addition to its integration and simplicity, the dialog resembles the heavily used dictionary tool (InterLex) in important ways. First, the default display provides the simplest functionality, and extended controls may be revealed or hidden by picking a menu command. This design enables users to adjust settings and immediately recover screen space. When they need more control for an extended period, all controls appear in a single window instead of drifting around the screen on a floating palette. Finally, the two dialogs present identical controls for morphological analysis, which has been available in Intermedia for nearly two years.

In sum, the interface has required minimal instruction. In fact, the single one-hour presentation of the research proved sufficient for current Intermedia users. From the user's point of view, the invisibility and currency of the indexing process provides for a seamless integration. The system might benefit from a relevance feedback capability, and I intend to experiment in that direction.

In addition to an interactive tool, Full Text has proven useful as a foundation for the automatic linking of documents and passages. In Intermedia, Auto Link has two functions. First, the application assists users in initiating a web on a topic. The Miltonist, for example, can quickly link all references to the angel Abdiel in *Paradise Lost* to an overview document with a module on typology. Inappropriate links can easily be deleted, and anchor extents can be edited at leisure. Second, the application can automatically resolve coded cross references in imported documents. The *Online Mendelian Inheritance in Man*, for example, contains such references as "See 10082," where 10082 is the number of the article on the "ACHOO Syndrome" (for Autosomal Dominant Compelling Helioophthalmic Outburst Syndrome). Instead of the opaque reference "See 10082", users should be presented with "See ACHOO Syndrome," with a link from the reference to the appropriate document. We have observed other documents, such as dictionaries, that include such cross references.

A full description of Auto Link will have to await another forum, but Figure 5 should give some indication of the functionality. To disambiguate article references from other numbers, I converted the references from the form "See 10082" to "See omim10082"; in addition, I appended the article number to the end of each article, in the form "art10082." The figure shows the dialog prepared to locate all documents containing identifier patterns such as "art10082." The ANCHOR LINKS IN SOURCE radio button specifies that anchors will be created at the start of these source documents. For each source document, Auto Link retrieves a list of the documents containing, e.g., "omim10082", which is the reference pattern. The ANCHOR LINKS IN DESTINATION radio button specifies that the reference pattern will be replaced by the name of the source document and that the name will be the endpoint of the link. In the example, then, the article on ACHOO Syndrome will have a single link marker at the top, which the user can select to view a list of all referring articles. The referring articles will have text such as "See ACHOO Syndrome" with links back to the ACHOO Syndrome article. Thus, the user is presented with a clear reference and a simple traversal mechanism. Moreover, the hypertext creator can perform much of the work automatically instead of working through the nearly 6,000 articles by hand.

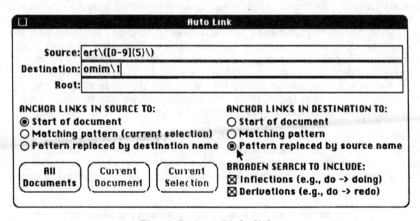

Figure 5. Auto Link dialog

Intermedia has been proven through use at IRIS and in Brown University courses since 1986. The full-text searching capabilities have been available at IRIS since October 1989 and will be put in the classroom with the next release.

The scale and diversity of use constitutes something of a trail by fire if not outright abuse. At IRIS, we have approximately thirty users, including software engineers, managers, and materials developers. We create more than 32,000 documents a year in our primary database, of which we delete approximately 85%. In all of our databases combined, we have over 17,000 active documents, consuming approximately 250 Mb of disk space. They include not just design documents but all of Shakespeare, two medical text books, a study of Chinese poetry, and two published hypertexts ("Exploring the Moon" and "The Dickens Web"). Documents and webs may be accessed by many users concurrently, and we rely on the system for much of our engineering teamwork. In addition to the IRIS installation, a Brown University classroom provides facilities for Biology and English courses, ranging from introductory to graduate level.

The environment provides challenges of type as well as scale. Users can create or import whatever documents they like. Thus, we at times have a single database with documents from many different domains. Second, we have a variety of applications, each with its own type of document. Applications currently include not just text and graphics but also timelines, animations, and videos.

Criticisms

In short, the ideas have been tested in working environments, and the response has been overwhelmingly positive. A few criticisms stand out. First, users need to search for **phrases**, not just conjunctions of terms. They have not responded well to descriptions of proximity operators, which introduce considerable syntactic complexity; but they do believe that the ability to search for a phrase such as "concept inferencing" would be a major improvement. The request may be to a large extent a consequence of the fact that they can search *The American Heritage Dictionary* for phrases when they use InterLex, the lexical reference. Adding such capabilities, however, would require the introduction of some operator, such as quotation marks, to distinguish phrases from lists of terms. Moreover, disk space requirements would increase substantially, making the full text capabilities less palatable to resource administrators. Currently, indexes consume about 50% as much as text-only documents; I estimate that full support for phrases would double the size of the index. Alternatively, the system could re-read documents to check for phrases, but searches would be considerably slowed by the additional overhead. All things considered, we believe that the current system sits well on the tradeoff curve, so only a change in the environment can justify the introduction of phrasal searching.

Second, there has been some discussion about the possibility of providing more flexibility in **sorting** the list of documents. Some would like to see the ability to sort by any combination of document attributes. The current system, however, provides an extremely simple set of controls, and no one has come to me with a real problem that they would like to solve.

Finally, the display of **merit numbers** has caused some confusion and many suggestions. At first, users think that the number is the count of occurrences of the specified term in the document. When they are told that the number represents a computed relevance, they are not sure what to think. The first response is usually that the order alone should be sufficient, but they quickly agree that the difference between 98 and 3 is significant, suggesting that, in the "Wordsworth Milton prpohecy" example, the "Biblical Typology" document has a lot more information on the topic than does the "Imagery" document. Without the numbers, the degree of difference would not be represented. To simplify the conceptual model, I present the computed relevance as a confidence factor ranging from 1 to 99%. For example, I am 98% certain that the "Biblical Typology" document will be worth examining.

CONCLUSION

Current computing systems typically support only mid-century information structures: simple hierarchies. Hypertext technologies enable users to impose many structures on document sets and, consequently, provide many paths to desired information, but they still require that users work their way through some structure. Full-text search eliminates this requirement by ignoring structure altogether. Once the user has broken through to an interesting structure, we can readily reconstruct the boundaries by constraining full-text search to a specified branch of the hierarchy. Thus, the user can selectively work through the document set, ignoring and exploiting the hierarchy at will. Finally, the architecture provided for full-text search readily supports automatic linking.

ACKNOWLEDGMENTS

Funding for this project was provided in part through research contracts with Apple Computer, Inc.

REFERENCES

Clitherow, P., D. Riecken., and M. Muller. 1989. VISAR: A system for inference and navigation of hypertext. *Hypertext '89 Proceedings*. New York: ACM.

Coombs, J. H., Fitzmaurice, G., and Utting, K. D.. "Selection manipulation protocol: An interface to application data." IRIS Technical Report 89-7, Brown University, Providence RI, 1989.

Consens, M. P., and A. O. Mendelzon. 1989. Expressing structural hypertext queries in GraphLog. *Hypertext '89 Proceedings*. New York: ACM.

Coombs, J. H. 1990. Cognitive tools: From dictionary to IRIS InterLex. In review.

Croft, W. B., and H. Turtle. 1989. A retrieval model incorporating hypertext links. *Hypertext '89 Proceedings*. New York: ACM.

Crouch, D. B., C. J. Crouch, and G. Andreas. 1989. The use of cluster hierarchies in hypertext information retrieval. *Hypertext '89 Proceedings*. New York: ACM.

Frisse, M. E., and S. B. Cousins. 1989. Information retrieval from hypertext: Update on the Dynamic Medical Handbook Project. *Hypertext '89 Proceedings*. New York: ACM.

Halasz, F. G. 1987. Reflections on NoteCards: Seven issues for the next generation of hypermedia systems. *Hypertext '87 Proceedings*. New York: ACM.

Landow, G. P. 1989a. Hypertext in literary education. *Computing in the Humanities,* 23. 173-98.

Landow, G. P. 1989b. Course assignments using hypertext: The example of Intermedia. *Journal of Research on Computing in Education,* 21. 349-65.

Lesk, M. 1989. What to do when there's too much information. *Hypertext '89 Proceedings.* New York: ACM.

Meyrowitz, N.. 1986. Intermedia: The architecture and construction of an object-oriented hypermedia system and applications framework. *Proceedings OOPSLA '86.* New York: ACM.

Remde, J. R., Gomez, L. M., and Landauer, T. K. 1987. SuperBook: An automatic tool for information exploration—hypertext? *Hypertext '87 Proceedings.* New York: ACM.

Salton, Gerard. 1989. *Automatic Text Processing.* Reading, MA: Addison-Wesley.

Utting, K., and N. Yankelovich. 1989. Context and orientation in hypermedia networks. *ACM Transactions on Information Systems,* 7. 58-84.

Walter, Mark. 1989. IRIS's Intermedia: Multiuser hypertext. *Seybold Report on Publishing Systems,* 18. August 7. 21-32.

Yankelovich, Nicole, Bernard J. Haan, Norman K. Meyrowitz, and Steven M. Drucker. 1988. Intermedia: The concept and construction of a seamless information environment. *IEEE Computer,* 21. 81-96.

MACHINE LEARNING AND VECTORIAL MATCHING
FOR AN IMAGE RETRIEVAL MODEL :
EXPRIM AND THE SYSTEM RIVAGE

Halin G., Créhange M., Kerekes P.

Centre de Recherche en Informatique de Nancy (CRIN) : CNRS UA 262,
BP 239 - 54506 Vandœuvre-lès-Nancy , Cedex - FRANCE.
Tél: 83 91 21 57. Electronic address : @halin.loria.crin.fr. or marion.loria.crin.fr

I. INTRODUCTION

Image retrieval is a field of general Computer Aided Information Retrieval. It is of great interest to us from two points of view. Not only in itself, but also as a particularly sensitive application area and testbed of various models and techniques which, although applicable in other fields, become much more spectacular in this one. It is especially clear for models and techniques which apply to the aspects of man-machine communication. We present some of our ideas in this domain, based on the realization and experimentation of the prototype RIVAGE, built for the EXPRIM project. It deals with an image database, stored for instance on a videodisk, coupled with an alphanumeric database, called the "descriptive database", which contains descriptions and possibly other knowledge about the images.

An attempt to make a system understand a user's need -thanks to a man-machine dialogue- may be viewed as a machine-learning problem (§ III.1). We show that it may even be considered as a mutual learning between man and machine, thanks to a **deep interactivity**, in which man and machine share responsibility. In the prototype RIVAGE, we have brought into action machine-learning techniques based, on the one hand, on "examples and negative examples" and, on the other hand, on the use of a taxonomy (the thesaurus). Examples and negative examples are given by the user's choices of images among the set of images the system proposes following a request. Since image visualization is instant, the set of proposed images is allowed to be large and the method we describe is very powerful.

At the kernel of the retrieving process is the means of matching between request and documents. Our first idea was to use boolean matching but after studies we have chosen vectorial matching. Actually, vectorial matching makes it possible to implement a more flexible and progressive partial matching and is a better support for a machine-learning process for retrieval.

This paper presents (§ III) a modelization of vectorial matching associated with the machine-learning process. It then describes the prototype RIVAGE (§ IV) through an object-oriented description of one of the main objects : the thesaurus. It closes (§ V) with an evaluation of it, following an experimentation by a documentalist and by users.

II. INFORMATION RETRIEVAL AND IMAGE RETRIEVAL

II.1. Relevance feedback

When you are looking for documents, you rarely find a satisfying set at the first try. Why ? For two main reasons. First, even if you can precisely define your need, the way you express it may not correspond with the descriptions of some relevant documents ; this may be for lexical or more semantic reasons [Chi 86]. But a second possible reason is that your need, particularly if its criteria are somewhat abstract, may not be clear or not completely thought out, and has still to be defined or adapted to the database content.

When a retrieval system has to fight against the first above reason, it must use a semantic knowledge, a very classic one being a thesaurus. This may help in combatting the second reason but is not sufficient. Techniques relying on relevance feedback are very effective. One might say that they provide noise to fight against silence : they propose to the user a pretty lenient answer to his request, ask him to choose, amongst the retrieved documents, which ones fit with his need, and then use this information to try to know his need better. This method has been studied and put into action by several authors [Sal 84] [v Rij 79]. It proves to be very effective ; but one great difficulty is to provide enough noise but not too much, since observing and judging proposed documents may be heavy when documents are litteral. Let us show that it becomes particularly pertinent for image retrieval.

II.2. Image specificities

A very frequent use of image retrieval is for illustration purposes. And the range of the illustrating ways is often broad. So, a pretty large freedom exists between the demand (the need) and the relevant images. Sometimes the user can and wishes to dictate his way of illustrating, so limiting this freedom a priori. But often he prefers to be guided by the base content and possibly by intuition to choose a way. Relevance feedback is particularly suitable in this case. In place of helping to bring to light an existing retrieval target, it aids in conceiving a new one.

To this argument concerning the image as "the object to retrieve", an argument relying on the nature of the retrieving objective, we may add very interesting arguments concerning the nature of the image information itself. First, an image may be a very dense information container. Secondly, its reading by man is extremely fast : this quality enables the organization of a relevance feedback based on a bold understanding of the needs ; noises may be numerous, unsuitable images will be quickly eliminated. A third fertile property of images is that viewing an image or a set of images, together or as a sequence, may entail imagination and reflexion. So, visualization may suggest to a searcher new ideas of illustrating his subject or a new understanding of the domain of his need [Hal 89a].

A last argument is that the means of storing images make it possible to intimately include visualization in the retrieval process since it may be done online.

II.3. The EXPRIM process : how to fight against silence by noise
(or how to lightly lie to learn truth)

The target of EXPRIM (EXPert to Retrieve IMages) is to aid a user, especially a "naive" one, in progressively retrieving images from an image database coupled with a descriptive database. The project has been supported by the European ESPRIT program and by the French PRC BD3 (Programme de Recherches Coordonnées "Bases de données de 3ème génération"). The EXPRIM process is conceived as the iteration of three phases : "before-visualization", "visualization" and "after-visualization" [Cre 89b].
- In the before-visualization phase, the system may help the user to formulate or reformulate his demand. Then the role of the system is to transform this primitive demand into a system query which is used to retrieve descriptions from the descriptive database. The result of this phase is an image set called : selected image set.
- The visualization phase gives the user the capability of friendly displaying and manipulating the selected images, classifying them and finally making a choice. The result of this phase is three image sets called : chosen image set, rejected image set, neutral image set.

- In the after-visualization phase, the system tries to understand the user's real needs, relying on the previous image choices. The result of this last phase is a new demand which may be, after the user's agreement or addition, submitted to a next "before-visualization" phase.

So, the process is based on two strong complementarities : one between user and system, and the other one between image and text. User and system are complementary because the latter only works on descriptions, whereas the former works on images (and possibly descriptions) ; moreover, the user judges and influences the system's decisions and completes them by visual inference. This shows the complementarity between images and descriptions.

The before-visualization phase often moulds the initial request in an enlarging sense to obtain a large selected image set, that is to say to produce noise (selection of non suitable documents) or to lightly lie. This noise is very useful because it will be the means of finding documents which have some relationship with the demand but were not really present in the user's mind. And the visualization phase makes it possible to eliminate the really non-relevant images and to keep the interesting ones, so suppressing some silences (non selection of suitable images). Moreover, the after-visualization phase makes it possible to try to recover (to learn) the reasons why these images fit the need and to teach these reasons to the user. Nothing surprising if we call on machine-learning techniques to realize this process.

III. THE IMAGE RETRIVAL MODEL (IRM) [Cre 89a] [Hal 88] [Hal 89b]

The IRM is based on a general learning process which allows the system to guide the user in his image quest. This general process has two principal components :
- the matching process which enables the proposition of an image set to the user,
- the reformulation process which proposes a possible formulation of his needs to the user.

In this paragraph we present the IRM at its different levels : first the learning process is globally explained, then in the two following parts we detail the two components : the matching process and the reformulation process.

III.1. The learning process

The learning we propose is a **learning from examples** thanks to the use of a taxonomy [Mic 83]. In this learning, the user's demand stands for one expression of the concept to learn, while the chosen image descriptions stand for concept positive examples and rejected image descriptions stand for negative examples. The considered method consists of representing the demand expression by an **expression level** built as a marking of terms with **expressivity weights** within the thesaurus which stands for a taxonomy. The mark attached to a term measures its ability to express the demand.

III.1.1. The general expression level evolution

Learning proceeds in two steps :
-The first one consists of making the expression level of the **demand** concept evolve as the retrieval progresses (cf every number except 5 in figure 1).
-The second step consists of using the expression level written in the thesaurus to build a new expression of the concept, that is to say a new demand (number 5 in figure 1).

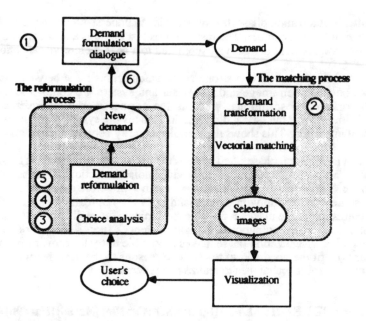

Key : numbers refer to stages of evolution or use of the expression level :
1 : Expression level initialization,
2 : Building of the first expression level,
3: Terms relevance calculation from the user's choices,
4 : Propagation of the relevance calculation to obtain a new expression level,
5 : New demand formulation from the new expression level,
6: Expression level adaptation according to interactions with the user.

Figure 1 : EXPRIM process and expression level evolution

III.1.2. The evolution of the expression level during the EXPRIM process :

The expressivity weights attached to the terms in the thesaurus are updated at different stages of the retrieval process (cf figure 1). We have proposed a calculation mode for this evolution.

Expressivity weight evolution during the "Before-Visualization" phase (fig. 1, number 2) :
The user, during the demand formulation, can attach a valuation to each term (cf § IV.1), this valuation allows the building of the first expression level : each term present in the demand has its expressivity weight set to the weight corresponding to the user valuation, or to a default value ; the same value is given for its specifics of whatever level. The repercussion towards the generics (not present in the demand) is done in such a way that the expressivity weights decrease as one climbs towards the thesaurus root.

Expressivity weight evolution during the "After-Visualization" phase :
To make the expression level evolve according to the user's choices, the system calculates for each term present in the selected image descriptions a relevance weight computed in a way close to relevance measures used in some information retrieval systems [Dil 80] [Sal 83b] [Sal 84] (figure 1, number 3). Then the expressivity weights are updated by taking into account the relevance weights so as to obtain a new expression level closer to the user's needs (figure 1, number 4).

Example of the thesaurus parts representative of the user's choices after an updating of the expressivity weights (the initial demand was "photo content = boat") :

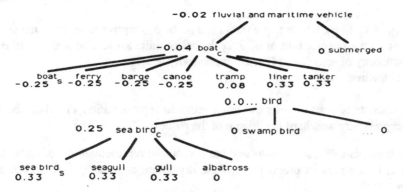

Figure 2 : a thesaurus part with expressivity weights

The expression level has been updated, by taking into account the term present in the chosen or rejected image descriptions.

New demand formulation in the "After-Visualization phase" (figure 1, number 5) :
The demand concept is now represented in the thesaurus in the form of an expression level. A thesaurus scanning is necessary to extract terms which best express the concept. A breadth first scanning is made : for every node of the tree the system compares its expressivity weight with a threshold ; if the weight is higher, the term is selected and the scanning stops for this tree part, if the weight is lower we go down the tree and apply the same treatment to the nodes of this level.

Example :
After a thesaurus scanning with a threshold of 0,20 we obtain, with the thesaurus part we have previously shown, the following new demand :
<u>Demand</u> *Photo content* = liner (0.33), tanker (0.33), sea bird$_c$(0.25).

Important remark : Let us remark that the method makes it possible to propose to the user new search criteria like *sea bird* which were completely absent from his first demand.

III.2. The matching process

The objective of such a process is to respond to a user's demand by a set of images (selected image set), which is sufficient but not superabundant, and without imposing on the user the need to have a precise knowledge of the desciptive base and of the domain.

The model we have developed to realize this process [Ker 90] is based on a thesaurus. The user's demand is first transformed into a request. Each document is then evaluated for the request. ; different strategies are used to satisfy the user's demand, guided by the number of images he wishes to see. Let us display the matching model as made up of a data model, a demand transformation and a vectorial matching (document evaluation).

III.2.1. The data model description

The data model is composed of a thesaurus model, a request model and a document model :

- The thesaurus is a set of semantic fields Sf_m. Each field is a set of units u_i linked by the generic/specific relation, forming a tree :

$TH = \{ Sf_m \}, \quad Sf_m = (\{u_i\}, r_m) \quad$ with :

$u_i = (t_i, SPE_i, g_i, AT_i, Ew_i)$, where t_i is a term used in the descriptive base, SPE_i the set of specific units of u_i, g_i the generic unit of u_i, AT_i the set of units associated whith u_i (terms having a certain similarity of sense), and Ew_i the expressivity weight ;

r_m is the root of the tree.

- The request consists of a set of units and has a vectorial representation Vr, where the jth coordinate is the expressivity weight of the jth unit of the request.

- The document consists of a set of units and has a vectorial representation Vd, where the jth coordinate is 1, in the present proposition, if the document contains the jth unit of the request, otherwise it is 0.

III.2.2. The demand transformation

A few facets enable the user to formulate his demand (cf § IV.1). The transformation consists of grouping all the terms of the different facets in the same request. Each term of the request is then substituted by all of its specifics in the thesaurus. At last, the request contains only specific terms which are leaves of the thesaurus. This property is linked with the fact that the image descriptions contain only thesaurus leaves (units with the property SPE=∅).

The obtained request is then used to evaluate the documents.

III.2.3. The vectorial matching (document evaluation)

The evaluation of a document D consists of measuring the **proximity** F(D,R) between the document and the request R ; let us call it the matching coefficient. We wish to have the following properties for the matching coefficient :

- $F(D,R) \in [0,1]$
- $F(D,R) = 1$ if D contains every term of R,
- $F(D,R) = 0$ if D contains no term of R,
- F(D,R) grows when the number of terms of R in D grows.

There are many suggestions for matching coefficients [Dun 81]. Our present solution is an adaptation of Jaccard's Coefficient [v Rij 79] :

$$F(D_i,R) = \frac{Vr.Vd}{Vr.Vp}$$

where Vp defines a document which perfectly fits the request (Vp=(1, 1,..., 1)).

III.2.4. The matching process : global view

The result of an interrogation step is a set of N images, where N is fixed by the user at the beginning of a step. The images having the highest matching coefficient are chosen at first. Let us see on figure 3 the whole process.

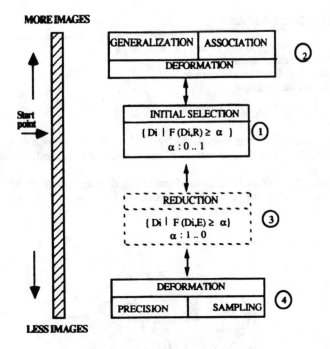

Figure 3 : the matching process.

1 : this is the starting point of the matching process. In the initial selection, an image Di is selected if its matching coefficient is greater than a fixed threshold α. The selection of the N images is realized by varying this threshold. If we c nnot satisfy this condition of N images, several phases of reduction or deformation make it possible to extend or reduce the selected image set.

2 : this deformation is used to change the request content. It uses the thesaurus so as to have more images. For doing that, it combines two strategies :
- generalization : substitution of a term by its generic,
- association : adding to the initial request the terms that are associated with terms already presented.

3 : in the reduction phase, the system eliminates images from the selection, using their proximity to the rejected images. This is possible by building an anti-request E which contains terms which caracterize the rejected images. This anti-request can be "learnt" by the system in the "after-visualization phase", or can also be built by the user. This point is currently a study point in this project.

4 : this deformation is used to have fewer images. The two following strategies are possible :
- precision : substitution of a term by a choice inside its set of specifics, or by adding more terms to make the request more precise ; this operation is realized thanks to a dialogue with the user,
- sampling : choosing some representative images in the selection for presenting to the user.

After the user visualization of this image set, the reformulation process can begin.

III.3. The reformulation process

The formulation process is composed of three steps :
- the relevance calculation,
- the expression level modification,
- the demand formulation.

III.3.1. The relevance calculation

The relevance calculation is computed by analysing the descriptions of the user chosen images and by attaching a relevance weight to each present unit in the following manner :

Let u be a thesaurus unit and t its term, S the selected image set, C the chosen image set, NC its cardinal, R the rejected image set, NR its cardinal, N the neutral image set and T the image descriptions which contain the term t.

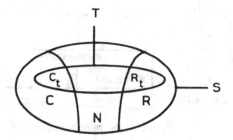

Let us call $C_t = T \cap C$, $R_t = T \cap R$ and NC_t, NR_t their respective cardinals.
The relevance weight Re_t of t is presently obtained by the formula :

$$Re_t = \frac{NC_t}{Max(NC,1)} - \frac{NR_t}{Max(NR,1)} .$$

This relevance calculation is then used for the expression level modification.

III.3.2. The expression level modification

The relevance weight repercussion is done in each semantic field of the thesaurus from the more specific units (the leaves) to the more general unit (the root). We propose the following calculation mode. Let u be a thesaurus unit, $u = (t, SPE, g, AT, Ew_t)$ and Re_t the relevance weight of t if the term has been found in the user's choice.

If $SPE = \emptyset$ (u is a leaf)
      then $Ew_t = Re_t$
      else   Let be $SPE = \{ u_i \}$ with $u_i = (t_i, SPE_i, g_i, AT_i, Ew_i)$, and $i = 1..n$

$$Ew_t = \frac{\sum_{i=1}^{n}(Ew_i * coef_i)}{\sum_{i=1}^{n} coef_i} ,$$

where coef$_i$ represents the importance in the thesaurus of the sub-concept (symbolized by the specific term) with regard to the general concept (symbolized by the generic term). In our experimentation coef$_i$ is equal to the rate of descriptions where the term or one of its specific terms appear.

III.3.3. The demand formulation

To formulate the new demand, it is necessary to scan the thesaurus. A scanning of every semantic field is done by starting from the root and processing to the leaves as explained in § III.1.2. A semantic field scanning is made by a recursive function "UnitSelection" with two parameters : a predefined threshold and a unit.

In our experimentation, each semantic field has a specific threshold which is equal to $\frac{Ew_{max}}{2}$, Ew_{max} being the maximum of the expressivity weights of the semantic field. This choice makes it possible to propose a sufficient number of terms in the new demand. Finally, the selected units associated with their expressivity weights are dispatched in the new demand facets and presented to the user.

III.4. Advantage of the method

The most important advantage of this method is being able to propose a global model which allows a flexible and continuous control of the matching between documents and request, and a semantic control of the request during the whole interrogation session. The two principal processes of IRM are really integrated together and they share information, as the expressivity weight.

Our first approach, based on the boolean logic, does not allow an easy use of the results of the reformulation process in the matching process. In addition to that, this solution generates rigidity in the matching. A solution could consist of an adaptation of some extended boolean logic propositions [Sal 83a] [Wal 79], but such a matching process does not offer an easy semantic control of the request.

This new approach makes it possible to do such things and also offers the possiblity to realize many other extensions e.g. the anti-request construction (cf § III.2.4), the use of some other weights as for example weight attached to terms in a description, weight attached to the demand facets ... All of these weigths may be considered as "nuances" attached to different kinds of information [Cre 89b].

The advantages of this method have been confirmed during the system RIVAGE experimentation.

IV. THE SYSTEM RIVAGE

The system RIVAGE represents the implementation of the process EXPRIM as a learning process. It has been written in an object oriented language which is called Smalltalk 80 [Gol 83]. This choice intends to eliminate the often insoluble problem of software communication and to favour the dialogue with the user by taking advantage of the reciprocal action facilities of Smalltalk. The object oriented programming offers qualities of modularity, reusability and extendibility which, added to the interactive programming environment, make the development of an interactive prototype much easier [Mey 88][Mas 89].

Let us show the system functions through the presentation of an interrogation session.

IV.1. The system functions : an interrogation session

(In this paragraph which describes an interrogation session, all the used objects are put in bold characters). When a user wants to retrieve images with our system, he may have no precise idea of the subject of his needs. The system offers the user the possibility to define progressively his need during an **interrogation session**. An interrogation session is composed of several **steps**, each step being composed of the three phases described in § II.3. The end of a session is reached when the user decides that he has obtained the images which correspond to his needs.

At the first **step** of a **session** the system proposes to the user different accesses to the image base which can be : to formulate a **demand**, to browse among an image sample and make a choice, to browse among the knowledge base, see images and then make a choice. Let us describe the first way. The user formulates a demand, by putting terms into **facets** which correspond to general characteristics of the photographs belonging to the photo base. He can also attach a qualitive valuation to each term as "important", "medium-important", "not-important". If he has no precise idea about terms which can illustrate his needs or about the content of a specific facet, he can have access to the domain knowledge, which is essentially composed by a **thesaurus**, to select terms or to see some images which are an illustration of a specific term. Then the user returns to his demand formulation to add some terms or to choose the *see images* option in the window associated pop-up menu, if he wishes to tell the system that the formulation is finished.

The system, to reach the images, makes a transformation of the demand ; it then obtains a **request** (cf III.2.2) which enables the selection of the **image descriptions** which are possible representations of the demand. If not enough or to many image descriptions correspond to the system request, a "deformation" phase begins (cf III.2.4). When the system has selected the fixed number of image descriptions in the **descriptive base**, this **set of selected images** is proposed to the user in the form of a list of description abstracts (title or legend). A new window appears on the screen ; when the user selects an abstract in the list, the system accedes, on the videodisk, to the corresponding image and displays it on the TV monitor. The full description is then accessible. Then the user can choose or reject this image by selecting the suitable option in the associated pop-up menu. When the user has finished his choice among the set of proposed images, he must select the option *end of visualization and choice analysis* which indicates to the system that the After-Visualization phase can begin.

Then the user can modify the proposed demand by adding new terms with specific valuation, by removing terms or by changing some proposed valuations.

IV.2. Data description

The facilities of programming in Smalltalk make it possible to represent the thesaurus, its behaviour and its caracteristics (inverted list of each term, expression level and all the links between terms) as one **object** with the operations needed to use it (term access, browsing, updating...). The descriptive base is also represented as one object with its specific operations (description access, image visualization, consultation). Many other objects have been defined like, for example : the user demand, the system request, ... All these objects are directly accessible in the programming environment and their structure can be modified at any time. The content of an object can be visualized in a predefined window associated with specific menus containing options which can act on the windowing object or on other objects of the system.

To describe the structure of these objects we have to use a conceptual model which enables the representation of complex objects. In the following we use some concepts, extracted from the semantic database conception model [Hul 87], to design the static structure of the thesaurus object. Let us represent it by figure 4 where one has defined three "abstractions" with the following representations :

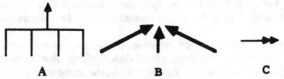

A stands for **aggregation** : grouping of a set of objects (components) giving an "aggregate" object,
B stands for **generalization** (and specialization in the top down direction),
C stands for **grouping** of several objects of same type into a collection.

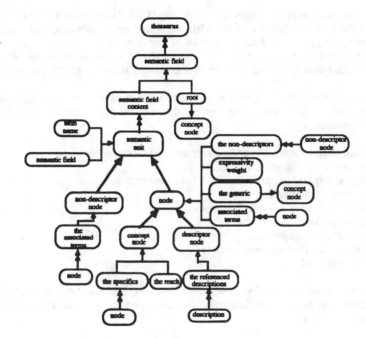

Figure 4 : the thesaurus object

Let us comment on the graphic description of the object **semantic unit** which is present in this structure. Indeed the **semantic unit** object may have several possible representations :
 - **non-descriptor node** object,
 - **node** object which may have two representations :
          - **concept node** object,
          - **descriptor node** object.

The **non-descriptor** allows the representation of the terms which may appear in a request but not in the image descriptions. The **node** represents all the other thesaurus terms.

To transform the thesaurus into a taxonomy form (cf III.1), we have differentiated between terms which express a concept (the generic terms, boat$_c$ in figure 2) and the others, which are specific representations of this concept (the leaves, boat$_s$ in figure 2). This thesaurus tranformation enables the description of the images with only leaf terms (terms which have no specific). It is for this reason that the **node** object is composed of two sub-objects : the **concept**

109

node and the **descriptor node** used to describe the images. These two sub-objects inherit properties and behavior from their generic object, this allows a structure factorisation. For example the **descriptor node** has the following properties : the term name, the semantic field, the non-descriptors, the expressivity weigth, the generic term, the associated-terms and the referenced descriptions ; in this list of properties only the last one is not inherited.

The reach of a concept node represents the number of images which contain one representation of the concept. The **referenced descriptions** object contains the set of descriptions which contain the considered node ; this object has the same role as the classic inverted files.

IV.3. Experimentation field

The data we deal with is extracted from the "Old Paris images" which is a real image collection of the French Ministry of the Culture, stored on a videodisc and complemented by a thesaurus and descriptions. The thesaurus of the French Ministry of the Culture, which contains 6000 terms with their semantic links, is stored in our application. We are testing our approach with this thesaurus and with the 1000 images we have in our possession.

An example will enable the reader to have an intuitive view of an interrogation session. After precising the initial user's need, we present the request proposed by the system during the course of the process :

User's initial need : <<images with water and old monuments>> ;
the user chooses 12 images and rejects 9 ;
first proposed request : <<bridge, river, ark, tower>> ;
the user accepts this request ;
the user obtains 3 other relevant images ;
second proposed request : <<stream>> ;
the user accepts this request ;
the user obtains 2 other relevant images ;
he stops the retrieval.

The system has been tested by a documentalist who has made many critical searches. This experimentation has made it possible to perfect the proposed method and to make an evaluation we are going to present.

V. THE SYSTEM EVALUATION

An evaluation of the system has been realized to measure system performance, in terms of recall and precision, and to compare them with those a documentalist would obtain with a usual boolean interrogation. To achieve that, we have defined an experimentation area consisting of a list of some representative demands (eight). For each demand we have searched manually in the image base for all possible relevant images.

V.1. The evaluation procedure :

The evaluation procedure consists of three successive interrogations : one done by a documentalist with boolean requests, two with the system RIVAGE, the first using a boolean matching model and the second using a vectorial one ; and finally the results obtained in each case are compared.

Each of the eight interrogations has been processed with no more than four steps. At the end of each session, we have calculated the obtained recall with regard to the existing relevant images and the just found relevant ones. From these different measures, we have defined an average recall (average of the eight recalls). These are the only compared quantitative results we give, precision being less important in such a system (cf § II.3.).

This quantitative comparison is not sufficient at all, and a comparison between the qualities of the different researches is also of great importance for such a system.

V.2. The different retrievals :

- Manual boolean interrogation by a documentalist conversing with the user
Quantitative : this form of interrogation gives very good results : average recall of 0,82.
Qualitative : such an interrogation cannot be realized by a non-specialist. A perfect knowledge of the document base and of its domain is required.

Let us see now the RIVAGE interrogation results with a user who doesn't have this knowledge.

- Interrogation within the system RIVAGE
Our first idea was to use a boolean matching model, where the system decides which operator to use. So, the user has to choose between two strategies : broad or precise. With regard to this choice, the system builds a boolean request from the user's demand.

Broad or "large" strategy :
In this form of interrogation, the system tries to obtain a lot of images.
Quantitative :   the results are good : recall of 0,70.
Qualitative : the main inconvenience is that the user is often required to choose between terms the system proposes for building a new request. Another inconvenience is that the system often proposes too many images to the user who is obliged to specialize his request.

Precise strategy :
Here, the system adjusts its strategy to obtain not too many images.
Quantitative :   the results are correct, recall of 0,60.
Qualitative : this strategy is very difficult to implement. The set of images proposed to the user is often too small and does not enable him to have a good idea of the base. These problems are due to the operator 'AND'.

- The IRM solution :
This solution, described in paragaph III.2, is based on a selection of images equiped with a matching coefficient.

Quantitative : the results we obtain, recall of 0,66, are judged very interesting, principally if we consider the quality of the reseach.
Qualitative : the user only sees the number of images he fixed at the beginning of the session. After the initial formulation of his request, he does not need any intervention on it. The whole interrogation is realized by choosing and rejecting images in the "visualization phase".

Thanks to the figure 5, let us compare the results we have obtained.

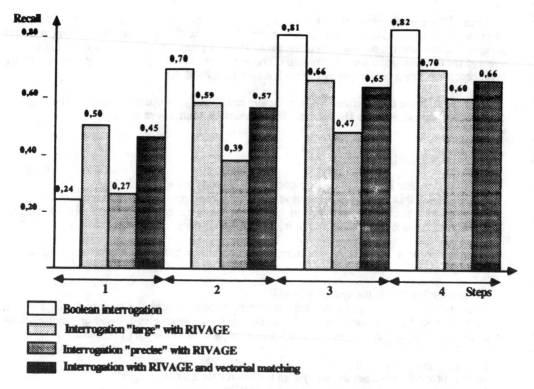

Figure 5 : the evaluation quantitative results.

This figure does not really illustrate the advantage of vectorial matching, as it only displays quantitative results. It shows that they are not significatively distinct from one another, apart from manual retrieval. This proves two things. First, the system has still to be improved, principally for its strategy, and we are working on this subject, made much easier by the adoption of vectorial matching. Secondly, the qualitative criteria are essential ; and they are greatly at the advantage of vectorial matching, as it will be shown in [Ker 90].

VI. CONCLUSION

We have presented the main ideas and models brought into action in the project EXPRIM and its prototype RIVAGE. They are based on the fact that retrieving images needs a deep interactivity and cooperation between man and machine and, thus, that the retrieval process may be viewed as a machine-learning process. We have also displayed a matching process based on a vectorial matching model ; we have recently implemented it and it has already proved to be of good quality. In particular, one of its main advantages is to be perfectly coherent with and integrated in the machine-learning process. Both together make a retrieval system having a great flexibility and where one may realize a continuous control on retrieving.

Moreover, we think that such a system will be a very good tool to control not only each session but even the improving of our strategy. Thus, it will be a factor for increasing the relevance of the results of our future realizations. This is connected with the study we are presently initiating on long-term machine-learning in the system, which will enable it to improve itself by running.

REFERENCES

[Chi 86]   Chiaramella Y., Defude B. Bruandet M.F. Kerkouber D.
           IOTA : A full text information retrieval system.
           Proceeding of ACM 1986 : Information Retrieval, PISE, pp 207-213.

[Cre 89a] Créhange M., Halin G.
           Image progressive retrieval from a Videodisk : A Machine Learning Problem.
           Conférence on Applications of Artificial Intelligence, Orlando, USA, Mars 89.

[Cre 89b] Créhange M., Foucaut O., Halin G., Mouaddib N., Foucaut J.F.
           **Semantics of user Interface for Image Retrieval : possibility theory and learning
           techniques.**
           Information Processing and Management Vol 25, n°6, pp 615-627, 1989.

[Dil 80]   Dillon M., Desper J.
           Automatic relevance feedback in boolean retrieval systems
           Journal of Documentation 1980, 36, pp 197-208.

[Dun 81]   Duncan A. Buell
           A general model of query processing in information retrieval systems
           Information Processing & Management Vol. 17, n° 5, pp 249-262, 1981

[Gol 83]   Goldberg A., Robson D.,
           Smalltalk 80 ; the language and its implementation.
           Addison-Wesley Reading, Massachussets, 1983.

[Hal 88a] Halin G., Mouaddib N., Foucaut O., Créhange M.
           **Semantics of user Interface for Image Retrieval : possibility theory   and
           learning techniques applied on two prototypes.**
           Proceedings of Conference RIAO 88, Boston (USA), Mars 1988.

[Hal 89a] Halin G., Créhange M.,
           Image Progressive Retrieval from a Videodisc.
           Proceedings of Opticalinfo '89, Amsterdam, Avril 1989.

[Hal 89b] Halin G.
           **Apprentissage pour la recherche interactive et progressive d'images :
           processus EXPRIM et prototype RIVAGE.**
           Thesis of the NANCY I University, Nancy, France, Oct 1989.

[Hul 87]   Hull R., King R.
           **Semantic Database Modelling : Survey, Applications and research
           Issues.**
           ACM Computing Survey, 19(3) : pp 202-260.

[Ker 90]   Kerekes P.
           **Implantation industrielle du système RIVAGE : interrogation souple   de la
           photothèque d'un centre de recherches**
           Mémoire CNAM, à paraître en 1990.

[Mas 89]   Masini G., Napoli A., Colnet D., Léonard D., Tombre K.
           Les langages à objets.
           InterEditions. Paris 1989.

[Mey 89]   Meyer B.
            Conception et programmation par objets, pour des logiciels de qualité
            InterEditions. Paris 1989.

[Mic 83]   Michalski R.S., Diettrich T.G.
            A comparative review of selected methods for learning from   examples.
            In Machine Learning, an Artificial Intelligence Approach, 1983 pp41-81.

[Sal 83a]   Salton G., Fox E.A., Wu H.
            Extended Boolean Information Retrieval.
            Communication of th ACM 26:11, Novembre 1983, pp 1022-1036.

[Sal 83b]   Salton G.,Fox E.A., Bukley C., Voorhees E.
            Boolean Query Formulation with relevance feedback.
            Tech Rep TR 83-539, Department of computer Science, Cornell University, Jan
            83.

[Sal 84]   Salton G., Voorhees E.
            A comparison of two methods for boolean query relevance feedback.
            Information Processing & Mangement Vol 20, n°5/6 pp637-651, 1984.

[v Rij 79] van Rijsbergen C.J.
            Information Retrieval,
            Second Edition, Butterworths, London 1979.

[Wal 79]   W.G. Waller & Donald H. Kraft.
            A mathematical of a weighted boolean retrieval
            Information Processing & Mangement Vol 15, pp239-245.

[Won 86a]   Wong SKM. & Ziarko W.
            A machine learning approach to information Retrieval.
            ACM Pise 86 pp 228-233.

Online Query Refinement on Information Retrieval Systems: A Process Model of Searcher/System Interactions

Hsinchun Chen[1], MIS Department, University of Arizona
Vasant Dhar[2], IS Department, New York University

Abstract

This article reports findings of empirical research that investigated information searchers' online query refinement process. Prior studies have recognized the information specialists' role in helping searchers articulate and refine queries. Using a semantic network and a Problem Behavior Graph to represent the online search process, our study revealed that searchers also refined their own queries in an online task environment. The information retrieval system played a passive role in assisting online query refinement, which was, however, one that confirmed Taylor's four-level query formulation model. Based on our empirical findings, we proposed using a process model to facilitate and improve query refinement in an online environment. We believe incorporating this model into retrieval systems can result in the design of more "intelligent" and useful information retrieval systems.

1 Introduction

Electronic text-based information storage and retrieval systems in the form of online catalogs, online bibliographic databases, and videotex that can store huge amounts of data and allow access via a terminal or a television set are changing the way we gather, process, and retrieve information. These systems provide a wide variety of information and services, ranging from daily updates of foreign and national news, movie reviews, law cases, and financial data on companies to journal articles, books, trademarks, and statistics. While archival information sources such as libraries are becoming increasingly computerized, access to such information is often difficult, due in large part to the indeterminate nature of the process by which documents are indexed and the latitude searchers have in expressing a query. For inexperienced searchers, the problem of finding documents that are relevant to a query can be difficult for three reasons:

1. it can require a significant amount of knowledge of the subject area in which information is sought,

2. it requires knowledge about the functionality of the information storage and retrieval system, and

3. it requires knowledge about the classification scheme employed in the information storage and retrieval system.

Searchers generally have limited knowledge about the classification scheme and the retrieval system. Since the purpose of the search itself is often to acquire knowledge about the subject area, searchers may not be clear about the subject area for which answers are being sought Searchers may have only a felt or conscious need which requires to be formalized and articulated. A human information specialist such as a reference librarian often assumes an active role in helping searchers refine and articulate their queries.

The focus of our research was to identify empirically how searchers refined their queries when using an online catalog. We compared the results with prior studies in which librarians' assistance was present. Based on our empirical findings, we proposed a process model for facilitating online query refinement.

[1]hchen@mis.arizona.edu, MIS, University of Arizona, Tucson, AZ 85721, USA
[2]vdhar@vx1.gba.nyu.edu, IS, NYU, NY, NY 10003, USA

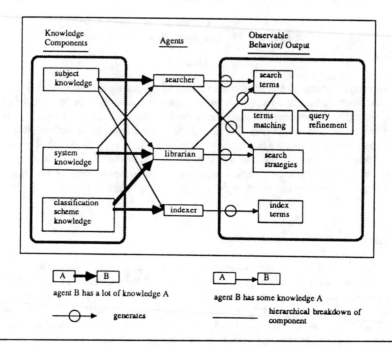

<figure>
Knowledge Components | Agents | Observable Behavior/ Output

subject knowledge → searcher
system knowledge → librarian
classification scheme knowledge → indexer

searcher → search terms
librarian → search strategies
indexer → index terms

terms matching   query refinement

A ⇒ B   agent B has a lot of knowledge A

A → B   agent B has some knowledge A

─○→   generates

─────   hierarchical breakdown of component
</figure>

Figure 1: A framework for information storage and retrieval

In Section 2, we present an information retrieval framework as the context for our research. We then describe our research design and method in Section 3. In Section 4, we discuss how searchers refined their queries in an online environment based on Taylor's theory of query formulation. In Section 5, we present a process model that aimed at facilitating online query refinement. We draw conclusion concerning our research in the final section.

2 Information Retrieval Framework

In this section, we present the information retrieval framework we developed. This framework, as shown in Figure 1, examines the human agents involved in the online information storage and retrieval environment, the types of knowledge these agents possess, and the unique characteristics of their indexing and search behavior.

2.1 Knowledge Components

Three types of knowledge are required for the information storage and retrieval process. First, classification scheme knowledge is used for indexing documents. Second, subject area knowledge is required for expressing a query. Lastly, system knowledge helps a user perform a fruitful and effective search in an online retrieval system. These three knowledge components are presented on the left hand side of Figure 1.

2.2 Agents

The three types of knowledge are typically distributed among three different parties to whom we refer as "human agents." These agents include *indexers*, who classify the documents based on some pre-determined classification scheme; *searchers*, who express their queries in their own terms; and *reference librarians*, who serve as intermediaries between searchers and retrieval systems.

Searchers generally do not have classification scheme knowledge and their knowledge of the subject area and the system functionality varies widely. Indexers generally have a great deal of classification scheme knowledge and some subject knowledge. They are, however, not concerned about the functionality of retrieval systems. Librarians must have all three kinds of knowledge, although they generally know more about the classification scheme and system than about various subjects. The relationships between the knowledge components and the agents are represented as links in Figure 1.

2.3 Indexing and Search Behavior

Indexing uncertainty and search uncertainty are the primary sources of information retrieval problems.

2.3.1 Indexing Uncertainty

The process of indexing is partly indeterminate. Evidence suggests that different indexers, all of whom are well trained in an indexing scheme, might assign different index terms to a given document (see the box labeled index terms in Figure 1). It has also been observed that an indexer may use different terms for the same document at different times [15] [24].

2.3.2 Search uncertainty

Search uncertainty refers to the latitude searchers have in adopting **search strategies** and choosing **search terms** (see the boxes on the right side of Figure 1) during the information retrieval process.

1. **Search Strategies:**

   Search strategy is often used to describe the plan or approach to the whole search. In a card catalog study, two strategies for searching have been identified: a "self-reliant" style where searchers generate their own search terms and a "catalog-oriented" style where searchers use the terms found in the card catalog [26]. Another study classifies the search strategy in terms of the critical decision points faced during the online search. Two types of decision points occur during the search: a decision to react to unfavorable results and a decision to revise search logic [16]. Bourne identifies two search strategies. In the "building-block" approach, one enters various terms as separate search statements. After the search results are derived, one combines all search statements into a single final statement using the Boolean operator, AND. This strategy contrasts with the "pearl-growing" strategy, in which one starts by searching on a few specific terms to retrieve initial citations. These citations are then examined carefully for new candidate search terms to be added in the subsequent searches [18].

2. **Search Terms:**

   A high degree of uncertainty with regard to search terms has been observed. Searchers tend to use different search terms for the same information sought. Studies have revealed that, on average, the probability of any two people using the same term to describe an object is about 10 percent [13] [12]. This fundamental property of language limits the success of various design methodologies for controlled vocabulary-driven interaction [12].

Due to the uncertainty in choosing the index and the search terms, generating an exact match between the searcher's terms and those of the indexer becomes difficult. Bates [2] argues that for a successful match, the searcher must somehow generate as much "variety" (in the cybernetic sense, as defined by [1]) in the search as is produced by the indexers in their indexing.

While indexers use the rule of specificity for indexing, searchers tend to approach a search by specifying broader terms first. There may be several reasons for this. One hypothesis is that searchers often do not have "queries," but what Belkin calls an "anomalous state of knowledge" [4]. Searchers often expect to refine this anomalous state into a query *through* an interactive process. The organization of a catalog or a system does not always facilitate this type of query refinement, however. In contrast, reference librarians appear to be particularly adept at performing this function.

Taylor suggests that a searcher's queries start from an actual but unexpressed need (visceral need). The visceral need is refined to a conscious description of the need (conscious need). This need is finally formalized as a statement (formalized need). However, the actual query presented to the information system may be compromised by the searcher's expectation of the system (compromised need) [28]. Based on Taylor's model, a similar model for describing query refinement during the pre-search interview between reference librarians and online searchers was developed by Markey [17]. We also used Taylor's theory to model the online query refinement process. Details are discussed in Section 4.

The importance of query refinement during the information retrieval process and the reference librarian's role in assisting this process are well recognized in earlier research. Nevertheless, prior studies did not investigate the functionality of the retrieval systems in assisting query refinement. In our research, we investigated online query refinement process in detail, and our findings were used to develop a process model for aiding online information retrieval.

3 Research Design

A field study was conducted in 1988 at New York University. Data collection techniques including think-aloud protocols, tape-recordings, interviews, and questionnaires were used. By studying the interactions between information searchers and an online catalog, we were able to identify the query refinement process which occurs. The online catalog system we studied, Bobcat, listed over 600,000 catalog records including all new materials acquired after 1973 and many older items previously listed in the card catalog. Journals were not listed. The system provided seven search options: title search, author search, combination of author and title search, subject search, call number search, keyword search, and Boolean search. These options are considered standard in most online catalog systems.

Thirty business school students ranging from Ph.D. candidates to freshmen participated in the study. These subjects were asked to perform a search for documents within a subject area of their own choosing. In general, the most frequently chosen option was subject search, followed by keyword search using index term (one word only). Before beginning their searches, subjects were requested to explain what they were looking for. They were also asked to think aloud during their searches. Their verbal protocols were tape-recorded, and the interactions between the searchers and the system were logged. The interactions lasted between 5 and 40 minutes. After the interaction, subjects were requested to state their queries again. A few follow-up questions pertaining to the search process and the problems encountered during the search also were asked.

Our study was based on information processing theory [19]. The technique we used to analyze the collected data was *protocol analysis*, a qualitative analysis technique frequently used in the Artificial Intelligence and Cognitive Psychology communities [11].

4 Levels of Query Refinement in Online Search

Based on the representation we developed for capturing the online query refinement process, we were able to describe the online query refinement process in terms of Taylor's theory. We conclude this section by discussing the differences between the way librarians assist in refining queries and the way information systems provide such help.

4.1 Representation of Search Process

The representation scheme we used for the analysis of the query refinement process is based on a *semantic network* and a *Problem Behavior Graph* (PBG). Both representations are widely used in the area of Artificial Intelligence. The semantic network is used to represent the semantic contents of searchers' queries. The PBG, on the other hand, depicts the flow of the online information retrieval process.

4.1.1 Semantic Network

The concept of a semantic network was first introduced by Quillian [21] as a general association mechanism for encoding the meaning of words. A semantic network represents knowledge by means of nodes and links: nodes represent objects, things, concepts, facts, etc.; links represent relationships among them. Semantic networks have been used in different applications, mainly in the area of natural language processing [23] [33] [6]. Recently, they also have been applied to the design of information retrieval systems [22] [9]. In particular, the online thesauri for retrieval systems, have been represented using a semantic network structure [10] [25].

Knowledge of a subject area can be captured and represented by a large semantic network of terms (concepts) where links are of two types: relations between non-index and index terms (USE links) and relations between general and specific terms (NT/BT links). These links exist in most thesauri, including the Library of Congress Subject Headings (LCSH) handbook (the classification scheme of the online catalog we studied). Figure 2 shows a portion of the semantic network corresponding to the LCSH classification scheme.

4.1.2 Problem Behavior Graph

In order to make the analysis of the online query refinement process more meaningful, we summarize the search process in terms of a Problem Behavior Graph (PBG). This representation describes problem-solving activities in a time sequence, from an initial state (a vague description of needs) to a goal state (a solution that satisfies the needs). This detailed representation of the problem-solving process is derived by first splitting up the user's interaction logs and verbal protocols into their *semantic elements*, which consists of *knowledge elements* and *operator elements* [19] [31]. The *knowledge elements* specify the kinds of knowledge the subject has about the task. The *operator elements* are a finite set of actions that take a state of knowledge as input and produce a new state of knowledge as output. Users typically use a finite number of operators to change the knowledge states. PBG, which was grounded on the information processing theory [19], has been used in a large body of research to study the human problem solving process. Examples of the domains that have been studied include: financial analysis [5], mathematical programming [20], scheduling [14], and conceptual data modeling [3]. We found it useful to represent the online information retrieval process in terms of PBG.

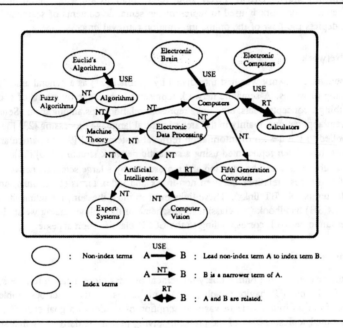

Figure 2: A sample network of LCSH terms

In the information retrieval context, the essential knowledge elements are the terms used to express the query. The operator elements are the moves or actions that change the content of the query. We refer to them as the *semantic operators*. As shown in Table 1, we observed five *semantic operators* used by searchers to move from one datum to the next. They are: ST (synonymous term operator, moves from a non-index term to its synonymous index term), BT (broader term operator, from specific to general term), NT (narrower term operator, from general to specific term), AT (adjacent term operator, from one term to another term which partially overlaps in meaning), and DT (disjointed term operator, from one term to another semantically different term). These operators were derived from our empirical studies. Details of how searchers used these operators in refining their queries are presented in Section 5.

In this subsection, we explain these operators in the context of the semantic network structure we proposed.

1. **ST:** The USE link in our semantic network leads from a non-index term to its synonymous index term. A searcher may follow this link to identify synonyms. These links are listed explicitly in the LCSH Handbook. For example, by following the USE link in Figure 2, a searcher can identify "Computers" as a synonym of "Electronic Brain."

2. **BT or NT:** The NT link leads from a broader term to a narrower term. BT link is the reverse of NT link. Following the NT (or BT) links we can determine the level of specificity of different terms. For example, by following the NT links in Figure 2, we know that "Electronic Data Processing" is more specific than "Computers," "Artificial Intelligence" is more specific than "Electronic Data Processing," and "Expert Systems" is more specific than "Artificial Intelligence." Both NT and BT links are transitive. Searchers may decide to broaden or narrow their queries by following these links.

3. **AT:** Terms which are not directly related via the USE or NT/BT links but have the same common ancestor (broader term) or descendant (narrower term) in the network are considered *adjacent* terms. We can determine the common ancestor or descendant of any two terms by activating all paths leading to/from the two terms in the network. The intersection of these paths is the common ancestor or descendant, respectively. For example, "Fuzzy Algorithms" and "Machine Theory" have a common ancestor, "Algorithms," reached by following the reverse direction of NT links (BT links) in Figure 2 for both terms. "Electronic Data Processing" and "Machine Theory" are adjacent because they have a common descendant, "Artificial Intelligence." Searchers may change their topic of interest from an initial term to its "adjacent" terms.

4. **DT:** This operator represents the transition from one term to another term which is semantically disjointed (i.e., one term cannot reach another via the links in the network). This generally represents a change of query from one topic to another disjointed topic.

Based on these primitives, we can construct a PBG to describe the progression of the state of the query through the problem space. Each node of the graph represents a particular state of knowledge for the searcher, and each arc represents an operator that was applied to transit to the next state. By superimposing the PBG on the semantic network, we get an interesting visual picture of the trajectory of the query. Figures 4 and 5 demonstrate two query processes using this scheme. We discuss them in the next subsection.

4.2 Taylor's Theory for Online Query Refinement

In a seminal article on query refinement, Taylor proposed four levels of query refinement that pertain to the client/information specialist interview session [27] [28]. These four levels are: visceral need, conscious need, formalized need, and compromised need. Changes of needs from one level to another are indicated in Figure 3. The librarian's role in assisting query refinement has been well recognized in the prior studies. We postulate

121

Semantic Elements	Description
Knowledge Element: TERM	Terms used by the searcher.

Operator Element:
    ST
    BT
    NT
    AT
    DT
	(Going from one term to another:)
	Synonymous Term
	Broader Term
	Narrower Term
	Adjacent Term
	Disjointed Term

Table 1: Semantic elements for query refinement

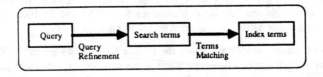

Figure 3: Taylor's theory of query refinement

that online information retrieval systems also assist searchers in refining or articulating queries, but possibly in a more passive way.

We represented the 30 searcher/system interactions in terms of the PBG and then analyzed these PBGs based on Taylor's model. Although our study was unable to identify the visceral need, it revealed the remaining three levels of needs. (However, the very existence of the searcher's query indicates the presence of the visceral need.) Definitions for the four types of needs in the online task environment are as follows [28]:

1. **Q1. Visceral need:** a vague sort of dissatisfaction, or a certain incompleteness in the searcher's picture of the world.

2. **Q2. Conscious need:** the conscious, within-brain description of the need. In our study, this was revealed in the searchers' think-aloud protocols during their online searches.

3. **Q3. Formalized need:** the formal statement of need. This is a searcher's query statement. In our study we elicited both presearch and postsearch query statements, using interviews.

4. **Q4. Compromised need:** the query as presented to the information system. This is disclosed by the actual search terms used by a searcher on the system. They were recorded in our log file.

The data collection techniques used in our study, namely, log file, tape-recording of the think-aloud protocols, and interviews, were useful for identifying the searchers' information needs at various levels. We observed numerous examples of query refinement from Q2 to Q3 and from Q3 to Q4.

Eight of the subjects changed the intent of their queries. Their postsearch statements of their information needs were significantly different from their presearch statements (a change in the formalized needs). These searchers' conscious needs emerged during the search and were formalized during the retrieval process. This query refinement process involved the formalization of the conscious needs (Q2-Q3).

Twenty-one (21) subjects' presearch and postsearch statements of information needs were unchanged (no changes in the formalized needs). However, the search terms used by these subjects varied during the search (although these terms were semantically close to the presearch and postsearch statements). This can be considered a process of forming a compromised need from a formalized need (Q3-Q4). The higher frequency of the second type of refinement (Q3-Q4) may have resulted from the searchers' attempts to provide search terms that the system could recognize and that represented their complete information needs. In the following subsections, we describe these two types of query refinement processes (formalize the conscious need, Q2-Q3, and compromise the formalized need, Q3-Q4) with examples.

4.2.1 Formalize the Conscious Needs: (Q2-Q3)

For eight of the subjects we observed, their presearch and postsearch query statements were significantly different (in terms of contents). The subjects' think-aloud protocols revealed their conscious needs, which involved needs that were different from what had been stated in their presearch statements. These conscious needs were formalized and then included in their postsearch statements.

Figure 4 illustrates how the content of one subject's query changed during the search process. The knowledge components (terms) involved in this interaction are represented using the semantic network structure we described earlier (see the ovals and the light arrows). The flow of the search process (in time sequence) is captured by a PBG (follow the heavy arrows from *Start* to *End*). The terms involved in the search are represented by the ovals in Figure 4. The concepts involved in the subject's presearch query statement (rectangular boxes) as well as the postsearch query statement (shaded ovals) are also shown in Figure 4.

Six groups of terms were mentioned in this query. Each group consisted of terms that comprised a *concept*. We refer to this as a *concept group*. In terms of semantic network representation, words that address a similar concept are connected via some links (the ST or NT links as shown in Figure 4). In this example, six concept groups were involved: Group 1 - "error" and "error – psychology" (connected by an NT link as shown in the upper right hand corner of Figure 4), Group 2 - "routine work" and "motor skills" (connected by an NT link), Group 3 - "data," "data entry," "data editing," "data processing," "data processing service center," "data processing service center – management," and "data reduction" (connected by the NT links), Group 4 - "ergonomics" and "human factors" (connected by an ST link), Group 5 - "learning," and Group 6 - "performance." The subject's presearch query statement was very fuzzy, "how people make errors." It mentioned only one concept in Group 1 (indicated by the rectangular box in Figure 4). Five new concepts were introduced during the search (Groups 2, 3, 4, 5, and 6). After the search, the searcher's query statement was: "the human factors in the routine work of data entry." It contained concepts in Groups 2, 3, and 4 (see the shaded ovals in Figure 4). We postulate that the searcher's own brainstorming and the incidental information displayed by the system resulted in a query refinement process similar to the one observed in the client/librarian interview session. However, because the searchers had little support from the system, this query refinement process was often time-consuming and ineffective.

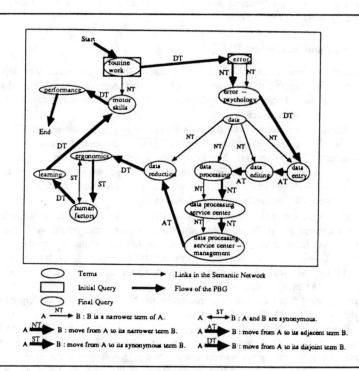

Figure 4: An example of formalizing the conscious needs

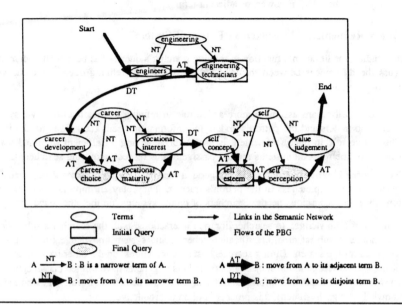

Figure 5: An example of compromising the formalized needs

4.2.2 Compromise the Formalized Needs: (Q3-Q4)

The contents of 21 subjects' presearch query statements had the same or similar meaning as their postsearch query statements. However, the search terms they used during the search varied. The search terms input to the information system (the compromised needs) were variations of their formalized needs. We posit that this was the result of the searchers' attempts to adjust to the system's vocabulary.

In terms of semantic network representation, searchers may move from one term to its synonymous terms (ST) in order to generate matches; to its broader terms (BT) in order to broaden the scope of their queries; to its narrower terms (NT) in order to focus their searches; or switch from one topic to another topic which overlaps partially in meaning (AT) in order to cover different aspects of their queries.

Figure 5 shows an example of how one searcher chose different search terms to express an unchanged (in terms of its meaning) query. Only one concept group was involved in this search, but this concept group contains a number of terms which are related to "planning" (see the ovals in Figure 5). The subject's presearch statement and postsearch statement addressed the same information need, "hierarchical planning" (see the shaded oval and the rectangular box in Figure 5), although different terms were chosen to express the query. After failing initially, the searcher tried other semantically close terms to generate matches. These terms included: "business planning," "multi-level planning," "large scale planning," and "organizational planning." (Follow the dark arrows from Start to End in Figure 5.)

There may be several hypotheses to explain this process. First, because of the controlled vocabulary used for document indexing, search terms used initially may not have produced any matches. So searchers were often forced to use different terms. Second, information displayed by the system may have suggested new clues for the search. Lastly, searchers may have found it more prudent to approach their queries from different angles (by using synonymous, broader, narrower, or adjacent terms).

4.3 Query Refinement: Librarian vs Retrieval System

In earlier studies, the librarian's function in refining searcher's queries has been well documented. In this section we discuss the differences between the way librarians assist in refining queries and the way online retrieval systems provide such help.

1. **The Role:** Librarians assume a more active role in refining queries than retrieval systems do. Librarians attempt to understand the patron's underlying information needs (conscious needs) in a very early stage. This active role in query refinement is useful for achieving an efficient (minimal wasted effort) search. Current online retrieval systems are too passive in this respect, requiring searchers to do too much.

   Experienced librarians, in particular, are good at identifying a patron's conscious needs by detecting inconsistency or incompleteness in the patron's queries. They play an important role in prompting patrons to formalize their conscious needs. Searchers of online systems, on the other hand, rarely have this support.

2. **Sources of Knowledge:** In searcher/librarian interactions, both the searcher's subject area knowledge and the librarian's subject area, classification scheme, and system knowledge contribute to the generation of new cues for the search. During searcher/system interactions, on the other hand, searchers can rely only on their own knowledge in the subject area (searchers in general have limited classification scheme and system knowledge) and incidental information displayed on the screen. For searchers who have little subject area knowledge (e.g., freshmen), this process is often unproductive.

   Librarians' classification scheme knowledge is often used to assist patrons in generating queries the information systems can recognize (compromised needs). Their knowledge about the system's controlled vocabulary, the cross-referencing structure, and the index principles employed helps patrons obtain a good surrogate for their formalized needs. In the searcher/system interactions, this process is essentially one of trial and error.

3. **User Modeling:** One capability which we found to exist only in the librarians was their ability to perform a user modeling function. For example, librarians may expect vagueness in the queries from inexperienced and less sophisticated searchers (e.g., freshmen). Librarians generally spend a considerable amount of time in sharpening queries from these clients. But when dealing with more sophisticated searchers (e.g., Ph.D. students), they may assume the searchers know exactly what they what. This *user modeling* function of the reference librarians has been reported in [7].

We summarize these differences between librarian and online system assistance in refining queries in Table 2. It is clear that in order to design more effective and useful online retrieval systems, query refinement functionality needs to be incorporated into the retrieval systems.

5 Process Model of Online Query Refinement

We derived some interesting empirical findings pertaining to how searchers refine their queries when using the retrieval system. These findings were used to develop a process model that can facilitate online query refinement.

Differences	Searcher/Librarian	Searcher/System
The Role	o Active	o Passive
Sources of Knowledge	o Subject Area, System, Classification Scheme	o Subject Area
User Modeling	o Yes	o No

Table 2: Librarian vs. system in query refinement

5.1 Two Approaches to Online Query Refinement

We observed that searchers refined their queries using two approaches to which we referred as **semantic-based browsing** and **retrieval by instantiation**.

5.1.1 Semantic-Based Browsing

Searchers may obtain their search terms by browsing the semantic network of concepts. From our empirical studies we identified a typology of *semantic operators* that searchers used for refining their queries. This typology included synonymous term (ST), broader term (BT), narrower term (NT), adjacent term (AT), and disjointed term (DT). The searcher's query refinement process can be viewed as a traversal (browsing) in this semantic network of concepts (terms, topics, etc.) using these five operators. Figures 4 and 5 illustrate this type of query refinement. We discuss these semantic operators below.

1. **Synonymous Term (ST):** In the searcher/system interactions, we observed a process where the synonymous terms were self-generated by the searchers when their initial terms matched too few citations. For example, as a consequence of having found no matches by using "human factors," a user next used a synonymous term, "ergonomics," to express his query.

2. **Broader Term (BT):** Searchers may change from terms which are more specific in meaning to terms which are more general. This change may be due in part to a searcher's misconception that citations classified under the specific terms should also be classified under broader terms. For example, a searcher who was looking for books about "statistical power" immediately changed her search term from "statistical power" to "statistics" after obtaining no matches from the first term.

3. **Narrower Term (NT)** Sometimes, searchers may decide to narrow their queries by choosing more specific terms. This occurred when a set of matched citations was too large. Searchers often had their own expectation of what a reasonable number of matched citations should be. For example, after deriving a huge set of matched citations under "statistics," a searcher immediately returned to a more specific term, "measurement." Searchers also used narrower terms when the initial term generated irrelevant citations.

4. **Adjacent Term (AT):** Searchers may change their search topic to one which partially overlaps with their initial terms in content. This occurred when few relevant citations were derived from their initial terms. These adjacent terms may capture aspects of the query which were not represented in the initial terms.

For example, a searcher switched from "economics of information" to "game theory" in two consecutive search stages in an attempt to explore the different aspects of the "bargaining problem."

5. **Disjointed Term (DT):** Searchers may change their search topic to another semantically disjointed topic. This occurred when multiple topics were involved in a query and when previously ignored conscious needs were revealed during the search. In an online retrieval system that has full Boolean capability, this type of query can be expressed using Boolean operators. Searchers, however, may have problems using these operators. In our study, four subjects attempted to use a Boolean search, while most subjects searched with single term (not using the Boolean search option) even though they had more than one topic in their query. For instance, a searcher used "hypertension" and "salt substitute" (two disjointed topics) in two separate steps in an effort to search for materials about "the effect of salt substitutes on hypertension" This query can be expressed by the Boolean logic: "hypertension AND salt substitute."

These five operators correspond to the various links of the semantic network structure we have proposed. The ST operators follow the USE links in the semantic network (see Figure 2). The NT and BT operators follow, in either direction, the NT or BT links. Terms which have a common ancestor or descendant (but not on a hierarchy of NT or BT links) are considered to have an AT relationship (going from one such term to another is considered as an AT operation). Terms which are not linked in the network are considered to have an DT relationship (likewise, going from one such term to another is considered as an DT operation). We believe that an online thesaurus that is based on this semantic network structure can help searchers refine their queries.

5.1.2 Retrieval by Instantiation

Detailed citation information can also help searchers obtain new cues for search. This includes: the title, the author, the publisher, and the index term of a book. In our studies, we frequently heard statements such as:

> This book is exactly what I am looking for.

> I am looking for books similar to this one.

By using information associated with the citations that are right on target, searchers can obtain other relevant citations. Searchers can use the index terms derived from the matched citations to perform a subject search. New relevant citations can be obtained. Searchers can examine the titles of the matched citations in order to elicit new search terms (title also reflects the content of a book). Searchers can find all books written by a particular author in the area (most authors work in a few specific areas). Searchers can sometimes find all new books published by a particular publisher (many publishers specialize in certain subject areas). This retrieval mechanism, which we referred to as **retrieval by instantiation**, has also been found useful in the design of other information retrieval systems [29] [30] [32].

5.2 A Process Model

Grounded on our empirical findings, we have developed a process model for assisting query refinement using online information retrieval systems. This process model consists of five stages as shown in Figure 6. They are: **Initial Query Stage, Terms Grouping Stage, Relevance Evaluation Stage, Terms Solicitation Stage**, and **Citations Instantiation Stage**. We discuss each of these stages below.

5.2.1 Initial Query Stage

A search session starts with the **Initial Query Stage** (see the box at the top of Figure 6). Two activities are involved in this stage. First, searchers express their queries by using a few search terms. These search terms

128

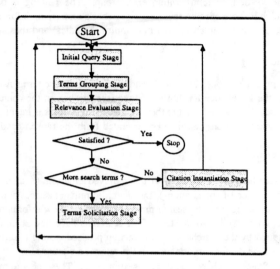

Figure 6: A process model for query refinement

represent the searchers' information needs. The searchers can use Boolean operators to combine their search terms.

Second, the search terms elicited are used to consult a semantic network-based online thesaurus (based on the LCSH Handbook). Non-index terms supplied by the searchers can be translated to index terms by tracing the USE links in this thesaurus. The output of this stage is a list of index terms (possibly combined by Boolean operators) which represent the searchers' queries.

5.2.2 Terms Grouping Stage

The **Terms Grouping Stage** consists of two processes. The first process focuses on grouping the index terms derived from the previous stage according to their contents (relationships to each other with respect to the semantic network) and generating new candidate terms from each group. The second process applies a few heuristics to rank these newly derived terms.

1. **Grouping:** Grouping of terms is accomplished by first instantiating all paths in the semantic network which lead to/from these terms. This operation is referred to as *spreading activation*. Terms which are connected via some paths are classified into the same *concept group*. Complex queries (e.g., a Ph.D. student's query relating to a dissertation topic) may often involve more than one concept group.

   An important by-product of this spreading activation process is a set of new terms found along the activated paths. These new terms can become good candidate terms for the searchers' queries.

2. **Ranking:** The concept groups derived are first ranked according to the total number of searcher-supplied terms (originators) in each group. A group with many originators is considered more important to the query than a group with fewer originators. We refer to this heuristic of ranking as the *principle of origination*.

Next, we rank the newly derived terms within each group. The ranking is based on the *principle of specificity*. A term which is more specific reveals the searcher's underlying information need better than its more general counterparts (an observation from our empirical studies) and thus should be ranked higher.

5.2.3 Relevance Evaluation Stage

The Terms Grouping Stage produces groups of ranked candidate terms. These terms need to be evaluated by the searchers, however. During the **Relevance Evaluation Stage** (see the box in the center of Figure 6), searchers select and rank those terms they think are relevant to their queries. This process is intended to reveal the searcher's conscious needs. A list of ranked citations can then be generated from the ranked candidate terms.

5.2.4 Terms Solicitation Stage

As shown in Figure 6, if searchers are satisfied with the retrieved citations (both in terms of the number of matched citations and the relevance of the citations), the search terminates successfully. On the other hand, if searchers are not satisfied with the results, the search process continues. New information needs to be supplied. The search moves on to the **Terms Solicitation Stage** if the searchers have new search terms to provide. When no search terms can be supplied by the searchers, the interaction proceeds to the **Citations Instantiation Stage**. This stage involves the use of the detailed information in the retrieved citations.

At the Terms Solicitation Stage searchers supply new search terms. These new terms are first translated into index terms. A *spreading activation* process using these new terms and the previous terms then follows. New candidate terms and citations can be generated. This iterative process ends when no new terms can be supplied by the searchers. This stage attempts to simulate the searchers' **semantic-based browsing** approach described earlier.

5.2.5 Citations Instantiation Stage

While the Terms Solicitation Stage aims at soliciting new terms from the searchers, the **Citations Instantiation Stage** instantiates the information embedded in the citations that have been selected by the searchers. It attempts to simulate the **retrieval by instantiation** approach for query refinement. The index terms assigned to the selected citations, in particular, provide good clues for the search. By performing a *spreading activation* process using the old terms and the index terms just derived, new relevant terms and citations can be obtained.

As shown in Figure 6, our proposed process model for online query refinement is iterative in nature. By applying the heuristics and the refining mechanisms in this model repeatedly, a retrieval system can better assist searchers in articulating and refining their queries.

6   Conclusion

Electronic information storage and retrieval systems have changed the way people retrieve information. Investors access financial data of companies via their terminal at home. Lawyers consult law cases by online browsing of databases. Researchers obtain information about relevant studies by using online catalogs and online bibliographic databases. While the amount of information available for online access increases dramatically, searches are often problematic. This may be due in large part to the difficulty involved in articulating and refining the searchers' underlying information needs. Human information specialists' role in refining queries has been well recognized in prior studies. In our research, we observed an online query refinement process consistent with Taylor's theory.

However, the process was passive and unproductive in comparison with the process when information specialists were present.

We observed that searchers refined their queries at the search term level with the aid of five semantic operators and at the citation level using author, title, publisher, and index term information. We proposed a semantic network representation to capture the subject area knowledge and developed a process model for query refinement. This model, we believe, can serve as a basis for designing more "intelligent" and useful information retrieval systems. We have incorporated this model into the design of a knowledge-based document retrieval system. Readers are referred to [8].

References

[1] W. Ross Ashby. *An Introduction to Cybernetics*. Methuen, London, 1973.

[2] Marcia J. Bates. Subject access in online catalog: a design model. *Journal of the American Society of Information Science*, 37(6):357–376, November 1986.

[3] D. Batra and J. G. Davis. A study of conceptual data modeling in database design: similarities and differences between expert and novice designers. In *Proceedings of the 10th International Conference on Information Systems (ICIS-89)*, pages 91–100, Boston, MA, December 1989.

[4] N. J. Belkin, R. N. Oddy, and H. M. Brooks. Ask for information retrieval: Part I. background and theory. *Journal of Documentation*, 38(2):61–71, June 1982.

[5] J. Marinus Bouwman. Human diagnostic reasoning by computers: an illustration from financial analysis. *Management Science*, 29:653–672, June 1983.

[6] R.J. Brachman. What's in a concept: Structural foundations for semantic network. *International Journal of Man-Machine Studies*, 9, 1977.

[7] Hsinchun Chen and Vasant Dhar. Reducing indeterminism in consultation: a cognitive model of user/librarian interaction. In *Proceedings of the 6th National Conference on Artificial Intelligence (AAAI-87)*, 1987.

[8] Hsinchun Chen and Vasant Dhar. A knowledge-based approach to the design of document-based retrieval systems. In *Proceedings of the 5th Conference on Office Information Systems*, Cambridge, MA 1990.

[9] Paul R. Cohen and Rick Kjeldsen. Information retrieval by constrained spreading activation in semantic networks. *Information Processing and Management*, 23(4):255–268, 1987.

[10] Timothy C. Craven. Thesaural relations in a concept-network management system for customizing of permuted index displays. *Information Processing and Management*, 20(5/6):633–610, 1984.

[11] K. Anders Ericsson and Herbert A. Simon. *Protocol analysis: verbal report as data*. The MIT Press, Cambridge, Massachusetts, 1984.

[12] G. W. Furnas, T. K. Landauer, L. M. Gomez, and S. T. Dumais. The vocabulary problem in human-system communication. *Communications of the ACM*, 30(11):964–971, November 1987.

[13] M. D. Good, J. A. Whiteside, D. R. Wixon, and S. J. Jones. Building a user-derived interface. *Communications of the ACM*, 27(10):1032–1043, October 1984.

[14] B. Huguenard, M. J. Prietula, and F. J. Lerch. Performance ≠ behavior: a study in the fragility of expertise. In *Proceedings of the 10th International Conference on Information Systems (ICIS-89)*, pages 101–117, Boston, MA, December 4-6 1989.

[15] J. Jacoby and V. Slamecka. *Indexer Consistency Under Minimal Conditions*. Documentation, Inc., Bethesda, MD, 1962.

[16] F. W. Lancaster. *Information Retrieval Systems*. John Wiley and Sons, Inc., 1979.

[17] Karen Markey. Levels of question formulation in negotiation of information need during the online presearch interview: a proposed model. *Information Processing and Management*, 17(5):215–225, 1981.

[18] Karen Markey and Pauline Atherton. *Online Training and Practice Manual for ERIC Data Base Searchers*. Syracuse, NY: ERIC Clearinghouse on Information Resources, ERIC: ED 160109, 1978.

[19] A. Newell and H. A. Simon. *Human Problem Solving*. Prentice-Hall, Englewood Cliffs, NJ, 1972.

[20] Wanda Orlikowski and Vasant Dhar. Imposing structure on linear programming: an empirical analysis of expert and novice models. In *Proceedings of the Fifth National Conference on Artificial Intelligence (AAAI-86)*, Philadelphia, PA, August 1986.

[21] M. R. Quillian. Semantic memory. In *Semantic Information Processing*, 1968.

[22] Peretz Shoval. Principles, procedures and rules in an expert system for information retrieval. *Information Processing and Management*, 21(6):475–487, 1985.

[23] R.F. Simmons. *Semantic Network: Their Computation and Use for Understanding English Sentences*. In Schank, R.C. and Colby, K.M. (eds.), Computer Models of Thought and Language, Freeman, 1973.

[24] Mary Elizabeth Stevens. *Automatic Indexing: A State-of-the-art Report*. U.S. Government Printing Office, Washington, DC, 1965.

[25] Gary W. Strong and M. Carl Drott. A thesaurus for end-user indexing and retrieval. *Information Processing and Management*, 22(6):487–492, 1986.

[26] R. Tagliacozzo and M. Kochen. Information-seeking behavior of catalog users. *Information Storage and Retrieval*, 6:363–381, 1970.

[27] Rober S. Taylor. The process of asking questions. *Am. Documen.*, 13:391–396, 1962.

[28] Rober S. Taylor. Question-negotiation and information seeking in libraries. *College and Research Libraries*, 29:178–194, May 1968.

[29] Bernd Teufel. Natural language documents-indexing and retrieval in an information system. In *ICIS'88 Conference Proceedings*, Minneapolis, MN, December 1988.

[30] F. N. Tou, M. D. Williams, R. Fikes, A. Henderson, and T. Malone. Rabbit: An intelligent database assistant. In *Proceedings of the National Conference on Artificial Intelligence*, 1982.

[31] D.A. Waterman and A. Newell. Protocol analysis as a task for artificial intelligence. *Artificial Intelligence*, 2:285–318, 1971.

[32] Michael David Williams. What makes rabbit run? *International Journal of Man-Machine Studies*, 21:333–352, 1984.

[33] W.A. Woods. *What's in a Link: Foundations for Semantic Networks*. In Bobror, G. and Collins, A. (eds.), Representation and Understanding: Studies in Cognitive Science, Academic Press, New York, NY, 1975.

A Direct Manipulation Interface for Boolean Information Retrieval via Natural Language Query

Peter G. Anick, Jeffrey D. Brennan, Rex A. Flynn, David R. Hanssen

Digital Equipment Corporation, 290 Donald Lynch Blvd., DLB5-2/B4, Marlboro, MA 01752-0749

Bryan Alvey, Jeffrey M. Robbins

Digital Equipment Corporation, 305 Rockrimmon Blvd. South, CXO3-1/Q3 Colorado Springs, CO 80919-2398

Abstract

This paper describes the design of a direct manipulation user interface for Boolean information retrieval. Intended to overcome the difficulties of manipulating explicit Boolean queries as well as the "black box" drawbacks of so-called natural language query systems, the interface presents a two-dimensional graphical representation of a user's natural language query which not only exposes heuristic query transformations performed by the system, but also supports query reformulation by the user via direct manipulation of the representation. The paper illustrates the operation of the interface as implemented in the AI-STARS full-text information retrieval system.

1. Introduction

The AI-STARS project is an on-going research program at Digital Equipment Corporation, investigating methods for improving full-text information retrieval. Our target audience is Digital's Customer Support Specialists, for whom ready access to on-line technical information is indispensable for quick and accurate handling of a wide range and heavy volume of customer inquiries. Specialists typically must conduct textual information searches while on the phone with the customer and without much time for planning a query. Hence system response time and ease of use are critical to effective use of information retrieval technology in this environment. Our aim is to exploit linguistic and domain knowledge to improve article indexing, query interpretation, and query reformulation.

Our starting point for this research is STARS, the text retrieval system currently in use at Digital's Customer Support Centers. STARS provides full-text retrieval, given a query expressed either as a Boolean expression or as a natural language string. In interviews with STARS users, we found that natural language query is by far the preferred input mode, since users need no training to express topics via the natural language methods of adjectival and prepositional phrase modification, relative clauses, nominal compounds, etc. But, unlike Boolean queries, which provide an explicit semantics defining the set of documents retrieved, natural language queries typically require some "behind the scenes" transformations before they can be matched against a document set. STARS, for example, performs word truncation to remove suffixes, removes noisewords, adds in synonyms, and finally converts the result into a Boolean expression for article matching.

When successful, natural language query is an ideal interface. However, our interviews revealed that natural language query users tend to be confused by system results that don't conform to their expectations of what "should" happen and they often request ways to override (supposed) system default behavior. Thus, the major advantage of natural language query, its avoidance of more cumbersome input languages such as Boolean expressions, is counterbalanced by the need for query-enhancing transformations which typically transpire without the user's awareness.

This state of affairs presents a challenge to projects like AI-STARS, which have the goal of implementing even more powerful "behind the scenes" intelligence. Our approach to this dichotomy is to augment a natural language query facility with a direct manipulation "Query Reformulation Workspace", which incorporates an explicit visual Boolean semantics. This window gives the user a view into the heuristic decisions made by the system and, at the same time, the ability to override, influence, or supplement those decisions.

This paper describes our interface design. We begin with an overview of some of the query reformulation techniques that are appropriate to natural language query systems and describe our implementation of those techniques. We then enumerate a set of design goals we believe a human interface should meet and present a design which comes close to satisfying those goals. We conclude with a discussion of the merits and shortcomings of our approach.

2. Reformulation Techniques

Reformulation techniques can be applied at both article indexing time and at query time to enhance the matching of natural language queries with articles. AI-STARS incorporates the following techniques.

- Stemming. AI-STARS utilizes a lexicon of known words, morphological paradigms, and orthographic rules in order to reduce morphologically inflected forms to their uninflected "citation" forms. This eliminates the need for the user to worry about truncating query terms to increase recall.

- Phrase construction. The lexicon also stores uninflected forms of known contiguous phrases, such as "database management system". This allows the system to recognize known phrases in a user query, obviating the need for the user to explicitly request that the terms be treated as a phrase. Articles are indexed by both the phrase as a whole and the individual components of the phrase.

- Expression canonicalization. Special expressions, such as release version numbers and date expressions, which have multiple surface realizations, are parsed and canonicalized. For example, the variant surface forms "version 5.1-a", "v5.1-a" and "v. 5.1a" are indexed by a single canonical form. This eliminates the need to construct and retrieve on a set of alternative forms at query time.

- Expression generalization. Certain expressions, such as version numbers, encode implicit generalizations. For example, "v5.0a" is a specialization of "v5.0" which is in turn a specialization of "v5". At indexing time, articles containing such expressions are indexed on each generalization of such an expression. This allows for the matching of articles with various levels of query expression specificity.

- Noiseword removal. Words unlikely to contribute to the content of a query, such as articles and prepositions, are automatically excluded from the query.

- Use of thesaurus relations. AI-STARS maintains a database of related terms. Synonyms may be ORed with terms in the query in order to improve recall. More specific terms may be substituted for more general terms to improve precision.

Numerous other reformulation techniques have been investigated in the context of other experimental natural language query systems. [DEBILI88] discusses spelling correction, "explicitation" of implicit concepts recognized via morpho-syntactic frames, and stemmatization relating words with their morphological derivatives. [SALTON75] and [DILLON83] have experimented with phrasal normalization, relating word collocations appearing in semantically similar but syntactically different constructions, such as "retrieval of information" and "information retrieval." [LANCEL88] associates word sequences with semantic filters. [SCHWARZ88] analyzes text into dependency trees reflecting head-modifier relations.

These techniques, while utilizing computational linguistics, stop short of attempting to do a full parse and deep understanding of either the query or text. Researchers [BOGURAEV82, RAU88] have explored this approach to indexing and query interpretation as well. However, our focus here will be on the former kinds of reformulation, those designed to enhance the mapping of a natural language input into a traditional Boolean query. In the STARS full-text system, for example, natural language queries are typically not sentences at all, but rather strings of words and phrases.

3. User Interface Design Goals

Given the context of a full-text information retrieval system which translates natural language queries into Boolean expressions, our aim was to augment the interface to allow the user better understanding of and control over the actual query formulation. We identified a number of design goals for an appropriate human interface for this task.

1. It should make explicit any "behind the scenes" operations done by the system. The results of morphological analysis and other forms of canonicalization should be viewable. If noisewords are removed, this should be made obvious.

2. It should accommodate ambiguity in natural language expressions. Since the system's default interpretation of a query may depend on ambiguity resolution, the interface should have a way to present the ambiguity and indicate the system's response to that ambiguity. For example, in a system which indexes and retrieves on phrases, a natural language input containing a phrase is automatically ambiguous between two interpretations, one matching articles which contain the contiguous phrase, the other matching articles which contain the component terms but not necessarily in contiguous positions.

3. It should provide a natural way of visualizing the Boolean expression created as a result of analyzing the natural language query.

4. It should facilitate query reformulation and experimentation, by making iterative adjustments to the query easy to perform. (e.g. Bates' search formulation tactics [BATES79]).

5. It should integrate smoothly with other information retrieval aids, such as a thesaurus.

4. AI-STARS User Interface

Our experimental realization of the above design goals takes the form of a direct manipulation "Query Reformulation Workspace". This has been implemented using X-windows on a DEC VAXstation as part of the AI-STARS prototype. As mentioned earlier, input to AI-STARS is in the form of a natural language expression. Each word is morphologically analyzed to identify its citation form (the uninflected form as it would appear in a dictionary); meaningful phrases, composed of two or more consecutive words, are recognized; special expressions are canonicalized and generalized; and noisewords are identified. By default, the system makes noisewords, generalizations, and those words that are components of phrases (as opposed to the entire phrases) "inactive", meaning that they are not included in the query executed against the article database. All other terms are initially "active".

The results of this analysis are displayed in the graphical "Query Reformulation Workspace." Figure 1 illustrates the appearance of the workspace after the user has entered the query "Copying backup savesets from tape under v5.0".

All citation forms (for words, phrases, special expressions, generalizations and noisewords) are laid out as tiles in two dimensions, in a chart, or spreadsheet-like, format. The citation forms for the tokens in the original query are displayed horizontally along the top of the chart, thereby defining columns of the chart. Phrases, multi-term special expressions, and ambiguous interpretations of the query terms are displayed below the corresponding items of the top line. The two-word phrase "BACKUP saveset", for example, is displayed in a single tile covering the two columns delineated by its component terms. The tiles of active query terms are indicated by reverse video. The

Figure 1 Initial Query

function words, "from" and "under" are inactive. Likewise, the components of the phrase "BACKUP saveset" are inactive, as is the generalized term, "version 5".

The two-dimensional layout provides a simple visual semantics for the Boolean interpretation of a query, while accommodating ambiguity that may exist in a natural language expression. Roughly, tiles which overlap vertically are ORed and those which do not are ANDed. The set of documents retrieved can be described as all those articles containing some combination of terms from any possible left-to-right path through the chart. We will characterize the semantics of the display more completely in section 6.

The Boolean expression corresponding to the displayed configuration of tiles in figure 1 is

("copy" AND "BACKUP saveset" AND "tape" AND ("v5.0" OR "version 5.0")).

As a result of applying the query, the user is informed of the number of articles matching the query and is given the option of viewing a list of their titles. Additionally, the number of postings for each term included in the query is displayed in the lower left-hand corner of the tile corresponding to that term. This feedback can suggest to the user which terms may require broadening or narrowing.

The workspace supports query reformulation via direct manipulation of the display. The system's default choices of active tiles are currently biased towards precision rather than recall. However, each term can be individually included in or excluded from the query by clicking on the tile (which toggles its activation). Figure 2 illustrates the display after the user has deactivated the term "copy" and activated the terms "BACKUP" and "saveset". The Boolean interpretation of this new configuration is

(((("BACKUP" AND "saveset") OR "BACKUP saveset") AND "tape" AND ("v5.0" OR "version 5.0")).

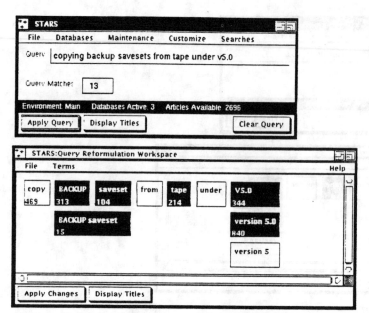

Figure 2 Query after changing activations

In addition to toggling activation of tiles, users can manipulate the search expression further by moving tiles from one column to another via mousing and dragging. For example, in figure 3, the user has moved the "tape" tile into the column below the tile "saveset", changing the configuration to mean

(((("BACKUP" AND ("saveset" OR "tape")) OR "BACKUP saveset") AND ("v5.0" OR "version 5.0")).

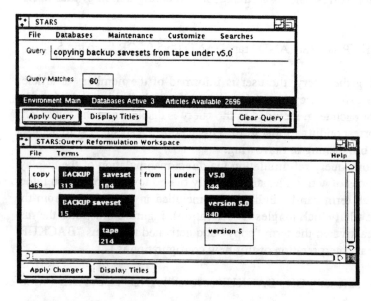

Figure 3 Query after moving tile

Note that the column previously containing "tape" is empty as a result of the move and is no longer displayed.

A tile can be made to extend across more or fewer columns by mousing and dragging the edge of the tile. These operations allow the user complete control over how the terms are to be ANDed or ORed with each other; the Query Reformulation Workspace thus serves as a visually appealing alternative to manipulating Boolean expressions in the form of parenthesized expressions or AND/OR trees.

5. Adding New Search Terms

It is well known that initial user queries rarely contain all the right terms to conduct a successful search [BATES86]. Many systems provide on-line thesauri [FREI83, MC-MATH89, THOMPSON89] or support relevance feedback [CROFT86, SALTON89] to supplement an initial query with further search terms.

The AI-STARS system maintains a database of related terms, which are made accessible from the Query Reformulation Workspace. A user can click on a term in the workspace to "select" it and then call on a "related terms" pop-up window to display terms that are related to the selected term in various ways: synonyms, terms containing the term (or a portion of the term) as a substring, phrases containing the term, and conceptually related terms.

In figure 4, the term "tape" has been selected (as indicated by the surrounding bolded rectangle) and the Terms window corresponding to the term "tape" has been displayed to the right of the Query Reformulation Workspace window.

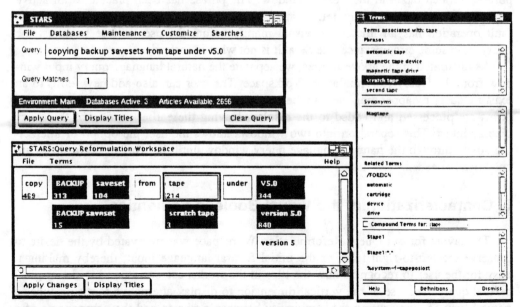

Figure 4 Query after term substituted from terms display

141

The Terms window is composed of four subwindows, each with its own operational semantics.

- For phrases containing the term, selecting an item from the Terms window has the effect of narrowing the query by substituting the item for the selected term in the workspace. This is achieved by placing the item as an active tile into the same column(s) as the workspace selected term and making the workspace selected term inactive.

- For synonyms, selecting an item from the Terms window broadens the query by adding the item as an active tile in the same column as the workspace selected term, without changing the activation of the workspace term.

- For conceptually related terms, selecting an item narrows the query by appending the item as an active tile after the last occupied column of the chart (visually establishing a new column).

- Compound terms are superstrings of the term which contain at least one non-alphabetic character. Such superstrings are common in a computer science domain, where many terms, such as error messages and facility names, are composed of mnemonic strings embedded in longer strings, using non-alphabetic characters as delineators. When being added to a query, compound terms are treated in the same manner as synonyms.

The association of a default semantics with each Terms subwindow minimizes user effort in augmenting a query, since a user need only select the term to be added, without first considering where the term should be placed in the configuration. In figure 4, the Query Reformulation Workspace has been updated to show the result of selecting the phrase "scratch tape" in the Terms window. The phrase has been placed, as an active term, in the column below the term "tape", which has been made inactive. As each default operation has an immediate visual manifestation, the user is free to adjust the query if, in some circumstance, the default is not what is desired.

As illustrated in the above figures, we separate the natural language query input window from the Query Reformulation Workspace. The user can also add new terms to an existing query by appending them to the original natural language query string. The new terms are processed and added to the display, leaving the earlier portion of the query display intact. This separation into two windows allows the user the option of interacting solely through the natural language query window until the workspace facilities are specifically needed.

6. Characterization of the Visual Boolean Semantics

The layout for our Query Reformulation Workspace was motivated by the desire to preserve the left-to-right form of the initial natural language input, thereby making it easy for the user to recognize how the tiles in the workspace correspond to the original textual query. The use of the vertical dimension to display alternative terms provides a natural way of representing the ambiguity between a phrase and the components of a phrase taken individually. Yet, as the previous sections illustrate, the set of tile manipu-

142

lations available permits the construction of arbitrarily complex visual displays. In this section, we describe the visual semantics of the workspace with a series of examples of increasing complexity.

One Column Groups

The simplest configurations are those in which none of the tiles span more than one column.

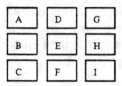

Each column constitutes a group of ORed terms. The ORs formed from each column are ANDed from left to right. This is a standard conjunctive normal form interpretation. We extend the conjunctive form to deal with situations where tiles have been deactivated. If a single tile in one of the columns above is inactive, it simply does not participate in the OR for its column. If all of the tiles in one column are inactive, we have chosen to ignore that column in the query. (The alternative choice would have been to make the query unsatisfiable.) A common situation producing inactive columns is the deactivation of function words, such as "from" and "under" in Figure 1.

Multi-column Groups

A multi-column group exists whenever a single active tile spans more than one column.

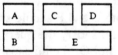

In this example, we consider tiles C, D and E to form a single multi-column group. Within this group, C and D do not overlap, but together they overlap completely with E. We therefore translate this group into the Boolean expression ((C AND D) OR E). The expression for this group is then included in the overall query as if it were a single-column group (the resulting query is [(A OR B) AND ((C AND D) OR E)]).

There are some multi-column groups where tiles are not necessarily displayed in the order in which the expression is generated.

In this configuration, D and F overlap completely, so they are ORed together before ANDing with C (and ORing the result of that with E). So, the resulting expression for this group is ((C AND (D OR F)) OR E).

Multi-column group with partial overlap

Sometimes some of the tiles in a multi-column group are inactive.

By analogy to the situation in which a column contains no active tiles, there are two ways the space left by tile D can be interpreted. Breaking down the group into two sub-groups (C and "D" as one subgroup, and E as the other), either the subgroup containing C cannot satisfy the query on its own, or it can. We have chosen the latter interpretation, i.e. to ignore the "column" occupied by D in the subgroup, so the Boolean interpretation for the whole group ends up being (C OR E).

Multi-column group with complex overlap

There are certain overlapping situations which are much harder to interpret.

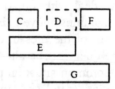

In this situation, we extend the notion of a group to include all of the tiles above. A more formal definition of a group is that it consists of all the active tiles in a series of adjacent columns, where each of the boundaries between these adjacent columns has at least one active tile spanning it, but the boundaries on either side of the the outermost columns in the group have no tiles spanning them.

The major question for such a group is how we would like it to be interpreted. It is clear that an article containing both E and F should satisfy the query. Likewise, an article containing both C and G should satisfy the query. It is not clear whether an article containing C and F, but neither E nor G, should satisfy the query. The algorithm which we use (and which is described in section 8) will allow this last possibility to satisfy the query. We believe that this is consistent with how we have interpreted the other configurations containing inactive tiles. Nevertheless, such situations are difficult to analyze.

Fortunately, such circumstances rarely occur. Where two terms overlap each other in the way that E and G do, they tend to represent competing concepts. For example, if the user typed in "operating system management," the system might know about the phrases "operating system" and "system management." It is unlikely that the user would want to query on both these concepts simultaneously.

7. Explicit Boolean operators

The visual Boolean semantics described above allow the expression of any propositional calculus expression formable using the connectives AND and OR. Even so, there are queries that cannot easily be expressed in our two-dimensional graphical language, such as ((A and B) or (C and D)). Visually representing this query would require repetitions of the same terms at different points along the horizontal axis, as shown here:

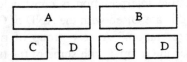

Furthermore, the traditional Boolean NOT operator is not available. While these are potential shortcomings of this approach, they may have little practical consequence. McAlpine and Ingwersen [MCALPINE89], for example, limit their query-by-forms search expression interface to conjunctions of ORed terms, arguing that this is sufficient in most cases.

Nevertheless, we are experimenting with the addition of an optional "escape hatch" to full propositional calculus, by allowing the user to include the Boolean operators AND, OR, and NOT directly in their natural language queries. When one of these terms is encountered in a query, it is treated as ambiguous between the English word and the Boolean operator, with the Boolean interpretation active by default. With the use of parentheses, this permits the formation of arbitrary Boolean expressions. Natural language sequences appearing between Boolean operators are interpreted as above.

8. An Algorithm for Interpreting Chart Configurations

We implement the visual Boolean semantics described in section 6 by employing a recursive divide-and-conquer strategy. Applied to any subgroup of terms generated from the tiles in the workspace, it generates a tree of nodes, where the internal nodes are Boolean query operators (AND, OR and NOT), and the leaves are the workspace terms. The "divide" part of the algorithm splits a group of terms into multiple smaller groups of terms, to which the algorithm can be re-applied. The "conquer" part groups multiple subtrees together into a single larger tree by supplying a new AND or OR internal node. Once a tree is generated for all the terms in the workspace, it can be interpreted directly to search the database of articles.

The same algorithm handles both the default workspace semantics and explicit Boolean terms as described in the previous sections. The process of splitting and regrouping terms recursively into a tree is not complicated for explicit Boolean terms, and is handled at the top levels of recursion.

The lower levels of recursion, which handle the default workspace semantics, involve 3 basic steps.

1. "Find-fewest-spanning-terms." Find the way to perform the recursive subdivide of a group of terms supplied to it. A group of terms spans a set of columns in the workspace. The algorithm finds a point between two of these columns that has the fewest number of terms spanning it. It splits the group of terms into 3 subgroups — Group 1 contains all terms that are to the left of the point, Group 2 contains all terms to the right, and Group 3 contains any terms that span the point.

2. Groups 1 and 2 together constitute a "compatible" interpretation of the query — i.e. the results of processing the default algorithm against Group 1 can be ANDed against the results of processing the algorithm against Group 2. If Group 3 is empty, this is all that needs to be done. Otherwise, Group 3 constitutes an "incompatible" interpretation: an alternative interpretation is constructed with Group 3 (see next item), and the results of this are ORed with the AND of Groups 1 and 2.

3. "Construct-alternate-interpretation." A new group of tiles is constructed by augmenting the spanning tiles in Group 3 with some of the tiles in Groups 1 and 2. The tiles that are included from Groups 1 and 2 are any that do not overlap with at least one of the tiles in Group 3. This creates a new group with potential term overlaps in it, but later recursions will resolve these overlaps correctly. Once a group is generated in this way, it is processed recursively.

In this specific implementation, there are three degenerate cases which constitute the stopping points of the recursion.

1. An empty column, which returns nothing (we ignore empty columns).

2. A single term — this is returned as a leaf node.

3. A group of multiple terms, which all span the same columns — these are ORed together.

After the tree is generated, nested Boolean AND nodes and nested Boolean OR nodes are merged, to reduce the number of Boolean operations on article sets further.

Example

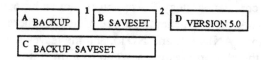

The starting group of terms is [A B C D]. "Find-fewest-spanning-terms" finds point 2 has no overlapping terms, and splits the group into Group 1, [A B C], and Group 2, [D]. Group 1 is re-analyzed, and point 1 is found as having 1 overlapping term -- we get Subgroup 1 as [A], Subgroup 2 as [B], and Subgroup 3 as [C]. Subgroups 1 and 2 are the second degenerate case — the terms are returned as nodes. Subgroup 1 and Subgroup 2 are mutually compatible, and are ANDed together

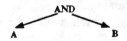

"Construct-alternate-interpretation" finds no terms in Subgroups 1 and 2 that can be included with Subgroup 3, so C is returned as the degenerate tree for the alternate interpretation, and this is ORed with the prior AND node, which gives

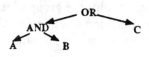

146

Finally, the results of this (the original Group 1) are compatible with Group 2, and they are ANDed together.

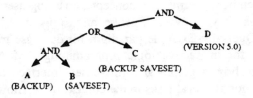

9. User Feedback

In a preliminary study of the effectiveness of the proposed interface, we observed a dozen users, already familiar with the STARS system, as they formulated queries using the AI-STARS interface. Users were able to manipulate the Query Reformulation Window appropriately after several minutes of explanation and experimentation. Their feedback indicated that "opening up the black box" simplified the task of query reformulation and made them more confident in the results of the search. For most realistic queries, the visual displays were readily interpretable with respect to their Boolean semantics. As alluded to in section 6, cases of "complex overlap" of tiles were difficult to decipher in the contrived examples we presented to the users. However, users did not encounter such cases while formulating queries on their own.

Further testing is required to generalize our findings to a large population. We are particularly interested in ease of learnability for novice STARS users, and comparisons of retrieval effectiveness with and without the reformulation window.

10. Performance

Our interface supports query reformulation via interactive iterative refinement. This mode of interaction requires quick query response times (i.e. within several seconds) to be most effective. Using a cache to speed up lexicon access, our current prototype, operating on a database of 3000 one-to-two page articles, satisfies our interactive response requirements. As we scale up to databases in the 100,000 to 500,000 article range (the size of the existing STARS database), we expect the major cost to come from performing I/O's on the inverted indices. For this reason, we have avoided including some of the more expensive operations sometimes available in information retrieval systems, such as term proximity constraints, word truncation, and wildcarding. Our hope is that the indexing of known contiguous phrases, morphological analysis, and the compound terms window make these search term operations largely unnecessary.

11. Related Work

A number of researchers have explored the use of graphics interfaces for information retrieval. Fischer and Nieper-Lemke [FISCHER89] support browsing and query formulation with a visually displayed concept hierarchy. Croft and Thompson [CROFT86] allow users to graphically navigate a knowledge base consisting of a semantic network of documents, terms, and concepts, enabling users to discover and indicate relevant items as they browse. Spenke and Beilken [SPENKE89] generalize Zloof's [ZLOOF77] Query-by-Example paradigm for database retrieval with a spreadsheet based interface for interactive logic programming. McAlpine and Ingwersen [MCALPINE89] show how a graphical forms-based interface can be applied over a wide range of information retrieval tasks in the context of a "knowledge worker support system."

Our approach to the graphical representation of natural language input has also been influenced by work in "chart parsing" [KAY80], for which a two-dimensional graphical layout can be exploited to display constituent structure.

12. Conclusions

Lynch [LYNCH87] has argued that the introduction of heuristics into information retrieval systems has an associated risk, that the "portion of the user community who understands how the information retrieval system really works and how to exploit the full power of the retrieval system thus will grow smaller and smaller." Corroborating this prediction, our analysis of users' problems with the STARS full-text retrieval system revealed that the benefits of natural language queries were somewhat undermined by the necessity of hidden query reformulation.

This paper has described an approach to opening up the "black box" that characterizes many information retrieval systems accessed via natural language query. The resulting interface is a hybrid that, we believe, reaps the benefits of both natural language queries and explicit Boolean query manipulation, while minimizing the drawbacks that each approach has on its own.

Informal off-line testing by Customer Support Specialists has tended to validate this hybrid approach. Users appear to learn the visual semantics quickly and enjoy the ease with which they can experiment with the form of a query. Thus, while we have not yet had the opportunity to test our prototype on a wide number of users in a realistic setting, we are optimistic about the effectiveness of this solution for our target user community.

We are also evaluating potential shortcomings of the current approach.

- The display method is best suited for relatively short queries, since the visual representation becomes less perspicuous as the number of tiles in the configuration increases. While this limits the size of practical queries, our experience suggests that most actual queries fall within the range accommodated by this approach.

- The existence of certain complex configurations containing partially overlapping tiles (mentioned above) may make it hard for users to map some configurations to their Boolean equivalents. Again, our experience to date suggests that truly complex configurations are rarely produced in real queries, and that the interpretations of simple cases of partial overlap are easily learned by experience.

- The current system is based on mapping to an exact match Boolean expression. While the ease of manipulating this expression removes some of the drawbacks of exact match retrieval, we have not yet considered how this approach might be adapted to an extended Boolean [SALTON83] or probabilistic [SALTON86] semantics.

In addition to such issues, future research will investigate extensions to the current set of workspace operations, the integration of structured data into a query via the workspace, and integration with other on-line retrieval aids.

As we build more intelligence into the system, enabling more system-initiated query reformulation, it will be interesting to see how well our model of user/system cooperation through the visual workspace scales up. It is our belief that the ability to display the results of system-initiated reformulation in a manner comprehensible to and easily correctable by a user will be a major factor in user acceptance of and confidence in more "intelligent" retrieval systems of the future.

References

[BATES86] Bates, Marcia J., Terminological Assistance for the On-line Subject Searcher, Proceedings of 2nd Conference on Computer Interfaces for Information Retrieval, 1986.

[BATES79] Bates, Marcia J., Information Search Tactics, Journal of the American Society for Information Science, July 1979.

[BOGURAEV82] Boguraev, B.K. and K. Sparck Jones, A Natural Language Analyser for Database Access, Information Technology: Research and Development, 1982,1,23-39.

[CROFT86] Croft, W. B. and R. H. Thompson, I3R: A New Approach to the Design of Document Retrieval Systems, COINS Technical Report 87-58, 1986.

[DEBILI88] Debili, Fathi, Christian Fluhr, and Pierre Radasoa, About Reformulation in Full-Text IRS, Proceedings of RIAO, 1988, 343-360.

[DILLON83] Dillon, M. and A. S. Gray, FASIT: A Fully Automatic Syntactically Based Indexing System, 1983, Journal of the American Society for Information Science, 34(2):99-108.

[FISCHER89] Fischer, Gerhard and Helga Nieper-Lemke, HELGON: Extending the Retrieval by Reformulation Paradigm, Proceedings of CHI, 1989, 357-362.

[FREI83] Frei, H. P. and J. F. Jauslin, Graphical Presentation of Information and Services: a User-Oriented Interface, Information Technology: Research and Development, 1983, 2(23-42).

[KAY80] Kay, M., Algorithm Schemata and Data Structures in Syntactic Processing, Xerox Palo Alto Research Center, Tech Report no. CSL-80-12, 1980.

[LANCEL88] Lancel, J. M. and N. Simonin, TEX-NAT: A Tool for Indexing and Information Retrieval, Proceedings of RIAO, 1988, 369-377.

[LYNCH87] Lynch, Clifford A., The Use of Heuristics in User Interfaces for Online Information Retrieval Systems, Proceedings of the American Society for Information Science, 1987, 148-151.

[MCALPINE89] McAlpine, Gordon and Peter Ingwersen, Integrated Information Retrieval in a Knowledge Worker Support System, Proceedings of the Twelfth Annual International ACM SIGIR Conference on Research and Development in Information Retrieval, 1989.

[MCMATH89] McMath, Charles F., Robert S. Tamaru, and Roy Rada, A Graphical Thesaurus-Based Information Retrieval System, International Journal of Man-Machine Studies, 1989, 31, 121-147.

[RAU88] Rau, Lisa F., Conceptual Information Extraction and Retrieval from Natural Language Input, Proceedings of RIAO, 1988, 424-437.

[SALTON89] Salton, Gerard, Automatic Text Processing: the Transformation Analysis, and Retrieval of Information by Computer, Addison-Wesley, 1989.

[SALTON86] Salton, Gerard, Another Look at Automatic Text Retrieval Systems, Communications of the ACM, 1986, 29, 648-656.

[SALTON83] Salton, Gerard, Edward A. Fox, and Harry Wu, Extended Boolean Information Retrieval, Communications of the ACM, 1983, 26, 1022-1036.

[SALTON75] Salton, G., C. S. Yang, and C. T. Yu, A Theory of Term Importance in Automatic Text Analysis, Journal of the American Society for Information Science, 1975, 26(1):33-44.

[SCHWARZ88] Schwarz, Christoph, The TINA Project: Text Content Analysis at the Corporate Research Laboratories at Siemens, Proceedings of RIAO, 1988, 361-368.

[SPENKE89] Spenke, Michael and Christian Beilken, A Spreadsheet Interface for Logic Programming, Proceeding of CHI, 1989, 75-80.

[THOMPSON89] Thompson, R. H. and W. B. Croft, Support for Browsing in an Intelligent Text Retrieval System, International Journal of Man-Machine Studies 1989, 30, 639-668.

[ZLOOF77] Zloof, Moshé M., Query-by-Example: a Data Base Language, IBM System Journal 16(4), 1977, 324-343.

Determining the Functionality and Features of an
Intelligent Interface to an Information Retrieval
System

System

Nicholas J. Belkin

School of Communication, Information & Library Studies
Rutgers University
4 Huntington Street
New Brunswick, NJ 08903
belkin@zodiac.rutgers.edu

Pier Giorgio Marchetti

European Space Agency - IRS
via Galileo Galilei
00044 Frascati
Italy
pmarchet@ifresal0.profs

ABSTRACT

In this paper, we propose a method for specifying the functionality of an intelligent interface to large-scale information
retrieval systems, and for implementing those functions in an
operational environment. The method is based on a progressive,
three-stage model of intelligent information support; a high-
level cognitive task analysis of the information retrieval problem; a low-level specification of the host system functionality;
and, derivation of explict relations between the system functions
and the cognitive tasks. This method is applied, by example, in
the context of the European Space Agency Information Retrieval
Service, with some specific suggestions for implementation of a
stage one intelligent interface to that system.

1. Introduction

In this paper, we consider the issue of design of intelligent
interfaces to existing information retrieval (IR) systems. In
particular, we address the following questions:

1. what should the functions of such an interface be; that
    is, what constitutes intelligence in such an interface;

2. what factors ought to influence the design of such an
    interface, and how; and,

3.   how could such an interface be implemented?

We address these questions here within the specific context of
the large operational IR system of the European Space Agency
(ESA-IRS, using ESA-QUEST), specifying an interface design which
takes account of its characteristics and constraints. However,
we intend this as an example of the application of our method,
which we believe, and attempt below to demonstrate, is general at
least to the class of large, operational IR systems. Our context
is such that we assume in our discussion that our interface will
be tightly coupled to the host system and as much as possible
supported by it in its basic functions. Thus we will be relatively unconstrained by factors such as telecommunication problems that other interfaces (e.g. Marcus, 1985; Robertson, et al.,
1986) have had to face, and will be able to make use of system
facilities which might otherwise be unavailable. Nevertheless,
it seems to us that our general procedures will be applicable to
the design of both host and remote interfaces.

2.   A Design Sequence for an Intelligent Interface

Our general approach to the problem of intelligent interface
design is to take a sequence of design steps, outlined below,
which lead to a design specification. This sequence is:

1.   The statement of a three-stage model of intelligent
      support for end users of operational IR systems;

2.   Specification of a cognitive task analysis for IR sys-
      tems in general (a high-level functionality specifica-
      tion);

3.   Specification of the underlying functionality of the
      host system (here, ESA-QUEST, the search facility for
      ESA-IRS);

4.   Establishment of explicit relationships between the
      cognitive task analysis and system functionality;

5.   Specification of an 'ideal' interface design, given the
      relationships between desired functions identified in
      the cognitive task analysis, and available (or possi-
      ble) system functionalities;

6.   Identification of environmental constraints and human-
      computer interaction design principles and specifica-
      tion of their effects on interface implementation;

7.   Design specification for implementation of a stage-one
      interface.

The body of this paper is the description, and some results, of
application of some aspects of this design sequence within our
specific context. Here, we present a rationale for this particular approach to the problem.

We begin with a staged model for intelligent interface design on the premises that:

a. the actual accomplishment of such an interface will
    need to proceed through some sequence of intermediate
    implementations due to operational constraints, and in
    order to respond to principles of formative design
    (Egan, et al, 1989); yet,

b. to maintain continuity of implementation and in the
    design process, we need some overall view of what the
    'ideal' intelligent interface should accomplish.

Thus, the stages, discussed in section 4, serve as a means to
integrate a series of interface designs and implementations
within an overall goal, maintaining consistency in design decisions.

In contrast to some other approaches taken to intelligent interface (or intermediary) design (see section 3), we attempt to
develop an abstract, functional model of what such an interface
should accomplish, in terms of the problem faced by the IR system
(which includes the user). This approach is based on the concept
of cognitive task analysis (Roth & Woods, 1988), and requires a
specification of the goal of the system and the decisions, tasks
or functions required to achieve that goal. The result of such
an analysis thus sets the 'ideal' requirements for the interface.
We present such an analysis in section 5.

The possibility for accomplishing our ideal interace is constrained to some extent by the functionality of the underlying
host system, in particular its data structures, available
knowledge sources and retrieval facilities. In this instance, we
accept that our interface will be to some existing such system,
which could conceivably be modified in some ways, but which will
remain basically static. Our view on how to deal with the constraints that this imposes is to specify, at a very low level,
that which the system can actually do, on the assumption that
combinations of low-level functions can lead to more complex
functionalities. In section 6, we indicate the form and content
of such a description.

Our next step is to attempt to relate the ideal functionality for
the interface to the possibilities afforded by the system. One
can view this as trying to move down in level of detail from our
cognitive task analysis, and up in level of detail from our system functionality specification, with the intention of meeting
somewhere in the middle with a specification of interface functionality which responds to the ideal level and is possible to
implement. This procedure requires compromises from each end, in
terms, for instance, of reduction of aspiration, and of identification of desirable system modifications. One point of this procedure is to identify these compromises in a principled way, so
that they can be considered as candidates for incorporation in
the interface at its various stages of implementation. We outline such a procedure and and examples of its resulting stage one
interface specification, in section 7.

Any interface to an IR system will be implemented within certain environmental constraints established, for example, by its users, the host's general policies, telecommunication and hardware issues, and so on. These constraints will have effects on which interface functions will be implemented at any stage of development, and on how they can be implemented. Furthermore, the actual implementation of any functions must take account of what we know of the constraints (e.g. ergonomic, cognitive) of human-computer interaction in general. Both types of constraints are extremely important, but our view is that they should be considered only insofar as they relate to a prespecified functionality. In section 8 we discuss some such constraints in our environment, and suggest how they could affect implementation of our interface design.

This sequence of activities leads to identification of a staged sequence of interface functionalities, and the subsequent direct specification of a stage one interface implementation. In section 9, we give some examples of an implementation of a stage one intelligent interface to the ESA-IRS system.

3. Interaction and the Function of the IR Interface

Much previous work in IR has considered the information retrieval process as a sequence of steps leading to a search statement, which is then put to the system. The system then responds to that statement, the user evaluates the response, and modification and iteration takes place as appropriate. In this view, interaction between the user and the other components of the system can take place at the various steps, but its primary locus is at the search statement reformulation stage. The prototype model for this view of IR is relevance feedback (e.g. Robertson & Sparck Jones, 1976).

An alternative view is one of progressive development or refinement of a search formulation (to include search strategy). This view was exemplified in the THOMAS system (Oddy, 1977), which was designed to allow the user to develop a search through interaction with the system, without necessarily establishing an explicit query formulation. More recently, Belkin & Vickery (1985), Ingwersen & Wormell (1986), and Bates (1986), among others, have suggested that the process of IR is inherently interactive, and that the user's interaction with the data base should be construed as a process during which a search, and query, is gradually constructed, through formulation and reformulation. The difference between this view of IR and the more traditional one lies primarily in the status of the query, which in the traditional view is taken as an explicit statement of the user's information requirement, but in the interactive view as a means to an eventual desirable response.

The former view of IR arises, it seems, from the original context of computerized IR systems, in which elaborate queries and search strategies were constructed through interaction between the user and a human intermediary, highly trained in the characteristics of the system to which the query would be put. After such a search formulation was constructed, the query would be put to the system, and after a delay of up to two weeks, a response would be sent to the requestor. This procedure effectively removed any possibility of direct interaction between user or intermediary, and the rest of the system, and reified the evolved query and search strategy. A similar procedure and attitude underlies the typical Selective Dissemination of Information (SDI) search profile, still very much in use.

Although there is substantial interaction in the development and formulation of the search in the traditional view, it has been almost exclusively between the user and the human intermediary, separated from the interaction between the search specification and the rest of the IR system. This separation has tended to be reflected in a general procedure for conducting IR in the current online environment, which sees much of search formulation taking place off-line, in interaction between user and intermediary, with only some modification due to interaction (primarily concerned with methods for reducing or increasing retrieved set size in Boolean systems) occuring online. This attitude has been reinforced by the pricing policy of most data base hosts, which has a large component of connect-time costs, and by the costs of telecommunication. This situation has led, in turn, to the development of front-ends (or, in general, interfaces) to commercial IR systems which typically support off-line query specification, but very little, if any, online interaction, apart from simplifying the native command language in various ways (see Hawkins & Levy, 1986, for a survey of such interfaces).

Our view is that for end-user searching in IR systems, one should incorporate all of the necessary functions performed by the human intermediary in interaction with the user in the interface or in the system itself, taking the view that the whole process is one of progressive, interactive search formulation. This is now the general approach taken by research in 'intelligent information retrieval' (e.g. Belkin, Brooks & Daniels, 1987; Croft & Thompson, 1987), in which wholly new IR systems are being designed; it seems to us that this approach applies equally to front ends or interfaces to existing systems. The context of our project supports this view, since our interface is planned to be embedded as much as possible in the host, and since ESA-IRS does not charge for connect time. These two conditions allow for development of an interface which actively supports user interaction with the system.

There are many front ends or interfaces to IR systems which are in production, in experimental condition, or proposed. Most of them are, from our point of view, concerned with mechanical issues which are not of great relevance to the intelligent interface problem. We mention here four such interfaces which do exhibit features which are of relevance to this program, and attempt to relate them to our work.

One of the first attempts at an intelligent interface for IR systems was the IIDA project (Meadow, Hewett & Aversa, 1982). This system was implemented on a mainframe connected to a single host search system, and its goals were two-fold; to provide tutorial assistance to end users in learning to use the host system; and, to intervene and offer assistance to users during the search process, by identifying patterns of searching behavior and suggesting alternative actions. The first goal was achieved off-line in tutorial mode, and also through online help facilities; the second was achieved by monitoring user-system interaction and offering help in cases such as syntactic errors and errors in search formulation and strategy.

At about the same time as IIDA, the CONIT interface was developed at MIT (Marcus & Reintjes, 1981). This interface took a somewhat different approach than that of the IIDA project, identifying the problem with which it was concerned as simplified access to a number of heterogeneous systems. The CONIT response to this issue was two-fold: to develop a simplified command language for the end user, which the system translated into the appropriate format for the particular system with which it was connected; and to offer both substantial off-line explanation of searching in general and of its commands, and also extensive online help facilities, based on explanations of its commands. A result of this project was the realization of the significance of support for the user in search formulation. This realization was the basis of various enhancements to CONIT, reported in Marcus (1985), which were aimed at helping the user to formulate a query in terms which could be interpreted by the host command language, yet did not require explicit Boolean formulation by the user.

A somewhat similar approach has been taken in the OAK project (Meadow, et al., 1989; Borgman, Case & Meadow, 1989), who developed an interface to the RECON retrieval system for the Department of Energy. An interesting aspect of this interface is that it was based on empirical studies of the proposed users of the system, which was a definite innovation in the design of front ends. The goal of this interface was to help the users to search in the one specific system for which the interface was designed. The approach to this goal was to provide two-stage support: stage one being a tutorial program in online searching in general and in searching using the specific front end system of OAK; stage two being a search assistance program which aimed to assist in the initial formulation of the search statement, and in search term and output evaluation. The most interesting part of the OAK interface from our point of view here, is the assistance program (OAKASSIST). The approach taken was to develop a new retrieval interface, based on the idea of the IR search as a set of facets, combined by the Boolean 'and', with each facet being a set of synonymous or related terms combined by the Boolean 'or'. Since two very difficult aspects of Boolean search languages are understanding the Boolean operators and remembering commands and using them appropriately, this interface attempts to do away with the necessity for these features. Thus, the user is prompted, through menus, to specify the search topic as a number of facets, with one window to each facet. Within each facet, the user is prompted to enumerate related terms, and receives some support through available facilities for browsing in indexes of terms. When the user has specified all of the desired facets and their terms, the front end combines them into the appropriate search formulation, which it sends off to the host system. There are also facilities in OAKASSIST to support the user in evaluating the retrieved documents.

One of the more recent interfaces to IR systems is called
TOMESEARCHER (Vickery, 1988). This system, based on an earlier
expert system for referral called PLEXUS (Vickery, et al., 1988),
is explicitly aimed at support for end users in query construction, in particular in selecting appropriate terms for searching.
This intelligent intermediary is designed to interface to a
variety of data bases; but for each data base it accesses it
requires substantial knowledge of various aspects of that data
base to be held in its own memory. The reason for this is that
the main feature of TOMESEARCHER is its support for off-line
search formulation, including help with establishing whether
terms that the user enters are likely to be useful given the
posting frequencies of terms in the data base. This front end
helps the user to formulate a query without forcing an explicit
Boolean formulation (much in the spirit of OAKASSIST, although
without its fairly sophisticated graphics and interaction mech-
nanisms), and attempts to take account of various user-defined
parameters, such as search output requirements.

These systems, it can be fairly said, represent the state of the
art in front ends to operational IR systems. Although they all
attempt to support query and search formulation, and they all
take some care in assisting interaction between user and front
end, none of them actually supports the progressive development
of query and search formulation through interaction directly with
the data base. Indeed, in most of them, it is extremely difficult for the user to take account of system feedback to modify
the query or search strategy. Thus, all of these front ends
still subscribe to the two-part model of IR. Nevertheless, they
also all exhibit features that we would expect to incorporate in
any intelligent interface, including the one which we propose
here.

These features include the concept of faceted search expression
without specification in Boolean terms, substantial help and
tutorial facilities, assistance in search term selection based on
characteristics of the data base itself, replacement of the
native host language with simpler and easier to use alternatives,
and responsive and easy to use interface characteristics. In
general, all of these front end systems attempt to support the
user in search formulation and evaluation of output, rather than
to do the search for the user, but all of them also attempt to
take some responsibility for dealing with the intricacies of
actually formulating and implementing a search.

What these front ends do not do is to support a truly interactive
IR system which includes user, intermediary and data base, nor do
they incorporate and emulate, except in some very default ways,
the knowledge and activities that human intermediaries bring to
IR systems. These in particular are the areas which we believe
are required for a really intelligent interface to IR systems;
below, we present an analysis which identifies the functions
which such an interface would need to perform, and suggest ways
in which these functions could be implemented.

4. A Three-Stage Approach to Intelligent IR Support

The attempt to provide truly intelligent support for end-users of
IR systems will naturally require several generations of interface implementation. We say naturally on two grounds. In the
first instance, we take the view that the principles of formative
design, as suggested by Egan, et al. (1989), are appropriate in
our situation. That is, we have some ideas about the bases on
which such a system should be built, but many details of the
implementation are unclear, as are the effects on performance of
specific aspects of our general system design. So we assume that
our interface will go through several iterations of design,
implementation, evaluation, redesign, and so on.

Our second reason for this statement has to do with operational
realities and implementation strategies. That is, the requirements on our host system of an ideal intelligent interface will
be substantial, and it is probably unrealistic to expect them to
be met immediately. Therefore, our expectation is that we will
need to begin with a less taxing interface, to test it, and only
after having gone through some formative design, to move on, if
justified, to a next generation of capabilities.

This strategy for implementation, although it responds to system
constraints, and also to design principles, also poses some problems. The most important of these, from our point of view here,
is that of maintaining consistency from generation to generation;
that is, making sure that any one implementation actually fits in
to our overall 'ideal' interface. To this end, we suggest the
following three-stage model toward intelligent information support.

Stage one we characterize as _efficient_ end-user support. At this
stage, we anticipate only that the interface mask the underlying
query language, and that the knowledge contained in the interface, that is used to direct the interaction with the user, is
primarily knowledge of the structure of the system. At this
stage, the interface maintains static models of, for instance,
the user and the system's functions.

The second stage, which we call _knowledge-based_ end-user support,
builds upon the first by incorporating a model of what constitutes a search strategy, and incorporating knowledge of system
functionality within the more flexible search strategy functionality. At this level, more active support is offered to the
user in the search formulation process, based on knowledge of the
topic of the search, as well as of the system functionality.
User models will probably be adaptive in some respects.

The third stage, _intelligent_ end-user support, will move to adaptive and interactive support of the user at the search-session
level. By this we mean that the interface will be able to adapt
its functions and operations to what it has learned of the user
during the course of the current search session. At this stage,
the interface's knowledge will be of system, topic and user, and
it will construct and maintain models of all of these which will
change during the course of the session, as required, and which

will be used to guide the interaction and to provide support to the user in search formulation and evaluation.

Our point in specifying these three stages is primarily so that when implementing the earlier stages, we construct them so that they respond to the anticipated requirements of the later stages, insofar as this is possible. Our task then, is to specify just what we consider the third stage of intelligent end-user support to require, in functional terms, and then to identify explicitly how the first stage of this ideal functionality can be implemented. In the next section, we propose a cognitive task analysis which leads to such functional specfication.

5. A Cognitive Task Analysis for Information Retrieval

5.1. Goals analysis

A cognitive task analysis (CTA) (Roth & Woods, 1989) is a specification of the functions and tasks that need to be performed in order to achieve some overall goal, and of the decisions that need to be made in the performance of those tasks. In order to identify the required functionality of our interface, we begin with a CTA for information retrieval, especially from the points of view of the user and the intermediary (whether human or computer) to the data base.

In order to establish a CTA, it is necessary first to establish an overall goal for the system. In the IR system setting, we can do this by defining a hierarchy of goals, and then specifying the level (or levels) of goals which we wish to attain (see Daniels, Brooks & Belkin, 1985). The advantage to this approach is that it allows one always to view any particular goal within its context, and also to relate specific tasks within one goal level to tasks which might be necessary at another. The goal hierarchy which we propose for IR is specified in figure 1, taken from Daniels, Brooks & Belkin, (1985).

LEVEL	GOAL
1	User leaves system
2	User is satisfied
3	Appropriate response to user
4	System is inappropriate, or Appropriate information
5	Effective search formulation

Figure 1. A goal hierarchy for information retrieval.

The overall goal of the IR system (the level one goal) is that the user leave the system. This is because the IR system is a support mechanism for users, to which they have recourse only when their own resources are inadequate for responding to some other problem or goal. That is, being in the IR system is not the user's normal or desired situation.

The user may leave for system for a variety of reasons, including frustration, boredom and satisfaction. We need to know the variety of possible reasons for leaving the system, in order to design against some of them, and in favor of others. In particular, we wish to consider that the goal at level two is that the user leaves the system because s/he is satisfied.

One way to achieve the level two goal is that the user obtains an appropriate response from the rest of the system. Other ways include the possibility that the user obtains an inappropriate response, which may not be recognized as such. We wish only to consider the 'appropriate response' branch, which becomes our level three goal for IR. By appropriate, we mean a response which responds to the user's goal and general situation.

One means to achieve the level three goal of an appropriate response is to offer the user information appropriate to the situation. Another, for instance, is to suggest to the user that the particular system in which s/he is interacting is not appropriate to the user's situation. From our point of view, it is at this level that we can begin to consider IR system functional design, and to specify overall goals to be achieved by the system. In particular, we wish to consider, of possible level four goals, those of 'appropriate information', and 'system appropriateness'.

Thus, we ask, what is required in order to achieve a response of appropriate information? One means, particularly reasonable in the IR system environment with which we are concerned, is by establishing an effective search formulation. We take this to be a goal specification at level five. In order to achieve our other level four goal (system appropriateness), we need somehow to establish a representation of the user's situation which it is possible to compare to some representation of the system's capabilities. Although, in principle, this branch of the IR goal hierarchy is extremely important, we will, for the moment, not consider it, and devote our attention to the goal of establishing an effective search formulation (we return later to the issue of system appropriateness, and will demonstrate that aspects of what one needs to do in order to achieve an effective search formulation can also be used for the purpose of establishing system appropriateness).

We can define our level five goal of effective search formulation by specifying the tasks which are required in order to accomplish it. For this, we take the general Distributed Expert-Based Information System (DEBIS) model (Belkin, et al, 1987), especially as proposed in Belkin, Seeger & Wersig (1983) and elaborated in Belkin, Brooks & Daniels (1987). These level five tasks (or goals), outlined in figure 2, we then consider as the activities in which the user and intermediary collaborate in order to achieve an effective search formulation.

Level 5: Effective Search Formulation

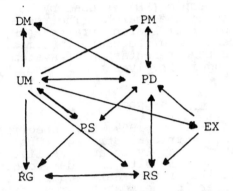

PM: Problem Mode; DM: Dialogue Mode; UM: User Model
PD: Problem Description; PS: Problem State; EX: Explanation
RG: Response Generator; RS: Retrieval Strategies

Arrows indicate logical (empirically established) and temporal relations. General sequence of events is from top to bottom, with iteration and recursion.

Figure 2. A problem structure for information retrieval (after Daniels, Brooks & Belkin, 1985).

In Belkin, Hennings & Seeger (1984), and in Daniels, Brooks and Belkin (1985), a very rough partial order was suggested for the accomplishment of the level five goals. Belkin (1988) also suggested temporal characteristics of clarification (explanation and related activities). Croft and Thompson (1987) specified and implemented an order of accomplishment (or plan) of a similar set of goals for their intelligent intermediary system I3R, which is based on a set of distributed functions similar to our level five goals. This order, or general plan, follows the general structure of figure 2, going from top to bottom. Thus, these results suggest that constructing an effective search formulation proceeds, in general, from the goals of identifying an appropriate level and type of dialogue, a model of the user, a model of the user's state in the problem-solving process, and a model of the user's problem, to the goals of establishing a representation of the user's search topic and developing and implementing an associated search strategy, and finally to the goals of constructing and presenting an appropriate response to the user. Throughout, the goal of explanation is invoked as required.

In this goal analysis, we can say that the first goal, of extablishing a suitable dialogue mode (DM), is achieved by user and intermediary in mutual agreement, and is of direct use to both. The models of the user (UM) and of the user's state in the problem solving process (PS) are used primarily by the intermediary in order to support other activities, such as deciding on system appropriateness (PM), determining output characteristics (RG), guiding explanation (EX), and so on. The model of the user's problem and search topic (PD) is used by both parties in formulating and developing the search. The representation of search topic and development of search strategy (RS) is a highly interactive process among the user, intermediary and data base, used by all. And the presentation of system output and evaluation by the user again involves and is used by both user and intermediary.

5.2. Search formulation support

Brooks (1986) and Daniels (1987) have specified details of Problem Description and Retrieval Strategy (Brooks) and User Modelling (Daniels) as they apply to an intelligent intermediary system. We draw on their results in order to specify the characteristics and details of the tasks required to accomplish active support for the user in the search formulation process. The specific tasks associated with search formulation support (and their associated level 5 goals) are:

Choice of interaction mode (DM);

General topic identification (PD);

Database selection (RS);

Specific search topic formulation (PD);

Query specification and representation (RS);

Search strategy formulation (RS);

Output constraints (RG);

Evaluation (All).

The accomplishment of these tasks is viewed as the evolving representation of a search topic and strategy in the context of an online IR system. It begins with the choice of interaction mode (having assumed relevance of system to the user's situation), and then moves to general topic identification. This result is used in order to define a context for specific search topic, query and search strategy formulation, and also as a means for data base selection. Once data bases have been selected, specific search topic formulation begins. This provides a basis for query specification, search strategy formulation and constraint identification, and is also used, as required, to reformulate the general search topic, or to make new decisions concerning data base selection. The result of query, strategy and constraint formulation leads to a search, whose results are used to support reformulation of any of the decisions which have led to the search. The whole process is iterated to completion, as decided by the us er, the reformulation decisions at any point being based on evaluation of system response in terms of user requirements.

Each of these tasks can be viewed as a set of problems which hinder the user in their achievement, with the goal of the intelligent interface being to provide support which helps the user to overcome these problems. This, in effect, specifies details of the activities the interface needs to perform to in effective search formulation support. In section 7, we present a structured description of these tasks (excepting interaction mode).

Accomplishment of these tasks will depend upon the functions which we have not discussed in detail here, especially user modelling and explanation. Daniels (1987) has specified details of the user model for an intelligent interface in a specific IR system context. Her results, and those of Brajnik, Guida & Tasso (1987), indicate that an effective user model will represent the user's goals (at various levels), the user's subject knowledge, the user's previous experience with IR systems, the user's status and the user's general background. These elements, singly and in combination, are used in accomplishment of all of the search formulation support tasks. For instance, choice of interaction mode will depend upon, among other things, the user's previous experience with IR systems in general, and with this system in particular; or, effective representation of a search topic will depend upon understanding what use the user intends to make of the retrieved information.

Similarly, effective interaction between user, interface and database, as required by the search formulation tasks, depends upon the user's understanding of the other components of the system and of her/his role in the system; explanation, or clarification, is the major means for ensuring that the user has appropriate understanding (Belkin, 1988). Whether explanation is offered to the user at any point, and what kind of explanation is offered, can be construed as dependent upon the interface's model of the user, and of its model of the user's understanding of the system.

Finally, we note that having models of the user's goals, experience, place in the problem solving process, problem and topic amount to a representation which can be compared to a model of the system's capabilities, in order to decide whether the system is appropriate to the user's situation. For instance, if the interface knows that the user is a junior high school student who has a class assignment to write a four-page essay on DNA, it would be appropriate to inform the user that s/he should not expect to find useful information on ESA-IRS. Depending on what kinds of knowledge the interface has, it might be able to suggest an appropriate alernative system, such as an encyclopaedia. Thus, we see that the Problem Mode function, associated with the level four goal of determining whether the IR system is appropriate for the user, is capable of being supported by tasks also associated with search formulation support.

6. Host System Functionality

We specify host system functionality in order to establish the basic operations and resources available to the host, and, eventually, interface. These define the capabilities of the system, which either the host or the interface must manipulate, in order to respond to the desiderata of the CTA. Here, we mention a few such functions within ESA-QUEST, which are germane to our stage one interface specification examples in subsequent sections, or which respond directly to the search formulation task description which follows.

ESA-QUEST has the standard host structure of inverted indices to its records, with all that this implies. In particular, this gives substantial statistical charaterization of its databases. Its resources include structured textual descriptions of its resident data bases, and online thesauri for some of them. ESA-QUEST has a number of pre-defined subject clusters of databases, and a facility for user-defined clusters, both types of which be be searched in cross-file mode.

Its searching facilities include all of the standard statements of searching for terms and combinations, and so on. It offers in addition a facility for doing quorum searching, which relaxes Boolean constraints and makes ranked output possible. It has a unique facility, called ZOOM, which does statistical characterization of terms associated with specified document sets. This is in general a frequency analysis of terms in various fields of the retrieved documents. ZOOM thus provides data for establishing statistical relations among terms, and between documents and terms. The information derived from ZOOM, in combination with general statistics of the database, can be used for probablisitic relevance feedback (Robertson, et al, 1986), and in other semi-automatic feedback modes (Ingwersen & McAlpine, 1989).

7. Relating Cognitive Task Analysis to System Functionality

In this section, we demonstrate, by example, how our methods can lead to specification of host and interface features for support of end-user search formulation. We do this by identifying the problems associated with each of the search formulation tasks identified in section 5.2, suggesting possible support mechanisms which respond to these problems, and drawing upon the host's functionalities to indicate methods and techniques for accomplishing these mechanisms. This exercise also leads to suggestion of areas of potential enhancement of host capabilities, by identifying problems for which the system's capabilities offer no potential support mechanisms. Below, we present a structured description of each of the search formulation tasks.

Identification of general search topic

Problems:

Terminology
Specification at appropriate level of generality
Matching topic specification to system capabilities

Non-restricted input
Categorization of system topics
User selection of topics
Structured topic display
System matching of input to topic structure and data base

Methods:

Rich aliasing, through establishment of a 'user thesaurus'
(Bates, 1986)
Display of hierarchically organized list of Questindex
topics, with optional display of databases associated with
topics
Display of frequency characteristics of topic terms in vari-
ous data bases
Display of relative importance of term in database, derived
from frequency characteristics of term, size of database,
etc.
Supporting user search and browsing in full text of ESA-
QUEST Directory of Data Bases and Services

Database selection

Problems:

Relationships between databases and topics unknown
User unfamiliarity with database characteristics
Relevance of database to topic, goals and desired level of
treatment
Whether to choose one or several databases.

Support:

Associate structured topic display with relevant databases
Match user topic input to database characteristics
Pre-specification of database topic groups
User specification of database clusters
User interaction with database descriptions and contents.

Methods:

Display of hierarchically organized list of Questindex
topics, with display of databases associated with topics
Display of frequency characteristics of topic terms in various data bases
Display of relative importance of term in database, derived
from frequency characteristics of term, size of database,
etc.
Supporting user search and browsing in full text of ESA-
QUEST Directory of Data Bases and Services
Display of QuestClusters (pre-specified groups of databases)
with term importance characteristics
Incremental construction of user-selected database cluster
for cross-file searching.

Initial formulation of search topic

Problems:

Difficulty in statement/specification of requirements
Vocabulary/terminology mismatch
Relationships among terms unknown, or mismatch between user
relationships and system relationships
Knowledge of subject area and literature
Relationship of problem to system and database characteris-
tics

Support:

Ease of input - not constrained to specification
Accept variety of input
Display of related terms and relationships within database
Display of topic/context groupings within database
Display of knowledge resources available to interface (from
interface and host)
Relationship of user input to system descriptions
Display of current state of topic selection

Methods:

Quasi-natural language input with support for concept/facet
specification
Model document as input, with document template for description; use SuperZoom to display controlled and uncontrolled
terms from retrieved set
Direct matching of input to system knowledge resources
(thesaurus, controlled terms, uncontrolled terms) with
display of conceptual and statistical relationships within
system
Direct manipulation-based browsing in displays of conceptual
and statistical relationships
Direct retrieval of example documents from selected terms;
direct choice of terms from examined documents

Query formulation

Problems:

Terminology
Matching of topic description to effective search statement
Effects of using specific formulations
Effects of changing formulations
Identifying appropriate formulations and changes

Support:

Progressive and interactive use of search topic description
for query formulation
Explicit demonstration of relations between input vocabulary
and system vocabulary
Display of, and choice from, structured system vocabularies
Structured query representation

Immediate retrieval from query formulations, with explicit
demonstration of cause
Example successful formulations

Methods:

Display of search topic description as it is being formu-
lated, with access to system terms related to those in topic
description semantically (through thesaurus) or statisti-
cally (through Zoom)
Rich aliasing
Thesaural and other index displays
Windows for construction of faceted query formulation
Explanation facilities for 'good' query construction
Ranking of retrieved documents
Direct retrieval of example documents from selected terms;
direct choice of terms from examined documents
Display of query formulations for topically related queries

Search strategy formulation

Problems:

Understanding search logic
Relating search logic to topic requirements
Understanding the results of logical operations
Understanding the relationship of lobical operations to
desired consequences
Identifying appropriate logical statements

Support:

Mask logic from user
Redisplay of search formulation for modification
Structured representation of query and search
Translate displayed topic and query representations into
displayed search structures
Relate retrieval results to characteristics of search stra-
tegy
Provide patterns for search formulation

Methods:

Quasi-natural language input
Continuous display of underlying search formulation, with
explicit relations to topic and query formulations
Visual display of effects of search formulation on retrieved
set, step by step
Search strategy formulation within windowed faceted struc-
ture
Templates for search strategy types, to be filled in by user
Ranked retrieval output

Evaluation and reformulation

Problems:

Understanding system response
Finding representative documents for evaluation
Relating output to desirable changes
Relating output to characteristics of search formulation
Incorporating appropriate modifications

Support:

Explanation of factors that led to response (visually and textually)
Ranked output of documents
Manipulable display of output related to query and search formulation
Suggestions for appropriate changes

Methods:

Graphic display of immediate history of response
Explanation of immediate history of response
Quorum searching
Graphic display of underlying search formulation, with explicit relations to topic and query formulations, and to response
Direct selection of items from retrieved set to be incorporated into search
Facility for indicating degree of relevance of response, for indicating characteristics of interest and undesirable characteristics, and for maintaining record of decisions
Semi-automatic relevance feedback based on user evaluations and on Zoom and thesaural structures, automatically invoked

8. Constraints on the Interface

The potential users of ESA-IRS are a large, international population, heterogeneous on many dimensions, including subject matter, backgrounds, working environments, IR system experience, computing experience, and so on. We can suppose that most of these users will be accessing the system in their work roles, many of them as direct end users, others as proxies or intermediaries or representatives of groups. There will be substantial variety among these users in the extent to which the access ESA-IRS and other IR systems. Their access to ESA-IRS will typically be through micro-computers or workstations connected via modems or local area networks to telecommunications networks on which ESA-IRS is a host.

ESA-IRS will remain a large, primarily centralized facility for access to a wide variety of data bases, but with, of course, a focus on those of relevance to the ESA mission. We assume that it will continue to be innovative in research and development policies concerning system enhancements, but also that it will maintain its basic structure and facilities. We also assume that the ESA-IRS policy of promoting user-system interaction (as, for instance, in pricing) will at least be maintained.

All of these factors, combined with general precepts for human-computer interaction in information systems, have a number of implications for ideal interface design and features. Among these, we mention especially:

the need to maintain a variety of access/interaction modes, to respond to the variety of users;

the significance of intelligent explanation facilities, again in response to user variety;

the ability to maintain long-term models of system users;

general interface flexibility, in terms of tolerance of a variety of data bases and search topics;

support for effective interaction, rather than merely for efficient or quick searching;

distribution of aspects of the interface between host and local access computers;

portability and generality of direct end-user interface software (for mounting on local machines);

window-based interfaces, with a variety of interaction modes, including direct manipulation, menus, forms, graphics, quasi-natural language and command languages.

These implications can be considered as aspects of our method for specification of interface design.

9.   Stage One Interface Implementation

Our design specification procedure, as outlined in the previous sections, suggests a general structure for a level one implementation of an intelligent interface to ESA-IRS. Here, we outline the characteristics of such an interface, and then offer an example of what implementation of this interface in support of one kind of activity would look like.

The intelligent interface would be one of three different interfaces available to the system, for choice by user or recommendation by interface (at any point in the interaction). These are: the native command language (ESA-QUEST); a form-filling menu interface based on a standard document template; and interface for search formulation support. The first of these is the current access mode, and the second is at present an internal prototype. This multiple interface structure responds to the variety of user preferences and IR experience, and responds to some extent to the Dialogue Mode goal.

The intelligent interface will be window based, with windows corresponding to the tasks to be performed in support of any one function. Multiple windows will be available at all stages, with a history window and a current search formulation window available at all times. This responds to requirements of interaction and clarity.

The basic mode of input will be unconstained natural language, which will be interpreted by the system as stemmed key words, with stop words removed. Word combinations will be variously interpreted according to specific function invoked. The other major method of input will be direct selection of displayed items, for instance by pointing and selecting items in a graphic display, or items in a document display. Input into predetermined formats, for instance search logic templates will also be supported. These input modes require keyboard and mouse (or similar) interaction. This responds to issues of vocabulary problems, and of interaction support.

The basic mode of display from the system will be graphic, giving a visualization of the structure of the search, a visualization of term relationships, a visualization of the history of the session, and so on. These visualizations are constructed on the basis of initial user input, and are intended for direct manipulation, modification and selection by the user. Thus, the user can change aspects of the visualization, when appropriate, can request information about any aspect of the visualization, can move to consider any aspect of the visualization, can invoke an action, and view its result by manipulation in the visualization, and so on. This form of presentation and interaction responds to various issues; one important one is that it provides a natural structure for showing the current state of the search, and the relationship of that to what has come before (and perhaps to what might follow); another is that it provides a powerful framework for browsing, which we consider to be a primary support functi on for search formulation.

The interface will maintain a long-term user model for each system user, which amounts to a tailored user profile. It will include data on total uses of the system, databases used, interaction modes used, explanation levels used, and user-specified preferences. The model will be used for initial choice of interaction mode, explanation level, level of search formulation support and choice of database selection method (direct or negotiated, for instance).

This suggests the basic environment of the stage one intelligent interface facility. Our next steps are to implement this environment in a prototype, to implement the specific functions suggested in the previous section within this environment, and to engage in an experimental formative design exercise with this prototype. This facility responds to our ideal design in several ways, but remains only a stage one implementation especially because it does not incorporate knowledge of the user within the session, and especially because it does not respond actively to the user's situation, but rather depends highly on user initiative. Below, we offer an example of how this stage one intelligent interface could deal with one specific aspect of search formulation support, even within its limited goals.

The ESA-QUEST retrieval system has already available a tool to be used for manual feedback that can incorporated in the interface for semi-automatic or automatic query reformulation, that is, the ZOOM facility. Possible uses of the actual tool have already been described by Robertson (1986), Ingwersen (1986), McAlpine & Ingwersen (1989).

How to extract from the host IR system all the potentiality already built in is an open question. Examining possible areas of improvements it came out that there is an area that could help the user in formulating his query that is not completely exploited; that is, thesaurus browsing. Several on-line biblio-graphic databases are enriched by an on-line thesaurus. Thesaurus creation entails a big effort from the file producer but often is difficult for an inexperienced user to benefit from its on-line availability. Again some attempts have been made in order to use the thesaurus for concept specification and automatic query for-mulation (see e.g. Giger (1988).

One aspect of an intelligent interface is to support terminology choice in problem description. We propose to implement this type of support by means of an interactive tool able to browse the thesaurus "before" the search action, when no set has been yet retrieved. As is well known in existing large information retrieval systems the thesaurus is available but its accessibil-ity and visibility are rather difficult for inexperienced users. In particular if the concept the user has in mind is expressed by term(s) or phrase(s) that are not thesaurus entries its is very difficult for the user to browse it.

In the basic functional implementation of the interface a key tool will be a browse function with the ability of finding (pointing to) thesaurus entries and from these entries browsing the thesaurus hierarchy. Of course the major effort has been put in finding in a completely automatic and transparent way concep-tually related terms that are entries in the thesaurus in case that the concept (term or phrase) that the user has in mind is not a thesaurus entry itself. This would make easy the concept identification stage in the PD phase by simple browsing of the thesaurus. In order to make the query formulation process as much as possible straightforward the possibility is given to the user either to simply browse the thesaurus or to search directly a term in the hierarchy thus retrieving a set.

Thus the core of the basic functional support that is being implemented on ESA-QUEST is a browse function capable of linking thesaurus entries to a term or phrase entered by the user before any search process is started, and thereafter in conjunction with the search. It is possible to think to several solutions to the problem. Since our environment (ESA-QUEST) entails mainly use of large bibliographic databases, our approach has been to use sta-tistical techniques. If the term (phrase) the user is entering is not in the thesaurus then a sample of the documents containing that term (phrase) is examined. The controlled keywords (control terms) of the documents in the sample are ranked according to their frequency in the sample of documents (this uses the ZOOM command). The top five controlled keywords that are also thesaurus entries are shown to the user. As stated above phrases (multiple terms) are accepted in input, but no real natural language processing is performed on them. This means that no verbs should be used and that (at least at this stage of the project) only a simple pre-processing is performed. In this pre-processing terms like "and" and "or" are treated as logical ANDs or ORs and the term "in" is transformed in a logical "AND". The kind of phrases the user can input are then analogous to the one the user can search for via the Common Command Language command "find". In figures 3-8 some examples of a basic interface dialogue using this browsing function are shown. The results make reference to the file INSPEC as loaded on ESA-QUEST in January 1990.

Figure 3 shows how the browse-thesarus option is chosen, and the desired term input. Figure 4 shows the conceptually related terms to micro computer, which have been determined by invoking ZOOM on the controlled terms in the documents in which the term micro computer occurs (in any field). Figure 5 indicates how browsing in the thesaurus itself is chosen, and figure 6 shows the resulting hierarchy. Figure 7 is the input of a full phrase for browsing (where 'in' is interpreted by the interface as logical AND), and figure 8 is the result of the frequency analysis of the set retrieved by the phrase, interpreted as search.

This sequence thus demonstrates some characteristics of the input and manipulation of the interface, and also, importantly, of the combination of various underlying host functions into automatic procedures for responding to user problems.

10. References

BATES, M.J. (1986). Subject access in online catalogs: a design model. Journal of the American Society for Information Science, v. 37: 357-376.

BELKIN, N.J. (1988). On the nature and function of explanation in intelligent information retrieval. In: Proceedings of the 11th ACM SIGIR International Conference on Research and Development in Information Retrieval, Grenoble, 1988. Grenoble, Presses Universitaires de Grenoble: 135-145.

BELKIN, N.J., BROOKS, H.M. & DANIELS, P.J. (1987). Knowledge elicitation using discourse analysis. International Journal of Man-Machine Studies, v. 27: 127-144.

BELKIN, N.J., HENNINGS, R.-D. & SEEGER, T. (1984). Simulation of a distributed expert-based information provision mechanism. Information Technology: Research, Development, Applications, v. 3: 122-141.

BELKIN, N.J., SEEGER, T. & WERSIG, G. (1983). Distributed expert problem treatment as a model for information system analysis and design. Journal of Information Science, v. 5: 153-167.

BELKIN, N.J. & VICKERY, A. (1985). Interaction in information systems. (Library & Information Research Report 35). London, The British Library.

BELKIN, N.J. et al. (1987). Distributed expert-based information systems: An interdisciplinary approach. Information Processing and Management, v. 23: 395-409.

BORGMAN, C.L., CASE, D.O. & MEADOW, C.T. (1989). The design and evaluation of a pront-end interface for energy researchers. Journal of the American Society for Information Science, v. 40: 99-109.

BROOKS, H.M. (1986). An intelligent interface for document retrieval systems: Developing the problem description and retrieval strategy components. Ph.D. Thesis, Department of Information Science, The City University, London.

CROFT, W.B. & THOMPSON, R. H. (1987). I3R: A new approach to the design of document retrieval systems. Journal of the American Society for Information Science, v.38: 389-404.

DANIELS, P.J. (1987). Developing the user modelling function of an intelligent interface for document retrieval systems. Ph.D. Thesis, Department of Information Science, The City University, London.

DANIELS, P.J., BROOKS, H.M. & BELKIN, N.J. (1985). Using problem structures for driving human-computer dialogues. In: RIAO '85. Actes of the Conference: Recherche d'Informations Assistee par Ordinateur, Grenoble, March 1985. Grenoble, I.M.A.G.: 131-149.

EGAN, D.E., et al. (1989). Formative design-evaluation of Super-Book. ACM Transactions on Information Systems, v. 7: 30-57.

GIGER, H.P. (1988). Concept Based Retrieval in Classical IR Systems. In: Proceedings of the 11th ACM SIGIR International Conference on Research and Developemtn in Information Retrieval, Grenoble, 1988. Grenoble, Presses Universitaires de Grenoble: 275-290.

INGWERSEN, P. & WORMELL, I. (1986). Improved Subject Access, Browsing and Scanning Mechanisms in Modern Online IR. In: Proceedings of the 9th ACM SIGIR International Conference on Research and Development in Information Retrieval, Pisa, 1986. New York, ACM: 68-76.

McALPINE, G. & INGWERSEN, P. (1989). Integrated information retrieval in a knowledge worker support system. In: Proceedings of the 12th ACM SIGIR International Conference on Research and Development in Information Retrieval, Cambridge, MA, 1989. New York, ACM: 48-57.

MARCUS, R.S. (1985). Development and testing of expert systems for retrieval assistance. In: Proceedings of the 48th Annual Meeting of the ASIS, vol. 22. White Plains, NY, Knowledge Industry Publications: 289-292.

MARCUS, R.S. & REINTHES, J.F. (1981). A translating computer interface for end-user operation of heterogeneous retrieval systems. I. Design & II. Evaluations. FIJournal of the American Society for Information Science, v. 32: 287-303; 304-317.

MEADOW, C.T., HEWETT, T.T. & AVERSA, E.S. A computer intermediary for interactive database searching. I. Design & II. Evaluation. FIJournal of the American Society for Information Science, v. 33: 325-332; 357-364.

MEADOW, C.T., et al. (1989). Online Access to Knowledge: System design. FIJournal of the American Society for Information Science, v. 40: 86-98.

ODDY, R.N. (1977). Information retrieval through man-machine dialogue. Journal of Documentation, v. 33: 1-14.

ROBERTSON, S.E. & SPARCK JONES, K. (1976). Relevance weighting of search terms. Journal of the American Society for Information Science, v. 27: 129-146.

ROBERTSON, S.E., THOMPSON, C.L., MACASKILL, M.J. & BOVEY, J.D.(1986). Weighting, ranking and relevance feedback in a front-end system. FIJournal of Information Science,, v. 12: 71-75.

ROTH, E.M. & WOODS, D.D. (1989). Cognitive task analysis: An approach to knowledge acquisition for intelligent system design. In: Topics in expert system design: Methodologies and tools, G. Guida & C. Tasso, eds. Amsterdam, North-Holland: 233-264.

VICKERY, A. (1988). The experience of building expert search systems. In: Online Information 88. Proceedings of the 12th International Online Information Meeting, London, December 1988. Oxford, Learned Information: 301-313.

VICKERY, A., BROOKS, H.M., ROBINSON, B.A. & STEPHENS, J. (1988). An expert system for referral. (Library and Information Research Report 66). London, The British Library.

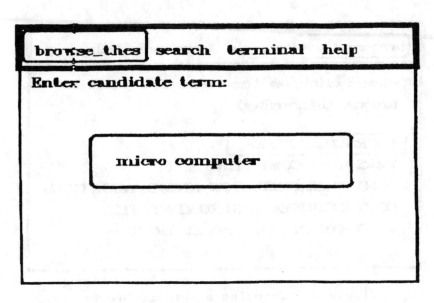

browse_thes | search terminal help

Enter candidate term:

micro computer

Figure 3. Choosing to browse the thesaurus,
          and specifying a starting term.

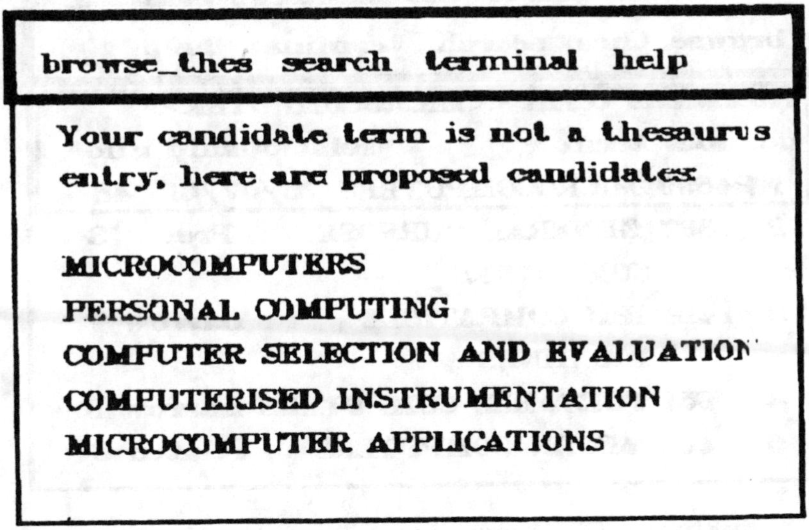

browse_thes search terminal help

Your candidate term is not a thesaurus
entry, here are proposed candidates:

MICROCOMPUTERS
PERSONAL COMPUTING
COMPUTER SELECTION AND EVALUATION
COMPUTERISED INSTRUMENTATION
MICROCOMPUTER APPLICATIONS

Figure 4. Display of related terms from
          thesaurus, derived from frequency
          analysis in retrieved document set.

```
┌─────────────────────────────────────────────┐
│  ┌──────────┐                                │
│  │browse_thes│ search  terminal  help        │
│  └──────────┘                                │
│                                              │
│  Please click on the term You want to        │
│  browse (hierarchy)                          │
│                                              │
│  ┌─────────────────────┐                     │
│  │ MICROCOMPUTERS      │                      │
│  └─────────────────────┘                     │
│  PERSONAL COMPUTING                          │
│  COMPUTER SELECTION AND EVALUATION           │
│  COMPUTERISED INSTRUMENTATION                │
│  MICROCOMPUTER APPLICATIONS                  │
│                                              │
└─────────────────────────────────────────────┘
```

Figure 5.   Choosing a term to browse
            from in the thesaurus.

```
┌─────────────────────────────────────────────┐
│                                              │
│  browse_thes   search   terminal   help      │
│                                              │
├──────────────────────────────────────────────┤
│ Thesaurus term <<MICROCOMPUTER>>             │
│ no. docs term          relationship r.no     │
│ 1 24699 MICROCOMPUTERS 75/07/01   48         │
│ 2   887 GENERAL PURPOSE        Prev   3      │
│         COMPUTERS                            │
│ 3  1412 IBM COMPATIBLE         narrow 7      │
│         MACHINES                             │
│ 4   951 PORTABLE COMPUTERS narrow 8          │
│ 5   486 ACORN COMPUTERS      related 6       │
│                                              │
└─────────────────────────────────────────────┘
```

Figure 6.   Thesaurus hierarchy display.

```
┌─────────────────────────────────────────┐
│ ┌──────────┐                             │
│ │browse_thes│ search  terminal  help     │
│ └──────────┘                             │
│ Enter candidate term:                    │
│                                          │
│        ┌─────────────────────────┐       │
│        │ text search in information│      │
│        │ retrieval               │       │
│        └─────────────────────────┘       │
│                                          │
│                                          │
└─────────────────────────────────────────┘
```

Figure 7.   Natural language phrase
             input for thesaurus browsing.

```
┌─────────────────────────────────────────┐
│ browse_thes  search  terminal  help      │
│                                          │
│  Your candidate term is not a thesaurus  │
│  entry, here are proposed candidates:    │
│                                          │
│  INFORMATION RETRIEVAL SYSTEMS           │
│  INFORMATION RETRIEVAL                   │
│  OPTICAL DISC STORAGE                    │
│  RECORDS MANAGEMENT                      │
│  INDEXING                                │
│                                          │
└─────────────────────────────────────────┘
```

Figure 8.   Thesaurus terms related
             to input phrase.

USING SYNTACTIC ANALYSIS IN A DOCUMENT RETRIEVAL SYSTEM THAT USES SIGNATURE FILES [1]

Ron Sacks-Davis

Peter Wallis

Ross Wilkinson

Department of Computer Science
Royal Melbourne Institute of Technology
GPO Box 2476V
Melbourne, VIC 3001
Australia

Abstract

Our work involves the study of the extent to which natural language processing techniques aid the automatic indexing and retrieval of documents. In this paper we describe the use of signature files in large text retrieval systems. We show that good performance can be obtained without requiring the significant overheads required for the inverted file technique. We examine the use of syntactic analysis of the text in all stages of retrieval and argue that an initial boolean query should be performed that provides a subset of documents, which are then ranked. We then give an algorithm for generating such queries, taking into account the syntactic structure of the queries.

1 Introduction

This paper describes a project that involves using a very fast document retrieval system that is based on signature file methods [Sacks-Davis 87], and measuring its retrieval performance using successively more sophisticated natural language processing techniques to aid the indexing and search processes. One of the important goals of our study is to quantify the improvements gained as a result of using natural language processing. Another goal is to determine an appropriate database system for performing document retrieval, when natural language processing is used. The approach that is most commonly adopted is to use inverted files. We compare the performance of inverted files with that of signature files.

Since it is not possible to compare a given query with one million raw text documents in an acceptable time, documents are *indexed* prior to query time and then the query is transformed and matched against the indexed terms. The standard way of indexing documents is to select key words or all significant words in a document. These techniques have a well developed history and literature [Salton 89]. The *effectiveness* of a text retrieval system can be measured in terms of recall and precision. Other important measurements include the time taken to index documents and the speed with which documents are matched against the query and retrieved.

In previous work, attempts have been made to use natural language processing in order to generate pairs or triples of words that better describe the documents. The attempt is to produce such pairs by analyzing the sentences in the documents, rather than simply using adjacency to generate the pairs. Thus the pair

---

[1] Supported by an AIRS grant from the Australian Commonwealth Department of Industry, Technology and Commerce

"computer science" will be extracted from "The science of computing is important" but not from "In all science, computing is becoming increasingly important." We duplicate these results but work under the requirement that the system works on a large document collection and works quickly. Thus, standard natural language processing techniques are probably not appropriate. If a parser takes one second per sentence, then it might take years to process a large document database. We are investigating the level of natural language understanding required to allow good retrieval under the constraint that it is also fast.

In section two we describe the way in which conventional information retrieval is performed. In the next section, we describe the signature file technique, and some modifications that improve performance. Next we compare the performance of the signature file methods and the more commonly used, inverted file method.

In the remaining sections we describe the ways in which we have investigated using natural language processing in the document retrieval process. We first consider using the significance of the parts of speech in the words used to form the queries. The second issue we address is how to rank a set of documents in order of their relevance to a given query. Finally, we ask how can we isolate a small subset of a document collection for further analysis. We end with conclusions and a brief discussion of further work.

2 Conventional Document Retrieval Using Inverted Files

To use a document retrieval system, a request is made and relevant documents are retrieved. Search requests are formulated by using terms that reflect the user's information needs. Often, queries are represented by Boolean expressions, consisting of search terms interrelated by the Boolean operators *and*, *or* and *not*. These expressions are evaluated in an inverted file environment by retrieving and merging the pointer lists corresponding to the terms contained in the query.

Another important search request specifies that two or more terms must appear together in a document within a certain number of words of each other. In particular, in order to search for phrases, it can be specified that the terms that make up the phrase must appear in adjacent positions in the sentence.

The limitations of conventional boolean retrieval are well known [Salton 89]. The size of the output obtained in response to a given query is difficult to control. No ranking of output documents in any order of relevance to the user query is provided. No provision is made for assigning weights which indicate the importance of a term in either the user queries or the documents. Ranking algorithms have been proposed to overcome these deficiencies. The basic approach consists of representing both documents and queries by sets of terms with associated weights and then comparing representatives. If the document and query representatives are considered as vectors in t dimensional space, where t is the number of unique terms in the document collection, then a vector similarity function, such as the *cosine measure*, can be used to compare document and query representatives. The cosine measure takes into account both the frequency of a term across the document collection, the *inverse document frequency*, and the frequency within the document, the *within-document frequency*. For these and other definitions see [Salton 89].

We can now describe an approach advocated in [Salton 85] for ranking and automatic feedback using complex similarity measures. A two-stage process is used. In the first stage, using the terms provided in the user search request, a Boolean query is formulated. This query is designed to retrieve T documents from the collection, T being a parameter of the method. During the second stage, all T documents are retrieved and are ranked using a similarity function.

For such a method, the important requirements of an indexing scheme include the ability to index documents on single words and dependent term groups such as phrases and to estimate the number of documents in the collection containing such syntactic units. Inverted file methods do not provide the capabilities to perform such functions particularly well. In the next section, we will describe a signature file implementation suitable for indexing document databases, and then we will compare the inverted file method with signature files on the basis of suitability for text processing.

3 Signature File Methods for Indexing Large Databases

Signature file methods are well described in the literature [Faloutsos 85]. With these methods the contents of a record are encoded to form a bit string or signature for the record. On query, the signatures rather than the original data are searched to obtain the matching records.

For each record, each term is hashed onto a bit string of say 500 bits. The hashed values of the terms are superimposed, or *ored*, to form a single bit string for the record, which is called its *signature*. The bit strings for all the records are collected to form the *signature file*. The pointers to the data file are stored with the bit strings for fast access.

The general architecture of the signature file method is given in figure 1. The index consists of a signature file and an array of N pointers to the data records. Upon query, the signature file is examined and a set of *record identifiers* for the possible matching records is obtained. These record identifiers can be used to look up the pointer array in order to obtain the physical address of these records. Since signatures are formed using superimposed coding, *false matches* may occur and must be identified.

For large files, the signatures are usually stored using the *bit slice* technique. With this technique, the signature file, considered as a bit array, is stored in transposed form. Another technique used for large data files is to form signatures for blocks of records, rather than single records. In fact, with a further refinement, called the *multi-organization method*, it is not necessary to form any record signatures, only block signatures are necessary. With this approach, k signature files, rather than a single signature file is formed. Each signature file consists of N_s block signatures where $N_s = N/N_r$ and N_r is the number of records per block. The length of a bit slice is then N_s bits. The way records are grouped to form blocks can vary in the k signature files and this provides the reason why individual record descriptors are not required. The reader is referred to [Kent 88], [Kent 89], and [Sacks-Davis 87] for a description of these techniques.

The cost of answering a query for the signature file method for which a single term is specified and for which there are α matching records can be estimated as $k + 2\alpha$ seeks. This assumes that the length of a bit slice, N_s, is less than the page size in bits. Since N_s represents the number of blocks rather than the number of records, this will be possible even for very large files. Typical values of k are 8-14. If the pointer array can be stored in memory, then the cost reduces to $k + \alpha$ seeks, close to optimal performance.

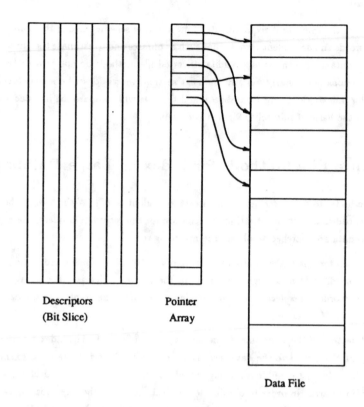

Descriptors   Pointer
(Bit Slice)   Array

Data File

Figure 1: One Level Bit Slice Signature File Implementation

4 A Comparison of Signature File Methods and Inverted File Methods for Information Retrieval Applications

In this section, we list some of the important requirements for supporting information retrieval applications. Inverted file schemes provide a good benchmark for measuring the performance of an indexing scheme due to their wide use [Salton 89]. Inverted file methods require that for each term that is used for indexing, a list of pointers to the occurrences of that term is maintained. An index of these terms, the term dictionary, is also maintained, typically organised as a B-tree. We now briefly compare these two techniques based on the requirements of a natural language based document retrieval system.

Indexing on Single Words, Adjacent Word Pairs and Dependent Term Groups are all handled as efficiently using signature file methods. Very little additional storage overhead is required compared to indexing only on single words. This is because the bits set in the signature file for the single words can also be used when searching for dependent term groups containing these. For example, in results reported in [Sacks-Davis 87] for a library database of 160,000 records, in order to index on every pair of adjacent words, an additional 15% storage overhead was required compared to indexing on single words only. Inverted file methods support indexing on single words very effectively, but are less able to support efficiently the indexing on word pairs and dependent term groups. Reasonable efficiency can be obtained however, if the address lists within the pointer file are modified to contain word offset information.

Indexing on Word Parts is also well supported using the signature file approach since it is possible to form signatures by setting bits for word parts as well as whole words. For inverted file methods, the indexing on word prefixes can be supported, provided the vocabulary is organised by an order-preserving data structure such as a B-tree. However, the support of general substring searches, such as the last k characters of a word is not well supported.

Support for Boolean Queries is provided in the in the inverted file environment by merging the pointer lists corresponding to each of the search terms. In a signature file environment, queries involving *and* and *or* operators are first transformed to an equivalent disjunctive normal form. The expressions involving only a conjunction of terms can be evaluated in the same way as single terms and bit vectors of matching records are formed for each of these expressions. These bit vectors can then be merged in order to evaluate the *or* expressions, and the records can then be retrieved and checked for false matches. A problem with signature file methods is the inability to efficiently evaluate *not* expressions. It is not possible to invert the bit vector computed for the expression that has to be negated, due to the possibility of false matches.

Storage Overheads for signature files are typically about 10-50% of the size of the data file, while inverted file methods generate overheads of 100%- 300% [Faloutsos 85]. For signature files implemented as bit strings, the signature size, b, and the number of bits set per term, k, can be chosen to achieve minimal storage overheads. In this case the resulting signatures have approximately half the number of bits set to one, and half the number of bits set to zero (the most storage-efficient encoding), and storage overheads of less than 20% can be indeed be achieved. However, for bit slice implementations, the query costs are dependent on the number of bit vectors that need to retrieved, namely k, and are independent of b. Hence it make sense to reduce k, requiring an increase in b (and hence the storage overhead) to maintain the same false match probability. Results based on simulation studies as well as practical implementations are presented in [Sacks-Davis 87].

Interactive Insertions and Updates are very fast for the bit string implementation of the signature file method, since all the information about a record that is stored in the index is stored in one place. However for both the signature file methods employing the bit slice storage technique, and for inverted file methods, information about a particular record is scattered over different parts of the index, and the cost of an interactive insertion is proportional to the number of terms per record. For each term that is indexed, k bits have to be set in the signature file for the bit slice implementations requiring up to k disk accesses, whereas for the inverted file method, for each indexed term, a B-tree has to be traversed and possibly updated, and pointer list also updated. Hence for both these methods, interactive updates are reasonably expensive.

Batch Insertions are an important option. When a database is initially loaded or is reorganised, a large number of documents must be inserted. A very important property of signature file method is that if insertions can be batched, very significant savings in insertion costs can be achieved. As we have seen, the costs for an interactive insertion is approximately ks disk accesses where s is the number of terms per record. With batch insertion, the cost can be reduced to approximately 2 disk accesses per record, independently of s. The technique is described in [Sacks-Davis 87] and relies on the availability of a memory buffer of typical size 256 Kbytes - 1 Megabyte in which signatures are formed. When a buffer is full, the signatures are flushed to disk resulting in large reductions in the number of disk accesses required.

Estimation of Term Frequencies differs depending upon the term. With the inverted file method, word frequencies can be stored in the vocabulary together with the terms themselves. For dependent groups of words such as phrases, and for conjunctions of words, frequencies are usually estimated assuming independent occurrence of the terms throughout the database. Thus if p_i is the probability that word w_i appears in a document, for $i = 1, 2, ..., t$, then the probability that the term (w_i and w_j) appears in a document is estimated as $p_i p_j$. For highly correlated terms this will lead to large underestimates. For signature file schemes, term frequencies can be estimated reasonably accurately for single words, word phrases and dependent term groups at a cost of k disk accesses per group.

Estimation of Within-Document Frequencies using the inverted file method is carried out by examination of the pointer lists associated with the relevant terms. No facility exists for the signature file methods for estimating within-document frequencies, since the bits in a signature reflect only the unique terms in a document. A term duplicate will not set any additional bits in a signature compared to the original term. If the restriction that a document is represented by a single signature is relaxed and a document is broken into segments, each with its own signature, then a knowledge of the number of segments containing a term can be used to estimate within-document frequencies [Croft 88].

Estimation of Document Lengths is performed poorly by both the inverted file method and the signature file method.

Support of Long Documents is required as a large database may have significantly variation in document length. Inverted file indexes are term-based so that the length of documents does not effect the basic structure of the index. Signature files, on the other hand, are document based; a separate signature is typically formed for each document. In an environment where documents are indexed on a few fields such as title, author, a set of keywords and an abstract, this approach to signature file indexing is quite satisfactory. However, if the full text of a document is to be indexed, and the length of documents can be large, it will be necessary to partition a document into segments of roughly equal length and form a signature for each such segment. The processing of queries may then involve the merging of results obtained for different segments within the same document.

A summary of this comparison is presented in Table 1.

	Inverted file	Signature File Bit String	Bit Slice
Indexing on Single Words, Adjacent Word Pairs and Dependent Term Groups	$\checkmark$	$\checkmark\checkmark$	$\checkmark\checkmark$
Indexing on Word Parts	$\times$	$\checkmark\checkmark$	$\checkmark\checkmark$
Support of Boolean Queries	$\checkmark$		
Storage Overheads		$\checkmark\checkmark$	$\checkmark$
Interactive Insertions and Updates	$\checkmark$	$\checkmark\checkmark$	$\times$
Batch Insertions		$\checkmark\checkmark$	$\checkmark\checkmark$
Estimation of Term Frequencies			
Estimation of Within Document Frequencies	$\checkmark$	$\times$	$\times$
Estimation of Document Lengths	$\times$	$\times$	$\times$
Support of Long Documents	$\checkmark$		
Support of Large Databases	$\checkmark\checkmark$	$\times$	$\checkmark\checkmark$

Table 1: Comparison of Inverted File Implementation, the Bit String Signature File Implementation and the Bit Slice Signature File Method (both single level and multilevel implementations); $\checkmark\checkmark$ = very good, $\checkmark$ = good; <blank> = average; $\times$ = poor.

5 Weighting Terms using Parts of Speech

Work of [Palmer 85] and [Smeaton 88] assumes that noun phrases occuring in a document are highly descriptive of the document. If so, it may well be the case that the heads of such noun phrases are more descriptive of documents than say, a present participle occuring in the same document with the same within document frequency and same document frequency.

We devised a series of experiments where each of a set of sentences in the queries were parsed and a part of speech assigned to each word that was not on the stop list. A distinction was also drawn between a noun appearing as a modifier and a noun appearing as a head. Each part of speech was assigned a weight and so if an adjective had a weight of 2 assigned to it, the word's document frequency was divided by 2 with a corresponding increase in inverse document frequency and significance of the word.

The document collection used for this test is a collection of 3,204 abstracts of articles that appeared in the Communications of the ACM. A set of 52 natural language queries were tried on this collection. This is the same collection used in [Fagan 87] and [Salton 89]. The results are given in table 2.

Head	Noun	Adjective	Verb	Pres_Pcple	Past_Pcple	Av. Precision
1	1	1	1	1	1	0.2293
0.5	1	1	1	1	1	0.2287
2	1	1	1	1	1	0.2276
4	1	1	1	1	1	0.2103
1	1	1	1	1.5	1	0.2304
1	1	1	1	2	1	0.2304
1	1	1	1	4	1	0.2297
1	1	1	1	8	1	0.2271
1	1	2	1	1	1	0.2289
1	1	1	2	1	1	0.2304
1	1	2	1	2	1	0.2300
1	2	2	1	2	1	0.2272
1	2	2	1	2	2	0.2294
1	4	4	1	4	4	0.2180

Table 2.

As can be seen, almost no improvement was obtained, and certainly no statistically significant improvement was obtained. It is interesting to note that increases in the weight of the heads actually degraded precision.

6 Using Pairs for Ranking

In this section we discuss what is an appropriate set of terms to describe a document in order to form a measure of the documents similarity to a set of terms that describe a query. We will assume that the cosine similarity measure is being used for this calculation. A number of different indexing sets have been proposed. A general discussion may be found in [Salton 89].

A simple strategy is to form a list of all the words appearing in the document, delete all the common words, including function (or closed class) words, stem the remaining words, and use the resulting set for indexing.

Stemming is the process of making all the terms "finding", "finder", "finds" and "find" equivalent. This strategy has the advantage of simplicity and provides reasonable performance. It is also the basis of most commercial information retrieval systems currently available.

A slightly more complicated strategy involves forming pairs of words that are adjacent, after stemming and removal of common words. The consequences of using this strategy are several. Firstly, the indexing time increase is negligible. Next, since pairs of words are less frequent than single words, their weight will be higher and thus dominate the similarity measure. We shall look at whether that is beneficial shortly. A serious disadvantage may be that the number of indexing terms generally at least doubles for a given document. The number of terms over the whole database may increase 10-fold. For retrieval systems that use inverted files, there is a significant increase in storage overhead, as word offsets need to be stored if adjacency calculations are required.

Since many pairs generated this way are poor indexing phrases, an approach is described in [Dillon 83] whereby only those adjacent pairs that satisfy certain syntactic constraints are allowed. Thus verb-adjective pairs might not be allowed but verb-noun pairs would be allowed.

Another strategy is to form pairs of words that are syntactically related. This approach was pursued in [Smeaton 88], based on the premise that noun phrases provide the best descriptions of information needs as described in [Palmer 85]. Smeaton wrote a parser of noun phrases in English and implemented the parser in Prolog. The pairs generated in this case would not necessarily be adjacent so that implementing this strategy would be prohibitively expensive of storage using an inverted file system, since the technique of storing word offsets is no longer applicable. As well, the time required for parsing 1,000,000 sentences, say, for indexing a large database would be prohibitive using the parser described.

For all the above three cases, improved recall and precision figures are obtained compared to indexing the database using single terms. However, in the work in [Fagan 87] it was shown that using adjacent pairs or syntactic pairs gave approximately the same results. If anything, adjacent pairs performed better. Thus the clear inference is that it is better to use adjacent pairs since the storage cost is lower and the processing time is lower.

We were interested to duplicate these results and obtained essentially the same results as in [Fagan 87]. We do not conclude, however, that syntactic parsing is inappropriate. If signature file techniques are used to index the documents, then direct indexing of both syntactic pairs and adjacent pairs can be achieved at low cost [Sacks-Davis 87]. As well, upon examination of the parser described in [Smeaton 88], we discovered that a simple Marcus parser could be used for the fragment of English grammar required, and because ambiguous parses most often give the same pairs, we were able to give priority to parses and thus produce a single parse. This fits in with the philosophy discussed in [Metzer 89] of only providing as detailed a parse as is needed. As a result we were able to parse text 30 times as fast as our NU-Prolog implementation of the grammar in [Smeaton 88]. Thus both objections to efficiently using syntactically formed pairs disappears.

To date, using the same CACM collection, we have no better results than those obtained in [Fagan 87] for adjacent pairs. However, since it is practical to use syntactically based parsing, it seems worthy of further investigation. Since it is the case that, depending upon the query, sometime syntactic pairs perform better, and sometimes adjacent pairs perform better, there is reason to believe that there may be an algorithm combining the two approaches that may be appropriate. Particular attention has been placed on generating good pairs. We hope to find ways of eliminating bad pairs, since this is often the cause of poor retrieval performance.

7   Boolean Query, then Ranking

To determine which documents are relevant to a given query, it is usual to assign a measure of similarity to each document for the given query. This similarity measure allows the documents to be ranked and the highest ranked documents to be returned to the enquirer. However, it is impractical to rank extremely large document collections, say of one million documents, in this manner. It is thus necessary to reduce the documents under consideration to a manageable subset before ranking. A strategy that has been used effectively is to first form a Boolean query that returns a set number of documents and then rank the documents in this subset.

To estimate the number of documents given by a Boolean query, the frequencies of all terms in the original query are required. An earlier section discusses the requirements of the database in this regard.

Finally, the number of documents returned by a query in disjunctive normal form (DNF) is obtained by simply adding the estimated frequency of the conjuncts.

In [Salton 85], an algorithm is described for returning a fixed number of documents to a given query by creating a Boolean query in DNF form, created from the set of terms in the original query. In outline, the algorithm is as follows.

The first approximation of the Boolean query is created. This is all the single terms related by *ors*. While the estimated number of retrieved documents is greater than the required number, the most frequently appearing term is removed, and if this reduces the estimated number of documents to below the desired figure, a set of more infrequent terms, such as pairs or triples are added. These pairs and triples are made up of previously removed terms. In this way a query, in DNF is generated that will return approximately the required number of documents.

Thus if a query is *"Intermediate languages used in the construction of compilers"*, a Boolean query *(construction or language or (compiler and intermediate))* might be formed.

The algorithm thus allows a small number of documents to be isolated in the document collection, ready for further processing and ranking. One problem with the algorithm is that the number of disjuncts in the DNF query is not controlled. Since the number of disjuncts is close to directly proportional to the time taken to answer a DNF query in both inverted file and signature file based retrieval systems, there is a risk that a DNF query may take longer than desirable to answer.

8   A Modified DNF Query Generation Algorithm

The desirability of being able to generate such queries is considerable with large databases, where exhaustively ranking the entire database is infeasible. However the algorithm in [Salton 85] takes no account of extra information that may improve performance. In particular, queries often take the form of sentences or phrases. (Even when using the algorithm in the context of relevance feedback, this is appropriate, since documents that are judged relevant consist of text.) As a result, the m single terms will have parts of speech and be related to other single terms by the structure of the text.

We propose a modification to the algorithm given in [Salton 85] that takes into account syntactic information. The syntactic information consists only of determining which single terms are modifiers of other single terms which are nouns. These nouns are the heads of noun phrases. Thus, in the previous query, *intermediate* modifies *language* and *compiler* modifies *construction*. Now we have a list of head words, each of which has zero or more modifiers. Thus (*language* and *construction*) are the head words in the above, and both are nouns.

Following the work described in [Palmer 85], we believe that noun phrases give the best querying terms, so the algorithm ideally selects a set of noun phrases to query upon, where each noun phrase is represented as a conjunction of a noun and some of its modifiers. Such a query may not always be possible, given the constraint of getting close to a given number of documents that are to be retrieved. We use a modified version of the algorithm given in [Salton 85] to get close to the desired result. We refer to this algorithm as SYN(tactically generated). Now, given a set of terms and their relationships, we generate the DNF query to retrieve T documents.

1. Find the frequency f(t) of each term t. Let q be the set of terms. (The *ored* elements of the list q represents the current query). Let p be an empty list of terms. Let E be the expected number of retrieved documents for the current query.

2. While (E > T) and (a non-head-noun remains in list q), remove the largest non-head-noun from q and add it to p.

3. While (E > T) (Only heads of noun phrases remain)

   - Select the disjunct that returns most documents and replace it by the disjunct *anded* with the most frequently occurring modifier of the head of this disjunct that has not yet been added.
   - If the selected disjunct has no outstanding modifiers, remove the disjunct from q and add it to p.

4. If there are any nouns in p, select the least frequent, and form the term, *anded* pair or *anded* triple, y, made up of elements of the list p and involving that noun that has f(y) + E - T closest to 0. If (f(y) + E) < 1.25T, add y to q.

5. If E < 0.75T, select the term, *anded* pair or *anded* triple, y, made up of elements of the list p that has f(y) + E - T closest to 0. If (f(y) + E) < 1.5T, add y to q.

Notice that the number of disjuncts using this algorithm is at most two more than the number of simple noun phrases in the query. We shall discuss the result of this restriction in a later section.

9   Using Pairs in DNF Queries

The above section introduced an algorithm in which the terms were words of a sentence. It has been shown in [Fagan 87] and [Smeaton 88] that using indexing documents using pairs of words as well as single words as retrieval terms improves retrieval performance. Therefore we wish to modify the algorithm to take this into account. The reason a modified algorithm may be desirable is that since the documents will contain not only single words but word pairs as index terms, it is desirable that the query do so also. Notice that the previous algorithm allows for *anded* terms, which indicate that both terms occur in the same document. We may now ask that they occur in the same document as part of a noun phrase. However, we must be careful to avoid certain queries. A query consisting of *operating and operating_system* word be a silly one: every document containing the term *operating_system* will certainly contain the term *operating*. (The underscore indicates that the word pair is indexed directly.)

The following algorithm (referred to as PAIRS), describes a strategy of trying first single terms, then a conjunction of single word terms, then the corresponding two-word term. Suppose that we have a query that has been transformed into a set of terms, including pairs of words, and that we know which words are nouns, and which words modify other words:

1. Find the frequency $f(t)$ of each term t. Let q be the set of single word terms. Let p be the list of two-word terms. Let E be the expected number of retrieved documents for the current query. The current query is the set of entities in q connected by *ors*.

2. While $(E > T)$ and (a non-head-noun remains in list q), remove the largest non-head-noun from q and add it to p.

3. While $(E > T)$

   - Select the disjunct that returns most documents.
   - If the disjunct is a single word (and thus a head-noun), replace it by a disjunction of conjunctions of two words that include the head and a word that, together with the head, form a two-word term.
   - If the disjunct is a conjunction of two words, replace the conjunction with the corresponding two-word term. Thus the selected two-word term is added to q and removed from p, and the selected disjunct is removed from q and added to p.
   - If the selected disjunct is a single word term and appears in no two-word terms, simply remove the disjunct from q and add it to p.
   - If the disjunct is a two-word pair, remove it from q and add it to p.

4. If there are any nouns in p, select the least frequent and form the term, pair of terms, or triple of terms, y, made up of elements of the list p and involving that noun that has $f(y) + E - T$ closest to 0. If $(f(y) + E) < 1.25T$, add y to q. No pair of terms or triple of terms may include a single word term and a two-word term that have a word in common.

5. If $E < 0.75T$, select the term, pair or triple made up of elements of the list p that has $f(y) + E - T$ closest to 0. If $(f(Y) + E) < 1.5T$, add it to the list q. No pair of terms or triple of terms may include a single word term and a two-word term that have a word in common.

10   Evaluation of the DNF algorithms

Both algorithms have been implemented and compared with the algorithm given in [Salton 85]. The comparison considers a number of different measurements. The most important and obvious requirement is that a large number of relevant documents are retrieved. The other important requirement is that they are retrieved quickly.

The same document collection and queries that were used in the previous experiments were used in this test.

	Desired no. of Documents	Retrieved no. of Documents	Recall	Precision	Disjuncts	Time
SFV	25	60	0.20	0.13	10.4	817
	50	84	0.34	0.10	18.7	1212
	100	135	0.50	0.08	29.1	2081
SYN	25	40	0.25	0.13	3.9	211
	50	67	0.34	0.10	4.3	423
	100	109	0.52	0.08	4.8	945
PAIRS	25	35	0.27	0.13	4.5	210
	50	59	0.39	0.11	5.0	420
	100	104	0.51	0.09	5.5	940

Table 3.

The figures are given in table 3, first for the algorithm of Salton, Fox and Voorhees [Salton 85] (SFV), and then using the algorithms SYN and PAIRS described here. It is a little difficult to compare the algorithms as the average number of documents returned differ significantly, although all attempt to return a fixed number, T, of documents. In order to make the comparison, we assume that only T documents are wanted for ranking, so that since all documents satisfy the Boolean query, we select the first T documents returned from the collection. Thus both the recall figures and the time figures for the actual runs are normalised by multiplying the actual figures by the number of documents required and dividing by the number of documents actually returned.

From the table it is clear that there is little difference with the normalised recall and precision results for SFV and SYN. We believe that the reason for this is that SYN selects a few good disjuncts, whilst the SFV algorithm generates a large number of disjuncts. A look at the column indicating the average number of disjuncts supports this view. However, when the two-word terms are introduced, a significant improvement in recall occurs - more relevant documents are found. Thus it appears that indexing on pairs is very helpful.

For SYN a significant saving is found in the speed with which the documents are retrieved. Since there are so many more disjuncts to evaluate using the SFV algorithm, the retrievals are two to four times slower, even after normalisation, for the range of T that we have considered. Thus, whether or not indexed pairs are available, syntactic analysis of the queries proves worthwhile.

It is worth noting that small changes to the database, the stemming algorithm, the calculation of the estimates, and the algorithm all have noticeable effect on the result. We thus view these figures as indicators of trends that need to be further investigated.

11 Conclusions

In this paper we described the implementation of a document retrieval system that uses natural language processing, supported by signature files.

We first characterized the database requirements of a natural language based document retrieval system. We then investigated the use of signature file techniques to satisfy these requirements. In section 4, we demonstrated a number of significant advantages over the widely used inverted file method.

We found that weighting terms on the basis of their part of speech did not aid retrieval. We have found no way of generating syntactically based pairs for indexing that improve on adjacent pairs, but both improved retrieval in comparison to single terms. We described two new algorithms for generating Boolean queries using syntactic parsing. Both of these algorithms represent an improvement over previous approaches. If the frequency of indexed pairs are available, the algorithm that takes advantage of this gives a significant improvement in recall. We are looking at ways of enhancing ranking methods using various syntactic techniques. It is worth noting that all techniques that we have described are usable for very large document collections.

References

[Croft 88]   W. B. Croft, P. Savino *Implementing Ranking Strategies Using Text Signatures* ACM Transactions on Office Information Systems, Vol. 6, No. 1, January 1988, pp. 42-62.

[Dillon 83]   M. Dillon, A. Gray *Fully Automatic Syntax-based Indexing* J. of the American Society for Information Science, Vol. 34, No. 2. March 1983, pp. 99-108

[Fagan 87]   J. L. Fagan *Experiments in Automatic Phrase Indexing for Document Retrieval: A Comparison of Syntactic Methods and Non-Syntactic Methods.* Ph. D. Thesis, Cornell University, 1987.

[Faloutsos 85]   C. Faloutsos *Access Methods for Text* ACM Computing Surveys, Vol. 17, No. 1, March 1985 pp. 49-74.

[Kent 88]   A. J. Kent, R. Sacks-Davis, K. Ramamohanarao *A Superimposed Coding Scheme Based on Multiple Block Description Files for Indexing Very Large Databases* In Proceedings of 14th. International Conference on Very Large Databases, August 1988, pp. 351-359.

[Kent 89]   A. J. Kent, R. Sacks-Davis, K. Ramamohanarao *A Signature File Scheme Based on Multiple Organisations for Indexing Very Large Databases* To appear: Journal of American Society for Information Science.

[Metzer 89]   D. P. Metzler, S. W. Haas, C. L. Cosic, L. H. Wheeler *Constituent Object Parsing for Information Retrieval and Similar Text Processing Problems* Journal of the American Society for Information Science, Vol. 40, No. 6, 1989, pp. 398-423

[Palmer 85]   P. Palmer, C. Berrut *Definition of a surface syntactical parser for natural language.* In Proceedings of ACSI, Montreal, 1985

[Roberts 79]   C. S. Roberts *Partial Match Retrieval via the Method of Superimposed Codes* Proceedings of the IEEE, Vol. 67, No. 12, 1979, pp. 1624-1642

[Sacks-Davis 87] R. Sacks-Davis, A. Kent, K. Ramamohanarao *Multikey Access Methods Based on Superimposed Coding Techniques.* ACM Transactions on Database Systems, Vol. 12, No. 4, December 1987, pp. 655-696.

[Salton 85]   G. Salton, E. A. Fox, E. Voorhees *Advanced Feedback Methods in Information Retrieval.* Journal of the American Society for Information Science, Vol. 36, No. 3, 1985, pp. 200-210

[Salton 89]   G. Salton *Automatic text processing.* Addison-Wesley, Reading, Massachusetts, 1989

A Dynamic Signature Technique
for Multimedia Databases

*F. Rabitti and *P. Zezula*

IEI-CNR, Pisa
Via S. Maria 46, 56126 Pisa, Italy

* Computing Center of Brno Technical University
Obrancu miru 21, 60200 Brno, Czechoslovakia

ABSTRACT

A signature file acts as a filtering mechanism to reduce the amount of data that needs to be searched during query evaluation. Even though several techniques for organizing and searching signature files have been proposed in literature, they have serious limitations when applied to multimedia databases, where integrated access methods to text and image content are neeeded.

A new signature technique, called Quick Filter, is proposed in the paper. According to this technique, signatures are divided into partitions, each of which holds signatures sharing the same characteristic key. As a result, it is possible to determine if the signatures in a partition satisfy a query by merely examining the key. Partitions not matching the key need not be searched. This method is based on dynamic hashing since signatures are hashed into partitions according to the keys and the file size, computed algorithmically from the signatures. Implementation of this technique is illustrated using an example and is verified by analytical performance evaluation.

The result is a signature technique which satisfies the requirements for access methods in multimedia databases: dynamicity, with respect to insertions and updates, good query processing performance on large databases for high-weight queries.

---

1. INTRODUCTION

The signature file access method and its applications have received in recent years a large attention in the literature, e.g. [TSIC-83], [CHRI-84], [CHRI-86], [FALO-87], [SACK-87], [CHAN-89], [LEEL-89], etc. The advantages of signatures over inversion for text data was confirmed several times [RABI-84], [CHRI-84]. The authors agree that the signature file overhead is usually less than 10% of the size of initial data, while the inversion requires space between 50% and 300% of the size [HASK-81]. Moreover, signature techniques are much more flexible for insertion and update operations [RABI-84].

However, the increasingly sophisticated studies on signature techniques presented in literature have been mainly applied to rather simplistic application environments. Most performance studies concern the search of words in text documents, where equiprobabilistic distribution of words is assumed [CHRI-84], [FALO-87]. Other studies focus more on integrated signature techniques for data attributes and text, with the obvious difficulty in performing range queries on numerical data using the signatures [FALO-86].

There is a new area of application which is attaining increasing importance, i.e. the area of multimedia databases. A crucial point of multimedia database is the integration not only of formatted data and text but also of images [RABI-87] [RABIb-89]. Image data must be treated, in the system, with the same level of functionality as the other data (i.e. formatted data and text). This means that the system must be able not only to store images and store relationships with other data, but also to allow queries addressing the image content [RABIa-89].

Multimedia databases require access strategies which are much more complex than the access strategies for formated record systems or text document systems [THAN-90]. Present signatures techniques cannot be satisfactorily exploited as integrated access methods for multimedia database systems since they do not satisfy the operational requirements of these systems, such as the dynamicity and the query processing performance. The purpose of this paper is to propose a new signature technique, called *Quick Filter*, which fits the operational requirements as an integrated access method to multimedia databases.

In Sec. 3, we give an example of a multimedia database application concerning the retrieval of multimedia documents and we discuss the shortcomings of current signature techniques when applied to this application environment. Then, we derive the requirements for new signature techniques suitable for new application environments with these characteristics. In Sec. 4, we present the quick filter signature technique, its implementation and use in query processing. Then we evaluate its performance, mainly in relation with the requirements previously defined for the multimedia databases.

2. PRELIMINARIES ON SIGNATURE TECHNIQUES

The very idea of the *signature file access method* is to extract and compress properties of data objects and store them in a separate file. The extracted pieces of data are called *signatures*. Queries are supposed to be transformable to the signature form too. A collection of the derived signatures is called the *signature file* or the *filter* because of its role during the query processing. Signatures are connected to the data objects through unique object identifiers (OID). The function of the filter is to find all OIDs of data objects qualifying for a given query. In fact, the signature file access method allows some *false hits* on the signature file level. This is why a signature file is called "filter". Therefore, a second step of query processing, called *false drop resolution*, is needed.

The novelty of this method is the invention of the filter. Since objects are accessible by the OIDs, any direct access method for storing the objects can be used. In general, an efficient filter is a filter with very few false hits and fast filtering process. From the implementation point of view, the problem can be solved by the appropriate design of a *signature extraction method* and a *data structure* for organizing signatures.

2.1. Signature Extraction Methods

Probably the best review and analysis of the signature extraction methods is in [FALO-87]. It also contains the performance comparison which is based on the estimation of the *false drop probability*. The false drop is the situation, during query processing, in which a signature seems to qualify a query, while the corresponding object does not qualify. However, [FALO-87] does not consider data structures and their effects on the query processing performance. Such comparison can be found in [ZEZUa-90]. The basic types of the signature extraction methods are known under the names of *Word Signature (WS)*, *Superimposed Coding (SC)*, *Bit-Block Compression (BC)*, *Run-Length Compression (RL)*.

In SC, each data object descriptor yields a bit pattern of size f where m bits have the value "1", while the others have the value "0". These bit patterns are OR-ed together to form the object signature. The number of ones in a signature S is the *signature weight*, designated as $w(S)$. If an object signature contains ones in the same positions as the query signature does, then the object signature qualifies for the query. The time required for comparing two SC signatures is very short, in particular for query signatures with low weights.

Since we are mostly going to concentrate on SC, we will not survey the other signature extraction methods. Interested readers are referred to [CHRI-84], [FALO-86], and [FALO-87].

2.2. Data Structures for Signature Filters

Even though the false drop is an important measure for comparing different signature extraction methods, the performance of signature filters depends mainly on the I/O cost, i.e. on the number of physical pages which must be accessed to evaluate a query. If the false drop is low, we can save a lot of accesses on the storage level. The efficiency of filtering is determined by the storage structures and access strategies which support the filtering process.

The most important storage structures for organizing signatures are: *Sequential Signatures (SS)*, *Bit-slice Signatures (BS)*.

SS is the basic organization, which is easy to implement and is space efficient. Insertions are easy to perform and exhaustive processing is efficient. Performance of query processing is not dependent on the query signature weight and the response time is linearly proportional to the size of the signature file. That is the reason why it is not convenient for very large files. Many deletions and updates may require the file reorganization.

BS, suggested in [ROBE-79], is the best organization for processing queries with low weights. Increasing the query weights requires additional block accesses and for this reason BS filter cannot be recommended for queries with very high weights. Maintenance is extremely time consuming. Th that is why BS is only suitable for stable archives, where insertions and updates are not permitted.

3. REQUIREMENTS FOR NEW APPLICATIONS

Although very sophisticated studies on signature techniques have been presented in literature, they have been usually applied to rather simplistic application environments. Historically, they were studied as access methods to formatted records (for secondary non-numerical key access) and text [FALO-86].

However, new application environments, such as office systems, multimedia databases, etc., require access strategies which are much more complex than the access strategies for formatted record systems or text document systems. In this section, we give an example of a new application environment, concerning the retrieval of multimedia documents, we present a way of defining signature for such application, and we discuss the shortcomings of current signature techniques in this context. Then, we derive the requirements for new signature techniques suitable to be applied to these new application environments.

3.1. Experience in the MULTOS Project

MULTOS (MULtimedia Office Server) is an ESPRIT Project in the area Office Systems. It supports basic filing operations, such as creation, modification, and deletion of multimedia documents, and the ability to process queries on documents. Documents are stored in databases, integrating also Optical Disk media, to allow the storage of very large amounts of data. Documents and may be shared by several users: facilities like authorization, version, and concurrency control are supported. MULTOS is based on a client/server architecture. Three different types of document servers are supported: *current server, dynamic server* and *archive server.* They allow filing and retrieval of multimedia documents based on document collections, document types and document content.

The MULTOS system must be able to answer queries at a high level of abstraction, where conditions on different document components, such as free text, formatted attributes and images, are intermixed. In order to support a fast document retrieval process, the query processor uses special access structures to the document content. In the actual system, specialized and independent access structures are defined for the different document components. B+ tree indexes are used for formatted attributes. Other B-trees are used to index objects contained in the images. Images are analyzed according to particular application domains and symbolic information, in terms of objects recognized in the image, is extracted as result of the analysis process [THAN-90]. Access to image content is then performed only using this symbolic information and not the original image (which can be a raster image or a graphical image). Image objects are characterized by the particular application domain and by the plausibility and belief of their recognition [THAN-90].

Signature techniques are used, instead, for text access. Superimposed coding of the words contained in the textual part of the document is used as text signature extraction method. As signature filter organization, sequential signatures are used in the *current server* (i.e. the server containing updatable documents, on magnetic storage, where a lot of insertions are expected) and bit-slice signatures are used in the *archive server* (i.e. the server containing stable documents, on optical storage, where only retrieval operations are allowed). The use of these signature filter organizations is consistent with the characteristics of the two MULTOS servers: sequential signatures are flexible for insertion and update operations but are slower to search, bit-slice signature are not flexible for modifications (no modification is allowed on the archive server) but are faster to search (in case of low-weight queries, see Sec. 4.4).

However, the lack of integration of the different access methods to the different document components makes the query optimization an extremely difficult problem to solve. In [BERT-88] the query processing in MULTOS is presented in detail, but only with respect to formatted attribute and text components in the documents (the extension of the system with queries involving also image document components was added later on in the second MULTOS prototype [THAN-90]) and considering only sequential signature organization (not bit-slice organization, also added later on). Query processing algorithms resulted very complex, and a similar analytical study on query optimization taking into account image access methods was never attempted (in the second MULTOS prototype organization, simpler heuristics have been used [THAN-90]).

A possible solution could be to use of a unique signature technique as an integrated access method. With this solution query processing would be much simplified, being limited to the exhaustive search of a single signature filter. In the sequel, we focus on the integration of the access structures to text and image document components into a single signature filter. We still prefer to treat formatted attribute using separated indexes (i.e. B+ trees), as in [BERT-88], due to the difficulty to treat effectively range queries using signatures.

3.2. Integrated Signature Creation

We propose here a simple approach to create a unique signature, by superimposed coding, for text and image document content description. Then, we will discuss the implications in terms of requirements on the organization of the signature filter and in terms of performance of signature search.

A unique signature block (of f bits) is allocated for a document. The signature of the textual part of the document is generated in the usual way: each word in the text sets to 1 m bits in the signature block. A scheme where each word triplet sets a bit can be used to decide which of the f bit are set by a word. This allows for search on parts of words of the text.

An image, after the image analysis process, is represented symbolically in terms of the contained objects. Each object can be in turn composed of other objects.

An example of symbolic representation of an image is the following (for simplicity we omit positional information associated with each object, which is anyway neglected in the signature generation):

$$I = O_1, O_2(O_4, O_5(O_6)), O_3(O_9, O_{10}), O_1, O_3(O_9, O_6, O_7))$$

In this example we notice that in image I five objects have been recognized: two simple objects (O_1 has been detected in two positions in the image) and three complex objects (O_2 and twice O_3). Notice that O_3 has been recognized in two different formats: once as (O_9, O_{10}) and once as (O_9, O_6, O_7). In fact, the image analysis process is based on a body of rules which may lead to many different ways in recognizing the same semantic object.

The signature for image I is obtained by superimposing the codes of the objects recognized in it. Then, the signature for I is superimposed with the signature of the text associated to I.

For each application domain, the signature of an image object is fixed as n specific bit positions in the complete signature block (f bits). The codes of all possible objects in the domain are specified in a look-up table, which may be updated to reflect the changes in the rules of image analysis process (e.g. rules for new semantic objects or rules expressing more ways of recognizing the same semantic object can be added). A simple object (e.g. O_1 in image I) will set only n bits in the image signature, as specified in the application look-up table. A complex object, instead, will set its n bit position and the bit positions associated with all the simpler objects which compose it in the symbolic representation of the image. For example, the signature of O_2, defined in I as ($O_4, O_5(O_6)$) is obtained superimposing the codes, obtained from the look-up table, of O_2, O_4, O_5, O_6.

The values of m and n must be evaluated in relation to f, taking into account the average text length, the average number of objects in each image, the number of semantic objects in the application domain, etc. to approach the target of 1/2 of ones in the resulting signature block.

Query signatures are obtained superimposing the codes of the words and image objects which the user is looking for in the database. Query processing is then performed with a unique exhaustive search of the unifies text and image signature.

We should briefly discuss here the inaccuracy introduced by this signature extraction method. False hits caused by superimposed coding in text signature has been extensively studied [CHRI-84]. In our case, a further source of false hits is due to the superimposed coding of image content. Although every object in the application domain has a unique n bit signature, coded in the look-up table, the superimposition of the codes for different objects, and their superimposition with codes of words in the text, can cause false hits. Therefore, it is necessary to perform false drop resolution on images checking the query on the symbolic representation of the image (completed with information of relative positions of the objects, plausibility and belief of recognition, etc.) linked to the image itself (either raster of graphical). Since the false drop resolution is necessary for images, in this step it is possible to check for other kind of information which is lost in the image signature but may be requested in the user query, such as presence of several instances of the same object (e.g. a house with at least four windows), relative position of the objects (e.g. a window above a door), recognition degree of the objects (e.g. a door recognized with minimum belief 0.8).

3.3. Requirements for a New Signature Technique

Let us to summarize the main requirements resulting for these signature techniques:

A)   must be used as *integrated* access method to multimedia databases (i.e. addressing text and image data).

B)   must be fast in the exhaustive search of *large* multimedia databases.

C)   must be suitable for *dynamic* environments, with frequent insertion and update operations.

D)   must be efficient for *high-weight* queries.

The last requirement is due to the fact that conditions on text and images are merged in a unique query signature and that conditions on image objects may often be transformed into equivalent queries with higher weight. Suppose that O_i is a complex image object. If it has a unique definition, in the application domain, or all its definitions are based on the same objects $O_1, \cdots, O_n$, a query on O_i can be expanded superimposing the codes of $O_i, O_1, \cdots, O_n$. In case of multiple definitions of O_i, with partially disjoint sets of composing objects, it is either possible to ask the user to choose the preferred interpretation or to limit the query signature construction only to the objects belonging to all the definitions of O_i (i.e. the intersection).

As signature extraction method, superimposed coding (*SC*) satisfies requirement A, as we have seen in the previous section on integrated signature creation. More complex is to choose an adequate filter data structure. Consider the candidates SS and BS:

SS: The sequential signature technique satisfy requirement C, is indifferent to requirement D (search speed is not dependent on query weight), but does not satisfy requirement B. In fact, since the search time is linearly proportional to the database size, the response time is bad for large databases.

BS: The bit-slice signature satisfy requirement B but not requirement D. In fact it is in general very fast in searching large databases but performance deteriorates in case of queries with high weight (see the performance comparison in Sec. 4.4). Moreover, it does not satisfy requirement C, since insertions and updates require very time consuming reorganizations.

From this discussion, we can conclude that new signature data structures are required to meet requirements B, C and D and thus be suitable for multimedia databases.

4. QUICK FILTER

We call *Quick Filter* our proposal of a new signature technique satisfying the previous requirements. This technique allows the handling of dynamic signature files and an efficient processing of high-weight queries. This technique comprises the organizational aspects of data as well as the processing procedures for efficient query execution. In the following sections we present the basic idea, a possible implementation, and performance evaluations.

4.1. The Basic Idea

The quick filter is an organization of signature strings, not slices like the Bit-slice organization. The basic units of access are pages of signatures. From this respect, quick filter is much closer to SS. However, in the quick filter similar signatures are placed in a page. The criteria for grouping signatures in pages and distributing pages within the signature file are based on hashing. This kind of organization has been presented for the first time in [ZEZU-89]. Here we present more implementation details as well as performance evaluations and comparisons with other filters.

The implementation of the idea described above concerns mainly two design problems. At first, it is the hashing function which should be applied to a signature in order to find a storage page into which the signature belongs. The second problem is the query processing algorithm with the ability to save some, preferably many, of the pages from access. Dynamic data environment is another important design assumption. Specific solutions to the problems will be discussed in the following section.

4.2. Implementation

One of the important functional requirements for the quick filter is the management of dynamic data. A dynamic hashing schema for organizing files of records having single attribute keys, called *linear hashing*, has been presented in [LITW-80]. The most important extensions of the work are *linear hashing with partial expansions* [LARS-80] and *recursive linear hashing* [RAMA-84].

4.2.1. Linear hashing

The hash function of linear hashing, let's say g, maps the keys onto the address space $\{0,1,2,...,n-1\}$ where $2^{h-1} < n \leq 2^h$, for some integer h. The value of h is called *level* of the file or hashing. A variation in h induces a variation in g. In fact, the function g must be a *split function*, which means that the following condition must hold:

$$g(K,h,n) = g(K,h-1,n) \text{ or,}$$
$$g(K,h,n) = g(K,h-1,n)+2^h,$$

for any key K from the file.

Briefly, the idea of linear hashing scheme involves a set of n *primary* (addressable) pages, each with zero or more overflow pages chained to it to form a list of pages. Assuming that the file level is h, then to insert a record with key K, the page address, p, is computed as $p=g(K,h,n)$. The record is stored in the primary page p except when an overflow occurs. In this case, it is stored in an overflow page linked to p. The occurrence of an overflow triggers an expansion of the address space from n to $n+1$ primary pages.

The expansion of the address space progresses by page splitting whenever an overflow occurs in a primary page. A pointer, denoted by SP, designates the primary page that is to be split next. Suppose a collision occurs in page p, for $0 \leq p < n$. The key, being inserted, is stored in an overflow page chained to p. Besides, a new primary page, number n, is allocated and the keys in the primary page SP, as well as its overflow keys, are rehashed and distributed between the pages SP and n. The number of primary pages now becomes $n+1$. The values of SP and h are synchronized as follows:

(1)   the file level h is increased just before the primary page 0 is split,

(2)   the pointer SP is advanced according to the assignment $SP = (SP+1) \mod 2^{h-1}$.

4.2.2. Hashing function for signatures

Now, since an object signature, S_i, $i=1,2,...,N$ (N is the number of signatures in the signature file), is a sequence of f binary digits $b_1,b_2, \cdots ,b_f$, let's suppose them to be the keys and let n be the number of allocated pages addressed from 0 to $n-1$. A hash split function of the

201

signatures can be defined for $h > 0$ as:

$$g(S_i, h, n) = \begin{cases} \sum_{r=0}^{h-1} b_{f-r} \, 2^r, & \text{if } \sum_{r=0}^{h-1} b_{f-r} \, 2^r < n; \\ \sum_{r=0}^{h-2} b_{f-r} \, 2^r, & \text{otherwise.} \end{cases}$$

(Eq. 1) Hashing function

For the initial condition, it is $h = 0$, $n = 1$, we define $g(S_i, 0, 1) = 0$.

In fact, what the hashing function g does is that it takes the h-bit, or the $(h-1)$-bit, suffix of S_i and interprets it as an integer value. The value of g is always a non-negative integer smaller than n.

The important corollary of this scheme is that N signatures can be stored in n pages in $O(n)$ page accesses and that pages with signatures can be accessed for the retrieval purposes by consecutive physical page accesses.

4.2.3. Exhaustive search

Sequential processing of the stored signatures is easy. The only thing we must do is to generate the page characteristics p in the range from 0 to $n-1$ and access the pages. If the pages are allocated on a continuous part of a dedicated disk memory, then the best thing we can do is to access them in the increasing (decreasing) order. However, sequential processing of hashed signatures is not as efficient as the processing of the sequential file. The main reasons are the overflow and a lower page load which can be for the linear hashing expected. Fortunately, the expected overflow is not high. Since signatures are usually not large, mostly less than 100 bytes, we can store many signatures in a page. For this case Litwin [LITW-80] reports practically no overflow with the page load of 50%. When the load was controlled and guaranteed to be 75%, the observed overflow was only 5%.

Furthermore, we can adopt a more efficient access strategy for the exhaustive search of signatures organized by linear hashing. All the primary pages can be accessed first in the most efficient way, i.e. with the increasing page number. Since the order of accessing signatures is not for the exhaustive search important, signatures in the overflow pages, if any, can be read in the second step, preferably in the batch access mode.

4.2.4. Search space reduction

The way how the linear hashing scheme can be exploited for a more efficient query processing is explained in detail in [ZEZU-89]. Briefly, since queries are translated into query signatures, they are also bit patterns of size f. The number of 1's in the query signatures ranges from m to $f/2$, supposing the signatures are designed as optimum. Let recall here that according to [FALO-87], optimum superimposed signatures have 50% 1's and 50% 0's. The *weight* of a specific query signature, $w(Q)$, depends on the number of terms specified in the query.

However, the typical query signature weight $w(Q)$ is usually smaller than $w(S_i)$, the weight of the i-th object signature S_i. But also in this case we can compute a characteristic key of Q as $p=g(Q,h,n)$. The value of p is in fact the smallest number of the primary page which must be accessed and its signatures tested for qualification. If $p=0$, all pages must be accessed, and exhaustive search must be used. The zero value of p also means that there are no 1's in the h-bit suffix of Q. But if there are some bits with value 1, the number of accessed pages can be decreased considerably.

For the sake of simplicity, we will suppose now that $n=2^h$. Let further assume that there is just one bit with value 1 in the h-bit suffix of Q. Then the number of accessed pages can be reduced to 2^{h-1} and the rest of the primary pages, which is also 2^{h-1}, do not have to be accessed. The reason is obvious since any h-bit binary integer with j bits having a fixed value, e.g. 1, in any specific position, can have at most 2^{h-j} different values.

According to this, if there is a query signature Q with j 1's in its h-bit suffix, $j=w(h(Q))$, it is enough to read only 2^{h-j} primary pages and their overflow areas instead of using the exhaustive search. This is the main idea of the implementation of the query processing algorithm of the quick filter. The actual numbers of read pages are decided by the Algorithm 1. The pages are accessed in the *semi-consecutive* page retrieval mode with the increasing page number, starting in the page number $g(Q,h,n)$.

Algorithm 1:

    1. $P := g(Q,h,n)$
    2. IF $h(Q) \cap P \equiv h(Q)$ THEN
         access the page P to match its signatures for qualification
    3. $P := P+1$
    4. IF $P<n$ THEN GOTO 2.
    5. END of the query processing

where:
    P is an h-bit binary integer,
    n is the number of addressable pages,
    h is the level of the file
    Q is the query signature,
    g is the hashing function,
    $h(Q)$ is the h-bit suffix of Q.

4.2.5. An example

Let's end up the implementation part of this paper with an illustration. For convenience, we use a set of six superimposed signatures. The size of each signature is f = 8. The data can be seen in the Figure 1. as a table consisting of six rows and eight columns. To demonstrate the searching ability of the quick filter we define the sample query signature Q as the following:

sample query signature Q: 00100010.

As we can see, there are just two once in our query signature, that means that the weight of the signature is w(Q) = 2.

	C1	C2	C3	C4	C5	C6	C7	C8
S1	0	0	0	1	1	1	1	0
S2	1	1	0	1	0	0	0	1
S3	0	0	1	1	1	1	0	0
S4	1	1	0	0	0	0	1	1
S5	0	0	1	1	0	1	1	0
S6	1	1	0	0	1	0	0	1

Figure 1. Sample Data of a Signature Filter

In Figure 2 we show how our sample data can be inserted into the filter and in Figure 3 how the sample query can be performed. We suppose that the capacity of a page is two signatures. The process of filling the filter is shown in seven steps. The step number 0 corresponds to the initial state when the filter is empty. The other steps show the content of the pages and the values of the file characteristics (split pointer SP, level of hashing h, and number of addressable pages n) always after inserting a signature. The signatures are inserted in the natural order, it is S1, S2, ... , S6.

Step 0.	P0: empty			$SP=0, h=0, n=1$
Step 1.	P0: S1			$SP=0, h=0, n=1$
Step 2.	P0: S1 S2			$SP=0, h=0, n=1$
Step 3.	P0: S1 S3	P1: S2		$SP=0, h=1, n=2$
Step 4.	P0: S1 S3	P1: S2 S4		$SP=0, h=1, n=2$
Step 5.	P0: S3	P1: S2 S4	P2: S1 S5	$SP=1, h=2, n=3$
Step 6.	P0: S3	P1: S2 S6	P2: S1 S5	P3: S4	$SP=0, h=2, n=4$

Figure 2. Inserting signatures organized by linear hashing

The resulting arrangement of the data can be seen in the Figure 3. The important feature of this organization is that all signatures in a page have the same suffix, the characteristic key, which in our case is two bits long. Considering the sample query, we can easily deduce that pages P0 and P1 cannot contain qualifying signatures, because none of their object signatures contain value "1" in the 7th position (column) as it is required by the query Q. In this way we can save page accesses and speed up the search. In our example we have to access two pages, P2 and P3, but we can save another two page accesses, namely to the pages P0 and P1.

P0: 00111100	P1: 11010001 11001001
P2: 00011110 00110110	P3: 11000011

Figure 3. Quick Filter

4.3. Performance Evaluation

It is the well known fact that every new suggestion for organizing data is not complete without appending it with qualitative evaluations. However, even though the quick filter is currently being implemented for experimental use as an access structure of MULTOS [THAN-90], no practical results are available at the moment. That is why we have decided to use modelling techniques to investigate the performance ability of quick filter.

We present two groups of performance tests, both of them based on block (page) access estimations. In the first group we study only the quick filter, namely its relationships among the type of query, size of the signature file and the efficiency of query processing. In the second group of performance analysis we compare the quick filter with the other access structures.

4.3.1. Quick filter analysis

It is not difficult to realize that the number of not accessed pages depends on the number of 1's in the h-bit suffix of Q, which in turn depends on the query weight and the size of h. Analytical formulas for estimating the number of pages which do not have to be accessed, provided the total number of pages n, level of hashing h, signature size f, and query weight $w(Q)$ are given, have been derived in [ZEZU-89]. From this article we present here a formula, see Eq. 2, for computing the expected number of 1's in the h bit suffix of Q. This formula has been used as the basic algorithm for our block access estimations.

$$E\left[\dot{w}(Q,h)\right] = \sum_{j=1}^{min\,[h,w(Q)]}\left[j\,\prod_{i=1}^{j}\frac{(h-i+1)\,(w(Q)-i+1)}{i\,(f-w(Q)+i)}\,\prod_{i=1}^{w(Q)-j}\frac{f-h-i+1}{f-i+1}\right]$$

(Eq. 2) Expected number of 1's in h-bit suffix of Q

The weight of a query depends on the application, namely on the way how queries are specified. Thus, the performance of query processing cannot be tuned by the database design.

Therefore the relationship between the query weight and the performance is very important so that embarrassment from imperfect or bad function of the filter can be avoided.

For the demonstration purposes we define *savings* as the percentage of accessed pages from the total number of addressable pages from which the filter is formed. In Figure 4, we can see dependences between the savings and the file size expressed in the number of pages. We show several curves representing query signatures composed of different numbers of terms, provided the total number of image descriptors $D=40$, signature size $f=600$ bits, and the number of bits which each term puts to one $m=10$.

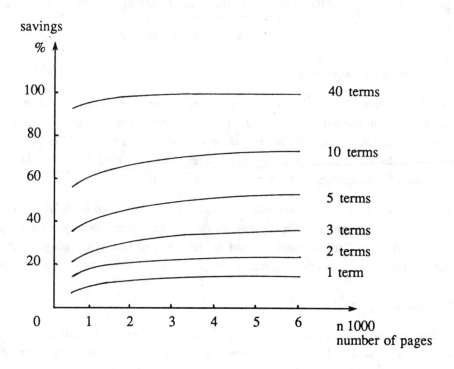

Figure 4. Percentage of savings depending on signature file size and query type
$f = 600, m = 10, D = 40$

The figure demonstrates mainly the advantage of quick filter when processing queries containing many terms, that is to say, the high weight queries. But you can also observe that the performance is better for large rather than small files and the fact is true for any type of query.

4.4. Comparison with other access structures

In this section we would like to show the performance of the quick filter in the relation to the performance of the other access structures namely, the sequential, and Bit-slice.

As we have indicated, we used the analytical approach. We computed two performance characteristics for the quick filter, the sequential, and the Bit-slice organizations. Actually, we

estimated the number of accessed pages needed for query evaluation and the space requirements, measured again in number of pages which the signature files occupied. Page size of
2K, 4 byte pointers to objects in the storage level, and the image signature weights of 120 bits,
were accepted as the model assumptions.

The specific features of the modeled storage structures were built on the following additional
assumptions. The pages of the sequential organization were filled with as many signatures as
they could contain. All the bit-slices of the Bit-slice organization started in new pages and no
page contained bits of more than one slice. Storage utilization for the quick filter was considered 75% and 5% of signatures was stored in overflow area.

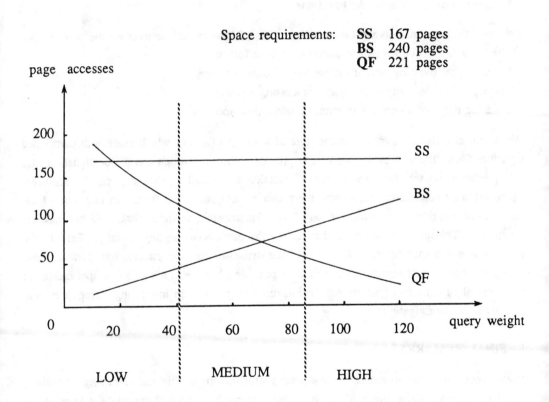

Figure 5. Comparison of signature file access structures
10,000 signatures, 2K pages, and image signature weight of 120bits

The results of the performance comparison are summarized in the Figure 5. According to
these, we can say that quick filter, QF, is a complementary access structure to the Bit-slice
organization. It is nearly always better than the sequential organization. The performance of
quick filter for the high-weight queries is far better than the performance of any other data
structure. But also for the medium weight queries, quick filter is a serious competitor even to

the bit-slice organization, not to mention the sequential organization for which the query processing requires approximately twice as many page accesses than quick filter.

Unlike with the bit-sliced access structure, maintenance of the quick filter can be handled easily, because the file can both grow and shrink linearly while the load stays very high. Since the signature patterns are generated by using the random number generator, the distribution of 1's and 0's within the signatures is uniform. The overflow is low and as a consequence of this, exhaustive search is nearly as good as the exhaustive search of the sequential signatures. High weight queries, however, need to access much less blocks than any other organization and in this respect quick filter shows considerable performance improvements.

4.5. Extensions and Research Directions

As a result of our analysis we can see three ways of how to further increase the performance of the quick filter. We suggest to concentrate the effort on:
- decreasing the overflow and/or increasing the loading factor,
- increasing the selectivity of the query processing algorithm,
- clustering pages of signatures to reduce random disk accesses.

We would also like to mention another related work, [LEEL-89], which deals with partitioned signature files. The aim of the work is to provide algorithms which can divide signature files into partitions, so that both search space reduction and parallel processing can be achieved. Three different partitioning algorithms are presented and compared there. In fact, one of the partitioning algorithms, called the *Fixed Prefix Partitioning*, is quite similar to our hashing function g. The main difference is that, unlike the partitioning algorithms in [LEEL-89], the function g is the split function. It can distribute dynamic sets of signatures into partitions and guarantee reduction of search space whenever possible. We are convinced that application of the other algorithms to dynamic file organizations may result in interesting storage structure designs worth investigation.

5. FINAL REMARKS

In this paper, we have introduced a new access structure for storing and retrieving signatures, based on hashing, called quick filter. Both the hashing function and the application of linear hashing as underlying data structure are defined and illustrated using an example. We have also presented the query processing algorithm with favorable performance characteristics. The query processing performance is investigated in terms of the number of pages accesses.

Results show that quick filter is mainly convenient in applications where large files are to be searched, insertions and updates are frequent and user queries mostly result in high weight signature queries. These characteristics fit the requirements, discussed in Sec. 3, for signature techniques to be used as integrated access methods to text and image data in multimedia databases.

REFERENCES

[BERT-88]
  Bertino E., Rabitti F., Gibbs S., *"Query Processing in a Multimedia Document System"*, ACM Trans. on Office Information Systems, Vol.6, N.1, pp. 1-41, 1988.

[CHAN-89]
  Chang W. W., and Schek H.J.: *"A Signature Access Method for the Starburst Database System"*. Proc. of VLDB-89, Amsterdam, The Netherlands, 1989, pp. 145 - 153.

[CHRI-84]
  Christodoulakis S. and Faloutsos C. *"Signature Files: An Access Method for Documents and its Analytical Performance Evaluation"*. ACM Transactions on Office Information Systems, Vol. 2, N. 4, pp. 267-288, 1984.

[CHRI-86]
  Christodoulakis S., et. al. *"Multimedia Document Presentation, Information Extraction and Document Formation in MINOS: A Model and a System"*. ACM Transactions on Office Information Systems, Vol. 4, N. 4, pp. 345-383, 1986.

[FALO-86]
  Faloutsos C. *"Integrated Access Methods for Message Using Signature Files"*. Proc. of the IFIP Working Conference on Methods and Tools for Office Systems, Pisa, Italy, 1986, pp. 135-157.

[FALO-87]
  Faloutsos C. and Christodoulakis S. *"Description and Performance Analysis of Signature File Methods for Office Filing"*. ACM Trans. on Office Information Systems, Vol. 5, No. 3, 1987.

[HASK-81]
  Haskin R.L. *"Special-purpose Processor for Text Retrieval"*. Database Engineering Vol. 4, No. 1, 1981.

[LARS-80]
  Larson P. *"Linear hashing with partial expansions"*. Proceedings of the 6th International Conference on VLDB, 1980, pp. 212-223.

[LEEL-89]
  Lee D.L. and Leng C. *"Partitioned Signature Files: Design Issues and Performance Evaluation"*. ACM Transactions on Office Information Systems, Vol. 7, No. 2, April 1989. pp. 158-180.

[LITW-80]
  Litwin W. *"Linear hashing: a new tool for files and table addressing"*. Proc. 6th International Conference on Very Large Databases, Montreal, 1980, pp. 212-223.

[RABI-84]
  Rabitti F. and Zizka J. *"Evaluation of Access Methods to Text Documents in Office Systems"*. Proc. 3rd Joint ACM-BCS Symposium on Research and Development in Information Retrieval, Cambridge, England, 1984.

[RABI-87]
  Rabitti F. and Stanchev P., *"An Approach to Image Retrieval from Large Image Databases"*, Proc. ACM-SIGIR 1987 International Conference on Research and Development in Information Retrieval, New Orleans, June 3-5, 1987.

[RABIa-89]
  F. Rabitti, P. Stanchev, *"GRIM_DBMS: a GRaphical IMage Data Base Management System"* Proc. IFIP TC-2 Working Conference on Visual Database Systems, Tokyo, April 1989, in "Visual Database Systems", edited by T. L. Kunii, North-Holland, pp. 415-430, 1989.

[RABIb-89]
  F. Rabitti, P. Stanchev, *"Image Database Management Systems: Applied Theories, Tools and Decisions"* Proc. of the Third International Conference on Automatic Image Processing, CAIP-89, Leipzig, GDR, September 1989, in "Computer Analysis of Images and Patterns", edited by K. Voss, D. Chetverikov, G. Sommer, Akademie-Verlag, Berlin, pp. 208-214, 1989.

[ROBE-79]

Roberts C.S. *"Partial Match Retrieval via the Method of the Superimposed Codes"*. Proc. of IEEE, Vol. 67, No. 12, pp. 1624-1642, Dec. 1979.

[RAMA-84]

Ramamohanarao K. and Sacks-Davis R. *"Recursive Linear Hashing"*. ACM Transactions on Database Systems, Vol. 9,No. 3, (September 1984), pp. 369-391.

[SACK-87]

Sacks-Davis K. and Ramamohanarao A. *"Multikey Access Methods Based on Superimposed Coding Techniques"*. ACM Transactions on Database Systems, Vol. 12, No. 4, December 1987.

[THAN-90]

"Multimedia Office Filing and Retrieval: The MULTOS Approach", edited by C. Thanos, North-Holland Series in Human Factors in Information Technology, North-Holland, 1990.

[TSIC-83]

Tsichritzis, D. et. al., *"A Multimedia Office Filing System"*. Proc. of VLDB-83, Florence, Italy, Oct. 1983.

[ZEZU-89]

Zezula P. *"Linear Hashing for Signature Files"*. In the book *"Network Information Processing systems"*, edited by K. Boyanov and R. Angelinov, Elsevier Science Publishers (North-Holland), IFIP, 1989, pp. 243-250.

[ZEZUa-90]

Zezula P. and Tiberio P., *"Engineering Signatures for Multimedia Data"*, submitted for publication.

[ZEZUb-90]

Zezula P., Tiberio P. and F. Rabitti, *"Quick Filter"*, IEI-CNR Tech. Rep. B4-07, Pisa, Febr. 1990.

Surrogate Subsets: A Free Space Management Strategy for the Index of a Text Retrieval System

F. J. Burkowski

Department of Computer Science
University of Waterloo
Waterloo, Ontario
Canada

ABSTRACT

This paper presents a new data structure and an associated strategy to be utilized by indexing facilities for text retrieval systems.The paper starts by reviewing some of the goals that may be considered when designing such an index and continues with a small survey of various current strategies. It then presents an indexing strategy referred to as surrogate subsets discussing its appropriateness in the light of the specified goals. Various design issues and implementation details are discussed. Our strategy requires that a surrogate file be divided into a large number of subsets separated by free space which will allow the index to expand when new material is appended to the database. Experimental results report on the utilization of free space when the database is enlarged.

INTRODUCTION

This paper will present a new data structure and an associated strategy to be utilized by indexing facilities for text retrieval systems. Typical applications [FAL87D], [CHR86] include the archiving and retrieval of natural-language documents contained in very large databases such as automated law [DEF88] and patent databases, electronic encyclopedias, abstracts, medical libraries, automated office filing and newspaper databases. In the more sophisticated systems, a computer network is used to communicate user queries to a document server which responds by sending a selection of documents back to the user workstation. Queries typically involve the inclusion of words or phrases in a syntax which defines a Boolean or relevance search that selects a hopefully limited set of documents that are germane to the information needs of the user. Query syntax may support the stipulation of words within various <u>text elements</u> of a document, for example, the query may request all newspaper articles containing "acid rain" WITHIN the headline AND "river pollution" WITHIN the main text.

Typically, during retrieval operations, words or phrases extracted from the query are presented to an <u>index</u> facility which maintains the text locations of all the significant words in the database. Depending on the needs of the application, the precision used to specify the location or address of a word may be extremely narrow (byte displacement in a text file) or very wide (the address of some text element, perhaps the document itself). In the former case we will consider the index entry for a word to have an <u>address granularity</u> of a byte while in the latter case the address granularity is some larger extent specified by the type of some particular text element (for example, a sentence, paragraph, chapter or the document itself). Naturally, the granularity of the address has an effect on the size of the index and on the nature of the queries that may be handled efficiently.

In response to a query the retrieval system will access the index, extracting from it all required address lists and it will then perform various manipulations on these lists in an attempt to determine the address of words which meet the constraints imposed by the query. These manipulations typically involve intersections, union and sorting operations. We will avoid any further discussion of these manipulations since this paper will deal primarily with index techniques.

This paper will assume that the words selected for indexing have been determined by the needs of the application. Techniques which consider the appropriate strategies for index word selection generally fall into one of two categories which serve to support either free-text search or keyword searching. These issues are discussed briefly in [STA86] and more extensively in [SAL86]. While not advocating any particular strategy we will generally assume index word selection is being done to support a free text search allowing the user to retrieve information from the database after defining queries which incorporate arbitrary combinations of document words. This assumption places the heaviest demands on the size and performance requirements of the index, keyword searching typically requiring fewer index entries.

ASSUMED ENVIRONMENT

The following list of assumptions will summarize the text retrieval environment that this paper considers:

1) Multi-user large database

    The multi-user environment will make frequent demands on the system which should strive to provide short response times while dealing with an index that is very large.

2) Dynamic Growth

    The database will grow with the addition of new material.

3) Flexibility

    Indexing techniques should *potentially* allow text inversion on every word of the database. The system should efficiently handle queries that contain word proximity constraints and phrases.

GOALS

1) Fast retrieval

    List manipulation aside, most of the time spent in retrieval arises from disk accesses to the index and so indexing techniques should focus on achieving low I/O counts.

2) Fast loading and appending

    The initial database load and subsequent database append operations should be done quickly and in a fashion that will least compromise retrieval ability.

3)   Efficient Free Space Management

During append operations the index will extend into free space areas. This should be done in a way that does not seriously compromise retrieval performance, append performance or the efficient utilization of the storage area.

It can be seen that these three goals are in a type of dynamic tension in that design tradeoffs which favour one goal tend to weaken the achievability of the other goals.

OTHER ISSUES: INDEX SIZE

An important consideration is the size of the index. This paper will assume that the primary use of the index will be the retention of word addresses within the text file. In this case, the size of the index is very dependent on the address granularity that is utilized. Small granularity addressing (say down to the text word or character level) will give a much larger index but the system functionality is greatly enhanced since proximity searching and detection of phrases are handled in a much more effective fashion.

Let us consider this dependency in more quantitative terms. We will develop formulae that establish the ratio of index size to overall text size under two scenarios:

A)   address granularity is a single byte

B)   address granularity is a text element with a minimum size of TE_s bytes.

The following notation will be used:

$$
\begin{aligned}
DB_s &= \text{database size in bytes} \\
w_s &= \text{average size of word (4.87 bytes)} \\
TE_s &= \text{text element size in bytes} \\
TE_v &= \text{average number of distinct words in a text element of size } TE_s \\
R_{sb} &= \text{ratio of index size to text size when address granularity is a single byte} \\
R_{te} &= \text{ratio of index size to text size when address granularity is a text element} \\
&\quad \text{of size } TE_s
\end{aligned}
$$

The value of w_s was obtained by calculating the average word length in a newspaper data base containing 250 megabytes of text. If we include the delimiter after each word, the word accounts for $1 + w_s = 5.87$ bytes on average.

With an address granularity of a single byte and assuming each address is stored in a sequence of bytes we get $DB_s \lceil (\log_2 DB_s)/8 \rceil / (1 + w_s)$ as the size of the index (ignoring any contribution necessary to define the structure of the index). Thus,

$$R_{sb} = \lceil (\log_2 DB_s)/8 \rceil / (1 + w_s) \tag{1}$$

Now with the wider granularity it is possible to save on the size of the address since it need only identify the text element to specify a word's location. Consequently the address size is $\lceil (\log_2(DB_s/TE_s))/8 \rceil$. More significantly we can eliminate duplicate words in the text element during the load activity, indexing only the distinct words. The number of distinct words V in a sequence of N consecutive words can be derived from the formula

$$V (\gamma + \ln V) = N \tag{2}$$

where $\gamma = 0.57721$ (Euler's constant). This formula (derived in [FAL84]) assumes that the distribution of words in text follows a Zipf distribution. Thus the size of the contribution made by the text element to the index is $TE_v \lceil (\log_2(DB_s/TE_s))/8 \rceil$ where

$$TE_v (\gamma + \ln TE_v) = TE_s /(1 + w_s) \quad \text{and so}$$

$$R_{te} = \lceil (\log_2(DB_s/TE_s))/8 \rceil / ((1 + w_s)(\gamma + \ln TE_v)). \tag{3}$$

As an example, let us consider 1 gigabyte of text stored on an optical disk. Equation (1) indicates that with single byte address granularity the index has a size that is 68% of the size of the text. In practice, since the addresses are in ascending order, we can use a simple front end compression scheme on the addresses to drop this to a smaller percentage providing a final size that is considerably lower than the frequently cited extreme of 300% mentioned in [HAS81].

If we consider a text element size TE_s to be equal to 1024 bytes then $TE_v = 40.72$. In this case equation (3) indicates an index of size 12% and again with front end compression this can be reduced even further.

SEARCHING FOR PHRASES WHEN THE ADDRESS GRANULARITY IS LARGE

With the above observations in mind it becomes extremely tempting to do a partial inversion of the text by employing this larger address granularity. Savings would be significant, especially for large multi-gigabyte text collections. The major problem is that these schemes have a good average response time but an unpredictable worst case response time [DEF89], very extended response times occurring when searching for a phrase which must be detected by a final document inspection since the search itself can only retrieve documents containing the phrase constituents in any order and in any location within the document.

Many examples of such an anomaly can be given, the worst situation being a phrase which is relatively rare in occurrence but which is comprised of words that are frequently used elsewhere in the text. We have performed indexing experiments using document level address granularity and have discovered many queries that support this claim. For example, in a newspaper collection of 95,000 articles a search for documents containing the phrase "John Turner" produces a very fast response fetching the first of 646 articles in less than 5 seconds. However, a search for documents with the phrase "the new John Turner" takes over 3 minutes because of the extensive document scanning (typically the word "new" appears in roughly one out of every three newspaper articles).

A Brief Overview of Current Access Methods

We will start by discussing some of the indexing techniques that have been used for text. This discussion is not meant to be a tutorial, but will instead describe these strategies from a perspective that will consider the performance and goals stated earlier. A more comprehensive description of the following strategies appears in [FAL85].

Inverted Lists

Inverted lists [TEO82] (pg. 344) can be implemented using a database dictionary [FAL85], and a postings file. A word from the query is found in the dictionary. The dictionary entry contains a pointer which selects a list of addresses specifying the text locations containing that word. All such lists are stored in the postings file. Organization of the dictionary can be done using a variety of techniques such as B-trees [BAY72], TRIES, or hashing. In most cases the technique will allow rapid updates to the dictionary when the database increases in size due to the appending of new documents. Accomodating list expansion in the posting file is a more challenging problem especially if one is concerned about space consumption on secondary storage.

Discussion

Inverted lists can exhibit very fast retrieval times provided the address list for a particular word is stored in contiguous areas of the disk. During load or append operations one or more addresses will be appended to various lists in the postings file and since these are spread over a large area of the disk there will be many disk seeks. Typically, one of two strategies is used:

1) The address lists in the postings file are retained in a series of chained buckets. When a bucket is filled, a pointer to a new bucket allows the list to expand. In addition to internal fragmentation the scheme has the drawback of extending the retrieval time due to the extra disk seeks across the noncontiguous buckets.

2) In an effort to maintain fast retrieval each list can be stored in a contiguous extent which has a length equal to 1 or more adjacent buckets. When new entries are about to overflow the extent the list can be copied to a longer free extent made available from a free space list. The original extent is returned to the free list manager. Retrieval is not compromised but the load process becomes quite extended due to the copying and overhead associated with the free list management.

Signature Files

Signature file techniques [BER87], [CHR84], [FAL87S], [STA86] typically require that each document be divided into "logical blocks" each containing a constant number D of distinct, non-common words. Each word is mapped to a word signature which is a bit pattern of length F (F=512, for example) with m bits set to "1", the rest being 0. Positions of the m "1" bits are determined by hashing techniques. The word signature derived from the D distinct words are then OR-ed together to form the *block signature* corresponding to the logical block. In the next figure we use small values (F=12, m=4, D=3) to illustrate the technique.

Word	Signature		
phantom	0 0 0 1	1 0 0 0	0 1 1 0
opera	0 0 0 1	0 1 1 0	0 0 0 1
webber	1 0 0 0	0 0 1 0	0 0 1 1
block			
signature	1 0 0 1	1 1 1 0	0 1 1 1

Illustration of a Block Signature for Three Words

Searching for a word is done by creating the word signature and then examining each block signature to see if that word signature has been included. Because of the hashing and due to the superimposition of the word signatures it is possible that a block signature appears to contain a word signature even though the corresponding word is not actually in the document. This occurence of a "false drop" will happen very infrequently if appropriate choices are made for m, F and D [TSI83], [CHR84].

Discussion

The main advantage of a signature file is the rapid update capability. Appending new information to the database will result in a simple extension of the signature file into the free space that follows it. Utilization of the free space is excellent since there is no possibility of fragmentation. Size of the index is small, quoted at 5 to 10% in [CHR84] when the logical block contains about 40 distinct words. Since the address granularity is essentially the size of the logical block, the signature file exhibits a size which is not surprisingly low. It is comparable to the size that would be achievable with inverted list schemes using the same address granularity (see equation (3)).

Superimposed encoding implies that proximity and phrase searches must be done with document filtering.

Retrieval is quite slow because of the extensive scanning. For example, a signature file that is 5% of the size of the text file will be 30 megabytes in length if the text is 600 megabytes long. Since disk transfer rates are typically one megabyte per second, the I/O time for accessing the signature file will be half a minute. Various modifications to superimposed encoding have been implemented [FAL87D], [ROB79] most with the goal of speeding up the retrieval strategy while trying to maintain the ease of update.

Bit-Slice Signature Files

Roberts [ROB79] stored signature files in a "bit-slice" fashion. The large array of bits comprising the signature file is transposed and stored in such a way that the bits from the i-th position of all the signatures are stored contiguously in a bit-slice. Since we need not check the j-th bit of any signature in the file if the j-th bit of the signatures derived from all the query words is "0", we can reduce the amount of scanning that is to be done. We need only scan those bit-slices that correspond to the bit positions in the query word signatures that are set to "1". This considerably speeds up the scan operation but the cost per query word is still rather high since it involves one disk seek for each "1" bit set in the word signature plus the bit-slice transfer time which may be longer than the seek time depending on the size of the signature file. Ease of update is still retained, but only if documents are appended in batches and the signature bits are buffered in main memory before being written out to the transposed signature file.

Signature Files with Concatenated Signatures

The surrogate file (essentially a signature file with concatenated word signatures) is a sequence of integers (bit strings of fixed length), each integer representing the *word signature* of a significant word contained in the main text of the database. Creation of the surrogate corresponding to a text element (for example, the entire document) involves three steps [LAR83]:

1.   Common words are removed using a list of *stop* words.

2.   A signature word is computed for each remaining word in the text element. In most cases, this is simply a hash function that maps words (character strings) onto integer values that are m bits long. A reasonable value for m would be between 16 and 24.

3.   Duplicate word signatures are eliminated.

Thus the surrogate file is a series of *signature groups* (see next figure below) appearing in the same order as the corresponding text elements. Each signature group is comprised of a series of word signatures derived from the words in the corresponding text element followed by the address of that element. When a user query is to be satisfied, words from the query are converted into word signatures and the surrogate file is scanned for these word signatures. Whenever a match occurs the address at the end of the group is extracted so that the corresponding text element can be eventually located. Since the hash encoding is not guaranteed to be a 1-to-1 mapping, it is possible that more than one text word maps to the same signature value. During a scan operation this multiple map can produce a *false drop* and an unrelated document of no interest to the user may be retrieved. This can be detected and rectified by having software check documents before they are passed to the user. As noted in [LAR83] false drops can be made to occur with very small frequency if signature words are long enough.

signature Group:

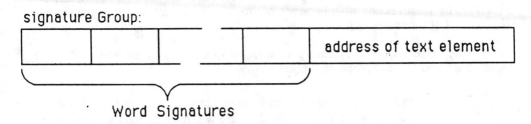

Word Signatures

Structure of a Signature Group

Note that if more documents are appended to the text portion of the database, the surrogate file is similarly extended by the appending of additional document signature groups. Retrieval operations are expected to be slow since the size of the surrogate file results in extensive transfer times and hence long scan times.

Surrogate Subsets with Anticipatory Expansion Space

We will now progress to the main content of this paper which describes an index strategy that we have dubbed *surrogate subsets*. The approach is intended to serve many of the goals presented earlier while maintaining both fast retrieval (without false drops) and fast update.

In an effort to minimize the scan time while retaining the property of an easy update, we adopt a technique which is a compromise strategy in that it has some of the properties of both inverted files and signature files with concatenated signatures. Our approach is most easily described as an extension of the concatenated signature scheme with the following modifications:

1)   As in signature files a word is represented in the index by a fixed length value or identifier which we will call a *marker*. A marker has the same appearance and functionality as a word signature. We use this different terminology to stress the fact that a marker is <u>not</u> created using hashing techniques but rather it is <u>assigned</u> during a database load, the assignment technique guaranteeing uniqueness. This will avoid the false-drop problem.

2)   The file of concatenated markers is subdivided into a reasonably large number of *subsets*. During the creation of the file a word marker is mapped to a particular subset and this subset will be the one that retains the marker group. During retrieval operations the same mapping is used when we wish to select the subset to be scanned when presented with the marker value derived from a given query word. The subset designation and marker value for each word are kept in a <u>database dictionary</u>. Note that within a subset there is a one-to-one mapping between markers and words.

3)   Each subset is followed by free space that allows for subset expansion during subsequent database appends.

This simple overview of the technique avoids any discussion of the free space assignment strategy which works by taking advantage of the predictable nature of the Zipf distribution of word frequencies in the database. This word frequency distribution is essentially determined by an initial <u>load</u> of a portion of the database and it is then used to predict free space requirements, the objective being to drastically reduce the occurrence of overflows of subsets. The final section of this paper outlines an experiment which reports on the effectiveness of the strategy.

We now describe the load, append and retrieval operations in more detail. In these discussions we will use the following notation:

$\{W_i\}_{i=1}^N$ is the set of distinct words in the text that are to be indexed. Each distinct word W_i from the database will have an entry at location i of the dictionary. This entry initially keeps track of the word frequency and later will retain the marker value and subset identifier assigned to the word.

$\{S_j\}_{j=1}^\sigma$ is the set of identifiers for the subsets in the surrogate file.

SID[i]   This dictionary entry retains the subset identifier S_j assigned to the word W_i.

MRK[i]   This dictionary entry holds the marker value assigned to the word W_i.

CNT[i]   This temporary dictionary entry retains the number of times W_i appears in the text of the initial load.

ESZ[]   This array keeps track of the current estimated size of all the subsets.

IXMIN(ESZ) This function returns the index of the minimum value in the array ESZ.

Other functions and arrays will be defined as we progress in the discussion.

The Load Activity

The initial load builds the index for an initial portion of the database. For example, in our experiments, we used the first 40 megabytes of a text database that was 250 megabytes long. From this first portion the loader can determine with reasonable accuracy the statistical properties of the word frequencies. While we could get by with a smaller initial load, it is more effective to use a larger portion. However, as the size increases, it become more difficult to handle other memory resident structures such as the word dictionary. The load activity progresses through the following phases:

1)   Pass I

The loader processes the text extracting from it the distinct words $\{W_i\}_{i=1}^{N}$ that are to be indexed. While doing this it builds a word dictionary which retains CNT[i] for each word W_i. When a word is taken from the text stream, the loader will attempt to find it in the dictionary. If found it increments CNT[i], if not found, a new entry is created with CNT[i]=1.

2)   Assignment of Subsets

The loader initializes all ESZ[] entries to 0. Entries in the dictionary are now processed in descending order with respect to the CNT[] value. This can be done through a sort vector SV[k] k=1,2,...,N created just prior to this step. SV[k] will be the index of the dictionary entry that is in position k after a descending order sort of CNT[].

For k=1,2,...,N the loader executes:

        SJ_TEMP = IXMIN(ESZ)
        SID[SV[k]] = SJ_TEMP
        increment ESZ[SJ_TEMP] by CNT[SV[k]].

When this is completed, CNT[] locations in the dictionary may be used for other purposes such as retention of the subset ID and marker values computed in the next steps. The assignment of subset identifiers is essentially analogous to the packing of a collection of boxes with articles of various sizes. We place the largest articles in the largest available space within the boxes, followed by the lesser size items

219

(always using the largest available box space) until we finish with the smallest articles. This heuristic approach will help ensure that subsets are fairly well balanced.

3) Assignment of Markers

The loader progresses through the dictionary <u>assigning</u> a marker value to each word W_i. Marker values will be <u>unique</u> within subsets (and hence there is never a false drop problem). The array NXTMRK[] keeps track of the next marker value to be assigned to a particular subset. Initially, all its entries are 0.

For k=1,2,...,N the loader executes:

MRK[k] = NXTMRK[SID[k]]
increment NXTMRK[SID[k]] by 1.

Marker values should be at least one byte in length, two if the number of subsets is small. The database designer must consider the anticipated vocabulary of the system and choose accordingly.

4) Pass II

In this second pass of the text, the surrogate subsets are created. For each word, the loader consults the dictionary to determine the subset selection and marker values to be used. For each word W_i in the text stream, the loader creates the pair MRK[i], ADRS[i] where MRK[i] is extracted from the dictionary and ADRS is the address of the word in the text stream. This information is appended to the end of the list held in the subset designated by SID[i]. In practice, the loader will record in another array the last MRK[ ] that was placed in a subset and if it is the same as the current MRK[i] then the MRK[i] value can be omitted. The loader also keeps track of the last address in a subset and enters ADRS[i] using an encoding that provides a type of front-end compression. In our experiments, address entries had a length of 1, 2, or 4 bytes the average length being between 1 and 2 bytes. Steering bits in the most significant part of an entry are used to distinguish markers and addresses of particular lengths.

5) Free Space Allocation

The ESZ array used in step 2 is also used in step 4 to provide a rough estimate of the size requirements for the subsets. The appropriate amount of free space can be preallocated for each subset in proportion to the values held in ESZ (ESZ[i]*6 is sufficient at this time). It is impossible to establish the exact space requirements that each subset will need to accomodate the first load since we cannot anticipate the space savings due to marker omission and front-end compression.

In this step, the loader can redefine the free space needs based on the true size of the subsets thus far. Let FS[S_j] denote the length of the free space that is to follow subset S_j and let the current length of S_j be given by CL[S_j]. Define

$$R = TL/PL \qquad (4)$$

where TL is the total length of the text that is to be indexed (this includes the portion of the text just loaded) and PL is the length of the text portion just loaded. The success of our allocation policy rests on the assumption that, on average, future appends will cause the subsets to grow to a final size which is R times larger than the current size, that is:

$$(CL[S_j] + FS[S_j]) / CL[S_j] = R. \tag{5}$$

Equations (4) and (5) essentially deal with average behaviour. Some subsets will not totally use the free space, others will need more. In our effort to reduce the overhead associated with overflow of the free space we can extend the free space by some small fraction of the free space size recommended by (5). With this approach

$$FS[S_j] = (R-1)(1+XTR) CL[S_j] \tag{6}$$

where XTR provides the extra extension of the free space. In a future section we report on recommended values of XTR. Once all the $FS[S_j]$ are determined the subsets can be shifted so that each one gets the calculated free space allotment.

If both index and text are to be kept on a single volume the loader can be informed about the volume capacity and will use this to calculate TL the maximum allowable length of text that can be both indexed and stored on the volume. With a little calculation it can be determined that:

$$TL = PL(VC + XTR*SC) / (PL + (1 + XTR)*SC) \tag{7}$$

where VC represents the volume capacity and SC is the sum of the lengths of the current subsets that is

$$SC = \Sigma \; CL[j].$$

The Append Activity

An append is similar to a load except that a two pass procedure is not needed. When a word is extracted from the text stream there are two possibilities:

1) The word is in the dictionary
   In this case the append program must recognize the commitment made by the prior assignation. If the word is found at location k then the pair MRK[k], ADRS[k] is entered into the subset just as in step 4 of the load activity.

2) The word is not in the dictionary
   In this case the word is entered into the dictionary at index i, for example, and SID[i] is assigned the subset identifier which designates the subset having the shortest current length. As before NXTMRK[] is used to determine the marker value to be assigned to MRK[i]. Having done this the subset entry can be made in the usual fashion.

It is important to realize that loading and appending can proceed at a very fast rate if suitable buffering is used. In our experimental database 4096 subsets were used. Each subset was given a buffer area equal in length to the size of a disk sector. When this buffer is filled it is written out to disk. Total buffer space required is 4096 x 512 bytes = 2 megabytes. The size of the buffer area was the primary restriction on the number of subsets used by the indexing scheme. Since the buffer area represents a "wavefront" of subset extension activity the disk writes tend to be more localized using this technique than that experienced in updating the typical inverted file.

Disk writes are also far less frequent. Considering front end compression and redundant marker omissions a word in the text will contribute about 3 bytes (on average) to the index. This means that on average we can process about 170 words in the text stream before a disk write to the index is required. The index scheme tends to be much less I/O bound than indexing done with inverted lists.

Retrieval Activity

The main concern during retrieval activity is the generation of an address list for each word in the query. When presented with a query word the search administrator task will consult the dictionary to find the subset and marker value assigned to that word. It will then scan the designated subset looking for any occurrence of the marker. Whenever the marker is found addresses following it are extracted and returned as part of the required address list.

Discussion

The surrogate subsets scheme just described has the following advantages:

1)   Fast Loading and Appending

   This is due to the buffering capability just described.

2)   Fast Retrieval

   Typically, the derivation of an address list for a query word requires one disk seek to pull out the dictionary entry, another disk seek to get to the subset and the equivalent of one more seek to scan the subset. As an example, consider a 200 megabyte text file to be stored on a 300 megabyte optical disk. With the subset building techniques described above, we can create an index that uses word level address granularity while occupying space that is about 40% of the size of the text. Actual size will depend on various decisions regarding exclusion of stop words from the index. The index will then be about 80 megabytes in size. This is distributed over 4096 subsets giving 20K bytes per subset (on average). With a disk transfer rate of 1 megabyte/second or 1K bytes/ms we can transfer this in 20 ms which is comparable to the time to do a disk seek.

3)   Good Space Utilization

   Because of the marker values, the total size of the index tends to be longer than that possible with inverted lists. However, the extra space required is somewhat ameliorated by the following considerations: Since index entries for low frequency words are intermingled with one another within a subset the average difference between successive addresses is smaller than the average difference seen when the addresses have their own "private" lists as in typical inverted files. This means that front end compression can be used more effectively introducing a compression factor which tends to offset the regular appearance of marker values in these subsets. Subsets holding high frequency words have far fewer marker values since there is a higher chance that successive index entries are for the same word and so the marker value is omitted as previously described.

Experimental Results: Choosing XTR

In the following experiment we sought to determine how the number of overflows varied with respect to XTR. A newspaper database comprised of 250 megabytes was created using one load activity of 44 megabytes followed by five append operations each adding in about 41 megabytes each. Subsets were established using the strategy defined in the previous sections but the free space areas following the 4096 subsets after the initial load were made extra large so that no overflows occurred during the subsequent appends. After the last append, data defining the final lengths of the various subsets were extracted and passed to a program which evaluated the number of overflows that would have been realized for various values of XTR in the range [-0.3, 0.5]. Results are summarized in the following plot:

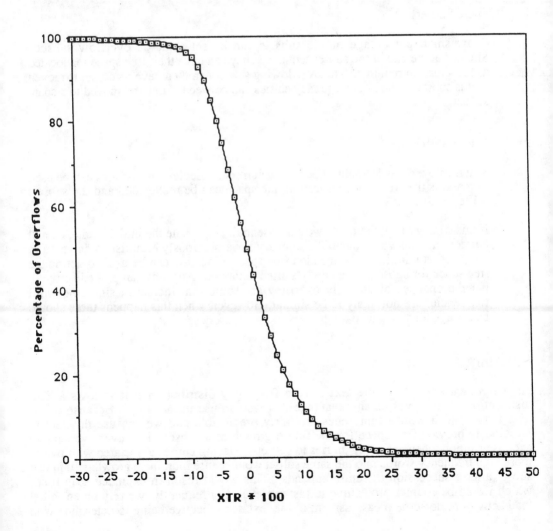

When XTR = 0, the number of overflows was 1940, slightly less than half the subsets. The significant feature about this plot is that the number of overflows rapidly decreases as XTR climbs to about 0.20 with relatively small gains after that. For example, with XTR = 0.10, 0.15 and 0.20 the number of overflows is 444, 188 and 86 respectively corresponding to 10.8%, 4.6% and 2.1% of the subsets. These figures indicate that small increases in the index size allocation produce substantial returns in reducing overflows. For example, if the size of the index is derived from equation (5) and amounts to 40% of the size of the text, then making it 48% the size of the text represents a 1/5 increase, ie. XTR = 0.20 and so we expect the overflows to drop to less than 2.1%.

Handling Overflows

Overflows will occur. For example, in a newspaper database the sudden popularity of a name or topic will generate many index entries for a subset that was perhaps initially considered to exhibit slow growth. Various strategies can be used to accomodate this situation:

1)   Spare Subsets

Some small percentage of the subsets can be set aside as overflow subsets. Situated at the end of the subset sequence, they can have their free space reallocated as the situation requires. The overflowing subset can then have its contents moved to this subset or the high frequency entries can be weeded out and moved to a spare subset.

2)   Subset Shift

When an overflow is about to occur the current subset length statistics can be used to reassess the free space allocation, the space can be reallocated and the subsets shifted accordingly.

If this strategy is put in place we can essentially eliminate the initial load. A small but comprehensive "standard" dictionary for a previously established database in conjunction with its recommended free space allocation can be used to define the free space for subsets in a newly started database. Appends can procede directly but the chances of an early overflow are somewhat increased since the word frequencies are not likely to be similar. However, when this happens there should be enough loaded data to do the reassessment just described.

SUMMARY

High frequency words in the text have a frequency distribution that follows a Zipf distribution. This gives us an advantage that we can use in indexing. Because of the distribution, such word occurrences are fairly predictable and we can use this fact to judiciously provide free space for the future growth of a subset. However, we have to exercise caution when assigning entries to subsets. Placing entries associated with two or more high frequency words into the same subset would cause inordinate growth within that subset after a succession of future appends. This would result in extended scan times which would be counter productive to fast retrieval. Consequently, we rely on an initial load activity to do some preassessment of the text, the objective being to determine with reasonable accuracy, those words that are high frequency and those that are not. The high frequency words can then be established in their own "private" subsets.

Because of the strategy used for the load activity, a low frequency word will share a subset with other low frequency words. There is an immediate benefit. While the growth of a subset containing one low frequency word (as in an inverted list scheme) is rather unpredictable, the growth of a subset with many low frequency words can be more accurately assessed since the <u>average</u> occurence of low frequency words in the database is much more predictable.

The net result is a tendency to build subsets that have a predictable growth. Furthermore, the subsets are as uniform as possible in length (within the constraints imposed by the uneveness of the distribution corresponding to the high frequency words). This not only aids storage utilization and scan time but also allows us to devise address compression strategies that are appropriate for each frequency level.

CONCLUSION

The indexing scheme presented in this paper provides retrieval times and storage utilization which is competitive with typical inverted list schemes but it provides an update capability which is significantly faster since it allows an easy expansion of lists into available free space. This is done without significantly compromising execution times for either retrieval or load activities. Furthermore, indexing can be done with word level address granularity thus promoting the rapid handling of queries dealing with proximity and phrases.

ACKNOWLEDGEMENTS

The author wishes to thank The Montreal Gazette for their provision of a large newspaper text collection which has been used in our experiments. I also wish to express gratitude to Mr. Dennis Ablett of Infomart in Toronto for his help in arranging the acquisition of this text. Finally I wish to thank Kent Chow of Sigscan Systems (Toronto) for work done in the programming and testing of the surrogate subset retrieval engine thus proving its effectiveness in various real-life text database applications.

REFERENCES

[BAY72]   BAYER, R. AND MCCREIGHT, E., Organization and maintenance of large ordered indexes, *Acta Informatica*, vol. 1, no. 3, 1972, pp. 173-189.

[BER87]   BERRA, P. B., CHUNG, S. M. AND HACHEM, N. I., Computer architecture for a surrogate file to a very large data / knowledge base, *IEEE Computer*, vol. 20, no. 3, 1987, pp. 25-32.

[CHR84]   CHRISTODOULAKIS, S. AND FALOUTSOS, C., Design considerations for a message file server, *IEEE Trans. Software Engineering*, Vol. SE-10, No. 2, Mar. 1984, pp. 201-210.

[CHR86]   CHRISTODOULAKIS, S. AND FALOUTSOS, C., Design and performance considerations for an optical disk-based, multimedia object server, *Computer*, Vol. 19, No. 12, Dec. 1986, pp. 45-56.

[DEF88]   DEFAZIO, S. AND GREENWALD, C., The Mead information retrieval system, *IEEE Compcon 88*, Feb. 1988, pp. 431.

[DEF89]   DEFAZIO, S., Private communication.

[FAL84]   FALOUTSOS, C. AND CHRISTODOULAKIS, S., Signature files: an access method for documents and its analytical performance evaluation, *ACM Transactions on Office Information Systems*, Vol. 2, No. 4, Oct. 1984, pp.267-288.

[FAL85]   FALOUTSOS, C., Access methods for text, *Computing Surveys*, Vol. 17, No.1, Mar. 1985, pp. 49-74.

[FAL87D]   FALOUTSOS, C. AND CHAN, R., Fast text access methods for optical disks: designs and performance comparison, UMIACS-TR-87-66, CS-TR-1958, Dept. of Comp. Sci. and Inst. for Adv. Comp. Studies, Univ. of Maryland, Dec. 1987, 29 pages.

[FAL87S]   FALOUTSOS, C. AND CHRISTODOULAKIS, S., Optimal signature extraction and information loss, *ACM Transactions on Database Systems*, Vol. 12, No.3, Sept. 1987, pp. 395-428.

[HAS81]   HASKIN, R. L., Special purpose processors for text retrieval, *Database Engineering*, Vol. 4, No. 1, Sept. 1981, pp. 16-29.

[LAR83]   LARSON, P. A., A method for speeding up text retrieval, *Proceedings of ACM SIGMOD Conference*, May, ACM, New York, 1983, pp. 117-123.

[ROB79]   ROBERTS, C. S., Partial-match retrieval via the method of superimposed codes, *Proc. IEEE*, 67,12, Dec. 1979, 1624-1642.

[SAL86]   SALTON, G., Another look at automatic text retrieval systems, *Communications of the ACM*, Vol. 29, No. 7, July 1986, pp. 648-656.

[STA86]   STANFILL, C. AND KAHLE, B., Parallel free-text search on the connection machine system, *Communications of the ACM*, Vol. 29, No. 12, Dec. 1986, pp. 1229-1239.

[TEO82]   TEORY, T. J. AND FRY, J. P., *Design of Database Structures*, Prentice Hall, Englewood Cliffs, New Jersey, 1982.

[TSI83]   TSICHRITZIS D. AND CHRISTODOULAKIS, S., Message files, *ACM Trans. Office Information Systems*, Vol. 1, No. 1, Jan. 1983, pp. 88-98.

Construction of a Dynamic Thesaurus and Its Use for Associated Information Retrieval

Haruo Kimoto   Toshiaki Iwadera

Nippon Telegraph and Telephone Corporation
Electrical Communication Laboratories
407C 1-2356 Take, Yokosuka-Shi
Kanagawa 238-03 Japan

Electronic mail: kimoto%nttnly.ntt.jp@relay.cs.net
Electronic mail: iwadera%nttnly.ntt.jp@relay.cs.net

Abstract

An information retrieval system based on a dynamic thesaurus was developed utilizing the connectionist approach. The dynamic thesaurus consists of nodes, which represent each term of a thesaurus, and links, which represent the connections between nodes. Term information that is automatically extracted from user's relevant documents is used to change node weights and generate links. Node weights and links reflect a user's particular interest. A document retrieval experiment was conducted in which both a high recall rate and a high precision rate were achieved.

The topics discussed in this paper:

Connectionist Model, Automatic Indexing, Information Retrieval, and Thesaurus.

1. Introduction

The development of word-processors, optical disk filing systems, and computer networks enables us to use large scale databases. In order to advance database systems, there are two problems that need to be addressed: document storing and document retrieval. For document storing, an automatic document classification system and an automatic indexing system have already been developed.[1][2] For document retrieval, many kinds of AI techniques are currently being studied. The AI techniques most commonly used in a database system are expert systems[3] and natural language processing systems.[4] Development of an expert system requires a rule base for each application. Natural language processing techniques have difficulties with syntactic analysis and semantic analysis.

In this paper, a new system is proposed which incorporates the connectionist model in a dynamic thesaurus. This system is designed to discover and use the interests of a user so that the results of document retrieval are more beneficial to that user. This new system is called the Associated Information Retrieval System (AIRS).

2. Basic Concept of the AIRS System

The general diagram of AIRS is shown in Fig.1. The distinctive feature of AIRS is that it determines the user's interests from user's sample relevant documents as term information. This term information is used to construct a dynamic thesaurus that generates associated keywords. These keywords are used to retrieve documents that precisely fit the user's own interest.

2.1 Term Information from User's Sample Relevant Documents

Term information consists of keyword information and keyword relation information. Keyword information consists of keywords and the ranking of each keyword, which is ranked according to the importance of that keyword in a particular sample relevant document. Keyword relation information consists of relation type and relation strength. These are shown in Fig.2.

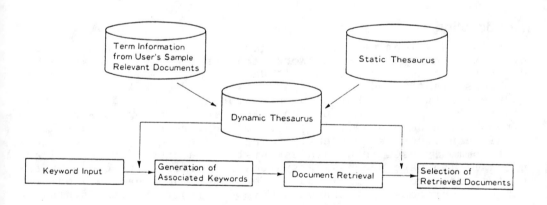

Fig. 1   The General Diagram of the Associated
Information Retrieval System (AIRS)

2.2 The Dynamic Thesaurus

The dynamic thesaurus is constructed based on a network structure. Each node of the network, which has a node weight, represents one term of the thesaurus. Each link represents a relationship between terms. The data structure of the dynamic thesaurus is shown in Fig.2. Nodes (Term and Node Weight) and Links (Relation and Link weight), which constitute the dynamic thesaurus, reflect a user's interest. The node weight of a term is calculated using the keyword ranking in term information. There are five kinds of relations between nodes. They are as follows:

a. Broader term relation
b. Narrower term relation
c. Use relation(Descriptor)
d. Used for relation(Synonym)
e. Co-occurrence relation

Relations of a, b, c, and d are obtained from the static thesaurus. Relation e, the co-occurrence relation, is obtained from keyword relations in term information. The co-occurrence relation is defined as the relation of keyword pairs that co-occur in the sample documents (See Fig.3).

There are a lot of small, separate networks in the initial state of the dynamic thesaurus, which, initially, is identical to the static thesaurus. The use of co-occurrence relations in the dynamic thesaurus makes it possible to personalize the thesaurus by modifying the node weights and links. AIRS uses the dynamic thesaurus to generate associated keywords from the input keywords of a user.

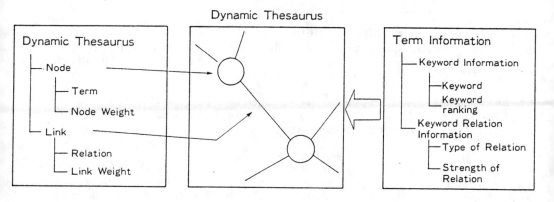

Fig. 2   Construction of The Dynamic Thesaurus
using Term Information

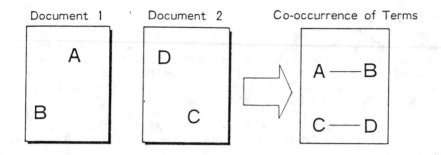

Fig. 3   Co-occurrence of Keywords
in Documents

2.3 Expected Effect of the AIRS System

The expected effects of AIRS are as follows:

(1) Associated keywords, which reflect the user's interest, are generated by the dynamic thesaurus.

(2) Both a high recall rate and a high precision rate are achieved by using these associated keywords for document retrieval.

(3) It is possible to use state transitions of the dynamic thesaurus to reflect a user's change of interest over time. Thus, document retrieval reflecting the user's prior interests is possible.

3. An Overview of the AIRS System

The general operating procedure of AIRS is described in this section. The configuration of the prototype system is shown in Fig.4. The system operates as follows.

Step 1. Term information is extracted au tomatically from the user's sample documents. Keywords, keyword ranking, and keyword co-occurrence information are extracted using the INDEXER system.[2]

Step 2. A static or traditional thesaurus is modified by term information to form the dynamic thesaurus. Links are generated and node ·weights are calculated while the dynamic thesaurus is being made.

Step 3. Associated keywords are generated from a user's input keyword using the dynamic thesaurus. The dynamic thesaurus starts with an input keyword and then selects associated keywords based on their node weights and links.

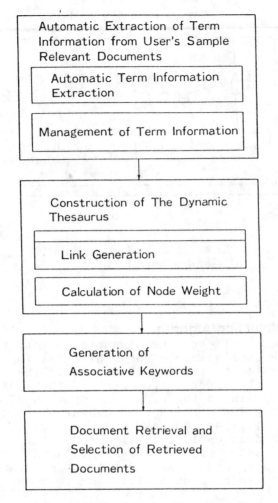

Fig. 4   AIRS Operating Procedure

Step 4.   Documents are retrieved using these associated keywords. Retrieved documents are ranked by using information in the dynamic thesaurus.

The following section describes each of these functions in detail.

4. Algorithms
4.1 Link Generation Algorithm
If two keywords occur in a document, links are generated between corresponding nodes in the dynamic thesaurus if no previous link exists between these two nodes (See Fig.5).

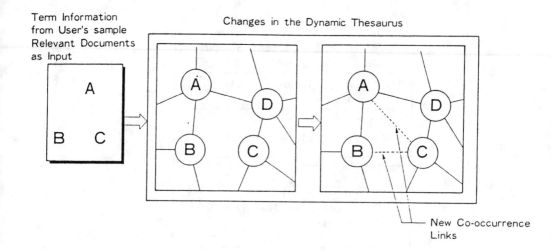

Term Information
from User's sample
Relevant Documents
as Input

Changes in the Dynamic Thesaurus

New Co-occurrence
Links

Fig. 5   Generation of Links

4.2 Node Weight Calculating Algorithm

Node weight reflects the importance of the keywords extracted from the user's sample documents. The importance of the keywords is calculated by the INDEXER system. The INDEXER system extracts and ranks keywords from each of the user's sample documents. Ranking is in the order of importance according to frequency and location in that document. In the formulas presented below, (1)-(4), D is the complete set of sample documents, and Ti denotes individual documents. Ki is the set of keywords extracted from Ti with the INDEXER system. KWij denotes individual keywords. Assume there are n documents and a total of m keywords in a document Ti; hence,

$$D = \{Ti\} \qquad (i=1,\ldots,n) \text{ and} \qquad (1)$$

$$Ki = \{KWij\} \qquad (j=1,\ldots,m). \qquad (2)$$

The importance of KWij to Ti is denoted as KI(ij). The value of KI(ij) is designed to decrease linearly as J, the ranking number, increases, and the sum of the value of KI(ij) (j=1 to m) equals one (for each i) for normalizing the importance; the closer the value of the keyword is to one, the more important the keyword is ranked. KI(ij) is calculated using formula (3):

$$KI(ij) = \frac{2TWi}{m*(m+1)}*(m+1-j), \qquad (3)$$

where TWi is the value given to Ti in D, and j is the ranking of KWij in Ti. TWi is calculated using the following formula:

232

$$TWi = \frac{DW}{n}, \qquad \text{(Constant)} \qquad (4)$$

where DW is the value of D given by a user.
After KI(ij) is calculated for each Ti, the node weight of node
1, denoted as NW1, is calculated as the sum of KI(ij) in D.

4.3 Associated Keyword Generation Algorithm

Associated keywords are intended to extend the keywords
inputted by the user. Associated keywords are obtained by
traversing the links and nodes of the dynamic thesaurus starting
with the node that corresponds to the user inputted keyword.
Hereafter, in this paper, the starting node is called the
"generation starting node," and the set of links and nodes
traversed in the associated keyword generation process is called
the "generation path." The traversing distance is defined as the
number of links traversed to generate an associated keyword. The
AIRS procedure for associated keyword generation is as follows:

Step 1: The traversing distance and the kinds of links to
traverse are preset. The threshold value of the node weight is
preset for selecting nodes, which are likely to be generated as
associated keywords. The distance between two nodes in the
dynamic thesaurus is defined as the number of links between those
two nodes.

Step 2: Starting from the generation starting node, acceptable
links are traversed up to the preset distance.

Step 3: All nodes in the generation path become candidates of
associated keywords.

Step 4: Among the candidate nodes, only those that have a node
weight larger than the threshold value are outputted as
associated keywords.

An example of the keyword generation process is given in
Fig.6. Assume that the traversing distance is set at three, that
all kinds of links can be traversed, and that the traversing is
limited to the enclosed area in Fig.6. The generation starting
node is node A. The generation path consists of nodes A, B, C,
and D, which also become candidate nodes. Finally, nodes A and
D, whose node weights are larger than the threshold value, are
selected as associated keywords.

5. Experimental Results

A prototype of AIRS was created. The configuration of the
prototype system is shown in Fig.7. An experiment was conducted
using this system. The results of this experiment are described
in the following sections as follows: First, the results of the
associated keyword generation are described in section 6. Then,
the results of the document retrieval process are described in
section 7.

233

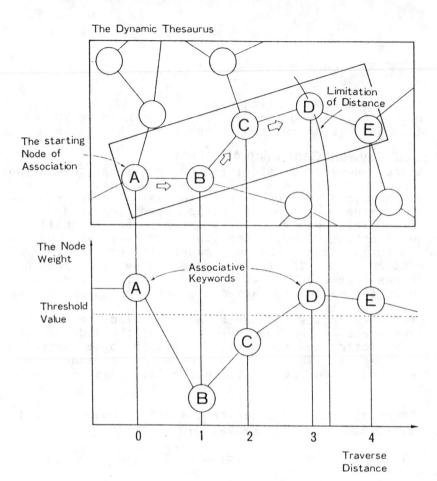

Fig. 6   Generation of
Associated Keywords
using links and node weight

6. Results of Associated Keyword Generation

Five newspaper articles were chosen as sample relevant documents for the experiment. These articles were then processed with the INDEXER system, which automatically extracts term information. A dynamic thesaurus was made from a static thesaurus and term information. Associated keywords generated from input keywords were evaluated against the keywords indexed in each relevant newspaper article. It was decided that if the associated keywords were a subset of the indexed keywords of a relevant document, then the associated keywords would be effective in

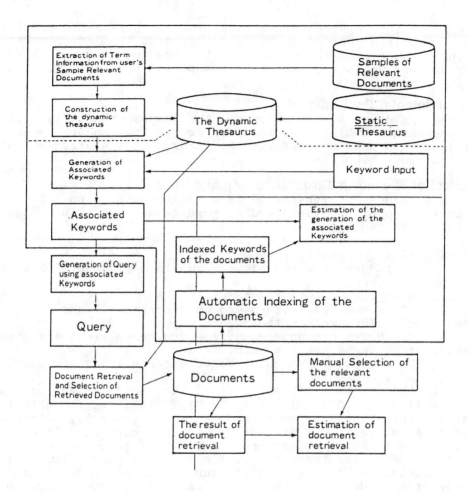

Fig. 7   Configuration of the AIRS Prototype

retrieving that document. The accuracy of associated keywords were measured by utilizing keyword recall rate and the keyword precision rate. Both a high keyword recall rate and a high keyword precision rate are necessary for accurate and effective document retrieval. The rates are defined as follows:

$$Kr = \frac{Nia}{Ni}, \text{ and}$$

$$Kp = \frac{Nia}{Na},$$

where Kr is the keyword recall rate; Kp is the keyword precision rate; Nia is number of the indexed keywords that are duplicated by the associated keywords; Ni is the number of indexed keywords; and Na is the number of associated keywords.

6.1 Experimental Environment

The prototype system processed the newspaper articles. Then, the thesaurus, which was made for retrieving these newspaper articles, was used as a static thesaurus. This static thesaurus contains about 8,000 terms.

6.2 Effect of Thesaurus Structure on Kp and Kr

Four kinds of thesauri were tested to find the most appropriate one for associated keyword generation. The thesauri tested are listed below.

Thesaurus A: The static thesaurus
   (Nodes are unweighed; no co-occurrence links are used)
Thesaurus B: The dynamic thesaurus
   (Nodes are weighed; no co-occurrence links are used)
Thesaurus C: The dynamic thesaurus
   (Nodes are unweighed; co-occurrence links are used)
Thesaurus D: The dynamic thesaurus
   (Nodes are weighed; co-occurrence links are used)

For all the dynamic thesauri the threshold value was set heuristically at 0.005. Table 1 and Fig.8 indicate the effect of each of these thesauri on Kp and Kr. At traversal distances greater than zero, Kr exceeds 70% if co-occurrence links are used. Kr is fairly constant and under 15% if co-occurrence links are not used or the traversal distance equals zero. Thus, links are very successful in accurately generating keywords. This is because the indexed keywords are extracted from those user relevant documents as one item in term information, and they are always linked with each other in the dynamic thesaurus. Thus, when one indexed keyword is inputted as a keyword, the other keywords which are indexed to the same document are always generated by traversing the links in the dynamic thesaurus.

Kp is about 30% to 50% when the thesaurus, whose nodes are weighed, such as B and D, are used, though Kp is 24% when only the input keywords are used. This means that the node weight is effective for improving Kp. Kp is highest for the type B thesaurus, where links are not used. This is because the type D thesaurus generates more and more keywords as the traversal distance increases. This suggests that the threshold value should increase with traversal distance.

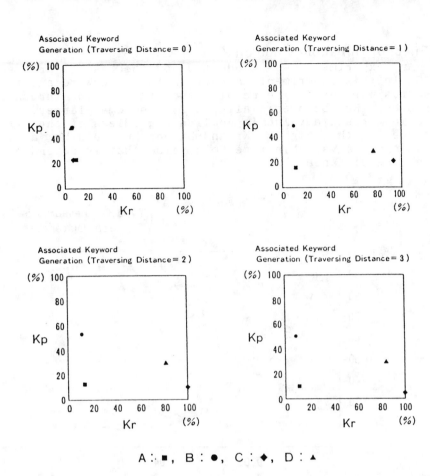

Associated Keyword
Generation (Traversing Distance= 0)

Associated Keyword
Generation (Traversing Distance= 1)

Associated Keyword
Generation (Traversing Distance= 2)

Associated Keyword
Generation (Traversing Distance= 3)

A ： ■ ， B ： ● ， C ： ◆ ， D ： ▲

Fig. 8　Relationships between various kinds of
Thesaurus Structures　(A, B, C, D) and
Associated Keyword Generation

. Table. 1　Effect of Thesaurus on Kr and Kp

Various Kinds of Thesaurus Structures	Usage of Generated Links	Usage of Node Weight	Traversing Distance							
			0		1		2		3	
			Kr	Kp	Kr	Kp	Kr	Kp	Kr	Kp
A : Static Thesaurus	✕	✕	9.60	24.00	12.82	15.24	14.36	12.68	12.95	10.10
B : Dynamic Thesaurus	✕	○	7.18	51.67	10.39	50.33	11.93	53.33	9.91	50.00
C : Dynamic Thesaurus	○	✕	9.60	24.00	94.00	21.78	100.00	9.28	100.00	5.81
D : Dynamic Thesaurus	○	○	7.18	51.67	77.08	29.18	83.08	28.85	83.38	28.85

6.3 Effect of Threshold Value on Kp and Kr

An experiment was conducted and the results are shown in Fig.9. In this experiment, a certain input keyword and the type D thesaurus were used. The results show that as the threshold value increases, Kr becomes smaller and Kp becomes larger. In AIRS, the same threshold value is applied regardless of the traversing distance. Both higher Kr and higher Kp could be achieved by introducing a variable threshold value that is dependent on the traversing distance.

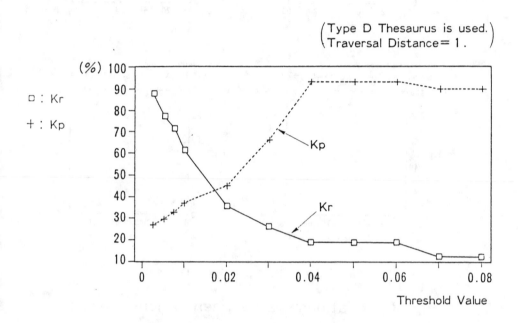

Fig. 9 Relationship between Threshold Value
and Document Retrieval

7. Results of Document Retrieval Using Associated Keywords

A document retrieval experiment was performed using the associated keywords generated by AIRS. The results of this experiment are described in this section.

7.1 Experimental Environment

The experiment used a database of 163 newspaper articles. The experiment was conducted three times. The different documents were retrieved in each time. The numbers of relevant documents used to extract term information are; three for the first experiment; five for the second experiment; three for the third experiment . Keywords were inputted by a user, and then the associated keywords were generated by AIRS as described in section 3. The document retrieval was performed using these associated keywords. The Boolean OR search strategy was adopted as a search strategy. Both a recall rate (Dr) and a precision rate (Dp) for the document retrieval were calculated. Three kinds of thesaurus structures were used in this experiment in order to find the most appropriate one among the three. They were the type A, C, and D thesauri. Two searchers attended the experiment.

7.2 Effect of Thesaurus Structure on Dr and Dp

An experiment was performed to find which type of thesaurus is most suited for document retrieval. The results of this experiment are shown in Fig.10 and Table 2. In Fig.10, the numbers attached to each point show which kind of thesaurus was used to get those particular data. The correspondence between the number and the type of thesaurus is as follows:

1: Thesaurus is not used.
2: Type A thesaurus is used.
3: Type C thesaurus is used.
4: Type D thesaurus is used.

The results show that when the type D thesaurus is used, both Dr and Dp are increased considerably. Thus, from the results of this experiment, the use of associated keywords generated by the type D thesaurus is the most effective for document retrieval.

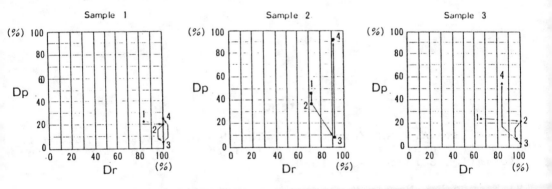

Fig. 10 The Relationship between various kinds of Thesaurus Structures and the corresponding results of document retrieval

Table. 2 Effect of Thesaurus on Dr and Dp

Various Kinds of Thesaurus Structures	Usage of Generated Links	Usage of Node Weght	Sample 1		Sample 2		Sample 3	
			Dr	Dp	Dr	Dp	Dr	Dp
1 : Retrieval Using only / User Input Keywords	—	—	83.33	20.83	72.73	47.06	66.67	28.00
2 : Static Thesaurus	×	×	100.00	20.00	72.73	38.10	100.00	24.00
3 : Dynamic Thesaurus	○	×	100.00	5.94	90.91	9.01	100.00	4.80
4 : Dynamic Thesaurus	○	○	100.00	24.00	90.91	90.91	83.56	55.56

8. Further Issues

The following are items that need to be researched in order to achieve higher Dr and Dp.

8.1 Construction of a Dynamic Thesaurus

8.1.1 Node weight calculating algorithm

The implemented system uses only the ranking of keywords, which are extracted from documents relevant to the user, as a means of measuring the importance of keywords. A more precise measurement would be possible if other information could be used such as keyword frequency, keyword location, syntactical information, and the time series information about a keyword.

8.1.2 Link generation and link weight calculating algorithm

The implemented system generates co-occurrence links whenever two keywords appear in the same relevant document. The generation of links should reflect the grammatical role of the keywords in the sentence, such as a subject-object relation. Furthermore, the link generation algorithm should generate various types of links, such as a cause-result link. Finally, all links should have a weight attached to them.

8.2 Associated Keyword Generation

During the traverse process in the dynamic thesaurus, the optimal node selection and optimal link selection should be calculated by using the node weight, the link weight, and so on.

References

[1] Hamill,K.A. and Zamora,A.: "The Use of Titles for Automatic Document Classification," Journal of the American Society for Information Science, Nov. 1980.

[2] Kimoto,H. Nagata,M. Kawai,A.:"Automatic Indexing System for Japanese Text," REVIEW of the Electrical Communications Laboratories, Vol.37, No.1, pp.51-56, 1989.

[3] Salton,G.: "Expert Systems and Information Retrieval," ASCM SIGIR Forum, Vol.21, No.3-4. 1987.

[4] Smeaton,A.F., Van Rijsbergen,C.J.: "Experiments on Incorporating Syntactic Processing of User Queries into a Document Retrieval Strategy," in Proceedings of the 11th ACM Conference on Research and Development in Information Retrieval, Presses Universitaires de Grenoble, pp31-51, 1988.

Knowledge based retrieval of office documents

Augusto Celentano[1], Maria Grazia Fugini[1,2], Silvano Pozzi[3]
[1] Dipartimento di Automazione Industriale, Università di Brescia
[2] Dipartimento di Elettronica, Politecnico di Milano
[3] CEFRIEL - Politecnico di Milano

Abstract

Document classification and retrieval systems for office applications require knowledge management to describe the semantics of documents related to procedural and domain dependent aspects of the office work to be described: operational dependencies, documents relationships and references to regulations and laws are concepts which are not explicitly stated in the text. This paper presents a semantic model for office documents classification and retrieval based on knowledge representation of the office procedural environment and of the application domain. Navigation along knowledge networks for document retrieval and browsing is described.

1. Introduction

Document management in office environments often relates the document contents to the procedures that manipulate the documents themselves and to the people who are involved in these procedures; classification and retrieval are based on the meaning and usage of documents, and require the support of knowledge about the operational aspects of the office and the embedding in the application domain. At first sight, meaning is coupled with the semantic properties described by the documents contents: some processing can be automatically driven by the text, with current technology, for narrow application domains [Hendrix 78, Croft 86, Salton 89]. Most of the document processing related to the classification and retrieval of documents, however, requires a deep insight into the information meaning, because the lexical and structural properties are not sufficient to reveal at the required level of accuracy the scope of a document in a given context, the relationships between a document and the procedures that manipulate it, the dependencies from the domain rules; in other words, the semantics of documents need to be represented in a broad and complex way if complex queries are to be supported by the retrieval system.

Procedural knowledge about the office system of which the document management system is a part, is useful to satisfy queries like "Retrieve the budget approval forms for projects carried by the Research Department during the last year". Documents are involved in a set of regulations and laws that belong to the application domain where the documents are located; *domain knowledge* is thus needed to satisfy queries like "Retrieve all documents to be completed to participate in a public competition".

In this paper, we address the issue of document retrieval based on document contents, on the office procedures that manipulate documents, and on the application knowledge. However, the retrieval system is kept centered around documents, that is, only documents are thoroughly represented in their structure and contents. All the other elements of the system are modeled to the minimum level required to retrieve documents. In the paper we present a document retrieval model that constitutes the basis for a system able to answer queries related to the application domain and to the procedural context where documents are used. We propose a knowledge based approach to document modelling and we give rationale for such a choice. In particular the retrieval model comprises three types of knowledge, namely: (1) knowledge about the structure of documents and about the relationships among documents (*static knowledge*), (2) knowledge about the relationships among the documents and the procedures which produce or use them (*procedural knowledge*), (3) knowledge about the relationships among documents and laws and regulations (either internal or external to the application domain) which constitute the theoretical and practical basis for document existence (*domain knowledge*).

1.1. Related work

In Information Retrieval systems knowledge based techniques are used in query processing, natural language understanding, text understanding and classification, to augment the identification of text contents. In RUBRIC [Mc Cune 85], production rules are used to map semantic concepts used for retrieval into text patterns. The goal of the system is to provide more automated and relevant access to unformatted textual databases. The idea of retrieval as an inference process is exploited in the OFFICER system [Croft 88], according to the approach proposed in [Van Rijsbergen 86]. Indeed the system treats retrieval as a process of plausible inference and uncertainty is part both of query specification and of the process of the query-document matching. The user is presented with a ranked list of documents satisfying his query, each document being labelled with a degree of relevance with respect to the presented information needs. Ranking strategies for documents are also described in [Gordon 88]: document descriptions are improved by repeatedly performing the description process basing on observation of the inquirers' requests. The idea of document re-description according to system adaptative capabilities of learning, for example using alternate search terms or modified relevance weights, has been variously investigated (for example in [Brauen 75] and [Furnas 85]).

In [Smith 89], a knowledge based system for bibliographic information retrieval is presented: a knowledge base describes topics within a certain domain, and a database describes the contents of documents according to these topics.

In some systems, a database supports document storage and retrieval, exploiting database mechanisms such as transaction management, back-up, concurrency control. In these systems, information in a document is seen as partially structured to simplify management and retrieval. An example is given in [Clifton 88], where basic search and retrieval capabilities of traditional information retrieval systems are coupled with database search mechanism: a document manipulation language is defined to query the document base, on which keyword indexes are constructed. In [Lynch 88], indexing techniques for document retrieval on top of the INGRES database system are described. Knowledge based classification of documents and automatic identification of the document conceptual structure is discussed in [Eirund 88].

In [Watters 89] the analogy between expert systems and retrieval systems is discussed: an information structure called concept space is introduced and a semantic model is defined to use the knowledge contained in this space. [Schwabe 90] presents a knowledge based browser that helps users to access a statistical database through a semantic model of the domain.

2. Rationale for knowledge based document modelling

Document retrieval aims at identifying documents whose contents match the meaning required by the user. From a logical point of view, the document retrieval process consists of the following steps:

* semantic document modelling, whiich produces the conceptual document;
* elaboration of user's information needs to formulate a query in terms of a set of semantic properties;
* match between the two semanticic representations to obtain the required documents.

In office environments, the relationships between document contents and semantics are often complex, since they heavily depend on how the documents are used, and on the reasons that justify them within specific procedures. In particular, in a document retrieval system two cases occur: (a) the semantics carried by a document is completely described by its contents, that is, the document alone is sufficient to identify its purpose and the role it plays in a specific office procedure; (b) the semantics carried by a document is mostly defined by its role in the office, by the relationships with other documents, and by the justifications provided by general rules such as regulations or law, information which is not contained in the document text.

The retrieval of information and documents in complex office environments relies in the two cases upon two different attitudes; both require identification of documents carrying a specific meaning, but the selection of documents according to their roles in the office, rather than according to the content alone, requires a description at the conceptual level of the environment where the documents are used. Therefore a wider scope document model is needed which enables to consider elements like procedures, agents, temporal events and to express relationships among such elements and the documents. Suggestions about the definition of a document retrieval model can come from the wide literature on office modelling [Newman 80, Pernici 89, Tsichritzis 85]. On the other hand we argue that a whole office model is not needed since, for example, an office model describes in detail the execution flow of procedures and the rules for their activation, which do not concern directly the processing of documents.

A formal representation of the concepts associated with the life and the evolution of the documents allows one to design document retrieval systems which overcome the limits of traditional information systems, that is, the inability to process in a uniform way and inside a unique information processing system queries or explorations related to different targets: *instances* of documents ("Retrieve all scientific paper about Information Retrieval and Office Systems"), *types* of documents ("What documents shall I submit to ask for a business trip"), document *usage context* ("Retrieve the procedure which has output the financial plan"). While they appear, from a design point of view, related to three distinct types of information systems, from the user point of view they are very similar.

An example is the identification of the documents that are necessary to exploit, say, a contract with the Public Administration. This search has two apparently similar but very different facets: if the search concerns a procedure to be executed, the target is a set of document *types* (since they must be filled in during the procedure execution), if the search concerns a specific procedure already completed, the target is a set of document *instances*. In the former case traditional information retrieval techniques are not sufficient; in fact, the search is closer to a database search (since the answer is a structured and short information, and concerns a domain, the types of the documents, which is classifiable in advance) or to an expert answering query system (if the office procedure involved is complex, and subjected to many logic constraints). The latter case can benefit of a knowledge based approach, because the knowledge about the relevance of a document as a component of a procedure can be described apart from the document itself. However, deep knowledge about why a document is used within a procedure is needed. Registration numbers or classification codes that usually link documents cannot always guarantee that all relevant documents will be retrieved; such tags are usually applied for classification reasons, and are unrelated to the deep knowledge about the document purpose; although supplementary tags can be used to include this information, the consequent growth of complexity of the resulting system seems inadequate to represent procedural contexts.

3. Knowledge representation for office document retrieval

The knowledge used by a system which aims at satisfying the document retrieval requirements above outlined can be classified in *static knowledge*, *procedural knowledge*, and *domain knowledge*. We call static the semantic information regarding the document types, the document contents, and the hierarchical relationships among document types and subtypes. We call procedural the knowledge about the office procedures, about their executors, and about elements (events) that trigger and halt the execution of the procedures. The application domain knowledge comprises the description of links between the documents and laws and regulations (either of the office and of the external world) which are part of the motivation for the existence of documents.

In the following of this section, we first present the elements of the document retrieval model; then, basing on this model, we present the static, procedural and domain knowledge used for document retrieval. As a reference example throughout the paper we will use the student application management system that supports the enrollment of students in the Master course of CEFRIEL[1]. The Master course is open to post-graduate

---

1   CEFRIEL is a research center supported by Industries, University and Public Administration in Milan.

students; as an exception, graduating students which have fulfilled their examinations can perform the graduation thesis at CEFRIEL. In order to join the Master course, an applicant must fill in a predefined applicant form, and forward this form to the secretarial office of CEFRIEL together with documents pertaining his/her curriculum and current employment. The arrival of applicant forms causes some dossiers to be opened which contain the documents presented by the applicant. Every applicant is examined by a Committee; students are ranked using the examination results and the curriculum: if the rank is satisfactory, the applicant is accepted (an admittance letter is sent to him/her), otherwise a non-acceptance letter communicates the rejection reasons. We focus our discussion on the interview phase of the enrollment: the candidate has to present a set of documents, is notified of an interview date, and the Committee eventually prepares a report of the interview with the evaluation of the candidates.

3.1 Document retrieval model

The basic elements of the document retrieval model are the following:

- document
- procedure
- agent
- event
- link.

These types are shown in figure 1 in a IS-A hierarchy of inheritance whose root element is the *object*. Document objects have properties describing their conceptually relevant portions. All the objects in the model belong to one type, types are instantiated through the *instance-of* link [Tsichritzis 82].

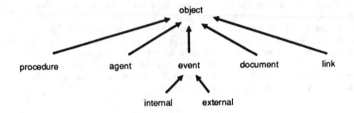

Fig. 1. Elements of the document retrieval model.

While the *document* element is described in detail in its contents and structure, all the other elements are represented in as much detail as is needed for the retrieval of documents. The *link* element is used to represent all the relationships that hold between elements of the model. Links connect pairs of elements of the model and have an attached semantics which is used for navigation in the model structures when retrieving documents. We have three types of links: *document, process* and *activity* link, discussed in the following sections.

3.1.1. Static knowledge

Any type of document in the office is modelled using a predefined set of basic objects (for example, document, letter, form and dossier) and exploiting typical class relationships (e.g. is-a, is-member, is-part relations) to establish classification hierarchies among documents in terms of specialization or membership. Any real document used in the office then results in an instance of a particular class. The properties of documents are structured according to basic constructs (e.g. part-of for the components, and set-of for repeated groups) that are drawn from the field of semantic modelling [Tsichritzis 82]. In figure 2, the IS-A hierarchy of documents used to model the reference example is depicted.

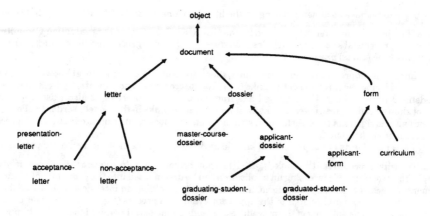

Fig. 2. IS-A hierarchy of documents used in the example.

Documents are inter-related through links. Figure 3 shows the link object and its specializations. In general, a link expresses a binary relationship between elements, has a direction, and a type.

Document links connect document pairs and represent relationships between document contents and structures, and between document types. Some predefined document links are shown in figure 3; they can be further specialized using the IS-A construct in order to be tailored to specific application environments.

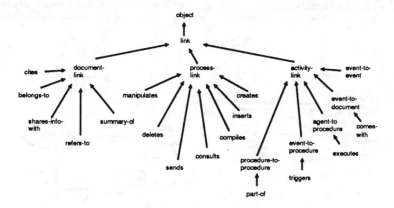

Fig. 3. The IS-A hierarchy of the *link* objects.

3.1.2. Procedural knowledge

The relationships among documents and the procedural properties associated to their meaning can be formalized through a network based model that shows how documents are created and accessed by office procedures, how events trigger the procedures, and who executes the procedures. This knowledge is called *procedural knowledge*, and allows users to retrieve documents basing on the life of documents in the Office System, that is, to answer queries like "Retrieve all documents forwarded by the CEFRIEL Secretary to the evaluation Committee".

The model of procedural knowledge includes *procedures*, *events* and *agents*. They are connected in a network through the link types called *process link* and *activity link*.

Process links connect procedures and documents, therefore bridging the procedural knowledge to the static knowledge. Considering the direction of the links to be from procedures to documents, figure 3 shows a sample set of predefined process links. The inverse links from documents to procedures also exist (e.g. is-input-of) although not shown in the figure; inverse links exist for all types of links in the model in order to allow a broader set of queries and navigations to be performed, such as "Retrieve documents that are input of the procedure of processing student applications".

Activity links put objects of the procedural knowledge in relation to each other, and more precisely:

- *procedures* with procedures: this link is used to split procedures into component phases or steps. For example, the procedure of processing an application can be decomposed into the procedure of examining the documents attached to the applicant form, in organizing and holding an interview with the applicant, and in preparing the documents related to the applicant evaluation process (e.g., rejection letter or opening of a student dossier). The splitting of the procedures depends on the detail required to classify documents, and is under the designer responsibility: the description of a procedure can proceed until the basic steps are reached. The basic type of link for performing this decomposition process is the *part-of* link. Other links between procedures model causal and temporal relationships between the execution of procedures.
- *events* with procedures: this link models the triggering of procedures by occurrence of events; events can be *internal* (they belong to the office environment) or *external* (they belong to the external world).
- *events* with events: this link models mainly temporal relationships (e.g., before, after, upon-completion) and causal relationships (e.g., derives-from, is-caused-by) between events.
- *agents* with procedures: this link represents the involvement of agents in the execution of procedures; in figure 3 the *executes* link is shown.
- *events* with documents: this link is intended to express the situation where an external event carries some documents with it, for example, the arrival of an applicant form at the CEFRIEL Secretarial Office; in figure 4, this event and the related document are shown as connected through the *comes-with* activity link.

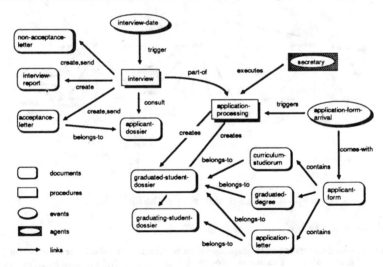

Fig. 4. The interview and application processing procedure.

Every type of link connects specific classes of entity, that is, every entity has a set of applicable links. Figure 4 shows a portion of the procedural knowledge related to our example (some document links are also shown, to illustrate the contents of some dossiers). The arrival of an application form is modeled by the *application-form-arrival* event which starts the enrollment procedure modelled by the *application-processing* procedure. This procedure is performed by the secretary and creates a *graduate-student-dossier* or a *graduating-student-dossier*. The *interview* node represents a procedure which is part of *application-processing*. The *interview-date* node represents an event. A sample external event is *application-form-arrival*, that represents the decision by a person to apply to the Master course. We model only the effect of such event on the office in terms of the triggering of the *application-processing* procedure. The documents involved in the interview procedure are connected to the procedures through process links.

3.1.3. Domain knowledge

The three levels of knowledge and the location of the model elements in these levels is shown in figure 5. The central region of the figure is the Document Retrieval System where static knowledge about documents is represented. The Office System region represents the procedural knowledge and contains procedures, internal events (e.g., the decision of holding an interview on a certain date), and agents (roles of office workers who create, manipulate, send, edit documents). Links connect documents in the Document region and connect elements of the procedural knowledge in the Office System region. Links also connect the Document Retrieval System and the Office System.

In the External World region, the application domain knowledge is represented through *external events* and *rules*. Activity links connect the External World and the Office System; the activity links used here are the event-to-procedure and the event-to-event links. The rules of the application domain are of two types:

- general rules
- navigation rules.

General rules concern the role of documents both in the procedural context of the office and in the context of laws and regulations of the external World. They contribute to the description of the meaning, role, motivation, and constraints of documents and of document relationships in the office. These rules are used as euristics that restrict the search of the documents relevant to a query.

Using a production rule approach, which seems suitable to describe relationships and constraints among concept, general rules describe cause-effect dependencies, implication, generalization, exclusion. Such dependencies can be established in a simple and consistent way also among concepts stated in documents which are not directly connected in the network.

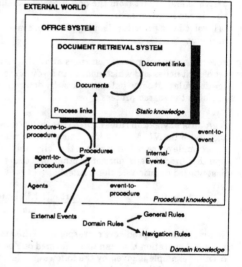

Fig. 6. Levels of knowledge for document retrieval.

An example of general rule is the rule stating the conditions under which an applicant can receive a scholarship for his Master fees: the applicant's age must be less than 25 and he must be unemployed, that is

$$\frac{applicant(X) \text{ and } age(X,A) \text{ and } less\text{-}than(A,25) \text{ and } unemployed(X)}{can\text{-}receive(X,scholarship)} \tag{1}$$

The predicate *unemployed(X)* means that X must certificate he/she is unemployed; this constrains the *applicant-form* document to contain a certificate of unemployment. This rule concerns the documents which must be provided by the applicant, and it can be seen as a link to a more general law which governs the issue of scholarships. A query where this rule is useful is the following:

"Which documents must be provided by a Master student?".

A simple but common example of retrieval based on operational meaning is to find all documents which must be processed to complete a specific procedure, such as a store inventory; all the documents whose usage is dictated by operative rules and regulations must be retrieved, although they do not mention the store inventory problem at all. Another example regards the update of documents in order to conform to the variations of laws and regulations: general rules allow one to retrieve documents which must be revised because a specific law has changed (this problem has been addressed in [Celentano 88] in the domain of automated document generation); the influence of a law on the set of documents handled in an office is far from being straightforward, especially in contexts inspired by principles of law rather than by specific detailed regulations.

Navigation rules are used for traversing the semantic network during the search process. These rules are the basis for selecting the next node in the knowledge network, starting form the current node. Nodes are connected in the network of the model through several types of links and, in general, from one node, links of various types need to be examined in order to satisfy a query. For example, a document node:

* belongs to a IS-A hierarchy, that puts its structure in relation with the structure of parent nodes;
* is part of a set of document links, that show the relationship of the document with other documents. Links arrive to and depart from the document: depending on the type of query, arriving and/or departing nodes should/can be examined;
* is involved in a procedural and application context that shows how the document is manipulated, by whom, and why.

In processing a query, navigation rules allow the retrieval system to decide which nodes can be considered in the set of next nodes and which nodes can be discarded because not relevant in the context of the current query. Navigation rules cut some paths of search by determining which nodes can be explored, and which of these nodes are useful in the search process.

A group of navigation rules express the *transitivity* of links, that is, given three nodes $N1, N2, N3$, connected through two links $N1$--$N2$, $N2$--$N3$, this group of rules is oriented to the computation of the link $N1$--$N3$.

An example of transitivity rule is the following, which says that if a document D is involved in a procedure $P1$, and this procedure is part of another procedure $P2$, then the document is involved also in $P2$ (we use a predicate-based notation for these rules):

$$\frac{\text{part-of(P1,P2) and manipulates(P1,D)}}{\text{manipulates(P2,D)}} \tag{2}$$

The *manipulates* predicate corresponds to the *manipulates* process link (see figure 3) which expresses the most general operation that can be performed on documents.

Another example is given by the following rule, which establishes a relationship between the executors of the procedures and the transitivity between components of procedures:

$$\frac{\text{part-of(P1,P2) and executes(X,P2) and not inhibited(X,P1)}}{\text{executes(X,P1)}} \tag{3}$$

where the *inhibited(X,P1)* predicate specifies that an agent X cannot execute procedure $P1$. In our example of figure 4, let us suppose that the following fact exists:

$$\text{inhibited(secretary,interview).} \tag{4}$$

This fact specifies that the secretary agent is not involved in the manipulation of documents related to the interview process. Using this fact, rule (3) above allows the retrieval system to skip some nodes in the search because excluded by this rule.

The following transitivity rule:

$$\frac{\text{executes}(X,P1) \text{ and manipulates}(P1,D) \text{ and authorized}(X,D)}{\text{manipulates}(X,D)} \quad (5)$$

states that agents are involved in the manipulation of all the documents relating to a procedure only if authorized to do so. Rule (5) states that the transitivity of the operations performed by agent X on the document D through an office procedure $P1$ is restricted to the authorizations of X for D. For example, if the following fact does not hold in the network of figure 4:

$$\text{authorized}(\text{secretary, curriculum-studiorum}) \quad (6)$$

the *secretary* agent is prevented from accessing the *curriculum-studiorum* document during the execution of the *application-processing* procedure.

Another group of navigation rules is oriented to stating the *order* of link processing by the system during a search. The search ordering is dynamically determined on the basis of the query terms, that is, of the terms contained in the query that are abstracted from the query through a query parser. Rules that establish the search order within each of the above classes can also be given. Search ordering rules highly depend on the system usage experience and should be varied under the control of a system administrator.

4. Retrieving Documents

The retrieval process identifies a mapping from a set of concepts contained in the user query, to a set of initially unknown documents. Relating to the semantic network which describes the document environment, the process is described by the following schema:

$$\text{Query} = \text{Starting Node(s)} = \text{Target Node(s)}$$

The Target Node is a (set of) document(s). The Starting Node is a (set of) entry point(s) in the network, that is, nodes that are directly identifiable in the phase of query parsing through their names. Starting nodes can be documents as well as other node types. Query processing is executed as a *navigation* along the three levels of knowledge of figure 5; navigation rules and general rules are used as search euristics.

4.1 Query Processing

As an example of query processing, let us consider the following query:

"Retrieve all documents used by the secretary for processing an incoming applicant request".

The retrieval process should return the set of documents connected to the *application-processing* node of figure 4 through process links, and the *applicant-form*. The documents used in the interview procedure should not be returned: we suppose that fact (4) mentioned in Sect. 3.1.3 holds and therefore the secretary does not take part in the interview procedure. The steps of the query processing are the following:

a) Query parsing. This step abstracts relevant terms from the query using a system thesaurus. The illustration of this step is beyond the purpose of this paper; we suppose that the terms:

secretary
applicant-form

are abstracted (applicant-form is found as a synonym of applicant request). Used by in the query is interpreted as a synonym of the inverse link manipulated-by, referring to the most general operations performed by a procedure onto documents.

249

b) IS-A network examination. The terms abstracted from the query are matched against the IS-A network of static knowledge in order to identify their types. For the terms of our query, the following result is returned:

```
secretary -> agent
applicant-form -> document
```

These matching terms become Starting Nodes of the query in the network.

c) Agent-to-procedure links examination. Since this query is procedure oriented because it contains an agent as a Starting Node, activity links departing from the *secretary* node are examined. The node *application-processing* is determined as the next node and reached. Because of rules (2) and (3), and of fact (4) above, the process link *part-of* between *interview* and *application-processing* is inhibited: therefore, the document links departing from the *interview* node will not be taken into account in the search.

d) Procedure-to-document links examination. The documents connected to *application-processing* are reached, namely the *graduated-student-dossier* and the *graduating-student-dossier.* These two documents are marked by the system as belonging to the retrieval set.

e) Examination of the applicant-form Starting Node. The Starting Node *applicant-form* and the links connected to it are taken into account. Because of the chain of links *comes-with* and *triggers*, *applicant-form* is an input of *application-processing* according to the following rule:

$$\frac{\text{comes-with}(Ev,D) \text{ and triggers}(Ev,P)}{\text{is-input-of}(P,D)} \qquad (7)$$

where D is a document, Ev is an event, and P is a procedure. The transitivity rule (5) causes the *applicant-form* to be inserted in the retrieval set.

The document links departing from applicant-form (*contains* links) are then traversed, leading to the three documents shown in figure 4. From these documents, the links *belongs-to* depart, leading to the dossiers which have already been marked in step d) as belonging to the retrieval set; therefore, the query terminates.

Another group of rules is used to determine the conditions applying to links according to the logical conditions that regulate the execution of the procedures. An example is given in figure 4 by the *application-processing* procedure; this procedure creates two dossiers, depending on the characteristics of the applicant (whether he/she holds a degree or is still a student):

$$\frac{\text{contains}(\text{applicant-form, graduated-degree, Person})}{\text{graduated}(\text{Person})} \qquad (8)$$

$$\frac{\text{graduated}(\text{Person})}{\text{creates}(\text{application-processing,graduated-student-dossier,Person})} \qquad (9)$$

$$\frac{\text{not graduated}(\text{Person})}{\text{creates}(\text{application-processing,graduating-student-dossier,Person})} \qquad (10)$$

4.2 Navigation Tool

The examples given in this section provide an idea of the use of navigation rules. In general, the process of retrieval proceeds by examining the entry points in the network and applying navigation rules and general rules to select relevant nodes and to progressively refine the retrieved set of documents. The retrieval process is a back-and-forth mechanism involving all the three levels of knowledge, that exploits both the semantics of links and the navigation rules.

The link object is the basis of the navigation process in the semantic networks. This navigation is performed by a Navigation Tool whose basic functionalities have been presented in [Celentano 89]. In order to answer a query, the Navigation Tool traverses the knowledge network searching for interesting nodes and determines, from one node, the links to be traversed in order to reach nodes that are relevant to solve the query. The

Navigation Tool manages also a user interface based on a browsing paradigm where the user is provided with a set of mechanisms for network visualization, orientation in the network, query history, search path recording.

The links carry much of the semantics necessary to explore the network nodes and to get orientation in the network ([Schwabe 90]). The link object has the following properties:

type   one of the types shown in figure 3
inverse   name of the inverse link type
status   traversed, to be traversed, being traversed, selected
presentation   graphical representation properties

The *status* property is used to distinguish among the actions that can be undertaken by the Navigation Tool, depending on the status of the links that are connected (depart or arrive) to the current node of the network. In particular, the *selected* value of the status means that the information associated to a link has been considered interesting by the user and therefore moved to a working area for further processing.

The *presentation* property describes how the link appears on the screen, according to its type. For example, IS-A links are shown by displaying the parent and the children objects: the presentation property describes the number of descendants in the IS-A hierarchy that are to be shown, how to see the parents and children properties, which information is maintained on the screen when scrolling up and down the hierarchy. Default presentations are given for predefined link types; however, the mechanism should be flexible enough to allow the system administrators to define the presentation modes for new link types.

4.3 User modeling

The system efficency may be improved by some considerations about the characteristics of the users interacting with the system. Work on user modeling employs, for instance, user stereotypes activated by questions [Croft 87b] to build views of the domain knowledge. The basic assumption, underlying also the work presented in [Belkin 87, Croft 87a] is that each end-user generally has an individual perspective of the application domain; studies focus on how the user can best describe this knowledge and how the system can take advantage of this knowledge.

Our approach, evaluated in the earliest phase of the research when the overall system architecture was designed, is to use a knowledge base of user profiles in order to instantiate a query environment. A user profile is manily based on:

- the user role in the office system and
- the query history kept by the system along search sessions (a query history record is kept up-to-date according to the user actions, such as saving a set of documents resulting from a query).

A possible approach to follow in the construction and dynamic update of the user profiles knowledge base has been presented in [Schreiber 89]; the inclusion of this issues in our prototype implementation is scheduled for the next implementation activities.

5. Implementation notes and concluding remarks

A knowledge based document model satisfies the stated requirements of document retrieval systems, covering a broad spectrum of situations typical of office environments. Beyond the information retrieval applications, additional benefits are gained in terms of understandability and uniformity of representation. The reasoning based on implication and logic inference allows one to approach the problem of identifying documents, procedures, and operational requirements in a uniform way: the retrieval of documents needed for completing a specific dossier, of documents to be issued before a specific date, of documents concerning a specific topic, are several facets of a unique semantic characterization which focuses, in different cases, the procedural, operational or informative meaning.

A prototype implementation of the model is currently carried on as part of the Master Course in the Office Automation Area of CEFRIEL, with the partnership of Bull HN. The implementation is still at an early stage, also due to the educational role associated with it. The project will take two years: in the current year the implementation has been restricted to the general framework of the model and to the definition of the browsing interface; the next activities will be focused on the implementation of the automatic processing of queries and retrieval.

The implementation is based on a system, developed by Bull, called KOOL (Knowledge Object Oriented Language), which is a Lisp based environment for development of knowledge management systems. KOOL runs on 386 based personal computers under the MS-Windows run-time system, thus providing a confortable and powerful graphical user interface. Following the object-oriented paradigm, KOOL provides constructs for defining hierarchies of classes and instances, and incorporates a rule-based inference engine which can be triggered by creation or modification of objects, allowing modeling of general relationships among objects.

The general framework of the system uses the basic constructs of KOOL to define classes and metaclasses for the predefined objects of the model: documents, agents, activities and events. Links are defined as object attributes, and methods are used to assure the consistency of inverse links.

Acknowledgments

We would like to thank the persons involved in the research activity of the Office Automation Area at CEFRIEL. Namely, G. Frigerio and A. Momigliano from Bull HN contributed to the development of the model and provided support to the KOOL programming environment. The students S. Camuffo, M. G. Carenzi, P. Gattoni, M. Lazzaretto of the Office Automation Area contributed to the definition of the model through a deep analysis of the CEFRIEL office environment: the example described in this paper has been extracted from their work. They are currently engaged in the prototype implementation.

References

[Belkin 87] N. Belkin and W.B. Croft, "Retrieval techniques", Annual Review of Information Science, M.E. Williams, Elsevier Publishers, n. 22, 1897

[Bertino 88] E. Bertino, F. Rabitti, and S. Gibbs, "Query processing in a multimedia document system", ACM Trans. on Office Information Systems, 6, 1, 1988

[Brauen 75] T. Brauen, "Document vector modification" in G. Salton, SMART Retrieval System Experiments in Automatic Document Processing, Prentice-Hall, 1975

[Brodie 84] Brodie M., Mylopolous J., Schimdt H.J., "On Conceptual Modeling: Perspectives from Artificial Intelligence, Databases, and Programming Languages", Springer-Verlag, 1984

[Celentano 88] A. Celentano, P. Paolini, "Knowledge Based Document Generation", in W. Lamersdorf (editor), Office Knowledge: Representation, Management and Utilization, Elsevier Science Publ. Co., North-Holland, 1988

[Celentano 89] A. Celentano, M.G. Fugini, S. Pozzi, "Semantic Retrieval of Documents: a Framework for a Knowledge-based System", AICA Conference, Trieste, 1989

[Clifton 88] C. Clifton, H. Garcia-Molina, and R. Hagmann, "The design of a document database", Princeton Univ., Dept. of Comp. Sc. Int. Rep. CS-TR-177-88, 1988

[Croft 86] W. B. Croft, "User specific domain knowledge for document retrieval", Proc. ACM Conf. on Research and Development in Information Retrieval, Pisa, 1986

[Croft 87a] W.B. Croft, "Approaches to intelligent information retrieval", Information Processing and Management, vol. 23, n. 4, 1987

[Croft 87b] W.B. Croft and R. Thompson, "I^{3}R: A new approach to the design of document retrieval systems", Journal of the American Society for Information Science, n. 38, 1987

[Croft 88] W. B. Croft, R. Krovetz, "Interactive retrieval of office documents", *Proc. ACM-IEEE Conf. on Office Information Systems*, Palo Alto, 1988

[Eirund 88] H. Eirund, K. Kreplin, "Knowledge Based Document Classification Supporting Integrated Document Handling", *Proc. ACM Conference on Office Information Systems*, Palo Alto, 1988

[Furnas 85] G.W. Furnas, "Experience with an adaptive indexing scheme", *Proc. ACM-SIGCHI Conf. on Human Factors in Comp. Sytems.*, S. Francisco, 1985

[Gordon 88] M. Gordon, "Probabilistic and genetic algorithms in document retrieval", *Comm. ACM*, 31, 10, 1988

[Hendrix 78] G. G. Hendrix, E. D. Sacerdoti, D. Sagalowicz, J. Slown, "Developing a natural language inteerface to complex data", *ACM Trans. on Database Systems*, 3, 2, 1978

[Lynch 88] C.A. Lynch, M. Stonebraker, "Extended user-defined indexing with application to textual databases", *Proc. 14th VLDB Conf.*, Los Angeles, 1988

[Marchionini 88] G. Marchionini, and B. Schneiderman, "Finding facts vs. browsing knowledge in hypertext systems", *IEEE Computer*, 1, 1988

[Mc Cune 85] B. P. Mc Cune, R. M. Tong, J. Dean, D. G. Shapiro, "RUBRIC: A System for Rule-Based Information Retrieval", *IEEE Transactions on Software Engineering*, SE-11, 9, 1985

[Newman 80] W. M. Newman, "Office models and office systems design", in N. Naffah (editor), Integrated Office Systems, *Nort-Holland*, 1980

[Peckham 88] J. Peckham, and F. Maryanski, "Semantic data models", *ACM Comp. Surveys*, 20, 3, 1988

[Pernici 89] B. Pernici, A.A. Verrijin-Stuart (editors), "Office Information Systems: the design process", *North-Holland*, 1989

[Salton 89] G. Salton, "Automatic Text Processing", *Addison Wesley*, 1989

[Schreiber 89] F.A. Schreiber, F. Barbic and S. Madeddu, "Dynamic user profiles and flexible queries in office document retrieval systems", Decision Support Systems, vol. 5, n. 1, Marzo 1989

[Schwabe 90] D. Schwabe, E. E. Mizutani, "A knowledge based browser to access complex databases", submitted to the *International Conference on Extending Database Technology*, Venice, March 1990

[Smith 89] P. J. Smith, S. J. Shute, D. Galdes, "Knowledge-based search tactics for an intelligent intermediary system", *ACM Trans. on Office Information Systems*, 7, 3, 1989

[Tsichritzis 82] D. C. Tsichritzis, F. Lochowsky, "Data Models", *Prentice-Hall*, 1982

[Tsichritzis 85] D. C. Tsichritzis (editor), "Office Automation - Concepts and Tools", *Springer Verlag*, 1985

[Van Rijsbergen 86] C.J. Van Rijsbergen, "A non-classical logic for information retrieval", *Computer Journal*, 29, 1986

[Watters 89] C. R. Watters, "Logic framework for information retrieval", *Journ. of the American Soc. for Information Science*, 40, 5, 1989

Evaluation of an Expert System for Searching in Full Text

by

Susan Gauch

Department of Computer Science
Wellesley College
Wellesley, MA 02181

ABSTRACT

This paper presents a prototype expert system which provides online search assistance. The expert system automatically reformulates queries, using an online thesaurus as the source of domain knowledge, and a knowledge base of domain-independent search tactics. The expert system works with a full-text database which requires no syntactic or semantic pre-processing. In addition, the expert system ranks the retrieved passages in decreasing order of probable relevance.

Users' search performance using the expert system was compared with their search performance on their own, and their search performance using the online thesaurus. The following conclusions were reached: 1) The expert system significantly reduced the number of queries necessary to find relevant passages compared with the user searching alone or with the thesaurus. 2) The expert system produced marginally significant improvements in precision compared with the user searching on their own. There was no significant difference in the recall achieved by the three system configurations. 3) Overall, the expert system ranked relevant passages above irrelevant passages.

1 INTRODUCTION

1.1 Online Search Difficulty

Information systems are undergoing a technological revolution. Massive quantities of online text are being produced using optical character recognition hardware, word processors, and computer publishing software. These large full-text databases, or *textbases*, are being stored and distributed on optical storage media. End-users are searching online databases themselves, with the use of personal workstations and modems. Soon, the inability of end-users to search effectively will be the main roadblock to the wide-spread use of online textbases.

Christine Borgman [Borgman, 1986] identifies two types of knowledge necessary to search: knowledge of the mechanical aspects of searching, and knowledge of the conceptual aspects. She concludes that whereas system mechanics are rarely a problem for any but very inexperienced and infrequent users, even experienced searchers have significant problems with search strategy and output performance. Similarly, Carol Fenichel [Fenichel, 1981] finds that even experienced searchers could improve their search results by using more system interaction to iterate their search.

Studies of inexperienced searchers find even more problems with search strategy. In one study [Borgman, 1987], a quarter of the subjects were unable to pass a benchmark test of minimum searching skill. Another experiment [Oldroyd, 1984] found that novices find some relevant documents easily, but they fail to achieve high recall and are unable to reformulate queries well.

David Blair [Blair and Maron, 1985] paints an even bleaker picture for searching full-text databases. Lawyers searching a legal database achieved only 20% recall, although they were attempting to do a high recall search. The factors, as identified by the authors, leading to this poor performance were poor searching technique, stopping the query iteration too soon, and the inability to search on inter-document relationships.

1.2 Research Overview

My goal is to demonstrate that an expert system can improve a novice searcher's retrieval from full-text databases. To this end, I have developed a expert system which automatically reformulates user queries and ranks the retrieved passages. The expert system incorporates a knowledge base of domain-independent search tactics, ranking rules, and has access to an online thesaurus.

1.3 Related Research

Bibliographic Expert Systems

Steven Pollitt [Pollitt, 1984] built an expert system to search the MEDLINE medical database for cancer literature. The knowledge base is tailored for the specific database queried. Peretz Shoval [Shoval, 1985] has developed an expert system which uses the users' initial search terms to identify nodes in a semantic network of search terms. The links from these nodes are used to identify new, potentially relevant, search terms. These new terms are given strength ratings and suggested to the user as possible alternative search terms. IR-NLI II [Brajnik et al, 1988] incorporates user modelling into a domain-independent bibliographic retrieval expert system. IOTA [Chiaramella and Defude, 1987] is a bibliographic expert system which incorporates a natural language interface. PLEXUS [Vickery and Brooks, 1987] is an expert system designed to help novice users find information about gardening. Natural language queries are accepted, and information is extracted to fill in frames.

Each of latter four systems uses an online classification of terms, similar to a thesaurus, as the source of domain knowledge. However, only PLEXUS and IOTA incorporate strategies to automatically reformulate queries, although that is not the main focus of those systems.

Full-Text Expert Systems

Fewer projects are aimed at providing intelligent assistance for full-text searching. One such system is RUBRIC [Tong et al, 1987], which has the user describe his query in terms of rules. These rules describe the domain knowledge for the system as a hierarchy of topics and subtopics.

I3R [Croft and Thompson, 1987] also requires the user to provide the appropriate domain knowledge. The query process is managed as a dialogue between the user and the system during which the user is asked to supply a semantic network, similar to a thesaurus, that describes the relationships among the concepts in his query. A full-text system that incorporates query reformulation assistance is under development at OCLC [Teskey, 1987]. The emphasis to date has been on provision of an intelligent online help function, but a few basic reformulation strategies are provided. The CODER system [Fox, 1988] incorporates natural language processing with expert systems techniques to produce a testbed for evaluating advanced information retrieval techniques. The expert system is used to identify the structure within electronic mail messages, and semantic relationships between messages.

Searching Studies

The most thorough catalogue of search tactics was compiled by Marcia Bates [Bates, 1979]. She outlined 29 search tactics in four areas: monitoring, file structure, search formulation, and term manipulation. Philip Smith [Smith, P. J. et al, 1989] conducted a similar study as the first step to building an online search intermediary for searching the environmental literature of Chemical Abstracts. By analysing the discourses and actions of 17 users and search intermediaries, he compiled a list of 19 search tactics. P. W. Williams [Williams, 1984] developed a model of all possible search situations and all possible responses, to be used as the basis of an expert system's knowledge base.

2 SYSTEM DESCRIPTION

The prototype search assistant system was implemented on a Sun3 workstation. It consists of five modules:

1) MICROARRAS [Smith et al, 1987], which serves as the full-text search and retrieval engine

2) a full-text database of over 188,000 words, containing a draft of "Computer Architecture, Volume 1 - Design Decisions" [Blaauw and Brooks, 1986]

3) a hierarchical thesaurus of approximately 7424 words specific to the textbase's domain

4) an expert system of 85 OPS83 rules and over 5,000 lines of C code, which interprets the user's queries, controls the search process, analyses the retrieved text, and ranks the search results

5) a user interface, which accepts the user's queries, presents requests for information from the expert system, and displays the search results.

The search process consists of a dialogue between the user and the expert system. The user enters the initial Boolean query and the number of passages he would like to retrieve. The query is parsed and translated into a request for information from MICROARRAS. MICROARRAS retrieves text passages from the full-text database and informs the expert system of the number of passages that satisfy the request. The expert system compares the number retrieved with the target number to decide how to reformulate the query.

To expand a search query, the expert system may use three different strategies, alone or in combination. First, it can expand individual search terms to the sets of words using the thesaurus. Words with the same stem, synonyms, broader, narrower, and similar words can be added iteratively. Second, it can relax contextual constraints. Since MICROARRAS provides considerable generality in terms of segmental contexts, search expressions may contain contextual parameters expressed in terms of any number of words, sentences, paragraphs, etc. to either the right or left of any term in the search expression. Thus, the expert system can increase the default number or type of such units to generate more potential hits. Finally, it can change the Boolean operators, making the query less restrictive by replacing ANDs with ORs or removing ANDNOTs.

To restrict a search, the expert system uses the same strategies as those described above, but in reverse. That is, it may add sets of search terms to those terms to be excluded from the retrieval passages, contract contexts, and replace ORs with ANDs. Changing the Boolean operators in this way will reduce the number of passages retrieved, in general, however, it is only likely to be useful when the user has used the incorrect Boolean operator in the original query.

Once an appropriate number of passages is identified, the expert system attempts to rank the passages in terms of probable relevance. It does this by performing a rudimentary content analysis on the passages retrieved by MICROARRAS and computing a relevance index for each. The relevance index for each passage is a function of the number of search terms actually found in that passage, the number of distinct types for each (for terms that are sets), and the number of different thesaural categories represented. Query structure, distance between search terms, and frequency of the search terms in the textbase as a whole are also taken into consideration. The retrieved passages are then sorted by their relevance indices and presented to the user in order of probable interest.

A major advantage of this architecture is the separation of strategic knowledge, contained in the knowledge base for the expert system, from domain knowledge, contained in the thesaurus. Now that the search strategy rules have been developed and tested with the existing textbase, the expert system can be tested with other content domains by simply providing a suitable thesaurus for the new textbase.

For a more complete description of the system's architecture and search strategies, see [Gauch and Smith J. B., 1989a]. In addition, [Gauch, and Smith, J. B., 1989b] contains a description of the implementation of the search strategies as rules in a knowledge base, and [Gauch, 1989] contains a complete description of the entire research project.

3 EVALUATION

Evaluating an interactive system is difficult. Jean Tague [Tague and Schultz, 1988] has defined a framework for evaluating information retrieval system interfaces. She identified three ways to measure the information retrieval system: informativeness, time, and user friendliness. Informativeness is measured by retrieval output (search effectiveness) and retrieval order (ranking). The search efficiency of the system is related to Tague's time factor. Finally, the user friendliness of the system can be evaluated by a post-search questionnaire.

My primary goal is to demonstrate that using an expert system to reformulate queries can improve search performance for novice searchers. Ideally, both their effectiveness and efficiency would be improved. The second, less important, goal is to show that the expert system can rank the retrieved passages in decreasing order of relevance.

To evaluate the expert system, subjects attempted to find relevant passages in response to high-level questions. They queried MICROARRAS with three interfaces with different capabilities: an interface whose only function was to accept contextual Boolean queries and display search results; a similar interface which also allowed the user to explore the online thesaurus; and a third which incorporated the searching expert system. Each subject's search performance with the three interfaces was monitored and compared.

3.1 Hypotheses

Hypothesis 1: The expert system improves the search effectiveness for a novice searcher.

Hypothesis 2: The expert system improves the search efficiency for a novice searcher.

Hypothesis 3: The expert system can rank the passages retrieved by the search in decreasing order of relevance.

The effectiveness of the retrieval output is evaluated by looking at recall (the number of relevant items found / the total number of relevant items in the database) and precision (the number of relevant items retrieved / the number of items retrieved). Two estimates of the number of relevant items retrieved are examined: the number of passages the users mark as relevant and the number of passages retrieved from the set of passages deemed relevant by the author.

The efficiency of the systems is measured by the number of Boolean queries the subjects entered for each of several high-level questions, and by the amount of time they spent searching for relevant passages for each question.

The ranking algorithm was evaluated by comparing the order of appearance of relevant passages after they have been ranked with a random order of appearance.

3.2 Method

Subjects

Twelve computer science graduate students participated as subjects in the study. All subjects were knowledgeable in the use of computers, but unfamiliar with online searching. Thus, they were representative of the anticipated users of future information retrieval systems.

Apparatus

Information Retrieval Systems

The *user-alone* configuration consisted of a Sun 3 running MICROARRAS and a rudimentary expert system. This expert system performed only the system control function, and did no query reformulation or ranking of retrieved passages. The user was prompted for a contextual Boolean query, this query was sent to MICROARRAS, and the number of passages retrieved was reported back to the user. The user could display the passages retrieved, if there were fewer than 25, or try another query.

The *user-thesaurus* version consisted of a Sun 3 with one window running MICROARRAS, as in the user-alone system, and a second window running a thesaurus access function. In the thesaurus window the user had access to all the thesaurus information available to the expert system. He could find out the stemname for a specific word's stemgroup. For any stemname, he could ask for the stemnames of the corresponding synonym, parent, sibling, or child stemgroups. These stemnames could be used in the user's query to MICROARRAS.

In the *user-expert system* version the user did not have access to the online thesaurus. Context and the addition of stemgroups were controlled by the expert system. Thus, the user entered a Boolean query and a target number of passages and the expert system reformulated the user's query to attempt to get close to the target number. The user was prompted to filter search terms found in the thesaurus, and to continue or abandon the current reformulation.

To keep the response time approximately the same as for the other two configurations it was necessary to run MICROARRAS remotely on the Sun 4 file server containing the textbase. The user worked with one window on a Sun 3 which ran the full version of the query reformulation expert system. The expert system communicated with MICROARRAS over the network. This setup was approximately twice as fast as when MICROARRAS was run on the user's Sun 3. This speed up was necessary, not because the expert system code itself was slow, but rather because the expert system tended to form very long queries involving many MICROARRAS categories, and MICROARRAS slows down linearly with the number of search terms in a query.

Questions

Three sets of five questions were devised. Each set contained one training question and four questions on which the subjects were monitored. The questions covered material ranging over the whole textbase. The number of relevant passages found by the author (see Definitions) follows each monitored question.

Query Set A

Practice:

What are some sources of error in floating point arithmetic?

Monitored:

1) How is computer architecture distinguished from the other computer design domains? (16)

2) What are some upward pressures on the level of a machine language? (16)

3) Fixed length multiplication produces a double length result. How have different machines handled this? (14)

4) How are interrupts handled? Do not consider techniques to disable them. (23)

Query Set B

Practice:

I/O devices have moving parts. What is the effect of this motion on the architecture of computers?

Monitored:

1) What are some design principles that lead to clean architectures? Do not consider the economic advantages of a quality design. (14)

2) What techniques have been used to reduce bit traffic? (10)

3) How are control structures implemented? (13)

4) What role does buffering play in I/O transfers? (22)

Query Set C

Practice:

Fragmentation of memory is one problem of using a segmentation scheme. How is paging used to fix this?

Monitored:

1) Discuss the two fundamentally different ways to formally specify an architecture. (19)

2) What are the effects of having two zeros, as in the sign magnitude representation of fixed point numbers? (7)

3) What is done to save state upon a procedure call? (15)

4) Besides I/O, where is concurrency practiced in the implementation? (16)

Procedure

Subjects were asked to try to find on the order of ten relevant passages from the textbase in response to the questions they would be given. They were informed that they might not always be able to find that many, and they were allowed to stop working on a query whenever they were satisfied that they had found as much as they could. The target number of ten was chosen because it was large enough to require a high recall search, yet small enough that the users would not become tired reading passages. For similar reasons, Carlo Vernimb [Vernimb, 1977] also used a target number of ten when developing an automatic query reformulation system for document retrieval.

Each subject worked with each of the three systems, in turn. This was done to compensate for the large individual differences found in searching ability [Borgman, 1987]. To compensate for learning during the experiment, the order of presentation of the three systems was counterbalanced among subjects. The subjects received a training session with each system before they began their monitored searches. When they had completed all three sessions, they were asked to fill out the questionnaire stating their preferences and opinions.

Data Collection

Raw Data

Data was collected in a trace file while the subjects worked with the system. Each communication from the subject to the retrieval system, and vice versa, was stored with a time stamp. Thus, timing information was collected along with the history of queries entered by the subject and the search results. When the subject chose to display the retrieved passages, those passages and the subject's relevance judgement of them were also stored.

Several parameters were chosen from the trace file to represent each subject's sessions. Measurements were taken on time, number of queries, and number of relevant passages. Before the variables to be compared are described, I will provide a few definitions.

Definitions

A *unique query* was any error-free query entered by a subject. If a subject entered a query which contained a typographic or logical error, and he indicated that he noticed the error by aborting the search and re-entering a corrected version, then the erroneous query was not considered a unique query. However, if the subject gave no indication that he was aware of the error, but instead moved on to a different query altogether, then the erroneous query was considered unique.

The *relevance weight* of a passage is the relevance number assigned to the passage by the subject. A *very relevant (user)* passage is one assigned a relevance weight of two. A *somewhat relevant (user)* passage has a relevance weight of one. A *relevant passage (user)* is one that is either very relevant or somewhat relevant, as judged by the user. An *irrelevant passage (user)* is a passage given a relevance number of zero.

It is necessary to have an estimate of the total number of relevant passages available for each question, in order to calculate recall. This estimate was calculated by forming the union, for each question, of the set of passages judged very relevant by any subject. Passages in this set judged irrelevant by the author were removed. The remaining passages form the *absolute retrieval set* and are called the *relevant passages*. It was necessary to remove some passages marked very relevant by a subject because, perhaps due to a misinterpretation fo the question or a misunderstanding of the passage, some subjects gave a relevance weight of two to irrelevant or marginally relevant passages. This tendency to oversestimate the relevance of passages may also be because, in some cases, subjects were unable to find the truly relevant passages, and thought that they had retrieved the best passages available when in fact they had not.

A *successful retrieval set* is a retrieval set containing at least five relevant passages. Since the subjects were attempting to find ten relevant passages, a successful retrieval set contains at least half the number for which they were looking. The textbase contained approximately the same number of relevant passages for each question, allowing the target number and size of the successful retrieval set to be held constant.

The *final retrieval set* was chosen as the last successful retrieval set. If a subject never retrieved a successful retrieval set for a given question, the retrieval set with the highest number of relevant passages, as judged by the subject, was chosen.

Variables

Total time per question is calculated from the entry of the subject's first query for the question until after the display, or decision not to display, of the final set of retrieved passages.

Number of queries per question is determined by counting the number of unique queries the subject entered for a given question.

Number of relevant passages (user) found per question is determined by counting the number of user indicated relevant passages in the final retrieval set for the question.

User precision is calculated for the final retrieval set using the standard formula of:

   number of relevant passages (user) retrieved / number of passages retrieved

Number of relevant passages found per question is determined by counting the number of passages in the final retrieval set for the question that are members of the absolute retrieval set.

Precision is calculated for the final retrieval set using the standard formula of

   number of relevant passages retrieved (absolute) / number of passages retrieved

Recall is calculated for the final retrieval set using the standard formula of

   number of relevant passages retrieved (absolute) / total number of relevant passages available

The *ranking balance point* (R) for each retrieval set (not just the final one) is calculated by

$$R = \frac{\sum_{i=1}^{n} i * relevance_i}{\sum_{i=1}^{n} relevance_i}$$

   where n = number of passages in the retrieval set
          i = position of the passage in the retrieval set
          $relevance_i$ = relevance weight of passage i

This calculates where the midpoint of the relevant passages lies, accounting for the relevance weight. The earlier in the retrieval set the relevant passages occur, the smaller their midpoint. For example, consider a retrieval set of five passages of which the first two are very relevant (weight = 2), the next two irrelevant (weight = 0), and the last passage somewhat relevant (weight = 1). The ranking balance point for this set would be:

$$(1*2) + (2*2) + (3*0) + (4*0) + (5*1) / 6 = 1.83$$

The *random balance point* (R) for each retrieval set is calculated by (n+1)/2 where n is the number of passages in the retrieval set. A random distribution of relevant passages in the set would have the midpoint (M) of the retrieval set as the balance point. Therefore, the random balance point for the set of five passages in the previous example would be 3.

The *best case balance point* (BC) for each retrieval set is calculated by applying the ranking balance point formula to the case where all very relevant passages preceded all somewhat relevant passages which in turn preceded all non-relevant passages in the set. In this case, the ranking balance point would be:

$$(1*2) + (2*2) + (3*1) + (4*0) + (5*0) / 6 = 1.5$$

The *normalized ranking balance points* were calculated from the ranking balance points by moving the random balance point to 0 and adjusting the range so that the best case balance point fell on 1, and the worst case balance point at -1. The normalization performed was:

Normalized ranking balance point (NR) = (M - R) / (M - BC).

For the example retrieval set, the normalized ranking balance point would be:

$$(3 - 1.83) / (3 - 4.5) = 0.78.$$

Summaries Calculated for Each System

For each system the means calculated were:

- number of queries per question
- time per question (seconds)
- number of relevant passages (user) per question
- user precision
- number of relevant passages (from absolute retrieval set)

- precision

- recall

For each ranking algorithm (the expert system's, and randomness) the normalized balance points were calculated.

3.3 Results

The means were compared to determine if their differences were statistically significant. Pairwise two-tailed t-tests were performed. A difference was considered significant if its probability of occurring due to chance was less than 5% at the 95% confidence level (a 10% chance at the 95% confidence level was considered marginally significant). Pairs of means with statistically significant differences are flagged with asterisks.

Search Effectiveness

All three systems retrieved comparable numbers of relevant passages. Whereas there seemed to be higher recall with the thesaurus, shown by a mean of 7.688 compared to a mean of 7.292 with the expert system, this difference was not significant ($p = 0.5333$).

- number of relevant passages (user)

  per question

  - user alone   7.375

  - user and thesaurus   7.688

  - user and expert system 7.292

All three systems produced comparable precision, based on the subject's relevance judgements.

- user precision

  - user alone   0.763

  - user and thesaurus   0.786

  - user and expert system 0.761

All three systems retrieved approximately the same number of passages from the absolute retrieval set.

- number of passages from absolute retrieval set
    - user alone   5.521
    - user and thesaurus   5.708
    - user and expert system   5.729

Recall was comparable across all three systems. There was a slight improvement in recall for the user and expert system configuration, but the advantage over the user-alone configuration was not significant ($p < 0.6988$).

- recall
    - user alone   0.364
    - user and thesaurus   0.368
    - user and expert system   0.379

The user and expert system configuration produced marginally significant improvements in precision when compared with the user-alone configuration.

- precision
    - user alone   0.530 *   ($p < 0.0817$)
    - user and thesaurus   0.576
    - user and expert system   0.604 *

Search Efficiency

The expert system was not significantly slower than the other two systems. However, the user was marginally significantly slower when using a thesaurus. However, MICROARRAS was being executed by a Sun 4 with the user-expert system configuration resulting in approximately a doubling of its speed.

- mean time per question (seconds)
  - user alone   474.5 *   ($p < 0.101$)
  - user and thesaurus   571.5 *
  - user and expert system   539.8

The expert system improved search efficiency, as measured by number of user queries over both the user alone and user plus thesaurus.

- number of queries per question
  - user alone   4.833 *   ($p < 0.0001$)
  - user and thesaurus   5.458 **   ($p < 0.0001$)
  - user and expert system   2.354 *,**

Ranking

The expert system ranked relevant documents more highly than would be predicted by randomness. The expert system's ranking was compared to a random distribution for 74 sets of retrieved passages.

- balance points
  - random   5.00 *   ($p < 0.0165$)
  - expert system   4.53 *
- normalized balance points (on range of -1 to +1)
  - random   0.000 *   ($p < 0.0025$)
  - expert system   0.195 *

3.4 Analysis

The first hypothesis, that the expert system can improve the search effectiveness for a novice user was partially supported by this study. The expert system produced marginally significant improvements in precision, and seemed to indicate improvements in recall, but these results were not significant. Providing the online thesaurus produced no improvement in search effectiveness.

The improvements in precision may result from the expert system applying better broadening techniques. The subjects, when searching alone, would often stop with a very broad query and examine a large set of retrieved passages (over fifteen) looking for relevant information. This type of strategy results in the lower precision observed when the subjects search on their own.

However, this browsing strategy also accounts for the ability of the subjects to produce recall comparable to the expert system. For example, in two questions with large absolute retrieval sets the subjects were able to retrieve, on average, 10 and 10.25 relevant passages on their own compared with the expert system's retrieval of 8 and 7.75 passages respectively. By using a target number of 10 for these broader questions, the expert system was operating at a disadvantage. More relevant information was easily found, judging by the high recall of the subjects, but the expert system did not even attempt to further broaden the query.

The second hypothesis, that the expert system can improve the search efficiency of novice searchers, was supported. Using the expert system significantly reduced the number of queries subjects needed to answer a given question. Subjects required fewer than half as many queries per question on average versus systems in which the user queried without it, a substantial improvement. The expert system reduced the amount of user effort required by decreasing the number of queries a user needs to design to express their information needs. If efficiency is measured in terms of total user time the expert system fares less well. The expert system was not significantly slower than either of the other two systems but it was necessary to run MICROARRAS on a faster machine to achieve this. However, this version of the expert system was designed with correctness rather than efficiency in mind, and there are several ways that it could be sped up.

Allowing the subjects to access the online thesaurus actually decreased the subjects' efficiency. They took significantly more time than when they searched on their own, and required no fewer queries. This allows us to conclude that the improvement in efficiency seen above was due to the expert system's searching knowledge base, not just the provision of an online thesaurus.

The third hypothesis that the expert system could rank passages in decreasing order of relevance was supported. Although the expert system did present relevant passages significantly earlier than would be predicted by randomness, the improvement was not large enough to be considered truly successful. The current algorithm needs to be evaluated with different weights or a somewhat different algorithm needs to be tried in order to further improve the ranking function. Decreasing the query term weights more quickly as the query terms move farther from the original may improve the ranking by placing more emphasis on the user's original search terms. Using a more sophisticated closeness factor, one that took into account to how many words apart the search terms were in the passage, as well as sentence and paragraph measures considered in this version, could also lead to improved ranking.

3.5 Questionnaire

The twelve subjects were asked which features of the expert system they liked best. The automatic addition of terms from the thesaurus was the most frequently mentioned (8 subjects), whereas the automatic context adjustment was the second most popular feature (3 subjects). Many subjects (8) mentioned the decreased amount of work needed to perform a search, with three of them specifically mentioning that they did not have to think as much. Other features mentioned which decreased the user effort were the simplified syntax, decreased typing, and the fewer queries to remember. ·

System slowness was the feature most disliked (6 subjects). Although the amount of time necessary to answer a question was no greater with the expert system (see Section 4.3.1),there was less work for the user so time seemed longer. The other main complaints concerned the user interface. The subjects were fairly evenly split between wanting the system to proceed more automatically, with less prompting from them (4 subjects), whereas others wanted the system to explain what it was doing and/or allow the user to direct it (5 subjects). These comments lead to the conclusion that if a usable system is to be built based on the success of this research prototype, the execution of the system must be sped up and more work on interface design is needed.

Almost all the subjects (10) found the user-expert system version the easiest to use, with the remaining two subjects split between the other two versions. Not surprisingly, given the comparable effectiveness of the three systems, the subjects were split on which system they felt gave the best results. Three voted for the user-alone version, two for the user-thesaurus, and three for the expert system. Three said it was a tie between the user-thesaurus and the expert system, and one abstained.

4   CONCLUSIONS

I have designed, implemented, and evaluated an expert system that automatically reformulates contextual Boolean queries for full-text information retrieval. Whereas more research is necessary to develop a better search assistant, I have demonstrated that a domain-independent online search assistant can be developed now. This is important because if more people can successfully search online textbases, and they can do so with less effort, the information stored in these textbases will become more widely disseminated.

Running the experiment suggested several possible refinements to the system. The experimental subjects had many useful comments, the bulk of which dealt with the desire for a more sophisticated user interface. Desirable changes include: provision of a non-Boolean query language; allowing users to adjust the amount of system interaction; having the user specify the type of search desired, rather than having him give a specific target number; and increasing the speed of the system by improving the way the expert system uses MICROARRAS. Improvements to the searching knowledge base were suggested by observing the expert system in use. Specifically, the order in which the search tactics are applied needs further investigation. Additionally, more narrowing techniques are needed, and expansion of multi-word phrases could be handled better. The thesaurus used for this textbase was developed manually. Research is needed in how to automatically this process. Finally, other ranking algorithms should be investigated.

REFERENCES

Bates, Marcia J., "Information Search Tactics", *Journal of the ASIS*, Vol. 30, No. 4, 1979. pp. 205-214.

Blair, David C., and Maron, M.E., "An Evaluation of Retrieval Effectiveness for a Full-Text Document-Retrieval System", *Communications of the ACM*, Vol. 28, No. 3, March 1985. pp. 289-299.

Blaauw G.A. and Brooks, Frederick P. Jr., *Computer Architecture, Volume 1-Design Decisions*, Draft, Spring 1987.

Borgman, Christine L., "Why Are Online Catalogs Hard to Use?", *Journal of the ASIS*, Vol. 37, No. 6, November 1986. pp. 387-400.

Borgman, Christine L., "Individual Differences in the Use of Information Retrieval Systems: Some Issues and Some Data", *Proceedings of the Tenth Annual International ACMSIGIR Conference on Research & Development in Information Retrieval*, C.J. von Rijsbergen and C.T. Yu (ed.), ACM Press, 1987. pp. 61-69.

Brajnik, G., Guida, G., and Tasso, C., "IR-NLI II: Applying Man-Machine Interaction and Artificial Intelligence Concepts to Information Retrieval", *Proceedings of the Eleventh Annual International ACMSIGIR Conference on Research & Development in Information Retrieval*, Y. Chiaramella (ed.), ACM Press, 1988. pp. 387-399.

Chiaramella, Y. and Defude, B., "A Prototype of and Intelligent System for Information Retrieval: IOTA", *Information Processing & Management*, Vol. 23, No. 4, 1987. pp. 285-303.

Croft, W. B. and Thompson, R. H., "I3R: A New Approach to the Design of Document Retrieval Systems",*Journal of the ASIS*, Vol. 38, No. 6, November 1987. pp. 389-404.

Fenichel, C. H., "Online Searching: Measures that Discriminate Among Users with Different Types of Experience", *Journal of the ASIS*, Vol. 32, No. 1, January 1981, pp. 23-32.

Fox, Edward A., Weaver, Marybeth T., Chen, Qi-Fan, and France, Robert K.,"Implementing a Distributed Expert-Based Information Retrieval System", *Proceedings of RIAO 88*, M.I.T., March 1988. pp. 708-726.

Gauch, Susan, "An Expert System for Searching in Full-Text", Doctoral Dissertation, Dept. of Computer Science, *Tech. Report* #TR89-050, University of North Carolina, Chapel Hill.

Gauch, Susan, and Smith, John B., "An Expert System for Searching in Full-Text", *Information Processing &Management*, Vol. 25, No. 3, 1989. pp. 253-263.

Gauch, Susan, and Smith, John B.,"Query Reformulation Strategies for an Intelligent Search Intermediary", Proceedings of the Annual AI Systems in Government Conference, Washington, D.C., March 1989.

Oldroyd, B. K., "Study of strategies used in online searching 5: differences between the experienced and the inexperienced searcher", *Online Review*, Vol. 8, No. 3, 1984. pp. 233-244.

Pollitt, A.S., "A `Front-End' System: An Expert System as an Online Search Intermediary", *ASLIB Proceedings*, Vol. 36, No. 5, May 1984. pp. 229-234.

Shoval, Peretz, "Principles, Procedures and Rules in an Expert System for Information Retrieval", *Information Processing &Management*, Vol. 21, No. 6, 1985. pp. 475-487.

Smith, John B., Weiss, Stephen F., and Ferguson, Gordon J., "MICROARRAS: An Advanced Full-Text Retrieval and Analysis System", *Proceedings of the Tenth Annual International ACMSIGIR Conference on Research & Development in Information Retrieval*, C.J. von Rijsbergen and C.T. Yu (ed.), ACM Press, 1987. pp. 187-195.

Smith, Phillip J., Shute, Steven J., and Galdes, Deb, *Proceedings of the Twelfth Annual International ACMSIGIR Conference on Research & Development in Information Retrieval*, N. J. Belkin and C. J. van Rijsbergen (ed.), ACM Press, 1989. pp. 3-10.

Teskey, Niall, "Extensions to the Advanced Interface Management Project", *OCLC Research Review*, July 1987. pp. 1-3.

Tong, Richard M., Applebaum, Lee A., Askmann, Victor N., and
Cunningham, James F., "Conceptual Information Retrieval using RUBRIC",*Proceedings of the Tenth Annual International ACMSIGIR Conference on Research & Development in Information Retrieval*, C.J. von Rijsbergen and C.T. Yu (ed.),ACM Press, 1987. pp. 247-253.

Vernimb, Carlo, "Automatic Query Adjustment in Document Retrieval", *Information Processing & Management*, Vol. 13, No. 6, 1977. pp. 339-353.

Vickery, A., and Brooks, Helen M., "PLEXUS-The Expert System for Referral", *Information Processing & Management*, Vol. 23, No. 2, 1987. pp. 99-117.

Williams, P.W., "A Model for an Expert System for Automated Information Retrieval", *Proceedings of the 8th International Online Meeting*, 1984. pp. 139-149.

Order Preserving Minimal Perfect Hash Functions and Information Retrieval *

Edward A. Fox   Qi Fan Chen   Amjad M. Daoud

Lenwood S. Heath

Department of Computer Science

Virginia Polytechnic Institute and State University

Blacksburg VA 24061-0106

April 27, 1990

Abstract

Rapid access to information is essential for a wide variety of retrieval systems and applications. Hashing has long been used when the fastest possible direct search is desired, but is generally not appropriate when sequential or range searches are also required. This paper describes a hashing method, developed for collections that are relatively static, that supports both direct and sequential access. Indeed, the algorithm described gives hash functions that are optimal in terms of time and hash table space utilization, and that preserve any a priori ordering desired. Furthermore, the resulting order preserving minimal perfect hash functions (OPMPHFs) can be found using space and time that is on average linear in the number of keys involved.

1 Introduction

1.1 Motivation: Sources of Static Key Sets

This work was in part motivated by our investigations of optical disc technology. In the last decade, developments in this area have had a revolutionary impact on computer storage,

*This work was funded in part by grants or other support from the National Science Foundation (Grant IRI-8703580), Online Computer Library Center, Inc., NCR Corporation, and the VPI&SU Computing Center.

lowering the price per unit of storage by three orders of magnitude, enabling many new computer and publishing applications, and encouraging a number of research investigations [FOX88b]. In publishing a series of CD-ROMs at VPI&SU, we have found the need for guaranteeing single-seek access to data, and have indeed included a demonstration of our earlier work with minimal perfect hash functions (MPHFs) on Virginia Disc One [FOX90].

Another reason for our work is to allow rapid access to objects in large network databases. Building upon earlier work with "intelligent" information retrieval in connection with the CODER (COmposite Document Expert/extended/effective Retrieval) system [FOX87], we observed the value of having the contents of machine readable dictionaries in an easy to manipulate computer form [FOX88a]. A large lexicon of this type should be useful to aid information retrieval by allowing automatic and semi-automatic query expansion [NUTT89]. Further, it should support a range of text understanding and other natural language processing activities [FRAN89]. However, these lexicons contain a large number of (relatively static) objects that must be rapidly located; rapid traversal of associational links is also required. We [CHEN89] elected to specify and build a Large External Network Database (LEND) and have indeed loaded over 70 megabytes of data into our current implementation. Further work is planned, showing how network databases of lexical data or other information often stored in semantic networks, as well as complex hyperbases (for hypertext and hypermedia), can be constructed to aid information retrieval [CHEN90]. All of these efforts make use of our work with MPHFs.

1.2 Minimal Perfect Hash Functions, Preserving Order

Our initial work with hash functions took a different tact from currently popular methods of dynamic hashing [ENBO88]. Those methods are suitable when it is acceptable to use extra space, and necessary to allow for frequent additions and deletions of records. While dynamic hashing generally does not preserve the original key ordering, there also exists order-preserving key transformations, which are appropriate for dynamic key sets as long as the key distributions are or can be made to be stable [GARG86]. In contrast, we made the very useful assumption that our key sets are static, and investigated published algorithms for finding minimal perfect hash functions (MPHFs), i.e., those where no collisions occur and where the hash table size is the same as the size of the key set (see review of earlier work in [DATT88]). Of those examined, one by Sager [SAGE85] had the best time complexity, $O(n^4)$, and seemed amenable to enhancement. With some small extensions we were able to handle thousands of keys, with an $O(n^3)$ algorithm for n unique keys [FOX89a]. By reformulating the problem, we developed an $O(n \log n)$ algorithm and tested it with a

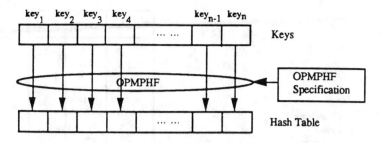

Figure 1: Order Preserving Minimal Perfect Hash Function

variety of key sets, including one with $n = 1.2$ million [FOX89b]. We have recently tested even better algorithms and will report on them in subsequent papers.

This paper, however, focuses on MPHFs that also have the property of preserving the order of the input key set. Because they are of special value for information retrieval applications, we elaborate on this part of our work. To make it clear what is implied, consider Figure 1. A function must be obtained that maps keys, usually in the form of character strings or concatenations of several numeric fields, into hash table locations. In brief, the ith key is mapped into the ith hash table location.

1.3 Applications for Information Retrieval

While there are numerous applications for our methods, it is appropriate to consider two that are particularly well known and important for information retrieval. First, there is the dictionary. Here the object is to take a set of tokens or token strings (words, phrases, etc.) and allow rapid lookups to find associated information (number of postings of a term, the "concept number" for that entry, pointers to inverted file lists, etc.). If OPMPHFs can be used for this purpose, in one disk access any dictionary item's record can be identified, and it is possible to rapidly find previous or subsequent entries as well. Thus, the dictionary can be kept in lexicographic order, and can be read sequentially or accessed directly. This application is illustrated in Figure 2a, where real data from the *Collin's English Dictionary* [HANK79] is given for illustrative purposes; this CED example is discussed later as well since some of our experimental studies were with a large set of keys in part derived from the CED.

A second application is for accessing inverted file data. Figure 2b illustrates selected data taken from the CISI collection [FOX83]. For a given term ID (identifier), it is usually necessary to find the number of postings, that is the number of documents in which the term occurs, and then to find the list of all those occurrences. All of this information has been included in a single file accessible by an OPMPHF. Normally, for a given term

a) Partial Dictionary from CED

Aveynn
Bulwer-lytton
Carl
Chunkking
Clouet
Euclidean
Han Cities
Indonesia.
Lagoomorpha
Sabbaths
antennae
burrows
debris
deposited
dentifrice

b) Partial Inverted File from CISI

Term Id	Doc Id	Weight
0	0	1
0	1271	3
1	0	102
1	11	1
1	16	3
1	17	3
....	....	....
....	....	....
9999	0	5
9999	447	1
9999	939	1
9999	988	1
9999	1250	1
9999	1429	2
10000	0	1
10000	177	1

Figure 2: Using OPMPHFs for Information Retrieval

ID, we obtain the document and frequency (of that term in that document) pairs for all occurrences. Assuming that document numbers have value at least 1, we use the simple trick of storing the postings data in the frequency field of an entry that has a given term ID and document number set to 0. Thus, we can, for a given term ID, build a key formed by concatenating the value 0 to it, find the postings in one seek, and read the document-frequency pairs that appear directly after. Various methods using unnormalized forms of the data are possible to effect space savings; the OPMPHF value can actually be an arbitrary value so that variable length records can be directly addressed [DAOUD90].

1.4 Summary of Earlier Work

Our earlier work has been discussed in [FOX89b], along with an overview of related work. We review the key concepts here. First, there is theoretical evidence that since MPHFs are rare in the space of all functions, a moderate amount of space is required to specify a given MPHF [MEHL82]. In a later paper we will describe MPHF methods that require space approaching the theoretical lower bound. In this paper (see section 3.1), a proof of the lower bound for OPMPHFs is given, and that bound is approached by the current algorithm. Thus, while readers might be concerned that using space to specify a function is contrary to the spirit of hashing, it is required based on theoretical analysis.

Second, the approach we take is to use a three step process of Mapping, Ordering, and Searching — following the suggestion by Sager [SAGE85]. We map the problem of finding a MPHF into one involving working with a random bipartite graph, where each given key is represented by an edge, and where randomness allows us to make use of important results from the theory of random graphs (see, for example, [BOLL85] and [PALM85]). Since in the original problem space we must avoid collisions among keys, in our graph we must identify dependencies between edges, which result when multiple edges share a common vertex. These dependencies are captured during the Ordering phase, which makes use of properties of the dependency graph, and which leads to an ordering of levels or groups of interdependent edges. If the Ordering phase is done well, then during the subsequent Searching phase, when the actual hash values are assigned so as to avoid collisions, a viable MPHF can be quickly specified.

To facilitate subsequent discussion, we adapt notation used in [FOX89b], relating to our work with MPHFs, and list it for reference in Figure 3.

Note that when $n = m$ the hash function is minimal, as desired, so in the following discussion n will be used instead of m. In the bipartite dependency graph G there are two parts having r vertices (numbered from 0 to $r - 1$ and from r to $2r - 1$, respectively), each part connected by n edges. One end of each edge associated with key k is at the vertex numbered by $h_1(k)$, and the other end is at the vertex numbered by $h_2(k)$. Thus, each edge is uniquely defined by the associated key. The function $h(k)$ is the one actually used with key k, and is easily computable from k, given a specification of g for all values in its domain.

Central to our algorithms is an analysis of the properties of the graph G, which is random since it is formed through use of the random functions $h_1()$ and $h_2()$. When the ratio (i.e., $2r/n$) is 1 or more, the graph has few vertices with high degree. When the ratio falls below 0.5, fewer vertices have low degree and the graph has larger connected components and more cycles. More detailed results are given in [FOX89b] for graphs with ratios as small as 0.4, but for OPMPHFs found using the current scheme, ratios are around 1.2. Other graph properties also are considered in the discussion below.

1.5 Outline of Paper

This paper is organized as follows. In section 2 we explain our approach, including three methods to find OPMPHFs, and then provide both details and an example for the third method. Section 3 gives analytical and experimental results, including lower bounds and

$U =$	universe of keys	
$N =$	cardinality of U	
$k =$	key for data record	
$S =$	subset of U, i.e., the set of keys in use	
$n =$	cardinality of S	
$T =$	hash table, with slots numbered $0, \ldots, (m-1)$	
$m =$	number of slots in T	
$h =$	function to map key k into hash table T	
$|h| =$	space to store hash function	
$G =$	dependency graph	
$r =$	parameter specifying the number of vertices in one part of G	
$ratio =$	$2r/m$, which specifies the relative size of G	
$h_0, h_1, h_2 =$	three separate random functions easily computable over the keys	
	$h_0: U \rightarrow [0, \ldots, n-1]$	
	$h_1: U \rightarrow [0, \ldots, r-1]$	
	$h_2: U \rightarrow [r, \ldots, 2r-1]$	
$g =$	function mapping $0, \ldots, (2r-1)$ into $0, \ldots, (m-1)$	
$h(k) =$	$\{h_0(k) + g(h_1(k)) + g(h_2(k))\} \bmod n$	
$=$	form of hashing function	
$v =$	vertex in G	
$K(v) =$	for a given v in the vertex ordering, the set of keys in that ordering level	
$VS =$	vertex sequence produced during the Ordering phase	
$t =$	length of VS	

Figure 3: Terminology from Earlier Work on MPHFs

other descriptive information about our methods, as well as confirming evidence from several runs with test collections. Section 4 gives timing results for our test collections, where a dictionary and an inverted file were implemented using an OPMPHF. Finally, we summarize our results in section 5.

2   Approach

This section describes our preferred method to obtain an OPMPHF. In section 2.1 we outline three methods to find OPMPHFs, and then focus on the third method, which requires less space than the other two. This method is fully described in section 2.2, and is illustrated with an example in section 2.2.4.

2.1   Three Methods to Find OPMPHFs

Based on our experience working on various versions of MPHF algorithms, we note that there are at least three ways to obtain an OPMPHF. The first two are straightforward extensions of our earlier research, but require a large amount of space to describe the OPMPHF. The third method, obtained after extensive study of graphs used with MPHFs, requires much less space but is rather complex.

2.1.1   Method 1: Acyclic Graphs

Method 1, the acyclic technique, involves constructing a bipartite graph G sufficiently large so that no cycles are present. This extends our earlier work described in [FOX89b], and is based on the use of a large ratio $(2r/n)$ which makes the probability of having a cycle approach 0 (see proof in section 3.2.1). If there are no cycles, we have sufficient freedom during the Searching phase to select g values that will preserve any a priori key order.

Our algorithm is basically the same as that described in [FOX89b] throughout the Mapping and Ordering phases. But because G is acyclic, we obtain an ordering of non-zero degree vertices v to yield levels $K(v)$ following certain constraints (see section 2.2.2), which only contain one edge (one key). This is achieved through an edge traversal (e.g., depth-first or breadth-first) of all components in G. Thus, in Figure 4, which shows an acyclic bipartite graph, an ordering obtained by depth-first traversal of first the left connected component and then the right might give the vertex sequence (VS) : $[v_1, v_5, v_0, v_2, v_6, v_3, v_7]$. The corresponding levels of edges are given in the edge sequence: $[\{\}, \{e_1\}, \{e_0\}, \{e_3\}, \{e_2\}, \{\}, \{e_4\}]$.

285

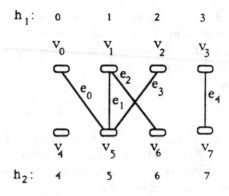

Figure 4: A Cycle Free Bipartite Graph

Notice that in this example, each level has at most one edge, which is only possible if G is acyclic.

During the Searching phase, a single pass through the ordering can determine g values for all keys in a manner that preserves the original key ordering. This is possible since with only one edge being handled at each level, there are no interdependencies that would restrict the g value assignments.

Although this approach is simple, it is only practical if a small acyclic graph can be found. Using our ratio, $2r/n$, we therefore give a lower bound on the number of vertices for a given set of n keys. Section 3.2.1 gives a detailed probabilistic account of the expected number of cycles in G, as a function of the ratio. If the average number of cycles, $E(Y)$, approaches 0, then by Chebyshev's inequality

$$P(Y \geq t) \leq E(Y)/t,$$

so the probability of a particular graph having cycles approaches 0. Thus, for sufficiently large ratio (e.g., $O(\log n)$), it will be very unlikely that G will have cycles. However, this ratio is very much larger than values required in the other two methods described below.

2.1.2 Method 2: Two Level Hashing

The second idea is to use two level hashing. Here the MPHF computed through the method in [FOX89b] is in the first level and an array of pointers is in the second. A hash value from the MPHF addresses the second level where the real locations of records are kept. The records are arranged in the desired order. This method uses at the first level $2r$, and at the second, n computer words for the OPMPHF. For large key sets, $2r \cong 0.4n$ is possible and feasible. Thus this method typically will use $1.4n$ computer words. Fig. 5 illustrates the two level hashing scheme. Note, however, that small OPMPHFs are much faster and more feasible to find using Method 3, which is discussed next.

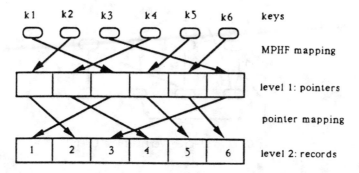

Figure 5: A Two Level OPMPHF Scheme

2.1.3 Method 3: Using Indirection

The third method is based on the idea of using G to store the additional information required to specify a MPHF that also preserves order. For n keys, if our graph has somewhat more than n vertices (i.e., if ratio > 1), then there should be enough room to specify the OPMPHF. In a random graph of this size, a significant number of vertices will have zero degree; we have found a way to use those vertices. The obvious solution is to use indirection. This means that some keys will be mapped using indirection, in this case using the composition:

$$h(k) = g\Big(\{h_0(k) + g(h_1(k)) + g(h_2(k))\} \bmod 2r\Big).$$

while on the other hand, the desired location of a key that is, as before, found directly is determined by:

$$h(k) = \{h_0(k) + g(h_1(k)) + g(h_2(k))\} \bmod n.$$

Note that we use the g function in two ways, one way for regular keys and the other way for keys that are handled through indirection.

Let us consider more closely the distribution of d, the number of degrees of vertices in G. The actual distribution is binomial and can be approximated by the Poisson:

$$
\begin{aligned}
E(X = d) &= \{2r\, e^{-n/r}(n/r)^d\}/d! \\
E(X = 0) &= 2r\, e^{-n/r}
\end{aligned}
$$

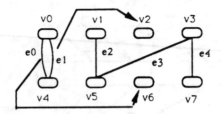

Figure 6: Zero Degree Vertices are Useful

When $2r = n$, about 13.5% of the vertices have zero-degree. If these zero-degree vertices can be used to record order information for a significant number of keys, then it is not necessary for G to be acyclic to generate an OPMPHF. Figure 6 is a brief demonstration of the idea. Note that keys associated with edges e_0 and e_1 can be indirectly hashed into zero-degree vertices v_2 and v_6. In general, an edge (key) is indirectly hashed when that situation is described by information associated with its two vertices, given by $h_1(k)$ and $h_2(k)$. Usually, indirection can be indicated using one bit that is decided at MPHF building time and that is subsequently kept for use during function application time.

Various schemes of indirection have been proposed and tested. In section 2.2, we describe our one bit algorithm capable of finding ordered hashing functions with high probability for large key sets with $ratio \cong 1.22$.

2.2 Method 3: Algorithm and Data Structures

This section outlines an algorithm using one indirection bit, which is an extension of the one in [FOX89b] used to find MPHFs. Our hashing scheme uses the OPMPHF class:

$$h(k) = g\Big(\{h_0(k) + g(h_1(k)) + g(h_2(k))\} \, mod \, 2r\Big),$$

when the indirection bit assoicated with the two vertices for this key have the same value, and otherwise uses

$$h(k) = \{h_0(k) + g(h_1(k)) + g(h_2(k))\} \, mod \, n.$$

The algorithm for selecting proper g values and setting mark bits for vertices in G consists of the three steps: Mapping, Ordering and Searching. By reducing the problem of finding an OPMPHF to these three subproblems, we can more easily and rapidly identify a usable hash function. Each step, along with implementation details, will be described in a separate subsection below.

2.2.1 The Mapping Step

This step is essentially identical to that discussed in [FOX89b]. The only addition is that the indirection bit must be included in the vertex data structure. Readers may elect to skip to the next subsection, or to follow the discussion below which is included for completeness.

The basic concept is to generate unique triples of form $(h_0(k), h_1(k), h_2(k))$ for all keys k. $h_0(), h_1(), h_2()$ are simple random functions. Since the final hash function should be perfect, all triples must be distinct. Following [FOX89b], we use random functions h_0, h_1, h_2 to build the triples so as to obtain a probabilistic guarantee on the distinctness of the triples. The probability that all triples will be unique is:

$$
\begin{aligned}
P &= nr^2(nr^2 - 1)\ldots(nr^2 - n + 1)/(nr^2)^n = (nr^2)_n/(nr^2)^n \\
&\cong e^{-n^2/2nr^2} \text{(by an asymptotic estimate from [PALM85])} \\
&= e^{-n/2r^2}.
\end{aligned}
$$

Since r is on the order of n, P goes to one as n approaches infinity.

The h_0, h_1 and h_2 values for all keys are entered into an array **edge** defined as

```
edge: array of [0...n - 1] of record
    h0, h1, h2: integer;
    nextedge1: integer;
    nextedge2: integer;
    final: integer
```

Here the combination h_0, h_1, h_2 field contains the triple. The nextedge$_i$ field $(i = 1, 2)$ indicates the next entry in the **edge** array with similar h_i value to the current entry. It is utilized to link together all edges joined to a vertex. The final field is the desired hash location of a key.

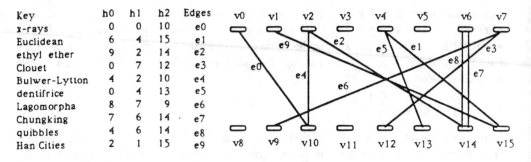

Key	h0	h1	h2	Edges
x-rays	0	0	10	e0
Euclidean	6	4	15	e1
ethyl ether	9	2	14	e2
Clouet	0	7	12	e3
Bulwer-Lytton	4	2	10	e4
dentifrice	0	4	13	e5
Lagomorpha	8	7	9	e6
Chungking	7	6	14	e7
quibbles	4	6	14	e8
Han Cities	2	1	15	e9

(a) The Key Set

(b) The Bipartite Graph

Figure 7: A Key Set and its Dependency Bipartite Graph G

The g function is recorded in another array **vertex** defined as

vertex: array of $[0 \ldots 2r - 1]$ of record
    g: integer;
    mark: bit;
    firstedge: integer;
    degree: integer

The g field in entry vertex[i] records the final g value for $h_1(k) = i$ if i is in $[0, r - 1]$ or the final g value for $h_2(k) = i$ if i is in $[r, 2r - 1]$. The mark field contains a bit of indirection information, as given above for either $h_1(k)$ or $h_2(k)$. The firstedge field in entry vertex[i] is the header for a singly-linked list of the keys having $h_1(k) = i$ if i is in $[0, r - 1]$ or the keys having $h_2(k) = i$ if i is in $[r, 2r - 1]$. The firstedge field actually points at an entry in the edge array indicating the start of the list and nextedge$_i$ for $(i = 1, 2)$ there connects to the rest of the list. The degree field is the length of the list or equivalently the degree of the vertex.

Thus, the **edge** and **vertex** arrays give a representation of a bipartite graph G, as illustrated in Figure 7(b) for the key set shown in Figure 7(a).

Appendix A shows a few detailed sub-steps of the Mapping phase. Step (1) builds the random tables that specify the h_0, h_1 and h_2 functions. Step (2) initializes the two key (edge) related fields of the **vertex** array. Step (3) constructs the graph representation for each key k_i. Step (4) validates the distinctness of triples. Step (5) enforces the repetition of the steps from (1) to (4) under the rare circumstance that triples duplicate. It is trivial to show that steps (1), (2) and (3) all take $O(n)$ time. Step (4) is linear on average also, because each vertex usually has quite small degree. Thus, the total Mapping step is $O(n)$.

2.2.2 The Ordering Step

In the Ordering step it is necessary to obtain a proper vertex sequence VS for use later in the Searching step. Specifically, VS specifies a sequence of the vertices so that, during searching, each related set of edges can be processed independently. For a given vertex in the ordering, v_i, these associated edges contained in $K(v_i)$ (i.e., at that level) are the backward edges, going to vertices that appear earlier in the ordering. Taking the bipartite graph in Figure 7 (b) as an example, we find one of the several possible vertex sequences to be

$$VS = [v_6, v_{14}, v_2, v_{10}, v_0, v_{13}, v_4, v_{15}, v_1, v_7, v_9, v_{12}]$$

with corresponding levels or edge sets

$$
\begin{aligned}
K(v_6) &= \{\}, K(v_{14}) = \{e_7, e_8\}, K(v_2) = \{e_2\}, K(v_9) = \{e_4\}, K(v_0) = \{e_0\}, \\
K(v_{13}) &= \{\}, K(v_4) = \{e_5\}, K(v_{15}) = \{e_1\}, K(v_1) = \{e_9\}, \\
K(v_9) &= \{\}, K(v_1) = \{e_6\}, K(v_{12}) = \{e_3\}.
\end{aligned}
$$

The graph constructed from vertices in VS plus edges in G is essentially a redrawing of G that excludes zero-degree vertices, as can be seen in Figure 8.

Finding a proper VS requires that we process vertices with many backward edges (i.e., with large $K(v_i)$), first. Thus we employ a variety of heuristics to quickly find such vertices early. The other key issue in finding a proper VS is to handle the fact that some edges must be involved in indirection while others will be involved in direct hashing. Since the assignment of a g value for vertex v_i fully determines the hash addresses of all keys in $K(v_i)$, given that the g values of each previously visited vertex has been set, it is in general true that at most one key in $K(v_i)$ can be order-preservingly hashed for a fixed g value at v_i. Thus, we must determine exactly which keys are indirectly hashed, if the Searching step is to proceed properly. In the scheme proposed, we attach one bit (namely the mark bit) in the Ordering step as well, to each vertex for the purpose. Then, when our hashing function is used, for key k we need ony consider the two indirection bits (stored in primary memory) attached to the two vertices $h_1(k)$ and $h_2(k)$.

Given the need to quickly find the proper VS and to decide the proper indirection bits for vertices in VS, it is essential that we obtain hints from the properties of the $K(v_i)$,

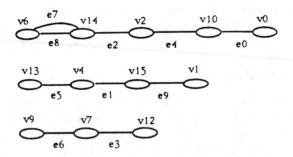

Figure 8: Redrawing of G based on a VS that excludes zero-degree vertices

such as their size. For a key in a level where $|K(v_i)| = 1$, the key can be directly hashed by setting the g value at v_i to

$$g(v_i) = [h_{desired}(k) - h_0(k) - g(v_s)] \bmod n.$$

Here $h_{desired}(k)$ refers to the desired hash address for key k, so that we can have an order preserving function.

For keys in $|K(v_i)| > 1$ levels, since at most one key can be direct, hashing of the other keys requires indirection. Since in our scheme indirect hashing is indicated by the indirection bits, all such keys have those bits set accordingly and thus are indirectly hashed. After considering the two cases, we conclude that a proper VS will be one that tends to maximize the number of $v_i s$ with $|K(v_i)| = 1$ and to minimize the number of $v_i s$ with $|K(v_i)| > 1$.

A practical way to obtain such a VS is to take into account the characteristics of G. Following standard graph terminology, we can refer to the set of edges (E_G) and the set of vertices (V_G), as given in Figure 9. Special attention must be given, though, to each connected component (C). Clearly, edges in a tree component (denoted by AC, which stands for "acyclic component") of G can be directly hashed if their vertices are included in VS by a simple depth or breadth first traversal. For example, in the bottom components in Figure 8, all five edges are direct. Since any vertex in an AC can be the root for a traversal and more importantly, since we have room left in such an AC to accommodate additional indirect keys, the ordering of vertices for AC is not performed until the Searching step. At that time, only one vertex in AC could accept an indirect key so that all other edges in the AC can be direct.

$E_G =$	edges of graph G
$V_G =$	vertices of graph G
$C =$	connected component in G
$AC =$	C that is acyclic. An isolated vertex is also an AC
$CCY =$	C that is cyclic
$CP =$	maximal subgraph of CCY containing only cut edges, each cutting CCY into at least one acyclic subcomponent
$CC =$	$CCY - CP$

Figure 9: Graph Terminology

For a cyclic component (denoted by CCY) such as the larger component at the top of Figure 8, three types of edges are distinguishable. First there are "bush" edges such as e_0, e_2, e_4 forming the bush part of CCY. In graph theory terms, any edges of this kind are cut edges of their component and removing one such bush edge will leave at least one subcomponent acyclic. We use cycle periphery (CP) to denote the maximal subgraph of CCY whose edges are bushes. Finally, we use CC to describe the portion of CCY left after CP. Note that in Figure 7(b), $V_{CP} = \{v_0, v_2, v_{10}, v_{14}\}$ and $E_{CP} = \{e_0, e_2, e_4\}$.

All edges in CP can be directly hashed if a vertex visiting strategy similar to that for tree component AC is used, and the roots for visiting are vertices shared by bush edges and non-bush edges. Since the existence of g values at the root is the only precondition for assignment of g values to other vertices in CP, edges in CP should be hashed well after the non-bush edges are handled.

The two other types of edges are non-bush edges of CCY, that can be direct or indirect, based on a specific ordering of vertices that these edges are connected to. In Figure 7(b), we only have indirect non-bush edges with $V_{CC} = \{v_6, v_{14}\}$ and $E_{CP} = \{e_7, e_8\}$. Intuitively, we see that keys where $|K(v_i)| = 1$ should be direct and those where $|K(v_i)| > 1$ should be indirect. However, due to the way in which the indirection bits are set, some keys where $|K(v_i)| = 1$ can also become indirect.

In summary, our strategy to obtain a good VS involves first identifying ACs, CPs and CCs. Second, we order vertices in CCs, then in CPs and finally in ACs. The implementation of the algorithm combines the ordering and searching for CPs and ACs in the Searching step to save one traversal of edges in CPs and ACs. In arranging vertices in CCs, a vertex whose $K(v_i)$ set is (currently) larger is chosen next in the ordering over a vertex whose $K(v_i)$ set is (currently) smaller. The arrangement of vertices in CPs and ACs is done purely through tree traversals.

The number of vertices of G for a fixed key set is an important factor affecting the quality of VS. First, $|VG|$ is theoretically bounded below by the number of keys n, as is shown in section 3.1. Any G with smaller than n vertices cannot be guaranteed to produce an OPMPHF. For G with $|VG| > n$, we have a tradeoff between the size of the OPMPHF and the ease of finding such an OPMPHF. Let S be the set of indirect keys. Then if G is large, $|S|$ becomes small implying both an easier indirect fit for S and a bigger OPMPHF. On the other hand, a small G will result in a big S, increasing the difficulty of finding an OPMPHF, though if one is found, it will be rather small. Of course, we have the final constraint that $|S|$ be less than the total number of ACs.

Having obtained VS_{CC}, we need to mark indirection bits for all vertices in the sequence. Though not necessarily yielding an optimal marking in terms of generating a minimal number of indirect edges, the method, described in detail in Appendix B, achieves satisfactory results. Step (3) in Appendix B works as follows. Suppose we are marking all edges in $K(v_i)$. Without loss of generality, assume v_i is in the first side of G and k_j is one of the keys in $K(v_i)$.

We determine the final mark bit $h_1[k_j]$.mark using the strategy of finding as many direct keys as possible in one scan of VS. Thus:

a) v_i.mark = 1 if $|K(v_i)| = 0$; or
b) v_i.mark = 1 if $h_2[k_j]$.mark = 0 and $|K(v_i)| = 1$; or
c) v_i.mark = 0 if $h_2[k_j]$.mark = 1 and $|K(v_i)| = 1$; or
d) v_i.mark = 0 if $|K(v_i)| > 1$ and all k_j.mark = 0
    and $|K(v_i)| = v_i$.degree; or
e) v_i.mark = 1 if $|K(v_i)| > 1$ and set all $h_2[k_j]$.mark = 1 if previously 0.

If v_i is on the second side, we just switch h_1 and h_2 for steps a) to e). A simple induction proof on the length i of VS_{CC} shows that (1) a direct edge only appears in a $|K(v_i)| = 1$ level if that edge is not forced to be indirect by (e); (2) all edges in levels with $|K(v_i)| > 1$ are indirect.

Our Ordering phase performs its job in three sub-steps (cf. Appendix B). First, all components in G are identified by assigning component IDs (CIds) as shown in Step (1) of Appendix B. VSTACK is a stack data structure that keeps all unidentified vertices adjacent to at least one identified vertex. Each time a vertex is popped from VSTACK, it gets a CId and its adjacent unidentified vertices are pushed into VSTACK. After the identification process, all zero-degree vertices will get a 0 CId and all other vertices get CIds greater than 0. Step (1) can be finished in $O(n)$ time because each non-zero vertex is in VSTACK only once, and pushing and popping operations take constant time.

Steps (2) and (3) recognize E_{CP} in each component by manipulating the degree field. Initially, Step (2) collects all vertices of degree one into VSTACK and sets their degree field to zero. Afterwards, Step (3) takes the VSTACK and tries to find more vertices whose degree could be reduced to one. Each time a vertex is popped, the degree of all its adjacent vertices is decreased. If some of them turn into degree one vertices, then they are pushed into VSTACK. The process will continue until no more vertices can have their degree values decreased. It can be seen that each time a vertex is popped, an edge in E_{CP} is found that connects the vertex to some earlier popped vertex. The final non-zero vertices left are just those in V_{CC}. The time complexity is easily determined. Since at most n vertices will get into VSTACK and each stack operation takes constant time, steps (2) and (3) together use $O(n)$ time.

Next, the vertices in V_{CC} are subjected to an ordering in Step (4) to generate a vertex sequence VS_{CC} for each CCY. In generating VS_{CC}, Step (4) uses a heap VHEAP to record vertices out of which a vertex with maximal degree is always chosen as the next vertex to be put into the sequence. The usage of VHEAP is analogous to Prim's algorithm for building a minimum spanning tree. Step (4) takes $O(n)$ time, on average, to finish the ordering.

Based on VS_{CC}, Step (5) marks all vertices in the sequence to maximize the number of direct keys in $|K(v)| = 1$ levels, and forces all keys in $|K(v)| > 1$ levels to be indirect. Step (5) is linear because the number of visits to vertices in VS_{CC} is bounded by the total of the degree values of those vertices.

2.2.3 The Searching Phase

The Searching step determines the g value for each vertex so as to produce an OPMPHF. The job is done in two sub-steps. First, g values for all vertices in the VS_{CC} generated by the Ordering step are decided. These g values will in turn hash all keys in E_{CC} to vertices in ACs. Then all the edges in E_{CP} and E_{AC} are processed to finish the searching.

A detailed description of the Searching phase is shown in Appendix C. Step (1) straight-forwardly assigns g values for VS_{CC}. The random probe sequence $s_0, s_1, \ldots, s_{n-1}$, the random permutation of the set $[0 \ldots n - 1]$, gives an ordered list of testing g values for each vertex. Step (1) classifies three kinds of v_i in the assignment: $|K(v_i)| = 0$, $|K(v_i)| = 1$ and k in $K(v_i)$ is direct, or $|K(v_i)| > 0$ otherwise. Each case is treated separately. Step (1) will use $O(n)$ time for a successful assignment. For the rare case that all possible g values cannot satisfy every single vertex, we start another run of the Mapping, Ordering and Searching steps.

Step (2) fits edges in CPs, by a depth-first traversal. The root vertices can be recognized by comparing the degree field of a vertex with the actual number of vertices adjacent to it. If they differ, then this vertex is a root vertex. The last two steps (3) and (4) are for edges in ACs with traversal root vertices either fixed during Step (1) or in ACs that have accepted no indirect edges. Step (3) can be done in linear time. Since only one edge is directly hashed during each visit of a vertex, steps (2) and (3) cannot fail.

2.2.4 An Example

We show in this section an example of finding an OPMPHF for the 10 key set listed in Figure 7(a) and the corresponding bipartite graph in Figure 7(b). It can be seen from Figure 7(b) that G has one CCY consisting of vertices $V_{CCY} = \{v_0, v_2, v_6, v_{10}, v_{14}\}$ and of edges $E_{CCY} = \{e_0, e_2, e_4, e_7, e_8\}$. G also has two trees AC_1 and AC_2 consisting of vertices $V_{AC1} = \{v_1, v_4, v_{13}, v_{15}\}$ and edges $E_{AC1} = \{e_1, e_5, e_9\}$ in AC_1, and vertices $V_{AC2} = \{v_7, v_9, v_{12}\}$ and edges $E_{AC2} = \{e_3, e_6\}$ in AC_2.

When the Ordering phase is carried out for G, it identifies CCY, AC_1 and AC_2 during Step (1) in Appendix B, and truncates bush edges in CCY in steps (2) and (3), leaving a sub-graph CC which has two edges $\{e_7, e_8\}$. In Step (4), vertices adjacent to these two edges are subject to ordering, producing a vertex sequence $VS_{CC} = \{v_6, v_{14}\}$. VS_{CC} is immediately involved in a marking process in Step (5), starting at v_{14}. Since $K(v_{14}) = 0$, we have $v_{14}.mark = 1$. v_6 obtains the same mark (bit 1) because $K(v_6)$ is of size 2 and v_{14} has been assigned bit 1.

During the Searching phase (Appendix C), g values will be assigned first to vertices in VS_{CC} in Step (1). v_{14} gets a random number 8. v_6 gets 3 so that keys e_7 and e_8 can be indirectly hashed to vertices v_7 and v_4. The remaining 8 edges are all direct. Vertices v_2, v_{10} and v_0 will obtain their g values in Step (2); they are all 5. Since neither AC_1 nor AC_2 has accepted any indirect edges, they are processed in Step (4). Vertices in AC_1 will get their g values in the sequence of $\{v_1, v_{15}, v_4, v_{13}\}$ and those in AC_2 $\{v_7, v_9, v_{12}\}$. The final g assignment for all vertices is illustrated in Table 1. To validate the OPMPHF based on the ranking of occurrence of keys in Figure 7(a), we list the h for each key in the fifth column of Table 2.

3 Analysis and Experimental Validation

To provide further insight into our algorithm, we provide analytical and experimental results in this section. In particular, section 3.1 discusses lower bound results for OPMPHFs.

vertex	0	1	2	3	4	5	6	7	8	9	10	11	12	13	14	15
g value	5	0	5	0	8	0	8	7	0	1	5	0	6	7	8	7
mark bit	0	1	0	1	1	1	1	1	1	0	1	1	0	0	1	0

Table 1: g Values Assignment to Vertices in Figure 7(b)

key	h_0	h_1	h_2	$h(k)$
x-rays	0	0	10	0+5+5 (mod 10) = 0
Euclidean	6	4	15	6+8+7 (mod 10) = 1
ethyl ether	9	2	14	9+5+8 (mod 10) = 2
Clouet	0	7	12	0+7+6 (mod 10) = 3
Bulwer-Lytton	4	2	10	4+5+5 (mod 10) = 4
dentifrice	0	4	13	0+8+7 (mod 10) = 5
Lagomorpha	8	7	9	8+7+1 (mod 10) = 6
Chungking	7	6	14	7+8+8 (mod 16) = 7, g(7) = 7
quibbles	4	6	14	4+8+8 (mod 16) = 4, g(4) = 8
Han Cities	2	1	15	2+0+7 (mod 10) = 9

Table 2: The Keys from Figure 7 and Their Final Hash Addresses

Section 3.2 deals with characteristics of graphs, giving formulas used to compute expected values of two random variables. Their actually observed values are also listed for comparison.

3.1 A Lower Bound on the Size of OPPHFs

Following the definition of a (N, m, n) perfect class of hash functions in [MEHL82], we define a (N, m, n) order-preserving perfect class H of OPPHFs as a set of functions h

$$h : [0 \ldots N - 1] \rightarrow [0 \ldots m - 1]$$

such that for any permutation of any subset S in N of size $|S| = n$, there is an h in H such that h is an OPPPHF for the permutation.

We show that the size of H (or the number of h in H) has a lower bound

$$|H| \geq \frac{\binom{N}{n} n!}{\left(\frac{N}{m}\right)^n \binom{m}{n}}.$$

The proof is based on a similar argument to that found in [MEHL82], in proving the lower bound for the (N, m, n) perfect class of PHFs.

Proof: Clearly, there are $\binom{N}{n}$ distinct subsets in N, each of size n. For each such subset S, there are $n!$ permutations (i.e., $n!$ different orderings). We need to show that at most $\left(\frac{N}{m}\right)^n \binom{m}{n}$ permutations out of the total $\binom{N}{n} n!$ can be order preserving and hashed by a single fixed h in H in order to prove claim (1) is correct.

It is trivial that if h is an OPPHF for a permutation P with elements in S, then any other permutation of S cannot be order preserving and hashed by h. It follows that the permutations for h to be OPPHF must come from different subsets. By applying the same argument in [MEHL82], we conclude the maximum number of permutations h can be is

$$\frac{\binom{N}{n} n!}{\left(\frac{N}{m}\right)^n \binom{m}{n}}. \text{ QED.}$$

In the case of OPMPHF, we have $n = m$ and $N = mr^2$. Thus

$$|H| \geq \frac{\binom{nr^2}{n} n!}{\left(\frac{nr^2}{n}\right)^n \binom{m}{n}}$$

20

Using asymptotic estimate $\binom{N}{n} \approx \frac{N^n}{n!}$

$$|H| \approx \frac{(nr^2)^n}{r^{2n}} = n^n$$

or $\log_2 |H| = n \log_2 n$. Therefore, $O(n \log_2 n)$ bits of space are required for $|h|$ or, equivalently, the number of g values should be larger than n.

3.2 Characteristics of G

This section gives probabilistic analysis on various random variables dealing with the characteristics of G. The actual values of these measures for a particular set of random graphs will also be given after each analysis.

3.2.1 Average Number of Cycles

In the following, we determine the number of cycles in our G — a bipartite graph having $2r$ vertices on each side and having m random edges. Let $\Pr(2i)$ be the probability of having a cycle of length $2i$ formed in a particular vertex set of $2i$ vertices, with i vertices being on each side. There are $i!(i-1)!/2$ ways to form distinct cycles out of these $2i$ vertices and $\binom{n}{2i}(2i)!$ ways to select $2i$ edges to form such a cycle. The remaining $n - 2i$ edges can go into G in $(r^2)^{n-2i}$ different ways. Thus in total there are $i!(i-1)!/2 \cdot \binom{n}{2i} \cdot (2i)! \cdot (r^2)^{n-2i}$ ways to form the $2i$ edge cycle in the vertex set. We have, given that there are a total of $(r^2)^n$ possibilities,

$$\Pr(2i) = \frac{\frac{i!(i-1)!}{2} \cdot \binom{n}{2i} \cdot (2i)! \cdot (r^2)^{n-2i}}{(r^2)^n}$$

$$= \frac{i!(i-1)! \cdot \binom{n}{2i} \cdot (2i)!}{2r^{4i}}$$

Let Z_{ij} be an indicator random variable. $Z_{ij} = 1$ if there is a $2i$ edge cycle in the jth vertex set of $2i$ vertices, $Z_{ij} = 0$ otherwise. Clearly, there are $\binom{r}{i}^2$ such sets in G. Each vertex set has the same probability of having $2i$ edge cycles.

Let X_i be a random variable counting the number of $2i$ edge cycles in G. We have

$$X_i = \sum_{j=1}^{\binom{r}{i}^2} Z_{ij} = \binom{r}{i}^2 \cdot \Pr(2i).$$

Define $Y_c = \sum_{i=1}^{r} X_i$ as another random variable counting the number of cycles in G of length from 2 to $2r$.

$$
\begin{aligned}
E(Y_c) &= \sum_{i=1}^{r} E(X_i) \\
&= \sum_{i=1}^{r} \binom{r}{i}^2 \cdot \Pr(2i) \\
&= \sum_{i=1}^{r} \binom{r}{i}^2 \cdot \frac{i! \cdot (i-1)! \cdot (2i)!}{2 \cdot r^{4i}} \cdot \binom{n}{2i} \\
&\cong \sum_{i=1}^{r} \left(\frac{r^i}{i!} \cdot e^{-\frac{i^2}{2r}} \right)^2 \cdot \frac{i! \cdot (i-1)! \cdot (2i)!}{2 \cdot r^{4i}} \cdot \left(\frac{n^{2i}}{(2i)!} \cdot e^{-\frac{(2i)^2}{2n}} \right) \\
&= \sum_{i=1}^{r} \frac{1}{2i} \cdot \left(\frac{n}{r} \right)^{2i} \cdot e^{-i^2 \cdot (\frac{1}{r} + \frac{2}{n})} \\
&\leq \sum_{i=1}^{r} \frac{1}{2} \left(\frac{n}{r} \right)^{2i} \\
&\leq \sum_{i=1}^{\infty} \frac{1}{2} \left(\frac{n}{r} \right)^{2i} \\
&= \frac{1}{2} \cdot \frac{\left(\frac{n}{r} \right)^2}{1 - \left(\frac{n}{r} \right)^2}
\end{aligned}
$$

Then,

$$E(Y_c) \leq \frac{1}{\left(\frac{r}{n} \right)^2 - 1}.$$

When $r = n \log n$, $E(Y_c) \to 0$ as $n \to \infty$.

Table 3 shows the existence of cycles in random graphs in a 1024 edge G. The number of vertices varies from 1638 to 3276 with the ratio ranging from 1.6 to 3.2.

Ratio	Vertices	Existence of cycle
1.6	1638	yes
1.8	1844	yes
2.0	2048	yes
2.2	2252	yes
2.4	2458	yes
2.6	2662	yes
2.8	2868	yes
3.0	3072	no
3.2	3276	no

Table 3: The existence of cycles in G containing 1024 edges

3.2.2 Average Number of Trees

This subsection includes a derivation of a formula counting the number of tree components in G, excluding zero-degree vertex components. Following [AUST60], we have the number of different trees in a bipartite graph G':

$$j^{i-1} \cdot i^{j-1}$$

Here the total $i + j$ distinct vertices are split into two groups: i vertices in one and the remaining j vertices in the other. These vertices are connected by $i + j - 1$ indistinguishable edges to form a tree. The formula counts the number of different such trees.

The expected number of trees of distinct edges of size from 1 to $\min(n, 2r - 1)$ in a bipartite graph G with r vertices in each side is

$$E(\text{Trees}) = \sum_{i=1}^{min(n,r)} \sum_{j=1}^{min(n,2r-1)-i+1}$$

$$\frac{\binom{r}{i}\binom{r}{j} \cdot j^{i-1} \cdot i^{j-1} \cdot \binom{n}{i+j-1} \cdot (i + j - 1)! \cdot (r^2 + i \cdot j - r \cdot (i + j))^{(n-i-j+1)}}{r^{2n}}$$

where the first summation is on i, ranging from 1 to $\min(n, r)$, and the second on j from 1 to $\min(n, 2r - 1) - i + 1$. It is easy to see that the term $\binom{r}{i} \cdot \binom{r}{j}$ is the number of ways to have all the combinations of i and j vertices on both sides. The following term $j^{i-1} \cdot i^{j-1}$ is the number of different trees constructible from these $i + j$ vertices. The next term $\binom{n}{i+j-1}$ allows us to select $(i + j - 1)$ distinct edges (keys) to participate in the tree.

No. Edges	E(AC)	Actual number
16	1.22	1
32	2.26	2
64	5.28	5
128	10.39	12
256	19.75	13
512	39.39	42

Table 4: Expected vs. Actual Number of Trees (ratio is set at 1.3)

Since these keys are distinct, there are $(i + j - 1)!$ ways to have the actual tree distinct. The next term $\{r^2 + i \cdot j - r \cdot (i + j)\}^{(n-i-j+1)}$ is the number of ways to have the remaining $n - i - j + 1$ edges freely go to G without being adjacent to any tree vertices. The last term, the denominator r^{2n} is the total number of ways to put n edges into G.

Table 4 shows the actual number of trees in G with various numbers of vertices and edges, and the expected values computed by the E(Trees) formula.

3.2.3 Observed Number of Indirect Edges

An adequate number of indirect edges is vital to a successful OPMPHF. Table 5 summarizes the observed components, observed trees, observed number of indirect edges generated by our one bit marking scheme, observed total number of zero degree vertices, and the observed total number of trees in G generated from a CISI vector collection of 74264 keys. The different ratios for G that were tested are 1.22, 1.3, 1.4 and 1.5.

It can be seen that most G will have only one or a few big cycle components and a couple of smaller tree components. Notice also that the number of indirect edges varies inversely with the size of G. This means more edges need to be indirect as G becomes smaller. On the other hand, a small G will have few vertices of zero degree or in tree components. Consequently, for our scheme to be successful we have to select a G that is not too small. A rough bound on the number of allowed indirect edges (keys) for our algorithm to be successful is $E(AC)$, i.e., the total number of zero vertices plus the total number of trees. The maximum number of indirect edges in a particular G is the total number of edges in non-tree components. Through the usage of mark bits, we can further lower that amount, given that the size of G is reasonably chosen.

Ratio	Components	Trees	Zero degree vertices	Indirect edges
1.20	4258	4257	16725	16536
1.25	4922	4921	18773	13914
1.30	5831	5830	20724	11789
1.40	7409	7407	24914	7365
1.50	9361	9360	29349	4510

Table 5: Number of Indirect Edges in a 74264 Edge G

4 Test Collections and Timing Statistics

Section 1.3 explains two applications of OPMPHFs for information retrieval. The first involved dictionary structures, and has led to our experimentation with dictionary key sets derived in part from the CED. Timing and other descriptive statistics from these runs with our OPMPHF algorithm are given in Table 6. On the other hand, Table 7 shows results for a set of 74,264 tuples based on the inverted files data for the CISI test collection. All of these runs were made on a Sequent Symmetry in the Department of Computer Science at VPI&SU, with 10 processors each rated at 4 MIPS and 32 megabytes of main memory. Since the algorithm used here is sequential, we used only one processor. Times were measured in seconds using the UNIX "times()" routine, and so are precise up to 1/60th of a second.

In Table 6, we show timings for runs on graphs with different numbers of edges (varying from 32 to 16384). Since the ratio is fixed at 1.25, the number of vertices in G is equal to 1.25*edges. We notice from Table 6 that the timing is approximately linear in the size of the key set, as is expected from our analysis. In Table 7, we list timings for runs on the 74,264 edge graph (CISI vector collection) with ratio varying from 1.22 to 1.5. Table 7 shows that as the ratio gets smaller (from 1.5 to 1.22), the Searching step takes more time to finish. This is because more indirect edges have to be packed into a smaller number of zero-degree or tree vertices.

5 Conclusion

In this paper, a practical algorithm for finding order-preserving minimal perfect hash functions is described. The method is able to find OPMPHFs for various sizes of key sets in almost linear time, with the function size remaining within reasonable bounds. The application of the method to dictionary and inverted file construction is also illustrated. Several

Edges	Prepare	Order	Search
32	0.27	0.02	0.00
64	0.37	0.02	0.03
128	0.38	0.02	0.03
256	0.43	0.07	0.08
512	0.52	0.10	0.12
1024	0.75	0.20	0.32
2048	1.19	0.37	0.65
4096	2.03	0.73	1.35
8192	3.48	1.52	2.53
16384	6.67	3.05	5.45

Table 6: Timing Results for Dictionary Collection

Edges	Prepare	Order	Search
1.20	26.08	13.80	72.10
1.25	26.18	13.85	23.33
1.30	26.23	13.78	14.78
1.40	26.40	13.60	10.35
1.50	26.38	13.38	9.45

Table 7: Timing Results for Inverted File Data

probabilistic analysis results on the characteristics of the random graph G are given. They are useful in guiding the proper selection of various parameters and providing insights on the design of the three main steps of the algorithm.

More experiments with the algorithm are planned. One direction is to find ways to make more edges direct so that an OPMPHF can be specified using a smaller ratio setting. Other possible interests are concerned with applications. Currently, we are using the scheme to index graph structured data. More benefits can be obtained when the scheme is applied to other fields.

Other experimentation is proceeding with a wide range of key sets. We are experimenting with a key set provided by OCLC that has more than 4 million unique keys, and so will be able to validate our approach with what are clearly very large databases.

Additional work with MPHF and OPMPHF algorithms is underway, using several somewhat different approaches. We have preliminary results regarding a MPHF method that uses much smaller function specifications and is quite fast. Subsequent papers will discuss this and other findings.

References

[AUST60]   Austin T. L. The Enumeration of Point Labeled Chromatic Graphs and Trees. *Canadian Journal of Mathematics* 12, 1960: 535-545.

[BOLL85]   Bollobs, B. Random Graphs. Academic Press, London, 1985.

[CHEN90]   Chen, Qi Fan. The Object-Oriented Network Database Model: Theory and Design for Information Retrieval Applications. Dissertation proposal, Department of Computer Science, Virginia Polytechnic Institute & State University, January, 1990.

[CHEN89]   Chen, Qi Fan. Proposed Specification for an Associative Network Database. Draft report, Department of Computer Science, Virginia Polytechnic Institute & State University, 1989.

[DATT88]   Datta, S. Implementation of a Perfect Hash Function Schemes. Master's report, Department of Computer Science, Virginia Polytechnic Institute & State University, 1988.

[DAOUD90]   Daoud, Amjad M. Efficient Data Structures for Information Retrieval Systems. Dissertation proposal, Department of Computer Science, Virginia Polytechnic Institute& State University, March, 1990.

[ENBO88]   Enbody, R. J. and Du H.C. Dynamic hashing schemes. *ACM Computing Surveys* **20**, 1988: 85-113.

[FOX90]   Fox, E.A., editor and project manager. Virginia Disc One. Produced by Nimbus Records, 1990, to appear. Blacksburg, VA: VPI&SU Press.

[FOX89a]   Fox, E.A., Chen, Q. F., Heath, L. and Datta, S. A More Cost Effective Algorithm for Finding Perfect Hash Functions. *Proceedings of the Seventeenth Annual ACM Computer Science Conference,* 1989, 114-122.

[FOX89b]   Fox, E.A., Heath, L.S. and Chen, Q. F. An $O(n \log n)$ Algorithm for Finding Minimal Perfect Hash Functions. TR 89-10, Department of Computer Science, Virginia Polytechnic Institute & State University. Submitted for publication, 1989.

[FOX88a]   Fox, E.A., J. Nutter, T. Ahlswede, M. Evens, and J. Markowitz. Building a Large Thesaurus for Information Retrieval. *Proceedings Second Conference on Applied Natural Language Processing,* Austin, TX, Feb. 9-12, 1988: 101-108.

[FOX88b]   Fox, E.A. Optical Disks and CD-ROM: Publishing and Access. In *Annual Review of Information Science and Technology,* Martha E. Williams (ed.), ASIS / Elsevier Science Publishers B.V., Amsterdam, **23**, 1988: 85-124.

[FOX87]   Fox, E.A. Development of the CODER System: a Testbed for Artificial Intelligence Methods in Information Retrieval. *Information Processing and Management* **23**, 1987: 341-366.

[FOX83]   Fox, E.A. Characterization of Two New Experimental Collections in Computer and Information Science Containing Textual and Bibliographic Concepts. TR 83-561, Department of Computer Science, Cornell University, Ithaca, NY, Sept. 1983.

[FRAN89]   France, R.K., E. Fox, J.T. Nutter, and Q.F. Chen. Building A Relational Lexicon for Text Understanding and Retrieval. *Proceedings First International Language Acquisition Workshop,* Aug. 21, 1989, Detroit, MI. 6 pages.

[GARG86] Garg, Anil K. and C. C. Gotlieb Order-Preserving Key Transformations. *ACM Transactions on Database Systems*, 11(2):213-234, June 1986.

[HANK79] Hanks, P., editor. Collins English Dictionary. William Collins Sons & Co., London, 1979.

[MEHL82] Mehlhorn, K. G. On the Program Size of Perfect and Universal Hash Functions. *Proceedings of the 23rd Annual IEEE Symposium on Foundations of Computer Science,* 1982: 170-175.

[NUTT89] Nutter, J.T., Fox, E.A., and Evens, M. Building a Lexicon from Machine-Readable Dictionaries for Improved Information Retrieval. *The Dynamic Text: 16th ALLC and 9th ICCH International Conferences,* Toronto, Ontario, June 6-9, 1989, revised version to appear in *Literary and Linguistic Computing.*

[PALM85] Palmer, E. M. Graphical Evolution: An Introduction to the Theory of Random Graphs. John Wiley & Sons, New York, 1985.

[SAGE85] Sager, T. J. A Polynomial Time Generator for Minimal Perfect Hash Functions, *Communications of the ACM,* **28**, 1985, 523-532.

6   Appendices

A   The Mapping Phase

Step   Description of Algorithm Step

1.   build random table for h_0, h_1 and h_2.
2.   for each v in $[0 \ldots 2r - 1]$ do vertex[v].firstedge = 0; vertex[v].degree = 0
3.   for each i in $[1 \ldots n]$ do
     edge[i].h_0 = $h_0(k_i)$; edge[i].h_1 = $h_1(k_i)$; edge[i].h_2 = $h_2(k_i)$
     edge[i].nextedge$_1$ = 0
     add edge[i] to linked list with header vertex[$h_1(k_i)$].firstedge;
          increment vertex[$h_1(k_i)$].degree
     add edge[i] to linked list with header vertex[$h_2(k_i)$].firstedge;
          increment vertex[$h_2(k_i)$].degree

4. for each v in $[0 \ldots r - 1]$ do
   check that all edges in linked list vertex[v].firstedge
   have distinct (h_0, h_1, h_2) triples.
5. if triples are not distinct then repeat from step(1).

B   The Ordering Phase

Step   Description of Algorithm Step

1. CId = 0 /* assign all vertices an ID 0. */
   for v in $[0 \ldots 2r - 1]$ do assign CId to v
   CId = 1
   for v in $[0 \ldots 2r - 1]$ do /*assign unique nonzero IDs to $CCYs$ and ACs. */
       if v has nonzero degree and its component ID equals 0 then
          initialize(VSTACK) /* process one component. */
          push(v, VSTACK) /* save the first vertex of the component. */
          do
             v = pop(VSTACK) /* get an unassigned vertex from VSTACK. */
             assign CId to v /* assign the ID. */
             for each w adjacent to v do
                /* if there are vertices unassigned, put them into VSTACK. */
             if component ID of w is zero and not in VSTACK then
                push(w, VSTACK)
             while VSTACK is not empty
          CId = CId +1 /* increase ID for next component. */
2. initialize(VSTACK) /* get all one-degree vertices into VSTACK. */ .
   for each nonzero degree v in $[0 \ldots 2r - 1]$ do
       if vertex[v].degree = 1 then
          push(v, VSTACK)
          decrement vertex[v].degree
3. while VSTACK is not empty do /* visit and truncate all edges in E_{CP}. */ .
       v = pop(VSTACK)
       for each w adjacent to v do
          if degree of w > 0 then decrease vertex[w].degree
          if vertex[w].degree = 1 then push(w, VSTACK)
4. make all vertices not SELECTED /* obtain a VS_{CC} for all V_{CC} vertices. */ .

$i = 1$;

for all nonzero degree and not SELECTED v in $[0 \ldots 2r - 1]$ do

    select v_i = a vertex of maximum degree > 0

    initialize(VHEAP); insert $(v_i,$ VHEAP)

    do

        v_i = deletemax(VHEAP)

        mark v_i SELECTED and put v_i into VS

        for each w adjacent to v_i do

            if w is not SELECTED and w is not in VHEAP then

                insert(w, VHEAP)

        $i = i + 1$

    while VHEAP is not empty

5.   for $i = 1$ to t do /* assign indirection bit to all vertices in V_{CC} */ .

Let $s = |K(v_i)|$ and w_j be any MARKED vertex adjacent to v_i.

Let t be the number of not MARKED vertices adjacent to v_i;

if $s = 0$ then vertex$[v_i]$.bit $= 1$

if $s = 1$ then

    if vertex$[w_1]$.bit $= 0$ then vertex$[v_1]$.bit $= 1$

    else vertex$[v_1]$.bit $= 0$

if $s > 1$ then

    if $i = 0$ and vertex$[w_j]$.bit $= 0$ for all w_j then vertex$[v_i]$.bit $= 0$

    else

        for all w_j do

            if vertex$[w_j] = 0$ then vertex$[w_j]$.bit $= 1$

        vertex$[v_i]$.bit $= 1$

C The Searching Phase

Step   Description of Algorithm Step

1. $R = \{\}$, $S = \{\}$ /* S is the set of component IDs of those occupied trees. */

                 /* R records the root vertices of trees in S. */

                 /*Both sets are empty at first. */

    for $i = 1$ to t do /* assign g values to V_{CC}s to have edges in E_{CC} indirectly hashed. */

        mark v_i ASSIGNED /* select the next vertex in VS_{CC} for g value assignment. */

        establish a random probe sequence $s_0, s_1, \ldots, s_{n-1}$ for $[0 \ldots n - 1]$

$j = 0$

<u>do</u>

Let W be the set of ASSIGNED vertices adjacent to v_i

collision = false

<u>if</u> $|K(v_i)| = 0$ <u>then</u> /* v_i is the first vertex of an un-assigned component. */

    vertex$[v_i]$.g = s_j; /* assign v_i's g entry the value s_j. */

<u>else</u>

<u>if</u> $|K(v_i)| = 1$ **AND** vertex$[v_i]$.mark $\neq$ vertex$[w]$.mark <u>then</u>

        /* if only one edge in the level and it is a direct edge, then assign the g value */

        /* to vertex v_i such that h_{final} of the edge can be computed directly. */

    let w be in W and k in $K(v_i)$

    vertex$[v_i]$.g = [edge$[k]$.final $-$ edge$[k]$.h$_0$ $-$ vertex$[w]$.g] mod n

        /* assign g value when k is direct */

    <u>if</u> edge$[k]$.final $\geq a$ <u>then</u> vertex$[v_i]$.g = edge$[k]$.final $- a$

    <u>else</u> vertex$[v_i]$.g = $n - a +$ edge$[k]$.final

<u>else</u>   /* all the edges in the level have to be indirect. Need to find */

        /* unoccupied zero-degree vertices or trees. */

    <u>if</u> v_i in $[0 \ldots r - 1]$ <u>then</u> /* distinguish which side v_i is on */

        <u>for</u> each k in $K(v_i)$ <u>do</u> /* v_i is on h_1 side. */

            $h(k) =$ edge$[k]$.h$_0$ + vertex$[$edge$[k]$.h$_2] + (s_j$ mod $2r)$

                /* obtain the location of indirect-to vertex. */

            <u>if</u> vertex$[h(k)]$ is occupied **OR** vertex$[h(k)]$.CId in S <u>then</u>

                collision = true /* the indirect-to vertex is occupied. */

    <u>else</u> /* the v_i is on h_2 side. */

        <u>for</u> each k in $K(v_i)$ <u>do</u>

            $h(k) =$ edge$[k]$.h$_0$ + vertex$[$edge$[k]$.h$_1] + (s_j$ mod $2r)$

            <u>if</u> vertex$[h(k)]$ is occupied **OR** vertex$[h(k)]$.CId in S <u>then</u>

                collision = true

    <u>if</u> not collision <u>then</u>

            /* if all indirect-to locations are not occupied, */

            /* set all of them occupied. */

        <u>for</u> each k in $K(v_i)$ <u>do</u>

            <u>if</u> vertex$[h(k)]$ is a zero-degree vertex <u>then</u>

                set vertex$[h(k)]$ occupied

        <u>else</u>

$$S = S \text{ UNION } \{\text{vertex}[h(k)].\text{CId}\}$$
$$R = R \text{ UNION } \{\text{vertex}[h(k)]\}$$
$\text{vertex}[h(k)].g = \text{edge}[k].\text{final}$ /* set the g value of for indirect key */
$i = i + 1$
<u>else</u> /* if this s_j causes any collisions, try next one. */
$j = j + 1$
<u>if</u> $j > n - 1$ <u>then</u>
fail
while collision

2. initialize(VSTACK) /* process E_{AC}. */ .
<u>for</u> $i = 0$ to $n - 1$ <u>do</u>
if v_i is both cycle and tree vertex <u>then</u>
/* identify starting vertices. */
<u>for</u> all w not ASSIGNED in step 1 and adjacent to v_i <u>do</u>
push(w, VSTACK)
<u>while</u> VSTACK is not empty <u>do</u> $v = $ pop(VSTACK)
/* directly hash all tree edges. */
mark v ASSIGNED
<u>for</u> w ASSIGNED and adjacent to v <u>do</u>
let k join v and w
$\text{vertex}[v_i].g = [\text{edge}[k].\text{final} - \text{edge}[k].h_0 - \text{vertex}[w].g] \bmod n$
<u>for</u> all w not ASSIGNED and adjacent to v and not in VSTACK <u>do</u>
push(w, VSTACK)

3. repeat (2) for all vertices in R. Each vertex in R will act as v_i in (2).

4. repeat (2) for arbitrary root vertices in ACs that have not accepted any indirect edges. Each such vertex will act as v_i in (2)

On the Interrelationship of Dictionary Size and Completeness

Hubert Hüther

Galgenbergstr. 13

D–6654 Kirkel-Limbach

West Germany

April 21, 1990

Abstract

When dictionaries for specific applications or subject fields are derived from a text collection, the frequency distribution of the terms in the collection gives information about the expected completeness of the dictionary. If only a subset of the terms in the collection is to be included in the dictionary, the completeness of the dictionary can be optimized with respect to dictionary size.

In this paper, formulas for the relationship between the frequency distribution of the terms in the collection and expected dictionary completeness are derived. First we regard one-dimensional dictionaries where the (non-trivial) terms occuring in the texts are to be included in the dictionary. Then we describe the case of two-dimensional dictionaries, which are needed for example for automatic indexing with a controlled vocabulary; here relationships between text terms and descriptors from the prescribed vocabulary have to be stored in the dictionary. For both cases, formulas for the interpolation and extrapolation with respect to different collection sizes are derived.

We give experimental results for one-dimensional dictionaries and show how the completeness can be estimated and optimized.

1   Introduction

Systems for automatic text analysis mostly are based on a dictionary or knowledge base. For tasks like automatic hyphenation or spelling checking, one-dimensional dictionaries are used, where the terms occuring in the texts (after the removal of stopwords) are stored in the dictionary. Two-dimensional dictionaries are needed for example for knowledge-based text analysis or automatic indexing with a controlled vocabulary. In this case, the dictionary contains relationships between terms from the text and concepts or descriptors from the controlled vocabulary. (In the following, we will use the terminology from the automatic indexing task for the discussion of the two-dimensional case).

When the information stored in the dictionary is derived from a collection of texts (documents), a relationship between the number of documents considered, the size of the dictionary and the completeness of the dictionary can be derived. In general, with an increasing number of documents, the completeness of the dictionary will improve. On the other hand, the effort spent for the dictionary construction process as well as the size of the dictionary increases. We will show how the completeness of the dictionary can be optimized with respect to these factors.

Our model differs from other approaches which use the length of (cumulated) texts and the number of occurrences of a term in the corpus as basic parameters. In order to assume the different occurrences of a single term to be independent of each other, we only distinguish between the occurrence and non-occurrence of the term in a document. Therefore, our basic parameters are the number of documents in the collection and the document frequency of a term, which is the number of documents in which the term occurs.

In this paper, the following problems are discussed:

- Completeness of a dictionary: For this purpose, measures for the dictionary completeness are defined. It is shown how these measures can be estimated from frequency distributions of the text collection the dictionary is derived from. Here the effect of different parameters in the dictionary construction process can be taken into account, too.

- Interpolation for different text collection sizes: If the dictionary size is restricted (e.g. for reasons of efficiency), one can derive the dictionary from a subset of the whole collection. For this problem, formulas for the interpolation of dictionary size and completeness are given. Furthermore, by choosing the size of the collection subset and parameters restricting the terms or term-descriptor pairs to be stored in the dictionary, the dictionary completeness can be optimized for a fixed dictionary size.

- Extrapolation with respect to text collection size: Having information about a text collection of fixed size, one is interested in estimating the completeness of dictionaries that could be derived from larger text collections (e.g. estimating the collection size needed for certain dictionary completeness). This problem is discussed only briefly here.

2 One-dimensional dictionaries

As a measure of completeness for one-dimensional dictionaries, we regard the expected number of terms per document which are not included in the dictionary. Let $T = \{t_1, t_2, t_3, \ldots\}$ denote the set of terms in the collection and $T_d \subset T$ the set of terms occurring in document d. With $p_i = P(t_i \in T_d)$ we denote the probability that a term $t_i \in T$ occurs in a randomly selected document d. For a subset of n documents of the collection we assume that we have a distribution of the document frequencies of terms. Regarding the terms that have currently the document frequency j, the expected number of these terms that will occur in the next document (that is, these terms change from frequency j to $j + 1$) is denoted by

$$E(j \rightarrow j + 1, n \rightarrow n + 1).$$

The probability that a term t_i has the document frequency j in n documents is

$$\binom{n}{j} p_i^j (1 - p_i)^{n-j}$$

For the probability that a term t_i will change from frequency j to $j+1$ when the document $n+1$ is considered, we get

$$p_i(j \rightarrow j + 1, n \rightarrow n + 1) = \binom{n}{j} p_i^j (1 - p_i)^{n-j} \cdot p_i.$$

This expression can be transformed to

$$p_i(j \rightarrow j + 1, n \rightarrow n + 1) = \frac{j+1}{n+1} \binom{n+1}{j+1} p_i^{j+1} (1 - p_i)^{n+1-(j+1)}.$$

For the expectation $E(j \rightarrow j + 1, n \rightarrow n + 1)$, we get

314

$$E(j \to j+1, n \to n+1) = \frac{j+1}{n+1} \sum_{i \geq 1} \binom{n+1}{j+1} p_i^{j+1} (1-p_i)^{n+1-(j+1)}$$

$$= \frac{j+1}{n+1} E_{n+1}(j+1).$$

There is $E_{n+1}(j+1)$ (also denoted as $E(j+1, n+1)$) the expectation for the number of terms that occurs exactly in $j+1$ documents of $n+1$ regarded documents (see also the formulas (3) and (4)). In the following, we will use the approximation

$$E(j \to j+1, n \to n+1) \approx \frac{j+1}{n} E_n(j+1).$$

Instead of this simple approximation, one can also apply formula (3) for extrapolation with $n' = n+1$ (see /Hü 90/). Assume that we have a frequency distribution for n documents, where #(j,n) denotes the number of terms that have document frequency j within the n documents. Then we can approximate $E(j \to j+1, n \to n+1)$ by

$$E(j \to j+1, n \to n+1) \approx \frac{j+1}{n} \cdot \#(j+1, n). \qquad (1)$$

For the expected number of new terms, we get from the above equation with $j = 0$

$$E(0 \to 1, n \to n+1) \approx \frac{1}{n} \cdot \#(1, n). \qquad (2)$$

These formulas answer the question of dictionary completeness for a given frequency distribution of a text collection. If the dictionary is to be restricted to terms that occur at least $j+1$ times in the collection, formula (1) gives the expected number of the terms with frequency j that will occur in a new document.

Formula (2) has been discussed by several authors before (e.g. /Ed 84/ and /KM 57/), where n has the meaning of the length of (cumulated) text. The more general formula (1) is published in /Hü 85c/ and /Hü 89/. In /Go 53/, for model of a frequency distribution the formula

$$E(q_j) = \frac{j+1}{n+1} \frac{E_{n+1}(j+1)}{E_n(j)}$$

is derived, where $E(q_j)$ denotes the expected ratio of a term which occur j times in a text of length n. However, this kind of application to texts will yield a bias, as words are not distributed randomly in a text. For example, when regarding a concatenation of documents, words with a low frequency tend to occur several times within the same document, instead of being distributed over the whole corpus. However, this bias for low term frequencies is not as serious as the deviations between model and reality in the case of the (frequently cited) model from Simon (/Sm 55/). While the latter model is inappropriate for low document frequencies, Good's model can be applied here, too.

Now we regard the problems of interpolation and extrapolation, where we want to derive the parameters discussed above for text collections of different size, given that we have the frequency distribution for n documents. Again #(l, n) denotes the number of terms with document frequency

l for n documents. For a subset with n' from the n documents of the whole collection, we want to derive the expected number $E(n', n, h(t, n') = k)$ of terms with document frequency k for n' documents. Similarly, we will compute the expected number $E(n', n, h(t, n') \geq k)$ with a document frequency of at least k for n' documents. In /Hü 84/ (see also /GT 56/, /Ka 65/ or /Br 75/), these expectations are derived as

$$E(n', n, h(t, n') = k) = \sum_{l \geq k} \frac{\binom{n'}{k}\binom{n-n'}{l-k}}{\binom{n}{l}} \cdot \#(l, n)$$

$$(0 \leq k \leq n, n' \leq n)$$

(3)

$$E(n', n, h(t, n') \geq k) = \sum_{l \geq 1} \left(1 - \sum_{m=0}^{k-1} \frac{\binom{n'}{m}\binom{n-n'}{l-m}}{\binom{n}{l}} \right) \cdot \#(l, n)$$

$$(1 \leq k \leq n)$$
$$(0 \leq n' \leq n)$$

(4)

In /Hü 84/ approximations of these exact formulas are derived by dividing the collection size into J $(J \in I\!N)$ intervals of equal length. For $j = n' \cdot J/n$, we get

$$E(j, J, h(t, j) = k) \approx E^*(j, J, h = k) =$$
$$\sum_{l \geq k} \binom{l}{k} \left(\frac{j}{J} \right)^k \left(1 - \frac{j}{J} \right)^{l-k} \cdot \#(l, J)$$

$$(0 \leq k \leq n)$$
$$(0 \leq j \leq J)$$

(5)

$$E(j, J, h(t, j) \geq k) \approx E^*(j, J, h \geq k) =$$
$$\sum_{l \geq k} \left(1 - \sum_{r=0}^{k-1} \binom{l}{r} \left(\frac{j}{J} \right)^r \left(1 - \frac{j}{J} \right)^{l-r} \right) \cdot \#(l, J)$$

$$(0 \leq k \leq n)$$
$$(0 \leq j \leq J)$$

(6)

(In the expectations noted here, j and J are used as simplified notations for $\frac{n \cdot j}{J}$ and n, respectively.)

With the formulas (3) und (4) (or (5) and (6)), the interpolation problem can be solved (see also the examples in section 4).

For the extrapolation problem, the same formulas can be applied. However, without additional mathematical methods, only expectations for the double collection size can be computed (see also /GT 56/, /Hü 89/, /Ka 65/, /Br 75/). A different approach for the extrapolation problem is described in /Hü 89/ and /Tz 88/.

3   Two-dimensional dictionaries

Like in the one-dimensional case, let p_i denote the probability that the term t_i occurs in a randomly selected document. $P(s_j|t_i) = p_{ij}$ is the probability that a document will be assigned the descriptor s_j manually, given that term t_i occurs in the document. For a fixed set of n documents, let $f(t_i)$ denote the document frequency of t_i, and $h(t_i, s_j)$ is the number of documents which have both term t_i and descriptor s_j.

If we regard the number of occurrences of the pairs (t_i, s_j) irrespective of the document frequency $f(t_i)$ of t_i, the methods described for one-dimensional dictionaries can be applied. For considering both the pair frequency and the term frequency we need appropriate formulas for the two-dimensional case.

For the probability $p_{ij}(h, f, n)$ that the term-descriptor pair (t_i, s_j) has the frequencies h and f for the n documents, we get the expression:

$$p_{ij}(h, f, n) = \binom{n}{f} p_i^f (1 - p_i)^{n-f} \binom{f}{h} p_{ij}^h (1 - p_{ij})^{f-h}$$

Then the probability that a pair (t_i, s_j) has the parameters (h,f,n) and that the term t_i will occur in a randomly selected document n+1 can be computed by:

$$\binom{n}{f} p_i^f (1 - p_i)^{n-f} \binom{f}{h} p_{ij}^h (1 - p_{ij})^{f-h} \cdot p_i$$

For the probability $p_{ij}(h \to h + 1, f \to f + 1, n \to n + 1)$ that the pair (t_i, s_j) with parameters (h,f,n) will have the parameters (h+1,f+1,n+1) after considering a randomly selected document n+1,we get:

$$p_{ij}(h \to h + 1, f \to f + 1, n \to n + 1) = \binom{n}{f} p_i^f (1 - p_i)^{n-f} \binom{f}{h} p_{ij}^h (1 - p_{ij})^{f-h} \cdot p_i \cdot p_{ij}$$

This can be transformed into:

$$
\begin{aligned}
p_{ij}(h &\to h + 1, f \to f + 1, n \to n + 1) = \\
&= \frac{f+1}{n+1}\binom{n+1}{f+1} p_i^{f+1}(1 - p_i)^{n-f} \frac{h+1}{f+1}\binom{f+1}{h+1} p_{ij}^{h+1}(1 - p_{ij})^{f-h} \\
&= \frac{h+1}{n+1}\binom{n+1}{f+1} p_i^{f+1}(1 - p_i)^{n+1-(f+1)}\binom{f+1}{h+1} p_{ij}^{h+1}(1 - p_{ij})^{f+1-(h+1)}
\end{aligned}
$$

The expectation E(h,f,n) for the number of pairs (t,s) with parameters (h,f,n) is given by the equation:

$$E(h, f, n) = \sum_{i \geq 1, j \geq 1} p_{ij}(h, f, n)$$

From this, we get for the expectation $E(h \to h + 1, f \to f + 1, n \to n + 1)$ of the number of pairs which have the parameters (h, f, n) and $(h + 1, f + 1, n + 1)$:

$$
\begin{aligned}
E(h &\to h + 1, f \to f + 1, n \to n + 1) \\
&= \sum_{i \geq 1, j \geq j} p_{ij}(h \to h + 1, f \to f + 1, n \to n + 1)
\end{aligned}
$$

This gives us the following relationship:

$$\boxed{E(h \to h+1, f \to f+1, n \to n+1) = \frac{h+1}{n+1} E(h+1, f+1, n+1)} \tag{7}$$

In a similar way, we can compute the probability $p_{ij}(h \to h, f \to f+1, n \to n+1)$ that with document n+1 the pair (t_i, s_j) will change from (h, f, n) to $(h, f+1, n+1)$:

$$p_{ij}(h \to h, f \to f+1, n \to n+1) = \binom{n}{f} p_i^f (1-p_i)^{n-f} \binom{f}{h} p_{ij}^h (1-p_{ij})^{f-h} \cdot p_i \cdot (1-p_{ij})$$

This can be transformed into:

$$p_{ij}(h \to h, f \to f+1, n \to n+1) =$$
$$= \frac{f+1}{n+1} \binom{n+1}{f+1} p_i^{f+1} (1-p_i)^{n+1-(f+1)} \frac{f+1-h}{f+1} \binom{f+1}{h} p_{ij}^h (1-p_{ij})^{f+1-h}$$
$$= \frac{f+1-h}{n+1} \binom{n+1}{f+1} p_i^{f+1} (1-p_i)^{n+1-(f+1)} \binom{f+1}{h} p_{ij}^h (1-p_{ij})^{f+1-h}$$

So we get the equation:

$$\boxed{E(h \to h, f \to f+1, n \to n+1) = \frac{f+1-h}{n+1} E(h, f+1, n+1)} \tag{8}$$

Formulas (7) and (8) correspond to formula (1) for the one-dimensional case. (In order to estimate $E(i, j, n+1)$ in both equations, one can use the approximation $E(i, j, n)/n \approx E(i, j, n+1)/n+1$. A different solution described in /Hü 90/ applies formula (9) by setting $n' = n+1$ for this purpose.) However, using these formulas as completeness measures for two-dimensional dictionaries is only appropriate under special conditions: As only a part of all possible pairs in a collection is meaningful (and therefore should be included in the dictionary), we need a decision procedure in order to distinguish "meaningful" from "meaningless" pairs. For most applications, only intellectual decisions would be appropriate here. Below, we will discuss more formal criteria for the inclusion of term-descriptor pairs in the dictionary.

First we present the formulas for the interpolation and extrapolation problems. The expected number $E(h', f', n', n)$ of pairs (t, s) with the parameters h' and f' for a subset of n' documents from the whole collection (n documents) can be computed as (/Hü 89/):

$$E(h', f', n', n) =$$
$$\sum_{h \geq h', f \geq f'} \frac{\binom{n'}{f'} \binom{n-n'}{f-f'}}{\binom{n}{f}} \cdot \frac{\binom{f'}{h'} \binom{f-f'}{h-h'}}{\binom{f}{h}} \cdot \#(h, f, n) \tag{9}$$
$$(0 \leq h' \leq f' \leq n' \leq n; 1 \leq h \leq f \leq n)$$

Dividing the collection size n into J intervals of equal length, we get for $j = n' \cdot J/n$:

$$E(h', f', j, J) =$$

$$\sum_{h \geq h', J \geq f'} \binom{h}{h'} \binom{f-h}{f'-h'} \left(\frac{j}{J}\right)^{f'} \left(1-\frac{j}{J}\right)^{J-f'} \cdot \#(h, f, J) \tag{10}$$

$$(0 \leq h' \leq f'; 1 \leq h \leq f)$$

If there is no method available for the separation of "meaningful" and "meaningless" pairs (t, s), one can use the parameters $h(t, s)$ and $h(t, s)/f(t)$ as criteria for the decision about the inclusion of a pair in the dictionary. For example, for the development of the indexing dictionary of the AIR/PHYS indexing system described in /B-S 88/, the following criteria were used:

- $h(t, s) \geq 3$

- $h(t, s)/f(t) \geq 0.3$

Instead of using the ratio $h(t, s)/f(t)$ as criterion, one can also regard the underlying conditional probability $P(s|t)$ that descriptor s will be assigned to a document, given that term t occurs in the document text. For the estimation of this probability, we get with formulas (7) and (8) a different derivation than in /Hü 89/ and /FH 89/:

$$p_{OPT}(h, f, t) = \frac{(h+1)E(h+1, f+1, n+1)}{(h+1)E(h+1, f+1, n+1) + (f+1-h)E(h, f+1, n+1)} \tag{11}$$

The approach based on formal criteria bears two new problems:

- Now we can only decide for a pair (t, s) occurring in a new document, whether it fulfills after this $n+1$-th document the criteria for the inclusion in the dictionary (e.g. $h/f \geq 0.3$ and $h \geq 3$). The completeness measure have to be modified appropriatly.

- The formulas (9) and (10) can be applied only when we have the full frequency distribution (with the numbers of pairs (t, s) with different parameters h and f that do not fulfill the formal criteria), or when we have also at least all numbers of pairs (t, s) with different parameter f. For reasons of efficiency, these pairs can be excluded at an early stage in the dictionary construction process, and therefore the corresponding frequencies are not computed in most cases (/F-S 86/).

4 Experimental results

Here we describe some experiments with one-dimensional dictionaries. As terms we use single words and noun phrases reduced to their standard forms by a stemming algorithm which yields the infinitive of verbs and the singular of nouns. In addition, the components of a phrase must occur within a distance of 8 words.

4.1 Example 1

In our first example we compare the completeness of dictionaries based on different collection sizes and show how the completeness can be optimized. The experimental data for this example is derived from a collection of 24 000 documents of the Food Science and Technology Abstracts from the years 1971 and 1972. Here the average length of a document is 87.3 words, with 39.2 different terms per document. In table 1, we give the number of different terms (types) with certain document frequencies for collection sizes ranging from 3 000 to 24 000 documents. The column named tokens contains the sum of the document frequencies of all terms.

table 1

docs	$f = 1$	$f = 2$	$f = 3$	$f = 4$	types	tokens
3 000	11 946	2 177	1 065	610	19 208	118 592
6 000	18 537	3 335	1 534	970	29 581	236 391
9 000	24 072	4 269	1 983	1 216	38 223	354 343
12 000	28 997	5 094	2 408	1 406	45 871	472 525
15 000	33 795	5 831	2 754	1 644	53 143	592 365
18 000	38 048	6 496	3 038	1 836	59 614	708 425
21 000	42 105	7 151	3 250	2 028	65 681	827 513
24 000	46 235	7 933	3 454	2 206	71 870	941 990

Numbers of document frequencies (FSTA)

From the numbers given in this table we can compute the expected number of new terms in a new document by applying formula (2). The corresponding results are shown in column headed $f = 1$ in table 2. Similarly, the other columns named $f = i$ give the expected number of terms which will occur for the i-th time in a randomly selected new document. The columns "$f \leq i$" give the corresponding sums of the other columns.

Table 2

docs	$f = 1$	$f \leq 1$	$f = 2$	$f \leq 2$	$f = 3$	$f \leq 3$	$f = 4$	$f \leq 4$
3 000	3.93	3.93	1.45	5.38	1.07	6.45	0.81	7.26
6 000	3.09	3.09	1.11	4.20	0.77	4.97	0.65	5.62
9 000	2.67	2.67	0.95	3.62	0.66	4.28	0.54	4.82
12 000	2.42	2.42	0.85	3.27	0.60	3.87	0.47	4.34
15 000	2.25	2.25	0.78	3.03	0.55	3.58	0.44	4.02
18 000	2.11	2.11	0.72	2.83	0.51	3.34	0.41	3.75
21 000	2.01	2.01	0.68	2.69	0.46	3.15	0.39	3.56
24 000	1.93	1.93	0.66	2.59	0.43	3.02	0.37	3.39

Expected numbers of new terms in a new document

Now we assume that we would derive dictionaries from the the different collections. We can either include all terms occurring in a collection, or we can restrict the dictionary to those terms that occur at least in i documents of the collection. In table 3, we list the completeness and the size of dictionaries based on different collections and restrictions. The size of a dictionary is given by the number of terms included, and the completeness is expressed by the expected number of missing terms per document. As an example, a dictionary derived from 3 000 documents with all terms included will contain 19 208 terms. In every new document, there will be 3.93 terms on the average that are not in this dictionary. On the other hand, a dictionary based on 18 000 documents and the terms with $f \geq 4$ will have a smaller size (12 032), but a higher completeness with only 3.75 "new" terms per document.

Table 3

docs	size	$f \geq 1$	size	$f \geq 2$	size	$f \geq 3$	size	$f \geq 4$
3 000	19 208	3.93	7 262	5.38	5 085	6.45	4 020	7.26
6 000	29 581	3.09	11 044	4.20	7 709	4.97	6 175	5.62
9 000	38 223	2.67	14 151	3.62	9 882	4.28	7 899	4.82
12 000	45 871	2.42	16 874	3.27	11 780	3.87	9 372	4.34
15 000	53 143	2.25	19 348	3.03	13 517	3.58	10 763	4.02
18 000	59 614	2.11	21 566	2.83	15 070	3.34	12 032	3.75
21 000	65 681	2.01	23 576	2.69	16 425	3.15	13 175	3.56
24 000	71 870	1.93	25 635	2.59	17 702	3.02	14 248	3.39

sets of documents - dictionary size - dictionary completeness

In most applications, the different frequency distributions shown in table 1 will not be available directly. If there is only a frequency distribution for the whole collection, the expected numbers for subsets of the collection can be computed by application of formulas (5) and (6). In table 4, the expectations for subsets of the collection (derived this way) are given. The comparison with the actual numbers (table 1) shows very little differences. Obviously there is no need to collect data for subsets of the collections, as the expectations derived from the whole collection are very good approximations of actual numbers.

Table 4

docs	$f = 1$	$f = 2$	$f = 3$	$f = 4$	types	tokens
3 000	12 034	2 205	1 027	618	19 272	117 749
6 000	18 724	3 348	1 562	936	29 756	235 498
9 000	24 326	4 272	1 988	1 199	38 432	353 264
12 000	29 337	5 089	2 352	1 421	46 128	470 995
15 000	33 950	5 843	2 677	1 621	53 176	588 744
18 000	38 267	6 557	2 972	1 810	59 751	706 493
21 000	42 349	7 248	3 234	1 999	65 959	824 241
24 000	46 235	7 933	3 454	2 206	71 870	941 990

Expectations for numbers from table 1

4.2 Example 2

As a second example, we regard a text collection of 392 000 documents from the physics data base PHYS of the Fachinformationszentrum Karlsruhe, West Germany. This text collection has been used for the construction of the indexing dictionary of the AIR/PHYS indexing system described in /B-S 88/. Here we consider only the terms of this dictionary which are noun phrases. For the generation of these phrases, the so called delimiter method described in /Lu 86/, /KR 86/, /JS 75/ was applied. For this collection the average document length is 103 words, with 57.8 different noun phrases per document.

In table 5, expectations for 12 subsets of different size are computed from the frequency distribution of the whole collection (by application of formulas (5) and (6)). Based on these numbers, dictionary size and completeness for different subsets and term frequency restrictions can be computed as shown in tables 6 and 7.

Table 5

docs	$f = 1$	$f = 2$	$f = 3$	$f = 4$	types	tokens
32 667	155 251	64 872	35 582	22 574	369 772	1 887 263
65 333	167 269	79 565	46 788	31 229	482 244	3 774 526
98 000	168 028	86 355	52 743	36 104	550 395	5 661 788
130 667	165 258	89 962	56 498	39 319	598 404	7 549 051
163 333	161 096	91 872	59 055	41 628	634 849	9 436 314
196 000	156 375	92 745	60 863	43 361	663 808	11 323 577
228 667	151 478	92 924	62 165	44 694	687 546	13 210 840
261 333	146 601	92 611	63 107	45 738	707 454	15 098 103
294 000	141 848	91 932	63 782	46 569	724 445	16 985 366
326 667	137 278	90 971	64 251	47 236	739 152	18 872 628
359 333	132 923	89 786	64 557	47 765	752 030	20 759 891
392 000	128 000	88 419	64 738	48 158	763 417	22 647 154

Expectations for numbers of document frequencies (PHYS)

Table 6

docs	$f = 1$	$f \leq 1$	$f = 2$	$f \leq 2$	$f = 3$	$f \leq 3$	$f = 4$	$f \leq 4$
32 667	4.75	4.75	3.97	8.72	3.27	11.99	2.76	14.75
65 333	2.56	2.56	2.44	5.00	2.15	7.15	1.91	9.06
98 000	1.71	1.71	1.76	3.47	1.61	5.08	1.47	6.55
130 667	1.26	1.26	1.37	2.63	1.30	3.93	1.20	5.13
163 333	0.99	0.99	1.12	2.11	1.08	3.19	1.02	4.21
196 000	0.80	0.80	0.95	1.75	0.93	2.68	0.88	3.56
228 667	0.66	0.66	0.81	1.47	0.82	2.29	0.78	3.07
261 333	0.56	0.56	0.71	1.27	0.72	1.99	0.70	2.69
294 000	0.48	0.48	0.63	1.11	0.65	1.76	0.63	2.39
326 667	0.42	0.42	0.56	0.98	0.59	1.57	0.58	2.15
359 333	0.37	0.37	0.50	0.87	0.54	1.41	0.53	1.94
392 000	0.33	0.33	0.45	0.78	0.50	1.28	0.49	1.77

Expectations for numbers of new noun phrases in a new document

Table 7

docs	size	$f \geq 1$	size	$f \geq 2$	size	$f \geq 3$	size	$f \geq 4$
32 667	369 772	4.75	214 521	8.72	149 649	11.99	114 067	14.75
65 333	482 244	2.56	314 975	5.00	235 410	7.15	188 622	9.06
98 000	550 395	1.71	382 367	3.47	296 012	5.08	243 269	6.55
130 667	598 404	1.26	433 146	2.63	343 184	3.93	286 686	5.13
163 333	634 849	0.99	473 753	2.11	381 881	3.19	322 826	4.21
196 000	663 808	0.80	707 433	1.75	414 688	2.68	353 825	3.56
228 667	687 546	0.66	536 068	1.47	443 144	2.29	380 979	3.07
261 333	707 454	0.56	560 853	1.27	468 242	1.99	405 135	2.69
294 000	724 445	0.48	582 597	1.11	490 665	1.76	426 883	2.39
326 667	739 152	0.42	601 874	0.98	510 903	1.57	446 652	2.15
359 333	752 030	0.37	619 107	0.87	529 321	1.41	464 764	1.94
392 000	763 417	0.33	635 417	0.78	546 998	1.28	482 260	1.77

sets of documents - dictionary size - dictionary completeness

If the scaling of dictionary size or completeness is not fine enough, a larger number of intervals for the subsets of the collection can be chosen. Furthermore, additional frequency restrictions (e.g. $f \geq 5$) can be considered.

5 Outlook

For the development of automatic indexing methods, the formulas (7) – (10) for two-dimensional dictionaries are more important than those for the one-dimensional case. As mentioned in section 3, there is a lack of appropriate empirical data for this kind of investigations, mainly because there are no complete frequency distributions available.

Another problem area is the notion of dictionary completeness: As a dictionary is only a means for automatic indexing and information retrieval, we would like to evaluate a dictionary in terms of indexing or retrieval quality. So the question is: What effect has the inclusion of a new term-descriptor pair in the dictionary on the final indexing or retrieval quality? Some concepts for an empirical investigation of this problem are described in /Hü 89/.

A different approach for the estimation of dictionary size and quality is described in /Hü 89/ and /Tz 88/: In contrast to the methods described in this paper, this approach only needs a sample of the whole collection in order to yield estimates for size and quality of dictionaries derived from the whole collection or subsets of it.

References

/B-S 88/ Biebricher, P.; Fuhr, N.; Knorz, G.; Lustig, G.; Schwantner M. (1988):
The automatic indexing system AIR/PHYS-from research to application.
In: Chiaramella, Y. (Ed.): Proceedings of the 1988 ACM Conference on Research and Development in Information Retrieval.
Presses Universitaires de Grenoble, (1988), 333-342

/Br 75/ Brookes, B.C. (1975):
A sampling theorem for finite discrete distributions.
J. of Documentation, 31, (1975), 26-35

/Ed 84/ Edmudson, H. P. (1984):
Mathematical models of text.
Information Processing & Management, 20, (1984), 261-8

/F-S 86/ Fuhr, N.; Jäger-Beck, R.; Schwantner, M. (1986):
Die Gewinnung von statistischen Relationen zwischen Terms und Deskriptoren.
In /Lu 86/.

/FH 89/ Fuhr, N.; Hüther, H. (1989):
Optimum Probability Estimation from Empirical Distributions.
Information Processing & Management, 25, (1989), 493-507

/Go 53/ Good, I.J. (1953):
The population frequencies of species and the estimation of population parameters.
Biometrika, 40,(1953), 237-264

/GT 56/ Good, I.J.; Toulmin, G.H. (1956):
The number of new species, and the increase in population coverage, when a sample is increased.
Biometrika, 43, (1956), 45-63

/Hü 84/ Hüther, H. (1984):
Wachstumsfunktionen berechnet mit Hilfe von eindimensionalen Häufigkeitsverteilungen.
(Interner Bericht DV-II-84-9), FB Informatik, TH Darmstadt, 1984

/Hü 85a/ Hüther, H. (1985):
Wachstumsfunktionen - Extrapolationen aus einer Häufigkeitsverteilung mit Hilfe einer theoretischen Häufigkeitsverteilung.
(Interner Bericht DV-II-85-5), FB Informatik, TH Darmstadt, 1985

/Hü 85b/ Hüther, H. (1985):
Erwartungswerte bei Häufigkeitenwechsel - Beziehung zu Extrapolationsformeln.
(Interner Bericht DV-II-85-14), FB Informatik, TH Darmstadt, 1985

/Hü 85c/ Hüther, H. (1985):
Eine theoretische Herleitung einer Häufigkeitsverteilung.
(Interner Bericht DV-II-85-10), FB Informatik, TH Darmstadt, 1985

/Hü 89/ Hüther, H. (1989):
Wachstumsfunktionen in der automatischen Indexierung.
Dissertation, FB Informatik, TH Darmstadt, 1989

/Hü 90/ Hüther, H. (1990):
Optimierung von Wörterbüchern.
(Interner Bericht DV-II-90-1), FB Informatik, TH Darmstadt, 1990

/JS 75/ Jaene, H.; Seelbach, D. (1975):
Maschinelle Extraktionen von zusammengesetzten Ausdrücken aus englischen Fachtexten.
(ZMD-A-29) Beuth Verlag, 1975

/Ka 65/ Kalinin, V.M. (1965):
Funkcionaly, svjazannye s raspredeleniem Puassona, i statističeskaja structura teksta [Functionals related to the poisson distribution, and the statistical structure of a text].
Trudy matematičeskogo instituta imeni V.A. Steklova 29., 1965, 182-197

/KM 57/ Koutsoudas, A. ; Machel, R. (1957):
Frequency of occurrence of words: a study of Zipf's law with application to mechanical translation.
University of Michigan Engineering Resaerch Institute, Publication 2144-147-T, University of Michigan, Ann Arbar, 1957

/KR 86/ Kienitz-Vollmer, B.; Reichardt, J. (1986):
Extraktion von Mehrwortgruppen im Projekt AIR/PHYS.
In /Lu 86/.

/Lu 86/ Lustig, G. (Hrsg., 1986):
Automatische Indexierung zwischen Forschung und Anwendung.
Olms Verlag, Hildesheim, 1986

/Sm 55/ Simon, H.A. (1955):
On a class of skew distribution functions.
Biometrika, 42, (1955), 425-40

/Tz 88/ Tzeras K. (1988):
Schätzfunktionen für die Relation Z.
Diploma thesis, FB Informatik, TH Darmstadt, 1988

Construction of Optimal Graphs for
Bit-Vector Compression

Abraham Bookstein and **Shmuel T. Klein**

Center for Information and Language Studies
University of Chicago, 1100 East 57-th Street
Chicago, IL 60637

The second author was partially supported by a fellowship of the Ameritech Foundation

Abstract:

Bitmaps are data structures occurring often in information retrieval. They are useful; they are also large and expensive to store. For this reason, considerable effort has been devoted to finding techniques for compressing them. These techniques are most effective for sparse bitmaps. We propose a preprocessing stage, in which bitmaps are first clustered and the clusters used to transform their member bitmaps into sparser ones, that can be more effectively compressed. The clustering method efficiently generates a graph structure on the bitmaps. The results of applying our algorithm to the Bible is presented: for some sets of bitmaps, our method almost doubled the compression savings.

1. Introduction

Textual Information Retrieval Systems (IRS) are voracious consumers of computer storage resources. Most conspicuous, of course, is the text itself, which constitutes the content of the database. But, to efficiently use the database, auxiliary structures must be created that themselves require a substantial ammount of space. Thus, mecanisms for compressing a wide range of data structures must be sought for the efficient operation of such systems [8]. To date, most attention has been given to, and progress made in, the area of text compression ([1], [11], [14]). In this paper, we shall describe and examine the possibilities of compressing bitmaps, a data structure often proposed for improving the performance of retrieval systems ([5], [16]).

Bitmaps occur often in information retrieval. They can represent the occurrences of a word in the sentences or paragraphs making up a text; they can indicate the documents associated with an index term; they appear as bit slices of a matrix of signatures; they might represent pixels in rows of a raster graphics display. They are useful; they are also large and expensive to store. Much work has been carried out on the compression of bitmaps, and this has been especially successful for those that are very sparse. But not all bitmaps are sparse, and even sparse bitmaps could benefit from further compression. This paper describes a method that complements existing compression techniques and improves their performance, at least for certain categories of bitmaps.

We concentrate here on sets of bitmaps such as are generally found in an IRS. How such bitmaps can be used to enhance the system is discussed in [2] and [4]. Each bit-position corresponds to a specified sub-unit of the database, henceforth referred to as a *segment*; below, a segment will refer to a paragraph of text, though, in other contexts, a full document (or even a set of documents) may be the preferred unit. For each different word (or index term) W in the database, there is a map $B(W)$, such that the i-th bit of $B(W)$ is 1 if and only if W appears in (or is assigned to) segment i. Such bitmaps can be compressed very efficiently. In part this is because they tend to be very sparse. That bitmaps compress better as they become sparser is expected theoretically. For suppose a bitmap can be considered as having been produced by a random bit generator, with the probability of a one bit being p (the theory can easily be extended to encompass more complex models of bitmap generation). Then the information content of a bit is given by:

$$H = -p \log p - (1 - p) \log(1 - p),$$

and, for a bitmap of ℓ bits, the quantity ℓH forms a lower bound on the number of bits needed to represent the bitmap. As is well known, H increases monotonically as p increases from 0 to .5, and then decreases monotonically as p continues growing. Since almost all of our bitmaps have p less than .5, we expect compression to improve as p decreases, that is, as the map becomes sparser. (For $p > .5$, we could complement the bitmap before proceding.) Thus we wish to be alert to opportunities for reducing the density of our bitmaps; this is the essence of the approach described in this paper.

Other factors also contribute to our ability to compress bitmaps effectively, as evidenced by the fact that actual IR bitmaps are more compressible than randomly generated bitmaps with the same density of 1-bits [3]. The reason for the better results is a *cluster-effect*: since the segment positions in the bitmaps are usually ordered by topic or chronologically, adjacent bits often correspond to segments treating the same or related subjects. Thus the appearance of a word in a given segment often implies that it also appears in neighboring segments. This effect is exploited by many compression methods, resulting in excellent reduction in storage requirements.

There is, however, another clustering possibility that has hitherto been overlooked, one involving sets of bitmaps (words), rather than sets of bits (segments) within a single bitmap. The occurrences of certain words, especially those taking part in well known phrases like Security Council or Curriculum vitæ, are sometimes strongly correlated accross segments in the sense that if one word appears in a certain segment, the other is also very likely to do so. Such pairs of bitmaps are likely to be quite similar. But identifying clusters of such highly associated words is not as direct as it was for bit clusters within a bitmap, because words and their associated bitmaps are generally arranged in lexicographical order, not in order of logical proximity. In this respect, IR bitmaps differ from self-clustered graphic bitmaps, in which adjacent (raster) rows are often similar. The objective of this paper is to show how to usefully identify clusters of correlated words, and then take advantage of these associations to squeeze out some additional compression.

In Section 2, we briefly review some known bitmap compression techniques and propose a new one that is simple and easy to implement; it will then be used as the compression component of a two-stage compression process described in Section 3. The first stage of the two stage process is to partition the bitmaps of our IR system into clusters of correlated bitmaps; the resulting clusters are then used to transform the original bitmaps into another set of bitmaps that are sparser and more effectively compressed in stage 2 of the process. In Section 4 we report on experiments testing the new method; the database we chose to study was the Hebrew Bible.

2. Bit-vector compression techniques

2.1 Overview of some known methods

Suppose we are given a bitmap v of length ℓ bits, of which s are ones and $\ell - s$ are zeros. In our applications, the maps are usually sparse, i.e., $s \ll \ell$. The simplest way to store v compactly for very small n is to **enumerate the positions** of the 1-bits. As one needs $d = \lceil \log_2 \ell \rceil$ bits to identify any position, this method would need sd bits for each map, which may well be much smaller than the ℓ bits required for the uncompressed original map. Alternatively, one could record the distances between successive 1-bits, that is, give the position of a 1-bit relative to the preceding 1-bit position rather than relative to the beginning of the vector. This is known as **run-length coding** (Schuegraf [12]). In its simplest form, the length of every run is encoded by a fixed length codeword; since this codeword must be large enough to accommodate the theoretical maximum run length, this is equivalent to the previous method.

Since, in simple run length coding, the space allocated for each run must be adequate for the largest possible run, such codes can be inefficient if many of the runs are of small or moderate length. The following variant, due to Teuhola [15], improves on simple run length coding by having a **variable length** representation of a **run length**. A run of r zeros is first broken up into successive blocks of zeros of exponentially increasing size; the first block is of size 2^k (for k a parameter selected to optimize this procedure), the second of size 2^{k+1}, etc., until a block is produced that extends beyond the run, i.e., is partially filled. The length of the run, r, can then be represented as follows: (a) each block in the sequence that is completely filled with zeros is represented in turn by a one, and (b) a zero is appended to the string of ones as delimiter. If t ones are present, then we know $2^k + 2^{k+1} + \cdots + 2^{k+t-1} \leq r < 2^k + \cdots + 2^{k+t-1} + 2^{k+t}$, that is: the first t blocks are filled with zeros, but the last potential block of 2^{k+t} zeros is either empty or partially filled. So, finally, (c) we can explicitly represent the number of zeros in the last block as a binary integer with $k + t$ bits. Thus a run of length r is encoded by $O(\log r)$ bits instead of $O(\log(\text{max length}))$.

Jakobsson [7] suggests the use of **Huffman coding** for bitmaps. The bit-vector is partitioned into blocks of fixed size k, and statistics are collected on the frequency of occurrence of the 2^k bit patterns. Based on these statistics, the set of blocks is Huffman encoded, and the bitmap itself is encoded as a sequence of such codewords. For sparse vectors, the k-bit block consisting of zeros only, and blocks with only a single 1-bit, have much higher probabilities than the other blocks, so the average codeword length of the Huffman code will be smaller than k.

Fraenkel & Klein [6] combine **Huffman coding with run-length coding**. Once again, a parameter k is chosen as a block size. However, since for very sparse vectors the probability of a block of k zeros is high, runs of blocks of k zeros receive special treatment. We first represent the succession of k-bit blocks comprising a bitmap as a sequence of two categories of symbols: beginning with the first block, if a k-bit block includes 1-bits, then we represent it by its own special symbol, as in the previous method. If it is a zero-block, then instead of representing the block itself, we represent the entire run of zero blocks which it starts by a string of integers as follows: suppose the run consists of r zero-blocks, with r represented in binary form as $r = \sum_{i \geq 0} a_i 2^i$, for a_i zero or one. Then the run is represented in the symbol sequence by the string of integers $n_0, n_1, \ldots$, where each n_i is a power of 2 in the representation of r for which $a_{n_i} = 1$; this in effect encodes the run lengths. Next, the frequency of occurrence throughout the bitmap file of each special and integer symbol is recorded, permitting a Huffman tree to be constructed for the $2^k - 1$ special symbols together with the integer symbols. Finally, the bitmap is Huffman encoded using this tree.

A **hierarchical method** for compressing a sparse bitmap was proposed by Wedekind & Härder [17]. The original bit-vector v_0 of length ℓ_0 bits is partitioned into r_0 equal blocks of k_0 bits each ($r_0 \cdot k_0 = \ell_0$), and the blocks consisting only of zeros are dropped. The resulting sequence of non-zero blocks does not by itself allow the reconstruction of v_0; we can, however, append a list of the indices indicating where these non-zero blocks occur in the original vector. This list of up to r_0 indices is itself kept as a bit-vector v_1 of $\ell_1 = r_0$ bits; there is a 1 in position i of v_1 if and only if the i-th block of v_0 is not all zeros. Now v_1 can be further compressed by the same method. In other words, a sequence of bit-vectors v_j is constructed, each bit in v_j being the result of ORing the bits in the corresponding block in v_{j-1}. The procedure is repeated recursively until a level is reached where the vector length reduces to a few bytes. The compressed form of v_0 is then obtained by concatenating, in order of decreasing i, all the nonzero blocks of the various v_i. The same method appears in Vallarino [16], who used it for two-dimensional bitmaps, but with only one level of compression.

The hierarchical method is refined by Choueka & al. [3], by adding a **pruning algorithm** that removes from the hierarchy-tree, branches pointing to very few segments. The algorithm partitions the set of 1-bits in v_0 into two subsets: the class of 1-bits which are efficiently handled by the hierarchical method; and the complementary class, consisting of more or less isolated 1-bits whose inclusion in the hierarchical tree structure would have been more expensive than their enumeration in an appended list. Either of these two classes may be empty. If the list is long enough, it is further compressed by a variant of prefix omission, to be decribed in more detail in the following sub-section.

It should be noted that since, for each map, the number of runs of zeros is equal to the number of 1-bits plus 1, the size of the compressed file obtained by the first few methods is clearly linearly related to the number of 1-bits in the original file. For the hierarchical and Huffman coding methods this relation is less evident, but has been empirically established. This observation is consistent with the theoretical argument presented in the introduction, and reinforces our intention to design a preprocessing stage that reduces the number of bits in a bitmap.

2.2 A simple new method

The following technique is a simple generalization of the prefix omission method suggested in [3] for the secondary compression of the list of 1-bits which were pruned from the tree. It can also be viewed as a variant of the hierarchical method, using only a single level of compression.

Choose an integer parameter k and partition the original vector v_0 of length ℓ_0 into blocks of 2^k bits. We shall assume that the number of 1-bits in the bitmap is s. As in the hierarchical method, construct a new vector v_1 of length $\lceil \ell_0/2^k \rceil$, in which bit i is zero if and only if block i of v_0 contains only zeros. However, now, instead of storing the non-zero blocks of v_0 themselves, we substitute for each block the string of indices of the 1-bits within that block. A priori k bits are sufficient for storing such a relative index; however we need an additional bit per index to serve as a flag, which identifies the boundary of each block. Therefore, in addition to the fixed overhead of storing the vector v_1, $k + 1$ bits are needed for representing each of the 1-bits of v_0. When a block has a small number of 1-bits, a significant saving in space could result.

We would now like to find k that optimizes the size of the block to be chosen, that is, the integer k^* that minimizes $f(k) = \lceil \ell_0 2^{-k} \rceil + (k + 1)s$, the size in bits of the compressed bitmap. Because of the appearance of the ceiling function in $f(k)$, finding the minimum value directly is difficult. Instead we shall search for an integer k_1^* that minimizes the related continuous function $f_1(k) = \ell_0 2^{-k} + (k+1)s$. Since f_1 is a convex function, k_1^* is an integer which satisfies

$$f_1(k_1^*) < f_1(k_1^* + 1) \quad \text{and} \quad f_1(k_1^*) \le f_1(k_1^* - 1).$$

Examining the left hand inequality, we find

$$\ell_0 2^{-k_1^*} + (k_1^* + 1)s < \ell_0 2^{-k_1^* + 1} + (k_1^* + 2)s,$$

or, $2^{-k_1^* + 1} < s/\ell_0$. Thus $k_1^* > \log_2(\ell_0/s) - 1$. Similarly, the right hand inequality is equivalent to $k_1^* \le \log_2(\ell_0/s)$. Combining the two, we find that k_1^* must satisfy

$$\log_2 \frac{\ell_0}{s} - 1 < k_1^* \le \log_2 \frac{\ell_0}{s},$$

so $k_1^* = \lfloor \log_2(\ell_0/s) \rfloor$.

If we have a file of m bitmaps, we want to use the same method for encoding each of them, so the optimal k will be determined by the average $\bar{s}$ of 1-bits per map. The total number of bits in the compressed file is thus

$$m \left\lceil \ell_0 2^{-\lfloor \log_2(\ell_0/\bar{s}) \rfloor} \right\rceil + S \left(\lfloor \log_2(\ell_0/\bar{s}) \rfloor + 1 \right), \tag{1}$$

for $S = m\bar{s}$, the total number of 1-bits in the bitmap set.

A priori, k_1^* need not equal k^*; however, it is easy to see that the cost of using k_1^* is identical to the cost of using k^*. To show this, first note that by the definition of the ceiling function, $f(k_1^*) < 1 + f_1(k_1^*)$. Since k_1^* minimizes f_1, $f_1(k_1^*) \le f_1(k^*)$. But f_1 cannot exceed f for any k, and in particular $f_1(k^*) \le f(k^*)$. Combining these results with the fact than k^* minimizes f, we get

$$f(k^*) \le f(k_1^*) < 1 + f(k^*).$$

We conclude that using k_1^* for the true optimum, k^*, results in an excess of less than one bit in storage for each bitmap. But $f(k)$ takes only integer values at integer k, so if the difference $f(k_1^*) - f(k^*)$ is smaller than 1, then it must actually equal zero: either $k_1^* = k^*$, or, at least, the storage implications are the same for both values $(f(k_1^*) = f(k^*))$.

For example, suppose $\ell_0 = 180$ and the indices of the 1-bits in v_0 are 36, 50, 53, 105 and 126. Thus $s = 5$, so we get that the optimal k is $\lfloor \log_2(180/5) \rfloor = 5$. There are $\lceil 180/2^5 \rceil = 6$ bits in v_1, each (except the last) corresponding to a block of 32 bits in v_0. There are three 1-bits in the second block, with relative indices 4, 18 and 21, and there are two 1-bits in the fourth block, with relative indices 9 and 30; the four other blocks are empty. Thus the following information would be kept:

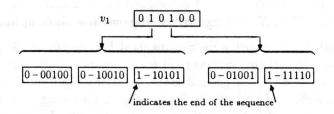

v_1

| 0 - 00100 | 0 - 10010 | 1 - 10101 | 0 - 01001 | 1 - 11110 |

indicates the end of the sequence

The number of bits necessary to store this map is thus $6 + 5 \times (5 + 1) = 36$. With $k = 4$ we would need $12 + 5 \times (4 + 1) = 37$ bits and with $k = 6$ we would need $3 + 5 \times (6 + 1) = 38$ bits. Note that if we list the relative indices of each sub-range in increasing order, the flag identifying the last index of each range is not always needed. In our example, for instance, the list of stored relative indices is 4, 18, 21, 9, 30, so clearly the sublist corresponding to the second 1-bit in v_1 consists of the last two elements. If, however, there were no 1-bit in position 105 of v_0, the list of stored relative indices would have been 4, 18, 21, 30, and the partition of this list into two increasing sub-lists is not uniquely determined.

3. Bitmap Clustering

3.1 Motivation

We have remarked several times above that sparser bitmaps are more effectively compressed. We will now describe a method for reducing the number of 1-bits by making use of a natural clustering of bitmaps. To do this, we take advantage of the fact that many bitmaps are associated in the sense that the presence of a 1-bit in one map increases the likelihood of a 1-bit occurring in the same position in the other. If two bitmaps X_1 and X_2 are strongly associated in this sense, then the bitmap $X_3 = X_1 \text{ XOR } X_2$ will very possibly have fewer 1-bits than, say, X_2. If we store X_1 and X_3, we can reconstruct X_2. The advantage of doing this is that we may be able to compress X_1 and X_3 more effectively than the original vectors. Since our intention when XORing two vectors is to reduce the number of 1-bits, it is useful to take as a measure of association between two vectors, the number of 1-bits in the XORed vector. But this quantity is the familiar *Hamming distance* between the two vectors. If the maps X_i and X_j are "close" in the Hamming distance sense, we would want to keep $\bar{X}_j$ and the pair $(\bar{x}_i, j)$ instead of $\bar{X}_j$ and $\bar{X}_i$; here $x_i = X_i \text{ XOR } X_j$, and a bar indicates that the maps have been compressed, say by the method presented in Section 2.2. Given the retained information, the original bitmap can then be recovered by first decompressing $\bar{x}_i$ and $\bar{X}_j$, which yields x_i and X_j, and finally XORing again, since $X_i = x_i \text{ XOR } X_j$.

As described above, the unchanged map X_j is compressed directly. However, X_j may itself be quite close to a third map, X_k, and therefore profitably XORed with that third map, producing the pair $(\bar{x}_j, k)$. Continuing in this manner we impose a structure on the bitmaps that can be represented as a directed graph, $G = (V, E)$,

333

where the vertices $V = \{X_1, \ldots, X_m\}$ correspond to the bitmaps and (X_i, X_j), the directed edge from X_i to X_j, belongs to E if and only if X_i is compressed as $(\bar{x}_i, j)$.

To be workable, the following restrictions must be imposed on G. (1) Any map can be compressed by XORing with at most one other map, so *the outdegree of every vertex is at most 1*. (2) In a general graph satisfying condition (1), it might be possible to form a chain of bitmaps $X_1, X_2, \ldots, X_k, X_1$, denoting that X_i is stored as $(\bar{x}_i, i+1)$ for $i = 1, \ldots, k-1$, and X_k is stored as $(\bar{x}_k, 1)$. However, this situation must be prohibited, if we want to be able to recover the original bitmaps: starting with an arbitrary node, the chain must terminate with an untransformed bitmap, that is, with a node with outdegree zero. In other words, *a legitimate graph must be cycle free*.

These conditions impose a strong structure on a legitimate graph. Let $R = \{r_1, \ldots, r_n\}$ be the set of vertices with outdegree zero, and define $T(r_i)$ as the set of vertices from which there is a directed path to r_i; $T(r_i)$ also includes r_i (connected to itself by the empty path). Since there are no cycles in G, a directed path starting at any vertex $X \in V$ must eventually terminate, reaching one of the vertices $r_i \in R$. Thus every $X \in V$ is in one of the $T(r_i)$. If $X \in T(r_i) \cap T(r_j)$ for $i \neq j$, then some vertex in the chain starting at X must have outdegree ≥ 2. Since this is impossible, the components $T(r_i)$ are disjoint and $\{T(r_i)\}$ is a partition of V into connected *clusters* of bitmaps. Further, there is no linkage between any pair $T(r_i)$ and $T(r_j)$: for suppose $X_1 \in T(r_i)$ and an edge (X_1, X_2) exists with $X_2 \in T(r_j)$. But then, since a path exists connecting X_2 to r_j, a path exists (through X_2) connecting X_1 to r_j. Such a node X_1 is a member of both $T(r_i)$ and $T(r_j)$, which is impossible. The $T(r_i)$ are thus isolated connected components in G; because of conditions (1) and (2), each $T(r_i)$ is an *oriented tree*, as defined by Knuth [9, Section 2.3.4.2].

Any forest of bitmaps can serve as the basis of our precompression operations. To maximize compressibility, however, we want to choose that forest among all possible forests that minimizes the total number of ones in the resulting bitmaps. (There could conceivably exist some maps which, because of their special internal structure, yield better compression than others which are sparser. But until a quantitative relationship can be derived between detailed bitmap characteristics and compression, sparseness is the best measure we have for bitmap compressibility.) We define the quantity to be minimized, that is, the total number of 1-bits in the roots plus the total number of 1-bits in the XORed bitmaps, as the *cost* C of the forest. Note that adopting this criterion prevents our XORing two vectors when the result would increase the number of 1-bits — for example, in the extreme case, the set of original bitmaps, with no XORed maps, is forest and thus a legitimate graph.

An exhaustive search generating all the possible graphs satisfying our constraints and checking for each the cost for the forest, must be ruled out on the grounds of computational expense, even if we have only a moderately large number m of bitmaps. Fortunately, such a search is unnecessary, as the problem is equivalent to another for which there are well known polynomial algorithms. To see this, we first recall that, except for the roots, the number of 1's in a XORed bitmap is just the Hamming distance between it and its successor in the directed graph. Thus, if we assign this distance as a weight to each edge, the cost of a forest is simply the sum of the weights of all edges in the graph plus the sum of the number of ones in each root. But we can further simplify the statement of the problem by noting that the number of ones in a map is its Hamming distance to the zero bitmap (the bitmap, all of whose values are zero), denoted by X_0. Thus, given any forest, if we introduce the zero bitmap and include the weighted edge between each root and X_0 (thereby transforming the forest into a tree), then the cost of the original forest is just equal to the sum of edge-weights over all the edges of the resulting tree in the enhanced graph. The latter sum will be called the *cost* of the tree. Since only the weights are significant when computing the cost, we can consider the tree as being non-directed. Such a simplification is well defined since the weight on an edge does not depend on its orientation (the Hamming distance is a symetric measure). Thus given any directed forest over the set of nodes V, we can define a non-directed tree over $V^* = V \cup \{X_0\}$ having the same cost.

The converse is also true. First note that given the set of vertices V^*, any (undirected) spanning tree on V^* defines a directed tree on V^*: the root of the directed tree in X_0; the directed edge (X_i, X_j) is in the directed tree if a path $(X_i, X_j, \ldots, X_0)$ exists in the undirected tree. Next, by removing X_0 and the edges incident on it from the directed tree, we obtain a directed forest G, on V. Furthermore, if the edge weights are as defined above, the cost of the forest is equal to the cost of the tree that induced it. Because of this equivalence, an optimal forest is associated with an optimal (lowest cost) tree. Thus our problem is equivalent to the following one: given a complete non-directed graph whose vertex set is the union of our bitmaps with X_0, and for which the weight on edge (i, j) is the Hamming distance between vertices i and j, find the tree for which the total edge weight is minimum. The directed forest induced by this tree is the solution to our problem.

More formally: we are looking for a graph G, which is a forest of oriented trees spanning the vertex set V, optimizing our problem. To find the graph G, we consider the weighted undirected graph $G^* = (V^*, E^*)$, where the set of vertices V^* is obtained by adjoining a new vertex, the zero vector X_0, to the set V of bitmaps; $E^* = V^* \times V^* - \{(X_i, X_i) : X_i \in V^*\}$ (ignoring order), that is, G^* is a complete graph from which self-loops are removed; and the weight $w(i, j)$ associated with the edge $(X_i, X_j) \in E^*$ is the Hamming distance between X_i and X_j. We then define as a legitimate sub-graph of G^* a non-directed tree T connecting all the vertices in V^*. Our task is to find the legitimate sub-graph for which the sum of all the weights of the edges in T is minimized — in fact, a minimum spanning tree (MST) of G^*. The MST in G^* now induces the optimal directed forest, G, on the original set of bitmaps, as described above. The vertices that were adjacent to vertex X_0 in T are the roots of the oriented trees in G. G is the optimal forest we were seeking.

Many algorithms for finding a MST for a non-directed graph appear in the literature, ranging from Kruskal's simple greedy algorithm [10], which has in our case complexity $O(m^2 \log m)$, to Yao's more involved technique [18], which would need $O(m^2 \log \log m)$ operations for our application.

3.2 Algorithm statement

Summarizing, we suggest the following procedure as the first stage for compressing a set of m bitmaps $X_1, \ldots, X_m$. This method in principle improves any given compression algorithm $\mathcal{C}$ for individual bitmaps, provided our assumption of strong correlation between some of the maps holds. As output, we get a table B of compressed bitmaps, the compressed form of X_i being stored in $B(i)$, $1 \le i \le m$. In addition, the algorithm produces a small table F of size m, defined by $F(i) = j$ if the map X_i is compressed as $(\bar{x}_i, j)$ (i.e., if X_j is the father of X_i in the oriented rooted tree T), or by $F(i) = 0$, if X_i is the root of one of the trees.

1. Choose a compression method $\mathcal{C}$ for an individual map: given a bitmap X, $\mathcal{C}(X)$ is the result of $\mathcal{C}$ applied to X.

2. Extend the set of bitmaps by adjoining X_0, the zero-vector.

3. (a) Using the Hamming distances as weights on the complete graph without self-loops having $\{X_0, X_1, \ldots, X_m\}$ as set of vertices, compute a minimum spanning tree T.

   (b) Consider T as an oriented tree rooted at X_0.

   (c) The subtrees of X_0 in T partition the original set of bitmaps.

4. (a) If X_i is a vertex adjacent to X_0 in T, then it is the root of one of the oriented trees: these bitmaps (one per tree) are compressed directly using $\mathcal{C}$.

$$B(i) \leftarrow \mathcal{C}(X_i)$$

$$F(i) \leftarrow 0$$

   (b) A bitmap X_i, which is not the root of a tree, has a directed edge to another bitmap X_j in the same tree; X_i is compressed by first computing $x_i = X_i \text{ XOR } X_j$ and then compressing x_i using $\mathcal{C}$.

$$B(i) \leftarrow \mathcal{C}(x_i)$$

$$F(i) \leftarrow j$$

In the case of a set of bitmaps of an IR system, the problems of compression and decompression are not exactly symetric. Compression is performed only once, during the construction of the system, and is applied to the entire set. Decompression, on the other hand, is practically never needed simultaneously for the entire set, but only for those maps associated with the keywords of a submitted query. We thus present the procedure decompress(i) which returns the original map X_i. It uses the function $\mathcal{C}^{-1}$ as the inverse of the compression function $\mathcal{C}$ — that is $\mathcal{C}^{-1}$ decompresses bitmaps which have been compressed by $\mathcal{C}$.

```
decompress(i)
        if  i = 0    return( C⁻¹(B(i)) )
        else         return( C⁻¹(B(i)) XOR decompress(F(i)) )
```

We see that the savings in storage space gained by our clustering procedure come at the expense of increased processing time. In order to recover the bitmap X_i, we need decompress all the maps forming the path from X_i to the root of the cluster X_i belongs to.

4. Example

The database we chose for testing our algorithm is the Hebrew Bible, consisting of 305514 words which are partitioned into 929 chapters. The number of different words is 39647. Following the suggestion in [4] that bitmaps should be constructed only for words which appear more often than some fixed frequency threshold, we restricted ourselves to the 1478 words which appeared in at least 20 chapters. As a text segment, we defined a set of four consecutive chapters. The resulting bitmaps were $\lceil 929/4 \rceil = 233$ bits long. The total number of 1-bits in the 1478 maps was 65734, or $\bar{s} = 44.47$ 1-bits per map.

We first used the compression technique of Section 2.2 by itself. The optimal parameter k was $\lfloor \log_2(233/44.47) \rfloor = 2$. From equation (1) we thus get that the total number of bits needed to store the set of bitmaps in compressed form is 284404. For the uncompressed file we would need $1478 \times 233 = 344374$ bits, so that the simple method yields 17.4% compression. This k is indeed optimal for this method, since with $k = 1$ we get 11.6% compression, and with $k = 3$ we get 10.8%.

We then applied Kruskal's MST algorithm, which partitioned the set of bitmaps into 716 clusters. Of these, 530 were singletons, i.e., maps which couldn't effectively be XORed with some other map and which were therefore compressed without transformation. The other 948 bitmaps were partitioned into 186 clusters, each containing at least two elements. Since in each cluster, the root is compressed directly, the number of bitmaps which were XORed before compression was $948 - 186 = 762$. For these, the total number of 1-bits decreased from 48590 to 33538, that is, by 31%.

Considering the entire file of bitmaps, the overall number of 1-bits decreased from 65734 to 50658, or to $\bar{s} = 34.27$ 1-bits per bitmap. The optimal parameter k was thus $\lfloor \log_2(233/34.27) \rfloor = 2$, as before. Substituting the values for m, S and $\bar{s}$ in equation (1), we find that the total number of bits needed to store the set of bitmaps if we use the clustering method of Section 3 is 239176. Relative to the noncompressed file this is a 30.5% reduction, and relative to using only the method of Section 2.2 without clustering, this is a 15.9% improvement.

It is interesting to compare this to the information theoretic estimate of compresibility mentioned in the introduction. The probability of a 1-bit in the original

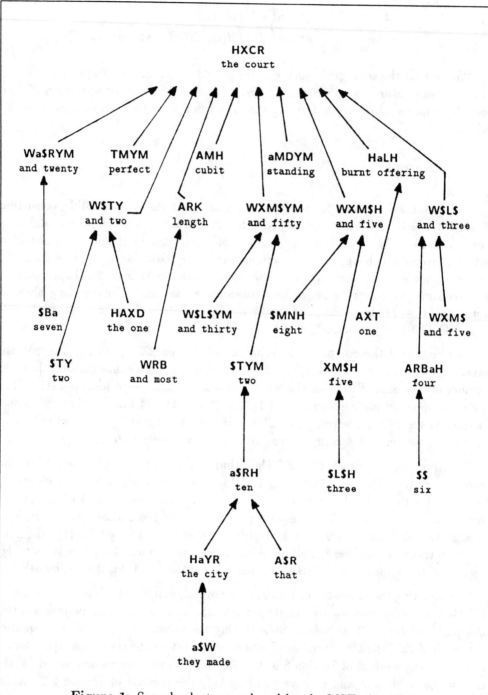

Figure 1: Sample cluster produced by the MST algorithm

file is 0.19, yielding an entropy per bit of $H = 0.703$. This means that if the 1-bits appear with the given frequency but independently from each other, the best possible compression would be 29.7%. Indeed, we got only 17.4% when the bitmaps were compressed individually. Introducing the clustering, we exploit the dependencies between different bitmaps, yielding compression savings of 30.5%, which is beyond those possible for independently generated maps.

While most of the generated clusters were small (two to four elements), some formed deep trees with tens of bitmaps, and the largest consisted of a tree of depth 15 with 112 vertices. A closer look at some of the larger clusters revealed interesting associations. Figure 1 shows a typical example. For each node in the tree, the Hebrew word is first given in English translitteration, using {`ABGDHWZXtYKLMNSaPCQRST`} respectively for {*aleph, beth, ..., tav*}, as well as the translation of the word into English.

In this cluster, 18 out of 28 words are numerals; these are clearly connected, as the Bible tends to give exact dimensions (note the words `length` and `cubit`) in certain detailed descriptions. See, for instance, Exodus 27:9–19, where a description of the court, the root of this cluster, is given. The depth of this tree is 5, which is therefore the maximal depth of the recursion for the decompression algorithm. Note also that the root of this cluster has a high in-degree. This was not always the case, as can be seen in the following example.

To present the second example, we use a more compact representation, based on pre-order traversal of a tree. A tree can be represented recursively by its root, followed by the list of its subtrees enclosed in parenthesis. To improve readability, the level of the root of a subtree in the full tree appears as subscripts to the parentheses. We now give only the English translation of the word at each node (many Hebrew words must be translated into several English words).

```
and they camped (1 night, and they saw, and they went out (2 the
men (3    and they came (4    from before, and he sent (5    and they
said, and he sat (6 and he, his people, and he went out )6,    and
he called (6 and he came (7 and now (8 please )8 )7,    and he gave
(7 in the hand of )7,    and he took (7 bread, and he did (8 two )8
)7 )6 )5, and they sat )4, and they went )3 )2 )1
```

The 25 elements in this cluster form a tree of depth 8, but no node has higher in-degree than 3. Note that most of the words are verbs related to motion, all in the past tense, and in third person singular or plural.

We also tried to apply the algorithm to sparser bitmaps, by defining a segment to be one, instead of four, chapters. The 1478 bitmaps then had a total of 95472 1-bits, so they were compressed with $k = 3$ and gave 59.9% compression. The clustering algorithm however produced only 300 bitmaps that were XORed; for these, the reduction in the number of 1-bits was about 21%, but nonetheless, the total number of 1-bits remained quite large at 85195 bits. The optimal k now shifted to be 4, and compression was improved by 7.5%; measured relative to the full file, a 62.9% reduction was achieved. In this case, the theoretical optimum for independently generated bitmaps with this 1-bit density is 63.8%.

In order to check the influence of the language of the database on the algorithm, we repeated the experiments with the *King James Bible*, again with a segment equal to one chapter. The improvement of the clustering method in this case was only 5.7%, again because only a small number of bitmaps (377 of 1454) were XORed. There were nevertheless some interesting clusters. For example: Asher ($_1$ Ephraim, Joseph, Manasseh, Simeon ($_2$ Levi, Reuben ($_3$ Gad)$_3$)$_2$, Zebulun ($_2$ Naphtali)$_2$, Issachar ($_2$ Benjamin, Dan)$_2$)$_1$. This cluster contains the names of all the tribes, except Judah. The latter appears in another cluster, together with words like Jerusalem, reign, reigned, kings, etc. Clearly, Judah differs from the other tribes, as his name often refers to the kingdom or land of Judah.

Summarizing our experiments, we see that the clustering algorithm works better when the bitmaps are not so sparse: very sparse vectors tend to have very few overlapping 1-bits, so that there is often no gain to be achieved by XORing. However, for the very sparse vectors, many of the known techniques already yield excellent results. Thus the clustering algorithm helps especially for those maps that are most difficult to compress.

5. Conclusion and Future Work

We have presented a new algorithm for transforming a set of bitmaps, which in principle may improve any previous compression method that does not take into account possible interrelationships among the different bitmaps. The experimental results suggest that the new method is particularly effective for bitmaps which are not extremely sparse. This may have several applications.

For example, bit-slices of signature methods are often chosen so that the density of 1-bits is $\frac{1}{2}$ [13]. Such vectors are almost impossible to compress individually. There may however be a possible gain by using clustering. Also, the possibility of compression would permit us to increase the size of the signature, resulting in more efficient retrieval, whitout affecting the space requirements [2]. Another application would be to IR bitmaps which have already been slightly compacted, such as the maps obtained by applying one iteration of the hierarchical bit-vector compression technique referred to in Section 2.1. Finally, there might be applications to areas outside of IR, such as image compression, where adjacent raster rows may be similar, or processing of genetic information, where different DNA strings often share long identical substrings.

REFERENCES

[1]   Bell T., Witten I.H., Cleary J.G., Modeling for Text Compression, *ACM Computing Surveys* **21** (1989) 557–591.

[2]   Bookstein A., Klein S.T., Using Bitmaps for Medium Sized Information Retrieval Systems, to appear in *Inf. Proc. and Management* (1990).

[3]   Choueka Y., Fraenkel A.S., Klein S.T., Segal E., Improved hierarchical bit-vector compression in document retrieval systems, *Proc. 9-th ACM-SIGIR Conf.*, Pisa; ACM, Baltimore, MD (1986) 88–97.

[4]   Choueka Y., Fraenkel A.S., Klein S.T., Segal E., Improved Techniques for Processing Queries in Full-Text Systems, *Proc. 10-th ACM-SIGIR Conf.*, New Orleans (1987) 306–315.

[5]   Faloutsos C., Christodulakis S., Signature files: An access method for documents and its analytical performance evaluation, *ACM Trans. on Office Inf. Systems* **2** (1984) 267–288.

[6]   Fraenkel A.S., Klein S.T., Novel Compression of sparse Bit-Strings, in *Combinatorial Algorithms on Words*, NATO ASI Series Vol **F12**, Springer Verlag, Berlin (1985) 169–183.

[7]   Jakobsson M., Huffman coding in Bit-Vector Compression, *Inf. Processing Letters* **7** (1978) 304–307.

[8]   Klein S.T., Bookstein A., Deerwester S., Storing Text Retrieval Systems on CD-ROM: Compression and Encryption Considerations, *ACM Trans. on Information Systems* **7** (1989), 230–245.

[9]   Knuth D.E., *The Art of Computer Programming, Vol I, Fundamental algorithms*, Addison-Wesley, Reading, Mass. (1973).

[10] Kruskal J.B., On the shortest spanning subtree of a graph and the Travelling Salesman Problem, *Proc. Amer. Math. Soc.* **7** (1956) 48–50.

[11] Lelewer D.A., Hirschberg D.S., Data Compression, *ACM Computing Surveys* **19** (1987) 261–296.

[12] Schuegraf E.J., Compression of large inverted files with hyperbolic term distribution, *Inf. Proc. and Management* **12** (1976) 377–384.

[13] Stiassny S., Mathematical analysis of various superimposed coding methods, *Amer. Documentation* **11** (1960) 155–169.

[14] Storer J.A., *Data Compression: Methods and Theory*, Computer Science Press, Rockville, Maryland (1988).

[15] Teuhola J., A Compression method for Clustered Bit-Vectors, *Inf. Processing Letters* **7** (1978) 308–311.

[16] Vallarino O., On the use of bit-maps for multiple key retrieval, *SIGPLAN Notices, Special Issue* Vol. **II** (1976) 108–114.

[17] Wedekind H., Härder T., *Datenbanksysteme II*, B.-I. Wissenschaftsverlag, Mannheim (1976).

[18] Yao A.C.C., An $O(|E|\log\log|V|)$ algorithm for finding minimum spanning trees, *Inf. Processing Letters* **4** (1975) 21–23.

Panel Session: Hypertext: "Growing Up?"

Panel Chair: M.E. Frisse, Washington University, St. Louis, USA;
Panelists: Maristella Agosti, Dipartimento di Elettronica e Informatica, Universita' di
Padova, Italy; Marie-France Bruandet, Equipe Systems Intelligents de Recherche
d'Informations, Grenoble, France; Udo Han, University of Freiburgh,West Germany;
Stephen F. Weiss, University of North Carolina at Chapel Hill, USA

Abstract:

This panel will employ two different
interpretations of the phrase "growing
up" to address areas of common interest
between hypertext and information
retrieval researchers. First, the panelists
will question whether or not hypertext is
"growing up" as a scientific discipline;
They will discuss characteristics that separate hypertext research from other related
disciplines. Second, the panelists will
discuss the problems encountered when a
hypertext system "grows up" in size and
complexity; They will discuss the very
real problems expected when representing
and integrating large knowledge bases,
accommodating multiple users, and distributing single logical hypertexts across
multiple physical sites.

The panelists will not lecture, but they
will advance a number of themes
including "the Myth of Modularity"
(Frisse), "New Architectures Employing
Hyperconcept Databases" (Agosti),
"Hypertext in Software Engineering"
(Bruandet), "Automatic Hypertext
Generation" (Hahn), and "Large-Scale
Hypertexts" (Weiss).

1. Overview

Hypertexts consist of a database of
discrete components (text, graphics,
video, audio), links connecting the text
components, and tools for creating and
navigating through the combination of
components and links [9,25,28].
Hypertext's flexible structure facilitates
creation of multiple unique "paths"
through a single corpus of literature.

These capabilities promote the use of
hypertext in areas as diverse as software
engineering, technical documentation,
and computer-assisted instruction.

A number of issues seem common to
most hypertext discussions. These
include assumptions of hypertext component modularity, the need for index
structures "external" to the hypertext, the
importance of link and component typing,
the utility of abstract models for
hypertext, and the feasability of automatic
generation of hypertexts from media
currently distributed in some other form.
Addressing the critical aspects of these
issues should lead to a number of
provocative questions regarding the
practical role hypertext can play in the
management of information.

2. Components and Links.

One of hypertext's principle features is
the ability to support direct machine-
supported links between discrete
hypertext components [9]. Although
hypertext components often play the role
of "tiny documents" and serve as the
fundamental unit of indexing and
retrieval, they differ from traditional
documents in their smaller size and
explicit relationships defined by the links.
Component size may diminish retrieval
performance because few concepts are
associated with each component. If the
components are derived from a larger
document, they may violate independence
assumptions because a concept formerly
expressed completely in one document is
now distributed across many
components.

Hypertext links serve three functions [10,12,16,29]. First, links denote associations between two highly related hypertext components. Second, links representing hierarchical structures allow for generalization and abstraction. Third, human computer interfaces can use links to facilitate visualization of relationships denoted by the hypertext.

3. Indexes "external" to the hypertext

Traditional hypertext link-based browsing is a search process whose performance is profoundly affected by the degree to which locally optimal choices result in a globally optimal hypertext path; performance deteriorates as a hypertext grows in size or becomes less formally structured. Halasz and others argue that in these circumstances browsing must be augmented with "global" search capabilities [11,12,13,21,23]. These capabilities require the addition of an index structure "external" to the components and links constituting the hypertext database. The added index structure allows quicker access to individual components and allows access directly to two or more documents unconnected by links if the components share some string, keyword or attribute. Agosti calls this structure, the "hyperconcept database" [1,2,3,4].

Hyperconcept databases allow one to infer new query terms on the basis of user queries and reader feedback [8,14]. In principle, one could employ a number of hyperconcept databases, each created by different indexing methods and each operating in parallel on the same hypertext database. Users or programs could then select at "run time" the hyperconcept database most appropriate to the circumstance.

4. Node and Link Types

The hypertext database and the hyperconcept database each can have different node and link types. Text nodes represent hypertext components in the hypertext database and topic nodes represent indexing concepts in the hyperconcept database. Cross-reference links are used in the structuring of hypertext database components; Semantic links make associations between topic nodes in the hyperconcept database; Connection links connect components in the hypertext database with topic nodes in the hyperconcept database.

5. Abstract Models

Hypertext systems have appeal to the software engineering field because they can combine database methods that provide direct data access with interface methods that permit document browsing [17, 24]. Software engineering applications, some believe, will require abstract models more complex than the simple directed graph model representing most hypertexts [7]; Models reported in the literature include those based on first-order logic [18], hypergraphs [30], Petri-nets [29], and object-oriented representations [22]. Abstract models would allow one to search on the basis of hypertext structure [10].

6. Automated hypertext generation

Many hypertexts are constructed from books or document collections. In these circumstances the text must be decomposed into individual components united by *structural links*. This process is dependent on modularity assumptions used to define component scope and indexing techniques used to represent the documents. When indexing, individual components are characterized and represented deterministically with structured data (e.g., author name, date of publication). Additional structured terms (auxiliary data) are produced by an index process in order to represent further the component's semantic content. Auxiliary data are neither complete nor unique descriptors of component content. The indexing process used to produce auxiliary data is not deterministic; The content can be interpreted and described in different ways depending on the observer's perspective and information needs. Accordingly auxiliary data pointers perform many of the same tasks as hypertext content links.

Automatic indexing remains a topic of active research in the hypertext field [5,11,12,14,15]. Salton and colleagues suggest that their approach towards full-text document retrieval can be used successfully to determine content links between hypertext components [27], but this claim is controversial. Hahn's TOPIC system employs a model of knowledge-based text condensation that transforms text-representation structures into more abstract thematic descriptions of text content. This process attempts to discard irrelevant knowledge structures and to retain only salient concepts. The topical structure of text is then represented in a hierarchical text graph which supports variable degrees of abstraction for text summarization as well as content-oriented retrieval of text knowledge. These text graphs provide a methodology for the automatic generation of hypertexts from full-text files. When applied to hierarchical hypertexts, these principles permit multiple levels of information granularity and abstraction - features useful to design and use of large-scale hypertext systems [19,20,26].

8. Discussion Topics

Hypertext developers often ignore link semantics when creating information retrieval systems for hypertexts and address information retrieval needs by equating hypertexts with a collection of unrelated "tiny documents." If each hypertext component has less information content than a conventional document and if the organizational information expressed through links is not considered, it becomes harder to argue that conventional methods will prove satisfactory. This argument would hold true even if very elegant external "hyperconcept databases" are applied to a hypertext.

Automatic hypertext production is difficult to achieve. Decomposing conventional text into a network of components requires many decisions which may impact greatly on component classification and hypertext use. Although success has been realized when documents are modular in nature and hierarchical in organization, it is not clear how these techniques can be generalized to other literature, nor is it clear how one can integrate multiple smaller hypertexts into a single larger hypertext.

Although abstract models have the potential to enhance retrieval from and understanding of hypertexts, very little work has moved from the speculative stage to the large-scale experimental stage. Among the many factors responsible for this slow movement is the lack of robust hypertexts of sufficient size and complexity to warrant full-scale research projects. The usual claim is that lack of information retrieval techniques impedes the delivery of large-scale hypertexts, but it may be instead that appropriate experiments are not available because large-scale hypertexts have not been made available to the appropriate researcher.

Controversy over the applicability to hypertext of techniques like Salton's will parallel that taking place when addressing full-text document collections [6]. It is possible however that in hypertext the discussions are impeded not so much by a lack of information retrieval techniques as by a lack of experimental methodology suitable to evaluate a retrieval technique's efficacy when applied to hypertext.

As hypertexts become larger, hypertext servers will be necessary. This necessity will require developers to understand how multiple users will share the same hypertext and how hypertexts can be distributed across multiple servers. In contrast to distributed file systems, distribution of hypertext components will be made arbitrarily in order to preserve transparency of the distributed system. This distribution scheme will produce an unbounded amount of interconnection among the hypertext components, and even small changes could place a tremendous burden on the network uniting the servers . Full transparency could bring unpredictable performance.

Citations

1. Agosti, M. Is hypertext a new model of information retrieval? In Proceedings of OnLine Information 88: 12th International Online Information Meeting. London, UK, 57-62,1988.

2. Agosti, M., R. Colotti, G. Gradenigo, P. Mattiello, A. Archi, R. DiGiorgi, B. Inghirami, R. Nannucci and M. Ragona. New prospectives in information retrieval techniques: a hypertext prototype in environmental law. In Proceedings of OnLine Information 89: 13th International Online Information Meeting. London, UK, 483-494,1989.

3. Agosti, M., F. Crestani and G. Gradenigo. Towards data modelling in information retrieval. Journal of Information Science. 25(6): (in press), 1989.

4. Agosti, M., G. Gradenigo and P. Mattiello. The hypertext as an effective information retrieval tool for the final user. In Proceedings of Pre-proceedings of the III International Conference on Logics, Informatics, and Law. Firenze, 1-19,1989.

5. Bernstein, M. An Apprentice That Discovers Hypertext Links. Eastgate Systems, PO Box 1307, Cambridge, MA 02238,1990.

6. Blair, D. C. and M. E. Maron. An Evaluation of Retrieval Effectiveness for a Full-text Document Retrieval System. Communications of the ACM. 28(3): 289-299, 1985.

7. Campbell, B. and J. M. Goodman. HAM: A General Purpose Hypertext Abstract Machine. Communications of the ACM. 31(7): 856-861, 1988.

8. Clitherow, P., D. Riecken and M. Muller. VISAR: A System for Inference and Navigation of Hypertext. In Proceedings of Hypertext'89. Pittsburgh, PA, 293-304,1989.

9. Conklin, J. Hypertext: an introduction and survey. IEEE Computer. 20(9): 17-41, 1987.

10. Consens, M. P. and A. O. Mendelzon. Expressing structural queries in GraphLog. In Proceedings of Hypertext'89. Pittsburgh, Pa., 269-292,1989.

11. Coombs, J. J. Hypertext, Full Text, and Automatic Linking. In Proceedings of SIGIR 90 (to appear). Brussells, 1990.

12. Croft, W. B. and H. Turtle. A retrieval model incorporating hypertext links. In Proceedings of Hypertext 89. Pittsburgh, PA, 1989.

13. Frisse, M. E. Searching for Information in a Hypertext Medical Handbook. Communications of the ACM. 31(7): 880-886, 1988.

14. Frisse, M. E. and S. B. Cousins. Information Retrieval from Hypertext: Update on the Dynamic Medical Handbook Project. In Proceedings of Hypertext'89. Pittsburgh, PA, 199-212,1989.

15. Frisse, M. E. and S. B. Cousins. Guides for Hypertext: An Overview. To appear in Artificial Intelligence in Medicine (Elsevier). Fall 1990.

16. Furuta, R. and P. D. Stotts. Programmable Browsing Semantics in Trellis. In Proceedings of Hypertext'89. Pittsburgh, Pa., 27-42,1989.

17. Garg, P. G. and W. Scacchi. A software hypertext environment configured software description. In Proceedings of International Workshop on Software Version and Configuration Control. Grassau, FRG, 1988.

18. Garg, P. K. Abstraction Mechanisms in Hypertext. Communications of the ACM. 31(7): 862-870, 1988.

19. Hahn, U. and U. Reimer. Automatic generation of hypertext knowledge bases: Conference on OFfice Information

Systems, Palo Alto. SIGOIS Bulletin. 9(2): 182-188, 1988.

20. Hahn, U. and U. Reimer. Knowledge-based text analysis in office environments: the text condensation system TOPIC. In Proceedings of Office Knowledge: Representation, Management and Utilization. Selected Full Papers based on Contributions to the IFIP TC 8/WG 8.4 International Workshop. 1988. Toronto, Ontario, 1988.

21. Halasz, F. G. Reflections on Notecards: Seven Issues for the Next Generation of Hypermedia Systems. Communications of the ACM. 31(7): 836-855, 1988.

22. Jarwa, S. and M-F.A.Bruandet. A hypertext model for information management in software management in software engineering. In Proceedings of DEXA'90, International Conference on Database and Expert Systems Applications. Austin, 1990.

23. Marchionini, G. and B. Shneiderman. Finding Facts vs. browsing knowledge in hypertext systems. Computer. 21(1): 70-89, 1988.

24. Norman, M. D. and D. S. Mayer. Context- a partitioning concept for hypertext. ACM Transactions of Office Information Systems. 5(2): 168-186, 1987.

25. Rada, R. Writing and Reading Hypertext: An Overview. Journal of the American Society for Information Science. 40(3): 164-171, 1989.

26. Reimer, U. and U. Hahn. Text condensation as knowledge base abstraction. In Proceedings of Fourth Conference on Artificial Intelligence Applications. San Diego, CA, USA, 1988.

27. Salton, G. Personal Communication.

28. Smith, J. B. and S. F. Weiss. An overview of hypertext. Communications of the ACM. 31(7): 816-819, 1988.

29. Stotts, P. D. and R. Furuta. Petri-net-based hypertext: document structure with browsing semantics. ACM Transactions on Information Systems. January: 1989.

30. Tompa, F. W. A data model for flexible hypertext data systems. ACM Transactions on Office Information Systems. 7(1): 85-100, 1989.

Complete Addresses of Panelists:

Maristella Agosti
Dept. Electronics & Informatics, Via Gradenigo, 6/a, 35131 Padova,Italy.
EMAIL: agosti@ipdunivx.unipd.it

Marie-France Bruandet and Sahar Jarwa
Laboratoire Genie Informatique, IMAG BP 53X 38041 Grenoble Cedex France.
EMAIL: bruandet@imag.imag.fr

Mark E. Frisse
Department of Internal Medicine (Box 8121), Washington University School of Medicine, 660 S. Euclid Avenue, St. Louis, MO. 63110 , USA.
EMAIL: frisse@informatics.WUSTL.EDU

Udo Hahn
Department of Math and Computer Science, University of Freiburgh,West Germany.
EMAIL: udo.hahn@informatik.uni-freiburgh.databasep.de

Stephen F. Weiss
Department of Computer Science, University of North Carolina, Chapel Hill, NC 27599
EMAIL: weiss@cs.unc.edu

347

Experiments with Query Acquisition and Use in Document Retrieval Systems

W. Bruce Croft and Raj Das

Department of Computer and Information Science

University of Massachusetts, Amherst, MA. 01003

Abstract

In some recent experimental document retrieval systems, emphasis has been placed on the acquisition of a detailed model of the information need through interaction with the user. It has been argued that these "enhanced" queries, in combination with relevance feedback, will improve retrieval performance. In this paper, we describe a study with the aim of evaluating how easily enhanced queries can be acquired from users and how effectively this additional knowledge can be used in retrieval. The results indicate that significant effectiveness benefits can be obtained through the acquisition of domain concepts related to query concepts, together with their level of importance to the information need.

1   Introduction

One of the most successful techniques developed for information retrieval is *relevance feedback* (Salton, 1968). This technique was developed in the context of statistical document retrieval, but it has also appeared in a slightly different form for database retrieval (Tou et al, 1982). In its simplest form, relevance feedback is used after an initial set of documents have been retrieved by comparing them to the query with a statistical ranking function (Salton, 1968, Van Rijsbergen, 1979). The person who generated the query then examines the top ranked documents and identifies which of these documents are relevant and which are not. The words and word frequencies in these documents are then used to modify the initial query and a new document ranking is formed. Retrieval experiments have shown that significant improvements in effectiveness can be obtained in this manner (for example, Sparck Jones and Webster, 1980; Salton and Buckley, 1988). One way of explaining the effectiveness of this technique is that it provides a simple method for acquiring more of the user's knowledge and using it to refine the query by adding related words and changing the relative importance of words.

Relevance feedback does, however, have some drawbacks. The principal ones are:

1. Identifying documents as relevant is a very crude way of identifying the information in the documents that is of particular interest. Many words from relevant documents that are unrelated to the information need can be included in the query.

2. Relevance feedback does not improve the initial search. If either no relevant documents or very few are found in the initial ranked list, users will be less likely to be satisfied with the system's performance.

In the I^3R document retrieval system (Croft and Thompson, 1987), emphasis is placed on the acquisition of a detailed model of the information need (or query) through interaction with the user. Analysis of an initial query and domain knowledge provide the basis for this interaction. The domain knowledge is used both to assist in the analysis of the query and to find related words and concepts. Since domain knowledge is typically not available for many applications, facilities are provided for users to provide this knowledge during query formulation. In addition, the relevance feedback process in I^3R is enhanced in that users not only specify the relevance of retrieved documents, but also the particular words and concepts that are important and their relationships to other concepts in the domain knowledge base.

There is obviously a contrast between what is expected from the user of a traditional statistical relevance feedback system and a system such as I^3R. The dialogue between the I^3R system and the user is designed to elicit as much as possible of the user's knowledge of the concepts mentioned in the query and of other domain concepts related to them. In a traditional system, the interaction with the users is minimized in that the only information they provide is the initial query (preferably in natural language) and relevance judgments. Increasing the amount and the complexity of the interaction with the users carries a penalty in terms of the effort required. The expectation is that this penalty will be more than offset by substantial improvements in retrieval effectiveness relative to simpler systems.

As we move to experimental systems that use knowledge-based and natural language processing techniques for document retrieval, the ability to interactively acquire domain and linguistic knowledge from users becomes crucial. This is because, in any real application, the knowledge that these techniques require will be incomplete or missing entirely. Given that some researchers believe that users are not even capable of providing more than the simplest information, the determination of what type of knowledge can be acquired interactively and how it can be acquired is a fundamental issue.

Our general approach is to acquire knowledge iteratively through interaction with the user. We also believe that acquisition should be done in the context of particular queries. The goal of finding relevant documents should motivate users to provide knowledge to the system. This can be contrasted to the approach of having a separate knowledge acquisition phase before the system can be used for any queries as, for example, in the IRACQ or TELI systems (Ayuso et al, 1988, Ballard and Stumberger, 1986). The knowledge that is acquired, together with the initial query, can be regarded as an "enhanced" query. Our research has focused on the following specific types of knowledge:

- Relative importance of query concepts.

- Complex query concepts (phrases).

- Domain knowledge (concepts related to the initial query concepts).

Each of these types of knowledge will be discussed in the next section.

The experimental methodology described in section 3 is designed to test the hypothesis that users of an information system can provide knowledge during query formulation that will improve retrieval effectiveness. The effectiveness of the enhanced queries will be compared both with simple queries and with queries modified using relevance feedback techniques. One of the major issues in designing a methodology is that the overall retrieval effectiveness can be affected by both the success of the techniques for acquiring enhanced queries from users, and the effectiveness of the retrieval techniques that use the additional knowledge in the enhanced query. In most cases, previous research and information retrieval models can be used to show why specific types of knowledge *should* improve the effectiveness of the system. A failure to obtain effectiveness improvements could then be regarded as a failure in knowledge acquisition. As some of the retrieval strategies we are using in this study are new, however, some changes to these strategies may be expected during the initial set of experiments and the separation of acquisition and use is not so straightforward.

Another feature of the methodology described here is that it is designed for evaluating complex, interactive retrieval systems. The evaluation of these types of systems using standard test collections has been recognized as a difficult problem, and as new, large collections of text become available for research, it becomes increasingly important to develop appropriate methodologies.

The fourth section of the paper contains the results of the experiments of experiments and a discussion. The appendix to the paper contains an example of the questionnaire that was used for query formulation.

2 Using Query Knowledge

2.1 Relative Importance of Query Concepts

The simplest type of knowledge a user can provide is to indicate, in a particular query, the words and phrases that are particularly important. In the I^3R system, this is done by using a pointing device to highlight these words and phrases in a natural language query (see Figure 1). For statistical document retrieval systems, this provides two types of information:

1. The relative importance of query words (or query term weights).

2. The important groups of words (phrases).

The way this information can be used is best described using the probabilistic model of retrieval, although the same information has been used effectively in systems based on the vector space model (Salton and McGill, 1983; Salton, 1986; Fagan, 1987). This section discusses the use of relative importance information, the next discusses phrases.

The probabilistic model of retrieval shows that the optimal ranking function for documents, given certain assumptions, is

$$P(Relevant|D)/P(NonRelevant|D)$$

where $P(Relevant|D)$ is the probability that a document is relevant given its representative D. Using Bayes' Rule we transform this ranking function to $R(D)/Q(D)$, where R(D) is the

351

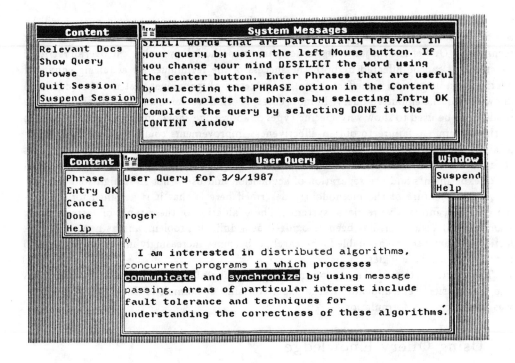

Figure 1: Selecting important words and phrases in I³R.

probability that a relevant document has representative D, and $Q(D)$ is the probability of a non-relevant document having representative D. $R(D)$ and $Q(D)$ are usually expanded by assuming that the terms are independent in the relevant and non-relevant sets of documents (Van Rijsbergen, 1979). The *approximation* to $R(D)$ derived in this way is

$$R'(D) = \prod_{i=1}^{n} p_i^{t_i}(1 - p_i)^{1-t_i},$$

where p_i is the probability that t_i is 1 in a random document from the relevant set of documents. A similar expression holds for $Q'(D)$, with the probability q_i being the probability that t_i is 1 in the non-relevant set of documents. Given these approximations, the ranking function can be shown to be

$$\sum_{i|qt_i=1} w_i t_i \tag{1}$$

where

$$w_i = \log\left[\frac{p_i(1 - q_i)}{(1 - p_i)q_i}\right]$$

and the summation is over all query terms The estimation of p_i and q_i can be done using information acquired during relevance feedback. Initially, however, this information is not available and the estimation of these parameters from document statistics results in a ranking function where w_i is approximated by the *inverse document frequency weight*, measured by $\log nd/frequency(t_i)$ (Croft and Harper, 1979). The parameter nd is the number of documents stored and $frequency(t_i)$ is the number of documents that contain t_i (sometimes called the term posting). An approximation for nd that is often used is the maximum term posting.

Another form of ranking function (1) can be developed that includes the within-document frequency information and has better performance (Croft, 1981, 1983). This ranking function includes a probability called the *term significance weight* that can estimated by normalizing the within document frequency for a term in a particular document. This weight, intuitively, measures the importance of a term in a given document whereas the inverse document frequency weight measures the importance of the term in the whole collection of documents. The actual definition of the term significance weight is $P(t_i = 1|D)$, which is the probability that term i is assigned to document representative D. For term i in document j, the term significance weight is referred to by s_{ij} and the resulting ranking function is

$$\sum_{i|qt_i=1} s_{ij}\, w_i\, t_i \tag{2}$$

Ranking function (2) is equivalent to the "tf.idf" form of the ranking function derived from the vector space model. We are also carrying out experiments with other forms of retrieval models (Fuhr, 1989), but these studies are beyond the scope of this paper.

Information about the relative importance of query terms can be used to get better estimates for w_i prior to relevance feedback. Specifically, instead of making assumptions about p_i values that result in w_i being essentially equivalent to the inverse document frequency weight, the relative importance information can be used to provide better estimates for p_i. There has been some research that indicates that user-defined query weights can be used effectively, although these experiments had many limitations (Salton and Waldstein, 1978; Harper, 1980).

From the acquisition point of view, it is not clear how many levels of importance can be specified by the users. It does seem unlikely that they can reliably specify numeric probability values. In I^{3}R, there are only two levels: important and default. In Harper's thesis (1980), he describes an experiment where 5 levels of importance are simulated. In the experiments reported here, 4 levels are used.

2.2 Phrases

Improvements to retrieval models that make an assumption of term independence have been suggested by Van Rijsbergen (1979) and Yu (1983). In general, these approximations result in ranking function (2) being replaced by

$$\sum s_{ij}\, w_i\, t_i + A \tag{3}$$

where A is a correction factor applied to documents that contain dependent terms. Experiments with these models have not, in general, led to significant performance increases. In another application of these models, Croft (1986) proposed using phrases identified in the query as dependent groups of terms. Documents that contain phrases receive an adjustment to the score they have obtained from retrieval strategy based on the independence model. The experiments using this approach, and the work by Smeaton on syntactic phrases, which used the same underlying retrieval model, showed improvements in retrieval performance (Smeaton and Van Rijsbergen, 1988). The details of the retreival model are given in the following subsection.

Another way of using phrases is to add terms representing phrases to the document and query vectors (Fagan, 1987). In Fagan's study, these extended vectors are then compared using a variation of the cosine correlation that separates the contributions of the words and phrases. Weights for the phrase terms are estimated from the weights of the words that make up the phrase rather than directly from the document collection. Fagan's results showed significant performance increases for some collections (such as CACM) and only small increases for others. Despite differences in implementation, the underlying use of phrases to correct a score resulting from an independence model is similar to the probabilistic approach. In our experiments, we have used both approaches.

2.2.1 A Probabilistic Phrase Model

If we restrict the phrases to two words, which has been shown to be the most effective in other studies, then we can use Van Rijsbergen's dependency model (1979) to calculate the correction factor in equation 3 as follows:

$$A = \sum (t_j \left[\log \left[\frac{(1 - c_i)}{(1 - d_i)} \right] - \log \left[\frac{(1 - c_i')}{(1 - d_i')} \right] \right] + t_i t_j \left[\log \left[\frac{c_i(1 - d_i)}{(1 - c_i)d_i} \right] - \log \left[\frac{c_i'(1 - d_i')}{(1 - c_i')d_i'} \right] \right])$$

where $t_i t_j$ is a dependent pair of terms, c_i, c_i' are $P(t_i = 1 | t_j = 1)$ in the relevant and non-relevant sets of documents respectively, and d_i, d_i' are $P(t_i = 1 | t_j = 0)$ in the relevant and non-relevant sets. The summation is over all pairs of terms identified as phrases. This could be rewritten as

$$A = \sum (t_j a_1 + t_i t_j a_2)$$

This makes it clear that documents containing both terms of a phrase receive a correction of $a_1 + a_2$. Documents containing only the second term in a phrase receive a correction of a_1. This can result in negative correction factors as we will see later.

We are then left with the problem of estimating c_i, c_i', d_i, d_i'. Similar to the way p_i and q_i are estimated, we can use the entire collection of documents to estimate the c_i', d_i' (the values in the non-relevant set), and estimate the values in the relevant set using constants in the initial retrieval and then a sample of relevant documents after relevance feedback. The maximum likelihood estimates are used in this study. They are

$c_i' =$ (no. of co-occurrences of t_i, t_j)/(freq. of occurrence of t_j)
$d_i' =$ (freq. of t_i - no. of co-occurrences)/ (size of collection - freq. of t_j)

	Phrase		
	t_1, t_2	t_1, t_2	t_3, t_4
Frequencies	191, 281	191, 281	140,226
No. of co-occurrences	31	31	13
c_i, d_i	.9, .6	.9, .3	.9, .4
c_i', d_i'	.11, .05	.11, .05	.06, .04
a_1	-0.57	-0.80	-0.77
a_2	0.37	0.91	0.92
A	-0.2	0.11	0.15

Table 1: Correction Calculation for 2 Phrases from CACM Collection (3730 documents)

An example of correction factors calculated for two phrases in the CACM collection (Salton, Fox and Wu, 1983) is shown in Table 1. Documents that contain only the second term of a phrase would receive a negative correction in each case. The first two columns show that the c_i, d_i estimates for relevant documents are important and can lead to negative corrections even for documents that contain both terms of a phrase.

2.3 Domain Knowledge

Knowledge-based systems rely on having a detailed model of the application domain. This domain knowledge can be quite complex, including arbitrary predicates on domain objects, causal relationships and temporal relationships. In the document retrieval application, however, our aim is to acquire this knowledge from the end users during retrieval sessions. This means that acquisition must be limited to types of knowledge that are both easily understood and directly applicable to retrieval. In the I^3R system and in this study, we aim primarily to capture the type of knowledge that is found in a thesaurus. More specifically, the domain knowledge is defined as concepts and relationships between them. The relationships we concentrate on are is-a (computer is-a device), **instance-of** (vax instance-of computer), **part-of** (processor part-of computer), **synonym-of** (program synonym-of software), and **related-to** (computer related-to hardware). The **related-to** relationship is very general and is used to describe relationships that could, in more detailed representations, be very complex. There are two approaches to acquiring this type of domain knowledge:

1. Ask the user to specify concepts that are related to query concepts and the types of relationships. This approach is very open-ended and does not provide much guidance. In I^3R, expert users are given this option both during query formulation and relevance feedback (Figure 2).

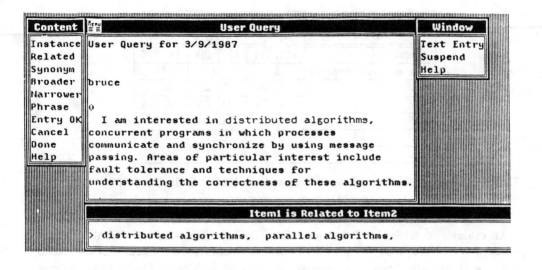

Figure 2: Domain knowledge specification in I³R: user relates two concepts formed as phrases.

2. Suggest possible related concepts and ask the user to clarify relationship types and validate the relationship. This approach is easier for the user, but more difficult for the system. Possible sources of related concepts include term clusters and information from relevance feedback (Harman, 1988).

The domain knowledge that is acquired can be used in the retrieval process in a number of ways. The typical use of this knowledge in a statistical retrieval system would be to expand the query with related concepts. This has been done in previous projects with mixed results (Salton, 1968; Sparck Jones, 1971), and this is the technique used in our initial experiments.

Another way of using this knowledge is in retrieval based on plausible inference (Van Rijsbergen, 1986, Croft et al, 1989). In this approach, retrieval is viewed as establishing plausible relationships between the query and the documents, and assessing the degree of plausibility. Domain knowledge obviously helps establish these relationships and, as such, takes part in the matching process. Rather than simply using it to expand the query, however, it is used as a source of evidence that is combined with evidence from statistical and NLP sources. The difference between using domain knowledge for query expansion and for plausible inference is clearer in the case where a significant domain knowledge base has been acquired. The knowledge base of concepts and relationships can be thought of as a network of nodes (representing concepts) and links (representing relationships). If we use this knowledge base to expand the query, then potentially every concept represented could be included if we follow all paths of links. The plausible inference process attempts to find connections between the concepts in the query and the concepts in particular documents. This approach is not pursued further in this paper.

2.4 Relevance Feedback

Relevance feedback provides much more information for the estimation of the probabilities in ranking function (2). The p_i estimates, in particular, can be improved greatly using the sample of relevant documents. It is also possible to modify the initial query by including words from the relevant documents. Salton and Buckley (1988) have recently done a series of experiments in which they establish that this type of query expansion, even by adding all words in the relevant documents, is very effective. In I^3R, it is also possible for the user to indicate important words and phrases in the text of relevant documents. Both techniques will be used in the experiments reported in this paper.

In order to establish that enhanced queries are more effective than simple queries, it is important to include relevance feedback. It may be, for example, that the words included through relevance feedback provide sufficient domain knowledge for effective retrieval. Our hypothesis is that enhanced queries will be more effective on the initial search and approximately the same effectiveness after feedback. This should result in more relevant documents being found overall.

3 Experimental Methodology

The approach used to acquire enhanced queries in the set of experiments reported here was to have people fill out a form designed for this purpose. The form was developed by looking at the performance and comments of a small group of users. Although there are disadvantages to this approach compared to acquiring queries through an interactive session with a retrieval system (for example, I^3R), we felt that it gave us more control and eliminated many factors that may affect performance, such as computer experience. We should emphasise that this form was designed to be used only in this study, and is not proposed as a subtitute for interactive query formulation. The lessons we learn from these experiments will be applied to the design of the next, larger study that will include interactive query formulation.

A limitation of our approach is the assumption that all users in the study have similar types of information needs. That is, we are assuming that all users want to see as many relevant documents as possible in the sample of documents they are shown, and that document abstracts can satisfy their need. This is a consequence of the artificial nature of the information needs in typical experimental settings.

A copy of one of the query forms we obtained in the study appears in the appendix. A person using this form is asked to provide some personal data and then increasingly detailed specifications of their information need. The initial query is a natural language statement of interest. The person then underlines important words and phrases in that query and indicates the importance of those concepts using a simple numerical level (1 to 3). This actually gives 4 levels of relative importance since those words not underlined are given a default value. The most complicated part of the form is a table where the person enters concepts from the initial query and then writes down related concepts, the relationship type, and the importance of the concepts. Finally, space is provided for criticism of the form and for comments on the difficulty of the specification process.

Once the form was filled out, the information from it was entered into a system which did the indexing and ran a variety of retrieval strategies based on the models discussed in the previous section. The top 10 documents in the ranking for each strategy were merged into a set in random order (to remove any bias toward the first documents seen) and shown to users for relevance judgments. Users were also asked to identify interesting concepts in the relevant documents. The relevance judgments were then used in a variety of feedback strategies, the top 10 documents for each strategy were merged (excluding documents already found by individual strategies), and this set was shown to users for more relevance judgments. Turnaround times were on the order of 2-3 days.

Comparison of the retrieval results is done using a matched-pair design (Robertson, 1981). In this design, the top ten documents in the ranking produced for a particular query by each pair of retrieval strategies are compared. The comparison, which simply identifies if one group of ten documents is better than the other, is on the basis of precision, or the number of relevant documents retrieved. This type of evaluation has the following advantages:

- It does not require full relevance judgments for each query. This is an important requirement for real system evaluation.

- It is realistic in the sense that users of a retrieval system will tend to examine only the top group of retrieved documents and are unlikely to make major distinctions based on the actual rankings in that top group. Traditional recall/precision tables are very sensitive to the initial rank positions and evaluate entire rankings.

- Significance measures can be readily used.

The disadvantage is, of course, that we do not obtain full recall/precision figures. Note that we can, however, estimate recall using the total number of relevant documents retrieved by all queries as has been done in many previous studies.

A total of 20 queries were processed for the experiments reported here. All experiments used a collection of abstracts from the *Communications of the ACM* between 1958 and 1985. Note that we are not using queries from the CACM test collection described in Salton, Fox and Wu (1983), and we have increased the coverage of the collection to include abstracts from 1979-1985.

Average number of terms in initial query (after stopword removal)	14.8
Average number of phrases in initial query	3.8
Average number of words in domain knowledge	9.4
Average number of phrases in domain knowledge	4.2

Table 2: Size of Queries and Domain Knowledge

Importance	% Use
Very Important	50.7%
Moderately Important	40.4%
Weakly Important	8.9%

Table 3: Use of Importance Levels for Words/Phrases

4   The Experiments

4.1   Acquisition Statistics

In this section, we present a number of statistics derived from the 20 forms that were filled out in the initial study. Of the 20 subjects, 5 were graduate students from a department of industrial engineering, 7 were graduate students from a computer science department, 5 were computer science undergraduates, 2 were graduate students from an electrical and computer engineeering department, and 1 was a graduate student from a department of education. Eleven of the subjects identified their degree of experience with the topic of the query as intermediate, 5 as expert, and 4 as novice. Eleven of the subjects have had some experience with IR systems, the other 9 have seldom or never used them.

Table 2 lists the average number of words and phrases that were provided as part of the initial query and the related domain knowledge. These figures clearly indicate that users (of the type in our study) are capable of providing enhanced queries. Table 3 lists the average use of the relative importance values used for words and phrases. The fact that the usage is heavily skewed towards the top two levels suggests that people may only distinguish a small number of levels of importance.

Table 4 shows the use of the relation types in the domain knowledge. This data shows a fairly even split in usage between **is-a** (in the form of broader-term and narrower-term), **synonym**, and **instance-of**. The other forms of relations were only used infrequently.

Finally, 11 of the subjects mentioned that they had some difficulty with query formulation. Most of the problems centered on the parts of the query form associated with the specification of domain knowledge. Based on their responses, the most difficult part of

Relation Types	% Use
Synonym	35.5%
Broader-Term	15.5%
Narrower-Term	13.7%
Instance-Of	18.4%
Part-Of	8.2%
Related-To	8.7%

Table 4: Use of Relation Types in Domain Knowledge

query formulation (for 5 of the 20 subjects) was identifying relation types in the domain knowledge.

4.2 The Initial Search

In this set of experiments, six retrieval strategies based on the models described in section 2 were used. These were:

Strategy 1: The baseline search using the independence model with tf.idf weights, as described in section 2.1.

Strategy 2: A search using phrases as described in section 2.2. The "phrases" were obtained using Fagan's approach, which is to use all pairs of words in the query and weight phrases by an average of the tf.idf scores of the individual terms.

Strategy 3: Same as strategy 1, but with p_i estimates based on user-specified relative importance values (0.5 for default, 0.6 for weakly important, 0.75 for moderately important, 0.9 for very important).

Strategy 4: A phrase search using the dependence model described in section 2.2.1, user-specified phrases, and estimates of p_i, c_i, d_i based on user-specified importance values.

Strategy 5: Same as strategy 4, but with words and phrases from domain knowledge included. Weights for domain knowledge words and phrases based on user-specified importance values.

Strategy 6: Same as strategy 3, but with words from domain knowledge (no phrases). Weights based on user-specified importance values.

The results are shown in Table 5. The average number of relevant documents found for each query by all strategies was 7.1. The average precision of the top 10 documents for each strategy is shown in Table 5. These figures show a 30% increase in precision for strategy 6 (including domain words) compared to the tf.idf baseline. We then carried out a series of

360

Strategy	Precision (20 queries)
Strategy 1	.37
Strategy 2	.35
Strategy 3	.40
Strategy 4	.35
Strategy 5	.41
Strategy 6	.48

Table 5: Results for Initial Searches

significance tests using a one-tailed sign test with $\alpha = .05$ (Siegel, 1956). The major results are as follows:

1. Neither of the phrase strategies were significantly different to the tf.idf strategy, or to each other. This suggests that we do not really understand how to use phrases. This is emphasised by the relative performance for strategies 5 and 6, where using words alone produced significantly better performance.

2. The use of user-specified importance weights with words (strategy 3) is significantly better than tf.idf at a level of .055.

3. The inclusion of domain knowledge leads to very significant performance increases. For example, in comparing strategy 6 with tf.idf, 12 of the queries performed better with strategy 6, and the other 8 queries had the same performance. Our experiments indicated that the user importance weighting was an important part of the success of this strategy.

4.3   Relevance Feedback

The main aim of these experiments was to see if a tf.idf search in combination with feedback significantly outperformed an enhanced query strategy with feedback. Five different relevance feedback strategies were used:

Strategy 7: Based on tf.idf search (strategy 1), all terms in relevant documents are added to initial query, and p_i estimates are based on occurrences in relevant documents. This strategy was designed to be similar to strategies described in Salton and Buckley (1988) that included all relevant document terms.

Strategy 8: Based on strategy 3, adding all terms from relevant documents to the initial query.

Strategy 9: Based on strategy 6, adding all terms from relevant documents to the initial query.

361

Strategy	Precision (20 queries)
Strategy 7	.20
Strategy 8	.22
Strategy 9	.23
Strategy 10	.29
Strategy 11	.38

Table 6: Results for Relevance Feedback

Strategy 10: Based on strategy 5, adding only words and phrases indentified by users in relevant documents to the initial query, and estimating p_i, c_i, d_i from relevant documents.

Strategy 11: Based on strategy 6, adding only words identified by users in relevant documents to the initial query.

The average number of relevant documents found for each query by all feedback strategies was 6. The average number of words identified by users in all relevant documents seen was 30.3. The average number of phrases identified was 12.9. The average precision for each feedback strategy is shown in Table 6. The major results from these experiments are:

1. Adding all terms from relevant documents was not as effective as using only words identified by the users. This is not the result obtained by Salton and Buckley (1988) and indicates that further work needs to be done to better understand the process of automatic query expansion.

2. Feedback strategy 11 was very effective. This means that not only does the enhanced initial query perform significantly better than tf.idf, it continues to perform better after feedback.

Another interesting piece of data is obtained by looking at the overlap between the words in the domain knowledge provided during query formulation and the words in the relevant documents used for feedback in strategy 7. Only 35% of the extra words provided by users were found in the relevant documents. This indicates that users are a potentially valuable source of domain knowledge and that a small sample of relevant documents will not necessarily contain the words that are important for describing the information need. It also indicates, however, that relevant documents are a good source of words to suggest to the users (Harman, 1988).

5   Conclusions

The results of this study indicate that enhanced queries significantly improve the effectiveness of retrieval strategies. The users in our study were able to provide a large amount of knowledge about the topic of their information needs, and retrieval strategies were able to make effective use of this knowledge. The most useful types of knowledge that were obtained (in terms of retrieval effectiveness) were domain concepts related to the query concepts, and the relative importance of concepts. The use of phrases was not successful. Other experiments indicate that this is caused by the inability of the phrase-based search strategies to make effective use of this knowledge.

Our future work will involve a larger study using interactive query formulation, rather than forms. We also intend to continue to study phrase-based search strategies, including the evaluation of new retrieval models for phrases with standard test collections.

Acknowledgments

This research was supported in part by NSF Grant IRI-8814790 and by contract AFOSR 90-0110 with the Air Force Office of Scientific Research.

References

Ayuso, D.; Shaked, V.; Weischedel, R. "An Environment for Acquiring Semantic Information." *Proceedings of the Twenty-Fifth Annual Meeting of the Association for Computational Linguistics*, 32-40; 1987.

Ballard, B.; Stumberger, D. "Semantic Acquisition in TELI: A transportable User-Customized Natural Language Processor". *Proceedings of the 24th Meeting of the Association for Computational Linguistics*, 20-29, 1986.

Croft, W. B. "Document Representation in Probabilistic Models of Information Retrieval". *Journal of the American Society of Information Science*, 32: 451-457; 1981.

Croft, W. B. "Boolean Queries and Term Dependencies in Probabilistic Retrieval Models". *Journal of the American Society for Information Science*, 37: 71-77; 1986.

Croft, W.B.; Harper, D.J. "Using probabilistic models of document retrieval without relevance information", *Journal of Documentation*, 35, 285-295, 1979.

Croft, W.B.; Thompson, R.T. "I³R: A New Approach to the Design of Document Retrieval Systems". *Journal of the American Society for Information Science*, 38: 389-404; 1987.

Croft, W.B., Lucia, T.; Cringean, J,; Willett, P. "Retrieving Documents by Plausible Inference: An Experimental Study". *Information Processing and Management*, 25, 599-614, 1989.

Fagan, J. *Experiments in Automatic Phrase Indexing for Document Retrieval: A Comparison of Syntactic and Non-Syntactic Methods*. Ph.D. Thesis, TR 87-868, Cornell University,

Computer Science Department, 1987.

Fuhr, N. "Models for retrieval with probabilistic indexing", *Information Processing and Management*, 25, 55-72, 1989.

Harman, D. "Towards interactive query expansion", *Proceedings of 11th ACM Conference on Research and Development in Information Retrieval*, 321-332, 1988.

Harper, D.J. *Relevance Feedback in Document Retrieval Systems: An Evaluation of Probabilistic Strategies.* Ph.D. Thesis, Computer Laboratory, University of Cambridge, 1980.

Van Rijsbergen, C. J. *Information Retrieval.* Second Edition. Butterworths, London; 1979.

Van Rijsbergen, C.J. "A Non-Classical Logic for Information Retrieval". *Computer Journal*, 29: 481-485; 1986.

Robertson, S.E. "The methodology of information retrieval experiment". In: Sparck Jones, editor, *Information Retrieval Experiment.* London: Butterworths, 9-31, 1981.

Salton, G. *Automatic Information Organization and Retrieval.* McGraw-Hill, New York; 1968.

Salton, G.; McGill, M. *Introduction to Modern Information Retrieval.* McGraw-Hill, New York; 1983.

Salton, G.; Buckley, C. "Improving Retrieval Performance by Relevance Feedback". Technical Report, Cornell University, 1988.

Salton, G; Waldstein, R.G. "Term Relevance Weights in On-Line Information Retrieval", *Information Processing and Management*, 14, 29-35, 1978.

Salton, G.; Fox, E.A.; Wu, H. "Extended Boolean Information Retrieval". *Communications of the ACM*, 26, 1022-1036, 1983.

Siegel, S. *Nonparametric Statistics*, McGraw-Hill, 1956.

Smeaton, A.; Van Rijsbergen, C.J. "Experiments on Incorporating Syntactic Processing of User Queries into a Document Retrieval Strategy". *Proceedings of ACM SIGIR International Conference on Research and Development in Information Retrieval*, 31-52, 1988.

Sparck Jones, K. *Automatic Keyword Classification for Information Retrieval.* Butterworths, London, 1971.

Sparck Jones, K.; Bates, R.G. *Report on a design for the 'ideal' test collection.* British

Library Report 5428, Computer Laboratory, University of Cambridge, 1977.

Sparck Jones, K.; Webster, C. *Research on Relevance Weighting*. British Library Report 5553, Computer Laboratory, University of Cambridge, 1980.

Tou, F.M. et al. "RABBIT: An intelligent database assistant". *Proceedings AAAI-82*, 314-318, 1982.

Yu, C.T.; Buckley, D.; Lam, K; Salton, G. "A generalized term dependence model in information retrieval". *Information Technology: Research and Development*, 4, 129-154, 1983.

Appendix: A Sample Query Form

Query Formulation Questionnaire

1. About the Questionnaire

This questionnaire asks you to create a query to a database of articles from the computer science journal *Communications of the ACM* (CACM). The database contains titles, abstracts, and related information on articles that appeared in CACM between 1958 and 1985. We would like you to think of a topic in computer science that you would be interested in reading CACM articles on, and write a query describing that topic. By a query we mean a description of the content of articles you are interested in rather than, for instance, the names of authors. The following is an example of a query:

> I would like papers about information retrieval that address issues in distributed databases. Also of interest to me would be articles about the use of parallel architectures in implementing retrieval (particularly commercial) systems.

We will be asking you to give a number of additional pieces of information about your query, as well as some data about yourself. This information will be used to retrieve titles and abstracts of CACM articles that are meant to address your interest. After this information has been retrieved, we will present you with a list of these titles and abstracts and ask you to judge whether each of them is in fact relevant to your query.

2. Personal Data

Name: *Jane Doe*
Age : *29*
Sex : *Female*
Dept: *Computer & Information Science*
Your degree of experience with the topic of your query
   (E)XPERT, (I)NTERMEDIATE, (N)OVICE: *E, I*
Your degree of experience with using text retrieval systems (i.e. computerized library catalogs, online bibliographic databases, etc.)
   (N)EVER, (SE)LDOM, (SO)METIMES, (F)REQUENT: *SO*

3. The Actual Query

In the space provided below please print or type your query:

> I am interested in articles about knowledge [3] based natural [3] language processing. I am also interested in articles that discuss the use of connectionist [2] techniques within the knowledge-based natural language [3] processing paradigm.

4. Important Words and Phrases in the Query

Please underline the important words and phrases of the query.

5. Providing a Ranking

Please categorize the words/phrases that you just underlined into one of three levels of importance. Put the appropriate number on top of the underlined words/phrases. If you feel that the word/phrase you underlined is very important to your query, please write down 3. If it is moderately important write down 2, and if less important write down 1.

6. Providing Related Words and Phrases

Please provide words/phrases that are related to the ones you underlined. For each **underlined** word/phrase in the query, please write down the word/phrase under the first heading in the following diagram, and list the **related** words/phrases under the second heading.

    Filling out the Relation Type and Importance Level Headings in the diagram will be described in Sections 7 & 8 respectively

Word/Phrase from Query	Related Words/Phrases	Relation Type	Importance Level
Knowledge-based	*semantic*	*Narrower-Term*	1
Knowledge-based	*pragmatic*	*Narrower-Term*	1
Knowledge-based	*meaning-based*	*Synonym*	2
Natural Language Processing	*Natural Language Understanding*	*Synonym*	3
Natural Language Processing	*NLU*	*Synonym*	3
Natural Language Processing	*NLP*	*Synonym*	3
Natural Language Processing	*Text Understanding*	*Part-Of*	3
Natural Language Processing	*Parsing*	*Instance-Of*	3
Natural Language Processing	*Conceptual Analysis*	*Instance-Of*	3
Connectionist	*Neural Network*	*Synonym*	3
Connectionist	*Artificial Neural Network*	*Synonym*	3
Connectionist	*ANN*	*Synonym*	3
Connectionist	*Relaxation Network*	*Instance-Of*	3
Connectionist	*Backpropagation Network*	*Instance-Of*	3

7. Identifying Relation Types

Please identify the relation types that exist between each of the words/phrases under the first heading of the table above and the related words/phrases you wrote under the second heading. Please choose one of the following relation types, and write it down under the third heading above. A few examples of the different relation types listed below are given below.

The Relation Types are:

SYNONYM, BROADER-TERM, NARROWER-TERM, INSTANCE-OF, PART-OF

If none of these relations appear to be appropriate, please use the generic relation RELATED-TO.

Examples of the different relation types:
    Two-Dimensional Array would be a SYNONYM for Matrix
    Data Structure would be a BROADER-TERM for Linked Lists
    Mouse would be a NARROWER-TERM for Pointing Devices
    VAX780 would be an INSTANCE-OF of Computers
    Keyboard would be PART-OF a computer

8. Providing a Ranking

Under the importance level heading in section 6 please categorize the extra words/phrase you provided into one of three levels of importance. If you feel that the extra word/phrase you provided is very important to your query, please write down 3. If it is moderately important write down 2, and if less important write down 1. This is identical to the information provided in Section 5, except that the importance levels are now being sought for the extra words/phrases.

9. Comments About the Questionnaire

Was this questionnaire difficult to fill out? Please feel free to comment on anything else about this questionnaire. For instance, was there any particular question that was difficult, confusing, ambiguous, etc.?

It would have been better if the table in section 6 were designed so that there was more space to fill in the related words for each word/phrase from the query.

The Automatic Generation of Extended Queries[*]

Carolyn J. Crouch, Donald B. Crouch and Krishna R. Nareddy

Department of Computer Science
University of Minnesota - Duluth
Duluth, Minnesota 55812

ABSTRACT

In the extended vector space model, each document vector consists of a set of subvectors representing the multiple concepts or concept classes present in the document. Typical information concepts, in addition to the usual content terms or descriptors, include author names, bibliographic links, *etc*. The extended vector space model is known to improve retrieval effectiveness. However, a major impediment to the use of the extended model is the construction of an extended query. In this paper, we describe a method for automatically extending a query containing only content terms (a single concept class) to a representation containing multiple concept classes. No relevance feedback is involved. Experiments using the CACM collection resulted in an average precision 34% better than that obtained using the standard single-concept term vector model.

INTRODUCTION

In document retrieval systems, the information contained in a document is generally represented by a set of descriptors or concept terms. This representation does not adequately reflect the variety of informational items contained in so-called *composite documents*. [FOX85] For example, a composite document may contain bibliographic information, citations, or author-assigned descriptive categories in addition to content terms. To enable systems to be developed which make use of this additional information, Fox proposed the extended vector space model. [FOX83] Before describing the extended model, we will briefly review the model on which it is based, namely, the vector space model.

---

[*] This work is being supported in part by the National Science Foundation under grant IRI 87-02735.

Vector Space Model

In the vector space model [SALT75], each document in the document collection is viewed as a set of unique words or phrases and is represented as a weighted term vector. The document collection as a whole thus represents a vector space of dimension m, where m is the number of words or phrases in the collection. In this model queries, like documents, are represented by weighted term vectors.

The weight assigned to a particular term in a document vector is normally indicative of the contribution of the term to the meaning of the document. Although many vector weighting schemes have been proposed [SALT88a], one of the most effective is *tf-idf* weighting, in which each term is represented by the product of its term frequency (the number of times the term occurs in the document) and a function of its inverse document frequency (the total number of documents in which the term appears). Thus, *tf-idf* weighting reflects the importance of a term within the document itself and within the document collection as a whole.

In the vector space model, the similarity between a pair of items (e.g., a document-query pair or document- document pair) is represented by the mathematical similarity of their corresponding term vectors. One measure of the similarity of vectors is the cosine measure, the cosine of the angle between the two vectors - the smaller the angle between the corresponding vectors, the greater the similarity of the two vectors. Conceptually, the items are viewed as points in the vector space, and the similarity of the items is inversely related to the distance between the two points.

The vector space model facilitates term weighting, the clustering of documents (grouping of similar documents), query formulation, ranking of retrieved documents, and relevance feedback. [SALT83] Clustering is of particular interest in our proposed work since it provides a means whereby extended query vectors can be constructed automatically.

Extended Vector Space Model

The vector space model can be modified to include concepts other than the normal content terms or descriptors. As noted, Fox developed a method for representing in a single, extended vector different classes of information about a document, such as author names, terms, bibliographic citations, *etc.* [FOX83] In the extended vector space model, a document vector consists of a set of subvectors, where each subvector represents a different concept class. Similarity between a pair of extended vectors is calculated as a linear combination of the similarities of corresponding subvectors. Figure 1 contains an example of the extended vector in this model.

Legend

d	a content term vector
o	an objective identifier vector (such as author name)
c	a citation vector
D	extended document vector
Q	extended query vector
α, β, γ	similarity coefficients (concept class weights)
v_i	weight of the i-th component in a v-type vector

Extended Vectors D and S

$$\mathbf{D} \equiv (\mathbf{d}_1, \ldots, \mathbf{d}_n, \mathbf{o}_1, \ldots, \mathbf{o}_m, \mathbf{c}_1, \ldots, \mathbf{c}_k)$$
$$\mathbf{Q} \equiv (\mathbf{d}_1, \ldots, \mathbf{d}_n, \mathbf{o}_1, \ldots, \mathbf{o}_m, \mathbf{c}_1, \ldots, \mathbf{c}_k)$$

Similarity of D and Q - S(D,Q)

$$S(D,Q) \equiv \alpha[\text{content term similarity}] + \beta[\text{objective identifier similarity}] + \gamma\,[\text{citation similarity}]$$

Fig. 1. - An Example of an Extended Vector

The extended model is intuitively appealing - the contents of documents can be represented more completely and search strategies can be formulated which take advantage of particular combinations of concept identifiers. In addition, the model has particular relevance to hypertext information retrieval in which various types of links connect document nodes. However, use of the extended vector model in a document retrieval environment does present several major problems, including

- construction of an extended search request, and
- selection of the coefficients for combining subvector similarities.

The work to be described in this paper focuses on a solution to the first problem.

Query Formulation

Document processing systems generally accept search requests expressed in one of two ways: (1) a natural language description of the query, or (2) a set of keywords representing the concepts inherent in the query. In the former case, automatic indexing processes translate a user's query from a natural language description to a term concept vector. [SALT88b] In the latter case, a user essentially constructs the term concept vector manually, albeit with the aid of controlled vocabulary lists and oftentimes with the assistance of a search intermediary.

In the extended vector environment, it is not known whether a user can formulate an extended query which consists of a variety of information types and which adequately expresses the user's needs. Similarly, it is not known what type of information should be provided to a user to assist in such a query formulation process. Because of these uncertainties, a more feasible approach to the construction of an extended query appears to be automatic construction. We propose to construct extended queries automatically from an initial query vector consisting only of content terms or descriptors.

RELATED WORK

Each of the two problem areas associated with the use of the extended vector space model have been investigated by Fox [FOX83] and Fox, *et. al.* [FOX88]. In this section we briefly review the approaches taken by these researchers and summarize their findings.

Automatic Query Construction using Feedback

Two strategies have been proposed for constructing extended queries. Each begins with a query vector that contains content terms only and uses relevance feedback (user assessments as to the relevance of retrieved documents) to construct an extended query vector.

The simpler strategy, which uses only a single feedback document, is as follows:

- Search the document collection using the content term query vector.

- Rank the documents according to document-query similarity values.

- Select the highest ranked, relevant document.

- Let the extended query vector be that extended document vector which represents the *most relevant* document.

Preliminary experiments were performed on the single document feedback method to test the validity of extended vector retrieval. [FOX83] The extended query vector was limited to pairs of concept types (subvectors), such as term-authors or term-cocitations. A search of the extended document collection was conducted using the extended query, and performance results were compared with those obtained for a search using only a single term concept vector. When calculating query-document similarity, various ad hoc weights were used for the coefficients of the concept subvectors. Modest improvement was obtained when extended query vectors were employed, but only when suitable weights were used for the subvectors. For example, searches of the CACM collection using extended queries consisting of terms and bibliographic links yielded an average 9% improvement in precision performance when equal weights were used for the two subvectors.

The single document feedback approach is limited in its performance effectiveness, since the highest ranked relevant document may not adequately reflect the information contained in the original query. Fox showed that a better extended query can be constructed if information contained not only in the original query but also in a larger set of retrieved documents is used to formulate the extended query.

The other query construction strategy takes such additional information into account. The algorithm is as follows:

- Search the document collection using the content term query vector.

- Rank the documents according to document-query similarity values.

- Select the 20 highest ranked documents and assess the relevance of each one.

- Generate an extended query vector using relevance feedback applied to the original query vector and the extended document vectors corresponding to the 20 retrieved documents. *Relevance feedback* [ROCC71] assigns weights to the components of the subvectors of the extended query vector based on the occurrence characteristics of these components in the set of relevant and nonrelevant retrieved documents.

Relevance feedback is known to yield good search results under certain conditions for the vector space model. Fox's tests of the multiple document feedback method revealed that improvement in performance is also gained when relevance feedback is used as the basis for constructing extended query vectors. For example, searches of the CACM collection performed using extended queries containing only equally weighted term and link subvectors yielded a 13% improvement over that obtained for a search using only a single term concept vector. This represents a gain of 5% in precision over searches using extended queries generated by the single document feedback method.

Fox's initial study revealed that reasonably good extended queries can be constructed using the information contained in the initial query vector and a set of documents retrieved by an initial search of the collection. His study also revealed the importance of proper selection of concept class weights in the query-document similarity function (weights α, β, γ in Fig. 1). This observation led to the second phase of Fox's work.

Coefficient Selection using Retrospective Analysis

Fox investigated the use of regression methods for deriving optimal weights for the coefficients of the subvectors in the composite similarity measure. Regression coefficients were calculated as follows:

- Search the document collection using the content term query vector.

- Rank the documents according to document-query similarity values.

- Select the 20 highest ranked documents and assess the relevance of each one.

- Do a retrospective analysis of these 20 documents to produce those weights which are best able to distinguish the previously identified relevant documents from the nonrelevant documents in the extended vector space.

Using regression weights instead of ad hoc weights considerably improved the performance of the extended query searches. For example, the CACM searches using the extended queries (term-link subvectors) constructed from 20 top-ranked documents yielded an average precision of 27%, an additional gain of 14% over extended searches without regression weighting.

Although regression weights lead to significant improvement in retrieval performance, it is not feasible in practice to calculate similarity weights using retrospective analysis. Furthermore, additional studies revealed that coefficient weights derived in the manner indicated are not generalizable; that is, for a given query, coefficients derived using an initial search of one-half of the collection did not necessarily yield good results when the other half of the collection was searched using the same regression weights in the composite similarity function. [FOX88]

Conclusions

The previous empirical results confirm that improvement in retrieval effectiveness can be obtained from the additional information contained in the extended vector model. However, for the model to be used in practice, additional work is needed. In particular, a procedure needs to be developed which constructs extended queries automatically without the use of relevance feedback. Relevance feedback requires user assessment of a large number of documents (for example, 20 documents as above).

In the following sections of this report, we describe a method of constructing an extended query which does not require user interaction, describe the factors which influence the design of the experiments, and present the results of experiments testing the validity of the proposed approach.

QUERY CONSTRUCTION WITHOUT RELEVANCE FEEDBACK

We propose to construct an extended query from a set of documents chosen by a search of the clustered collection using the initial content term query vector. No relevance judgments are made of the documents contained in clusters. The method is as follows:

- Cluster the document collection using only content term document vectors.

- Search the clustered collection using the content term query vector.

- Select the cluster(s) *most similar* to the query.

- Let the original query vector represent the content term subvector in the extended query. Form the other types of subvectors in the extended query from the corresponding subvectors of the extended document vectors identified in the clustered search.

This approach augments the original query with extended information contained in the documents returned by a search of the clustered collection. The content terms of the original query are not modified; rather, additional information from the other concept types is used to augment the query, producing as a result a query in extended vector format. No relevance assessments are made of the documents retrieved by the search and relevance feedback is not used to formulate the extended query.

Our query construction strategy is tested using facilities provided by the SMART information retrieval system. [SALT71] SMART provides a general framework for conducting retrieval experiments. It contains a number of document collections and corresponding sets of queries which may be used for experimentation. The means exist within the system for evaluating the effectiveness of the retrieval process for both normal (content term) vector searches and for extended vector searches.

EXPERIMENTAL FACTORS

A number of important factors which affect query construction and retrieval must be considered in the design of the experiments. In particular, the document collections and the document hierarchies generated by the clustering technique determine the quality of the information available for query construction. Additionally, the weights assigned to concept class subvectors in the composite similarity measure influence the overall retrieval process.

Document Collections

The document collection used in these experiments is CACM. Although Fox's earlier work also included the ISI collection, we did not use it in our initial study. The extended documents in ISI contain only three subvectors: content terms, author name(s) and cocitation information   Fox found the author subvector to be useless for extending queries. Removing this identifier leaves only a single subvector for extension. CACM, on the other hand, uses seven subvectors in its representation of extended document vectors.

CACM consists of information about 3,204 articles which appeared in *Communications of the ACM* from 1958 through 1979. It has been used by a number of researchers and often serves as a standard for testing retrieval performance. The CACM collection contains a set of extended document vectors and a set of single content term query vectors. Relevance judgments have been made for each of the queries by users familiar with the collection. Table 1 summarizes the characteristics of this collection. A detailed description and a history of this collection are contained in [FOX88].

Clustering the Documents

As previously noted, a principal advantage of the vector space model is that algorithms exist for structuring a collection of document vectors in such a manner that similar documents are grouped together. A cluster hierarchy can be represented by a tree structure in which terminal nodes correspond to single documents and interior nodes (*clusters*) to groups of documents. Each cluster is represented by an artificial or typical element called the centroid. A search of the clustered file is more efficient than the normal retrieval process. In a clustered search, the query is compared first to the centroids to determine those clusters most similar to the query and then to documents contained within the cluster(s) found most similar.

Since the objective of this experiment is to construct extended queries from the extended documents corresponding to the document identifiers returned by a clustered search of the content term vectors, we want to form a document hierarchy using a clustering algorithm which

---

Table 1 - Characteristics of the Extended CACM Document Collection

DOCUMENTS

Total Number of Documents	3,204
Number of Terms	17,139
Document Subvectors - Type & Average Length	
Author	1.4
Computing Reviews Category	1.2
Date	1.0
Content Term	22.5
Bibliographic Coupling	4.2
Bibliographic Link	2.7
Cocitation	3.7

QUERIES

Total Number of Queries	52
Avg. No. of Terms per Query Vector	10.7
Avg. No. of Relevant Documents per Query	15.3
Avg. No Relevant in 10 Most Similar Documents	2.8
Avg. No Relevant in 20 Most Similar Documents	4.7

produces *tight* clusters. A tight cluster contains only documents which are very similar (closely related) to one another. Our premise is that if the content term vectors are closely related, then the additional information concepts contained in the corresponding extended document vectors can be considered to be closely related. The complete link clustering algorithm, one of a class of agglomerative, hierarchical clustering algorithms, is known to produce small, tight clusters. [VOOR85, VOOR86, VANR79].

The theoretical properties of agglomerative, hierarchical clustering methods are well known. [LANC67, JARD68] These methods initially view the items to be clustered as singleton clusters. The two most highly similar clusters are successively merged until only one cluster remains. In the complete link method, the similarity between two clusters is defined as the *minimum* of the similarities between all pairs of documents, where one document of the pair is in one cluster and the other document is in the other cluster. Since the criteria for joining two clusters is very restrictive, the complete link method tends to form small, tight clusters.

In our experiments, the content term document vectors are clustered using the complete link clustering algorithm. The documents in each cluster are represented by a single content term centroid vector. Theoretically, the length of a centroid vector associated with each of the resulting document clusters is equal to the number of unique terms or word types contained in the collection at large. In practice, it is not necessary to use the complete centroid vector, since most component weights are very small. Based on previous work done by Voorhees [VOOR85], we reduce the centroid vectors to the 250 most heavily weighted (i.e., most frequent) content terms in the centroid. The centroid vectors themselves are weighted using normalized tf-idf weights, where the term-frequency component is based on the rank weight of that term.

The CACM complete link cluster hierarchy is searched using Voorhees' so-called *top-down individual* method. [VOOR85] In the top-down method, the user specifies the number of documents to be returned by the search. Clusters highly similar to the query are successively retrieved until sufficient documents have been found to satisfy the user's request.

Extending the Term Query Vector

We extended queries using ten retrieved documents returned by the clustered search. As Table 1 indicates, the average number of relevant documents per query in the set of ten highest ranked documents returned by a normal vector search of CACM is 2.8. In forming an extended query, the content terms of the original query become the concept term subvector of the extended query; the other subvectors are formed from the ten extended documents corresponding to those found by the clustered search.

Building the query vector extensions involves using the extended portions of the selected documents; that is, each non-content-term subvector of those documents is combined to produce a corresponding subvector for the query. The weighting of components within each of these subvectors is binary (i.e., if a component occurs at least once in any subvector, its presence in the corresponding query subvector is indicated by a 1). At this point, an extended query consists of a set of subvectors with binary weights for all the components of the non-content-term subvectors and term frequency weights identical to those in the original query for the components in the content term subvector. Each component of the extended query vector is then multiplied by a function of its inverse document frequency and the weights are normalized on a subvector basis. Such a query retains the information for the search request formulated by the user and augments his/her original query with information contained in a set of documents which in all likelihood are related to the query.

Searching the Extended Collection

As shown in Fig. 1, in the extended vector environment, query-document vector similarity is computed as a linear combination of the similarities of corresponding subvectors in the two extended vectors. We chose to use inner product as the similarity measure for comparing query-document subvectors. The inner product is a function of the number of corresponding non-zero components in each subvector.

When calculating a composite similarity value, the contribution made by of each of the subvectors is determined largely by the individual concept class weights (weights α, β, γ in Fig. 1). In our experiments, we used various *ad hoc* weights for the subvectors to determine the impact such weights have on the retrieval performance of the automatically constructed extended query vectors.

Experiments and results are presented in the next section.

EXPERIMENTAL RESULTS

Using the facilities of the SMART system, the effectiveness of the extended queries can be tested by comparing the performance results obtained when the extended queries are used to search the extended document collection to the results obtained when the original queries are used to search the single content term documents. The retrieval performance of an individual query is measured by averaging the precision values at recall levels of 0.25, 0.50 and 0.75 for a search of the collection. A composite measure of retrieval performance is obtained by averaging the 3-point precisions of all fifty-two queries.

In the first experiment, we wanted to ascertain the validity of the method proposed for extending queries. Each of the fifty-two queries in the collection was extended using the specified construction method based on documents chosen from a clustered search. Since retrieval performance is affected by the weights of the the subvectors in the similarity measure, we designed a set of runs in which the concept class weights are varied over a range of values.

Table 2 contains the range of weights which were used for each concept type. For any combination of weights used in the composite similarity function, the sum of the weights must always equal one. Based on Fox's results which showed that some concept classes are more effective than others in extended queries, we chose weights in a manner such that more importance was always given to content terms and links. We imposed an upper limit of 0.75 on the content term subvector weight, since greater weights tend to make an extended query behave like the original query from which it was derived. We also imposed the additional constraint that weights be distributed such that each extended query contain at least three different types of concept subvectors. As may be noted from Table 2, in each case two of these subvectors are terms and links. We felt that in general one should not initially attempt to prioritize the other five concept classes in terms of their contributions to the extended vector.

Application of these constraints produced a set of approximately 500 different combinations of composite weight assignments; within this set, the number of subvectors comprising an extended query ranged from three to a maximum of seven (the total number of concept types available in the CACM collection). The average length of an extended query in terms of the number of subvectors was 4.7. Runs corresponding to each of these combinations of weights were made for each of the 52 queries; 3-point averages were obtained. The extended queries performed substantially better than the original set of queries for *every* combination of weights in

Table 2 - Weights for Concept Classes

Concept Class	Lower Limit	Upper Limit	Step Size
Author	0.0	0.05	0.05
Computing Reviews Category	0.0	0.15	0.05
Date	0.0	0.10	0.05
Content Term	0.50	0.75	0.05
Bibliographic Coupling	0.0	0.05	0.05
Bibliographic Link	0.15	0.45	0.05
Cocitation	0.0	0.05	0.05

the set of 500. The minimum precision improvement was 11.7% and the maximum was 33.8%. The average improvement of all 500 combinations was 22.9%. These results confirm that very effective extended queries can be constructed automatically with no relevance feedback.

The experimental results are summarized in Table 3. The base case represents the retrieval results obtained using the original query and document vectors which contain only content terms. To consolidate the results of the 500 combinations of subvector weights, the results of the 500 runs were sorted in ascending order of improvement in precision and grouped according to the range of improvement (<16%, 16%-18%, 18%-20%, ... , 30%-32%, and >32%). For each group, the weights of the concept classes and the percent improvement were averaged over the number of combinations contained within the group. These averages are reflected in Table 3. The number of combinations within each of the ten groups is shown in the first column of the table. As may be noted, terms, links and Computing Review categories are the most important subvectors within an extended query. However, as Table 3 reveals, each concept contributes additional

Table 3 - Performance Results for 52 Extended Queries

% Range	No of Cases	Author	CR Category	Date	Terms	Coupling	Link	Cocitations	Average Precision	Percent Improvement
	1				1.00				0.2643	
11≤%<16	53	0.03	0.00	0.06	0.62	0.05	0.23	0.01	0.3038	14.93
16≤%<18	73	0.02	0.00	0.05	0.59	0.05	0.27	0.03	0.3096	17.13
18≤%<20	47	0.02	0.01	0.03	0.60	0.04	0.28	0.02	0.3146	19.03
20≤%<22	49	0.02	0.04	0.04	0.60	0.05	0.23	0.01	0.3199	21.04
22≤%<24	79	0.05	0.05	0.05	0.60	0.00	0.25	0.00	0.3261	23.38
24≤%<26	37	0.02	0.08	0.03	0.57	0.06	0.21	0.03	0.3303	24.98
26≤%<28	51	0.02	0.11	0.04	0.55	0.06	0.21	0.02	0.3360	27.11
28≤%<30	55	0.02	0.11	0.04	0.56	0.02	0.22	0.03	0.3406	28.88
30≤%<32	37	0.02	0.15	0.04	0.56	0.02	0.21	0.01	0.3462	30.99
32≤%<34	16	0.02	0.15	0.03	0.55	0.02	0.19	0.04	0.3509	32.77

The header spans: **Combination Cases - Average Weights** (Author, CR Category, Date, Terms, Coupling, Link, Cocitations) and **Performance** (Average Precision, Percent Improvement).

information which enhances the search performance over the normal query.

These combinations of weights took advantage of the knowledge that terms and links should be weighted more highly in the composite similarity function. We ran two experiments which did not assume this information. In one experiment, we weighted each concept subvector equally, including the content term subvector, and obtained an average 3.1% improvement over the base case. In practice it is reasonable to assume that more importance should be given to the content term subvector. However, it may not be realistic to assume any additional information is known about the relationships between other subvector categories. In our second experiment we varied the weight assigned to the term subvector in the composite similarity measure while distributing the remaining weight equally over the other six concept classes. The results of these runs are shown in Table 4. As may be noted, the performance improvement over the base case ranged from 17.5% to 25.8%.

These experiments confirm that the proposed method for automatically extending queries yields significant improvement even when one may not know the relationship between various concept classes.

Table 4 - Performance Results for Equally Weighted Non-Content-Term Subvectors

Terms Subvector Weight	Precision	Percent Improvement
0.50	0.3318	25.54
0.55	0.3326	25.84
0.60	0.3275	23.91
0.65	0.3210	21.45
0.70	0.3146	19.03
0.75	0.3105	17.48

SUMMARY

We have described a method of generating extended queries automatically without the use of relevance feedback. The method is based on an initial clustering of the document collection (using content terms only) and the extraction of extended vector characteristics from the document cluster(s) that are found to be most similar to the original content term query. With only rudimentary knowledge of how the different concept classes should be weighted in terms of their contributions to the extended query, substantial improvements in retrieval effectiveness are generated. When the best case concept class weights are applied, an improvement in precision greater than 30% is achieved by the extended queries over the original content term queries (based on the three point average).

The results of these experiments are promising and indicate that more effort should be directed at work in the extended vector environment. We plan to continue this research to provide additional insight into the role that extended queries can play in the design of search strategies.

REFERENCES

[FOX83]   E. A. Fox, Extending the Boolean and Vector Space Models of Information Retrieval with P-Norm Queries and Multiple Concept Types. Ph.D. Dissertation, Department of Computer Science, Cornell University (1983).

[FOX85]   E. A. Fox, Composite Document Extended Retrieval - An Overview. In *Proceedings of the Eighth Annual International ACM SIGIR Conference*, Montreal (1985).

[FOX88]   E. A. Fox, G. L. Nunn and W. C. Lee, Coefficients for Combining Concept Classes in a Collection. In *Proceedings of the Eleventh Annual International ACM SIGIR Conference*, Grenoble (1988).

[JARD68] N. Jardine and R. Sibson, The Construction of Hierarchic and Non-hierarchic Classifications. *The Computer Journal*, 11:2 (1968).

[LANC67] G. N. Lance and W. T. Williams, A General Theory of Classification Strategies: I. Hierarchical Systems. *The Computer Journal*, 9:4 (1968).

[ROCC71] J. J. Rocchio, Jr., Relevance Feedback in Information Retrieval. In G. Salton, Editor, *The SMART Retrieval System: Experiments in Automatic Document Processing*, Prentice-Hall, Inc., Englewood Cliffs, New Jersey (1971).

[SALT71] G. Salton, The SMART Project - Status Report and Plans. In G. Salton, Editor, *The SMART Retrieval System: Experiments in Automatic Document Processing*, Prentice-Hall, Inc., Englewood Cliffs, New Jersey (1971).

[SALT75] G. Salton, A. Wong and C. S. Yang, A Vector Space Model for Automatic Indexing. *Communications of the ACM*, 18:11 (1975).

[SALT83] G. Salton and M. J. McGill, *Introduction to Modern Information Retrieval*. McGraw-Hill Book Company, New York (1983).

[SALT88a] G. Salton and C. Buckley, Term Weighting Approaches in Automatic Text Retrieval. Information Processing and Management, 24:5, (1988).

[SALT88b] G. Salton, *Automatic Text Processing*. Addison-Wesley Publishing Co., Reading, Massachusetts (1988).

[VANR79] C. J. van Rijsbergen, *Information Retrieval*, second edition. Butterworths, London (1979).

[VOOR85] E. M. Voorhees, The Effectiveness and Efficiency of Agglomerative Hierarchic Clustering in Document Retrieval. Ph.D. Dissertation, Department of Computer Science, Cornell University (1985).

[VOOR86] E. M. Voorhees, Implementing Agglomerative Hierarchic Clustering Algorithms for Use in Document Retrieval. Technical Report 86-765, Department of Computer Science, Cornell University (1986).

Term Clustering of Syntactic Phrases

David D. Lewis
W. Bruce Croft
Computer and Information Science Department
University of Massachusetts, Amherst, MA 01003

April 30, 1990

Abstract

Term clustering and syntactic phrase formation are methods for transforming natural language text. Both have had only mixed success as strategies for improving the quality of text representations for document retrieval. Since the strengths of these methods are complementary, we have explored combining them to produce superior representations. In this paper we discuss our implementation of a syntactic phrase generator, as well as our preliminary experiments with producing phrase clusters. These experiments show small improvements in retrieval effectiveness resulting from the use of phrase clusters, but it is clear that corpora much larger than standard information retrieval test collections will be required to thoroughly evaluate the use of this technique.

1 Introduction

A primary goal of information retrieval (IR) research has been the development of methods for converting the original words of a document into a set of more effective content identifiers. Several of these representation methods make use of relationships between words in the original text. *Term clustering* attempts to group terms with related meanings, so that if any one appears in a query all can be matched in documents. *Syntactic phrase indexing* uses syntactic parsing to find groups of words in particular syntactic relationships, and indexes a document on these groups. Both of these methods have yielded mixed results in past experiments.

Reliably producing better representations requires understanding the important characteristics of representations and how they are change under different transformations [20]. Transformations applied to natural language text should take into account the fact that text contains more distinct words than is optimal for the statistical classification methods used in IR, and that as indexing terms these words are redundant, noisy, and infrequent. From a semantic standpoint, words are ambiguous identifiers of content, and are perhaps broader in meaning than is desirable.

Term clustering is a method which groups redundant terms, and this grouping reduces noise and increases frequency of assignment. If there are fewer clusters than there were original terms, then dimensionality is reduced as well. However, semantic properties suffer, since ambiguity can only be increased and meaning broadened.

Syntactic phrase indexing has exactly opposite effects. Each word in a phrase provides a context which disambiguates the other, and the meaning of a phrase is narrower than that of its component words. However, statistical properties suffer, since a large number of terms, many of them redundant and infrequently assigned, are created.

The strengths of these two methods are complimentary, which leads us in this paper to investigate combining them. We begin by surveying previous research in both areas. Following that, we discuss the specifics of our syntactic phrase generator and the phrases formed.

We then turn to the clustering of phrases. While the low frequency of occurrence of phrases makes them desirable to cluster, it also makes traditional similarity measures based on co-occurrence in documents untenable. We have instead formed clusters based on co-occurrence in semantically coherent groups of documents defined by controlled vocabulary indexing. These initial experiments produced only small performance improvements, and indicated that much larger corpuses will be necessary to produce high quality phrase clusters.

2   Previous Research

In this section we survey previous research on term clustering and syntactic indexing, as well as work near the intersection of the two areas. Our goal in this survey is to identify what has been learned about these techniques and how they might be combined.

2.1   Term Clustering

Term clustering is the application of cluster analysis [1] to forming groups of terms drawn from an existing text representation. From a pattern recognition viewpoint, term clustering is a form of *feature extraction*—a way of transforming an initial set of features into a new set that is more useful for classifying patterns (in this case, documents) [15]. It is therefore related to other feature extraction methods that have been used in IR, such as document clustering and factor analysis.

Any cluster analysis method requires that some similarity (or dissimilarity) measure be defined on the items to be clustered. Term clustering in IR has usually, though not always, defined similarity in terms of the degree to which two terms occur in the same documents.

Term clustering has been widely researched, with the largest body of work performed by Sparck Jones [35,32,36]. She investigated the effect of clustering strategies, term similarity measures, and vocabulary characteristics on the performance achieved with a clustered representation. Some of her most important conclusions were that clusters should be restricted to relatively infrequent and highly similar terms, clusters should be used to supplement the original terms rather than replace them, and that clustering was unlikely to be effective if the relevant and non-relevant documents were not well separated on the input representation. The particular shape of clusters formed and the particular measure of similarity between terms was not found to have a significant effect. Of the several collections she experimented with, only one had its retrieval performance significantly improved by term clustering.

Similar early experiments were performed by Salton and Lesk [27], Lesk [18], and Minker, et al [23]. Salton and Lesk compared statistical term clustering with manually constructed thesauri on three test collections. No significant performance improvements were found for the term clustering, in comparison with significant improvements for two out of three collections for the manual thesauri.

Lesk's experiments were, strictly speaking, with association lists rather than clusters, the difference being that a term A can be considered similar to a term B without the reverse holding. Lesk expanded both query and document descriptions with similar terms of moderate collection frequency, but achieved no large performance improvements. Lesk studied the term similarities that were actually produced and concluded that the small size of his collections (40,000 to 110,000 words) meant that the similarities were local to the collections, and were not good indications of the general meanings of the words.

Minker and colleagues experimented with two collections, and with three different text representations for each. Terms from all six representations were clustered using a variety of graph-theoretic algorithms. Like Sparck Jones, Minker found that small clusters performed the best, but he found no significant performance improvements over indexing on terms.

All of the above researchers used co-occurrence in documents as the basis for term similarity. Other similarity measures include co-occurrence in syntactic relationships with particular words [14] and presence in pairings between queries and relevant documents [40]. Crouch recently achieved significant performance improvements on two collections by first clustering documents, and then grouping low frequency terms that occurred in all documents of a document cluster [7].

2.2 Research on Syntactic Phrase Indexing

The use of syntactic information for phrasal indexing has been surveyed elsewhere [9,31,21], so we discuss this area only briefly. These techniques break down into two major classes: template-based and parser-based.

Dillon and Gray's FASIT system [8] is typical of template-based phrasal indexers. Adjacent groups of words from documents are matched against a library of templates, such as <JJ-NN NN> (adjective noun), and <NN PP NN> (noun preposition noun), and those matching some template are retained. Most templates in FASIT and other template-based systems are oriented toward finding contiguous words which represent noun phrases. Phrases are normalized by stemming and removal of function words. Klingbiel's MAI system used a similar strategy [16], while the TMC Indexer [24] and LEADER [13] combined limited parsing with templates.

Parser-based strategies attempt to analyze entire sentences or significant parts of them in producing syntactic phrases. Fagan [9], for example, used the PLNLP parser to completely parse the text of two test collections and extract indexing phrases. The sophistication of the

PLNLP grammar enabled Fagan to handle complex noun phrases with prepositional and clausal postmodifiers, as well as some adjectival constructions. Fagan also used a number of hand-built exclusion lists of words which signaled that a phrase should not be generated or should be generated in a special fashion.

On two test collections Fagan's syntactic phrases produced improvements of 1.2% and 8.7% over indexing on words alone. Despite the care with which Fagan's phrases were formed, this was less than the improvement (2.2% and 22.7%) provided by very simple statistically defined phrases. Furthermore, Sembok's system [30] achieved similar results to Fagan using only a very simple noun phrase grammar. Smeaton's method [31] provided a somewhat smaller improvement over single word indexing than the above two systems, but required parsing only of noun phrases in queries, followed by looking for co-occurrence of phrase components in documents.

In summary, experiments on syntactic phrase formation have not found it superior to statistical phrase formation, and have not found much correlation between the sophistication of phrase formation and the resulting performance improvements.

2.3 Integration of Syntactic Phrase Indexing and Clustering

While there has been extensive research on both term clustering and syntactic phrase indexing, the two techniques have not been directly combined before. Of course, almost all phrase generation systems in effect do a small amount of clustering when they normalize phrases, mainly through stemming. The FASIT system combined all phrases which had a particular word in common into a group, a very simple form of clustering which did not appear to be very effective. Antoniadis, et al describe a similar method, but it is not clear if it was actually used in their system [2].

More traditional statistical clustering techniques have been used in at least two IR interfaces to suggest terms, including syntactically formed phrasal terms, that a user might want to include in their query. The LEADER system formed cliques of phrases based on co-occurrence in full document texts, and the REALIST system used unspecified statistical techniques to provide lists of strongly correlated terms [37]. Neither study presented any performance data resulting from the use of these strategies, however.

Salton [28] investigated indexing documents on *criterion trees*. These were equivalent to hand-constructed clusters of syntactic structures, with individual words replaced by class labels from a manually constructed thesaurus. A related strategy is Sparck Jones and Tait's [34] generation of groups of alternative indexing phrases from a semantic interpretation of a query. The phrases generated by this method only contained words from the query, but a thesaurus could have been used, as with criterion trees. Neither of these methods were tested on large enough collections to draw firm conclusions about their efficacy, and neither thoroughly addresses the statistical problems with syntactic phrases.

Lochbaum and Streeter have recently reported on the use of a factor analysis technique, singular value decomposition (SVD), to compress term-document matrices [22]. They found that the inclusion of some noun phrases in addition to single words improved the performance achieved with the compressed representation. Since SVD can be viewed as simultaneously performing a term clustering and a document clustering, this result is suggestive that term clustering of phrases will provide an improved representation.

SVD can take advantage of dependencies among both terms and documents, but has the disadvantage that it is currently too computationally expensive for use with large document collections. Another advantage of term clustering over SVD is that prior knowledge about likely term groupings is more easily incorporated into a clustering similarity function than into the term-document matrix.

2.4 Summary

Previous research in the areas of term clustering and syntactic indexing has revealed a few important guidelines, and considerable evidence that many other choices are not of much significance. With respect to term clustering, the particular clustering algorithm used has not been found to make much difference, as long as clusters are small and composed of low frequency terms.

There is some evidence that the method by which the similarity of terms is judged can have an important effect. Crouch's strategy, for instance, partially addresses the dilemma that infrequent terms are the ones that most benefit from clustering, but are also the most difficult to get accurate co-occurrence data on.

Probably the most surprising result of research on syntactic phrase indexing is that the linguistic sophistication of the phrase generation process appears to have little effect on the performance of the resulting phrase representation. An open question is whether parser-based approaches are superior to template-based ones, but at least so far both approaches have been found inferior to statistical phrases.

Since it seems unlikely that individual statistical phrases are better content indicators than individual syntactic phrases, this suggests that it is the poor statistical properties of syntactic phrases (high dimensionality, noise, etc.) that are at fault. Clustering of syntactic phrases is a natural approach to improving these properties. While there is no direct evidence available on the performance of syntactic phrase clustering, the SVD results are encouraging.

3 Extracting Syntactic Phrases

This section first describes a particular goal for phrase formation and how our system approximated this ideal. We then show some of the strengths and weaknesses of the system by the analysis of an example sentence. Finally, we present statistics on phrase formation for the CACM-3204 corpus.

3.1 Syntactic Analysis Technology

One factor that makes previous research on syntactic indexing hard to evaluate is the wide range of heuristic techniques used in generating syntactic phrases. Since none of these variations has proven strikingly superior to others, we opted for a definition of phrases which was as simple as possible linguistically. We defined a syntactic phrase to be any pair of non-function words in a sentence that were heads of syntactic structures connected by a grammatical relation. Examples are a verb and the head noun of noun phrase which is its subject, a noun and a modifying adjective, a noun and the head noun of a modifying prepositional phrase, and so on. This is essentially the definition used by Fagan [9], except that we form phrases from all verbal, adverbial, and adjectival constructions, and do not maintain exclusion lists of specially treated words.

It is important to distinguish the definition of syntactic phrases used by a system from the actual set of phrases produced. Current syntactic analysis systems are far from perfect, so any definition of syntactic phrases which is not of the form "syntactic phrases are what my program produces" can only be approximated. Even the PLNLP parser used by Fagan produced a correct analysis of only 32% of a typical set of sentences [29], and that system was the result of a large-scale corporate development effort.

In designing our phrase generation system we attempted to generate all phrases that suited our definition, while avoiding the complexity and ambiguity of producing a full parse for each sentence. Our approach was to parse only the constituents of a sentence below the clause level. The analysis of a sentence, therefore, was a sequence of noun phrases, adjective phrases, adverb phrases, verb groups, and miscellaneous punctuation and function words. Since much of the complexity of most grammars is in rules to capture clause level structure, we were able to restrict ourselves to a grammar of only 66 rules.

Limiting the complexity of analysis does not limit the need for a large lexicon, since every word still had to be interpreted. We used the machine-readable version of the Longman Dictionary of Contemporary English (LDOCE) [3], which provided syntactic categories for about 35,000 words. By using a morphological analyzer for inflectional suffixes we extended the effective vocabulary of the system to perhaps 100,000 words. Even so, a substantial number of words encountered in text were not present in the dictionary. These tended to be compound words, proper nouns, or very technical terms. These unknown words were assumed to be ambiguous between the categories **noun**, **verb**, and **adverb**, and were allowed to be disambiguated by the grammar.

Parsing was performed by a chart parser operating in bottom-up mode[1]. The bottom-up parsing strategy produced a large number of overlapping parse trees covering parts of the sentence. The parser then selected a small set of non-overlapping trees which together covered the entire sentence. Phrase formation used these trees in two ways. Phrases were generated from complete constituents by means of annotations to each grammar rule. These annotations indicated which components of a tree corresponding to that rule should be combined into a phrase.

It sometimes was desirable to produce phrases from neighboring constituents as well. For instance, if a verb group was followed by a noun phrase, we wanted to combine the verb with the head noun of the noun phrase. Heuristics for forming phrases under these circumstances, including the handling of conjunction, punctuation, and function words,

---

[1] The parser was designed and implemented by John Brolio at the University of Massachusetts, who also was the principal designer of the syntactic grammar.

were encoded in a small (5 state) pushdown automaton.

Note that the two words in a phrase were considered to be unordered, and no distinction was made between phrases formed from different syntactic structures.

3.2   An Example of Phrase Generation

As an example, consider the following sentence from the CACM-3204 collection:

Analytical, simulation, and statistical performance evaluation tools are employed to investigate the feasibility of a dynamic response time monitor that is capable of providing comparative response time information for users wishing to process various computing applications at some network computing node.

A complete and correct analysis of this sentence would be extremely complex and would have to be distinguished from a large number of plausible alternatives. However, the partial syntactic constituents produced by our system capture most of the structure necessary to produce reasonable phrases. The greatest advantage of this approach is that reasonable analyses can be produced for any sentence. In Figure 1 we show the phrases that would be produced from a perfect parse of the sentence, and those that were produced by our system. Bracketed phrases are ones that would not have been produced by a perfect system, though some are reasonable indexing phrases.

The phrases generated from this example sentence exhibit some of the strengths and weaknesses of our system. For instance, the words *analytical, statistical, evaluation,* and *feasibility* were not present in the lexicon. Grammatical constraints were able to disambiguate *evaluation* and *feasibility* correctly to nouns, while *analytical* and *statistical* were incorrectly disambiguated to nouns. However, the incorrect disambiguations did not affect the generation of phrases, since premodifying nouns and adjectives are treated identically.

The presence of a word in LDOCE did not guarantee that the correct syntactic class would be assigned to it. The words *tool, dynamic, time, monitor, provide/providing, comparative, wish* and *process* all had multiple syntactic classes in LDOCE. Of these, *dynamic, providing, comparative, wishing,* and *process* were disambiguated incorrectly. The only case where phrase generation was seriously interfered with was in the interpretation of *providing* as a conjunction.[2] This meant that the phrases *providing information* and *providing users* were not generated. The interpretation of *wishing* and *process* as nouns, and the resulting interpretation of a clausal structure as a noun phrase, while atrocious from a linguistic point of view, had a relatively minor effect on phrase generation.

3.3   Phrase Statistics

For the experiments reported in this paper we parsed and generated phrases from the titles and abstracts of 1425 documents, totaling 110,198 words, from the CACM-3204 collection. We used only those documents which have *Computing Reviews* categories assigned to them,

---

[2] One price of using a machine-readable dictionary as a syntactic lexicon is the occasional odd classification.

DESIRED PHRASES	PHRASES PRODUCED
analytical tools	<analytical employed>
simulation tools	<employed simulation>
statistical tools	statistical tools
performance evaluation	<performance tools>
evaluation tools	evaluation tools
tools employed	tools employed
employed investigate	employed investigate
investigate feasibility	investigate feasibility
feasibility monitor	feasibility monitor
response time	<response monitor>
time monitor	time monitor
dynamic time	<dynamic monitor>
monitor capable	
capable providing	<capable feasibility>
providing information	<capable information>
comparative information	comparative information
response time	<response information>
time information	time information
information users	<information wishing>
	<information applications>
users wishing	users wishing
wishing process	<wishing applications>
process applications	process applications
various applications	various applications
computing applications	computing applications
process node	<applications node>
	<wishing node>
network node	network node
computing node	computing node

Figure 1: Desired and Actual Phrases (Before Stemming) for Example Sentence.

Collection Frequency (in 1425 Docs)	Unstemmed		Stemmed	
	Number of Distinct Phrases	Total Phrase Occurrences	Number of Distinct Phrases	Total Phrase Occurrences
1	41500	43612	32470	34689
2	3399	7336	4056	8866
3	906	3015	1284	4299
4	370	1687	576	2584
5	169	963	309	1735
6	124	850	218	1503
7	57	443	108	855
8	47	458	90	814
9+	128	2157	281	5176
Total	46700	60521	39392	60521

Table 1: Statistics on Phrase Generation for 1425 CACM Documents

since our current clustering strategy requires that controlled vocabulary indexing be available for documents. Table 1 breaks down the phrases generated according to the number of times they occurred in these 1425 documents.

As expected, the number of phrases was very large, and relatively few phrases had many occurrences. We used the Porter stemmer [26] to stem the words in phrases, which increased phrase frequency somewhat. These stemmed phrases were used for all the experiments reported in this paper.

4   Clustering Phrases

Given the few differences found between text representations produced by different clustering algorithms, we chose to form the very simple clusters that Sparck Jones referred to as *stars* [32]. These clusters consist of a seed item and those items most similar to it. A fixed number of nearest neighbors, a minimum similarity threshold, or both can be used. Here are some randomly chosen example clusters formed from CACM phrases when clusters were restricted to a size of 4:

{ <*linear function*>, <*comput measur*>, <*produc result*>, <*log bound*> }
{ <*princip featur*>, <*draw design*>, <*draw display*>, <*basi spline*>, <*system repres*> }
{ <*error rule*>, <*explain techniqu*>, <*program involv*>, <*key data*> }
{ <*substant increas*>, <*time respect*>, <*increase program*>, <*respect program*>}

The seed phrases are underlined above. Some clusters contain more than 4 elements, since elements with negligibly greater dissimilarity to the seed than the fourth element were

393

also retained.

The clusters formed rarely contained any exact synonyms for the seed phrase. This is not surprising since, of the large number of phrases with a given meaning, one will usually be considerably more frequent than the others. Given the relatively small size of the CACM corpus, only the most frequent of the synonymous phrases will have more than one occurrence. Since we required that a phrase must occur at least in at least two documents to be clustered, synonymous phrases were almost never clustered. However, some good clusters of closely related phrases were formed, along with many accidental clusters of essentially unrelated phrases.

The rest of this section discusses how clusters were formed and how they were used in scoring documents. Section 5 will then discuss our experimental results.

4.1 Co-occurrence In Controlled Vocabulary Indexing Categories

The dilemma between the desire to cluster infrequent terms and the lack of information on which to judge their similarity is even more severe for phrases than for words. Given that only 1.8% of the distinct phrases in our corpus occurred more than 5 times, it was unreasonable to expect that many phrases would have any substantial number of co-occurrences in documents.

Crouch's strategy of looking for co-occurrence in document clusters was a promising alternative, but we were conscious of the fact that document clustering itself does not necessarily produce meaningful clusters. Therefore, instead of producing document clusters, we made use of the document clustering implicit in the controlled vocabulary indexing of the CACM collection. A total of 1425 of the CACM documents, are indexed with respect to a set of 201 *Computing Reviews* (*CR*) categories [11,19]. Of those categories, 193 are assigned to one or more documents. Since *CR* categories are arranged in a three-level hierarchy, we assumed that whenever a document was assigned to a category it was also assigned to all ancestors of that category.

Some method was then required for clustering the phrases based on their presence in the *CR* categories. Crouch found the set of low frequency terms in each of the documents in a cluster and took the intersection of these sets. The large and quite variable size of the *CR* clusters makes this strategy inappropriate for us. Instead we viewed each *CR* category as a feature on which a phrase could take on a value between 0 and 1. We used the value n_{pc}/n_c, where n_{pc} was the number of occurrences of phrase p in category c, and n_c was the total number of occurrences of all phrases in category c. This treated multiple occurrences of a phrase as being more significant than single occurrences, and also normalized for the large differences in the number of documents, and thus phrases, appearing in the different categories.

The cosine correlation was used to compute the similarity between feature vectors for different phrases. This had the effect of normalizing for overall phrase frequency. All phrases occurring in 2 or more documents were used in clustering, expect when otherwise mentioned in results.

4.2 Weighting of Clusters

The point of forming clusters, of course, was to use them in retrieval. This required a method for incrementing the scores of documents based on the presence of phrases and clusters of phrases in queries and documents. We chose to use the same weighting methods used by Fagan for phrases and by Crouch for clusters, since these methods have shown some effectiveness in the past.

Fagan [9,10] assigned a two-word phrase a weight (in both queries and documents) equal to the mean of the weights of its component stems. The stem weights themselves are computed as usual for the vector space model. The inner products were computed separately for terms and phrases and then added together, potentially with different weightings.

Crouch [7] used a very similar method for clusters, giving them a weight in a query (or a document) equal to the mean of the weights of the cluster members in the query (or the document). The resulting weights were then multiplied by 0.5 in both documents and queries, for an overall downweighting factor of 0.25 for clusters with respect to single terms.

Combining these gave the following similarity function to be used for ranking documents:

$$SIM(q, d) = (c_s \cdot ip(q_s, d_s)) + (c_p \cdot ip(q_p, d_p)) + (c_c \cdot ip(q_c, d_c))$$

where ip is the inner product function, q_s, q_p, and q_c are the weight vectors of stems, phrases, and phrase clusters for queries, d_s, d_p, and d_c are the vectors for documents, and c_s, c_p, and c_c are the relative weights of stems, phrases, and documents.

5 Experiments

The main goal of the experiments reported here was to discover whether applying clustering to phrases from a small corpus would result in an improved text representation. Another goal was to explore whether the factors which have been found to be most important in clustering of words also have a strong impact on clustering of phrases. These include the size of clusters formed, the frequency of items clustered, and the maximum dissimilarity tolerated between cluster members. A secondary goal was to gather preliminary data on the efficiency of syntactic phrase clustering, given the likelihood than larger scale clustering would have to be investigated. We report on each of these goals in the following sections.

All retrieval results are based on the full CACM collection of 3204 documents. We used only the 50 queries which do not request documents by particular authors, and for which there are one or more relevant documents.

5.1 Effectiveness of Syntactic Phrase Clusters

Our first concern was whether the clusters of syntactic phrases formed from this small corpus would be sufficient to improve retrieval performance. Table 2 compares recall and precision figures for 4 sizes of clusters to the figures for single terms (stems) and single terms combined with syntactic phrases. Clusters produce a slightly smaller improvement than phrases, and neither is significantly better than the use of single terms alone.

Recall Level	Precision					
	Clusters + Terms				Phrases + Terms	Terms
	Size 2	Size 4	Size 8	Size 12		
0.10	55.5	55.5	57.9	57.1	58.1	56.3
0.20	43.2	42.0	42.2	41.9	45.4	41.0
0.30	37.7	37.0	36.5	36.2	38.0	35.7
0.40	31.1	30.5	30.8	30.0	30.2	29.6
0.50	23.3	23.3	22.2	22.3	23.4	22.0
0.60	19.5	19.3	18.2	18.3	19.0	18.8
0.70	13.5	13.3	13.3	13.3	13.7	13.8
0.80	9.2	9.4	9.4	9.3	9.5	9.9
0.90	5.5	5.8	5.6	5.6	5.6	6.1
1.00	4.2	4.1	4.1	4.1	4.1	4.7
Avg. Prec.	24.3	24.0	24.0	23.8	24.7	23.8
Change	+2.1%	+0.8%	+0.8%	+0.0%	3.8%	

Table 2: Performance Using Clusters and Terms

Using both clusters and phrases (Table 3) provides the most improvement. These results would be classified as "noticeable" (> 5.0%) but not "significant" (> 10.0%) according to Sparck Jones' criteria [33]. We investigating varying the weighting of the cluster and phrase vectors (c_c and c_p, respectively), but found only trivial and inconsistent improvements resulting from any values besides 1.0. In particular, reducing weighting of clusters to Crouch's value of 0.25 caused a small decrement in performance, providing some evidence that clusters of phrases are better content indicators than clusters of words.

5.2 Factors Affecting Phrase Clustering

In our survey on term clustering, we mentioned a number of factors that had been found in the past to impact the effectiveness of term clustering. We have already mentioned the effect of cluster size. Sparck Jones found small, tight clusters, of size 2 to 4, to be most effective, and our results are in agreement with this. We also found that using clusters of phrases in addition to phrases, rather than instead of phrases, was most effective. This again is in agreement with Sparck Jones' results on clustering of single terms.

Another approach to forming tight clusters would be to require that phrases have no greater than a fixed dissimilarity with the seed phrase. This causes some phrases not to cluster at all. We investigated several dissimilarity thresholds for cluster membership, but found only trivial improvements, and some degradations, in performance.

Another factor which has been found to impact term clustering is the frequency of the terms being clustered. The exclusion of high frequency terms from clusters was found by Sparck Jones in particular to be important in achieving an effective term clustering. Maximum frequency thresholds used by Sparck Jones included 20 out of 200 (10%) documents,

Recall	Precision					
	Clusters + Phrases + Terms				Phrases	
Level	Size 2	Size 4	Size 8	Size 12	+ Terms	Terms
0.10	57.4	60.0	59.3	58.5	58.5	56.3
0.20	46.4	46.4	46.1	45.0	45.4	41.0
0.30	38.8	39.5	38.9	37.7	38.0	35.7
0.40	31.3	31.1	31.1	30.8	30.2	29.6
0.50	23.0	23.1	23.1	23.1	23.4	22.0
0.60	19.3	19.5	19.5	19.5	19.0	18.8
0.70	13.9	13.9	13.8	13.7	13.7	13.8
0.80	9.6	9.8	9.7	9.6	9.5	9.9
0.90	5.7	5.7	5.7	5.7	5.6	6.1
1.00	4.2	4.2	4.2	4.2	4.1	4.7
Avg. Prec.	25.0	25.3	25.1	24.8	24.7	23.8
Change	+5.0%	+6.3%	+5.5%	+4.2%	+3.8%	

Table 3: Performance Using Clusters, Phrases, and Terms

20 out of 541 documents (3.6%), and 25 out 797 documents (3.1%) [36].

Since only 8 stemmed phrases occurred in more than 45 (3.2%) of the 1425 documents used for clustering, it was questionable whether omitting frequent phrases would be useful. We experimented with forbidding phrases which occurred in more than 45 documents from participating in clusters, and found this actually produced a slight decrease in performance. Forbidding phrases occurring in more than 30 documents produced a larger decrease. Examining the 8 phrases of frequency greater than 45 shows that even here there are several which are moderately good content indicators (<oper system>, <comput program>, <program languag>, <comput system>, <system design>) as well as several fairly bad ones (<paper describ>, <paper present>, and <present algorithm>). Therefore, omitting the most frequent phrases does not appear to be an appropriate strategy when clustering phrases.

One can also argue that very infrequent phrases should be omitted from clusters. If a term does not occur a sufficient number of times then we will have not have enough data on its distribution to accurately cluster it. Most work on term clustering has required that terms occur in 2 or more documents to become part of a cluster, but higher thresholds conceivably could result in more accurate clusters.

We investigated requiring that phrases occur in at least 3, 4, 5, or 6 documents in order to be clustered. These were fairly severe restrictions considering the low frequency of phrases, resulting in reducing the number of phrases available for clustering from 6922 to 2866, 1582, 1015, and 706 respectively. Small performance improvements resulted for some of these restrictions in combination with some cluster sizes. However, the improvements vanished when clusters were used in combination with phrases as well as terms. These results do help confirm that the small amount of frequency data available on phrases was a major impediment to forming effective clusters.

5.3 Efficiency

Our results suggest that the use of corpuses much larger than CACM-3204 will be necessary if phrase clustering is to be an effective technique. This means that efficiency of clustering will be of considerable importance. We therefore conducted some preliminary investigations into efficiency methods.

The use of an inverted file to speed up the finding of nearest neighbors is a technique that has been applied to both document clustering [5,39] and term clustering [25]. The main advantage cited for this technique is the avoidance of calculating the large number of similarity values of 0 present in typical term-term or document-document matrices. These 0 values arise in term-term matrices when similarity is based on co-occurrence in documents, since most pairs of terms will not occur together in any document.

The term-term (i.e. phrase-phrase) similarity matrix in our experiments has few 0 values since some of the CR categories contain very large numbers of phrases. Most of the similarity values will be very small, however, since normalization by category size, in combination with the cosine similarity measure, ensures that co-occurring in large categories has only a small impact on similarity.

This normalization for category size means that the k nearest neighbors of a seed phrase will almost always share some relatively specific CR category with the seed. We can therefore adapt the technique, first proposed for document ranking [4], of searching inverted lists in order of their length and testing at the end of each list whether any unseen item can possibly be more similar than the k best items already seen. Using this technique we found that only 7.2% of phrases needed to be examined on average when forming clusters of size 2, which is similar to the reductions achieved when term-term matrices contain mostly 0's. Even so, a full clustering run took about 40 hours on a Texas Instruments Microexplorer workstation, so additional attention to clustering efficiency will clearly be necessary for larger corpora.

6 Analysis and Future Work

The small performance benefits reported above are disappointing, but not really surprising. The fact that a high proportion of the occurrences of phrases were of phrases which occur only once or twice means that a corpus on the order of 100,000 words is simply inadequate for producing phrase clusters. We have experiments underway on a corpus of over 1 million words of newswire text previously used in tests of a text classification system [12]. We have also obtained corpora of 100 million words and more for future work.

Since standard IR test collections of large size are not currently available, the effectiveness of phrase clusters may have to be evaluated for retrieving documents which were not themselves used in forming the clusters. Previous researchers have suggested that the regularities captured by term clustering are collection dependent [35,18], which would interfere with this strategy. However, the combination of decreased ambiguity of phrases in comparison to words, combined with the use of a very large corpus, will, we believe, make phrase clusters of more general applicability.

To the extent that the CACM corpus allowed us to study the properties of phrase clustering, we found it to behave for the most part like clustering of single terms. The most notable exception was that excluding even the highest frequency phrases led to a degradation in performance. One possible explanation is that the corpus used is too small to manifest the frequency differences that would allow low quality phrases to be excluded. It should also be noted, however, that most of the results which argue against the clustering of high frequency terms assume ranking by coordination level. The use of inverse document frequency weighting may make exclusion of high frequency terms less important. A final possibility is that collection frequency is not as good an indicator of quality for phrases as it is for single terms. This view is supported by the fact that Fagan [9] found only trivial improvements in retrieval performance were possible from excluding high frequency syntactic phrases.

The exclusion of low quality phrases is clearly an important issue both for phrasal indexing and clustering of phrases. The fact that our performance improvements for syntactic phrases on the CACM collection are less than Fagan's (3.8% vs. 8.7%) suggests that his list of over 250 low content adverbs, verbs, and nouns, which triggered special purpose phrase generation heuristics, were successful in increasing the quality of phrases generated.

Some words which should be excluded from phrases can be defined linguistically, such as partitives (e.g. *half* in *eliminate half of the documents*). But many other words should be excluded from some corpuses and not from others. For instance, Fagan sensibly excluded the words "case," "property," and "development" from phrases for the computer and information science test collections he worked with, but this would not be appropriate in a collection of articles on real estate law. Word sense disambiguation methods might be useful in avoiding this problem [17].

The same distributional information used for clustering might also be usable to identify low quality phrases. In our experiments we noticed a tendency for low quality, high frequency phrases to appear under many different manual indexing categories, while high quality, high frequency phrases had most of their occurrences in a few categories. For instance, the low quality phrase <*paper describ*> occurs in 57 documents with a total of 104 *CR* categories assigned, while the higher quality phrase <*oper system*> occurs in 59 documents but only under 78 categories. Of course, as with clustering, a large text corpus is needed to obtain this distributional information.

Another potential source of high quality phrases is the user of the IR system [6]. While the user cannot control which phrases take part in clusters, he or she can control which phrases are extracted from the query, and thus used to match clusters. If we restrict the phrases used in the CACM queries to ones identified by a human as meaningful[3], the performance of phrases and clusters increases considerably (Table 4).

Besides better methods for generating phrases and clusters of phrases, there is also a

---

[3] The set of phrases used was generated by a graduate student who was not involved in the experiments on syntactic phrase formation.

	Precision					
Recall	Clusters + Terms				Phrases	
Level	Size 2	Size 4	Size 8	Size 12	+ Terms	Terms
0.10	60.7	61.9	61.5	61.4	61.4	56.3
0.20	45.8	45.9	45.9	45.9	45.2	41.0
0.30	40.6	40.3	39.8	39.8	39.5	35.7
0.40	34.2	33.4	33.5	33.5	33.2	29.6
0.50	25.0	25.1	25.2	25.2	25.3	22.0
0.60	19.8	20.7	20.7	20.6	20.9	18.8
0.70	13.8	14.6	14.5	14.6	14.6	13.8
0.80	9.4	10.2	10.0	10.0	10.0	9.9
0.90	5.6	6.3	6.2	6.3	6.2	6.1
1.00	4.2	4.9	4.9	4.9	4.9	4.7
Avg. Prec.	25.9	26.3	26.2	26.2	26.1	23.8
Change	+8.8%	+10.5%	+10.1%	+10.1%	9.7%	

Table 4: Performance With Human-Selected Query Phrases

need for a better understanding of how to use them. The lack of theoretical underpinnings to heuristic weighting schemes such as Fagan's for phrases and Crouch's for clusters make it hard to have confidence that they will be effective on new collections. On the other hand, existing probabilistic retrieval models are inadequate for use with phrases and clusters, particularly in handling the known dependencies between terms and phrases and terms and clusters. Network models [38] and probabilistic models incorporating explicit dependencies are two promising alternatives [6].

7 Conclusions

Term clustering is a natural approach to remedying the poor statistical properties of syntactic phrases. Our preliminary experiments offer some encouragement that the technique is practical, though it is clear that much larger corpuses will be necessary to draw strong conclusions about the technique's potential to improve retrieval performance. A better understanding is also needed of methods for selecting appropriate phrasal identifiers, and of scoring documents based on phrase and cluster matches.

Acknowledgments

We thank Longman Group, Ltd. for making available to us the typesetting tape for LDOCE, in the formatted version produced by Bran Boguraev at the University of Cambridge. This research was supported by the NSF under grant IRI-8814790, by AFOSR under grant AFOSR-90-0110, and by an NSF Graduate Fellowship. Anil Jain, Mike Sutherland, and Mel Janowicz provided advice on cluster analysis, and the work of our collaborator on syntactic parsing, John Brolio, was invaluable. Raj Das generated the hand-selected phrases for the CACM queries. All responsibility for errors remains with the authors.

References

[1] Michael R. Anderberg. *Cluster Analysis for Applications*. Academic Press, New York, 1973.

[2] Georges Antoniadis, Geneviève Lallich-Boidin, Yolla Polity, and Jacques Rouault. A French text recognition model for information retrieval system. In *Eleventh International Conference on Research & Development in Information Retrieval*, pages 67–84, 1988.

[3] Bran Boguraev and Ted Briscoe. Large lexicons for natural language processing: Utilising the grammar coding system of LDOCE. *Computational Linguistics*, 13(3–4):203–218, 1987. Special Issue on the Lexicon.

[4] C. Buckley and A. F. Lewit. Optimization of inverted vector searches. In *ACM SIGIR Conference on Research and Development in Information Retrieval*, pages 97–110, 1985.

[5] W. Bruce Croft. Clustering large files of documents using the single-link method. *Journal of the American Society for Information Science*, pages 341–344, November 1977.

[6] W. Bruce Croft and Raj Das. Experiments with query acquisition and use in document retrieval systems. In *Thirteenth Annual International ACM SIGIR Conference on Research and Development in Information Retrieval*, 1990.

[7] Carolyn J. Crouch. A cluster-based approach to thesaurus construction. In *Eleventh International Conference on Research & Development in Information Retrieval*, pages 309–320, 1988.

[8] Martin Dillon and Ann S. Gray. FASIT: A fully automatic syntactically based indexing system. *Journal of the American Society for Information Science*, 34(2):99–108, March 1983.

[9] Joel L. Fagan. *Experiments in Automatic Phrase Indexing for Document Retrieval: A Comparison of Syntactic and Non-Syntactic Methods*. PhD thesis, Department of Computer Science, Cornell University, September 1987.

[10] Joel L. Fagan. The effectiveness of a nonsyntactic approach to automatic phrase indexing for document retrieval. *Journal of the American Society for Information Science*, 40(2):115–132, 1989.

[11] Edward A. Fox, Gary L. Nunn, and Whay C. Lee. Coefficients for combining concept classes in a collection. In *Eleventh International Conference on Research & Development in Information Retrieval*, pages 291–307, 1988.

[12] Philip J. Hayes, Laura E. Knecht, and Monica J. Cellio. A news story categorization system. In *Second Conference on Applied Natural Language Processing*, pages 9–17, 1988.

[13] Donald J. Hillman and Andrew J. Kasarda. The LEADER retrieval system. In *AFIPS Proceedings 34*, pages 447–455, 1969.

[14] Lynette Hirschman, Ralph Grishman, and Naomi Sager. Grammatically-based automatic word class formation. *Information Processing and Management*, 11:39–57, 1975.

[15] J. Kittler. Feature selection and extraction. In Tzay Y. Young and King-Sun Fu, editors, *Handbook of Pattern Recognition and Image Processing*, pages 59–83. Academic Press, Orlando, 1986.

[16] Paul H. Klingbiel. Machine-aided indexing of technical literature. *Information Storage and Retrieval*, 9:79–84, 1973.

[17] Robert Krovetz and W. Bruce Croft. Word sense discrimination using machine-readable dictionaries. In *Twelfth Annual International ACM SIGIR Conference on Research and Development in Information Retrieval*, pages 127–136, 1989.

[18] M. E. Lesk. Word-word associations in document retrieval systems. *American Documentation*, pages 27–38, January 1969.

[19] David D. Lewis. A description of CACM-3204-ML1, a test collection for information retrieval and machine learning. Information Retrieval Laboratory Memo 90-1, Computer and Information Science Department, University of Massachusetts at Amherst, 1990.

[20] David D. Lewis. *Representation and Learning in Information Retrieval*. PhD thesis, University of Massachusetts at Amherst, 1990. In preparation.

[21] David D. Lewis, W. Bruce Croft, and Nehru Bhandaru. Language-oriented information retrieval. *International Journal of Intelligent Systems*, 4(3):285–318, 1989.

[22] Karen E. Lochbaum and Lynn A. Streeter. Comparing and combining the effectiveness of latent semantic indexing and the ordinary vector space model for information retrieval. *Information Processing and Management*, 25(6):665–676, 1989.

[23] Jack Minker, Gerald A. Wilson, and Barbara H. Zimmerman. An evaluation of query expansion by the addition of clustered terms for a document retrieval system. *Information Storage and Retrieval*, 8:329–348, 1972.

[24] Paul M. Mott, David L. Waltz, Howard L. Resnikoff, and George G. Robertson. Automatic indexing of text. Technical Report 86-1, Thinking Machines Corporation, January 1986.

[25] T. Noreault and R. Chatham. A procedure for the estimation of term similarity coefficients. *Information Technology*, pages 189–196, 1982.

[26] M. F. Porter. An algorithm for suffix stripping. *Program*, 14(3):130–137, July 1980.

[27] G. Salton and M. E. Lesk. Computer evaluation of indexing and text processing. *Journal of the Association for Computing Machinery*, 15(1):8–36, 1968.

[28] Gerard Salton. *Automatic Information Organization and Retrieval*. McGraw-Hill Book Company, New York, 1968.

[29] Gerard Salton and Maria Smith. On the application of syntactic methodologies in automatic text analysis. In *Twelfth Annual International ACM SIGIR Conference on Research and Development in Information Retrieval*, pages 137–150, 1989.

[30] Tengku Mohd Tengku Sembok. *Logical-Linguistic Model and Experiments in Document Retrieval*. PhD thesis, Department of Computing Science, University of Glasgow, August 1989.

[31] A. F. Smeaton and C. J. van Rijsbergen. Experiments on incorporating syntactic processing of user queries into a document retrieval strategy. In *Eleventh International Conference on Research & Development in Information Retrieval*, pages 31–51, 1988.

[32] K. Sparck Jones and E. O. Barber. What makes an automatic keyword classification effective? *Journal of the American Society for Information Science*, pages 166–175, May-June 1971.

[33] K. Sparck Jones and R. G. Bates. Research on automatic indexing 1974 - 1976 (2 volumes). Technical report, Computer Laboratory. University of Cambridge, 1977.

[34] K. Sparck Jones and J. I. Tait. Automatic search term variant generation. *Journal of Documentation*, 40(1):50–66, March 1984.

[35] Karen Sparck Jones. *Automatic Keyword Classification for Information Retrieval*. Archon Books, 1971.

[36] Karen Sparck Jones. Collection properties influencing automatic term classification performance. *Information Storage and Retrieval*, 9:499–513, 1973.

[37] G. Thurmair. A common architecture for different text processing techniques in an information retrieval environment. In *ACM SIGIR Conference on Research and Development in Information Retrieval*, pages 138–143, 1986.

[38] Howard Turtle and W. Bruce Croft. Inference networks for document retrieval. In *Thirteenth Annual International ACM SIGIR Conference on Research and Development in Information Retrieval*, 1990.

[39] Peter Willett. A fast procedure for the calculation of similarity coefficients in automatic classification. *Information Processing and Management*, 17:53–60, 1981.

[40] Clement T. Yu and Vijay V. Raghavan. Single-pass method for determining the semantic relationships between terms. *Journal of the American Society for Information Science*, pages 345–354, November 1977.

Optimizations for Dynamic Inverted Index Maintenance

Doug Cutting and Jan Pedersen

Xerox Palo Alto Research Center
3333 Coyote Hill Road
Palo Alto, California

Abstract

For free-text search over rapidly evolving corpora, dynamic update of inverted indices is a basic requirement. B-trees are an effective tool in implementing such indices. The Zipfian distribution of postings suggests space and time optimizations unique to this task. In particular, we present two novel optimizations, *merge update*, which performs better than straight forward block update, and *pulsing* which significantly reduces space requirements without sacrificing performance.

Inverted Indices

Most standard free-text search methods in Information Retrieval (IR) can be implemented efficiently through the use of an inverted index. These include standard boolean, extended boolean, proximity, and relevance search algorithms. [7]

An inverted index is a data structure that maps a word, or atomic search item, to the set of documents, or set of indexed units, that contain that word — its *postings*. An individual posting may be a binary indication of the presence of that word in a document, or may contain additional information, such as its frequency in that document and an offset for each occurrence, required for various non-boolean search algorithms. In the following, we will simplify this situation by assuming that each word *occurrence* indexed has a corresponding posting. This approximation has the advantage of being amenable to analysis.

Since access to an inverted index is based on a single key (i.e. the word of interest) efficient access typically implies that the index is either sorted or organized as a hash table. In the following we will assume that keys are sorted. For hashing schemes, the interested reader is directed to [6].

As a part of an operational IR system, properties beyond formal description become important. This paper is concerned with the following performance criteria:

- Block Update Speed: The time required to index documents.

It is presumed that a practical IR system will be manipulating indices too large to conveniently fit in main memory, and hence that the inverted index will be represented as a data structure on secondary storage. Since insertion in a sorted structure is at best a $\log n$ operation, where n is the number of previously indexed postings, we will measure performance by the number of references to secondary storage. This is further justified by noting that these sorts of computations are typically completely dominated by disk access time.

- Access Speed: The time required to access the postings for a given word.

This parametrizes search performance, and, hence, is extremely user-visible. Again, access time is inherently $\log n$, but may require fewer than $\log n$ disk accesses.

- Index Size: The amount of storage required for the inverted index.

Since some record must be made for each posting, the inverted index must be proportional to the number of postings. This proportionality constant is referred to as the *indexing overhead*, or the size of the index expressed as a percentage of the size of the entire corpus.

- Dynamics: The ease with which the inverted index is incrementally updated.

This is particularly important for rapidly evolving corpora. Insertion is typically more common than deletion. Many indexing schemes presume a static corpus. [2, 7] These may be updated only by reconstructing the entire index. We will only discuss incrementally updatable indices in this paper.

- Scalability: The relation between the above and corpus size.

  Indexing algorithms should scale gracefully with increasing corpus size. In particular, main memory usage should be independent of corpus size.

We assume that each of the above are important, and seek methods which perform well on all these axes.

B-trees are a file-based data structure particularly appropriate for the implementation of dynamically modifiable inverted indices. The following will analyze the use of B-trees in this task and suggest several novel time and space optimizations.

B-trees

Conceptually, a B-tree maintains an ordered sequence as an n-ary branching balanced tree, where the tree resides on secondary storage rather than in main memory. [1, 5, 6] Nodes in the tree are represented as disk *pages*, and rebalancing algorithms insure insertion, examination and deletion of entries in $O(\log_b N)$ disk accesses where b is the *branching factor* of the B-tree and N is the number of entries contained in the B-tree. The quantity $\log_b N$ is referred to as the *depth* of the B-tree. Entries may also be enumerated in sorted order in time proportional to N, requiring roughly N/b disk accesses.

The branching factor b is related to both the page size and the average size of entries, but is typically fairly large, say around 100. This means that any entry in such a B-tree containing a million entries may be accessed in three disk accesses. This may be improved by retaining some of the B-tree nodes or pages in main store. Since each page contains b entries on average, holding one page in memory requires storage proportional to b. If the root page is kept in core then we can reduce by one the number of disk accesses required for any operation — at the cost of storing just b entries. To make another similar gain we must cache all the immediate children of the root. In general, the cost of access is

$$\log_b N - \log_b C, \text{ for } N \geq C \tag{1}$$

disk accesses, where C is the number of entries stored in core, or the *cache size*. Note, we are describing an upper-nodes caching strategy. Other strategies, such as an LRU (least recently used) cache, have similar performance characteristics. [5]

If $C = N$, then the entire B-tree is represented in core, and no disk accesses are required. If $C = N/b$, all the non-terminal nodes are cached in core, and any access operation may be performed with just one disk

access. In our example, with $b = 100$, a B-tree of size $N = 1,000,000$ is of depth 3, and a cache of size $C = N/b = 10,000$ guarantees random access with just one disk operation.

Although the typical inverted index operation is random access to the postings for a given word, the sorted enumeration property of a B-tree may be exploited for prefix wild-carding. Suppose words are sorted in lexicographic order, then words with a common prefix are adjacent in the B-tree. If $b \log_b N$ storage is allocated to hold the path of pages between the root and the current point in an enumeration, a disk operation need only occur every b adjacent entries.

Naive B-tree Indexing

A B-tree inverted index clearly addresses the issues of access speed, dynamic update, and scalability. Access to any given entry requires no more than $\log_b N$ disk accesses, B-trees are intrinsically updatable, and access times may be reduced through the use of relatively small page caches. However, we have yet to discuss the time required for a block update or the space occupied by a B-tree index. In the following we will analyze block update time in terms of the number of disk *reads* required. An actual update will, of course, also requires disk *writes*, but each read will require no more than one write, hence the total cost of an update operation is no worse than proportional to the number of disk reads.

A simple approach to constructing a B-tree inverted index is to consider each entry to be a pair of the form

$$\langle word, location \rangle$$

ordered first by *word* and second by *location*. Thus, an entry is just a posting ordered so that the postings for the same word are adjacent. Random access to all the postings for a given word is simply B-tree enumeration, requiring a disk access for every b postings. Index update with this representation requires a B-tree insert for every word instance in the new text. Thus, by (1), indexing n words of new text requires

$$n(\log_b N - \log_b C) \tag{2}$$

disk reads.

Removal of references to a document can be accomplished at the same expense as insertion, providing the document is still available. If the tokens comprising the document are no longer available, then an exhaustive enumeration of the index is required to find and remove references to it.

A Speed Optimization

It has been shown that the number of disk accesses required to perform an update can be reduced by caching the upper nodes of the B-tree in core. If, instead, this core memory is used as a buffer for postings, which is merged with the B-tree when full, many more disk accesses can be eliminated. Equation (2) gives the expected number of disk reads to insert n new postings using a page cache containing room for C entries. If these same n postings are buffered and sorted by word in core, then, rather than having n instances, we have w words, each with an associated list of postings. (The time required to sort in core is ignorable, since it requires no disk accesses and is, in any event, much less than the time required to sort n postings via B-tree inserts.) At merge time, we must insert these w entries into the B-tree. Since the postings for a given entry typically fit on a single B-tree page, this is approximately equivalent, in disk access time, to w inserts in sort order. If we assume that these entries are uniformly distributed over the set of keys, each ordered insert will require an average advance of N/w entries through the B-tree.

Suppose $\log_b N$ pages are held in core to hold a path between the root and a leaf. Then the cost of each such advance can be estimated as follows. Consider the *sub*-B-tree defined by the span to be advanced over. This B-tree contains, by definition, N/w entries of which the leftmost path is in core. To access the last entry in the span we must bring the rightmost path into core. This requires $\log_b(N/w)$ disk transactions. Hence

$$w(\log_b(N/w)) = w(\log_b N - \log_b w) \qquad (3)$$

disk accesses are required on average to index n postings with this technique.

If n is large the frequency distribution of unique words will approximately follow Zipf's law.[8] In other words

$$f(w)r(w) \approx z \qquad (4)$$

for some constant z, where $f(w)$ is the frequency of word w in the set of n instances and $r(w)$ is the rank of $f(w)$ among the frequencies of all words in that set of postings. Note that in this approximation z is both the vocabulary size and the frequency of the most frequent word. It follows that

$$n \approx \sum_{r=1}^{r=z} z/r \approx z \int_{r=1}^{r=z} 1/r \, dr = z \ln z. \qquad (5)$$

In other words, the vocabulary size, z, grows much less rapidly than the number of word occurrences, n, and can, in fact, be estimated given n.

To demonstrate that memory is better utilized in a buffer than in a page cache, we must show that for constant C the cost in disk accesses, (2), denoted by X, is greater than (3), denoted by Y. This may be expressed by equating the number of postings n with C, since the same memory may either be allocated to a page cache or to store postings in a buffer. From these considerations and (5) we have

$$X = z \ln z (\log_b N - \log_b(z \ln z)), \qquad (6)$$

and

$$Y = z(\log_b N - \log_b z). \qquad (7)$$

Clearly,

$$Y = X/\ln z + z \log_b(\ln z). \qquad (8)$$

Suppose, $X > Y$, then, by substitution of (8),

$$X > X/\ln z + z \log_b(\ln z),$$

or, by rearrangement,

$$\frac{X}{z \ln z}(\ln z - 1) > \log_b(\ln z).$$

After substituting in (6) and rearranging terms, this reduces to

$$(\ln z - 1)(\log_b N - \log_b(z \ln z)) > \log_b(\ln z)$$

or

$$\log_b N > \log_b z + \log_b(\ln z)\frac{\ln z}{\ln z - 1}. \qquad (9)$$

Exponentiating both sides leads to

$$N > z(\ln z)^{\frac{\ln z}{\ln z - 1}} \qquad (10)$$

In other words, $X > Y$ iff inequality (10) holds. Now, since $z \ln z = n = C$ and (2) is only valid if $N \geq C$, we have $N > z \ln z$. For substantial z, the exponent $\ln z/(\ln z - 1)$ will be close to unity. Hence, for the update case, we can expect $X > Y$.

For the example under consideration, $b = 100$, $N = 1,000,000$ and $z \ln z = 10,000$, and $z \approx 1,383$. Hence $X \approx 10,000$ and $Y \approx 1,977$. Indeed, from (6), we expect

$$X = \ln z(Y - z \log_b(\ln z)). \qquad (11)$$

Hence, substantially fewer disk accesses are required if memory is used as buffer for sorting and subsequently merging postings into an existing B-tree inverted index than if it is allocated as a B-tree page cache and updates are preformed in occurrence order.

case		predicted		observed		
		z	reads	z	reads	writes
100	cache	30	200	74	302	260
	merge		68		216	201
1,000	cache	191	1,500	420	2,587	2,038
	merge		355		931	867
10,000	cache	1,383	10,000	3,421	16,012	13,605
	merge		1,977		5,049	4,890
100,000	cache	10,800	50,000	14,105	70,721	63,530
	merge		10,620		7,795	9,100

Experimental Results

Table (1) contains the results of experiments which demonstrate the effectiveness of the merge optimization. Initially a B-tree was created containing the postings for a corpus with one million word instances. Its branching factor, b, averaged 100, and its depth was three. We ran cached and merged updates of 100, 1000, 10,000, and 100,000 new postings. The B-tree cache size, C, and the merge buffer size for each trial was set equal to the number of new postings.

The predictions were based on equations (5), (6), and (7). The observed results for the merge case are higher than expected due to the inaccuracies of Zipf's law in predicting vocabulary size, z. The observed results for both cases are also slightly higher than expected because equations (6) and (7) do not account for page reads due to B-tree rebalancing. Writes exceed reads in one case due to the creation of new pages.

Space Optimizations

There is obvious redundancy in the 'naive' indexing scheme presented above; each word instance requires a reference to the word itself. If, instead, the set of postings for a word is decomposed into the word and a sequence of locations, then much of this redundancy is eliminated. There is a small overhead in performing this grouping, since any representation for a sequence of locations requires some record of its length, or a termination. A prefix length indication is preferred since it can then serve as a record of the marginal, or corpus, frequency. In other words, in addition to requiring a 'cell' for each word and for each location of that word, one additional cell is required to note the total number of locations.

For example, in the naive case, words of frequency one occupy two cells, while the revised representation requires three cells; words of frequency two require four

cells in both representations. In general, the naive representations requires $2N$ cells for N postings, while, by (5), grouping requires

$$\sum_w (2 + f(w)) \approx W(2 + \ln W)$$

cells, where W is the vocabulary size of the same N postings. Since $W \ln W \approx N$, this is smaller than $2N$ if $2W < N$, which is true if $\ln W > 2$ or $W > 7.39$. The ratio of cells required for the two strategies is

$$\frac{2W(1 + \ln W/2)}{2W \ln W} = 1/\ln W + 1/2, \qquad (12)$$

or slightly over $1/2$. Hence, grouping postings reduces space requirements by almost 50%.

If words are represented as integers, as would be the case if a lexicon is built to provide a 'word to number' mapping, and locations are also integers, then all cells may be presumed to be roughly equivalent in size. In this case, the space analysis above refers to the real sizes of the respective indices.

Heap Update

A grouped index may be implemented by considering variable-length B-tree entries of the form

$$\langle word, F, \langle location \rangle^* \rangle, \qquad (13)$$

where F is the marginal frequency of $word$ and $location$ refers to the corpus position of a single posting. As only one entry exists per unique word, the B-tree's ordering function need only examine $word$. A difficulty immediately arises, however, for words with a large number of postings. Recall that, by definition, the maximum size for any B-tree entry is one B-tree page; if the locations sequence overflows this limit no recourse is available. Indeed, if l is the number of locations that fit on one B-tree page, then from (5), we expect a corpus of size $l \ln l$

postings to overflow this limit for the highest frequency word.

This situation may be ameliorated by indexing tuples of the form

$$\langle word, F, pos \rangle \tag{14}$$

where *pos* indicates a position in an auxiliary data structure, known as a *heap file*, where the sequence of locations can be found. As is suggested by its name, a heap file is simply a binary file manipulated as if it were main memory. Continuous chunks of this memory are allocated as necessary for the storage of arbitrary data, in this case location sequences. Update is accomplished either in place, or if sizes change sufficiently, by allocating a new chunk to hold the updated sequence and freeing the old chunk. This implies that the chunks comprising a heap file are maintained by a dynamic storage allocation algorithm.

One such algorithm, the *buddy system*, allocates chunks in sizes that are powers of two. [4] This arrangement insures that chunks are on the average 75% full, which is comparable to the storage utilization of B-trees.

Access to an individual postings list for representation (14) requires no more than $\log_b W + 1$ disk reads; $\log_b W$ to read in the B-tree entry followed by one more to access the heap at *pos*. Block update proceeds by, for each new instance encountered, appending a new location to the end of the chunk at *pos*, computed by adding F to *pos*, and incrementing F. An additional cost is incurred when a chunk is filled, since its contents must be copied to a freshly allocated twice-larger chunk, and the old chunk deallocated. Since chunks are allocated in powers of two, a location sequence of length f must be copied no more than $\log_2 f$ times. This amortized per instance cost of $(\log_2 f)/f$ additional accesses is sufficiently small to be ignorable. Hence, the block update time is proportional to

$$n(\log_b W - \log_b C + 1) \tag{15}$$

for n postings. The 'merge' optimization mentioned above may also be applied in this case to reduce n at the expense of the B-tree page cache.

The space requirements for representation (14) are similar to (13) with one additional cell to hold the heap file pointer. Hence, N postings occupy

$$W(3 + \ln W)$$

cells. The ratio with respect to the naive indexing strategy is

$$3/(2 \ln W) + 1/2,$$

which is only slightly greater than (12).

Pulsing

Use of a heap file solves the B-tree page overflow problem at the cost of slightly increased access time and slightly larger overall index size. Yet, B-tree overflows will only occur for the relatively few high frequency words. This observations leads one to consider buffering postings directly in the B-tree, and overflowing to a heap file only when necessary, a technique known as *pulsing*. Essentially, a threshold t is chosen which determines the maximum number of locations which are to be stored immediately. Updates are made directly in the B-tree, and only after t new instances of a word are seen are their t locations *pulsed* to the heap. In other words, at most, the t newest posting for any given word appear directly in the B-tree; any additional postings are found in the heap file.

In this representation B-tree entries have the form

$$\langle word, F, l, \langle doc \rangle^{\star}, pos \rangle \tag{16}$$

where *word*, F and *pos* are as in (14), and l is the length of the locations $\langle doc \rangle^{\star}$. By convention, l and *pos* need not be provided when F is less than t as a space-saving measure.

For words, w, of frequency $f(w) < t$, all postings are directly accessible. Hence, the cost of access is no more than $\log_b E$, where E is the effective number of postings in the B-tree, $E \leq N$. We can estimate E by computing the number of occurrences of words whose frequencies are less than or equal to t. From (5) we have

$$f(w) \leq t \text{ iff } r(w) \geq W/t.$$

It follows that

$$E = \sum_{\{w:\, f(w) \leq t\}} f(w) \approx$$

$$\int_{W/t}^{W} \frac{W}{r} \, dr = W \ln t \tag{17}$$

If $f(w) > t$, than the cost of access is no more than $(\log_b E + 1)$. Since $W \ln t$ postings reside directly in the B-tree, we will avoid heap file access with probability

$$p = \ln t / \ln W.$$

Hence, the expected access time is no worse than

$$p \log_b E + (1 - p)(\log_b E + 1) = \log_b E + (1 - p).$$

In other words, in comparison to (14), access is accelerated by the hit rate p, but potentially penalized by the larger B-tree size, E. In particular, the ratio of access times is

$$\frac{\log_b W + 1}{\log_b E + (1-p)} = \frac{\log_b W + 1}{\log_b W + 1 + (\log_b(\ln t) - p)}$$

This ratio is greater than one iff

$$\log_b(\ln t) < p \quad \text{or} \quad t < e^{b^p}.$$

However, $t < b$ since we cannot buffer more postings than the B-tree page size directly in the B-tree.

From the above, with the introduction of a page cache, block update has expected cost proportional to

$$n(\log_b E - \log_b C + (1-p)). \tag{18}$$

Representation (16) also occupies less space than (14) since heap file indirection can be avoided with probability p. For an entry with $f(w) \le t$, we use $2 + f(w)$ cells. An entry with indirection uses $4 + f(w)$ cells. Hence the space occupied for N postings is

$$\sum_{\{w:f(w)\le t\}} (2 + f(w)) + \sum_{\{w:f(w)>t\}} (4 + f(w)) \approx$$

$$\int_{W/t}^{W} (2 + W/r))\ dr + \int_{1}^{W/t} (4 + W/r)\ dr =$$

$$W \ln W + 2W(1 + 1/t) - 4 \tag{19}$$

The threshold, t, may be selected to generate a desired 'hit' probability, p. For our example, $N = 1,000,000$ and $W \approx 88,000$. To achieve a hit rate of 25% we require $t = \sqrt[4]{W}$, or $t \approx 17$. In other words, use of pulsing with a threshold of 17 reduces the frequency of access to the heap file by 1/4.

Delta Encoding

A typical inverted index operation randomly accesses the postings for a given word. However, these postings are typically processed linearly. In other words, an inverted index need not provide easy random access to individual postings. This suggests that the sequence of postings may be compressed in any fashion that requires no worse than linear time to decode.

A pulsing strategy arranges for locations to be stored in the order indexed. If each location is represented as an integer, and these integers are allocated in an increasing manner, then a particularly simple compression scheme we term *delta encoding* is possible. [5] Rather than storing an actual location the difference between it and the previous location, a delta, is stored instead. This yields a sequence of much smaller integers than the original sequence of locations.

In itself this is uninteresting unless integers are encoded in such a way that small integers occupy less space than large integers. A typical scheme for performing such an encoding employs the high order bit of each byte to indicate whether another byte need be read. Thus, with eight-bit bytes, the numbers 0-127 may be represented in one byte, 128-16384 in two bytes, and so on. [3] Thus, if a word occurs on average every 64 locations, each location will, on average, occupy only one byte.

In order to easily incrementally append new locations at the end of an existing chunk of locations (i.e. without having to decode the entire chunk) the size of each block and the last location in it must also be maintained. These can be maintained in the B-tree or at the beginning of each block. The former is preferred as it minimizes the amount of the block which must be touched. As with other information about the chunk, e.g. its position in the heap, these need not be stored at all for words whose marginal frequency is less than the threshold t.

There is one application in which random access to individual postings is desirable; that is deletion. A compression strategy, such as delta encoding will require us to read the entire postings list for a word to delete a single entry, and will require us to rewrite it since the sequence of postings will have changed. In other words, space and access time is optimized at the expense of this relatively rare operation.

Conclusion

For free-text search over rapidly evolving corpora, dynamic update of inverted indices is a basic requirement. B-trees are an effective tool in implementing such indices and may be optimized to reduce access and update time and to minimize size. A speed optimization, *merge update*, performs better than straight forward block update and two space optimizations, *pulsing* and *delta encoding* significantly reduce space requirements without sacrificing performance.

410

References

[1] R. Bayer and E. McCreight. Organization and maintenance of large ordered indices. *Acta Informatica*, 1:173–189, 1972.

[2] Harman. D. and G. Candela. A very fast prototype retrieval system using statistical ranking. *SIGIR Forum*, 23(3,4):100–110, Summer 1989.

[3] H. S. Heaps. Storage analysis of a compression coding for a document database. *INFOR*, 10(1):47–61, February 1972.

[4] D. Knuth. *The Art of Computer Programming*, volume 1: Fundamental Algorithms. Addison-Wesley, 1968.

[5] D. Knuth. *The Art of Computer Programming*, volume 3: Sorting and Searching. Addison-Wesley, 1973.

[6] G. Salton. *Automatic Text Processing*. Addison-Wesley, 1989.

[7] G. Salton and M. McGill. *Introduction to Modern Information Retrieval*. McGraw-Hill, 1983.

[8] G. K. Zipf. *Human Behavior and the Principle of Least Effort*. Addison-Wesley, 1949.

Partitioned Posting Files:
A Parallel Inverted File Structure
for Information Retrieval

Craig Stanfill
Thinking Machines Corporation
245 First Street
Cambridge MA 02154

ABSTRACT

This paper describes algorithms and data structures for applying a parallel computer to information retrieval. Previous work has described an implementation based on overlap encoded signatures. That system was limited by 1) the necessity of keeping the signatures in primary memory, and 2) the difficulties involved in implementing document–term weighting. Overcoming these limitations requires adapting the inverted index techniques used on serial machines. The most obvious adaptation, also previously described, suffers from the fact that data must be sent between processors at query–time. Since interprocessor communication is generally slower than local computation, this suggests that an algorithm which does not perform such communication might be faster. This paper presents a data structure, called a partitioned posting file, in which the interprocessor communication takes place at database–construction time, so that no data movement is needed at query–time. Algorithms for constructing the data structure are also described. Performance characteristics and storage overhead are established by benchmarking against a synthetic database.

1 Introduction

Parallel computing has the potential to provide fast, cost–effective access to databases of virtually unlimited size. Systems based on parallel adaptations of the serial inverted file structure are particularly promising in this respect. Information retrieval systems provide two major components: an inquiry system which searches the database, and a maintenance system which allows the database to be constructed and updated. It is desirable that a retrieval system meet the following criteria:

— It should provide interactive response (under 5 seconds).
— The fully formatted database should entail minimal storage overhead.
— Formatting the database should not consume excessive resources
— The database should remain available during updates.

There exists an inverted index algorithm for the Connection Machine which delivers over 400 times the performance attainable on a serial machine (Sun–4). A retrieval system based on this algorithm and associated data structures appears capable of satisfying all of the above constraints for databases as large as one Terabyte (2^{40} bytes) using current hardware.

1.1 Previous Work

Initial parallel implementations of information retrieval were based on overlap–encoded signatures [1][2]. Overlap encoding is subject to some very specific constraints:

— If the signature file does not fit in primary memory the I/O load will prevent interactive access [3].

—   Only binary document weights can be supported [4][5].

Within the above constraints, signature files deliver excellent performance [6][7]. However, these constraints somewhat limit the usefulness of the method.

It has been suggested that parallel inverted files might not be subject to the above limitations (e.g. [3]). Preliminary results have indicated that at least one inverted file structure might be suitable for use with up to 64K processors and databases up to one Terabyte [7].

1.2 Paper Organization

This paper presents partitioned posting files, a new adaptation of the inverted file structure to parallel computers. Creation, update, and document ranking algorithms are described. Section 2 presents some background in information retrieval and parallel computing. Section 3 describes how the serial inverted file structure may be adapted to parallel computing. Section 4 presents the algorithms for scoring and ranking documents. Section 5 briefly describes the algorithms needed to build and maintain the database. Section 6 contains some measurements of system performance according to the four criteria presented above. Section 7 summarizes the results.

2 Background

2.1 Information Retrieval

A document is represented as a set of weighted terms. The weights indicate the importance of each term within the document. The terms may correspond to words, or to word–stems, or to phrases, or to high–level concepts. The extraction of terms and assignment of weights is generally done automatically [8]. Queries also consist of weighted terms, and are generally produced by a combination of automatic and manual methods [9].

The operation of a retrieval system can best be described in terms of the *vector model*. A database consists of a set of documents and a vocabulary of N terms T_i. A document D is represented as a vector of length N such that $D_i > 0$ only if T_i is present in D. Queries(Q) have the same representation. Retrieval is based on some measurement of document–query similarity. This paper will assume the *cosine similarity measure*:

$$\frac{D \cdot Q}{\|D\| \|Q\|}$$

$\|D\|$ stands for the Euclidean norm and the inner product is used. Information retrieval systems based on this model must determine which documents are most similar to a given query. The data structures and algorithms needed to accomplish this task are the sole concern of this paper.

2.2 Data Parallel Computing

This paper assumes the data parallel computing model used in the Connection Machine[(R)] System. The model includes a serial host computer and a large number of processing elements (PE's or processors). Data structures are distributed uniformly across the processing elements, and may be

414

thought of as vectors. There are three aspects of computation: serial computation, local parallel computation, and non–local parallel computation. Serial computation consists of arbitrary operations on scalars. Scalars may be freely promoted to vectors by broadcasting their value to the processing elements. Local parallel computation consists of arbitrary element–wise computations applied to the contents of the PE's memories. In this mode, the processing elements may be thought of as a set of independent machines operating on scalar quantities stored in their local memories. Processing elements may temporarily deactivate themselves. Non–local parallel computation consists of operations that move data either from one processor to another or from the processing elements to the host. Non–local computations may be as simple as permuting the data or as complex as sorting it.

I/O is provided by a high–throughput disk system. The Connection Machine uses a parallel disk array called the Data Vault™ mass storage system. Each such unit provides up to 20 Gigabytes of storage with a transfer rate of 25 Megabytes per second. Data Vault files are vector–structured: each location in the file stores one byte/word from each processing element in the machine.

3 Adapting Inverted Files to Parallel Computing

This section will start with an explanation of inverted files on serial machines, and proceed through various methods of adapting them to parallel computation, ultimately arriving at a data structure called a *Segmented Posting File*.

3.1 Serial Inverted Indexes

This paper presumes that the database has been indexed, and each document reduced to a set of tokens of the form:

$$<document–id, term–id, weight>$$

where: *document–id* is an integer uniquely identifying a document; *term–id* is an integer uniquely identifying a term; and *weight* is a number representing the importance of the term. This structure is referred to as a *posting*.

Consider, for example, the following set of documents:

This is the first document   *This be document two*   *I am document three*   *I am fourth*

One might assign document id's sequentially, and word id's alphabetically:

(R) Connection Machine is a registered trade mark of Thinking Machines Corporation.

0	am	6	is
1	be	7	the
2	document	8	this
3	first	9	three
4	fourth	10	two
5	I		

The set of postings shown below is produced. The position indicator is for convenience only. Weights are omitted from the diagram for compactness sake[1].

Position	0	1	2	3	4	5	6	7	8	9	10	11	12	13	14	15
Doc ID	0	0	0	0	0	1	1	1	1	2	2	2	2	3	3	3
Term ID	8	6	7	3	2	8	1	2	10	5	0	2	9	5	0	4

The first step in producing an inverted file is sorting these tokens by term identifier:

Position	0	1	2	3	4	5	6	7	8	9	10	11	12	13	14	15
Doc ID	2	3	1	0	1	2	0	3	2	3	0	0	0	1	2	1
Term ID	0	0	1	2	2	2	3	4	5	5	6	7	8	8	9	10

The positions of the first and last occurrences of each term are next recorded in a table called the *data map*.

ID	Word	Start	End	ID	Word	Start	End
0	am	0	1	6	is	10	10
1	be	2	2	7	the	11	11
2	document	3	5	8	this	12	13
3	first	6	6	9	three	14	14
4	fourth	7	7	10	two	15	15
5	I	8	9				

The word identifiers in the tokens are now redundant and are dropped. The result is a *inverted file*, which may be stored on disk.

Position	0	1	2	3	4	5	6	7	8	9	10	11	12	13	14	15
Doc ID	2	3	1	0	1	2	0	3	2	3	0	0	0	1	2	1

A query consists of a set of terms and weights, for example *3 * document + 2 * this*. Evaluating a query takes place in three stages: initialization, scoring, and ranking. Initialization consists of allocating one score register (called a *mailbox*) for each document and zeroing it:

0	0	0	0

Scoring is next. Each term is used to access the data map, so that the positions of the first and last postings are known. In the query shown above, the term *document* occupies positions 3 through 5, and the term *this* occupies positions 12–13. The appropriate portions of the posting file are then brought into primary memory.

---

1. Many of these words, such as *am* and *I* are stop words and would normally be dropped. They are retained here for the sake of the example.

Term	Weight	Postings		
Document	3	0	1	2
This	2	0	1	

The system now has available the identifiers of all documents containing *Document* and *This*, and the weight assigned to those terms in their documents. The final step is to iterate through these query terms, incrementing the mailboxes they reference.If the weights in the postings from the above example are all 1, then the following scores will end up in the mailboxes:

5	5	3	0

Finally, the mailboxes are scanned to locate the highest–ranking documents. Typically the top 20–40 documents might be retrieved.

3.2 Parallel Inverted Indexes, Implementation 1

A parallel algorithm described in [10] takes the posting file, in the form described above, and places it in a Connection Machine so that adjacent entries in the posting file are in adjacent processors. For example, in a 4–processor machine the data structure shown below would be produced (processors run left to right; the memory in each processor runs top to bottom).

2	3	1	0
1	2	0	3
2	3	0	0
0	1	2	1

In the initialization stage mailboxes are assigned so that the mailboxes for consecutive documents map to consecutive processors:

0	0	0	0

To start processing the query, the location of the postings for each query term must be determined. On a machine with p processors, location n of the serial posting file maps to memory location $\left\lfloor \frac{n}{p} \right\rfloor$ in processor $n \bmod p$. In the above example, the postings for *document* occupy positions 3 through 5 of the serial posting file. These locations map to row 0 processor 3 through row 1 processor 2 of the parallel file. These location–ranges are then broken into groups that do not span row boundaries. Thus, the postings for *document* occupy processor 3 of row 0, and processors 0 through 1 of row 1.

Word	Weight	Row	Start	End
Document	3	0	3	3
	3	1	0	1
This	2	3	0	1

The I/O system is then called on to move these postings into memory. As noted above in the section on parallel computing, the I/O system operates by writing vectors (rows of data) to disk, and reading vectors into memory. With this class of I/O system it is not possible to issue a read starting in the

417

middle of a row of data, or to have data from different rows transferred to memory in one operation.[2]

The algorithm then iterates through the rows of this table. For each (weight, row, start, end) quadruple, those processors having processor ID's between *start* and *end* will access the posting at memory location *row*. The term's weight in the query will be multiplied by the weight in the posting. The result will be used to increment the contents of the appropriate mailbox. This last step involves sending data between processors.

In this example, the postings for *document* occupy processor 3 of row 0, and processors 0 and 1 of row 1. Execution starts by considering row 0. First, the algorithm notes that only processor 3 contains row–0 postings for *document*; all other processors are deactivated. Second, this processor accesses the DOC ID's and document weights of row 0. Third, the document weight just found is multiplied by the query weight, which is 3. Fourth, the processor notes that it is dealing with document 0, the mailbox for which is in processor 0. Finally, the processor sends a message to processor 0, telling it to add 3 to the mailbox for document 0.

Processor ID	0	1	2	3
Doc ID's, Row 0	***	***	***	0
Weights, Row 0	***	***	***	1
Posting weight * Query weight	***	***	***	3
Send with Add				
Mailboxes Before	0	0	0	0
Mailboxes After	3	0	0	0

Execution now considers row 1. First, the algorithm notes that only processors 0 and 1 contain row–1 postings for *document*; once again all other processors are deactivated. Second, DOC ID's and document weights for row 1 are accessed. Third, the document weight is multiplied by the query weight. Fourth, each processor determines the location of its document's mailbox. Finally, each processor sends a message to increment the proper mailbox.

Processor ID	0	1	2	3
Doc ID's, Row 1	1	2	***	***
Weights, Row 1	1	1	***	***
Posting weight * Query weight	3	3	***	***
Send with Add				
Mailboxes Before	3	0	0	0
Mailboxes After	3	3	3	0

On the Connection Machine, incrementing the mailboxes is accomplished via an instruction called *send–with–add*. This operation is the dominant cost of this algorithm, each such step taking 3 milliseconds.[3]

3.3 Parallel Inverted Indexes, Implementation 2

The *send–with–add* step may be eliminated if, rather than storing the postings in sequential order and *send*'ing them to the correct processor at query–time, they are stored in the correct processor to begin

---

2. Such operations *are* possible with a different classes of I/O system having one disk per processing element.
3. In [6] the time to perform this operation was estimated at 1 millisecond.

with. Within a single processor, the postings will be in order of ascending word identifier. This file structure starts with the same set of tokens used to construct serial inverted indexes:

Position	0	1	2	3	4	5	6	7	8	9	10	11	12	13	14	15
Doc ID	0	0	0	0	0	1	1	1	1	2	2	2	2	3	3	3
Term ID	8	6	7	3	2	8	1	2	10	5	0	2	9	5	0	4

Each document is assigned a processor. For example, given a machine with two processors, documents 0 and 2 might be assigned to processor 0, and documents 1 and 3 might be assigned to processor 1. The tokens are then moved to the correct processor, sorted by ascending term ID.[4]

Row	Processor 0		Processor 1	
	Term ID	Doc ID	Term ID	Doc ID
0	0	2	0	3
1	2	0	1	1
2	2	2	2	1
3	3	0	4	3
4	5	2	5	3
5	6	0	8	1
6	7	0	10	1
7	8	0		
8	9	2		

A problem with the representation at this point is that the postings for a given term are not guaranteed to be in the same row of data. This is called *misalignment*. For example, the postings for term 8 are located in row 7 of processor 0 and row 5 of processor 1. As noted above, the class of I/O system being considered here does not permit different rows of data to be read in a single operation. The result is that all rows of postings from the first occurrence of the term through last must be transferred to memory (in the example above rows 5 through 7 would need to be read). Unless countermeasures are taken, this misalignment grows without bound as the database size increases.

3.4 Segmented Posting Files

This problem may be controlled by segmenting the posting file. Each segment has a lower bound and an upper bound. Each segment contains only postings with word identifiers between those two bounds, inclusive. Furthermore, the upper bound of each segment is no greater than the lower bound of the next. For example, the database above might be divided into four segments defined by the bounds (0 ...2) (2 ... 4) (5 ... 6) (7 ... 8) and (9 ... 10). Segment boundaries are stored on the host computer.

To create a segmented posting file, it is first necessary to select a blocking factor l, which will be the number of rows of postings per segment.[5] Let l be this length (in the present example $l = 2$). The smallest word-id in row l is determined by using a *global–minimum* operation, and used as the upper

---

4. The actual implementation on the Connection Machine is somewhat more complex. It takes advantage of programming techniques which allow groups of 32 processors to access each other's memory. Using this technique, a 64K–processor CM may be regarded as having 2048 32–bit processors rather than 65,536 bit–serial processors, at least from the point–of–view of algorithmic analysis.

5. It is not strictly necessary to use fixed–length segments, but doing so seems to cause no harm, and simplifies the software.

bound for a new segment All postings in rows *0 ... l–1* which are no greater than the bound are moved into the new segment. This step is repeated until no data remains. For example, the smallest value in row 2 of the unsegmented posting file is 2. All postings in rows 0 and 1 of the unsegmented file which are no greater than 2 are transferred to the segmented file, and the bounds are noted. This yields the following segment:

Row	Bounds		Processor 0		Processor 1	
	Low	High	Term ID	Doc ID	Term ID	Doc ID
0	0	2	0	2	0	3
1			2	0	1	1

The following data remains in the unsegmented file:

Row	Processor 0		Processor 1	
	Term ID	Doc ID	Term ID	Doc ID
2	2	2	2	1
3	3	0	4	3
4	5	2	5	3
5	6	0	8	1
6	7	0	10	1
7	8	0		
8	9	2		

This process is repeated until all postings have been transferred. The result is the segmented posting file shown below:

Row	Bounds		Processor 0		Processor 1	
	Low	High	Term ID	Doc ID	Term ID	Doc ID
0	0	2	0	2	0	3
1			2	0	1	1
2	2	4	2	2	2	1
3			3	0	4	3
4	5	6	5	2	5	3
5			6	0		
6	7	8	7	0	8	1
7			8	0		
8	9	10	9	2	10	1

It is immediately obvious that the above data structure does not fully utilize the available space: the file contains sufficient space for 18 postings, of which 16 are actually used, for a utilization of 89%. Section 6 will present an estimate of the utilization which is likely to be seen in practice.

There now remains the question of what to do with the term identifiers in the posting file. For the serial implementation and the first parallel implementation, a data map precisely defines which postings are associated with which terms. The term identifiers are thus unneeded and are dropped. With segmented posting files, the upper and lower bounds of the segment do not uniquely determine the term associated with each posting. Thus the term identifiers cannot simply be dropped. Instead, the lower bound of each segment is subtracted from each term identifier. The resulting *term tag* can generally be represented with considerably fewer bits than the full term ID. With a Terabyte of data and 8–row segments, 1–2 bits generally suffice. The document identifier can also be compressed.

When a posting file is created, the low–order bits of the document are used to select a processor. These low–order bits are now redundant, and can be dropped. The remaining high–order bits are called the *document tag*. For the sample database, this yields the following:

	Scalar Data		Vector Data			
Row	Low	High	Term Tag	Doc Tag	Term Tag	Doc Tag
0	0	2	0	1	0	1
1			2	0	1	0
2	2	4	0	1	0	0
3			1	0	2	1
4	5	6	0	1	0	1
5			1	0		
6	7	8	0	0	1	0
7			1	0		
8	9	10	0	1	1	0

The scalar portion of this data structure resides in the host's primary memory; the vector data will generally be stored on parallel secondary storage, and moved into memory one segment at a time.

4 Algorithms

4.1 The Scoring Algorithm

Given this data structure, queries can be executed without moving data between processors. First, each processor allocates and zeros–out one mailbox for each document it has been assigned. Second, the table of segment boundaries is consulted to determine which segments need to be loaded into primary memory. The tags corresponding to each term are then determined. For the sample query *Document * 3 + This * 2*, the following table results:

Term	Weight	Segment	Term ID	Low Bound	Tag
Document	3	0	2	0	2
		1	2	2	0
This	2	4	8	8	0

To begin processing, each processor allocates and zero's out one mailbox for each document it has been assigned. In this example, each processor has two mailboxes.

Mailboxes	0	0
	0	0

The first segment (segment 0) is then loaded into primary memory.

Term Tag	Doc Tag	Term Tag	Doc Tag
0	1	0	1
2	0	1	0

Each processor then loops through the rows in the segment, looking for postings with the correct term tag (2 at this point). When one is found, the document tag is used to determine which of the 2 mailboxes in that processor is incremented. In the present example, processor 0 finds a matching term

tag in the second row of the segment. This posting has document tag 0, corresponding to mailbox 0.
At this point, the query weight (3) is multiplied by the document weight (not shown here; assumed to be 1 in this example), and the product used to increment the appropriate mailbox.

Mailboxes	3	0
	0	0

Next, segment 1 (the final segment for *document*) is loaded.

Term Tag	Doc Tag	Term Tag	Doc Tag
0	1	0	0
1	0	2	1

The low bound for segment 1 is 2, and *document* has Term–ID 2, so the algorithm will look for postings with term–tag 0. Each processor finds one such tag in row 0 of this segment. The document tags are again used to index the mailboxes, yielding the following result:

Mailboxes	3	3
	3	0

4.2 The Ranking Algorithm

The output of the above algorithm is a set of mailboxes containing document scores. The mailboxes may be viewed as a 2–dimensional array, with rows corresponding to locations within processor memory and columns corresponding to processors. To illustrate this aspect of the system, a new example will be used, in which there are 4 processors and 16 documents, which would be stored thus:

3	8	16	7
99	4	34	87
18	97	2	1
0	45	18	6

The first step is to determine the document identifier corresponding to each mailbox. As noted above, the least–significant bits of a document ID select a processor, and the most significant bits become the document tag, which is used to select a mailbox within a processor's memory. The document identifiers corresponding to each mailbox are as follows:

0	1	2	3
4	5	6	7
8	9	10	11
12	13	14	15

The document identifier is then appended to the score, producing an array of surrogates.

3.0	8.1	16.2	7.3
99.4	4.5	34.6	87.7
18.8	97.9	2.10	1.11
0.12	45.13	18.14	6.15

The maximum element of each row is then determined using a *global_maximum* operation:

max	Surrogates			
16.2	3.0	8.1	16.2	7.3
99.4	99.4	4.5	34.6	87.7
97.9	18.8	97.9	2.10	1.11
45.13	0.12	45.13	18.14	6.15

The maxima are stored on the serial host. They are scanned to find the maximum of the maxima. In this case, the maximum element is 99.4, which indicates that document 4 had a score of 99. The surrogate for document 4 is then zero'ed out, and the maximum for its row re-computed:

max	Surrogates			
16.2	3.0	8.1	16.2	7.3
87.7	0	4.5	34.6	87.7
97.9	18.8	97.9	2.10	1.11
45.13	0.12	45.13	18.14	6.15

This process is repeated until sufficient documents have been found. The cost is one global maximum operation per row of mailboxes plus one global maximum per document to be identified.

5 Building and Maintaining the Segmented Posting Files

Segmented posting files can be constructed by a combination of sorts and merges. The starting point is a set of postings, ordered by document identifier, stored one token per processor.[6]

Doc ID	0	0	0	0	0	1	1	1	1	2	2	2	2	3	3	3
Term ID	8	6	7	3	2	8	1	2	10	5	0	2	9	5	0	4

The low-order bits of the document identifier are extracted to determine the destination processor for each posting.

Doc ID	0	0	0	0	0	1	1	1	1	2	2	2	2	3	3	3
Term ID	8	6	7	3	2	8	1	2	10	5	0	2	9	5	0	4
Dest Processor	0	0	0	0	0	1	1	1	1	0	0	0	0	1	1	1

These are then sorted, using the destination processor as the primary key and the term identifier as the secondary key.

Doc ID	2	0	2	0	2	0	0	0	2	3	1	1	3	3	1	1
Term ID	0	2	2	3	5	6	7	8	9	0	1	2	4	5	8	10
Dest Processor	0	0	0	0	0	0	0	0	0	1	1	1	1	1	1	1

The postings are assigned locations within their processors by 1) grouping the postings by destination processor; and 2) enumerating the postings in each group.

Doc ID	2	0	2	0	2	0	0	0	2	3	1	1	3	3	1	1
Term ID	0	2	2	3	5	6	7	8	9	0	1	2	4	5	8	10

---

6. This assumes the virtual processing model used in the Connection Machine's instruction set, in which the machine can be dynamically configured to simulate arbitrarily large numbers of processors. Thus, one might have 64K processors simulating 16 million virtual processors. If this is kept in mind, no confusion should result when the number of processors seems to shift in mid-example from 16 to 2.

Dest Processor	0	0	0	0	0	0	0	0	0	1	1	1	1	1	1	1
Enumeration	0	1	2	3	4	5	6	7	8	0	1	2	3	4	5	6

A single *send* instruction suffices to move the document and term identifiers to the correct location within each processor. The result is a set of unsegmented postings as shown in Section 3.3 These postings are then segmented, compressed, and written to secondary storage using the methods described in Section 3.4.

The amount of data which can be handled by this method is limited by the primary memory of the machine. Larger amounts of data may be handled by using the above method independently on relatively small sections of the database, then merging the resulting files. If d_1 documents can be handled in one pass of the sort algorithm, and the database contains d_2 documents, then the database can be formatted in time proportional to $d_2 \log_2 \frac{d_2}{d_1}$. An outline of the merge algorithm is as follows.

The data from the two files to be merged is read into primary memory, unpacked, and segments are appended to produce an unsegmented file. Let l be the blocking factor (rows per segment) for the database. The smallest word identifiers in the $l'th$ row of the two input files is determined, and the smaller of the two is chosen as an upper bound. All postings in rows 0 through $l-1$ having term ID's no greater than this bound are copied from the two input files into a new segment. At this point each processor has two sorted runs of postings, one from each input file. These two sequences are merged, producing a single ordered sequence. The results are packed and written to secondary storage.

Once the database has been built, it is important to be able to update it. The best strategy is to maintain two segmented posting files: a large one which is disk resident and contains the bulk of the data, and a second which is small enough to fit into primary storage. As new documents are added to the database, they are inserted into the memory–resident file. The memory resident file can then be probed independently of the disk–resident file, and the results combined. When the memory–resident file grows excessively large, the algorithm sketched above can be used to merge it with the disk–resident database. Details of how this may be done without disrupting service are still being studied.

6 Performance

This section will establish 1) that segmented posting files do not consume excessive amounts of secondary storage; 2) that constructing a segmented posting file does not take excessively long; and 3) that queries against segmented posting files are fast enough to support interactive access to databases in the range of 1 Terabyte using existing hardware. Its performance will also be compared with several alternative implementations.

6.1 A Synthetic Database

Evaluation of these algorithms will be done using a synthetic database and query load described in [10]. This has the advantage that 1) the database may be easily replicated by other researchers; 2) the parameters of the database (such as size) may be altered to explore the behavior of retrieval algorithms; 3) large quantities of disk need not be tied up; and 4) generation of the database can be selective: given a 10–term query, only that portion of the posting file needed to evaluate that query needs to be synthesized.

The lexicon for the database consists of n terms, t_1 through t_n. Term t_i occurs in the database with frequency $\frac{c_1}{i}$ (occurrences per megabyte), in accordance with Zipf's law. Terms 1 through s are *stop words*, and are not put into the posting file. It is assumed that the terms found in queries have the same frequency distribution as the terms in the database, omitting stop–words. For a query Q this gives us:

$$\Pr(Q_j = i) = \begin{cases} i < s & 0 \\ otherwise & \frac{c_2}{i} \end{cases}$$

The following values are used for these parameters:

n	200,000
s	550
c_1	9778
c_2	.1696

A database is synthesized by specifying the number of documents and size of the full text in Megabytes. If there are N_{doc} documents and b bytes of data in the database, then (on the average) $\frac{bc_1}{i}$ occurrences of term i are generated and randomly assigned document identifiers between 0 and $N_{doc} - 1$. Queries are generated by a similar mechanism. To study extremely large databases, postings for a subset of the terms will be generated. For example, if a query contains term number 5000, then postings might be generated for terms 4500 through 5500, allowing the portion of the segmented posting file relevant to the query to be generated.

6.2 Measurement 1: In–Memory Database Formatting

The first measurement seeks to arrive at an upper bound on the time required for in–memory database formatting.[7] Databases of 10, 20, 40, 80, and 160 Megabytes were synthesized, and the formatting algorithm described in Section 5 applied to the database, using a 4K–processor Connection Machine. Postings for 4–megabyte subsets of the database were synthesized using the above distribution. Each such segment yielded approximately 250,000 postings (about 61 per processor). These segments were independently sorted and converted to segmented posting files. The files were then merged to produce segmented posting files of the size noted.

DB Size	Sort Time	Merge Time	Utilization	Formatted Size	Overhead
10 MB	18.8 sec	4.5 sec	88.8%	4.8 MB	48%
20 MB	28.2 sec	11.8 sec	90.3%	7.0 MB	35%
40 MB	56.2 sec	37.7 sec	92.2%	13.6 MB	34%
80 MB	112.4 sec	100.1 sec	92.9%	26.4 MB	33%
160 MB	216.5 sec	231.4 sec	93.5%	49.2 MB	31%

DB Size   Size of the database synthesized and converted

---

7. The times reported in this section are for relatively untuned code; better performance may be anticipated in the future. The times are reported only to establish an upper bound on the cost of formatting a database.

Sort Time	Total time required to sort the data and convert it to segmented posting file format, in 4 Megabyte chunks.
Merge Time	Total time needed to merge the 4–Megabyte chunks, omitting disk time.
Utilization	The percentage of the segmented posting file which was actually occupied. The remainder was lost due to unused slots at segment boundaries.
Formatted Size	Size of the segmented posting file.
Overhead	Ratio of the formatted size to the full database size.

Holding sort–time constant, the amount of data processed in each sort step is proportional to the number of processors. Thus, whereas 4K processors can process 160 MB in 216 seconds, 64K processors could process 2.56 Gigabytes in the same amount of time. For a terabyte of data, 400 such sort–steps would be required, for a sort–time of approximately 90,000 seconds (about a day). It is not possible to accurately extrapolate the merge time that would be required for a full–sized database. If we assume that merge time accounts for 90% of the work on a Terabyte of data (as opposed to 50% for the small database considered above), then perhaps 10 days of merge–time would be required. Clearly, more work is required to validate the feasibility of the merge step, but the above results are encouraging.

Storage consumption does not appear to be a significant limitation for this algorithm: at 160 MB, storage utilization is well over 90%, and the posting file is less than 1/3 the size of the full text. Furthermore, utilization improves (and overhead falls) as the database grows.

6.3 Measurement 2: Blocking Factors and Database Size

The next measurement studies how blocking factors (the number of rows of postings in each segment of the posting file) affects storage utilization. For a 100 MB database, postings for all 200,000 words in the lexicon were generated. For a 64 GB database, postings were generated for 312 terms. The database was then segmented using blocking factors of 64, 8, and 1. Apparently, utilization improves with larger blocking factors and larger databases. On the basis of this measurement, a blocking factor of 8 seems reasonable.[8]

DB Size	Blocking Factor	Utilization
100 MB	64	94.3%
	8	85.6%
	1	66.1%
64 GB	64	97.2%
	8	93.2%
	1	86.1%

6.4 Measurement 3: Query Performance

This measurement establishes the performance of the scoring and ranking algorithms. First, a query is generated using the query–term distribution specified in the benchmark definition. Second, for

---

8. As noted above, the implementation of this file structure on the Connection Machine allows groups of 32 processors to share memory, and segmentation was actually done by groups rather than individual processors. Thus, with a blocking factor of 1, there are actually 32 postings in each segment, and with a blocking factor of 8 there are 256 postings per segment.

each query, a database was synthesized and formatted, restricting posting generation to only those terms close enough to a query–term to affect segment boundaries. The in–memory performance of scoring and ranking was then measured using 10–term queries, extracting the 20 highest–ranking documents

DB Size	Posting Rows	Data Transfer	Scoring Time	Ranking Time
64 GB	482	7.5 MB	200 ms	740 ms
8 GB	104	1.8 MB	42 ms	130 ms
1 GB	80	1.5 MB	37 ms	60 ms

The test was done using 64 GB of data and a 4K–processor machine. Multiplying both the size of the database and the number of processors by 16, one arrives at a Terabyte of data and a 64 K–processor machine. The above measurement indicates that the compute portion of a query against a Terabyte of data takes less than one second. I/O time was not measured, but can be estimated from the data transfer figure noted above. A Connection Machine with 64K processors can support I/O rates of up to 200 MB/second using 8 Datavaults. The amount of data to be transferred for a query against a Terabyte database would be 16 * 7.5 Megabytes, or 120 Megabytes, giving a transfer time of 600 milliseconds. Thus, the I/O problem should be ultimately solvable. More work is required in this area, particularly studying I/O latency effects.

6.5 Comparison of Methods

The serial inverted file algorithm was benchmarked on a Sun–4/280. The scoring step took 5.75 seconds for 100,000 postings. The ranking step took 2.20 seconds for 100,000 mailboxes. Assuming 10 Kilobyte documents (as we have been doing here) , a Terabyte of text would contain 10 million documents. Using the distributions discussed above, each query term references about 3 million postings. Extrapolating from these numbers, it appears that searching such a Terabyte of data on a Sun–4, using a 10–term query, will take in excess of 400 seconds. This figure exceeds the desired interactive response time by two orders of magnitude. The performance of the signature algorithm has also been estimated, assuming (unrealistically) that something like 250 Gigabytes of primary memory is available. The performance of the previous non–segmented inverted algorithm has also been estimated. The segmented algorithm seems to be the fastest of these methods, particularly on the scoring portion of the task.

Implementation	Scoring Time (sec)	Ranking Time (sec)	Total Time (sec)
Inverted Index, Sun 4	176.00	241.00	417.00
Signatures, 64K CM2	1.00	3.61	4.61
Inverted Indexes Algorithm, 64K CM2	1.35	.74	2.09
Segmented Algorithm, 64K CM2	.20	.74	.94

At this point, it is clear that the time required to score documents has been reduced so severely that further improvement will have to be attained by improving the ranking time. I/O is not included in the above figures and, as noted above, remains a major issue. However, the I/O load for inverted files is fundamentally independent of the algorithm used to process the file once the relevant postings have been transferred to memory, so the above comparisons remain important.

7 Conclusions

This paper has presented a new parallel representation for text databases called partitioned posting files. The following claims have been supported by measurements against a synthetic database:

1.   The algorithms are fast enough to permit interactive access to databases of 1 Terabyte.

2.   Overall, the parallel algorithms are approximately 400 times faster than comparable algorithms running on a fast serial machine.

3.   The file structure does not involve excessive storage overhead.

4.   Building and maintaining the file structure is probably feasible.

Considerable work remains to be done. First, I/O issues pertaining to querying and formatting the database need to be addressed. Second, better estimates of the time to build and update the database are required. Finally, the ranking algorithm is now the slowest part of the system, and requires more detailed examination.

REFERENCES

[1]   Stanfill, C. and B. Kahle, "Parallel Free–Text Search on the Connection Machine System," *Communications of the ACM*, Volume 29 Number 12, December 1986, pp. 1229–1239.

[2]   Pogue, C. and P. Willett, "Use of Text Signatures for Document Retrieval in a Highly Parallel Environment," *Parallel Computing* Volume 4, 1987, pp. 259–268.

[3]   Stone, H., "Parallel Querying of Large Databases: A Case Study," *IEEE Computer*, October 1987, pp. 11–21.

[4]   Salton, G., and C. Buckley, "Parallel Text Search Methods," *Communications of the ACM*, Volume 31 Number 2, February 1988, pp. 202–215.

[5]   Croft, B., "Implementing Ranking Strategies Using Text Signatures," *ACM Transactions on Office Information Systems*, Volume 6 Number 1, January 1988, pp. 42–62.

[6]   Stanfill, C., "Parallel Computing for Information Retrieval: Recent Developments," Technical Report DR88–1, Thinking Machines Corporation, Cambridge MA, January 1988.

[7]   Stanfill, C., "Information Retrieval Using Parallel Signature Files", *IEEE Data Engineering Bulletin*, 1990.

[8]   Salton, G., "Automatic Text Analysis," *Science* Volume 168, 1970, pp. 335–343.

[9]   Salton, G. and C. Buckley, "Term Weighting Approaches in Automatic Text Retrieval," Technical Report 87–881, Department of Computer Science, Cornell University, 1987.

[10]   Stanfill, C., R. Thau, and D. Waltz, "A Parallel Indexed Algorithm for Information Retrieval," *Proceedings, ACM Conference on Research and Development in Information Retrieval*, June 1988, pp 88–97.

Parallel Text Searching In Serial Files Using A Processor Farm

Janey K. Cringean[1], Roger England[3],
Gordon A. Manson[2] and Peter Willett[1,4]

Departments of Information Studies[1] and Computer Science[2], University of
Sheffield, Western Bank, Sheffield S10 2TN, U.K. and National Transputer
Support Centre[3], Sheffield Science Park, Arundel Street, Sheffield S1 2NS, U.K.

[4] to whom all correspondence should be addressed.

Abstract. This paper discusses the implementation of a parallel text retrieval system using a microprocessor network. The system is designed to allow fast searching in document databases organised using the serial file structure, with a very rapid initial text signature search being followed by a more detailed, but more time-consuming, pattern matching search. The network is built from transputers, high performance microprocessors developed specifically for the construction of highly parallel computing systems, which are linked together in a processor farm. The paper discusses the design and implementation of processor farms, and then reports our initial studies of the efficiency of searching that can be achieved using this approach to text retrieval from serial files.

1 Introduction

The last few years have seen a proliferation of interest in the use of *parallel processing* techniques, where some or many processors operate together so as to reduce the elapsed time required for a computational task. The use of multiple processors can bring about substantial increases in performance, as well as providing some degree of fault tolerance (and hence graceful degradation in the case of a system malfunction) and a facile upgrade path (since increased computational demands can be met simply by acquiring additional processors).

There have been several attempts to classify the many ways in which parallelism may be implemented in a computer system (Flynn, 1972; Handler, 1977; Hockney & Jesshope, 1988; Shore, 1973; Skillicorn, 1988). Of these, the most common is that developed by Flynn (1972), which classifies computer systems in terms of the multiplicity of the instruction stream and of the data stream. Four possible architectures are recognized:

- SISD, or single instruction stream, single data stream.

- SIMD, or single instruction stream, multiple data stream.

- MISD, or multiple instruction stream, single data stream.

- MIMD, or multiple instruction stream, multiple data stream.

Of the four classes, MISD is difficult to conceptualize and is usually regarded as a null class, while SISD represents the serial architecture that has formed the basis for nearly all computers since their initial development over forty years ago. SIMD machines are computers in which the same instruction is executed in parallel across some, or many, processors simultaneously. Examples include pipelined vector processors and array processors (Hockney & Jesshope, 1988; Sharp, 1987). The latter type of machine, which contains thousands of simple, bit-serial processing elements, is particularly well suited to the processing of large databases and there have been many reports of the use of two types of array processor, the Distributed Array Processor and the Connection Machine, for database processing applications (see, e.g., Carroll *et al.*, 1988; Waltz *et al.*, 1987): a review of this work is presented by Willett and Rasmussen (1990).

MIMD computers are characterised by multiple processors capable of independent operation; this allows a greater architectural variation than is the case with SIMD machines, and requires a greater range of organisational problems to be overcome if efficient computation is to be achieved (Dubois *et al.*, 1988; Gajski & Peir, 1985; Patton, 1985). The most widely applied sub-categorisation of MIMD computers depends on the degree to which the processor memories are coupled. In tightly coupled systems, all of the processors share a global memory through some central switching network or a high-speed bus that links the processors together. In loosely coupled systems, conversely, each of the processors in the network has a local memory and communicates with other processors by passing messages; thus facilities for highly efficient inter-processor communication are required. There are several ways in which message passing MIMD computers can be built: we are interested here in what are often referred to as *multicomputers*, *multicomputer networks* or *microprocessor-based multiprocessors*. A multicomputer consists of a large number of low-cost, high-performance microprocessors, each of which has some local memory and which can communicate with other such processors over some type of network (Athas & Seitz, 1988; Fox *et al.*, 1988; Reed & Fujimoto, 1987).

There have been a few reports of the use of multicomputers for text retrieval (Cringean *et al.*, 1988; Cringean *et al.*, 1989a; Sharma, 1989; Stewart & Willett, 1987; Walden & Sere, 1989). Cringean *et al.* (1989b, 1990) review the work to date and give a detailed specification of a multicomputer system that is designed for text scanning in serial files and that is intended to be used in conjunction with conventional PC-based equipment. The system uses an initial text signature search to reduce the number of documents that need to undergo the detailed and time-consuming pattern matching search. It is in the pattern matching stage that the parallel processing capabilities of the multicomputer come most obviously into play, using the *processor farm* approach to distributed processing (as described in Section 3 below). The present paper reports the results of initial experiments using this multicomputer system for serial text scanning.

2 The Transputer

The multicomputer networks considered here are based on the INMOS Transputer. A transputer is a high-performance processor developed especially for use in multiprocessor systems (Hey, 1988; Pritchard *et al.*, 1987). Each transputer consists of a processor with its own memory and links to connect it to other transputers, all on a chip less than a centimetre square. In fact, the transputer is a generic name for a family of devices. Each device contains some selection of the following architectural features capable of operating concurrently with other features:

- a high performance (up to 20 MIPS) 16-bit or 32-bit RISC central processor, including hardware support for simulated concurrency on a single processor; this special hardware facilitates fast process-switching which is orders of magnitude faster than time-slicing facilities on conventional non-parallel machines.

- very fast RAM, typically of size 4 Kbytes.

- external memory interface, with either multiplexed address and data buses for economy of device pins and price, or non-multiplexed for performance.

- some number (typically two or four) of serial communication link processors, for bi-directional communication between pairs of devices within the family. The links operate at speeds of 5, 10 or 20 Mbits/sec., and can achieve data transfer rates up to 1.7 Mbytes/sec. unidirectionally, and 2.3 Mbytes/sec. bidirectionally.

- further special function co-processors, currently including a floating point processor and disk controller.

The most important of these features are the links, which enable transputer devices to be used as building blocks in the construction of low-cost, high performance multiprocessing systems. Communication takes place only between pairs of devices and is distributed throughout a multiprocessing system, thus overcoming the classic von Neumann bottleneck of limited bandwidth which is often encountered in bus-based multiprocessing systems. It should be noted that even simple, single processor applications can make use of the concurrent operation of the CPU and link processors;

at any one instant, the CPU might be processing one item of data, one link transferring from disk to memory the next item of data, and a further link transferring from memory to disk the previous calculated result.

There are several different classes of transputer device. The two of most importance in the context of this paper are:

- T414 – this is a 32-bit processor, containing 2 Kbytes of RAM and four links operating at up to the maximum data rates previously quoted.

- T800 – this is a T414 processor with the addition of a concurrent 64-bit floating point processor that has been formally verified to conform to the ANSI IEE 785 standard and can sustain up to 2.3 Mflops/sec.

The particular transputer equipment that we have been working with is a model M40 Meiko Computing Surface. This is a modular transputer system that allows the network topology to be determined by the user. A Computing Surface may be configured as a general purpose computing resource or be optimised to a specific function using any mixture of subsystem boards to populate the expansion slots of the M40. Our work has used the following subsystem boards:

- MK014: Local Host board, incorporating a T414 transputer with 3 MBytes of external RAM, IEEE 488 and dual RS232 I/O interfaces.

- MK021: Mass Store, incorporating a T800 transputer with 8 MBytes of fast parity-checked RAM.

- 4×MK009: An MK009 Quad Computing Element system incorporates 4 T800 transputers, each with 256 Kbytes of external RAM; thus 4 boards provide 16 T800 transputers.

Transputer systems are designed in terms of an interconnected set of *processes*, i.e., subcomponents of the overall computational task. These processes are executed using one or more *processors*, i.e., individual transputers in the present context. Each process can be regarded as an independent unit of design, which communicates with other processes along point-to-point links called *channels*. The internal structure of each process can be in terms of a set of communicating processes. In fact, a complete program can be considered as a process made up of other communicating processes. This is reflected in the design of the language occam [1], which has been developed in conjunction with the transputer (May & Taylor, 1984) and which has been used for all of the work described in this paper. Programs can be developed in occam to run on an individual transputer or a network of transputers. When occam is used to program an individual transputer, all program code is placed on one transputer and the

---

[1] occam is a trademark of the INMOS Group of Companies.

432

processor shares its time between the concurrent processes; channel communication is implemented by moving data within memory. When occam is used to program a network of transputers, one or several processes may be allocated to each processor; communication between processes on different transputers is implemented directly by transputer links.

Having introduced the transputer and the process model of computation, the next section describes the processor farm approach to distributed computing that we have adopted for our studies of serial text retrieval.

3 Implementation Of Processor Farms

Database searching involves accepting an input stream of data records, D, and then carrying out some sort of matching operation, $M(D, R)$, which outputs a results stream, R, containing the records from D which match the query. Cringean et al. (1988) discuss several different ways of distributing these matching operations across a multicomputer network and conclude that the *processor farm*, or *processor pool*, approach to distributed computation (Hey, 1988; Pritchard et al., 1987) is the most appropriate for this type of application.

The farm approach involves decomposing the input datastream, D, into n sub-streams,

$$d_1, d_2, \ldots d_i, \ldots d_n \ (1 \le i \le n),$$

where n is the number of processors. The matching operation, M, is then replicated to give a series of identical processes, i.e., sub-components of the overall computational task,

$$M_1(d_1, r_1), M_2(d_2, r_2), \ldots M_i(d_i, r_i), \ldots M_n(d_n, r_n),$$

each of which outputs a result stream, r_i. Two main processes are required: one to decompose the datastream and to replicate M and the other to combine the n individual sets of results; in what follows, we shall refer to these as the *distributor* and the *collector* processes, respectively.

We can represent a processor farm logically by the flow diagram of Figure 1. Each worker process requests a data packet from the distributor process, performs the matching operation on that data, and sends the results to the collector process. The distributor process sends a data packet to an individual worker process whenever that process requests work. However, the network shown in Figure 1 cannot be implemented directly using transputers because there are only four links per transputer at present. Networks must therefore be designed to allow this logical model to be mapped onto a feasible physical network. One of the simplest physical networks that can be implemented with transputers is the *single linked chain*. In a single linked chain, the transputers are linked to each other in a simple, linear array, so that some transputer, T_j, in the body of the chain of n transputers is connected to two other transputers, T_{j-1} and T_{j+1} $(1 < j < n)$, as depicted in Figure 2.

If we wish to implement a processor farm based on a single chain, then data must be passed down the chain in one direction and results must be passed up the chain in the opposite direction along the transputer's bi-directional links. The distributor and collector processes are often executed on a single controlling processor, as in Figure 2. This processor is connected *via* one of its four links to the transputers which make up the farm and by another link to a host machine (typically a PC or a workstation) that provides terminal and file system support. Because it is attached to the host machine, this processor is called the *root* processor.

This physical network is not as simple as the logical model of the farm, where the distributor and collector have direct access to every worker process. In the case of a single linked chain the distributor and collector have direct access only to the worker process at the top of the chain, as is shown in Figure 2. Therefore, additional processes are required to allow a message to be forwarded from one transputer to another *via* other transputers in the network. The workers must therefore be able to do more than request some work, input a work packet, perform some work and output a result. They have to be able to input a work packet, decide whether it is intended for them, then either perform some work and output a result or pass the message further down the chain. Because all the functions of a single transputer can work independently of the others, it is possible to allow communication and decision making to be performed on one work paçket at the same time as work is being performed on another.

A slightly more complicated network is the *triple chain*, as shown in Figure 3. In this case, instead of having just a single chain attached to the root processor there are three chains, thus using all available links on the root processor. This network has the advantage that messages have a smaller average distance to travel without the network being too complicated.

4 System Design

4.1 Introduction

Our work in Sheffield seeks to evaluate the efficiency of nearest neighbour searching in transputer networks, using *text signature* representations to increase the efficiency of scanning in files of documents that are organised using the serial file structure, rather than the inverted file structure that provides the basis for the great majority of current text retrieval systems. A text signature is a fixed-length bit string in which bits are set to describe the contents of a document or query. These bit strings are created by applying some hashing-like operation to each of the terms describing a document or query, each such operation causing one or more bits in the string to be set (Faloutsos, 1985). Signature matching operations are probabilistic in character since a match at the bit string level is a necessary, but not sufficient, condition for a match at the word level. Thus, *false drops*, i.e., matches at the bit level that do not correspond to matches at the word level, can always occur. The elimination of such mis-matches requires the use of a second-level, pattern matching search which is carried out for just those documents that match at the signature level (so that the computationally demanding text scanning is applied only to small numbers of documents). There is a further problem with text signatures, this being the fact that the setting of a particular bit in a signature indicates merely the possible presence of a term in a document or query, this giving no information about the location of the word in the document or query or of how frequently the word occurs (Salton & Buckley, 1988). Thus, the specification of proximity or adjacency information in a query or the use of some types of frequency-based weighting schemes will again require the use of a second-stage search. For these reasons, we believe that it is imperative that retrieval systems based on text signatures should include the second-stage pattern matching search after the signature search; if this is not the case, then the undoubted efficiency of text signatures will be achieved only at the cost of reductions in effectiveness. Since pattern matching is very demanding of computational resources, it is thus an obvious candidate for the application of parallel processing techniques, as discussed in the remainder of this paper.

4.2 Implementation of nearest neighbour searching

In brief, the problem tackled is that of searching in a serial file for a query using a nearest neighbour retrieval algorithm. In common with most such retrieval systems, we will allow the query to be input at a keyboard as a natural language statement of need. The words in the query are compared with a stopword list and the remaining, content bearing words are then stemmed to conflate morphological variants. The stems are hashed into a bit string to form the query signature and this is then matched with a set of analogous signatures that represent each of the documents in the database. The documents are ranked in order of decreasing similarity with the query and the most similar documents then passed on for the second-stage pattern matching search, which is carried out using Horspool's version of the Boyer-Moore algorithm (Horspool, 1980). This search is used to produce the final ranking that is presented to the user. The similarity is calculated by means of the vector dot product, with the query terms being weighted using inverse document frequency (IDF) weighting. A basic data flow diagram for this process is shown in Figure 4.

The IDF-based similarity calculation that forms the basis for the final ranking is based on the matching of the actual stems that are present in the document and query texts. An analogous calculation can also be carried out during the signature search, although the calculated similarity value cannot be as accurate because less information is available (Mohan & Willett, 1985). If the bit or bits that are set in the query signature for some stem are also set in the document signature then the similarity is incremented by the IDF weight for that query stem; note that this procedure assumes the availability of a dictionary that contains the frequencies of occurrence of all of the words in the database (Croft & Savino, 1988). However, the many-to-one nature of the hashing procedures that are used in signature generation means that a match at the bit level indicates only the *possible* presence of the query stem in the document. Hence, the similarity which is calculated corresponds to the maximum possible similarity between the query and the document; the actual value will be somewhere between zero and this upperbound value.

We can then compare this calculated upperbound value with the actual similarity values that have already been calculated for earlier documents in the text scanning part of the search process. If the user wishes to see, e.g., twenty documents and the similarity value of the twentieth document in the ranking at that moment is higher than the upperbound calculated from the bit string of the document currently being considered, then there is no possibility that the current document can have a similarity value which would bring it into the ranking. There is therefore no need to send it forward for the pattern matching search. In order to implement this analysis of the bit strings, the threshhold value of similarity for the number of documents the user wishes to see must be passed back to the bit string search process, as shown in Figure 4, at intervals during the searching process.

4.3 Parallel implementation

As has already been stated, although the text signature search is very rapid, the second-level text searching stage is very time-consuming. It is this stage, therefore, for which we require a parallel solution. We have already stated that the processor farm model of distributing the computation is the most appropriate for this type of application. Therefore, the parallel implementation of text searching in a serial file can be represented by simply replacing the process called 'Compare texts' in

Figure 4 by the processor farm shown in Figure 1. Here, the two inputs to the farm are the required documents and the query stems, the work packet is the query and a document with which it is to be compared, and the required result is the text of a document for which the calculated similarity value is sufficiently large for it to be considered for inclusion in the final list of documents that is presented to the user at the end of the search. A physical implementation using a single chain processor farm is shown in Figure 5. The process 'Read required docs.' of Figure 4 is done before any processing takes place and the documents are stored in memory on a separate transputer board, which acts as the distributor and collector for the farm. All other processes are performed on the root transputer, with the text signatures also being read and stored in memory before the processing starts. The reader is referred to the papers by Cringean *et al.* (1989b, 1990) for a more detailed description of the logical processes required for serial text scanning and of the way in which these processes are implemented using a physical processor farm.

5 Efficiency Of Searching

The previous sections have described the implementation of serial text scanning on a transputer-based multicomputer system. This system is now operational in our laboratory and has been demonstrated at the Thirteenth International Online Information Meeting in London in December, 1989. In this section, we present the initial results from an ongoing study into the efficiency of retrieval that can be obtained from this system.

5.1 Measurement of performance

The measurement of computer performance is a controversial subject (even on conventional, serial processors) since the observed performance for an application is strongly affected by both the algorithm and the architecture (Hockney & Jesshope, 1988). Probably the most widely used measure of performance for parallel processors, and the one which is used in the following results, is an application-dependent one, the *speed-up*. The speed-up for P processors, S_P, is defined as

$$S_P = \frac{T_1}{T_P}, \tag{1}$$

where T_1 and T_P are the times to carry out an algorithm on one and P processors respectively. In the ideal case, $S_P = P$; all of the processors are fully utilized and the system is said to exhibit a *linear speed-up*, i.e., the speed-up varies directly with the number of processors that are available.

It must be emphasised that linear speed-up represents an upperbound to the performance of a parallel system: the actual degree of speed-up that can be obtained is controlled, at least in part, by Amdahl's law (Amdahl, 1967; Gustafson, 1988; Quinn, 1987). This states that if a given problem has a fraction f of sequential operations, then the maximum speed-up which can be achieved with a parallel computer of P processors is

$$S_P \leq \frac{1}{(f + \frac{(1-f)}{P})}. \tag{2}$$

This suggests that, unless very little serial processing is required, the running time for a system with both serial and parallel operations will be dominated by the serial processing.

In the context of the transputer-based document retrieval system considered here, the requisite computation can be sub-divided as follows:

- Serial processing. The main serial component is the initial preprocessing of the query. Two other serial components are the first-stage scan of the text signatures, which is carried out on the root transputer, and the communication of the texts of the documents passing this scan over the network to the transputers in the farm. However, the fact that they are performed at the same time as the main parallel processing element makes it difficult to specify whether these are important as serial components.

- Parallel processing. This is the second-stage pattern matching search, where many document texts can be processed in parallel by the transputers in the farm.

The observed level of performance will thus be determined in large part by the relative proportions of these two types of processing.

The speed-up is a system-oriented measure of performance. Of more interest to the actual user of a retrieval system is the *response time*, i.e., the time that elapses between the submission of a query and the display of (hopefully) relevant documents at the terminal. It is thus of importance to note not only the speed-up relative to a single transputer but also the absolute time for a search.

5.2   Experimental results to date

The dataset used in our experiments contains the titles and abstracts of the 6,004 documents that formed the input to the 1982 issues of *Library and Information Science Abstracts* (LISA) database. Associated with these documents is a set of 35 natural language queries, which were collected from students and staff in the Department of Information Studies, University of Sheffield by Ms. A. Davies as part of her 1982 MSc dissertation project.

438

Timing figures were obtained for searches in the LISA dataset with the 35 queries. Four sets of runs were carried out with the single chain processor farm as shown in parts (a) to (d) of Table 1. The first of these used text signatures in which all of the bits in the document bit strings had been set to '1', so that none of the documents were eliminated in the first stage of the search and so that the maximum possible amount of work was done by the network. The other runs used 128-bit, 256-bit and 512-bit text signatures, so that progressively less pattern matching would need to be carried out by the farm, as shown by the figures at the bottom of the tables, giving the number of documents that matched the query at the signature level and were passed on for text searching. The text signatures were created by hashing the stem of each non-stopword in a document or query onto a single bit position in the bit string. The number of documents shown to the user at the end of the search also determines how much pattern matching needs to be done; this number was set at 1, 5, 10 or 20. When all of the documents undergo the text search, i.e., when all of the bits are set to '1', the run times are little affected by the number of documents that are displayed and thus just a single figure has been listed in Table 1(a), that for 10 documents.

It is clear from an inspection of the figures in Table 1 that the search time reduces as the number of transputers is increased. More importantly, the response times for the best results obtained here are consistent with the basic assumption underlying our work, *viz.* that parallel processing can provide a mechanism for interactive access to serial files of documents. A comparison of the figures in parts (b), (c) and (d) with those in part (a) demonstrates the great decrease in times when text signatures are used. This is not only because documents are eliminated in the first stage of the search but also because, even when documents are sent for text searching, some processing can be eliminated. This is possible because it is not necessary to search in the text of a particular document for query terms whose bit position is set to '0' in the text signature of that document. This effect can be observed in Table 2, which shows the reductions in the number of documents searched and in the search times compared with the searches in which all the bits were set to '1'. The greater reductions in search times compared to the reductions in the number of documents searched can be attributed to the fact that the second-stage text searching has been optimised to make as much use of the information in the text signatures as possible. This is a particularly effective strategy when large numbers of documents are required by the user; the reduction in search time is nearly twice the reduction in documents searched when 20 documents are required by the user.

A rather less satisfactory state of affairs is evident if we consider the speed-ups, rather than the response times. When no signatures are used, i.e., when the maximum amount of text searching takes place, then near-linear speed-up behaviour is observed for networks containing up to around eight or twelve transputers; thereafter, there is very little further increase in speed-up. This is somewhat disappointing since our previous simulation studies had suggested that near-linear speed-ups should be obtainable with much larger farms than those used here (Cringean *et al.*, 1988). The speed-up behaviour becomes still more disappointing as longer and longer text signatures are used; indeed, there is very little speed-up at all when the 512-bit text signatures are used (although the actual response times here are very fast indeed).

It was thought that the problem could be a bottleneck in distributing the documents to the farm and that this might be alleviated by using the triple chain farm to reduce the average distance travelled by the messages, i.e., having three chains attached to the document store transputer instead of just the one shown in Figure 5. Four sets of runs were therefore carried out with a triple chain farm as shown in parts (a) to (d) of Table 3. The same parameters were used as for the previous runs except that the number of worker transputers was chosen so that all three chains were of equal length.

When all of the documents undergo the text search, i.e., when all of the bits are set to '1', the run times are longer with small numbers of transputers than in the case of the single chain because the use of the triple chain introduces overheads associated with the distribution of the documents. However, the response times when the farm is large are a considerable improvement on the single chain results. In this case, the speed-up is much more satisfactory than before. With a network of 15 worker transputers it is possible to get a speed-up of nearly 13, which is fairly close to the ideal linear speed-up. This verifies our assumption that the previous disappointing results had been due to a distribution bottleneck.

However, the speed-up behaviour is still disappointing when long text signatures are used; when the 512-bit text signatures are used there is again very little speed-up at all and little improvement in the response times over the single chain farm.

One point that should be made about these results is that they have been obtained in nearest neighbour searches where the natural language queries have been converted to a set of right-hand truncated word stems. The signature generation method used has been optimised for efficient searching using this particular type of query representative, and the signature search is thus very successful in eliminating documents from the pattern matching search. However, these signatures could not be used to eliminate documents if other types of pattern matching needed to be carried out, e.g., searches for left-hand truncated terms, embedded don't care characters and arbitrary substrings. Accordingly, very many more documents would have to be passed on for pattern matching, with a consequent substantial improvement in the speed-up behaviour. The results in Table 1 thus represent a lower bound for the speed-up which can be obtained when such text signatures are used.

We would also expect to obtain greater speed-up than those obtained to date if a more appropriate type of signature for these sorts of pattern matching operations were to be used, e.g., one based on the presence of trigrams. Text signatures based on the trigrams of non-stopwords were created by hashing each trigram to a single bit position in the bit string. A bit was also set for each word stem, as before. The length of the bit string was chosen so that approximately half of the bits were set to '1', since this is theoretically the most efficient arrangement; thus, the bit string length was 352. Searches were then performed using the original queries and modified queries in which wildcard characters were inserted at appropriate places, usually at the end of query terms. For words which did not contain wildcard characters, the appropriate IDF weighting was calculated as before: for words containing wildcard characters, an estimated IDF weight was calculated by assuming the term frequency was the average frequency of the terms in the document collection. This means that there is a graceful degradation in retrieval effectiveness from the case when no terms contain wildcards to the case when all terms contain them.

Table 4 contains the results of searches using these trigram text signatures. It is evident from comparison of Tables 4(a) and 4(b) that, as expected, both the response times and the speed-ups increase when wildcards are used in queries. It can also be observed that the response times are much greater than with the previous text signatures and the speed-ups are much lower. This was, at first, surprising because we had expected at least an improvement in speed-up because more text searching is being carried out (as is shown by a comparison of the numbers of documents searched here and in Table 3(c), where 256-bit signatures are used). However, it has now been realised that, by using text signatures, we have created another bottleneck. The original bottleneck was caused by a problem in distributing the documents from the document store transputer. Now we have a bottleneck in getting the document numbers sent out from the root transputer to the document store transputer quickly enough. With the trigram signatures, many more bit positions have to be checked for each term than previously. Thus, there is a greater delay between sending out the document numbers of those documents which need to be searched by the processor farm. Accordingly, the farm cannot be used to full effect. This could only be counteracted by having several processors searching the text signatures simultaneously and feeding document numbers into the document store transputer. A method of distributing text signature searching over several processors has been described by Walden and Sere (Walden & Sere, 1989).

A further unexpected, and possibly related, result is that there is no consistent trend in the variation of speed-up as the number of documents shown to the user is varied. This was again rather surprising, since, as more documents need to be displayed, so more documents need to be sent for text searching, and previous experience would have suggested to us that the speed-up should increase. However, with all the above results, as expected, the search time reduces as the number of documents required by the user decreases; this is because there is a higher threshhold similarity value when fewer documents are required.

6 Conclusions

The main conclusions of our experiments are as follows:

- The use of a transputer-based system allows very rapid searches based on serial files to be carried out, with response times that are comparable to those obtainable from PC-based inverted file systems.

- At least some speed-up has been obtained using parallel hardware under all the conditions investigated here.

- If no documents are eliminated at the first stage of the search, near-linear speed-up can be achieved with up to fifteen transputers.

- Large text signatures significantly reduce the search time, but there is also a marked reduction in the speed-up that can be achieved.

- The use of a single chain processor farm resulted in a bottleneck in the distribution of documents to the farm; this was alleviated by use of a triple chain network.

- The use of trigram signatures increases the response time and reduces the speed-up because it introduces a delay and thus creates a new bottleneck in the system.

Our results would thus suggest that transputer networks have at least some potential for allowing PCs to be used for interactive nearest neighbour searching in serial document files. That said, much further work is required to identify how such networks should be used to maximise the efficiency of searching. At present, we are investigating alternative ways of distributing the processes over the transputers at the top of the farm.

Acknowledgements. We thank the British Library for funding this work under grant number SI/G/814, the Library Association for the provision of the LISA data, and Mr. Andy Jackson, Mr. Glenn Miller, Mr. Geraint Jones and Dr. Jon Kerridge of the National Transputer Support Centre for technical support.

References

Amdahl, G. (1967). The validity of the single processor approach to achieving large scale computing capabilities. *AFIPS Conference Proceedings, 30*, 483-485.

Athas, W.C. & Seitz, C.L. (1988). Multicomputers: message-passing concurrent computers. *Computer, 21*(8), 9-24.

Carroll, D.M., Pogue, C.A. & Willett, P. (1988). Bibliographic pattern matching using the ICL Distributed Array Processor. *Journal of the American Society for Information Science, 39*, 390-399.

Cringean, J.K., Manson, G.A., Willett, P. & Wilson, G.A. (1988). Efficiency of text scanning in bibliographic databases using microprocessor-based multiprocessor networks. *Journal of Information Science, 14*, 335-345.

Cringean, J.K., Lynch, M.F., Manson, G.A., Willett, P. & Wilson, G.A. (1989a). Parallel processing techniques for information retrieval. Searching of textual and chemical databases using transputer networks. *Proceedings of the Thirteenth International Online Information Meeting*, 447-462.

Cringean, J.K., England, R., Manson, G.A. & Willett, P. (1989b). *Best Match Searching in Document Retrieval Systems Using Transputer Networks*. London: British Library Research and Development Department.

Cringean, J.K., England, R., Manson, G.A. & Willett, P. (1990). Implementation of text scanning using a multicomputer network. Part I. System design. Submitted for publication.

Croft, W.B. & Savino, P. (1988). Implementing ranking strategies using text signatures. *ACM Transactions on Office Information Systems, 6*, 42-62.

Dubois, M., Scheurich, C. & Briggs, F.A. (1988). Synchronisation, coherence and event ordering in multiprocessors. *Computer, 21*(2), 9-21.

Faloutsos, C. (1985). Access methods for text. *ACM Computing Surveys, 17*, 49-74.

Flynn, M.J. (1972). Some computer organisations and their effectiveness. *IEEE Transactions on Computers, C-21*, 948-960.

Fox, G.C., Johnson, M.A., Lyzenga, G.A., Otto, S.W., Salmon, J.K. & Walker, D.W. (1988). *Solving Problems on Concurrent processors. Volume I. General Techniques and Regular Problems* Englewood Cliffs: Prentice Hall.

Gajski, D.D. & Peir, J.K. (1985). Essential issues in multiprocessor systems. *Computer, 18*(6), 9-27.

Gustafson, J.L. (1988). Reevaluating Amdahl's Law. *Communications of the ACM, 31*, 532-533.

Handler, W. (1977). The impact of classification schemes on computer architectures. In *Proceedings of the 1977 International Conference on Parallel Processing* (pp. 7-15). New

York: IEEE.

Hey, A.J.G. (1988). Reconfigurable transputer networks: practical concurrent computation. *Proceedings of the Royal Society, A326*, 395-410.

Hockney, R.W. & Jesshope, C.R. (1988). *Parallel Computers 2. Architecture, Programming and Algorithms.* Bristol: Adam Hilger.

Horspool, R.N. (1980). Practical fast matching in strings. *Software - Practice and Experience, 10*, 501-506.

May, D. & Taylor, R. (1984). occam - an overview. *Microprocessors and Microsystems, 8*, 73-79.

Mohan, K.C. & Willett, P. (1985). Nearest neighbour searching in serial files using text signatures. *Journal of Information Science, 11*, 31-39.

Patton, P.C. (1985). Multiprocessors: architecture and applications. *Computer, 18*(6), 29-40.

Pritchard, D.J., Askew, C.R., Carpenter, D.B., Glendinning, I., Hey, A.J.G. & Nicole, D.A. (1987). Practical parallelism using transputer networks. *Lecture Notes in Computer Science, 258*, 278-294.

Quinn, M.J. (1987). *Designing Efficient Algorithms for Parallel Computers.* New York: McGraw-Hill.

Reed, D.A. & Fujimoto, R.M. (1987). *Multicomputer Networks: Message-Based Parallel Processing.* Cambridge, MA: MIT Press.

Salton, G. (1989). *Automatic Text Processing: the Transformation, Analysis and Retrieval of Information by Computer.* Reading, MA: Addison-Wesley.

Salton, G. & Buckley, C. (1988). Parallel text search methods. *Communications of the ACM, 31*, 202-215.

Sharma, R. (1989). A generic machine for parallel information retrieval. *Information Processing and Management, 25*, 223-235.

Shore, J.E. (1973). Second thoughts on parallel processing. *Computers and Electrical Engineering, 1*, 95-109..

Skillicorn, D.B. (1988). A taxonomy for computer architectures. *Computer, 21*(11), 46-57.

Stewart, M. & Willett, P. (1987). Nearest neighbour searching in binary search trees: simulation of a multiprocessor system. *Journal of Documentation, 43*, 93-111.

Walden, M. & Sere, K. (1989). Free text retrieval on transputer networks. *Microprocessors and Microsystems, 13*, 179-187.

Waltz, D., Stanfill, C., Smith, S. & Thau, R. (1987). Very large database applications of the Connection Machine system. *AFIPS Conference Proceedings, 56*, 159-165.

Willett, P. & Rasmussen, E.M. (1990). *Parallel Database Processing. Text Retrieval and Cluster Analysis using the Distributed Array Processor.* London: Pitman.

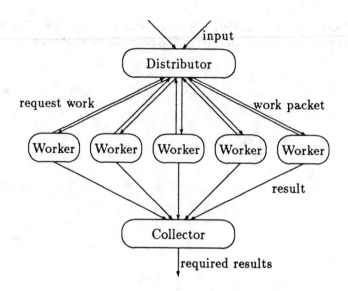

Figure 1: Flow diagram of processor farm with five worker processors. Rounded boxes indicate processes.

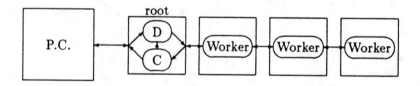

Figure 2: Single linked chain network with both the distributor process (D) and the collector process (C) on the root processor. Rounded boxes indicate processes and squares indicate physical processors.

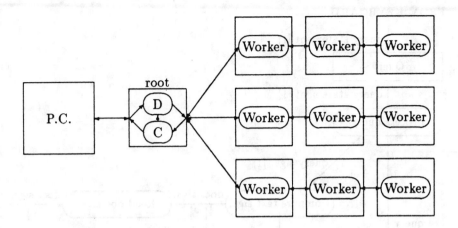

Figure 3: Triple chain network with both the distributor process (D) and the collector process (C) on the root processor. Rounded boxes indicate processes and squares indicate physical processors.

FROM KEYBOARD

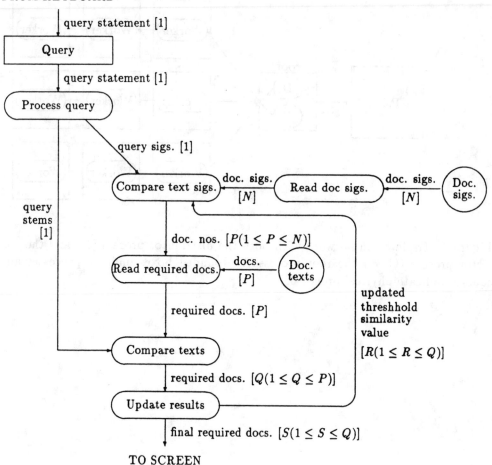

Figure 4: Basic flow diagram of two-level text searching in a serial file. Circles indicate disk storage media, rounded boxes indicate processes, and the rectangle indicates data input to the system from external sources; numbers in square brackets represent the number of times data units are transferred from one process to another.

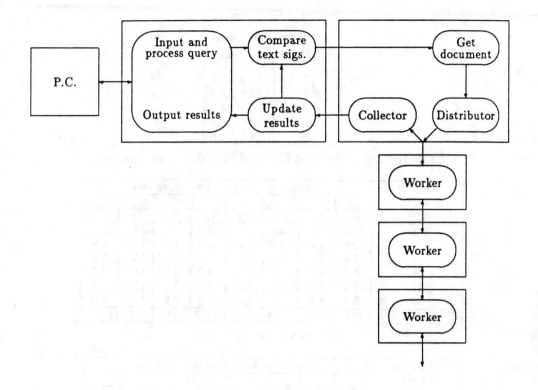

Figure 5: Physical implementation of parallel text searching using a single chain processor farm with processes placed on processors in a transputer network. Rounded boxes indicate processes and rectangles indicate processors.

Number of workers (P)	T_P	S_P
1	125.6	–
2	63.5	2.0
4	32.8	3.8
8	18.3	6.9
12	14.9	8.4
16	14.2	8.8

(a) No text signatures used (100% of 6004 documents searched)

Number of workers (P)	Number of documents shown to user							
	1		5		10		20	
	T_P	S_P	T_P	S_P	T_P	S_P	T_P	S_P
1	24.3	–	32.4	–	35.5	–	39.3	–
2	12.5	1.9	16.9	1.9	18.9	1.9	21.9	1.8
4	6.8	3.6	9.5	3.4	11.1	3.2	13.8	2.8
8	5.2	4.7	7.6	4.2	9.2	3.9	12.1	3.2
12	5.3	4.6	7.6	4.2	9.2	3.9	12.1	3.2
16	5.3	4.6	7.7	4.2	9.3	3.8	12.2	3.2
Docs. searched	1976 (33%)		2934 (49%)		3307 (55%)		3680 (61%)	

(b) 128-bit text signatures

Number of workers (P)	Number of documents shown to user							
	1		5		10		20	
	T_P	S_P	T_P	S_P	T_P	S_P	T_P	S_P
1	6.8	–	12.0	–	14.7	–	18.7	–
2	4.0	1.7	6.8	1.8	8.6	1.7	11.7	1.6
4	3.1	2.2	4.7	2.6	6.1	2.4	8.9	2.1
8	3.1	2.2	4.6	2.6	6.0	2.4	8.8	2.1
12	3.1	2.2	4.6	2.6	6.0	2.4	8.8	2.1
16	3.1	2.2	4.7	2.6	6.1	2.4	8.9	2.1
Docs. searched	613 (10%)		1222 (20%)		1521 (25%)		1883 (31%)	

(c) 256-bit text signatures

Number of workers (P)	Number of documents shown to user							
	1		5		10		20	
	T_P	S_P	T_P	S_P	T_P	S_P	T_P	S_P
1	2.8	–	4.5	–	6.0	–	9.0	–
2	2.6	1.1	3.7	1.2	4.9	1.2	7.3	1.2
4	2.6	1.1	3.6	1.2	4.7	1.3	7.1	1.3
8	2.6	1.1	3.6	1.2	4.7	1.3	7.1·	1.3
12	2.7	1.0	3.6	1.2	4.7	1.3	7.1	1.3
16	2.7	1.0	3.6	1.2	4.8	1.2	7.2	1.2
Docs. searched	149 (2%)		387 (6%)		540 (9%)		751 (12%)	

(d) 512-bit text signatures

Table 1: Mean search time in seconds, T_P, and speed-up, S_P, for searching the LISA dataset using a single chain processor farm (averaged over 35 queries).

Number of docs. shown	RD	RT
1	67%	81%
5	51%	74%
10	45%	72%
20	39%	69%

Table 2: Mean percentage reduction in documents searched, RD, and reduction in time, RT, for searching with 1 worker transputer in the LISA dataset (averaged over 35 queries) using 128-bit text signatures (compared to times when all bits set to '1').

Number of workers (P)	T_P	S_P
1	137.0	–
2	68.8	2.0
3	46.1	3.0
6	23.9	5.7
9	16.6	8.3
12	13.0	10.5
15	10.9	12.6

(a) No text signatures used (100% of 6004 documents searched)

Number of workers (P)	Number of documents shown to user							
	1		5		10		20	
	T_P	S_P	T_P	S_P	T_P	S_P	T_P	S_P
1	28.3	–	37.9	–	41.4	–	45.5	–
2	14.3	2.0	19.3	2.0	21.4	1.9	24.3	1.9
3	9.7	2.9	13.1	2.9	14.8	2.8	17.4	2.6
6	5.2	5.4	7.2	5.3	8.5	4.9	11.0	4.1
9	3.9	7.3	5.4	7.0	6.6	6.3	9.1	5.0
12	3.6	7.9	4.8	7.9	6.0	6.9	8.5	5.4
15	3.6	7.9	4.8	7.9	5.9	7.0	8.4	5.4
Docs. searched	2010 (34%)		2985 (50%)		3366 (56%)		3756 (63%)	

(b) 128-bit text signatures

Number of workers (P)	Number of documents shown to user							
	1		5		10		20	
	T_P	S_P	T_P	S_P	T_P	S_P	T_P	S_P
1	7.9	–	14.0	–	17.0	–	21.4	–
2	4.4	1.8	7.5	1.9	9.3	1.8	12.6	1.7
3	3.4	2.3	5.5	2.5	6.9	2.5	9.9	2.2
6	2.8	2.8	4.0	3.5	5.1	3.3	7.8	2.7
9	2.8	2.8	3.8	3.7	4.9	3.5	7.6	2.8
12	2.8	2.8	3.8	3.7	4.9	3.5	7.6	2.8
15	2.8	2.8	3.8	3.7	4.9	3.5	7.6	2.8
Docs. searched	613 (10%)		1231 (20%)		1542 (26%)		1910 (32%)	

(c) 256-bit text signatures

Number of workers (P)	Number of documents shown to user							
	1		5		10		20	
	T_P	S_P	T_P	S_P	T_P	S_P	T_P	S_P
1	2.9	–	4.9	–	6.5	–	9.8	–
2	2.6	1.1	3.7	1.3	4.8	1.4	7.5	1.3
3	2.6	1.1	3.5	1.4	4.6	1.4	7.1	1.4
6	2.6	1.1	3.5	1.4	4.5	1.4	7.0	1.4
9	2.6	1.1	3.5	1.4	4.5	1.4	7.0	1.4
12	2.6	1.1	3.5	1.4	4.5	1.4	7.0	1.4
15	2.6	1.1	3.5	1.4	4.5	1.4	7.0	1.4
Docs. searched	149 (2%)		390 (6%)		545 (9%)		760 (13%)	

(d) 512-bit text signatures

Table 3: Mean search time in seconds, T_P, and speed-up, S_P, for searching the LISA dataset using a triple chain processor farm (averaged over 35 queries).

Number of workers (P)	Number of documents shown to user							
	1		5		10		20	
	T_P	S_P	T_P	S_P	T_P	S_P	T_P	S_P
1	13.5	–	18.8	–	21.5	–	25.5	–
2	9.9	1.4	11.6	1.6	13.1	1.6	15.9	1.6
3	9.6	1.4	10.6	1.8	11.7	1.8	14.2	1.8
6	9.6	1.4	10.5	1.8	11.6	1.9	14.0	1.8
9	9.6	1.4	10.5	1.8	11.6	1.9	14.0	1.8
12	9.6	1.4	10.5	1.8	11.6	1.9	14.0	1.8
15	9.6	1.4	10.5	1.8	11.6	1.9	14.0	1.8
Docs. searched	653 (11%)		1172 (20%)		1421 (24%)		1722 (29%)	

(a) No wildcards in queries

Number of workers (P)	Number of documents shown to user							
	1		5		10		20	
	T_P	S_P	T_P	S_P	T_P	S_P	T_P	S_P
1	15.6	–	21.6	–	24.9	–	29.1	–
2	10.7	1.5	12.7	1.7	14.2	1.8	17.0	1.7
3	10.1	1.5	11.1	1.9	12.2	2.0	14.5	2.0
6	10.1	1.5	10.9	2.0	11.9	2.1	14.1	2.1
9	10.0	1.6	10.9	2.0	11.9	2.1	14.1	2.1
12	10.1	1.5	10.9	2.0	11.9	2.1	14.0	2.1
15	10.0	1.6	10.9	2.0	11.9	2.1	14.1	2.1
Docs. searched	692 (12%)		1182 (20%)		1438 (24%)		1722 (29%)	

(b) Wildcards in queries where appropriate

Table 4: Mean search time in seconds, T_P, and speed-up, S_P, for searching the LISA dataset with trigram text signatures using a triple chain processor farm (averaged over 35 queries).

An Architecture for Probabilistic Concept-Based Information Retrieval*

Robert M. Fung, Stuart L. Crawford, Lee A. Appelbaum and Richard M. Tong

Advanced Decision Systems
1500 Plymouth Street
Mountain View, California 94043-1230

Abstract

While concept-based methods for information retrieval can provide improved performance over more
conventional techniques, they require large amounts
of effort to acquire the concepts and their qualitative
and quantitative relationships.

This paper discusses an architecture for probabilistic
concept-based information retrieval which addresses
the knowledge acquisition problem. The architecture
makes use of the probabilistic networks technology
for representing and reasoning about concepts and includes a knowledge acquisition component which partially automates the construction of concept knowledge bases from data.

We describe two experiments that apply the architecture to the task of retrieving documents about terrorism from a set of documents from the Reuters news
service. The experiments provide positive evidence
that the architecture design is feasible and that there
are advantages to concept-based methods.

1 Introduction

In this paper we describe some preliminary research
on the use of probabilistic networks for information
retrieval. In particular, we introduce an architecture

*This work was funded by ADS' Internal Research and De-
velopment Program.

for probabilistic, concept-based information retrieval
(henceforth PCIR) that can be used to automatically
generate relationships between concepts, and then
reason about them given the evidence provided by
individual documents. This is in contrast to our previous research on concept-based methods [12, 16, 17],
in which we were primarily interested in issues related
to reasoning about concepts and not so much concerned with issues related to the construction of the
relationships. Our long-term goal, however, continues to be the development of techniques that can form
the basis for an effective system to assist users in sorting through large volumes of time sensitive material.
We have in mind such applications as the day-to-day
monitoring of newswires for specific topics of interest.

The architecture of a generic concept-based system
is shown in Figure 1. A knowledge base contains a
set of concepts together with their qualitative (i.e.,
structural) and quantitative relationships with other
concepts. Queries specify a user's information need
in terms of these concepts. When a new document
is presented with respect to a particular query, features are extracted from the document. The features
currently used are the presence or absence of certain
key words, and these features constitute evidence for
the presence of concepts in the document. Using the
features extracted from the document and the system knowledge base, inference is performed to assess
the impact of the evidence on the belief in the query
concept. The documents are sorted by belief and
retrieved by a user-specified rule (e.g., retrieve the

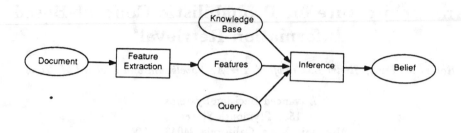

Figure 1: *Generic Concept-Based Architecture for IR*

"best" ten).

Thus, concept-based methods view information retrieval primarily as a problem of evidential reasoning. However, while they can provide improved performance over more conventional techniques, they do require large amounts of effort to acquire the concepts and their relationships. Our current research attempts to address this weakness with the use of new probabilistic methods to represent, reason about, and learn the relationships between concepts. While probabilistic methods have been recognized as an important evidential reasoning technology with well-defined semantics (*e.g.*, frequency, strength-of-belief) and solid theoretical foundations, they have often been passed over because of their computational complexity. Their use in information retrieval has also been limited, although many authors have recognized the benefits of employing such techniques [2, 11, 14].

The probabilistic network technology [7, 13] is a recent development which is computationally tractable. A probabilistic network is a graph of nodes and arcs where the nodes represent uncertain variables and the arcs represent relationships between the variables. Computationally efficient algorithms have been developed which perform inference. The technology has been applied to a wide variety of problems including medical diagnosis, machine vision, petroleum exploration, military situation assessment, and multi-target tracking.. Some initial work has applied this technology to information retrieval in hypertext [3, 5].

Because of the clear semantics behind probabilistic networks, it is possible to identify and quantify relationships between variables through experience (*i.e.*, data). CONSTRUCTOR [6] is a system for building probabilistic networks from data. It serves as the primary mechanism for learning about the relationship between concepts.

In the following section of the paper, we discuss both probabilistic networks and the CONSTRUCTOR system in more detail, and then, in Section 3, we describe the PCIR architecture. In Sections 4 and 5, we present the results of two exploratory experiments that show how we might use these techniques for concept-based retrieval. We conclude, in Section 6, with some comments and conclusions on the utility of the ideas we have presented.

2   Component Technologies

The two major component technologies of PCIR are probabilistic networks and CONSTRUCTOR.

2.1   Probabilistic Networks

Probabilistic networks is a technology for representing and reasoning with uncertain beliefs, and is based on the well-established theory of Bayesian probability. A successor to decision tree technology, probabilistic networks have been shown to be to be more understandable and computationally more tractable than the older technology. These advantages are achieved primarily through one innovation: the explicit representation of relevance relations between factors modeled in the network.

There are two major types of probabilistic networks, Bayesian networks which contain directed arcs and Markov networks which contain undirected arcs. Both types are used in PCIR. There are two types of nodes: state and evidence nodes. A state node represents a mutually exclusive and collectively exhaustive set of propositions about which there is uncertainty. A state node is represented graphically by a circle. For example, whether a document is or is not about terrorism may be uncertain. To model this situation, the two propositions "this document is about terrorism" and "this document is not about terrorism" could be represented by a state node in a probabilistic network. An evidence node represents an observation and is represented graphically with a rectangle. For example, the observation that the word "bombing" is contained as a document may be represented as a evidence node in a probabilistic network.

Relationships between nodes in probabilistic networks are indicated with arcs. In a Bayesian network, a node's relationship with its *predecessors*[1] is what is modeled in a probabilistic network. Each node contains a probabilistic model of what is expected given every combination of predecessor values. For example, the predecessor of the *shooting* node in Figure 2 is the *killing* node. The probabilistic model for the *shooting* node is shown in Table 1. The model can be interpreted as saying that when the concept **killing** is present in a document, the concept **shooting** will probably be in the document and that when the concept **killing** is not present in a document then the concept **shooting** will probably not be found in the document.

In a Markov network, relationships between nodes are also indicated with arcs but represented in a different way. Probabilistic models are associated with the cliques (*i.e.*, maximally connected subset) of a network instead of individual nodes.

Relevance relations are specified by the connectivity

---

[1] The set of nodes which have an arc which points to a given node are that node's predecessors.

Table 1: $p(shoot|kill)$

	¬shoot	shoot
¬kill	0.9	0.1
kill	0.1	0.9

of the network—what arcs are placed between what nodes, and in what direction. The concept of relevance in a Bayesian network is related loosely with graph separation and can be illustrated by examination of Figure 2. If it is known that the concept **killing** is present in a document, then the structure of the network implies that any other known information (*e.g.*, the concept **terrorism** is present in the document) will be irrelevant to beliefs about whether the **shooting** is present in the document. This is because the node *killing* separates the node *shooting* from every other node in the graph. Similarly, if it is known that the concepts **politician** and **terrorism** are both present in a document then any other piece of known information is irrelevant to whether the concept **subject** is present in the document. These relevance relations are useful not only from a qualitative point of view, but are also useful in reducing the amount of quantitative information needed and the amount of computational resources needed in inference.

Useful inferences can be made given a probabilistic network that represents a situation and evidence about the situation. For example, given the network representing the terrorism query and the evidence (*i.e.*, extracted features) from a document, one can infer an updated belief that the document is about terrorism. Several techniques are available for making inferences (*i.e.*, reaching conclusions) from a network and evidence. Shachter [15], Pearl [13], and Lauritzen and Spiegelhalter [10] all describe approaches to inference with probabilistic networks. Each approach has its advantages and disadvantages. For this work, we used the distributed algorithm [1, 9].

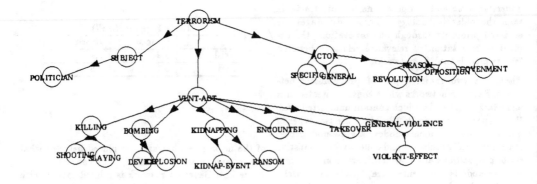

Figure 2: *Probabilistic Network for Terrorism*

2.2 CONSTRUCTOR

The CONSTRUCTOR system [6] induces discrete, probabilistic models from data. These models contain a quantitative (*i.e.*, probabilistic) characterization of the data but, perhaps more importantly, also contain a qualitative structural description of the data. By qualitative structure we mean, loosely, the positive and negative *causal* relationships between factors as well as the positive and negative *correlative* relationships between factors in the processes under analysis. CONSTRUCTOR has as a primary focus the recovery of qualitative structures since structure not only determines which quantitative relationships are recovered, but also because such structure have been found to be cognitively stable [8] and thus are valuable in explaining the real world processes under analysis.

The CONSTRUCTOR system is built upon techniques and research results from the fields of probabilistic networks, artificial intelligence (AI), and statistics. The probabilistic network technologies are central to the CONSTRUCTOR system since they not only provide the representation language for CONSTRUCTOR results but, more importantly, provide the conceptual impetus—the identification of conditional independence relations—that drives the CONSTRUCTOR system.

From the field of AI we have made use of heuristic search methods. These methods provide the primary problem solving paradigm of CONSTRUCTOR and allow for a computationally efficient implementation. From classical statistics, we make use of the χ^2 test for probabilistic independence and from the newer field of computer-intensive statistical analysis [4] we make use of *cross-validation* to prevent "overfitting" of models to data.

The CONSTRUCTOR algorithm works by finding the complete set of (graphical) neighbors for each feature in the data set. The neighbor relations for each feature can then be used to identify the structure of a belief network. The complete set of neighbors for a feature is called the Markov boundary. The neighbors are identifiable as the smallest set of features such that all other features are conditionally independent of that feature given any fixed set of values for the feature's neighbors.

Network identification involves successively finding the *neighbors* of each attribute in the training set. Despite these observations, managing the exponential process of finding neighbors is the primary challenge for the network identification task. Finding the

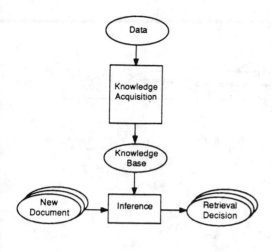

Figure 3: *PCIR Architecture*

neighbors for every attribute in a training set is an iterative search process based on finding the Markov boundary for each attribute.

3 Architecture

The PCIR architecture is shown in Figure 3. The major difference between it and the generic architecture in Figure 1 is the addition of the knowledge acquisition component. The rest of this section will discuss the PCIR knowledge base, the inference component and the knowledge acquisition component.

3.1 Knowledge Base

Central to the idea of a concept-based approach to information retrieval is a knowledge base which contains knowledge about relationships between concepts and features extractable from the document. In the PCIR architecture, the knowledge base takes the form of a set of probabilistic networks and can be obtained directly from a user or from the knowledge acquisition component of PCIR. The knowledge base

consists of concept networks and concept-evidence relationships. A concept network relates concepts to other concepts. A concept-evidence relationship relates a concept to a subset of the features that will be extracted.

For example, the terrorism concept network shown in Figure 2 contains 24 concepts and requires the specification of 47 quantitative parameters. Also included in the knowledge base are 61 concept-evidence relationships which require the specification of an additional 64 parameters. The relationships encoded by both sets of parameters are intuitive and include:

- If the concept **terrorism** is in a document, it is almost twice as likely that the concept **violent act** will be in the document compared with the case that the document does not contain the concept **terrorism**.
- If the concept **bombing** is in a document, it is nine times as likely that the concept **explosion** will be in the document compared with the case that the document does not contain the concept **bombing**.
- If the concept **explosion** is in a document, it is four times as likely that the word "explosion" will occur in the document compared with the case that the document does not contain the concept **explosion**.

3.2 Inference

Given a document, a concept of interest and some decision criteria, the function of the inference component is to use the knowledge base created by the knowledge acquisition component to first judge the likelihood that the document contains the concept of interest and secondly to use that likelihood and the decision criteria to make a decision about retrieval of the document. Figure 4 shows the functional flow for the inference component.

The first step in the inference process is to extract a set of features from the document. Each feature must have values which are well-defined and must be mutually exclusive and exhaustive. The features currently used by PCIR are words that have been deemed to be relevant (by a PCIR user) to the set of concepts in the PCIR knowledge base. For example, the words

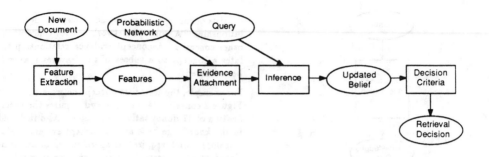

Figure 4: *PCIR Inference*

"explosive" "blast" and "explosion" would likely be deemed relevant to the concept **explosion**. The features currently used in PCIR are binary-valued. The values represent whether or not a particular word is present or absent in a document.

The result of feature extraction is a set of feature values. These feature values are instantiated as evidence nodes in the PCIR network and are attached to the appropriate state nodes (*i.e.*, concepts) in the network. The likelihoods which are required for the evidence nodes are derived from the concept-evidence relationships stored in the knowledge base.

The third step of the process is to perform probabilistic inference on the modified network. Given a concept of interest, the inference process computes the posterior distribution (*i.e.*, updated belief) of the concept given the evidence (*i.e.*, feature values) in the network. Since the concept of interest can be any of concepts in the network, a single network can serve to answer many queries.

The fourth step of the process is to apply the given decision criteria to the updated belief that the concept of interest is in the document. The decision criteria may be a simple threshold or may require comparison with the beliefs from other documents (*e.g.*, best n).

The probabilistic networks technology provides a probabilistic, model-based approach to deriving the strength of belief that a document contains a particular concept. By probabilistic, we mean that the domain knowledge of relationships between concepts and evidence is represented in probabilistic terms (*i.e.*, frequencies) and inference is performed with respect to the laws of probability. By model-based, we mean that the domain knowledge is represented as much as possible, in terms of behavioral models of cause and effect. For example the arc between the nodes *killing* and *shooting* in Figure 2 represents the belief that the presence of the concept **killing** in a document will with some probability, "cause" the presence of the concept **shooting**.

A model-based approach stands in contrast with an evidential-accrual approach, such as in RUBRIC [12, 16, 17]. The flow of reasoning in evidence-accrual approaches is directly from effect to cause (*i.e.*, evidence to conclusions). Evidence is accrued to the first level of conclusions which in turn act as evidence for the next higher layer of conclusions. In contrast, the flow of reasoning in model-based reasoning approaches can be viewed as a two pass process. In the first pass, reasoning flows from cause to effect in order to set up expectations for the evidence. And in the second pass, these expectations are compared with the actual evidence, and the comparisons are transmitted back from the effects to the causes.

In applying belief networks to information retrieval, one major decision was required—what states should the nodes represent. We choose to follow RUBRIC by assigning two states to each node in a network, where the states represent that a concept is present or absent in a document. Given this choice of states the probability distributions of a network represent beliefs about how the presence of sets of concepts in a document "causes" or "correlates with" the presence of other concepts in the document. For example, the model shown in Figure 2 shows that the presence of the concept **terrorism** in a document "causes," to some (probabilistic) degree, the inclusion of the concept **terrorist actor** to be in the document.

3.3 Knowledge Acquisition

While concept-based approaches such as RUBRIC are able to provide good results, the effort needed to acquire the knowledge bases needed by such approaches from experts requires substantial resources. PCIR provides an approach to reducing the effort needed for knowledge acquisition.

Given a set of documents, a set of features, and a set of concepts, the function of the knowledge acquisition component is to develop a knowledge base which establishes relationships between concepts and features. Figure 5 shows the functional flow for the knowledge acquisition component.

The user of PCIR must provide the inputs to the knowledge acquisition component. The inputs are a set of documents, a set of features, and a set of concepts. The document set is a population of documents which should be representative of the documents which will be faced in retrieval. The Reuters document collection used to generate the terrorism network contains 730 documents.

A set of concepts must be identified. Usually the concepts are identified through association (by the user) to the concept on which it is anticipated most retrievals will be performed. For example, the concepts included to generate the terrorism network were associated with the concept **terrorism**.

Given these inputs, there are two steps required to create a CONSTRUCTOR data set: feature extraction and concept specification.

Feature extraction is exactly the same process as in the inference component and is performed for each document in the document set.

Concept specification is the most user-intensive process in the architecture. The user must specify for each document in the data set which of the concepts in the concept specification are contained in the document.

Appending the concept specification and the feature values for each document creates a data set which can be processed by CONSTRUCTOR. The data set consists of an array of values. Each row represents the concepts and features present in a particular document. Each column represents a particular feature or concept.

The result of processing the data set through CONSTRUCTOR is a probabilistic network that can act as the knowledge base for the inference component.

If the user desires, a threshold decision criteria can be obtained for a particular concept of interest by passing each of the documents through the inference component of PCIR. A threshold can then be chosen by the user which provides for an appropriate tradeoff between precision and recall.

4 Experiments

Two simple experiments were performed with the Reuters database. The first experiment entailed building a probabilistic network where both the structure of the network and the probability distributions were given by a "user" (the principal author). In the second experiment, a probabilistic network was built using the Reuters database as input to the knowledge acquisition component of PCIR.

4.1 "Hand-constructed" Network

A simple network was built around the **terrorism** concept, using as a model a RUBRIC concept tree

461

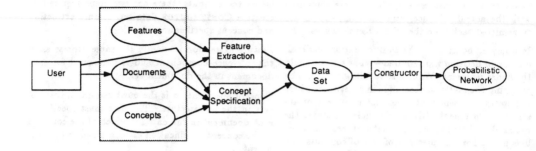

Figure 5: *PCIR Knowledge Acquisition*

built for **terrorism**. The network contains 23 concepts and was developed in a hierarchical fashion similar to the RUBRIC concept tree. The *terrorism* node was broken down into an *actor* performing a *violent act* on some *subject*. Similarly, *violent act* was broken down into different types of violent acts etc.. This network required 47 independent probability assessments. Except for the prior distribution on the *terrorism* node which was set to the frequency of terrorist documents in the document set, the probabilities were assessed qualitatively by the "user."

A set of 61 features (*i.e.*, words) were extracted from each document. Each of these features requires a concept-evidence relationship to be present in the knowledge base. (These relationships are not shown.) Each of the 61 words were assigned by the user to a single concept and probabilities were specified for the events that a word appears in a document given their assigned concept is present in a document.

Because of the difficulty of the knowledge acquisition task, several assumptions were made to reduce the number of parameters needed to be specified for this network. The assumptions included the hierarchical structure of the network as well as a constant likelihood that a word does not appear given its assigned concept does not appear in a document. The latter

assumption effects the posterior probabilities so that they are not "normalized." However the assumption does not effect the separation of the populations.

Using the concept-evidence relationships, evidence was attached to the probabilistic network in Figure 2. The mean and standard deviation of the posterior probability for both documents about terrorism and documents not about terrorism is shown in Table 2. It can be seen that the posterior probability of documents about terrorism is significantly higher than for the documents not about terrorism.

The precision and recall results for a range of possible thresholds are shown in Figure 6. In the middle range both precision and recall are approximately 50%. While RUBRIC results are significantly better, much less effort was expended on this experiment and the results are competitive with conventional techniques.

The goal of the experiment was to assess the feasibility of using probabilistic networks as the evidential reasoning mechanism in a concept-based information retrieval scheme. This experiment seems to suggest that this is feasible. Some effort was made to see if some parameter modification might easily improve performance. To this end the feature sets of relevant, unretrieved documents and irrelevant,

Table 2: *"Hand-constructed" results*

	avg	std dev
terrorism	.035	.03
¬terrorism	.015	.008

Table 3: Concepts

unnamed terrorist	named terrorist	assassination
politician	government	opposition
reason	takeover	encounter
kidnap event	ransom	explosion
bombing	device	shooting
killing	violent act	violent effect

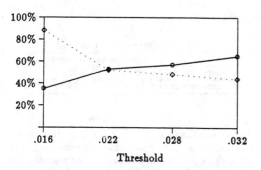

Figure 6: *Precision (solid line) & Recall (dotted line) vs. Threshold.*

retrieved documents were examined. While several modifications where made, no significant performance improvements were found. This points out the difficulty of knowledge acquisition from experts, not only in the initial acquisition stage but also in the knowledge base tuning stage.

4.2 Using CONSTRUCTOR

For this experiment, each of the 730 Reuters documents was tagged according to whether or not the document was "about" terrorism. Decisions about the relevancy of each document to the **terrorism** concept were made by a independent pair of readers. A total of 50 documents were judged to contain the concept **terrorism** and the other 680 were judged not to contain the concept **terrorism**. A set of 82 words was selected as the feature set. The presence or absence of each of the 82 words was determined for each document in the document set. In addition, 18 concepts were chosen as being possibly relevant to the concept of terrorism. The concepts are shown in Table 3. The two readers were also asked to indicate which of the 18 different concepts were relevant to

each of the 730 Reuters documents.

CONSTRUCTOR was first run with a data set made up of the 18 concepts plus the **terrorism** concept. The resulting Markov network is shown in Figure 7. Nodes for which there is not a path to the *class* node (*i.e.*, terrorism) are not shown. Many of the arcs have intuitive interpretations which are supported by the underlying probability distributions found in the data.

- "A bombing causes an explosion."
- "A shooting is a violent act."
- "A killing is a violent act."
- "A terrorist event is present if two or more of the concepts **bombing, named terrorist, killing** or **kidnapping** is present except for the combination **named terrorist** and **killing**."

The concept-evidence relationships were derived for each of 8 concepts in the network, by running CONSTRUCTOR on a data set which included one of the concepts and the words associated with the concepts. Given these results, the knowledge base was complete.

To test the network's performance, each of the 730 documents was processed by the inference component of PCIR using the CONSTRUCTOR-derived knowledge base. The mean and standard deviation of the posterior probability for both documents about terrorism and documents not about terrorism is shown in Table 4. It can be seen that the posterior probability of documents about terrorism is significantly higher than for the documents not about terrorism and that separation of the populations is well-defined.

The precision and recall results for a range of possible thresholds are shown in Figure 8. In the middle range both precision and recall are in the 70% to 80% range.

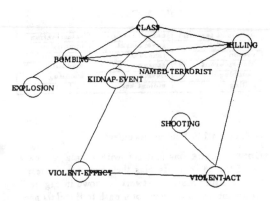

Figure 7: CONSTRUCTOR *Network for Terrorism*

Table 4: CONSTRUCTOR *results*

	avg	std dev
terrorism	.45	.21
¬terrorism	.036	.09

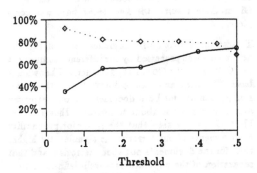

Figure 8: *Precision (solid line) & Recall (dotted line) vs. Threshold.*

Table 5: $p(explosion|bombing)$

	¬explosion	explosion
¬bombing	0.98	0.02
bombing	0.59	0.41

Table 6: $p(terrorist|terrorism)$

	¬terrorist	terrorist
¬terrorism	0.98	0.02
terrorism	0.64	0.36

As this was the first application of CONSTRUCTOR to real data, the robustness and intuitiveness of the relationships and the performance of the resulting network provided experimental evidence that the CONSTRUCTOR approach has merit.

Many of the relationships that were found are quite robust and had similar structures. Consider Table 5, and Table 6 as examples. In both these tables, the relations between the nodes can be interpreted as noisy if-then statements:

- "If the concept **bombing** is *not* in a document, then the concept **explosion** will *not* be in the document"
- "If the concept **terrorism** is *not* in a document, then the concept **terrorist** will *not* be in the document"

On the other hand, the contrapositive versions of these statements which are perhaps more intuitive, are not true. It is not true that:

- "If the concept **bombing** is in a document, then the concept **explosion** will be in the document" or
- "If the concept **terrorism** is in a document, then the concept **terrorist** will be in the document"

While many of the structural relationships and their corresponding quantitative relationships in the network are intuitive, there are some complicated relationships present in the network which are quite subtle. For example, consider the relationship between the concept **killing** and the concept **terror-**

ism. Whereas the other neighbors of **terrorism** (*i.e.,* **bombing**, **kidnap**, and **named-terrorist**) have strong, uncomplicated relationships with **terrorism**, the concept **killing** seems to have a relatively small effect by itself but seems to act as a magnifier of the positive influence of the other neighbors. This can be seen in Table 7 and was borne out when the frequencies of these events were examined in the raw data. Such subtle relationships may be the cause of the CONSTRUCTOR network's improved performance over the "hand-constructed" network and it is easy to imagine that such relationships would take much effort to find manually.

5 Conclusions

We believe that the experimental results presented above provide positive evidence that the PCIR architecture design is feasible. The choice of probabilistic networks for the knowledge base representation provides for an intuitive and well-defined semantics for acquiring knowledge either from an expert or automatically. The first experiment shows that reasonable performance can be obtained through use of probabilistic networks as the evidential reasoning mechanism for concept-based information retrieval. The second experiment reinforces this conclusion while also showing that partially automating the knowledge acquisition task is possible.

The central hypothesis of concept-based methods for information retrieval is that the representation of, and reasoning about, unobservable concepts is effective both from an organisational and from a computational point of view. We feel that a secondary contribution of this work is positive evidence for this hypothesis. All the evidence stems from the assumption that the CONSTRUCTOR-induced network is close to being correct and the fact that the network is sparse (*i.e.,* has few arcs). Out of the 153 possible arcs between the 18 concept nodes of the graph, only 12 of the arcs are instantiated. In addition, there are the 82 connections to the 82 evidence (*e.g.,* feature) nodes. In contrast, consider the situation if all the concept nodes except the *terrorism* node were removed from the graph by probabilistic manipulation. The resulting graph would be extremely dense. This

would correspond to the situation of deriving probabilistic relations between **terrorism** and the features directly.

Three advantages for concept-based methods can be seen from this analysis. First, concepts organize information into a small number of manageable concept-to-concept and concept-to-feature relations. This makes both manual and automatic knowledge acquisition easier. Secondly, concepts reduce the computational complexity of inference. Probabilistic inference is inherently easier in sparse networks than in dense networks. Thirdly, concepts make the automatic knowledge acquisition problem tractable by dramatically reducing the sampling problem. The probability tables of dense networks are exponentially larger than the probability tables for sparse networks. Dense networks will therefore spread the examples in the training set over a much larger space. Undersampling can be a serious problem in such situations. On the other hand, sparse networks do not suffer from such problems.

As a secondary point, we feel that not only are concepts useful computationally, but the robustness of the relationships between concepts seen in the CONSTRUCTOR-induced network provides strong evidence for the psychological intuition that these concepts are cognitively significant in people's thought processes.

The most visible drawback of this research is the amount of work needed by a user to identify what concepts are present for each document in a large document set. However, we think a scenario in which a user incrementally performed this is certainly feasible. Also, if the concepts of interest are not in a special domain, this work can be done by relatively untrained people. A research goal is to identify concepts automatically by clustering.

We think that the results are promising and intend to pursue further research in this direction. Further experimentation with the Reuters document set and the terrorism query is planned. Another area of research is experimentation with different document sets, different features, and different concepts. The CONSTRUCTOR algorithm itself is new and evolving. Improvements to the algorithm could be the source of important improvements to PCIR.

Table 7: $p(terrorism|bombing, kidnap, killing, terrorist)$

				¬terrorism	terrorism
¬bombing	¬kidnap	¬killing	¬terrorist	0.994	0.006
¬bombing	¬kidnap	¬killing	terrorist	0.85	0.15
¬bombing	¬kidnap	killing	¬terrorist	0.96	0.04
¬bombing	kidnap	¬killing	¬terrorist	0.61	0.39
bombing	¬kidnap	¬killing	¬terrorist	0.68	0.32
bombing	kidnap	¬killing	¬terrorist	0.02	0.98
bombing	¬kidnap	killing	¬terrorist	0.44	0.56
¬bombing	kidnap	killing	¬terrorist	0.51	0.49
bombing	¬kidnap	¬killing	terrorist	0.24	0.76
¬bombing	kidnap	¬killing	terrorist	0.05	0.95
¬bombing	¬kidnap	killing	terrorist	0.8	0.2
bombing	¬kidnap	killing	terrorist	0.53	0.47
¬bombing	kidnap	killing	terrorist	0.07	0.93
bombing	kidnap	¬killing	terrorist	0.003	0.997
bombing	kidnap	killing	¬terrorist	0.03	0.97
bombing	kidnap	killing	terrorist	0.02	0.98

References

[1] CHANG, K. C., AND FUNG, R. M. Node aggregation for distributed inference in bayesian networks. In *Proceedings of the 11th IJCAI* (Detroit, Michigan, August 1989), pp. 265–270.

[2] CROFT, W. B., AND HARPER, D. J. Using probabilistic models of document retrieval. *Journal of Documentation 35* (1979), 285–295.

[3] CROFT, W. B., AND TURTLE, H. A retrieval model incorporating hypertext links. In *Hypertext'89 Proceedings* (November 1989), pp. 213–224.

[4] EFRON, B. Computers and the theory of statistics: thinking the unthinkable. *SIAM Rev-21* (1979), 460–480.

[5] FRISSE, M. E., AND COUSINS, S. B. Information retrieval from hypertext: update on the dynamic medical handbook project. In *Hypertext'89 Proceedings* (November 1989), pp. 199–212.

[6] FUNG, R. M., AND CRAWFORD, S. L. Constructor: empirical acquistion of probabilistic models. In *AAAI-90* (July 1990).

[7] HOWARD, R., AND MATHESON, J. Influence diagrams. In *The Principles and Applications of Decision Analysis, vol. II*, R. Howard and J. Matheson, Eds., Menlo Park: Strategic Decisions Group, 1981.

[8] KAHNEMAN, D., SLOVIC, P., AND TVERSKY, A. *Judgement under uncertainty: Heuristics and biases.* Cambridge University Press, Cambridge, 1982.

[9] KIM, J. H., AND PEARL, J. A computational model for combined causal and diagnostic reasoning in inference systems. In *Proceedings of the 8th International Joint Conference on Artificial Intelligence* (Los Angeles, California, 1985), pp. 190–193.

[10] LAURITZEN, S. L., AND SPIEGELHALTER, D. J. Local computations with probabilities on graphical structures and their application in expert systems. *Journal Royal Statistical Society B 50* (1988), 157–224.

[11] MARON, M. E., AND KUHNS, J. L. On relevance, probabilistic indexing and information retrieval. *Journal of the ACM 7* (1960), 216–244.

[12] McCUNE, B. P., TONG, R. M., DEAN, J. S., AND SHAPIRO, D. G. RUBRIC: a system for rule-based information retrieval. *IEEE Transactions on Software Engineering SE-11*, 9 (1985), 939–945.

[13] PEARL, J. *Probabilistic Reasoning in Intelligent Systems: Networks of Plausible Inference.* Morgan Kaufmann Publishers, 1988.

[14] ROBERTSON, S. E., VAN RIJSBERGEN, C. J., AND PARKER, M. F. Probabilistic models of indexing and searching. In *Information Retrieval Research*, R. N. Oddy, S. E. Robertson, C. J. van Rijsbergen, and P. N. Williams, Eds., London: Butterworth, 1981.

[15] SHACHTER, R. D. Intelligent probabilistic inference. In *Uncertainty in Artificial Intelligence*, L. Kanal and J. Lemmer, Eds., Amsterdam: North-Holland, 1986.

[16] TONG, R. M., APPELBAUM, L. A., AND ASKMAN, V. N. A knowledge representation for conceptual information retrieval. *Int. J. Intelligent Systems 4*, 3 (1989), 259–284.

[17] TONG, R. M., AND SHAPIRO, D. G. Experimental investigations of uncertainty in a rule-based system for information retrieval. *Int. J. Man-Machine Studies 22* (1985), 265–282.

A NEW METHOD FOR INFORMATION RETRIEVAL, BASED ON THE THEORY OF RELATIVE CONCENTRATION

by

L. EGGHE

LUC, Universitaire Campus, B-3610 Diepenbeek, Belgium [°] and
UIA, Universiteitsplein 1, B-2610 Wilrijk, Belgium

ABSTRACT

This paper introduces a new method for information retrieval of documents that are represented by a vector. The novelty of the algorithm lies in the fact that no (generalized) p-norms are used as a matching function between the query and the document (as is done e.g. by Salton and others) but a function that measures the relative dispersion of the terms between a document and a query. This function originates from an earlier paper of the author where a good measure of relative concentration was introduced, used in informetrics to measure the degree of specialization of a journal w.r.t. the entire subject.

This new information retrieval algorithm is shown to have many desirable properties (in the sense of the new Cater-Kraft wish list) including those of the original cosine-matching function of Salton. In addition the property of the cosine-matching function that, if one only uses weights 0 to 1, one is reduced to Boolean IR, is refined in the sense that one takes into consideration the broadness or specialization of a document and a query. Our new matching function satisfies these additional properties.

[°] Permanent address

Acknowledgement : The author is indebted to Prof. Dr. R. Rousseau for stimulating discussions on this subject and to Prof. Dr. G. Salton for pointing out a few errors in an earlier version of this paper

I. INTRODUCTION

A popular and efficient model for information retrieval is based on the vector space concept for documents as well as queries as discussed e.g. in [9], [10]. In this model one uses the vector space (of documents resp. of queries) not only for the representation of these documents (resp. queries), but also for matching them, i.e. calculating the "similarity" between a document and a query, based on (generalized) , p-norms ($p \in [1,+\infty]$) in an N-dimensional space. These similarities are then used to produce a ranked output of documents, the highest similarity values ranked lowest (hence the corresponding documents appearing earlier in the retrieved list). The information retrievel process is then terminated by introducing a certain threshold value, under which one does not consider the documents with a lower similarity value. Possibly, on the retrieved set, one can repeat the above procedure in order to express new interesting key-words (expressing in fact an AND-relation), in order to limit the output of the search.

I.1. The Vector-space model of Salton

Presenting a bit more detail, the above method can be mathematically illustrated as follows (cf. [9]). Let D be the document space, being a subset of $[0,1]^N$ (the Cartesian product - N times - of the interval $[0,1]$) and where N is the total number of key-words that can be used in the system (e.g. a thesaurus). Hence, N is usually very high. In this setting any document $d \in D$ is represented by a vector

$$d = (d_1, ..., d_N),$$

where $d_i \in [0,1]$, for every $i = 1, ...,N$. Each d_i expresses the weight of the ith key-word in document d. Similarly, let Q be the query space, being again a subset of $[0,1]^N$. In principle, any element of $[0,1]^N$ can be considered as a query and any element of $[0,1]^N$ can be considered as a vector representation of a document. Hence one might as well put $D = Q = [0,1]^N$ which indicates a kind of equivalence between documents and queries.

A simple matching function between a query $q \in Q$ and a document $d \in D$ can be expressed as follows [9], where $q = (q_1, ..., q_N)$ and $d = (d_1, ..., d_N)$

$$\text{Cos}(d,q) = \frac{\sum\limits_{i=1}^{N} q_i d_i}{\sqrt{\sum\limits_{i=1}^{N} q_i^2} \sqrt{\sum\limits_{i=1}^{N} d_i^2}} = \frac{\sum\limits_{i=1}^{N} q_i d_i}{||q||_2 \, ||d||_2} \qquad (1)$$

The name Cos is chosen because formula (1) expresses indeed the cosine of the angle between d and q, considered as N-dimensional vectors.

When $||q||_2 = ||d||_2 = 1$, formula (1) reduces to the simple form :

$$\text{Cos}(d,q) = \sum\limits_{i=1}^{N} q_i d_i \qquad (2)$$

This method of Salton is very good since it has many desirable properties :

I.1.1. There is complete symmetry (equivalence) between a document and a query. This I consider to be an (at least theoretical) advantage. This cannot be said of the generalized Salton-Fox-Wu p-norm similarities as discussed in [10]. Furthermore, as shown by Rousseau [8] many other undesirable properties can be revealed of these p-norm matching functions. For this reason they are not used in the sequel.

I.1.2. Given a query $q = (q_1, ..., q_N)$, Cos (d,q) increases if the document $d = (d_1, ..., d_N)$ ressembles more and more q (culminating in the fact that Cos (q, d=q) = 1, the maximal value of Cos). This is a property that also appears in the new "wish list" of Cater and Kraft [3]. It improves an earlier requirement (cf. [2]) that the matching function should increase (for fixed q) when the weights in d increase.

The latter property is reached via the former by putting $q = (1,1, ...,1)$ in the Cater-Kraft wish. Furthermore, following the Cater-Kraft wish, if a weight $q_i \neq 1$, then the matching function should not increase for document weights d_j increasing from q_i to 1.

It should however be emphasized that the property stated in this subsection I.1.2. is not yet defined in an exact mathematical way. The reason for this is that both q and d are N-dimensional vectors and that there are several ways to define "ressemblance". In this article we will restrict ourselves to the case of $q = (0, ..., 0, q_j, 0, ..., 0)$ (i.e. one $q_j \neq 0$). In this case, the Cater-Kraft wish is that $Cos(d,q)$ increases for $|d_j - q_j|$ decreasing (q_j fixed and d_j variable here). Supposing, as we can, that $||q||_1 = ||q||_2 = 1$ (hence $q_j = 1$) we must show that $Cos(d,q)$ increases for $1 - d_j$ decreasing, hence for d_j increasing.

This is so because $Cos(d,q) = \dfrac{d_j}{||d||_2}$ and if d_j increases

from d_j to $d_j + \Delta$ (Δ such that $d_j < d_j + \Delta \leq 1$), we have, denoting $d' = (d_1, ..., d_{j-1}, d_j + \Delta, d_{j+1}, ..., d_N)$, that

$$\frac{d_j}{||d||_2} \leq \frac{d_j + \Delta}{||d'||_2}$$

as is easily calculated when squaring both sides.

I.1.3. For weights 0 and 1 in q and d, the matching is equivalent to a Boolean OR-relation. Indeed, suppose that in q and d there are k common 1's, then, upon a constant $c > 0$ (only dependent on the number of 1's in q and d), we find $Cos(d,q) = ck$, i.e. expressing the OR-relation between the terms in q.

I.1.4. The other requirements of the wish list of Cater and Kraft ([3], 23-24) are more linked with the successive application of the model (1), in order to reach more intricate queries. As such, the Salton model satisfies all these requirements.

So Salton's vector model is very good. It furthermore uses inproducts (or, as in [10] generalized p-norms), being logical ingredients when working with the vector representation of documents and queries. There is, however, one negative remark that can be made on model (1) : its insensitivity for the degree of broadness (or narrowness) of a query or a document : we will explain this now.

I.1.5. Insensitivity w.r.t. the degree of broadness or narrowness of queries and documents

Consider the following situation (A) : $q = (1,0,...,0)$ and $d = (0, ...,0,1)$. It is clear that Cos $(d,q) = 0$, as any good matching should be : both the document and the query are very specialized (narrow) but on a different key-word. Consider now the following (in practice unrealistic) situation (B) : $q = (1,0,...,0)$ and $d = (0,1,...,1)$. Note that we work here in dimension N, N being the number of key-words in e.g. a thesaurus; so N is very high in practice. Here again Cos $(d,q) = 0$ although document d deals with "everything" (since $d \approx (1,1, ...,1)$ since N is very large). Now it is perfectly logical to require here that the matching value between d and q should be strictly positive. As a more realistic example one could consider (situation (C)) $q = (1,0,...,0)$ and $d = (0,...,0,1,1,1)$. Certainly, if $N \geq 4$, Cos $(d,q) = 0$, yet d is a broader document in (C) than in (A). We would like to require that the matching function between d and q   (in situation (C)) is low (and indeed very close to zero of N is high) but not zero. In the same way one can require in a logical way that the matching function of situation (D) (unrealistic in practice) : $q = (1,...,1,0,...,0)$ (where there are M < N numbers 1) and $d = (0,...,01,...,1)$ (where there are M numbers 0), is not zero. Restating situation (D) in a more realistic way we could require that in the situation (E) : $q = (1,1,1,0,...,0)$ and $d = (0,...,0,1,1,1)$ (where $N \geq 6$), the matching function between d and q is small (very close to zero) but not zero. Note that Cos $(d,q) = 0$ in all the above situations.   In the same way one can notice a kind of "roughness" of Cos for other matching values (which are not zero).

One of the referees of this paper argued that (comparing situations (A) and (B)), in the latter case d contains more wrong terms than in the former case. This is so but in our viewpoint, all indexations must have the same total weight, so both (0,1,...1) and (0,...,0,1) deal with the wrong terms w.r.t. q = (1,0,...0) and from this point of view both (0,1,...,1) and (0,...,0,1) are equally wrong w.r.t. q (i.e. we work with relative weights).

But then we can make the remark that, in a fine-tuned ranked output, we would like to see (0,1,...,1) to have a smaller rank than (0,...,0,1) w.r.t. the query q since the former deals with a much broader subject than the latter, allthough, admitted, both must rank very high.

In fact, throughout the paper we will work with documents d and queries q with a total term weight of one (see II.1). So instead of (0,1,...,1) we work with

$$(\ 0, \frac{1}{N-1}, ..., \frac{1}{N-1} \ ) \qquad (N = \text{length of the vector}).$$

At least from a theoretical point of view (but not only from this view) one can wonder if there exist matching models (between documents and queries) that give more different values for different situations d and q. This is indeed the case as will be demonstrated in section II. To reach this goal we still use the vector representation for documents and queries : $d = (d_1, ..., d_N)$, $q = (q_1, ..., q_N)$, but (surprisingly) do not use any functions from vector analysis. Instead we use a modification of a measure that I introduced in [4], improving an older measure of Pratt [7]. All these measures have their roots in informetrics and econometrics, and this makes the application in information retrieval even more intriguing.

We will first repeat the necessary functions from [4] in the next subsection.

I.2. The measure of relative concentration [4]

Concentration measures are well-known and go back to the index of Gini [6] in econometrics; see also [1] and [5], to give just two references (the latter in the connection with informetrics). They all have the purpose of expressing the inequality occurring in a sequence of positive numbers

$$x_1, ..., x_N$$

(yielding e.g. zero in case all x_i are equal and one in case $x_1 = 1, x_2 = ... = x_N = 0$).

If one has two situations :

(I) $x_1, ..., x_N$

(II) $y_1, ..., y_N$

one can wonder "how much concentrated is situation (I) with respect to (or in comparison with) situation (II)" ? In [7], Pratt gave a first attempt to solve this problem, yielding however a measure that had several drawbacks. Based on Pratt's measure of relative concentration, we constructed a refined model which does not have any of the drawbacks of Pratt's measure. The definition is as follows :

I.2.1. Egghe's measure of relative concentration

Denote by π_N the set of all permutations from $\{1,...,N\}$ into itself, i.e. the set of all bijections

$$\varphi : \{1,...,N\} \rightarrow \{1,...,N\}.$$

Let $(x_i)_{i=1,...,N}$ and $(y_i)_{i=1,...,N}$ be two situations to be compared.

Upon normalization we may suppose that :

$$\sum_{i=1}^{N} x_i = \sum_{i=1}^{N} y_i = 1$$

Then the measure of relative concentration of Egghe can be defined as follows :

$$C_r = \frac{\max_{\varphi \in \pi_N} \sum_{i=1}^{N} \varphi(i)(x_i - y_i)}{N-1}, \tag{3}$$

475

where max denotes the maximum over all permutations $\varphi \in \pi_N$.
$\varphi \in \pi_N$

In [4] the following properties (also needed in the sequel) are proved :

(i) C_r yields the same value for two indistinguishable situations. Two situations $((x_i)_{i=1,\ldots,N} , (y_i)_{i=1,\ldots,N})$ and $((x'_i)_{i=1,\ldots,N} , (y'_i)_{i=1,\ldots,N})$ are called indistinguishable if there exists a $\psi \in \pi_N$ such that $x_i = x'_{\psi(i)}$ and $y_i = y'_{\psi(i)}$ for every $i = 1,\ldots,N$.

(ii) $0 \leq C_r \leq 1$ in all situations.

(iii) C_r is extreme (0 resp. 1) for the extreme situations :

   (A) In case $(x_1,\ldots,x_N) = (y_1,\ldots,y_N)$, then $C_r = 0$.

   (B) In case $(x_1,\ldots,x_N) = (0,\ldots,0,1,0,\ldots,0)$ (1 on the ith coordinate) and $(y_1,\ldots,y_N) = (0,\ldots,0,1,0,\ldots,0)$ (1 on the jth coordinate) and if $i \neq j$, then $C_r = 1$.

In the next section we will modify C_r a bit in order to become a measure of relative term dispersion. Furthermore, interpretations of properties (i), (ii) and (iii) in information retrieval (IR) will be given. Additional properties, important for IR will be proved. Finally examples will be given.

II. INFORMATION RETRIEVAL USING A MEASURE OF RELATIVE TERM DISPERSION

We continue with the representation of documents and queries in terms of vectors in $[0,1]^N$. We furthermore assume that for any document

$$d = (d_1,\ldots,d_N) : \sum_{i=1}^{N} d_i = 1$$

and the same for any query

$$q = (q_1,\ldots,q_N) : \sum_{i=1}^{N} q_i = 1.$$

This can always be obtained by normalization. This requirement is necessary in order to compare matching values : we want all our documents and queries to have the same "total weight" (being one). It is clear from property (iii) above that C_r itself cannot be used as a matching function in IR : Case (iii) (A) could be interpreted as a document d and a query q such that $q = d$ and hence we would require 1 to be the matching value. In the same way we would expect the value 0 in the case of (iii) (B). So we define :

II.1. Measure of relative term dispersion

Let $q = (q_1,...,q_N) \in [0,1]^N$ and $d = (d_1,...,d_N) \in [0,1]^N$ be any query and any document (respectively) such that

$$\sum_{i=1}^{N} q_i = \sum_{i=1}^{N} d_i = 1.$$

Then the measure of relative term dispersion is defined as :

$$D_r (d,q) = D_r = 1 - \frac{\max\limits_{\varphi \in \pi_N} \sum\limits_{i=1}^{N} \varphi (i) (d_i - q_i)}{N-1} \tag{4}$$

We will now show several good properties from the point of IR and, further on, calculate some examples (showing that D_r is a measure that is easily calculated).

II.2. IR- properties of D_r

We start with the properties derived from C_r, as described in subsection I.2.1.

II.2.1. D_r is independent of the order of the key-words in the thesaurus. This is essential in IR and follows from (4) and (i) in subsection I.2.1.

II.2.2. $0 \leq D_r \leq 1$ in all situations. This follows from (4) and (ii) in subsection I.2.1. This yields a good scale of measurement and comparison (in view of the rankings of documents).

II.2.3. D_r is extreme for the extreme situations :

(A) In case $q = (q_1,...,q_N) = d = (d_1,...,d_N)$ we have that $D_r (d,q) = 1$

(B) In case $q = (0,...,0,1,0,...,0)$ (1 on the ith coordinate) and $d = (0,...,0,1,0,...,0)$ (1 on the jth coordinate) where $i \neq j$, then $D_r = 0$.
This means that if d and q are "as different as possible", D_r must be zero. "As different as possible" means : both d and q are extremely narrow in topic (only one key-word has a value different from zero) and deal with a different key-word.

These properties, thus coming from the theory of concentration, are good IR-properties. We note that also Cos satisfies these requirements. It will be a refinement of property II.2.3 (B) that will be a drawback of Cos (see further). We now check the "natural" IR-properties as described in subsections I.1.1. through I.1.4.

II.2.4. (cf. I.1.1.) : We show that for any d and q :

$$D_r (d,q) = D_r (q,d) \tag{5}$$

showing the complete symmetry (equivalence) between a document and a query.

<u>Proof</u> : Let $\psi \in \pi_N$ be such that

$$D_r(d,q) = \frac{\sum\limits_{i=1}^{N} \psi(i) (d_i - q_i)}{N-1}$$

Let $\psi' \in \pi_N$ be such that

$$\psi'(i) = N - \psi(i) + 1$$

for every $i = 1,...,N$.   Then

$$\sum_{i=1}^{N} \psi(i)(d_i - q_i) = \sum_{i=1}^{N} \psi'(i)(q_i - d_i)$$

This shows that

$$D_r(q,d) \geq D_r(d,q)$$

An analogous reasoning yields

$$D_r(q,d) \leq D_r(d,q)$$

Hence (5).

This property hence gives us the complete equivalence between documents   and queries. We could (if we wished) forget about the difference and concentrate   only on the matching between two documents or between two queries. This, however, yields the same theory with the same degree of complexity. So, for the sake of clarity, we continue to compare documents d with queries q.

II.2.5. (cf. I.1.2.) : Given a query $q = (q_1,...,q_N)$, D_r (d,q) increases if the document $d = (d_1,...,d_N)$ ressembles more and more q. Stated in this general way, this is clear for D_r, culminating in D_r (q,q) = 1. Using the more exact mathematical definition (as given in I.1.2. and proved for Cos) we can also show here :

Proposition :

Given $q = (0,...,0,q_j,0,...,0)$ with $q_j \neq 0$, we have that D_r (d,q) increases for $|d_j - q_j|$ decreasing (q_j fixed and d_j variable here).

Proof :

Since we assumed $\sum_{i=1}^{N} q_i = \sum_{i=1}^{N} d_i = 1$, we have that $q_j = 1$ and that d_j

can vary modulo the constraint $\sum_{i=1}^{N} d_i = 1$

In this case we have (supposing $(d_1,..., d_N)$ increasing, which is not a limitation) :

$$D_r (d,q) = 1 - \frac{1}{N-1} [(d_j-1) + \sum_{i=1}^{j-1} (i+1) d_i + \sum_{i=j+1}^{N} i d_i]$$

Hence D_r (d,q) increases if

$$d_j - 1 + \sum_{i=1}^{j-1} (i+1) d_i + \sum_{i=j+1}^{N} i d_i \qquad (6)$$

decreases for decreasing $|d_j - q_j| = 1 - d_j$, hence for increasing d_j. At first glance (6) implies the contrary but this is not so : if d_j increases then since

$\sum_{i=1}^{N} d_i = 1$, the same amount is subtracted from some or all of the d_i ($i \neq j$).

This forces (6) to decrease, concluding the proof.

II.2.6. (cf. I.1.4.) : The remarks made in I.1.4. are also valid for our model.

II.2.7. (cf. I.1.3. and I.1.5.).

In this subsection we discuss the properties I.1.3. and I.1.5. in a combined way since they are linked. It is not at all surprising that Saltons Cos-matching function is relatively insensitive w.r.t. the examples given in I.1.5. Indeed, properties I.1.3. and I.1.5. are contradictory as is easily seen (e.g. all five examples in I.1.5. must yield a matching value of zero if I.1.3. is valid). So, since Cos satisfies I.1.3. it must lack the sensitivity described in I.1.5. Conversely, if we want a matching function with certain sensibility properties as in I.1.5., then property I.1.3. cannot be satisfied.

There is however a way out of this dichotomy : if we can show that in the cases encountered in practice, I.1.3. is approximately valid, while the sensitivity of I.1.5. is also ensured, then we can say that the problem is solved. This can be done for our matching function D_r.

A. Suppose $q = d = (\underset{i}{\underbrace{1,\ldots,1}}, 0,\ldots,0)$, where there are i numbers $\underset{i}{1}$.

Then, as follows from II.2.3 (A) , $D_r(d,q) = 1 = i\,\dfrac{1}{i}$

This expresses that, in case q and d contain the same key-words with equal weight (as is always so in Boolean IR), then D_r expresses an OR-relation between these terms. In this case, I.1.3. is perfectly satisfied.

B. Also, in the case that $q = (1,0,\ldots,0)$ and $d = (0,\ldots,0,1)$ we have that $D_r(d,q) = 0$ as follows from II.2.3 (B) and this is also in accordance with I.1.3.

C. Now I.1.3. requires that in all cases (classical Boolean cases with only the zero weight and equal non-zero weights, such that the total weight is 1, as assumed) :

$$d = (\underbrace{\frac{1}{M},\ldots,\frac{1}{M}}_{M},0,\ldots,0)$$

and

$$q = (0,\ldots,0, \underbrace{\frac{1}{N\text{-}M'},\ldots,\frac{1}{N\text{-}M'}}_{N\text{-}M'}),$$

where $M \leq M'$, that

$$D_r(d,q) = 0,$$

(as is the case for Cos) insensitive to the broadness of d and q (as expressed by the values of M and M' in $\{1,\ldots,N\}$).

This is not very reasonable. What one should have is that for any fixed $M < M'$, $D_r(d,q) > 0$ but $\lim\limits_{\substack{M' \to N\text{-}1 \\ N \to \infty}} D_r(d,q) = 0$.

Indeed, M resp. N-M' represent the number of key-words in d resp. q and N the total number of key-words (e.g. in a thesaurus). So indeed, in practice, $M' \approx N \approx N\text{-}1$ and N is very high. This is proved now.

Proposition :

Let d and q be as above, for $M < M'$, $M, M' \in \{1,\ldots,N\}$. Then $D_r(d,q) > 0$ and

$$\lim\limits_{M' \to N\text{-}1} D_r(d,q) = \frac{M}{N\text{-}1} \tag{7}$$

and hence, for any fixed $M < M'$:

$$\lim\limits_{\substack{M' \to N\text{-}1 \\ N \to \infty}} D_r(d,q) = 0 \tag{8}$$

Proof : If

$$d = (\underbrace{\frac{1}{M}, \dots, \frac{1}{M}}, 0, \dots, 0)$$

and

$$q = (0, \dots, 0, \underbrace{\frac{1}{N-M'}, \dots, \frac{1}{N-M'}})$$

as above, such that $M \le M'$, then

$$D_r(d,q) = D_r(q,d) = 1 - \frac{1}{N-1} \left[-\frac{\sum\limits_{i=1}^{M} i}{M} + \frac{(M'+1) + \dots + N}{N-M'} \right]$$

$$= 1 - \frac{1}{2} \frac{N^2 - NM - M'^2 + M'M}{N^2 - NM' - N + M'} > 0$$

Keeping M constant this gives

$$\lim_{M' \to N-1} D_r(d,q) = \frac{M}{N-1}$$

From (7), (8) follows immediately.

The results shown in this subsection II.2.7. show that for general Boolean queries q and documents d, occurring in practice,

$D_r(d,q) \approx$ the number of common key-words in q and d,

so that the requirement I.1.3. is valid (approximately) in practice.

This finishes our theoretic IR-study of the matching·function D_r. In conclusion we can say that this method of IR via the relative term dispersion measure is a good alternative to Salton's cosine function, and that the former is more sensitive than the latter. Especially from theoretical point of view, the link between IR and the theory of relative concentration [4] is remarkable.

In subsection II.2.3. we proved (based on [4]) that D_r is extreme for the extreme situations. We can also show the converse that D_r is extreme only in the extreme cases :

Proposition :

If $D_r (d,q) = 0$, then, up to a common permutation for d and q, $d = (0,...,0,1)$ and $q = (1,0,...,0)$.

Proof :

If :

$$D_r (d,q) = 1 - \frac{1}{N-1} \max_{\varphi \in \pi_N} \sum_{i=1}^{N} \varphi (i) (d_i - q_i) = 0$$

then :

$$\max_{\varphi \in \pi_N} \sum_{i=1}^{N} \varphi (i) (d_i - q_i) = N - 1 \qquad (9)$$

Rearrange $(d_i - q_i)_{i=1,...,N}$ such that it is an increasing sequence.

Then it follows from (9) that

$$\sum_{i=1}^{N} i (d_i - q_i) = N - 1 \qquad (10)$$

(10) implies that $d \neq q$ and hence that $d_1 - q_1 < 0$ (since

$$\sum_{i=1}^{N} d_i = \sum_{i=1}^{N} q_i = 1 \quad \text{and since} \quad (d_i - q_i)_{i=1,...,N} \quad \text{increases}).$$

Further, $d_2 - q_2 < 0$, $d_3 - q_3 < 0$, ... would imply that

$\sum_{i=1}^{N} i (d_i - q_i)$ is strictly smaller than in the case the total of the negative weights in

$(d_i - q_i)_{i=1,...,N}$ is located in $d_1 - q_1$.

In the same way, $d_N - q_N > 0$. Further $d_{N-1} - q_{N-1} > 0$, $d_{N-2} - q_{N-2} > 0$, ...

would imply that $\sum_{i=1}^{N} i (d_i - q_i)$ is strictly smaller than in the case the total

of the positive weights in $(d_i - q_i)_{i=1,...,N}$ is located in $d_N - q_N$.

Furthermore, the situation $(d_1 - q_1 < 0, 0, ..., 0, d_N - q_N > 0)$ gives the

highest value $N - 1$ for $\sum_{i=1}^{N} i (d_i - q_i)$ if $d_1 - q_1 = -1$ and $d_N - q_N = 1$

(cf. subsection I.2.1. (iii)) and any enlargement of $d_1 - q_1$ above -1 gives a lower

value for $\sum_{i=1}^{N} i (d_i - q_i)$, since $\sum_{i=1}^{N} i (d_i - q_i) = N (d_N - q_N) - (d_1 - q_1)$

and since $\sum_{i=1}^{N} d_i = \sum_{i=1}^{N} q_i$. This proves the proposition.

Corollary II.3.2. :

$\quad D_r (d,q) = 0$ implies $Cos (d,q) = 0$

Proof :

This follows readily from the above proposition.

In the examples in the next section we will see that the converse of corollary II.3.2. is not true. This is again an illustration of the fact that Cos is a bit rougher IR-method than D_r.

<u>Proposition II.3.3.</u> : If D_r (d,q) = 1, then $d = q$.

<u>Proof</u> :

D_r (d,q) = 1 implies that

$$\sum_{i=1}^{N} \varphi(i) \, (d_i - q_i) = 0,$$

for every $\varphi \in \pi_N$. If not all $d_i - q_i = 0$, then $I_1 \neq \emptyset$ and $I_2 \neq \emptyset$ where

$$I_1 = \{ i \in \{1,...,N\} \mid\mid d_i - q_i < 0 \}$$
$$I_2 = \{ i \in \{1,...,N\} \mid\mid d_i - q_i > 0 \}$$

Define $\psi \in \pi_N$ as follows (this definition allows some freedom in the choice of ψ; any choice within these limits will do) :

$$\psi : \quad I_1 \rightarrow \{1,..., \# \, I_1\}$$
$$I_2 \rightarrow \{N - (\# \, I_2 - 1),..., N-1, N\}$$
$$\{1,...,N\} \setminus (I_1 \cup I_2) \rightarrow \text{the remaining values in } \{1,...,N\}$$

(# denotes the number of elements in the set).

Then :

$$\sum_{i=1}^{N} \psi(i) \, (d_i - q_i) > 0$$

Indeed :

$$\sum_{i=1}^{N} \psi(i) \, (d_i - q_i)$$

486

$$= \sum_{i \in I_2} \psi\,(i)\,(d_i - q_i) + \sum_{i \in I_1} \psi\,(i)\,(d_i - q_i)$$

$$\geq (N - (\# I_2 - 1)) \sum_{i \in I_2} (d_i - q_i) + (\# I_1) \sum_{i \in I_1} (d_i - q_i)$$

But $\displaystyle\sum_{i=1}^{N} (d_i - q_i) = 0;$ hence

$$\sum_{i \in I_1} (d_i - q_i) = - \sum_{i \in I_2} (d_i - q_i)$$

So

$$\sum_{i=1}^{N} \psi\,(i)\,(d_i - q_i) \geq \sum_{i \in I_2} (d_i - q_i)\,[N - (\# I_2 - 1) - \# I_1] > 0,$$

a contradiction.   Consequently, all $d_i = q_i$ and hence $d = q$.

Corollary II.3.4. :

$D_r\,(d,q) = 1$ if and only if Cos $(d,q) = 1$

Proof :   **Only if**

This follows from the above proposition.

If

It is well known (and easy to prove) that Cos $(d,q) = 1$ together with

$\displaystyle\sum_{i=1}^{N} d_i = \sum_{i=1}^{N} q_i\ (=1)$ implies $d = q$.   Hence the proof follows from II.2.3 (A).

III. **EXAMPLES**

The above theoretical considerations show that D_r is easily calculated. The next practical examples show this once more. We also calculate Salton's Cos matching function and compare the ranked output of documents.

III.1. <u>Example 1</u>

$$D = \{ d_1, d_2, d_3, d_4, d_5, d_6, d_7, d_8, d_9, d_{10}, \},$$

where :

$$d_1 = (0.9, 0.1, 0, 0, 0)$$
$$d_2 = (0, 0.9, 0.1, 0, 0)$$
$$d_3 = (0, 0, 0.9, 0.1, 0)$$
$$d_4 = (0, 0, 0, 0.9, 0.1)$$
$$d_5 = (0.7, 0.2, 0.1, 0, 0)$$
$$d_6 = (0, 0.7, 0.2, 0.1, 0)$$
$$d_7 = (0, 0, 0.7, 0.2, 0.1)$$
$$d_8 = (0.4, 0.3, 0.2, 0.1, 0)$$
$$d_9 = (0, 0.4, 0.3, 0.2, 0.1)$$
$$d_{10} = (0.2, 0.2, 0.2, 0.2, 0.2)$$

and

$$q = (0.7, 0.3, 0, 0, 0)$$

We have the following results (example of calculation   :

$$D_r (d_4, q) = 1 - \frac{1}{4} (-0.7 - 2 \times 0.3 + 3 \times 0 + 4 \times 0.1 + 5 \times 0.9) = 0.1).$$

i	$D_r(d_i,q)$	$\cos(d_i,q)$
1	0.8	0.956
2	0.325	0.391
3	0.1	0
4	0.1	0
5	0.9	0.982
6	0.4	0.375
7	0.175	0
8	0.725	0.886
9	0.475	0.287
10	0.625	0.587

This yields the ranked output.

via D_r	Via Cos
d_5	d_5
d_1	d_1
d_8	d_8
d_{10}	d_{10}
d_9	d_2
d_6	d_6
d_2	d_9
d_7	d_3, d_4, d_7
d_3, d_4	

Both methods yield good IR-rankings, but they are not the same. Note that our method does not place documents d_3, d_4 and d_7 on the same (last) rank : d_7 is preferred (although ranked low). The reason for this is : all three documents give weights to the "wrong" key-words, but d_7 deals with a broader topic than d_3 and d_4 and hence is less specified in these wrong (i.e. not requested) key-words.

We keep D in the above example but give q' = (0,0.6,0.2,0.2,0). We now find :

i	$D_r (d_i,q')$	$\cos (d_i,q')$
1	0.25	0.100
2	0.725	0.932
3	0.325	0.333
4	0.275	0.300
5	0.4	0.287
6	0.9	0.985
7	0.425	0.369
8	0.625	0.661
9	0.825	0.936
10	0.65	0.675

This yields the ranked output.

via D_r	Via Cos
d_6	d_6
d_9	d_9
d_2	d_2
d_{10}	d_{10}
d_8	d_8
d_7	d_7
d_5	d_3
d_3	d_4
d_4	d_5
d_1	d_1

III.3. Example 3

We keep D in the above example but give $q'' = (0,1,0,0,0)$ a simple Boolean query. Now we find :

i	$D_r (d_i, q'')$	Cos (d_i, q'')
1	0.1	0.110
2	0.9	0.993
3	0.025	0
4	0.025	0
5	0.225	0.272
6	0.625	0.952
7	0.1	0
8	0.4	0.547
9	0.5	0.730
10	0.5	0.447

This yields the ranked output.

via D_r	Via Cos
d_2	d_2
d_6	d_6
d_9, d_{10}	d_9
d_8	d_8
d_5	d_{10}
d_1 , d_7	d_5
d_3 , d_4	d_1
	d_3 , d_4, d_7

Note that both retrieval methods perform alike (but, even in this Boolean case, not the same). Note also that $D_r(d,q) < Cos(d,q)$ as well as $D_r(d,q) > Cos(d,q)$ can occur. Finally one can see that $Cos(d,q) = 0$ does not imply $D_r(d,q) = 0$.

Documents d_1 and d_7 are ranked equal in our method, but their (low) matching value (0.1) is calculated differently : d_1 has only weight 0.1 for the requested key-word and is rather specific since d_1 contains only two key-words with non-zero weights. Document d_7 does not contain the requested key-word but deals with a broader topic (3 key-words with non-zero weights).

Documents d_3 and d_4 are ranked lowest (as is the case in both procedures) : they both have non-zero weights on not-requested key-words. But, contrary to Salton's method, their matching value is not zero (although very small : 0.025) since they deal with two key-words and hence are broader than a document such as $d = (0,0,0,0,1)$: here we find $D_r(d,q") = 0$.

REFERENCES

[1]   Allison, P.D., Measures of inequality.
American Sociological Review, 43, 865-880, 1978.

[2]   Buell, D.A. and Kraft, D.H., A model for a weighted retrieval system.
Journal of the American Society for Information Science, 32, 211-216,
1981.

[3]   Cater, S.C. and Kraft, D.H., A generalization and clarification of the Waller-
Kraft wish list.
Information Processing and Management, 25, 15-25, 1989.

[4]   Egghe, L., The relative concentration of a journal with respect to a subject
and the use of online services in calculating it .
Journal of the American Society for Information Science, 39, 281-284,
1988.

[5]   Egghe, L. and Rousseau, R., Elements of concentration theory.
Informetrics 89/90. Proceedings of the 2nd international Conference on
Bibliometrics, Scientometrics and Informetrics, London (Canada), L. Egghe
and R. Rousseau (eds.), Elsevier, Amsterdam, 1990 (to appear).

[6]   Gini, C., Il diverso accrescimento delle classi sociali e la concentrazione
della ricchezza.
Giornale degli Economisti, serie 11, 37, 1909.

[7]   Pratt, A.D., A measure of class concentration.
Journal of the American Society of Information Science, 28, 285-292, 1977.

[8]   Rousseau, R., Extended Boolean retrieval : a heuristic approach ?
Proceedings of the 13th international conference on research and
development in information retrieval, Brussels (Belgium), to appear, 1990.

[9]   Salton, G., Automatic information organisation and retrieval.
Mc Graw-Hill, New York, 1968.

[10] Salton,G., Fow, E.A. and Wu, H., Extended Boolean information retrieval.
Communications of the Association for Computing Machinery, 26, 1022-
1036, 1983.

Extended Boolean Retrieval: a Heuristic Approach ?

Ronald Rousseau

Speciale Licentie Documentatie- en Bibliotheekwetenschap
UIA, Universiteitsplein 1, B-2610 Wilrijk, Belgium

and

Katholieke Industriële Hogeschool West-Vlaanderen
Zeedijk 101, B-8400 Oostende, Belgium

Abstract

We show that the similarity measures for p-norm retrieval, as defined by Salton, Fox and Wu have some undesirable mathematical properties. We propose a new function that remedies some of these drawbacks. Still, even for this new similarity measure the extended Boolean model has some properties which can only be described as 'heuristic'.

1 Introduction

The predominant approach of currently operating information retrieval systems is based on Boolean logic. The assumptions underlying Boolean retrieval systems and practical elaborations have, however, been severely criticized (see e.g. [BOOK 82], [COOP 83], [ROUS 86]). It goes without saying that no one expects actual systems to be an exact expression of the ideal inspiring their construction, but, as Bookstein [BOOK 82] puts it: 'It has been suggested that in this case, the ideal diverges so far from reality that restricting ourselves to Boolean systems has become a very serious impediment to providing adequate service'. (See also [MARO 82].)

One possible solution consists in giving up the Boolean logic entirely and using Salton's vector model [SALT 83c]. In this case, both the stored records (representing documents) and the information requests are treated as vectors in some higher dimensional space, say $\mathbf{R}^n$. In the vector processing system, both the document and the query terms can be weighted in accordance with the presumed importance of the terms, and a similarity computation makes it possible to obtain a ranked output.

In an attempt to retain as much as possible of the essential features of classical Boolean retrieval while making it more flexible, the use of fuzzy set theory has been proposed (see e.g. [TAHA 76], [BOOK 80], [BUEL 81], [BOOK 82], [BUEL 82],

[BOOK 85], [ROUS 85]). Yet a lot of the criticisms raised against Boolean models is also valid for models based on fuzzy set theory [ROBE 78], [BOOK 82]. In essence, one may say that the fuzzy set approach shares the assumptions of conventional Boolean retrieval, simply generalising them to present a ranked output.

Finally, also the probabilistic retrieval approach rejects the Boolean framework. In this model the system is able to compute the probability that a document is relevant for a user, based on the presence or absence of potential clues assigned to a document (see e.g. [ROBE 76],[ROBE 77],[BOOK 82], [BOOK 85]). It was however pointed out by Salton [SALT 88] that there is little chance that the probabilistic approach will outperform the vector processing method as long as the term independence and binary indexing restrictions are maintained. On the other hand, more sophisticated probabilistic models generally need much more data to function, entailing practical problems concerning computer storage and retrieval times. Recent methods in this field seem however, to be able to overcome these problems [FUHR 89].

In 1983, Salton, Fox and Wu [SALT 83b] introduced a new, extended Boolean retrieval model, which is intermediate between the fuzzy model and the vector processing model. The query structure inherent in the Boolean approach is preserved (i.e. the use of the logical connectors AND, OR and NOT), while at the same time weighted terms may be incorporated into both queries and stored documents. The retrieval output can be ranked in strict similarity order with the user's query.

Tests [SALT 83b],[FOXE 86] have shown that the extended system produces better retrieval output than the Boolean or the fuzzy retrieval methods while its greater flexibility puts it at an advantage in respect to vector processing methods. It has further been shown [SALT 83a] that it is possible to automatically generate p-norm queries.

A more detailed description of the p-norm retrieval method follows in the next section.

2 The p-norm model

Consider a set of terms $A_1, A_2, \ldots, A_n$ and let d_i, $0 \le d_i \le 1$, represent the weight of term A_i in some document D. Then this document can be represented by a vector in $I^n = [0,1] \times \ldots \times [0,1]$. Hence $D = (d_1, d_2, \ldots, d_n) \in I^n \subset \mathbf{R}^n$. Also a query vector Q is denoted by a (non-zero) vector in I^n : $Q = (q_1, q_2, \ldots, q_n)$, where q_i, $0 \le q_i \le 1$, denotes the weight of term A_i in the query. A generalized Boolean OR-query, Q_{or}, can now be written as

$$Q_{or(p)} = [(A_1, q_1) \, or^{\,p} (A_2, q_2) \, or^{\,p} \ldots or^{\,p} (A_n, q_n)],$$

where $1 \le p \le +\infty$.

Similarly, a generalized AND-query, Q_{and}, is written as:

$$Q_{and(p)} = [(A_1, q_1) \, and^{p} (A_2, q_2) \, and^{p} \ldots and^{p} (A_n, q_n)].$$

The OR- and AND-similarities (to be used as retrieval status values) between a document D and a query Q are defined as:

$$sim(D, Q_{or(p)}) = (\frac{\sum_{i=1}^{n} q_i^p d_i^p}{\sum_{i=1}^{n} q_i^p})^{1/p} \tag{1}$$

and

$$sim(D, Q_{and(p)}) = 1 - (\frac{\sum_{i=1}^{n} q_i^p (1 - d_i)^p}{\sum_{i=1}^{n} q_i^p})^{1/p} \tag{2}$$

Formulae (1) and (2) can be rewritten as follows:

$$sim(D, Q_{or(p)}) = \frac{\| QD \|_p}{\| Q \|_p} \tag{3}$$

and

$$sim(D, Q_{and(p)}) = 1 - \frac{\| Q(1 - D) \|_p}{\| Q \|_p} \tag{4}$$

where QD and Q(1-D) are the vectors obtained as the result of coordinatewise multiplication of Q and D (resp. Q and 1-D, where 1 denotes the vector with all coordinates equal to 1) and the p-norm of a vector $X = (x_i)_i$ is defined as

$$\| X \|_p = (\sum_{i=1}^{n} x_i^p)^{1/p} (\text{for} p < +\infty) \text{and} \| X \|_\infty = \max_i (x_i). \tag{5}$$

From formulae (1) and (2) (or (3) and (4)) we immediately see that

$$0 \leq sim(D, Q_{and(p)}) \leq sim(D, Q_{or(p)}) \leq 1.$$

Problem 1 *Given two different document vectors D and E in I^n, do there exist queries Q_1 and Q_2 and a number $p \in [1, +\infty]$ such that*

$$sim(D, Q_{1,or(p)}) < sim(E, Q_{1,or(p)})$$
$$\text{and} sim(D, Q_{2,or(p)}) > sim(E, Q_{2,or(p)}) ?$$

We also consider the analogous problem for AND-clauses.

The answer to this problem is easy. If there exists a pair (i,j) such that $d_i < e_i$ and $d_j > e_j$, then we consider Q_1 such that $(Q_1)_k = \delta_{ik}$ (Kronecker delta: $\delta_{ik} = 1$ if i=k and $\delta_{ik} = 0$ if $i \neq k$) and Q_2 such that $(Q_2)_k = \delta_{jk}$. Then

$$sim(D, Q_{1,or(p)}) = d_i < sim(E, Q_{1,or(p)}) = e_i,$$

for every p, and

$$sim(D, Q_{2,or(p)}) = d_j > sim(E, Q_{2,or(p)}) = e_j,$$

for every p. Furthermore, in the case of AND-clauses:

$$sim(D, Q_{1,and(p)}) = 1 - (1 - d_i) = d_i < sim(E, Q_{1,and(p)}) = e_i$$

for every p, and

$$sim(D, Q_{2,and(p)}) = 1 - (1 - d_j) = d_j > sim(E, Q_{2,and(p)}) = e_j,$$

for every p. If, for every i: $d_i \leq e_i$, then by the monotonicity of power functions:

$$\forall Q, p : sim(D, Q_{or(p)}) \leq sim(E, Q_{or(p)})$$

and

$$\forall Q, p : sim(D, Q_{and(p)}) \leq sim(E, Q_{and(p)}).$$

In this case document E is never ranked after document D.

Next we will consider a more delicate problem.

Problem 2 *Given two different document vectors D and E in I^n, and a query vector $Q \in I^n$, do there exist numbers p and $s \in [1, +\infty]$ such that*

$$sim(D, Q_{or(p)}) < sim(E, Q_{or(p)})$$

and

$$sim(D, Q_{or(s)}) > sim(E, Q_{or(s)}).$$

In other words: is it possible to alter the ordering of retrieved documents, only by changing the p-value? We will also consider the analogous problem for AND-clauses.

Before trying to solve this problem, we will give some examples, showing that the answer to Problem 2 can be both positive and negative, depending on the vectors D, E and Q.

Examples

1. A case where the answer to Problem 2 (OR-case) is positive. Set $D = (0.4, 0.4)$, $E = (0, 0.45)$ and $Q = (0.5, 0.5)$. Then, for p = 3, we find $sim(D, Q_{or(3)}) = 0.4$ and $sim(E, Q_{or(3)}) = 0.357$, so

$$sim(D, Q_{or(3)}) > sim(E, Q_{or(3)}).$$

On the other hand, for p = 6, we find: $sim(D, Q_{or(6)}) = 0.4$ and $sim(E, Q_{or(6)}) = 0.4009$, so

$$sim(D, Q_{or(6)}) < sim(E, Q_{or(6)}).$$

2. A case where the answer to Problem 2 (OR-case) is trivially negative.
Set $D = (0.9, 0)$, $E = (0.1, 1)$ and $Q = (q_1, q_2)$, where $q_1 \leq q_2$. Then

$$sim(d, Q_{or(p)}) = \frac{(0.9)(q_1)}{\| Q \|_p}$$

Table 1: Similarity values

p	$sim(D, Q_{or(p)})$	$sim(E, Q_{or(p)})$
1.0	0.62250	0.63175
1.5	0.62026	0.63616
1.7	0.61940	0.63779
1.8	0.61898	0.63857
2.0	0.61815	0.64008
3.0	0.61432	0.64642
4.0	0.61104	0.65091
5.0	0.60828	0.65388
6.0	0.60601	0.65570
7.0	0.60415	0.65670
10.0	0.60044	0.65708
20.0	0.59645	0.65365
40.0	0.59519	0.65139
∞	0.59500	0.65100

and

$$sim(E, Q_{or(p)}) = \frac{((0.1)^p q_1^p + q_2^p)^{1/p}}{\| Q \|_p} \geq \frac{q_2}{\| Q \|_p}.$$

Here we have a situation where, for all $p \in [1, +\infty]$:

$$sim(D, Q_{or(p)}) < sim(E, Q_{or(p)}).$$

3. Another case where the answer to Problem 2 (OR-case) is negative.
Set D = (0.49,0.49,0.68,0.85,0.70)
E = (0.55,0.44,0.75,0.93,0.55)
Q = (0.25,0.225,0.2,0.175,0.15)
Then $sim(D, Q_{or(p)}) < sim(E, Q_{or(p)})$, as indicated by Table 1.

We would like to make three observations here. First, concerning Example 1, we note that if for all $i = 1, \ldots, n$, $d_i = d$ (a constant), for all queries Q and all $p \in [1, +\infty]$, $sim(D, Q_{or(p)}) = sim(D, Q_{and(p)}) = d$. This has also been observed in [SALT 83b].

Second, concerning Example 3, we see that the value of $sim(E, Q_{or(p)})$ is not monotone in p, as suggested in [SALT 83b], p.1025, equation(8). Our example even shows that not all similarity values lie between the values for the extreme cases $p = 1$ and $p = +\infty$: in this particular example the similarity value attains a maximal value for $p \approx 10$. We will return to this observation later on.

Finally, the 'anomalous' behaviour of p-norms is well-known among mathematicians and has been described e.g. in [EGGH 88] upon which some of the above examples are modelled.

Next we formulate a generalisation of Problem 2.

Problem 3 *Given two different document vectors D and E (different from 1), a query vector Q, and a positive real number $r \in \mathbf{R}_0^+$, does there exist a number $p \in [1, +\infty]$ such that*

$$F(p) = \frac{sim(D, Q_{or(p)})}{sim(E, Q_{or(p)})} = r.$$

We will also consider the analogous problem for the function

$$G(p) = \frac{sim(D, Q_{and(p)})}{sim(E, Q_{and(p)})}.$$

Problem 3 generalizes the previous problem in the sense that Problem 2 asks for the special cases r_1 and r_2, where $r_1 < 1$ and $r_2 > 1$. We note that

$$F(p) = \frac{\| QD \|_p}{\| QE \|_p} \tag{6}$$

and

$$G(p) = \frac{\| Q \|_p - \| Q(1 - D) \|_p}{\| Q \|_p - \| Q(1 - E) \|_p} \tag{7}$$

The next proposition gives a partial answer to Problem 3, hence also to Problem 2.

Proposition 1 *If $F(1) \leq r \leq F(\infty)$ or $F(\infty) \leq r \leq F(1)$, then the answer to Problem 3 (OR-case) is positive.*

Proof. This follows immediately from the continuity of the function F and the fact that a continuous function attains all intermediate values on a connected set. (This is Bolzano's theorem; for a proof we refer to [DIEU 69], 3.19.8).

Similarly, we can state the following result for AND-clauses.

Proposition 2 *If $G(1) \leq r \leq G(\infty)$ or $G(\infty) \leq r \leq G(1)$, then the answer to Problem 3 (AND-case) is positive.*

Corollary 3 *If $F(1) < 1$ and $F(\infty) > 1$, or, if $F(1) > 1$ and $F(\infty) < 1$, then the answer to Problem 2 (OR-case) is positive. Hence, it is possible to change the ranking of the output by manipulating p.*

Corollary 4 *If $G(1) < 1$ and $G(\infty) > 1$, or, if $G(1) > 1$ and $G(\infty) < 1$, then the answer to Problem 2 (AND-case) is positive.*

In the case where the functions F and/or G are monotone, we have more precise information. For this, we recall the following result of Marshall, Olkin and Proschan.

Proposition 5 *[MARS 67] (see also [MARS 79], p.130). If X and Y are vectors in R^n, if $x_1 \geq x_2 \geq \ldots \geq x_n > 0$, if $y_1 \geq y_2 \geq \ldots \geq y_n > 0$ and if y_i/x_i is decreasing in $i = 1, \ldots, n$, then*

$$h(p) = \frac{\| X \|_p}{\| Y \|_p}, \quad p \in \,]0, +\infty]$$

is decreasing in p.

So, in order to apply Proposition 5, we consider only those coordinates for which $q_i \neq 0$ (this has no influence on the value of the similarity measure) and rearrange the coordinates in such a way that $q_1 d_1 \geq q_2 d_2 \geq \ldots \geq q_n d_n$. If now $q_n d_n \neq 0$ and if the sequence (e_i/d_i) is decreasing, then F(p) is decreasing. Hence, in this case, we know that F(p) does not attain r-values outside the interval $[F(\infty), F(1)]$. In particular, if both $F(\infty)$ and $F(1)$ are greater than 1 (or both are smaller than 1) the ranking of D and E for this OR-query can not be reversed by adapting p. Note that we can also apply Proposition 5 to the function $1/F(p)$.

It is interesting to remark that the proof of Proposition 5 is based on the use of majorisation, a partial order (also called the Lorenz dominance order) which plays an important part in concentration studies in econometrics and informetrics ([MARS 79], [EGGH 89], [EGGH 90]).

An example of the application of the Marshall-Olkin-Proschan proposition for OR-queries.

Set D = (0.75,0.7,0.3), E = (1,0.6,0.25) and Q = (0.6,0.6,1). Then QD = (0.45,0.42,0.3) and $(e_i/d_i)_i$ = (4/3,6/7,5/6); hence $F(p) = \frac{sim(D,Q_{or(p)})}{sim(E,Q_{or(p)})}$ is decreasing. As $F(1) = \frac{1.17}{1.21} = 0.967$ and $F(\infty) = 0.75$, we conclude that for this query Q, D is always ranked after E.

In the case F (or G) are not monotone nothing much can be said in general. Indeed, the next example (Table 2) shows that even in the case of an unweighted query, for dimension three (n = 3) and for $F(1)$ and $F(\infty)$ both larger than one, it is possible that for some values of p, $F(p) < 1$. This shows that the ranking of the documents for this query can be reversed.

It is also possible that the ranking reverses several times, as shown by the example of Table 3. Finally, we show that the Marshall-Olkin-Proschan pro-

position can also be used for the analysis of AND-clauses. Set $\| Q \|_p = a;\, \| Q(1 - D) \|_p = b$ and $\| Q(1 - E) \|_p = c$. Then $a \geq c$ and $G(p) = \frac{a-b}{a-c} = 1 - \frac{(b/c)-1}{(a/c)-1}$. If e.g. b/c is decreasing (in p) and a/c is increasing (hence c/a is decreasing), we see that G(p) is increasing. From Proposition 5 we know that b/c is decreasing if Q(1-D) is ordered decreasingly, $q_n(1 - d_n) \neq 0$ and $((1 - e_i)/(1 - d_i))_i$ decreases. Similarly, c/a is decreasing if Q(1-E) is ordered decreasingly, $q_n(1 - e_n) \neq 0$ and $(1 - e_i)_i$ increases.

An example.

Table 2. An example where F(p) is not monotone: for some values of p, F(p) takes values greater than one and for others it takes values smaller than one. D = (0.8,0.6,0.3), E = (0.75,0.7,0.01), Q = (1,1,1).

p	$sim(D, Q_{or(p)})$	$sim(E, Q_{or(p)})$	$F(p)$
1.0	0.5667	0.4867	1.164
1.2	0.5745	0.5184	1.108
1.5	0.5857	0.5537	1.058
1.7	0.5927	0.5715	1.037
1.8	0.5962	0.5791	1.029
2.0	0.6028	0.5923	1.018
3.0	0.6314	0.6341	0.996
4.0	0.6535	0.6563	0.996
5.0	0.6709	0.6701	1.001
6.0	0.6849	0.6796	1.008
7.0	0.6962	0.6866	1.014
10.0	0.7207	0.6998	1.030
20.0	0.7574	0.7179	1.055
40.0	0.7783	0.7308	1.065
∞	0.8000	0.7500	1.067

Table 3. An example where the mutual order of two documents changes several times (depending on the p-value).
D = (0.99,0.53,0.84,0.54,0.42,0.19,0.40,0.11,0.03,0.02)
E = (0.98,0.80,0.69,0.59,0.30,0.20,0.17,0.16,0.14,0.10)
Q = 1

p	$sim(D, Q_{or(p)})$	$sim(E, Q_{or(p)})$	$F(p)$
1.0	0.4070	0.4130	0.9855
1.2	0.4328	0.4348	0.9953
1.5	0.4669	0.4663	1.0013
1.7	0.4870	0.4861	1.0020
1.8	0.4965	0.4955	1.0019
2.0	0.5142	0.5137	1.0010
3.0	0.5863	0.5882	0.9968
4.0	0.6403	0.6413	0.9983
5.0	0.6825	0.6808	1.0024
6.0	0.7162	0.7116	1.0064
7.0	0.7435	0.7367	1.0093
10.0	0.8007	0.7906	1.0128
20.0	0.8840	0.8742	1.0111
40.0	0.9347	0.9252	1.0102
∞	0.9900	0.9800	1.0102

Set D = (0.8,0.6,0.3), E = (0.65,0.5,0.4) and Q = (1,0.45,0.1). Then

1-D = (0.2,0.4,0.7)

1-E = (0.35,0.5,0.6)

Q(1-D) = (0.2,0.18,0.07)

Q(1-E) = (0.35,0.225,0.06).

Hence, Q(1-D) and Q(1-E) are ordered decreasingly, 1-E is ordered increasingly, and $((1 - e_i)/(1 - d_i))_i$ decreases. So, we conclude that G(p) increases. As $G(1) = \frac{1.55-0.45}{1.55-0.635} = 1.202$ and $G(\infty) = \frac{1-0.2}{1-0.35} = 1.231$, we conclude that for this AND-query Q, D is always ranked before E.

3   Further remarks and problems with p-norm retrieval

As a result of our investigations we note the following problems with the extended Boolean model as proposed by Salton, Fox and Wu.

1. From (1),(2),(3) and (4) we see that for OR-clauses as well as for AND-clauses, documents (D) and queries (Q) do not play a symmetric role.

2. Assume that A_1 and A_2 are perfect synonyms and consider $D_1 = (d, d)$ and $D_2 = (0, d)$. For queries $Q_1 = (1, 1), Q_2 = (1, 0)$ we find: $sim(D_1, Q_{j,or(p)}) = d$, $j = 1, 2$; yet $sim(D_2, Q_{1,or(p)}) = \frac{d}{2^{(1/p)}}$ $(p \neq \infty)$ (but $sim(D_2, Q_{1,or(\infty)}) = d$) and $sim(D_2, Q_{2,or(p)})$ is even 0 for every p. This seems to indicate that, at least for $p \neq \infty$, OR-queries involve some 'AND'-aspects. This observation is also confirmed by [SALT 83b], Table III, where an OR-query for $p = 3$ is interpreted as: 'The presence of several terms from a given class is worth more than the presence of only one term'.

3. We find it difficult to give an intuitive interpretation of the similarity formula for AND-clauses.

4. The functions $sim(D, Q_{and(p)})$ and $sim(D, Q_{or(p)})$ are not monotone in p.

5. The ranking of two documents is influenced by the used p-value (this in itself may or may not be an asset, for changing p may be considered as a method of fine-tuning the retrieval process), but this happens in a rather unpredictable way as shown from our investigations of Problems 2 and 3.

On the other hand, the extended Boolean model definitely has positive aspects, among which we mention:

1. It yields an ordered output.

2. For p = 1 it coincides with the vector model; for $p = \infty$ it coincides with the fuzzy model.

3. Experiments have shown its potential.

4 A suggestion for improvement of the Salton-Fox-Wu model

Since AND-clauses seem very difficult to handle and since OR-clauses are in reality AND/OR-clauses we propose to use only one formula, based on the existing one for OR-queries. It has moreover been observed in [FOXE 86] that p-norm results depend primarily on the p-value for the OR operator and are little effected by the p-value of the AND operator. Note also that we do not use the Boolean operator NOT.

We propose to use the following measure, denoted as SIM, to compute the p-similarity between a document D and a simple query Q:

$$SIM_p(D,Q) = \| DQ \|_p = (\sum_{i=1}^{n} d_i^p q_i^p)^{1/p}, \text{for} 1 \le p < \infty$$

and

$$SIM_\infty(D,Q) = \max_i(d_i q_i). \tag{8}$$

This measure has the following mathematical properties.

1.

$$0 \le SIM_p(D,Q) = SIM_p(Q,D) \le m, \tag{9}$$

where m is the minimum between the number of terms in the query Q, and the number of terms used to index the document D. This shows that SIM is bounded by 0 and m and is symmetric in D and Q. Moreover,

$$SIM_p(D,Q) \le \| D \|_p \text{ and } SIM_p(D,Q) \le \| Q \|_p. \tag{10}$$

2. For $p = 1, SIM_1(D,Q) = \sum_{i=1}^{n} d_i q_i$. This is precisely the simple vector processing model where the similarity between a document and a query is measured by the inner product between the document term weights and the query weights.

3. For $p = \infty, Q = 1, SIM_p(D,Q) = max(d_1,\ldots,d_n)$. This is precisely the formula for the fuzzy set model in the case of unweighted OR-queries. In the case of $0 - 1$ values for document terms, this boils down to classical Boolean retrieval.

4. As SIM_p is essentially a p-norm, $SIM_p(D,Q)$ is strictly decreasing in p, unless all the $d_i q_i$ but one are zero [JENS 06],[HARD 52] p.28.

5. As $F(p) = \frac{sim(D,Q_{or(p)})}{sim(E,Q_{or(p)})} = \frac{SIM_p(D,Q)}{SIM_p(E,Q)}$, all inconsistencies shown in our investigations of Problems 2 and 3, still hold for SIM.

5 Computation of query-document similarities in the SIM-system

The computation of a particular retrieval status value for a complex query is done as follows.

If terms $A_1, \ldots, A_{n(1)}$ are to be retrieved with weights $Q_1 = (q_1, \ldots, q_{n(1)})$ where $p = p_1$; and terms $(A_{n(1)+1}, \ldots, A_{n(1)+n(2)})$ with weights $Q_2 = (q_{n(1)+1}, \ldots, q_{n(1)+n(2)})$, where $p = p_2$, then this query is denoted as $(Q_1(p_1)\&Q_2(p_2))$.

$SIM(D, Q_1(p_1)\&Q_2(p_2))$ is then computed as:

$$(\sum_{i=1}^{n(1)}(d_i q_i)^{p_1} + \sum_{i=n(1)+1}^{n(1)+n(2)}(d_i q_i)^{p_2})^{1/P} \tag{11}$$

with

$$P = \frac{n(1)}{n(1) + n(2)} p_1 + \frac{n(2)}{n(1) + n(2)} p_2 \tag{12}$$

We require all A_i to be different, so that the same term can not be weighted by two different weights.

It is now easy to see that

$$SIM(D, Q_1(p_1)\&Q_2(p_2)) = SIM(D, Q_2(p_2)\&Q_1(p_1))$$

(commutativity), and that

$$SIM(D, Q_1(p_1)\&Q_2(p_2))\&Q_3(p_3)) =$$
$$SIM(D, Q_1(p_1)\&(Q_2(p_2)\&Q_3(p_3)))$$

(associativity).

6 Conclusion

We have shown that the formulae used in the p-norm retrieval model show some undesirable mathematical properties. Consequently, we propose to use a different similarity measure. Although the measure proposed here remedies some of the problems encountered by the use of the Salton-Fox-Wu retrieval measure, it still has some unexpected (and sometimes unpredictable) features. On the other hand, the Salton-Fox-Wu model has shown its superiority above other classical models. So, we suggest further experiments using the original as well as our new similarity measure. If retrieval results are consistently superior then there is no practical reason not to use the extended Boolean model. We only have to admit that it is not a 'mathematical' but rather a 'heuristic' model. Otherwise, one should abandon this model and use different, but (seemingly) equally promising approaches such as other generalisations of the vector space model [WONG 87],[WONG 89],[FOXE 88] or the Topological Information Retrieval System (TIRS) [CATE 87] based on the Waller-Kraft [WALL 79] and Cater-Kraft [CATE 89] wish lists for information retrieval.

Acknowledgement
We like to thank Leo Egghe for stimulating discussions and helpful suggestions concerning this article.

References

[BOOK 80] Bookstein A. Fuzzy requests: an approach to weighted Boolean searches. Journal of the American Society for Information Science, 31:240-247,
1980.

[BOOK 82] Bookstein A. Recent developments in the theory of information retrieval. Stockholm papers in library and information science. Royal Institute
of Technology Library, Stockholm, 1982.

[BOOK 85] Bookstein A. Probability and fuzzy-set applications to information
retrieval. Annual Review of Information Science and Technology, 20: 117-
151, 1985.

[BUEL 81] Buell D. and Kraft D. Performance measurement in a fuzzy retrieval
environment. In: Proceedings of the 4th Annual ACM SIGIR Conference,
56-62, 1981.

[BUEL 82] Buell D. An analysis of some fuzzy subset applications to information
retrieval systems. Fuzzy Sets and Systems, 7: 35-42, 1982.

[CATE 87] Cater S.C. and Kraft D.H. TIRS: a topological information system
satisfying the requirements of the Waller-Kraft wish list. Proceedings of the
10th annual ACM SIGIR Conference, 171-180, 1987.

[CATE 89] Cater S.C. and Kraft D.H. A generalization and clarification of the
Waller-Kraft wish list. Information Processing and Management, 25: 15-25,
1989.

[COOP 83] Cooper W. Exploiting the maximum entropy principle to increase retrieval effectiveness. Journal of the American Society for Information Science,
34: 31-39, 1983.

[DIEU 69] Dieudonné J. Foundations of modern analysis. Academic Press, New
York, 1969.

[EGGH 88] Egghe L. A norm problem, its solution and its application in econometrics and bibliometrics. Preprint 1988.

[EGGH 89] Egghe L. and Rousseau R. Transfer principles and a classification of
concentration measures. Preprint 1989. (JASIS, to appear).

[EGGH 90] Egghe L. and Rousseau R. Elements of concentration theory. In: Informetrics 89/90, L. Egghe and R. Rousseau (eds), Elsevier, Amsterdam,
1990.

[FOXE 86] Fox E.A. and Sharan S. A comparison of two methods for soft Boolean
operator interpretation in information retrieval. Preprint 1986.

[FOXE 88] Fox E.A., Nunn G.L. and Lee W.C. Coefficients for combining concept classes in a collection. Proceedings of the 11th Annual ACM SIGIR Conference, 291-307, 1988.

[FUHR 89] Fuhr N. Models for retrieval with probabilistic indexing. Information Processing and Management, 25: 55-72, 1989.

[HARD 52] Hardy G., Littlewood J.E. and Polya G. Inequalities. Cambridge University Press, Cambridge (UK), 1952.

[JENS 06] Jensen J.L.W.V. Sur les fonctions convexes et les inégalités entre les valeurs moyennes. Acta Mathematica, 30: 175-193, 1906.

[MARO 82] Maron M.E. Associative search techniques versus probabilistic retrieval models. Journal of the American Society for Information Science, 33: 308-310, 1982.

[MARS 67] Marshall A., Olkin I. and Proschan F. Monotonicity of ratios of means and other applications of majorization. In: Inequalities, O. Shisha (ed.), Academic Press, New York, 1967, 177-190.

[MARS 79] Marshall A. and Olkin I. Inequalities: theory of majorization and its applications. Academic Press, New York, 1979.

[ROBE 76] Robertson S. and Sparck Jones K. Relevance weighting of search terms. Journal of the American Society for Information Science, 27: 129-146, 1976.

[ROBE 77] Robertson S. The probability ranking principle in IR. Journal of Documentation, 34: 294-304, 1977.

[ROBE 78] On the nature of fuzz: a diatribe. Journal of the American Society for Information Science, 29: 304-307, 1978.

[ROUS 85] Rousseau R. On relative indexing in fuzzy retrieval systems. Information Processing and Management, 21: 415-417, 1985.

[ROUS 86] Rousseau R. De Boolese benadering bij geautomatiseerde gegevensopzoekingen: vooronderstellingen en kritiek. (A review and a criticism of the Boolean approach to online information retrieval.) Bibliotheek- en Archiefgids, 62: 67-73, 1986.

[SALT 83a] Salton G., Buckley C. and Fox E.A. Automatic query formulations in information retrieval. Journal of the American Society for Information Science, 34: 262-280, 1983.

[SALT 83b] Salton G., Fox E.A. and Wu H. Extended Boolean information retrieval. Communications of the Association for Computing Machinery, 26: 1022-1036, 1983.

[SALT 83c] Salton G. and McGill M.J. Introduction to modern information retrieval. McGraw-Hill, Auckland [etc], 1983.

[SALT 88] Salton G. On the relationship between theoretical retrieval models. In:
Informetrics 87/88, L. Egghe and R. Rousseau (eds), Elsevier, Amsterdam,
1988, 263-270.

[TAHA 76] Tahani V. A fuzzy model of document retrieval systems. Information
Processing and Management, 12: 177-188, 1976.

[WALL 79] Waller W. and Kraft D.H. A mathematical model of a weighted Boolean retrieval system. Information Processing and Management, 15: 235-245,
1979.

[WONG 87] Wong S.K.M., Ziarko W., Raghavan V.V. and Wong P.C.N. On modeling of information retrieval concepts in vector spaces. ACM Transactions
on Database Systems, 12: 299-321, 1987.

[WONG 89] Wong S.K.M., Ziarko W., Raghavan V.V. and Wong P.C.N. Extended
Boolean query processing in the generalized vector space model. Information
Systems, 14: 47-63, 1989.

AUTHORS INDEX

ALVEY, B., 135.
AMMERSBACH, K., 63.
ANICK, P.G., 135.
APPELBAUM, L.A., 455.
BELKIN, N.J., 151.
BOOKSTEIN, A., 327.
BRENNAN, J.D., 135.
BUCKLEY, C., 45.
BURKOWSKI, F.J., 211.
CELENTANO, A., 241.
CHEN, H., 115.
CHEN, Q.F., 279.
CHIARAMELLA, Y., 25.
COOMBS, J.H., 83.
CRAWFORD, S.L., 455.
CREHANGE, M., 99.
CRINGEAN, J.K., 429.
CROFT, W.B., 1, 349, 385.
CROUCH, C.J., 369.
CROUCH, D.B., 369.
CUTTING, D., 405.
DAOUD, A.M., 279.
DAS, R., 349.
DHAR, V., 115.
EGGHE, L., 469.
ENGLAND, R,. 429.
FLYNN, R.A., 135.
FOX, E.A., 279.
FRISSE, M., 343.
FUHR, N., 45.
FUNG, R.M., 455.

FUNGINI, M.G., 241.
GAUCH, S., 255.
HALIN, G., 99.
HANSSEN, D.R., 135.
HEATH, L.S., 279.
HOPPE, H.U., 63.
HUTHER, H., 313.
IWADERA, T., 227.
KEREKES, P., 99.
KIMOTO, H., 227.
KLEIN, S.T., 327.
LEWIS, D.D., 385.
LUTES-SCHAAB, B., 63.
MANSON, G.A., 429.
MARCHETTI, P.G., 151.
NAREDDY, K.R., 369.
NIE, J. 25.
PEDERSEN, J., 405.
POZZI, S., 241.
RABITTI, F., 193.
ROBBINS, J.M., 135.
ROUSSEAU, R., 495.
SACKS-DAVIS, R., 179.
STANFILL, C., 413.
TONG, R.M., 455.
TURTLE, H., 1.
WALLIS, P., 179.
WILKINSON, R., 179.
WILLETT, P., 429.
ZEZULA, P., 193.
ZINSSMEISTER, G., 63.

Ouvrage imprimé aux
PRESSES UNIVERSITAIRES DE BRUXELLES asbl
avenue Paul Héger, 42
1050 Bruxelles